Lecture Notes in Computer Science 12772

More information about this subseries at http://www.springer.com/series/7409

Pei-Luen Patrick Rau (Ed.)

Cross-Cultural Design

Applications in Arts, Learning, Well-being, and Social Development

13th International Conference, CCD 2021
Held as Part of the 23rd HCI International Conference, HCII 2021
Virtual Event, July 24–29, 2021
Proceedings, Part II

Springer

Editor
Pei-Luen Patrick Rau
Tsinghua University
Beijing, China

ISSN 0302-9743   ISSN 1611-3349   (electronic)
Lecture Notes in Computer Science
ISBN 978-3-030-77076-1   ISBN 978-3-030-77077-8   (eBook)
https://doi.org/10.1007/978-3-030-77077-8

LNCS Sublibrary: SL3 – Information Systems and Applications, incl. Internet/Web, and HCI

This Springer imprint is published by the registered company Springer Nature Switzerland AG
The registered company address is: Gewerbestrasse 11, 6330 Cham, Switzerland

Foreword

Human-Computer Interaction (HCI) is acquiring an ever-increasing scientific and industrial importance, and having more impact on people's everyday life, as an ever-growing number of human activities are progressively moving from the physical to the digital world. This process, which has been ongoing for some time now, has been dramatically accelerated by the COVID-19 pandemic. The HCI International (HCII) conference series, held yearly, aims to respond to the compelling need to advance the exchange of knowledge and research and development efforts on the human aspects of design and use of computing systems.

The 23rd International Conference on Human-Computer Interaction, HCI International 2021 (HCII 2021), was planned to be held at the Washington Hilton Hotel, Washington DC, USA, during July 24–29, 2021. Due to the COVID-19 pandemic and with everyone's health and safety in mind, HCII 2021 was organized and run as a virtual conference. It incorporated the 21 thematic areas and affiliated conferences listed on the following page.

A total of 5222 individuals from academia, research institutes, industry, and governmental agencies from 81 countries submitted contributions, and 1276 papers and 241 posters were included in the proceedings to appear just before the start of the conference. The contributions thoroughly cover the entire field of HCI, addressing major advances in knowledge and effective use of computers in a variety of application areas. These papers provide academics, researchers, engineers, scientists, practitioners, and students with state-of-the-art information on the most recent advances in HCI. The volumes constituting the set of proceedings to appear before the start of the conference are listed in the following pages.

The HCI International (HCII) conference also offers the option of 'Late Breaking Work' which applies both for papers and posters, and the corresponding volume(s) of the proceedings will appear after the conference. Full papers will be included in the 'HCII 2021 - Late Breaking Papers' volumes of the proceedings to be published in the Springer LNCS series, while 'Poster Extended Abstracts' will be included as short research papers in the 'HCII 2021 - Late Breaking Posters' volumes to be published in the Springer CCIS series.

The present volume contains papers submitted and presented in the context of the 13th International Conference on Cross-Cultural Design (CCD 2021) affiliated conference to HCII 2021. I would like to thank the Chair, Pei-Luen Patrick Rau, for his invaluable contribution in its organization and the preparation of the Proceedings, as well as the members of the program board for their contributions and support. This year, the CCD affiliated conference has focused on topics related to cross-cultural experience and product design, cultural differences and cross-cultural communication, as well as design case studies in domains such as learning and creativity, well-being, social change and social development, cultural heritage and tourism, autonomous vehicles, virtual agents, robots and intelligent assistants.

I would also like to thank the Program Board Chairs and the members of the Program Boards of all thematic areas and affiliated conferences for their contribution towards the highest scientific quality and overall success of the HCI International 2021 conference.

This conference would not have been possible without the continuous and unwavering support and advice of Gavriel Salvendy, founder, General Chair Emeritus, and Scientific Advisor. For his outstanding efforts, I would like to express my appreciation to Abbas Moallem, Communications Chair and Editor of HCI International News.

July 2021   Constantine Stephanidis

HCI International 2021 Thematic Areas and Affiliated Conferences

Thematic Areas

- HCI: Human-Computer Interaction
- HIMI: Human Interface and the Management of Information

Affiliated Conferences

- EPCE: 18th International Conference on Engineering Psychology and Cognitive Ergonomics
- UAHCI: 15th International Conference on Universal Access in Human-Computer Interaction
- VAMR: 13th International Conference on Virtual, Augmented and Mixed Reality
- CCD: 13th International Conference on Cross-Cultural Design
- SCSM: 13th International Conference on Social Computing and Social Media
- AC: 15th International Conference on Augmented Cognition
- DHM: 12th International Conference on Digital Human Modeling and Applications in Health, Safety, Ergonomics and Risk Management
- DUXU: 10th International Conference on Design, User Experience, and Usability
- DAPI: 9th International Conference on Distributed, Ambient and Pervasive Interactions
- HCIBGO: 8th International Conference on HCI in Business, Government and Organizations
- LCT: 8th International Conference on Learning and Collaboration Technologies
- ITAP: 7th International Conference on Human Aspects of IT for the Aged Population
- HCI-CPT: 3rd International Conference on HCI for Cybersecurity, Privacy and Trust
- HCI-Games: 3rd International Conference on HCI in Games
- MobiTAS: 3rd International Conference on HCI in Mobility, Transport and Automotive Systems
- AIS: 3rd International Conference on Adaptive Instructional Systems
- C&C: 9th International Conference on Culture and Computing
- MOBILE: 2nd International Conference on Design, Operation and Evaluation of Mobile Communications
- AI-HCI: 2nd International Conference on Artificial Intelligence in HCI

List of Conference Proceedings Volumes Appearing Before the Conference

1. LNCS 12762, Human-Computer Interaction: Theory, Methods and Tools (Part I), edited by Masaaki Kurosu
2. LNCS 12763, Human-Computer Interaction: Interaction Techniques and Novel Applications (Part II), edited by Masaaki Kurosu
3. LNCS 12764, Human-Computer Interaction: Design and User Experience Case Studies (Part III), edited by Masaaki Kurosu
4. LNCS 12765, Human Interface and the Management of Information: Information Presentation and Visualization (Part I), edited by Sakae Yamamoto and Hirohiko Mori
5. LNCS 12766, Human Interface and the Management of Information: Information-rich and Intelligent Environments (Part II), edited by Sakae Yamamoto and Hirohiko Mori
6. LNAI 12767, Engineering Psychology and Cognitive Ergonomics, edited by Don Harris and Wen-Chin Li
7. LNCS 12768, Universal Access in Human-Computer Interaction: Design Methods and User Experience (Part I), edited by Margherita Antona and Constantine Stephanidis
8. LNCS 12769, Universal Access in Human-Computer Interaction: Access to Media, Learning and Assistive Environments (Part II), edited by Margherita Antona and Constantine Stephanidis
9. LNCS 12770, Virtual, Augmented and Mixed Reality, edited by Jessie Y. C. Chen and Gino Fragomeni
10. LNCS 12771, Cross-Cultural Design: Experience and Product Design Across Cultures (Part I), edited by P. L. Patrick Rau
11. LNCS 12772, Cross-Cultural Design: Applications in Arts, Learning, Well-being, and Social Development (Part II), edited by P. L. Patrick Rau
12. LNCS 12773, Cross-Cultural Design: Applications in Cultural Heritage, Tourism, Autonomous Vehicles, and Intelligent Agents (Part III), edited by P. L. Patrick Rau
13. LNCS 12774, Social Computing and Social Media: Experience Design and Social Network Analysis (Part I), edited by Gabriele Meiselwitz
14. LNCS 12775, Social Computing and Social Media: Applications in Marketing, Learning, and Health (Part II), edited by Gabriele Meiselwitz
15. LNAI 12776, Augmented Cognition, edited by Dylan D. Schmorrow and Cali M. Fidopiastis
16. LNCS 12777, Digital Human Modeling and Applications in Health, Safety, Ergonomics and Risk Management: Human Body, Motion and Behavior (Part I), edited by Vincent G. Duffy
17. LNCS 12778, Digital Human Modeling and Applications in Health, Safety, Ergonomics and Risk Management: AI, Product and Service (Part II), edited by Vincent G. Duffy

38. CCIS 1420, HCI International 2021 Posters - Part II, edited by Constantine Stephanidis, Margherita Antona, and Stavroula Ntoa
39. CCIS 1421, HCI International 2021 Posters - Part III, edited by Constantine Stephanidis, Margherita Antona, and Stavroula Ntoa

http://2021.hci.international/proceedings

13th International Conference on Cross-Cultural Design (CCD 2021)

Program Board Chair: **Pei-Luen Patrick Rau,** *Tsinghua University, China*

- Kuohsiang Chen, China
- Na Chen, China
- Wen-Ko Chiou, Taiwan
- Zhiyong Fu, China
- Toshikazu Kato, Japan
- Sheau-Farn Max Liang, Taiwan
- Rungtai Lin, Taiwan
- Wei Lin, Taiwan
- Dyi-Yih Michael Lin, Taiwan
- Robert T. P. Lu, China
- Xingda Qu, China
- Chun-Yi (Danny) Shen, Taiwan
- Hao Tan, China
- Pei-Lee Teh, Malaysia
- Lin Wang, Korea
- Hsiu-Ping Yueh, Taiwan
- Run-Ting Zhong, China

The full list with the Program Board Chairs and the members of the Program Boards of all thematic areas and affiliated conferences is available online at:

http://www.hci.international/board-members-2021.php

HCI International 2022

The 24th International Conference on Human-Computer Interaction, HCI International 2022, will be held jointly with the affiliated conferences at the Gothia Towers Hotel and Swedish Exhibition & Congress Centre, Gothenburg, Sweden, June 26 – July 1, 2022. It will cover a broad spectrum of themes related to Human-Computer Interaction, including theoretical issues, methods, tools, processes, and case studies in HCI design, as well as novel interaction techniques, interfaces, and applications. The proceedings will be published by Springer. More information will be available on the conference website: http://2022.hci.international/:

General Chair
Prof. Constantine Stephanidis
University of Crete and ICS-FORTH
Heraklion, Crete, Greece
Email: general_chair@hcii2022.org

http://2022.hci.international/

Contents – Part II

Social Change and Social Development

Culture, Arts and Creativity

The Strategies of Experiential Design in the Creative Life Industry

Shu-Hua Chang(✉)

Department of Arts and Creative Industries, National Dong Hwa University, Hualien, Taiwan
iamcsh0222@gms.ndhu.edu.tw

Abstract. In 2002, the Taiwan government promoted the creative life industry as one of the cultural and creative industries. In terms of the various types of creative life industry, one of the challenges for operators is how to design valuable experiences through the service process. The purpose of this study is to examine the strategies of experiential design in the creative life industry within the experiential-based framework proposed by Pine and Gilmore's concept of the experience economy, and service design. In this study, data were collected from two different creative life industry contexts: traditional industry restructuring and upgrading and lifestyle developing categories. This study finds that the experiential realms at different touchpoints in the service process complement one another, and recommends that creative life enterprises carefully evaluate the association among different experiential realms at different service touchpoints in order to create greater experiential value by using limited resources.

Keywords: Experience economy · Experiential design · Creative life industry · Customer journey maps · Service design

1 Introduction

1.1 Research Background

In 2002, the Taiwan government promoted the creative life industry as one of the cultural and creative industries. This industrial policy is based on traditional production-oriented industries, and encourages small and medium-sized enterprises to use creative, scientific and technological, and human elements to develop a composite business model with products, services, activities, and space. The creative life industry is defined as an industry that uses creativity to integrate core knowledge of the life industry and provide in-depth experiences and high-quality aesthetics; these include the food culture experience, life aesthetic experience, natural ecological experience, fashion experience, cultural heritage experience, and craft experience. The theory of the experience economy [1–3] was also applied for the promotion of the creative life industry in Taiwan.

The creative life industry is seen as a provider of experiences, wherein experiential values can be created through various elements within related services, products, space, and activities [4]. The theory of the experience economy was proposed by Pine

© Springer Nature Switzerland AG 2021
P.-L. P. Rau (Ed.): HCII 2021, LNCS 12772, pp. 3–17, 2021.
https://doi.org/10.1007/978-3-030-77077-8_1

and Gilmore [1–3]: the authors argue that consumers want more than just products and services; they also want to "experience" and engage themselves in a personal way and gain unforgettable experiences. According to Pine and Gilmore [1–3], the experience-oriented businesses use service as a stage and products as props to engage consumers. Thus, experience designers should offer not only products or services, but also experiences and memories. Pine and Gilmore [1–3] also state that creating and providing experience is one of the ways in which producers can survive in an increasingly competitive environment.

1.2 Purpose

The framework of Pine and Gilmore's experience economy is seen to be valid for measuring customer experiences in various industries, such as tourism and hospitality, festivals, the creative life industry, etc. [5–13]. However, few studies have examined the strategies of experiential design with the experience realms developed by Pine and Gilmore [1–3] from a service design [14, 15] perspective in the creative life industry.

In terms of the various types of creative life industry, one of the challenges for operators is how to design valuable experiences through the service process. In this study, data were collected from two different creative life industry contexts: traditional industry restructuring and upgrading (Kuo Yuan Ye Museum of Cake and Pastry; Chihsing Tan Katsuo Museum) and lifestyle developing categories (The One Nanyuan Land of Retreat and Wellness; Gaeavilla Resort).

The purpose of this study is to contextualize the strategies of experiential design in the creative life industry by using the experiential-based framework proposed by Pine and Gilmore [2], and service design. Previous studies have not examined tourism experiences in the experience realms developed by Pine and Gilmore [1–3] from a service design perspective in the creative life industry. Hence, this study contributes a framework upon which the creative life enterprises may build their ability of experiential service design, to enhance their competitiveness.

2 Literature Review

2.1 Experience Economy

According to Pine and Gilmore's experience economy theory, an experience can be classified by the level of customer involvement (active or passive participation) and customers' connection with products and services (absorption or immersion). Based on this perspective, four realms of experience comprise the main components: entertainment (passive and absorption), education (active and absorption), aesthetics (passive and immersion), and escapism (active and immersion). What customers want is not just consumer products and services, but also an unforgettable experience by experiencing the process of a product or service. The authors propose that including more realms of experience increases the likelihood of producing an experience "sweet spot". When experience realms are designed into the business processes, they create memorable environments that will help generate memories of the brand for consumers. Hence, creating and delivering experiences will be a way for enterprises to survive in an increasingly competitive future [16].

Examining the experience economy's literature in the field of tourism, Pine and Gilmore view experience as a core aspect of creating differentiation between tourism products and destinations [17]. On the other hand, the creative industries play an important role in supporting narratives of content and experience creation, such as the development of local themes, cultural routes, and culinary experiences. Because of the diversity and unpredictability of consumer demand, the innovation of content and experience becomes important. The shift toward the experience economy has led to a demand for creative skills and content that can support the development of fascinating experiences for consumers [18].

Pine and Gilmore's framework of experience [2] is considered to be valid for measuring customer experiences in tourism industries. Oh, Fiore, and Jeoung [5] modified four realms of experience using the conceptual framework by Pine and Gilmore [2], and developed a measure to capture tourism experiences in the bed-and-breakfast industry. Previous studies have employed the realms of experience to examine customer experiences in various tourism fields, such as cruises [6], film festivals [7], festival and cultural tourism [8, 9], wine tourism [10], creative life industries [11], temple tourism [12], and rural tourism [13].

Quantitative measures help to evaluate the customer experience in tourism. However, exploring the nature of experience in various tourism industries assists in enriching the theoretical framework of the experience economy. The framework of experience was used to analyze the nature of customer experience in areas such as wine tourism [19] and casinos [20]. The qualitative study of the tourism experience has focused on the psychological aspect of the experience elements, but has failed to explore the design of experience elements for service systems. Therefore, this study will fill this research gap.

2.2 Service Design

The purpose of service design is to make a service more useful, feasible, effective, and attractive, to meet customer expectations [21]. Service design is defined as the integration of tangible and intangible cues to provide customers with a holistic service experience [14]. Ostrom et al. [22] proposed that great service experiences increase customer satisfaction and brand loyalty. However, most organizations fail to use an effective and systematic approach to design their service.

Stakeholder maps, customer journey maps, user diaries, empathy mapping, and service blueprints are mostly proposed as service design tools. For the sake of competitiveness, service providers should pay attention to the mood, behavior, and expectations of customers, and design a good experience through touchpoints [23]. Service design methods have been used in the relevant literature to examine tourism experiences, such as user diaries [24], personas and service blueprints [25], and customer journey maps [4]. A customer journey map is a valuable visualized experience from users' perspective, which provides a holistic overview of the factors influencing customers' experience. Customer satisfaction is influenced by service quality at all moments of touchpoints. Similarly, moment maps can be used to observe the many opportunities and threats as the customer navigates the customer experience through service stages [26]. The user-centered, co-creative, sequencing, evidencing, and holistic features are proposed by Stickdorn and Schneider [14] as five important principles for service design.

Pine and Gilmore [1–3] proposed five steps for experience design: defining themes, combining experiences with positive cues, eliminating negative cues, associating the experience with memorability, and integrating sensory stimulation. The authors also pointed out that even if the realms of experience are determined, service operators need to make good use of all kinds of experiential cues, combined with sensory design, to enhance customer experiences. Therefore, the use of service design in the experience realms can help build a complete service experience framework.

3   Research Methods

A case study is generally applied during the exploration of a question to understand the "why" or "how" [27]. The evidence obtained from multiple cases is often regarded as providing powerful materials applicable to descriptive analysis or establishment of theory [28]; however, the execution of multiple case studies may also require more resources and time [27].

There has been a relatively small number of studies on the strategic elements of experiential design, especially on the multi-domain operations in the creative life industry and the integration of service design with experience. Few studies have examined the essence of experience in the tourism industry by means of a qualitative research approach. Therefore, a qualitative, multiple-case research design is deemed to be suitable for this study.

Four enterprises in the creative life industry were invited to participate in the study via email. In selecting the four participants, two primary focuses in the creative life industry development were taken into consideration: namely, traditional industry restructuring and upgrading and lifestyle categories; and the operational performance of the enterprise and feasibility of data collection. In terms of the restructuring and upgrading of traditional industry, the research objects comprise the Chihsing Tan Katsuo Museum and the Kuo Yuan Ye Museum of Cake and Pastry (Shilin Branch), while in terms of lifestyle developing, the research objects are the Gaeavilla Resort and The One Nanyuan Land of Retreat and Wellness. All of these enterprises had been in operation for over 15 years and, due to their remarkable operational performance, received the "excellent creative life enterprise" award from the Industrial Development Bureau of the Ministry of Economic Affairs.

3.1   Data Collection

To examine the strategies of experiential design in the development of creative life industry, the study interviewed the enterprise owner or professional manager, who is responsible for decision-making and plays an administrative and representative role in the creative life business of the research objects. The study conducted purposive sampling in order to obtain abundant evidence-based materials concerning the relevant sources [29]. The main aim of purposive sampling is to select active participants applicable to the research requirement, rather than to underscore the size of the representative sample [30].

The interview questions were designed based on the literature on the experience economy. During the interviews, the researcher first explained the definition of the components of experience (entertainment, education, aesthetics, and escapism) to the interviewee. The purpose of a semi-structured and one-on-one interview is to collect useful and meaningful information by asking additional questions based on the information provided by the interviewee during the interview. The interview questions included: "What is the main idea of the business value?"; "What types of experience (e.g., entertainment, aesthetics, education, and escapism) do you hope to offer to the customers and why?"; and "How will the experience type be embodied through the products or service design?" In the study, we interviewed four business owners or professional managers, labeled B1 to B4, and all the content of the interviews was recorded and converted into transcripts and notes for further data analysis.

3.2 Data Analysis

The study uses the four components of experience—entertainment, education, escapism, and aesthetics—as the theoretical framework for the textual analysis of the interviews. Based on the studies of Dye [31], Elo and Kyngas [32], and Zhang and Wildemuth [33], the data analysis process was divided into four steps. First, the words in the textual record of the interviews were classified into smaller content units [31] and organized based on the interview questions; the interviewees' answers were also examined for the analysis and encoding of the information related to the questions. Second, the features frequently observed in the record were selected, and the seemingly relevant concepts and codes were categorized into the same group in order to form a category with an experimental statement in which different phenomena correlated with one another [32]. The credibility of the study is affected by the data in each category, and the formation of categories in the study was conducted on the basis of concept and experience [31]. Third, the codes were classified according to more extensive themes, and the dispersed codes that possessed relevant significance were gathered in the same theme. The researcher formulated each general theme after analyzing the textual context of the theme. Fourth, the code consistency in each theme was evaluated to ensure that the theme would fully represent the primary code and correspondingly correlate with the designated category [32]. Through repeatedly reading the content of the interviews based on the four components, the researcher obtained a solid understanding of the concepts proposed by the interviewees and classified the themes according to the four realms of experience [1–3].

4   Results

The study collected the design components of experience in the creative life industry through conducting interviews. The themes, categories, codes, and corresponding experience stages of the strategies of experiential design, all of which are organized using the aforementioned data analysis method, are shown in Table 1. To visualize the experiential design components, the study used the customer journey maps in service design to create the experiential design service journey maps, as shown in Fig. 1. Generally speaking, in terms of the industrial understanding and methods of providing experience in the creative life business, the experiential types in the same category manifest the same primary focus. For instance, the Gaeavilla Resort and The One Nanyuan Land of Retreat and Wellness, both of which highlight an lifestyle developing, focus on providing an experience of escapism and aesthetics, in which education and entertainment serve as an extended part. On the other hand, the two corporate museums—the Chihsing Tan Katsuo Museum, and the Kuo Yuan Ye Museum of Cake and Pastry (Shilin Branch)—focus more on education and entertainment than aesthetics. Also, the study finds that the experiential design components in the creative life industry are inseparably interconnected, which corresponds to Pine and Gilmore's idea that the experiential components do not repel one another [1].

Table 1. Summary table of elements of experiential design within experience stages

Experience realm			
Experience stage	Concept and code generated from interview transcripts	Category	Theme
Entertainment			
Activity participaion	Joyful cake and tea time with traditional music	Joyfulness in cultural activity	Making cultural activity entertaining
Field visiting	Fun in sharing cake and pastry culture using different languages		
Activity participation	Fresh experience of making cake using traditional techniques	Freshness in cultural experience	
Field visiting	Fun in wearing traditional wedding costume	Fun in experiencing cultural ritual	Gamification of interactive devices
Field visiting	Fun in the embroidered ball throwing ritual		
Activity participation	Fun in fish rubbing game device design	Fun interactive devices	
Activity participation	Making visiting more fun with the bonito cooking game machine		
Education			
Field visiting	Introducing the whole process of making bonito	Knowledge of the industrial culture	Professional introduction of information
Field visiting	Knowledge of the cake and pastry of different cultures		
Field visiting	Introducing the Hakka/Baroque building and garden building culture	Knowledge of the architectural culture	

(*continued*)

Table 1. (*continued*)

Field visiting	Introducing the herbs in the garden and experiencing aroma-therapy in the room, cooking, and food and agriculture education	Knowledge of the plant ecology	
Activity participation	Learning about cake and pastry engraving culture	Production artistry practice	Demonstration of cultural authenticity
Activity participation	Bonito flake making experience		
Activity participation	Applying bonito to making takoyaki	Food education design experience	Creative application in life
Activity participation	Applying herb planting to herb cooking classroom		
Shopping	Bonito dish tasting	Creative dish tasting	
Dining	Integrating local Oriental Beauty Tea into dish design, and learning about local products		
Aesthetics			
Field visiting	Integration of seasonal beauty into the space	Beauty of nature	Integration in spatial design
Field visiting	Green building		
Field visiting	Artistic creation for the space	Beauty of art	
Field visiting	Diverse architectural art forms	Beauty of mix and match	
Field visiting	Integration of fire-damaged remains into spatial design	Beauty of nostalgia	
Field visiting	Garden tea table scenario design	Scenario activity design	Sensory aesthetics activity design
Activity participation	Aesthetics of handmade shaped cake and pastry	Handmade activity design	
Escapism			
Field visiting and accommodation	Special essential oil spa and aroma-therapy experience	Thematic service facility	Comprehensive lifestyle design
Field visiting and accommodation	Herbal bath facility in architecture made of cypress		
Field visiting, activity participation, dining, and accommodation	Herbal aroma-therapy space, cooking, food and agriculture education, yoga, and sleeping	Richness of thematic lifestyle design	
Field visiting, activity participation, dining, and accommodation	Local creative dishes in the oriental park, art and culture activity, and traveling and lodging		

Experience stage

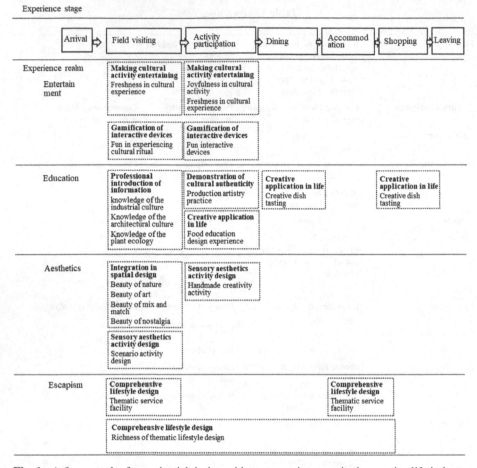

Fig. 1. A framework of experiential design with customer journeys in the creative life industry

4.1 Journey Design for Customers Seeking an Entertaining Experience

The restructuring and upgrading of traditional industry in the creative life business involves both entertaining and educational experience design, of which the former aims to enhance the customers' interest in visiting and learning. The entertaining experience comprises "making cultural activity entertaining" and "gamification of interactive devices". The first theme, "making cultural experience entertaining," consists of "joyfulness in cultural activity" and "freshness in cultural experience". Considering that the customers are unfamiliar with some aspects of the culture, in order to enable them to experience the culture in a pleasant atmosphere, making the cultural activity a joyful experience is necessary. As interviewee B4 stated: "Eating cake and drinking tea is part of the Taiwanese culture. We provide different products and play some light Chinese music to let the tourists chat with each other in a relaxed mood". He also pointed out that: "Tourists visiting Taiwan from overseas often want to learn some Taiwanese language, and it is a good chance for us to communicate and share what we know with them, which is kind of fun". In terms of "freshness in cultural experience", some special production techniques can be integrated into the experiential activities, through which the customers can personally take part in the activity and gain a sense of freshness and joyfulness. For instance, the Kuo Yuan Ye Museum of Cake and Pastry uses the traditional cake-making techniques to devise an entertaining and reminiscent cake-making activity, in which the customers get to experience innovative baking techniques. As interviewee B4 told us: "It reconstructs the early cake-making techniques in Taiwan, and the customers can touch the flour with their hands. We find that in an experience like this, being able to touch the raw materials is something that can leave a strong impression in the customers' minds".

The second theme, "gamification of interactive devices", comprises "fun in cultural and ritualistic experience" and "entertaining interactive devices", both of which can facilitate customer participation and arouse joyfulness. In terms of "fun in cultural and ritualistic experience," the customers can have fun by taking part in activities such as wearing traditional costume and embroidered ball throwing, which is a part of the wedding ritual. Interviewee B4 mentioned that: "We provide some traditional costumes for the customers to wear, and they can have fun playing games like this". Furthermore, with the "entertaining interactive devices", the customers can take part in an interactive experience, such as the bonito cooking-game machine, through which the customers can learn about the making of bonito dishes by playing the interactive game, and the fish engraving game, where they can learn more about fish. The interactive experience, however, is designed to give the customers an educational experience through playing.

4.2 Journey Design for Customers Seeking an Educational Experience

The design of the educational experience comprises three dimensions: "professional introduction of information", "demonstration of cultural authenticity", and "creative application in life". In terms of the Chihsing Tan Katsuo Museum and the Kuo Yuan Ye Museum of Cake and Pastry (Shilin Branch), both of which highlight the traditional industry restructuring and upgrading, the educational experience plays a major role. By contrast, in the Gaeavilla Resort and The One Nanyuan Land, both of which highlight the lifestyle developing, the educational experience is secondary to the aesthetic experience. The first theme, "professional knowledge", is mainly embodied in the introduction to the bonito industry culture, cake and pastry culture, park building culture, and herbal ecology, and their application in life. For instance, during the customers' visit to the Chihsing Tan Katsuo Museum, they would be given an introduction to the process of making bonito and gain an insight into the local fishery industry. As for the Kuo Yuan Ye Museum of Cake and Pastry, the cake and pastry culture is closely associated with different stages of life, such as weddings and funerals. As interviewee B3 stated: "We let the customers understand their culture. Especially when we introduce our cake and pastry culture to foreigners, something fun always happens. For example, the Korean tourists find that they also have something similar in their own country. What kind of cake and pastry do they have there? And how is their cake and pastry culture different from that of Taiwan? During the introduction and our chat with them, they also get to retrieve their long-lost cake and pastry culture".

The second theme, "demonstration of cultural authenticity", includes experiences such as cake and pastry culture learning and practice, and bonito flake making, which constitute the "production artistry practice" category. The primary focus of the theme is to extract certain parts of the industrial culture of the traditional or endangered industry, and to enhance the educational value by letting the customers take part in the demonstration activity. For instance, the Kuo Yuan Ye Museum of Cake and Pastry integrates the traditional engraving technique into cake and pastry making, from which customers can learn about the cake and pastry engraving culture. The Chihsing Tan Katsuo Museum allows the customers to experience the authentic bonito flake making process through a demonstration.

The third theme, "creative application in life," comprises the categories "food education design experience" and "creative dish tasting". Traditional local raw materials are integrated into the creative design of daily life. In this way, the customers can learn about the value of the combination of traditional industrial and cultural assets and modern life creativity. In "food education design experience", the customers can learn about using bonito in making takoyaki and applying herb planting in the cooking class. In "creative dish tasting," the customers are shown the process of making bonito dishes, and get to taste a creative dish made of local ingredients. The study finds that the creative dish made of local ingredients can give the customers a better understanding of the local products and how the ingredients can be used or cooked in daily life. As interviewee B2 shared that: "Using locally featured agricultural products, such as the Oriental Beauty Tea and dried persimmon, in developing a series of creative dishes gives the tourists a better knowledge of local products while enjoying the delicacies".

4.3 Journey Design for Customers Seeking an Aesthetic Experience

The aesthetic experiential design comprises two themes: "integration in spatial design" and "sensory aesthetics activity design". The first theme, "integration in spatial design" consists of "beauty of nature," "beauty of art," "beauty of mix and match," and "beauty of nostalgia". Overlooking the Central Mountain Range, the Gaeavilla Resort integrates the natural environment into its spatial design. The herb planting area, the herb maze, the guest rooms, the dining room, the herbal hydrotherapy pool, and the swimming pool are all combined with the natural environment of the green hill, displaying the natural beauty of the seasonal changes. Moreover, the exhibition of artworks in the public space and guest rooms also combines the beauty of both nature and art. As regards the architectural design of The One Nanyuan, the Taiwanese cypress was used as the building material; this was combined with the oriental park landscaping design of the Hakka, Jiangnan, and local Hakka culture to create a mixed-and-matched architectural style. In addition, inspired by the characteristic September wind of the area, the institute also invited an artist to use cypress to build a public artwork titled "Wind Eaves" as a highlight of modern art on the grassland of the park. Furthermore, the Chihsing Tan Katsuo Museum retains the structure of the old factory and uses the fire-damaged remains as decorative elements in the space, with the intention of evoking a sense of "rising from the ashes" in the viewers, and showing the aesthetics of culture and nostalgia.

The second theme, "sensory aesthetics activity design," is demonstrated in two categories: "scenario activity design" and "creativity activity design". Customers are expected to perceive the aesthetics of life in the creative life business through the design of sensory experience. The One Nanyuan has a large ecological hinterland, and the tourist activities and lodging experience in the park provide leisure activities full of the oriental humanistic spirit. For instance, the heaven-and-earth tea table activity in the park offers creative tea and food inspired by the Oriental Beauty Tea from Hsinchu. In this way, the customers are not simply drinking tea but experiencing the aesthetics of the heaven-and-earth tea table in the park. Moreover, the Kuo Yuan Ye Museum of Cake and Pastry (Shilin Branch) enables the customers to develop their own aesthetics by means of handmade shaped cake and pastry. The aesthetic experience of designing handmade cake and pastry also serves as a practical and educational cake and pastry-making experience, in which education and aesthetics nicely complement each other.

4.4 Journey Design for Customers Seeking an Escapist Experience

In terms of the escapist experience, "thematic service facility" and "richness of thematic lifestyle design" comprise a "comprehensive lifestyle design". Both the Gaeavilla Resort, which highlights herbal life experience, and The One Nanyuan, which provides an oriental park experience, focus on offering an escapist experience. The "thematic service facility" refers to the facility offering a leisure and lifestyle-related experience in which the customer can be personally immersed. As interviewee B1 mentioned that "[…] the introduction first helped customers understand our park, herbs, and the environment for the body and mind, so that they could freely choose to use the facility while clearing their own mind; […] after staying with us, they no longer need to go out, and they can enjoy all kinds of experience and all herbal facilities here".

Examples of "richness of thematic lifestyle design" include applying diverse herbal designs to field service, and a secluded leisure design in mountain areas. The One Nanyuan merges the architectural style of Jiangnan (China), Hakka (Taiwan), and Baroque (Europe); it offers park tours, accommodation services, special events, and a personal housekeeping service, so that the customers can immerse themselves in the idyllic life and enjoy a supreme experience of retreat and wellness. The Gaeavilla Resort integrates organic herbs into different types of experience, such as the aromatherapy space in the room, cooking, food and agricultural education, and yoga. From a business perspective, escapism and aesthetics nicely complement each other and put the aesthetics of lifestyle into practice by means of an environment that is far away from the city and merged with nature. In this way, the customers get to experience the aesthetics of a life away from the hustle and bustle.

5 Discussion

This study finds a conflict between the fact that the creative life business develops its major experiential pattern and other extended experiential patterns based on its business orientation, and the experience economy's idea that the "sweet spot" of consumer experience can be formed once the experience encompasses the four experiential realms: entertainment, education, aesthetics, and escapism [1–3]. In addition, the creative life business uses specific touchpoints in its experiential design, with the aim of optimizing the consumer experience. From the perspective of service design, a business should conduct efficient touchpoint design by means of crucial moment mapping in the service journey when executing complicated and diversified service experience design [26]. The study proposes the following discussions, which are expected to be of value for the formulation of experiential design strategies in the creative life industry.

First, the design of aesthetic experience in the creative life industry corresponds to Pine and Gilmore's [1–3] idea that in addition to visual immersion, the design of sensory aesthetics activity is also a crucial design strategy. The study finds that in the creative life industry, the building itself or the natural environment can be applied to landscaping and creating the beauty of nature. The use of artworks with a relevant theme, or mixing different architectural styles in the space, can convey the unique aesthetics of the business. On the other hand, proper preservation of the traditional architectural remains enhances the historical beauty of the architecture, showing the business operator's humanistic efforts in preserving the traditional architectural culture. The design of sensory aesthetics activity is advantageous to the innovative service scheme; it enables customers to personally and fully take part in the practical creation of aesthetics through various channels, such as food and drink, field visiting, and activities offered by the creative life enterprise. For instance, the heaven-and-earth tea table activity in The One Nanyuan offers creative tea and food inspired by the Oriental Beauty Tea from Hsinchu; in this way, the customers are not simply drinking tea, but also experiencing the aesthetics of the heaven-and-earth tea table in the park. Nevertheless, due to the abstract nature of the life aesthetics experience, the "crucial moment mapping" design of the touchpoints, which play a significant role in the customers' aesthetic experience, should be carefully examined and strengthened, for the purpose of enhancing the overall quality of the customers' aesthetic experience.

Second, in terms of the design of the entertainment experience in the studied cases, such an experience is neither a major nor an independently existing experience in the creative life industry. The design strategies of the entertainment experience mostly focus on making it part of the educational experience, for the purpose of educational entertainment. An effective combination of traditional or modern life culture and modern lifestyle can arouse joyfulness in the customers with the help of an entertaining design in the service touchpoints. The finding of the study corresponds to Pine and Gilmore's [1] theory that the experiential realms are not mutually exclusive. The entertainment experience in the creative life industry mostly focuses on experiential activities or field visiting, with traditional cake-making practice and interactive games being some of the examples. The finding of the study also corresponds to the essence of experience in the field of tourism and leisure, with the vineyard and food demonstration in wine tourism being an example [19].

Third, the enterprises share a similar view regarding the strategies of educational experience, in which the customers can be absorbed. These strategies, including the professional introduction of information, demonstration of cultural authenticity, and creative application in life, involve touchpoints such as field visiting, experiential activities, and shopping. A professional, amiable, and entertaining introduction given by the tour guide or staff also plays a crucial role in the educational experience of the creative life industry. In other words, the guiding staff plays the role of an actor and needs to possess performance ability [1–3]. The design of activities or courses that encourage the customers' learning also corresponds to the research findings in the field of tourism and leisure: examples include the wine tasting and making class in wine tourism, cooking and craft practice class [19], and gambling game learning [20].

Fourth, the idea of escapism refers to the customers' active participation in the transaction and intense immersion in their surroundings [1–3]. The study finds that the Gaeavilla Resort and The One Nanyuan, both of which highlight an lifestyle developing, place much emphasis on designing an escapist experience in which the customers are expected to be actively immersed in the thematic life experience in the space, through the rich design and diversified service facilities offered by the business operator. In this way, the customers get to experience a different time and space. This finding of the study corresponds to that of the study on wine tourism, both of which indicate that the customers can have a better understanding of the escapist aspect by taking part in a great number of activities offered at the end of the trip [19]. Furthermore, the study finds a strong link between escapism and aesthetic experience design in the creative life industry. The aesthetics of the creative life business's building design and the sense of seclusion of the building and its surroundings, along with the unique service facilities, can facilitate the customers' active participation and immersion in the spatial experience. As a result, much attention should be given to the consistent quality of different touchpoints, such as guest welcoming, field visiting, experiential activities, accommodation and dining; all of which may affect the customers' idea about immersion in an escapist experience.

6 Conclusion and Suggestions

The experience economy theory plays a significant role in tourism studies, most of which focus on examining consumer behavior from an experiential perspective, with the aim of assisting the tourism industry in enhancing its experiential value. This study explored the experiential design in the creative life industry from a business perspective; its findings can be of great value for the application of the experience economy to the creative life industry, in both an academic and professional sense. At the professional level, most creative life enterprises are medium-sized or small enterprises, and therefore have limited resources and a limited scale. The four enterprises investigated in the study all manifest an above-average operational performance, and the design strategies and components of experience proposed by the study can be of value for assessment of the experiential design of other creative life enterprises. At the academic level, in terms of the experiential design of the enterprises focusing on lifestyle developing, the study's finding that escapism and aesthetics can complement each other enriches Pine and Gilmore's [1–3] theory regarding the significance of experiential realms. Moreover, the study visualizes the experience design components by means of customer journey maps based on the service design theory; this embodies the effective combination of service design instruments and experience economy theory, as well as the service design principles, in order to provide user-centered, sequencing, co-creative, evidencing, and holistic services [14]. This study finds that the experiential realms at different touchpoints in the service process complement one another, and recommends that creative life enterprises carefully evaluate the association among different experiential realms at different service touchpoints in order to create greater experiential value by using limited resources.

The study's findings can be of value to the practical and theoretical development of experiential design in the creative life industry. Nevertheless, the study has not extended its analysis to investigating the customers' opinions on the experience. Thus, it is suggested that future studies examine customers' perception of the experiential design of the creative life enterprises. In addition, the study finds a gap in the significance of the four experiential design components in the creative life industry, and suggests that future studies assess the experience offered by the creative life enterprises.

Acknowledgments. The authors gratefully acknowledge the support for this research provided by the Ministry of Science and Technology, Taiwan, under Grants MOST 109-2221-E-259-007. The authors also wish to thank those who contributed to the research.

References

1. Pine II, B.J., Gilmore, J.H.: Welcome to the experience economy. Harvard Bus. Rev. **76**, 97–105 (1998)
2. Pine II, B.J., Gilmore, J.H.: The Experience Economy: Work is Theatre & Every Business a Stage. Harvard Business School Press, Boston (1999)
3. Pine II, B.J., Gilmore, J.H.: The experience economy: Competing for customer time, attention, and money. Harvard Business Review Press, Boston, MA (2019)
4. Chang, S.-H., Lin, R.: A service design framework for brand experience in the creative life industry – a case study of the millennium gaea resort Hualien in Taiwan. In: Rau, Pei-Luen Patrick. (ed.) HCII 2020. LNCS, vol. 12192, pp. 3–15. Springer, Cham (2020). https://doi.org/10.1007/978-3-030-49788-0_1
5. Oh, H., Fiore, A.M., Jeoung, M.: Measuring experience economy concepts: tourism applications. J. Travel Res. **46**(2), 119–132 (2007)
6. Hosany, S., Witham, M.: (2010) Dimensions of cruisers' experiences, satisfaction, and intention to recommend. J. Travel Res. **49**(3), 351–364 (2010)
7. Park, M., Oh, H., Park, J.: Measuring the experience economy of film festival participants. Int. J. Tour. Sci. **10**(2), 35–54 (2010)
8. Lee, J.S., Lee, C.K., Choi, Y.J.: Examining the role of emotional and functional values in festival evaluation. J. Travel Res. **50**, 685–696 (2011)
9. Mehmetoglu, M., Engen, M.: Pine and Gilmore's concept of experience economy and its dimensions: an empirical examination in tourism. J. Qual. Assur. Hosp. Tour. **12**(4), 237–255 (2011)
10. Quadri-Felitti, D.L., Fiore, A.M.: Destination loyalty: effects of wine tourists' experiences, memories, and satisfaction on intentions. Tour. Hosp. Res. **13**(1), 47–62 (2013)
11. Chang, S.H., Lin, R.: Building a total customer experience model: applications for the travel experiences in Taiwan's creative life industry. J. Travel Tour. Mark. **32**(4), 438–453 (2015)
12. Song, H.J., Lee, C.-K., Park, J.A., Hwang, Y.H., Reisinger, Y.: The influence of tourist experience on perceived value and satisfaction with temple stays: the experience economy theory. J. Travel Tour. Mark. **32**(4), 401–415 (2015)
13. Kastenholz, E., Carneiro, M.J., Marques, C.P., Loureiro, S.M.C.: The dimensions of rural tourism experience: impacts on arousal, memory, and satisfaction. J. Travel Tour. Mark. **35**(2), 189–201 (2018)
14. Stickdorn, M., Schneider, J.: This is Service Design Thinking: Basics, Tools, Cases. John Wiley & Sons, New York (2012)
15. Stickdorn, M., Frischhut, B.: Service Design and Tourism: Case Studies of Applied Research Projects on Mobile Ethnography for Tourism Destinations. Books on Demand GmbH, Norderstedt (2012)

16. Martins, M.: Gastronomic tourism and the creative economy. J. Tour. Herit. Serv. Mark. 2(2), 33–37 (2016)
17. Carvalho, R., Costa, C., Ferreira, A.: Review of the theoretical underpinnings in the creative tourism research field. Tour. Manag. Stud. 15(SI), 11–22 (2019)
18. OECD: Tourism and the Creative Economy, OECD Studies on Tourism. OECD, Paris (2014)
19. Quadri-Felitti, D., Fiore, A.M.: Experience economy constructs as a framework for understanding wine tourism. J. Vacat. Mark. 18(1), 3–15 (2012)
20. Shim, C., Oh, E.J., Jeong, C.: A qualitative analysis of South Korean casino experiences: a perspective on the experience economy. Tour. Hosp. Res. 17(4), 358–371 (2017)
21. Mager, B.: Service design as an emerging field. In: Miettinen, S., Koivisto, M. (eds.) Designing Services with Innovative Methods, pp. 28–42. Taik Publications, Helsinki (2009)
22. Ostrom, A.L., et al.: Moving forward and making a difference: research priorities for the science of service. J. Serv. Res. 13(1), 4–36 (2010)
23. Cook, L.S., Bowen, D.E., Chase, R.B., Dasu, S., Stewart, D.M., Tansik, D.A.: Human issues in service design. J. Oper. Manag. 20(2), 159–174 (2002)
24. Lee, G., Tussyadiah, I.P., Zach, F.: A visitor-focused assessment of new product launch: the case of Quilt Gardens Tour[SM] in Northern Indiana's Amish Country. J. Travel Tour. Mark. 27(7), 723–735 (2010)
25. Trischler, J., Zehrer, A.: Service design: Suggesting a qualitative multi-step approach for analyzing and examining theme park experiences. J. Vacat. Mark. 18(1), 57–71 (2012)
26. Shaw, C., Ivens, J.: Building Great Customer Experiences. Palgrave Macmillan, London (2002)
27. Yin, R.K.: Case Study Research: Design and Methods, 3rd edn. Sage, London (2003)
28. Benbasat, I., Goldstein, D.K., Mead, M.: The case research strategy in studies of information systems. MIS Q. 11(3), 369–386 (1987)
29. Patton, M.Q.: Qualitative Evaluation and Research Methods. Sage, London (1990)
30. Kensbock, S., Jennings, G.: Pursuing: A grounded theory of tourism entrepreneurs' understanding and praxis of sustainable tourism. Asia Pac. J. Tour. Res. 16(5), 489–504 (2011)
31. Dey, I.: Qualitative Data Analysis: A User-friendly Guide for Social Scientists. Routledge, London (1993)
32. Elo, S., Kyngäs, H.: The qualitative content analysis process. J. Adv. Nurs. 62(1), 107–115 (2008)
33. Zhang, Y., Wildemuth, B.M.: Qualitative analysis of content. In: Wildemuth, B. (ed.) Applications of Social Research Methods to Questions in Information and Library Science, pp. 308–319. Libraries Unlimited, Westport (2009)

ISDT Case Study of Cultivation of Employees' Creativity in Cultural and Creative Industries

Hao Chen[1(✉)], Chao Liu[1(✉)], Yu-Chao Liang[2(✉)], Rungtai Lin[3(✉)], and Wen-Ko Chiou[2(✉)]

[1] Graduate Institute of Business and Management, Chang Gung University, Taoyuan City, Taiwan
[2] Department of Industrial Design, Chang Gung University, Taoyuan City, Taiwan
wkchiu@mail.cgu.edu.tw
[3] Graduate School of Creative Industry Design, National Taiwan University of Arts, New Taipei City, Taiwan
rtlin@mail.ntua.edu.tw

Abstract. Objective: This study will design and develop an APP prototype with the theme of transcendental meditation to help cultivate and enhance the creativity of employees in the cultural and creative industry. Background: The work of employees in the cultural and creative industry involves the creation of new ideas and contents. These people are creative and value originality at work, expression of personal will, and a thirst for continuous innovation. Transcendental meditation is a simple, natural and relaxing technique that enables the mind to experience higher levels of thought processes. As a new concept, method and strategy framework, ISDT (I-Sustainability Design Thinking) conforms to the demand of cultivating innovative talents in the current world. Methods: This study takes the design and development of a mobile application platform as a case study, and this platform is dedicated to using transcendental meditation training methods to enhance the creativity of creative industry employees. This case study adopts the form of a workshop, recruiting 28 creative design students to discuss the core issues and concepts of the product under the guidance of ISDT theory, and complete the development of the product prototype. Results: First, analyze the driving factors in the fields of society economy and technology from a macro perspective, and get the potential opportunity gap. Then analyze the user's scenarios from a micro perspective, so as to get the key themes. Finally, a prototype concept of the product is developed and evaluated. Conclusions: ISDT description can effectively bridge the differences in cross-domain communication, provide a common orientation, user-centered, and comprehensive consideration of all stakeholders to establish a common goal of sustainable development.

Keywords: I-sustainability design thinking · Transcendental meditation · Creativity

© Springer Nature Switzerland AG 2021
P.-L. P. Rau (Ed.): HCII 2021, LNCS 12772, pp. 18–30, 2021.
https://doi.org/10.1007/978-3-030-77077-8_2

1   Introduction

With the development of science and technology, the world will soon enter the era of Artificial Intelligence Internet of Things (AIoT). AIoT will replace many repetitive routine tasks. Human beings should re-examine how AIoT affects our work and life in order to achieve win-win cooperation and sustainable development between humans and computers (Wu et al. 2019). Human beings are emotional, empathetic, compassionate, and creative in a way that AIoT is unable to do that. AIoT will replace humans to undertake repetitive labor, and at the same time humans can also use AIoT to make it a good tool to express emotions and realize creativity. The vigorous development of our cultural and entertainment creative industry is inseparable from the rapid progress of science and technology behind it. Therefore, by then, mankind will rely on AIoT to become more creative (Mitchell 2019). With a unique mind and spirit, human beings will do work that only humans are good at, and will win with creativity and compassion. The arrival of the AIoT era will liberate humans from routine work, and its arrival will also remind humans why they are humans (Yigitcanlar and Cugurullo 2020).

However, before the arrival of the AIOT era, are human beings ready for this? Mankind urgently needs a set of systematic sustainable development theories and methods to help people improve their creativity and spirituality. The current focus of creative industry is to promote educational innovation and cultivate creative employees. The work of employees in the cultural and creative industry involves the creation of new ideas and contents. These people are creative and value originality at work, expression of personal will, and a thirst for continuous innovation. If a company wants to survive in the market competition, it must constantly surpass its previous achievements. It also needs employees to come up with new ideas and find more efficient, economical and effective ways of working, which is by no means easy. As employees struggle to find creative solutions, so does stress. In addition to reducing the anxiety and other negative emotions of the creative class, it is more important to study whether it can improve their creativity from the perspective of positive psychological enhancement. Transcendental meditation is a simple, natural and relaxing technique that enables the mind to experience higher levels of thought processes, and the content and methods of transcendental meditation are easy to understand and operate, which are consistent with the working characteristics of creative industries.Therefore, we put forward the theory of I-Sustainability Design Thinking (ISDT), and based on this theory, we developed a prototype of mobile application integrating Transcendental Meditation training methods so as to enhance the creativity of creative industry employees.

1.1   I-Sustainability Design Thinking

The concept of ISDT is put forward on the basis of sustainable design, transition design, and design thinking theory, combines and the philosophy of I Ching from the East, which together constitute the theoretical framework of ISDT.

The Book of Changes (I Ching) is the crystallization of ancient philosophy and human wisdom from the East. By observing the natural phenomena such as the sun, the moon and the stars, the change of the four seasons, and the growth of all things, as well as social phenomena such as rise and fall, success or failure, sorrow and joy, separation and union, the ancients summed up the basic principles and human nature laws behind these phenomena, in order to find the way of harmonious coexistence between human beings and nature, human beings and society (Yuduo et al. 2011).

Design thinking is a powerful approach to new product development that begins with understanding unmet customer needs. It's a human-centered design process that approaches problem-solving with understanding the user needs. Design thinking encompasses concept development, applied creativity, prototyping, and experimentation. When design thinking approaches are applied to business, the success rate for innovation has been seen to improve substantially (Brown 2008).

Transition design is a kind of sustainable design will require new design approaches informed by different value sets and knowledge. Transition calls for a commitment to work iteratively, at multiple levels of scale, over longer horizons of time, and view a single design or solution as a single step in a longer transition toward a future-based vision (Irwin 2018). Transition design is also a process and methodology for making connections. Transition designers have the skill, foresight, and ability to connect different types of solutions (service design or social innovation solutions) together for greater leverage (solutions' ability to co-evolve) and impact because they are connected to, and guided by, a longer-term objective or vision. This approach is highly transdisciplinary, collaborative, and rooted in an understanding of how change within complex systems manifests. Visions of a sustainable future enlarge the problem frame to include social and environmental concerns and compel designers to design within long horizons of time (Irwin 2015). The difference and innovation between transition design and previous sustainable design lies in: (a) its deep grounding in future-oriented visions; (b) its transdisciplinary imperative; (c) its understanding of how to initiate and direct change within social and natural systems; and (d) its emphasis on the temporality of solutions. Transition design is conceived as a new area of design methodology, practice, and research. Transition visions stimulate new thinking and cause designers to look for knowledge in new places that, in turn, leads to shifts in their mindset and posture. All of these will give rise to new ways of designing (Irwin et al. 2015).

1.2   Transcendental Meditation and Creativity

Transcendental meditation is a form of meditation, a yoga technique developed by the Maharishi Mahesh Yogi in India. The practice involves sitting quietly, closing your eyes, and silently reciting "words" to remove distractions. Transylvania meditation is believed to be a form of exercise that increases energy, reduces stress levels, and benefits both the body and the mind (Domino 1977). Physically, transcendental meditation is different from waking, sleeping, dreaming, and hypnotic states. As a result, tension levels decrease, heart rate slows, blood pressure drops, oxygen consumption decreases, and alpha waves in the electroencephalogram increase (Venditti et al. 2015). Transcendence refers to the complete cessation of human thinking activities and the existence of only clear pure consciousness, which is called "fourth consciousness" or "pure consciousness" in religious psychology. In the "pure consciousness", no thought or matter exists, and the human body feels in a state beyond time and space. Religious psychology calls this state "the state of emptiness" or "the state of ego" (Wallace 1970). Maharish's "transcendental meditation" is to make people forget themselves. This is not a loss of memory, but a return of consciousness to the depths of the mind, to experience a feeling of complete absence of thought activity (i.e. pure consciousness). When experiencing pure consciousness, the breath becomes soft, the mind and body enter a deep rest, the whole body is completely relaxed, but the inner consciousness is still awake (Mahone et al. 2018). Transcendental meditation is a simple, natural and relaxed technology, which enables the mind to experience a higher level of thinking process and is consistent with the creative labor characteristics of the creative class. Besides, the practice content and method of Transcendental meditation are easy to understand and operate, which are in line with the creative labor characteristics of the creative class (Travis et al. 2018).

Creativity, refers to insight, remote association, or an individual's ability to produce novel, strange and useful ideas or products. It is generally accepted that creativity refers to the ability to produce creative products that are novel (e.g., original, unexpected) and appropriate (e.g., valuable, appropriate to the requirements of the relevant task) (Lebuda et al. 2016). Creativity is indispensable to the development of human civilization and plays a vital role in the field of human cultural life. Creativity is responsible for so many new inventions and discoveries, from alternating current theory and penicillin to post notes, ice cream cones and nylon prongs. So in today's innovation-encouraging economy, engineers, economists and government officials are eager to find ways to boost creativity (Zhang et al. 2020). In the early 17th century, with the prevalence of meditation in the Western world, more and more people began to study the effects of meditation in physiological and behavioral aspects, including the impact of meditation on human creativity. The importance of creativity means that we should study how to enhance its affective and cognitive processes. Mindfulness, emotion and creativity are related (Csikszentmihalyi et al. 2018). A wide body of research has indeed shown that meditation training enhances creative thinking and creative performance as well as improves the ability to solve insight problems and facilitates creative elaboration (Yang et al. 2019). Experienced meditators also outperform others in verbal fluency and are better at finding novel solutions to a given problem (Henriksen et al. 2020). Importantly, meditation has a positive effect on creativity regardless of the length of practice (Henriksen et al. 2020), which means that even short meditation can effectively stimulate creative abilities (Ding et al. 2014).

2 The ISDT Process

The ISDT Process uses the cooperative mandala painting based on the philosophy of I Ching as the thinking guiding program, and combines the double-diamond model (Fig. 1) procedure of the design thinking, and has gone through two processes of convergence and divergence of thinking. First, analyze the driving factors in the fields of society economy and technology (S.E.T.) from a macro perspective, and get the potential opportunity gap (POG). Then analyze the user's scenarios from a micro perspective, so as to get the key themes to be solved and the urgent functions to be satisfied. Finally, a prototype of the product is developed and evaluated.

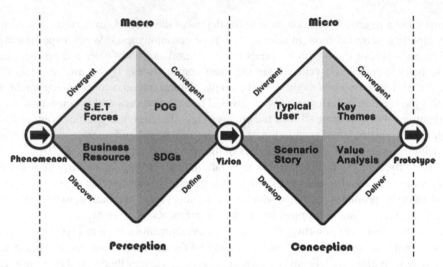

Fig. 1. ISDT double-diamond model

3   Methods

3.1   Case Study

This study takes the design and development of a mobile application platform as a case study, and this platform is dedicated to using transcendental meditation training methods to enhance the creativity of creative industry employees. This case study adopts the form of a workshop, recruiting 28 creative design students to discuss the core issues and concepts of the product under the guidance of ISDT theory, and complete the development of the product prototype.

3.2   ISDT Workshop Process

Cooperative Mandala Coloring
Cooperative mandala coloring (Fig. 2) as a kind of team work, was completed by several participants together under the guidance of the thoughts of the I Ching. Its process is full of labor division and cooperation, change and adaptation, personality publicity and overall harmony of unity (Liu et al. 2019; Liu et al. 2020).

Macro Factors Analysis
Firstly, participants can diverge their thinking and ideas through brainstorming, and find as many macroscopic influences and driving factors as possible from the perspectives of S.E.T. respectively (Cagan et al. 2002). Write these factors on yellow sticky notes and group them by topic similarity on a flat surface. Then, the convergence analysis of these factors was carried out to find the top10 driving factors, and write them down on pink sticky notes (Fig. 3).

Fig. 2. Cooperative mandala coloring

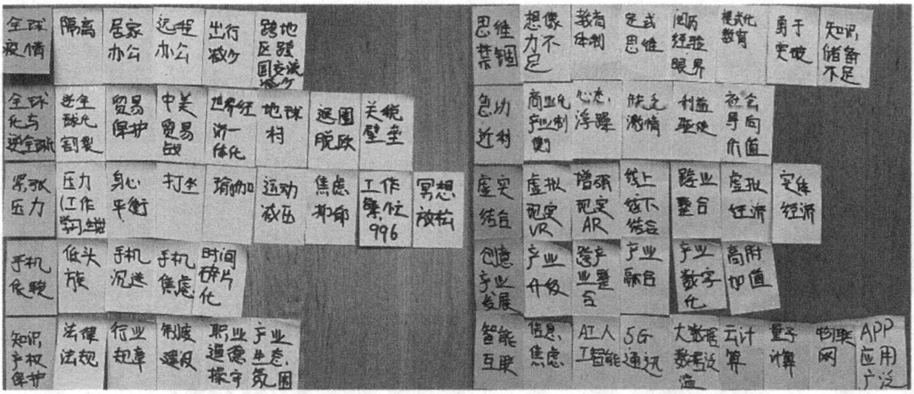

Fig. 3. Macro S.E.T. top10 forces

By following similar divergent and convergent thinking steps described above, the main business sources are obtained (Fig. 4).

According to the 17 sustainable development goals (SDGs) formulated by the United Nations, the relevant SDGs of this case study are identified (Fig. 5).

Fig. 4. Business resources

Fig. 5. SDGs of United Nations and goals of this case study

Micro Factors Analysis

According to the product opportunity gap generated by the above macro factor analysis, the typical user of the product and the usage scenarios story of the typical user (Fig. 6) are set from the micro perspective through divergent thinking, and the demand conditions and value proposition of the product are described in each usage scenario (Fig. 7).

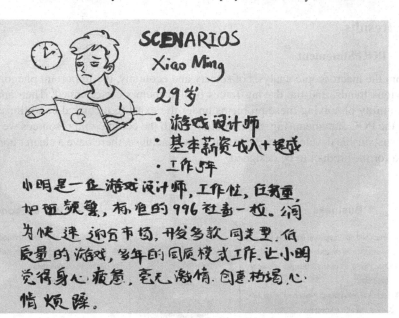

Fig. 6. Typical user settings for the product

Fig. 7. Usage scenarios story

4   Results

4.1   POG Statement

From the macroscopic analysis of society and economy, the important phenomena, the obvious trends, and the driving forces behind them were obtained. Then analyze the possibility of solving these problems under the existing technical conditions, so as to get the POG statement (Fig. 8). Combining with the commercial resources we have and the sustainable development goals that want to achieve, there have a clearer concept and idea for the product to be designed.

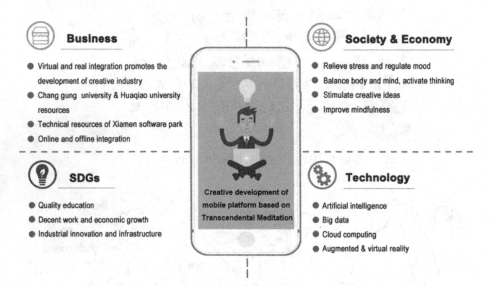

Fig. 8.   Product ideas and POG statement

4.2   Top10 Key Themes

According to the results of the micro scenario analysis, combined with the S.E.T. top10 driving forces of the macro analysis, Top10 key themes to be solved by the product were finally obtained (Table 1).

4.3   Value Analysis

Through value analysis, we further clearly define what the designed product is, what main functions it has, what needs it meets, and what value propositions are put forward (Table 2).

4.4   Business Model

Based on all the above, the business model canvas of the product is proposed to form the prototype concept of the product (Table 3).

Table 1. Top10 key themes

High working pressure	Long working hours	Heavy task	Frequent overtime	Squeezing into leisure time	Difficulty in maintaining balance
Negative emotions are hard to relieve	Negative emotions at work	Negative emotions in life	Lack of relief to vent emotions	Anxiety and depression	
Hard to break out stereotype	Insufficient knowledge reserve	Routine work	Solidification of thinking mode	Lack of imagination	Inspiration dried up
Used to mobile phones	Time fragmentation	Phubber	Information anxiety	Mobile app is widely used	
Money worship	Impetuous mentality	Lack of creative passion	Commercial thinking	Profit-driven	
Improve mindfulness	Balance body and mind	Relieve pressure	Activate thinking	Stimulate creativity	Regulating emotion
Promote the development of creative industries	Industrial integration	Industrial upgrading	Industrial digitalization	Cross-industry integration	Increasing the added value of industry
Innovation is the most important in AI era	Break through routine work	Value of innovation			
Intelligent connectivity enriches information	Intelligent filtering of material	Information analysis	Information integration	Cloud database	
Combine virtual and real to promote creativity	Virtual reality	Augmented reality	Online and offline integration		

Table 2. Value proposition

Creative development platform based on transcendental meditation
Transcendental meditation guidance platform
Mindfulness promotion platform
Body and mind balance emotional regulation platform
Creative development platform
Intelligent information material sharing platform
Online and offline intelligent interconnection platform
Virtual and real integration of inspiration platform

Table 3. Business model canvas

Key partners	Key activities	Value proposition	Customer relationship	Customer segments
• Chang Gung University • Huaqiao University • Xiamen Software Park • Transcendental Meditation Center • Mindfulness training institutions • Interconnection of information materials	• Transcendental meditation training • Mindfulness training • Emotion regulation • Stimulate inspiration and creativity • Material information sharing	• Transcendental meditation guidance platform Mindfulness promotion platform • Body and mind balance emotional regulation platform • Creative development platform • Intelligent information material sharing platform • Online and offline intelligent interconnection platform • Virtual and real integration of inspiration platform	• Customer problem information feedback system • Customer maintenance management system	• Practitioners of cultural and creative industries • Other personnel engaged in innovation and creativity related work
	Key resources • Chang Gung University • Huaqiao University • Xiamen Software Park • Transcendental Meditation Center • Mindfulness training institutions		**Channels** • App store platform promotion • WeChat, Weibo, Facebook, Twitter and other social platforms promotion • TikTok and other short video platform promotion • Professional Community Promotion • Online and offline integration and promotion	

Cost structure	Revenue stream
• Mobile application development • Product iterative upgrade and maintenance • Intelligent platform system construction • Customer maintenance management system construction • Database construction • Promotion and marketing cost • Cost of online and offline activities	• Revenue from fee-paying members • Advertising revenue • Revenue from sales of information materials • Training benefits

5 Discussion

With the ISDT design method, workshop members can freely express their ideas and concepts, effectively integrate different viewpoints, and start from different perspectives. For example, S.E.T forces analysis, combined with the heterogeneous characteristics of cross-field teams, can acquire a large number of multi-oriented concepts in a short period of time and integrate them into a common goal (Cagan et al. 2002). Therefore, ISDT can effectively connect different professional fields and achieve communication and thinking patterns through users' observation and sharing of life experience. Because the personnel, features and objects of ISDT are based on real life, so everyone has the opportunity to touch, see, or even experience it personally. Therefore, it is easy to resonate between the team and remove the standard of each field in a short time. Doctrine, so that engineering is no longer just a rigid technical theory; design is no longer an ethereal imagination (Nardi 1992).

The narration of scenario stories can help the team establish a set of common beliefs, goals and operating principles, and can balance the relationship between team members. The scenario story method is to explore the idea of the product from the user's point of view through an imaginary story in the process of product design and development. Through the use of scenario simulation, to explore and analyze the interaction between people and the product relationship (Kishita et al. 2020). Therefore, the user is the common focus and goal in a cross-domain team, and the operating process of the scenario story method is actually user-centric. In the stage of concept development, team members do not need to infiltrate a lot of professional knowledge, but only need to share and discuss their personal life and experiences during the discussion process (Park et al. 2020). Since these things are derived from everyone's life and their own experience, it is easy to resonate among the teams, and in a short period of time to remove the standardize in each field and most of the problems caused by the bias in a certain field, which would otherwise reduce the team, making the factors that would have reduced the team's creativity become factors that improve the team's creativity (Uwasu et al. 2020).

6 Conclusion

In summary, the ISDT description can effectively bridge the differences in cross-domain communication, provide a common orientation, user-centered, and comprehensive consideration of all stakeholders to establish a common goal of sustainable development. The results of the case study found that ISDT can strengthen the user-oriented concept of the team, increase the team creativity, and effectively improve the maturity and clarity of the product concept. ISDT has a positive impact on communication, design learning, and consensus and thinking among team members in cross-field collaborative design, thereby enhancing team innovation and creativity and strengthening user-oriented conceptual and sustainable development goals.

References

Brown, T.: Design thinking. Harvard Bus. Rev. **86**(6), 84 (2008)

Cagan, J., Cagan, J.M., Vogel, C.M.: Creating Breakthrough Products: Innovation from Product Planning to Program Approval. Ft Press, Upper Saddle River (2002)

Csikszentmihalyi, M., Montijo, M.N., Mouton, A.R.: Flow theory: optimizing elite performance in the creative realm. In: Pfeiffer, S.I., Shaunessy-Dedrick, E., Foley-Nicpon, M. (eds.) APA handbook of giftedness and talent, pp. 215–229. American Psychological Association, Washington, DC (2018)

Ding, X., Tang, Y.-Y., Tang, R., Posner, M.I.: Improving creativity performance by short-term meditation. Behav. Brain Func. **10**(1), 1–8 (2014)

Domino, G.: Transcendental meditation and creativity: an empirical investigation. J. Appl. Psychol. **62**(3), 358 (1977)

Henriksen, D., Richardson, C., Shack, K.: Mindfulness and creativity: implications for thinking and learning. Thinking Skills Creativity **37**, 100689 (2020)

Irwin, T.: Transition design: a proposal for a new area of design practice, study, and research. Des. Cult. **7**(2), 229–246 (2015)

Irwin, T., Tonkinwise, C., Kossoff, G.: Transition design: an educational framework for advancing the study and design of sustainable transitions. Cuadernos del Centro de Estudios en Diseño y Comunicación N°105 **23**, 31–65 (2015)

Kishita, Y., Mizuno, Y., Fukushige, S., Umeda, Y.: Scenario structuring methodology for computer-aided scenario design: An application to envisioning sustainable futures. Technol. Forecast. Social Change **160**, 120207 (2020)

Lebuda, I., Zabelina, D.L., Karwowski, M.: Mind full of ideas: a meta-analysis of the mindfulness–creativity link. Pers. Individ. Differ. **93**, 22–26 (2016)

Liu, C., Chen, H., Chiou, Wen-Ko., Lin, R.: Effects of mandala coloring on mindfulness, spirituality, and subjective well-being. In: Rau, Pei-Luen Patrick. (ed.) Cross-Cultural Design. Methods, Tools and User Experience: 11th International Conference, CCD 2019, Held as Part of the 21st HCI International Conference, HCII 2019, Orlando, FL, USA, July 26–31, 2019, Proceedings, Part I, pp. 543–554. Springer International Publishing, Cham (2019). https://doi.org/10.1007/978-3-030-22577-3_39

Liu, C., Chen, H., Liu, C.-Y., Lin, R.-T., Chiou, W.-K.: Cooperative and individual mandala drawing have different effects on mindfulness, spirituality, and subjective well-being. Front. Psychol. **11**, 2629 (2020)

Mahone, M.C., Travis, F., Gevirtz, R., Hubbard, D.: fMRI during transcendental meditation practice. Brain Cogn. **123**, 30–33 (2018)

Mitchell, M.: Artificial Intelligence: A Guide for Thinking humans. Penguin, London (2019)

Nardi, B.A.: The use of scenarios in design. ACM SIGCHI Bull. **24**(4), 13–14 (1992)

Park, K.-Y., Park, H.-K., Hwang, H.-S., Yoo, S.-H., Ryu, J.-S., Kim, J.-H.: Improved detection of patient centeredness in objective structured clinical examinations through authentic scenario design. Patient Educ. Counsel. (2020)

Travis, F., et al.: Effect of meditation on psychological distress and brain functioning: a randomized controlled study. Brain Cogn. **125**, 100–105 (2018)

Uwasu, M., Kishita, Y., Hara, K., Nomaguchi, Y.: Citizen-participatory scenario design methodology with future design approach: a case study of visioning of a low-carbon society in Suita city, Japan. Sustainability **12**(11), 4746 (2020)

Venditti, S., Verdone, L., Pesce, C., Tocci, N., Caserta, M., Ben-Soussan, T.: Creating well-being: increased creativity and proNGF decrease following Quadrato Motor Training. BioMed Res. Int. **2015**, 1–13 (2015)

Wallace, R.K.: Physiological effects of transcendental meditation. Science **167**(3926), 1751–1754 (1970)

Wu, Y.C., Wu, Y.J., Wu, S.M.: An outlook of a future smart city in Taiwan from post–Internet of things to artificial intelligence Internet of things. In: Smart Cities: Issues and Challenges, pp. 263–282, Elsevier (2019)

Yang, X., Cheng, P.-Y., Lin, L., Huang, Y.M., Ren, Y.: Can an integrated system of electroencephalography and virtual reality further the understanding of relationships between attention, meditation, flow state, and creativity? J. Educ. Comput. Res. **57**(4), 846–876 (2019)

Yigitcanlar, T., Cugurullo, F.: The sustainability of artificial intelligence: an urbanistic viewpoint from the lens of smart and sustainable cities. Sustainability **12**(20), 8548 (2020)

Yuduo, L., Yi, Q., Donghua, W., Yao, L.: Implications of I Ching on innovation management. Chin. Manag. Stud. **5**, 394–402 (2011)

Zhang, W., Sjoerds, Z., Hommel, B.: Metacontrol of human creativity: the neurocognitive mechanisms of convergent and divergent thinking. Neuroimage **210**, 116572 (2020)

The Museum of Dreams: Exploring a "Dreaming" Visual Experience via Machine Vision and Visual Synthesis

Judy Zixin Li[1]([⊠]) and Aven Le Zhou[2]

[1] New York University, New York City, NY, USA
[2] Xi'an Jiaotong - Liverpool University, Suzhou, People's Republic of China
`le.zhou@xjtlu.edu.cn`

Abstract. In this paper, we will be introducing an art installation titled "The Museum of Dreams,"—which is an interactive system incorporating AI and machine learning techniques to create a "dreaming" experience for the participant and the audience. It's a screen-based installation connected to a webcam placed on top of the screen and facing towards the participants. When the participants approach the installation, the system will read their movement and then translate the data, synchronize and generate images with varying shapes with vivid colors and smooth gradients in real-time.

Keywords: Interactive installation · Machine vision · Visual synthesis

1 Background

With the development of technology in recent years, AI has not only played roles increasing the efficiency of getting tasks done and performing tasks that were used to be done by humans. Meanwhile, it has also become a tool that is used by artists to produce artworks. For example, the machine learning model Deep Dream [1] was originally created by computer scientists to learn more about the interpretation of neural networks. The model allows humans to understand what the neural networks are seeing. Deep Dream is able to process input images, and by enhancing and over-interpreting the images, the images are then transformed to have a dream-like and abstract appearance. But, Deep Dream is used by scientists and engineers; the over-interpreted images it has created lead to a unique aesthetic. Soon Deep Dream is widely accepted and used by artists and designers to create artworks (Fig. 1).

A dream is an intriguing subject that differs from reality. We see, feel, and explore our bodies and our surroundings magically in dreams. However, when we wake up, we often do not remember. Nor can we be in reality and dreaming at the same time. What if we can see ourselves from a mirror in reality with a dream-like simulation or synchronization? How will our bodies be presented differently? What forms can our bodies be taken to? With machine learning capability, machines can now see (machine vision) and generate content (visual synthesis). How will the machines see and imagine our presents, can they help to translate and represent our body and movements into dreams and help us explore dreams in reality or fuse our dreams and the reality?

P.-L. P. Rau (Ed.): HCII 2021, LNCS 12772, pp. 31–39, 2021.
https://doi.org/10.1007/978-3-030-77077-8_3

Fig. 1. Selected generated results (with post-processing by Adaptive Style Transfer)

In this paper, we will be introducing an interactive art installation titled "The Museum of Dreams,"—which is an interactive system incorporating AI and machine learning techniques to create a "dreaming" experience for the participant and the audience. It's a screen-based installation connected to a webcam placed on top of the screen and facing towards the participants. When the participants approach the installation, the system will read their movement and then translate the data, synchronize and generate images with varying shapes with vivid colors and smooth gradients in real-time (Fig. 2).

Fig. 2. Selected generated results

2   Introduction

Dreams differ from yet probably exist parallel with reality, and we sense and explore ourselves and the world in another dimension in dreams. But we cannot be present in both reality and the dream simultaneously. However, in our proposed installation, participants will see themselves in the other dimension - the dreams as they see in the mirror and screen yet physically present in reality. What will the two parallel worlds lead us to? In the proposed system, dreams are explored with the help of machine learning techniques - a machine vision neural network named Posenet [2], as well as our customized algorithm, and another machine learning technology - a visual synthesis neural network named Adaptive Style Transfer [3], via open-source software Processing [4] and the creative Machine Learning platform - RunwayML [5]. Posenet takes image input to track the user's body movements and computes the result in real-time; and with our customized algorithms, we translate these movements to colorful graphics consisting of shapes and later apply adaptive style transfer to further synchronize the generated images into different pre-trained painting styles and so to make the final output more vivid art pieces.

The system is set up with a computer connected to a webcam and a screen. The webcam is placed on top of the screen and facing towards the participant. As the viewer approaches the screen, the webcam will send life data to the program. Posenet will then pick up the movement of the user's body parts. The movement of the user will then be translated into life images on the screen. When viewers move, they can see their bodies in the vision of an algorithm moving in synchronization. The outcome that the system generates are images of varying shapes with vivid colors and smooth gradients which change in real-time as the user moves. These images are then put together as a collection (Fig. 3).

Fig. 3. Selected generated results

3 System Overview

The proposed system contains three parts, the computer vision part for tracking the real-time human position and body movements; the customized algorithm for the visual content generation; and visual synthesis for style translation. The first part is a computer vision software and hardware system - the webcam and the Posenet algorithm which is capable of capturing the live video, and the Posenet algorithm can estimate the position of key body parts and sends the data of the position to our customized algorithm. The customized algorithm then incorporates this data by making the size of visual elements on the screen change in relation to the value of the key body parts coordinate of the viewer to generate live images in real-time with the viewer's movement. Finally, selected image outcomes are fed through Adaptive Style Transfer for further effects (Fig. 4).

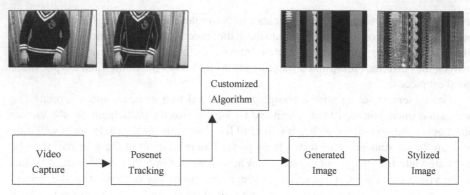

Fig. 4. System design

3.1 Posenet

Posenet is a machine learning model that can be used to estimate the pose of humans in real-time. To use Posenet, an image or a video is required, and we use a webcam with a live feed video. When Posenet detects a person's body, it will try to estimate where the key body parts of the body. And the algorithm will detect the pose and denote the joints as key points. These key points are each assigned a number that can be accessed later. For example, the nose is assigned "0" as the index number, the left eye is assigned "1" and the right eye is assigned "2". Currently, Posenet can detect 17 key points ranging from facial features such as nose to ankles and wrists. There is also a "pose confidence score", which ranges from 0 to 1, giving information on how confident Posenet is in estimating a pose. In the proposed system, we used a webcam to provide the live video feed to Posenet, and we have used several key points such as the nose and the eyes. Posenet will detect how the position of these key points changes over time.

3.2 The Customized Algorithm

The Customized Algorithm is one of the core generative functions of this system. To create the graphics, we coded a variety of shapes that filled sections of the screen. These shapes are then filled with gradient colors. To make the system interactive, we wanted to make the shapes on the screen respond to the viewer's movement. To do this we used the data from Posenet. The algorithm takes in a series of data from Posenet. This data is the numeric value of the key body points, which are coordinates on the viewer's body. The numeric value of the key points' coordinates will change as the viewer moves his/her body. These values are then used to control the graphic on the screen. These were achieved by assigning these values as the width of specific shapes that make up the graphic.

3.3 Adaptive Style Transfer

Adaptive Style Transfer is also a machine learning model and is quite different from Posenet. This model takes in an image as the input. Then it will apply a style to the input image, transforming the image into a new one. The style that this model can apply to the input image depends on which samples of artwork the model has been trained on. For example, the model can be trained on the artworks of the Monet, therefore producing output images in Monet's impressionist style. Style transfers are examples of generative adversarial networks (GAN) [6], where two neural networks are continually competing to produce the final output. In our system, after the program produced the images of the user's body movements, some of these images were selected and processed by Adaptive Style Transfer. The Adaptive Style Transfer then applied the styles of artists onto these images. The outcomes are enhanced images with oil paint texture and brush strokes.

4 System Implementation

To create this system, the machine learning library Posenet and Adaptive style transfer are used through the RunwayML platform and the software Processing, which is used for the major creative programming of the system.

4.1 Runway ML

Runway is a software and platform that provides its users access to various machine learning models such as StyleGAN [7] and Deep Dream. In this system, we have used Runway to access machine learning models such as Posenet and Adaptive Style Transfer.

To gain access to Posenet on Runway, we first searched for the model on the search bar. After finding the model, we created a new work-space for the model on Runway. The model will then ask for an input, which the user can select; for our system, we selected the camera as the input. Then, by pressing the "Run" button, the model can be run, and the output can be previewed on the Runway interface. To use the model in our algorithm, the Runway library is imported to Processing while making sure the Posenet model is running on Runway.

The work flow using Adaptive Style Transfer is similar. After finding the Adaptive Style Transfer model, we created a new work-space for it. For the input, we selected results from our system's output. Then we selected the specific artists' style that we want the Adaptive Style Transfer to transform the image into. There are several options for the artist, such as Gauguin, Reorich and Cezanne. After the input has been processed, it will show on the output section of the Runway interface. Finally, the output is exported to image files.

4.2 Processing

For this system, we were able to code the customized algorithm using software called Processing. Processing provides a programming environment, which is now used by many artists, designers to create new media arts. Processing is a software sketchbook, which we can write our code in. Each program written on Processing is called a sketch. After the program is finished, it can be run by pressing the "Run" button on the Processing interface. A new window will then open on Processing, showing the visual result of the program. It is also possible to import libraries and other tools into Processing, allowing a greater capability of the program. In our system, for example, we have imported the Posenet library into Processing.

4.3   Creative Coding for Generative Visual System

With the webcam turned on and the key points shown on the participant's body as dots and lines (Skeleton representation) moving on the screen, the program is able to take in data from Posenet on the position of key points and is feeding it to the generative visual system we built - The visual elements of the system. The coordinates of the key points on the user's body are assigned to the height and width of shapes, so as the user moves, the shapes will move in a random manner. The shapes are then filled in with gradient colors. To do this, the "Lerp Color" function on Processing is used. This function calculates a color between two colors at specific increments, thus creating gradients. After getting the visuals in place, we altered the system's color scheme and asked some users to choose their own color scheme as well, which created varying results of the final generated image.

4.4   Physical and Hardware Setup

The setup of this system was relatively minimal, which consists of a screen, a webcam, and a computer. The participant stands in front of the installation and moves. The webcam will pick up the movement of the viewer, and generate the visuals moving in real-time with the movements of the user on the screen. Unfortunately due to the pandemic, we did not get an opportunity to showcase the system with a more formal setup to a larger crowd of audiences (Fig. 5).

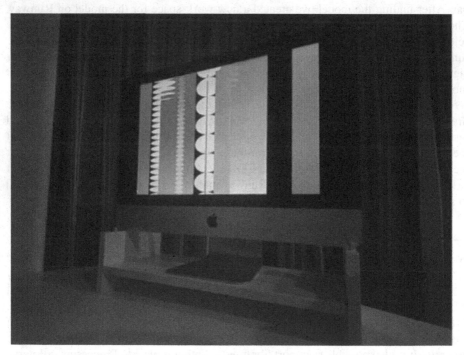

Fig. 5. Physical setup

5 Social Impact

Fig. 6. Selected generated results

The system was relatively easy to interact with, as it only required the viewer to move in front of the screen. It could also take some time for some users to make sense of what they are seeing on the screen. Several viewers have interacted with the system, they range in age and background. They usually realized that the movements on the visuals matched their body movements and were amazed. One young-age participant did not hesitate to dance and was excited to see her body in another form, moving in a different way in the screen. A participant commented that although he did not know how to draw, this system helped him create artwork (Fig. 6).

5.1 Interactions and Feedback

Our system was interacted by ten viewers. Unfortunately, the installation was not yet formally exhibited, so the participants were mostly friends and family. The system was relatively easy to interact with, as it only required the viewer to move in front of the screen. It took some time for some users to make sense of what they see on the screen.

> "This is something I have not experienced before. It is very cool to be part of the creation process of an artwork." -- A middle-aged man.

> "I love how the installation can move as I move, it is almost like we are dancing together!" -- An eight-year-old girl.

> "I do not know how to make artworks and have never painted before. But with this installation, I am able to create the artwork without the need for prior knowledge on art-making." -- A middle-aged lady.

This system has given its viewers a glimpse of machine vision by visually displaying how an AI captures human forms. It is exciting to see AI being used in making art, as it is different from the traditional ways of making art such as oil painting and sketching. we are also looking forward to seeing how art-making methods will continue to evolve in the future. This project has also given us thoughts and reflects more on humans' role in relation to AI in the creative processes.

5.2 More on Human-AI Collaboration

People live in a world filled with visual content such as digital images and video and are continually intaking different information and expressions. But when it comes to themselves, they have no easy way to express their thoughts or feelings and present themselves visually. Some artists apply image synthesis techniques to create visual artwork, and some apply image-to-image translation algorithms to create visuals with AI techniques. And many others work with visual synthesis techniques in different ways to express themselves. But it's less so for the average, especially the amateurish creators.

There are tools based on traditional algorithms or neural networks for artists and help them to create artwork. But when amateurish creators try to use them, they will always quickly meet the steep part of the learning curve. The excitement could fade out soon, but immediate frustrations will come in as a replacement rather than enjoying making. The SoTA techniques in visual synthesis with deep learning have started to bring in a new trend in the professional art world and potentially contribute to previously addressed problems. What if anyone without professional knowledge of fine art can paint a painting with just a quick sketch of ideas or even some words to describe the sparks in mind? What if participants only need to pass in some "parameters" or critical decisions, and the neural network will understand and help visualize their artistic expressions? Or like what we tried in this proposed system, participants will explore and visually present their bodies and dreams as art pieces?

6 Future Work

As mentioned before, due to the pandemic, unfortunately, we could not have a formal setup exhibition space. This had some impact on the user's experience with this system. If we get the opportunity, we will set up the system in a dark environment, with a larger screen or projection, making the experience more immersive and dream-like (Fig. 7).

Fig. 7. Ideal setup

Right now, there are some lags with the visuals at times. It would be beneficial if these lags could be improved, optimized the program and the performance is the next attempt. Currently, the visuals are not very smooth and organic. We would like to make the visuals more organic in the future to relate to the organic form of human bodies more. There are many to explore in this piece, looking at it as an art installation as well as a research topic.

References

1. Google AI Blog: Inceptionism: Going Deeper into Neural Networks. https://ai.googleblog.com/2015/06/inceptionism-going-deeper-into-neural.html, Accessed 01 Feb 2021
2. Kendall, A., Grimes, M., Cipolla, R.: Posenet: a convolutional network for real-time 6-dof camera relocalization. In: Proceedings of the IEEE International Conference on Computer Vision, pp. 2938–2946 (2015)
3. Sanakoyeu, A., Kotovenko, D., Lang, S., Ommer, B.: A style-aware content loss for real-time HD style transfer. In: Ferrari, V., Hebert, M., Sminchisescu, C., Weiss, Y. (eds.) ECCV 2018. LNCS, vol. 11212, pp. 715–731. Springer, Cham (2018). https://doi.org/10.1007/978-3-030-01237-3_43
4. Processing Homepage. https://Processing.org/, Accessed 01 Feb 2021
5. Runway AI, Inc. Homepage. https://runwayml.com/, Accessed 01 Feb 2021
6. Goodfellow, I.J., et al.: Generative adversarial networks (2014). arXiv preprint arXiv:1406.2661
7. Karras, T., Laine, S., Aila, T.: A style-based generator architecture for generative adversarial networks. In: Proceedings of the IEEE/CVF Conference on Computer Vision and Pattern Recognition, pp. 4401–4410 (2019)

From Imitation to Innovation: A Case Study of an Amateur Artist

Rungtai Lin[1]([✉]), Yikang Sun[2], and Andrew Yu[3]

[1] Graduate School of Creative Industry Design, National Taiwan University of Arts,
New Taipei City, Taiwan
rtlin@mail.ntua.edu.tw
[2] School of Fine Arts, Nanjing Normal University, Nanjing, Jiangsu, People's Republic of China
[3] Andrew Art Studio, City of Buena Park, Orange County, CA, USA

Abstract. Imitation is a human instinct, and it is an effective way for humans to learn new things. Imitation is an effective method in the process of learning painting. With the advent of the era of national aesthetics, everyone has the opportunity to become creators. Generally speaking, they have not received professional training, so they are called "Amateur Artist". This research takes the process of learning painting by an amateur artist with an engineering background as an example and selects 10 groups of his imitated paintings as experimental samples for questionnaire survey and analysis. A total of 322 interviewees from domestic and foreign have participated. The result shows that: (1) Although this amateur artist didn't start learning painting until he was 70, he has quickly mastered the expression skills of painting through imitation. So that part of his work can even surpass the original. (2) The interviewees' understanding of the "painting" does not affect their confidence and reason for judging the "original". They rely more on their intuition to make judgments. (3) Whether the interviewees like the "original works" has little relevance to the attributes they judge they are "original works". This research can be provided as a reference for readers who are learning painting or planning to treat painting as leisure. The author looks forward to the emergence of more and more amateur artists, forming a trend of national aesthetics.

Keywords: Amateur artist · Painting creation · Imitation · Innovation · Cognition and communication · National aesthetics

1 Introduction

Facing the advent of elderly society, many people start to have dreams after retirement. For these people, dreaming is the most beautiful, pursuing dreams practically, and building dreams come true. In their spare time, they use paintbrushes and cameras to record life and beauty. They use the light and breezy breath to depict the experience of life, and use simple and straightforward brushstrokes to depict pure art. They put the core concept of "be yourself and be at ease" to the fullest in their artistic creations, calling them: Amateur artists, it is not an exaggeration. Many people start to come into contact with art after retirement, perhaps just to pass the time in the beginning as one of their

© Springer Nature Switzerland AG 2021
P.-L. P. Rau (Ed.): HCII 2021, LNCS 12772, pp. 40–52, 2021.
https://doi.org/10.1007/978-3-030-77077-8_4

leisure interests; and the process of these amateur artists from learning various art fields to self-creation is a topic worthy of in-depth discussion.

Most people have a certain stereotype of aesthetics or design. They think that it is the profession of an artist or designer, which is out of reach! However, please recall how you decided to buy a bag, a piece of clothing, or any daily necessities. This decision-making process is actually related to your beauty. The sense of beauty is innate, but we have specialized and gifted it, thinking that this talent is exclusive to a specific few artist, but this does not mean that we have to give up our intuitive feeling of beauty. As Picasso said: "Every child is an artist. The problem is how to remain an artist once he grows up. [17]" In the era of national creativity, anyone has the opportunity to become a creative expert. It has nothing to do with whether he/she has received professional training in art or design, because techniques can be mastered through training, and "imitating" is one of the most effective ways. Those works that arouse the viewer's interest and resonance often lie in their whimsy (Connotation) and different forms of expression (Denotation).

This article takes the process of learning painting and the creation of an amateur artist with an engineering background as an example, and analyzes the desirability of his thinking method of starting to learn painting with "imitating" and applying his engineering qualities to creation. His perception and recognition of the theme of his creation have made up for the shortcomings in his technique performance caused by his short time in a painting. From the beginning of "an accident" to "self-affirmation", he used the simplest techniques to create works full of connotation and stories. In addition to the need for the same cognitive experience between the artist and the viewer, how to further resonate with the viewer requires further research.

Although art emphasizes uniqueness, this creative mode may not be suitable for everyone. But this article hopes to inspire all amateur artists and their creations, and let more people understand the charm and value of artistic creation. This research can be provided as a reference for readers who are learning painting or planning to treat painting as leisure. The author looks forward to the emergence of more and more amateur artists, forming a trend of national aesthetics.

2 Literature Review

2.1 Amateur Art and National Creativity

Amateur art is usually defined as visual art that is created by a person who lacks the formal education and training that a professional artist undergoes [2, 5, 7, 15]. When all kinds of creative or painting materials and tools become more and more abundant, anyone who wants to create can put them into creation anytime, anywhere. Because they have not received the basic training of the academic school, they can express their ideas more freely and casually, without worrying about some restrictions, such as what to draw first? How to compose the picture, how to shape it, etc. Many studies have conducted in-depth research on the creative mode, communication mechanism, display method of amateur artists, and the viewer's cognition of works interpretation [3, 9, 11, 14], which provides a lot of inspiration for this article.

Jones believes: "We are living in an era of uncertainty. For many people in the world, uncertainty is characterized by fear and violence. Because of these uncertain times, when designing self, culture, and future, the need for creativity has become more urgent [10]". Although in the field of art and design, the main voice is still controlled by professionals, consumers are often in a relatively passive position. However, people's cognition of beauty comes from nature. Their needs and desires for "beautiful things" even put themselves into artistic creation, forming a force that cannot be underestimated.

In the era of national aesthetics, anyone can participate in the creation of "beauty", and they can get satisfaction and happiness from creativity too [12]. National aesthetics contains huge economic benefits. It connects many different industries and develops in coordination to form a benign development model. If it is said that the original intention of the amateur artists to create is to cultivate temperament, leisure, and entertainment, and enrich life, then the proposal and promotion of the national creative concept will further enrich the art and humanities to every level of society. It pays more attention to people's psychological and spiritual satisfaction [16]. In short, national creativity emphasizes "Create from Function to Feeling". It allows art to penetrate into every aspect of life.

2.2 Knocking on the Door of Creativity Through Imitating

Imitating is the theory of artistic creativity, which can be proved by the following few words of painting or design masters. For example, Picasso said: "Good artists copy, great artists steal [4]", and A German industrial design master Dieter Rams believes: "Imitation is the sincerest form of flattery! [6]" According to these points of view, the creative process should be based on close imitation of the masterpieces of past creators. Everyone who learns to paint will practice basic skills by imitating different classic paintings to improve their creative ability. The "imitating" in the initial stage adopts a "complete copying" method, but it is different from taking photos or photocopying.

Imitating other people's works allows beginners to quickly become familiar with and master different materials, tools, and expressions. This process can effectively train their hand, eye, and brain coordination. In the process of imitating, there is usually no need to add personal thoughts. After a period of imitating, creators can combine their ideas and choose suitable methods for creation according to different themes. At this time, the inspiration and inspiration obtained from the past imitated works are "decoding" by the creator, and then "coding" according to their ideas and creative goals, and then transformed into a new work [1, 8].

Perhaps not every creator has received professional training, but the feeling of beauty and the accumulation of personal experience have made them gradually knock on the door of creativity. The expression of creativity is not limited to the form of expression, but pays more attention to the ingenuity and connotation behind the creativity. If imitating is the study and application of the external form (Denotation) of painting creation, then creativity depends more on the internal meaning of the work and the creator's thought (Connotation). For creators, this gradual process "from imitation to innovation", is a shortcut for them to enter the art world.

Imitating, which is different from "copying" in general understanding. No matter what materials or tools are used, imitation is a process by which people understand and become familiar with the expression techniques, composition, and style of the work. Although there are not many personal opinions in this process, it can still encourage imitators to think. And "copying", such as photocopying, is more focused on collection or dissemination. Those who simply copy the work do not have a deep understanding of the copied work, or simply like the original work. In addition, the use and effects of different tools and materials cannot be effectively mastered if people have no practical experience and simply use them.

2.3 Brief Introduction of Amateur Artist in This Study

The amateur artist selected for this study has an engineering background and now lives in California, USA. He practiced calligraphy with his father since he was a child, and he never painted after middle school. After half a year of retirement at the age of 70, he started to learn painting by a chance. He chose to start by imitating the master's paintings. The masters he chose came from different countries with different styles, such as French neo-impressionism master Paul Signac, Dutch post-impressionism master Van Gogh, Renaissance masters da Vinci and Michelangelo, American landscape painter and printmaker Winslow Homer, and Jean-François Millet from the Barbizon School. At the same time, he taught himself the background of the relevant painters and the relationship between them and the works, in order to better understand the connotation of the copied paintings. Figure 1 shows the painting chosen by the artist for the first time of imitating, and he imitated it three times successively. The process of imitating was done by himself.

Judging from the imitated works, his mastery of the original works and technical expression ability is not inferior to professional painters. As practice makes perfect, the last two imitating works not only take less time but also it can be seen that the artist has slowly added his own understanding of the painting. He also used the lens to faithfully record the entire process of imitating (Fig. 2).

Original   The 1st imitated   The 2nd imitated   The 3rd imitated

Fig. 1. The first imitated by amateur artist, 2018.

Fig. 2. Full record of the first imitating process by amateur artist, 2018.

3 Method

3.1 Experimental Samples

The experimental samples are taken from 10 copy works completed by the artist in the past 2 years. Among them, 1 sample was imitated 3 times and the other 2 samples were imitated twice. The styles of the original works are quite different and come from different periods. The basic information and pictures of the original work are shown in Table 1.

Table 1. Experimental samples

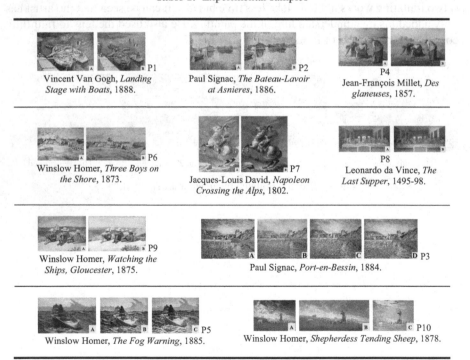

Vincent Van Gogh, *Landing Stage with Boats*, 1888. P1

Paul Signac, *The Bateau-Lavoir at Asnieres*, 1886. P2

Jean-François Millet, *Des glaneuses*, 1857. P4

Winslow Homer, *Three Boys on the Shore*, 1873. P6

Jacques-Louis David, *Napoleon Crossing the Alps*, 1802. P7

Leonardo da Vince, *The Last Supper*, 1495-98. P8

Winslow Homer, *Watching the Ships, Gloucester*, 1875. P9

Paul Signac, *Port-en-Bessin*, 1884. P3

Winslow Homer, *The Fog Warning*, 1885. P5

Winslow Homer, *Shepherdess Tending Sheep*, 1878. P10

3.2 Questionnaire Design

The questionnaire consists of 2 parts: the first part is the basic information of the interviewee; the second part asks the interviewee to make intuitive judgments on the "original", and compare the difference between the "original" and "imitated" works. Finally, the interviewees were asked to select their favorite paintings. The questionnaire will not tell the interviewee which one is the original, and the numbering is random (Table 2).

Table 2. Questionnaire content (Take P1 as example).

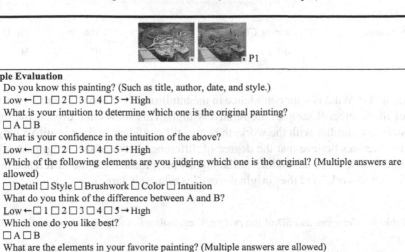

Sample Evaluation

1. Do you know this painting? (Such as title, author, date, and style.)
   Low ←☐ 1 ☐ 2 ☐ 3 ☐ 4 ☐ 5 → High
2. What is your intuition to determine which one is the original painting?
   ☐ A ☐ B
3. What is your confidence in the intuition of the above?
   Low ←☐ 1 ☐ 2 ☐ 3 ☐ 4 ☐ 5 → High
4. Which of the following elements are you judging which one is the original? (Multiple answers are allowed)
   ☐ Detail ☐ Style ☐ Brushwork ☐ Color ☐ Intuition
5. What do you think of the difference between A and B?
   Low ←☐ 1 ☐ 2 ☐ 3 ☐ 4 ☐ 5 → High
6. Which one do you like best?
   ☐ A ☐ B
7. What are the elements in your favorite painting? (Multiple answers are allowed)
   ☐ Detail ☐ Style ☐ Brushwork ☐ Color

3.3 Interviewees

A total of 322 people participated in the questionnaire, 247 come from domestic (85.09%) and the other 48 come from overseas (14.91%). All questionnaires are valid after inspection. Table 3 shows the distribution of different interviewees.

4 Results

4.1 Overall Assessment

Table 4 shows the average and standard deviation of interviewees' evaluations of different samples. The samples are divided into two types, single and multiple imitating, so different types of samples have different numbers of questions. The results show that: (1) Regarding the question "Q1-Do you know this painting? (Such as title, author, date, and style.)", except for P4 and P8, the other 8 samples got relatively low scores. It can be seen that the interviewees are not very familiar with these samples. (2) Regarding the

Table 3. The distribution of different interviewees. (N = 322)

1. Gender		2. Age				
Male	Female	18–30	31–40	41–50	51–60	61 and Above
115	207	66	59	64	78	55

3. Background							
Pedagogy	Humanities	Fine Art	Design	Sociology	Science	Engineering	Other
30	14	45	95	26	14	39	59

4. Education				
High School	Junior College	Bachelor	Master	Ph. D.
29	40	112	91	50

question "Q3-What is your confidence in the intuition of the above?", except for P3, the scores of the other 9 samples are relatively high. This shows that even if the interviewees are not familiar with the work, they are still confident in their intuitive judgment. (3) Interviewees believe that the degree of difference between the "original work" and "imitated work" is in the middle of the high, which means that the difference between the "imitated work" and the "original work" is relatively large.

Table 4. The mean and SD of interviewees' evaluations of different samples. (N = 322)

	Q1	Q3	Q5	Q6	Q7	Q8	Q9	Q10
P1	1.866 (1.075)	3.28 (1.054)	3.373 (0.936)	—	—	—	—	—
P2	1.988 (1.141)	3.149 (1.069)	3.245 (0.923)	—	—	—	—	—
P3	1.947 (1.111)	2.863 (1.085)	3.748 (0.948)	2.981 (1.026)	2.894 (1.051)	3.379 (1.023)	3.438 (1.004)	2.584 (1.077)
P4	3.929 (1.186)	4.137 (1.008)	3.814 (1.015)	—	—	—	—	—
P5	2.075 (1.15)	3.186 (1.095)	3.891 (1.04)	3.919 (0.986)	2.724 (1.074)	—	—	—
P6	2.143 (1.225)	3.186 (1.153)	3.36 (0.97)	—	—	—	—	—
P7	3.447 (1.339)	3.773 (1.106)	3.693 (1.066)	—	—	—	—	—
P8	3.981 (1.235)	3.879 (1.111)	3.531 (1.147)	—	—	—	—	—
P9	2.096 (1.184)	3.177 (1.183)	3.54 (1.026)	—	—	—	—	—
P10	2.127 (1.26)	3.121 (1.203)	3.96 (0.977)	4.14 (1.045)	4.298 (0.919)	—	—	—

Table 5. The proportion of interviewees correctly identifying the "original work" and the number of votes for their favorite work. (N = 322)

Samples	Original	Votes	Q1	Q3	Votes of favorite
P1	B	274 (85.09%)	1.86 (1.075)	3.32 (1.065)	B/218 (67.7%)
P2	A	256 (79.5%)	2.03 (1.136)	3.16 (1.027)	A/217 (67.39%)
P3	B	222 (68.94%)	1.91 (1.083)	2.97 (1.082)	B/177 (54.97%)
P4	B	304 (94.41%)	3.99 (1.140)	4.21 (0.939)	B/276 (85.71%)
P5	A	270 (83.85%)	2.05 (1.141)	3.25 (1.068)	A/225 (69.88%)
P6	B	285 (88.51%)	2.13 (1.235)	3.23 (1.158)	B/281 (87.27%)
P7	B	299 (92.86%)	3.52 (1.317)	3.83 (1.080)	A/275 (85.4%)
P8	B	292 (90.68%)	4.11 (1.160)	3.97 (1.090)	B/287 (89.13%)
P9	B	248 (77.02%)	2.13 (1.210)	3.29 (1.175)	B/247 (76.71%)
P10	B	292 (90.68%)	2.10 (1.252)	3.15 (1.200)	A/266 (82.61%)

Table 5 shows the proportion of all interviewees correctly identifying the "original work" and the number of votes for their favorite work. The results show that: (1) The most favorite works of the interviewees are "original works", but the number of votes is slightly lower than the number of people who made correct judgments. (2) Although most of the interviewees can correctly determine which work is the "original", there is still a certain percentage of interviewees who regard "imitated work" as the original and their favorite work. In summary, although this amateur artist has not studied painting for a long time, he has already mastered certain expression skills. Further analysis of his painting skills will be further analyzed with several repeatedly imitated samples below.

Generally speaking, familiarity with the work will directly affect people's confidence and basis for further judging the original work. If people are not familiar with the work, they tend to make relevant judgments based on "intuition", and the confidence index of judgment is usually not very high. However, there are also situations where interviewees are confident in their judgment, regardless of whether they are familiar with the work. Table 6 shows the relationship between the interviewee's understanding of the work and the confidence in judging the original work. The results show that: (1) There are significant differences between the interviewees' familiarity with the ten groups of works and their confidence in identifying the original works. (2) Except for P8, the average of the interviewees' familiarity with the other 9 groups of works are lower than the average of their confidence in identifying the original works. Generally speaking, the confidence of the interviewees in identifying the original works is relatively high.

4.2 Analysis of Repeatedly Imitated Sample

The artist imitated the samples P3, P5, and P10 many times, among which P3 has imitated 3 times. The Interviewees' cognition and judgment on "repeatedly imitated sample" are worthy of further discussion. Take sample P3 as an example (Fig. 3).

Table 6. The relationship between the interviewee's familiarity with the works and the confidence in judging the original work. (N = 322)

	Items	Means (SD)	MD (SD)	t	Cohen's d
Pair 1	P1-Q1	1.87 (1.08)	−1.41 (1.295)	−19.585***	1.091
	P1-Q3	3.28 (1.05)			
Pair 2	P2-Q1	1.99 (1.14)	−1.16 (1.253)	−16.64***	0.927
	P2-Q3	3.15 (1.07)			
Pair 3	P3-Q1	1.95 (1.11)	−0.92 (1.226)	−13.406***	0.747
	P3-Q3	2.86 (1.09)			
Pair 4	P4-Q1	3.93 (1.19)	−0.21 (0.962)	−3.881***	0.216
	P4-Q3	4.14 (1.01)			
Pair 5	P5-Q1	2.07 (1.15)	−1.11 (1.263)	−15.797***	0.88
	P5-Q3	3.19 (1.09)			
Pair 6	P6-Q1	2.14 (1.22)	−1.04 (1.311)	−14.287***	0.796
	P6-Q3	3.19 (1.15)			
Pair 7	P7-Q1	3.45 (1.34)	−0.33 (1.086)	−5.387***	0.3
	P7-Q3	3.77 (1.11)			
Pair 8	P8-Q1	3.98 (1.24)	0.1 (0.92)	1.999*	0.111
	P8-Q3	3.88 (1.11)			
Pair 9	P9-Q1	2.1 (1.18)	−1.08 (1.265)	−15.327***	0.854
	P9-Q3	3.18 (1.18)			
Pair 10	P10-Q1	2.13 (1.26)	−0.99 (1.304)	−13.674***	0.762
	P10-Q3	3.12 (1.2)			

Q1: Do you know this painting? (Such as title, author, date, and style.), Q3: What is your confidence in the intuition of the above?; *$p < .05$, *** $p < .001$.

Fig. 3. The repeatedly imitated sample P3 (B is the original work).

Among the four paintings in P3, number B is the original. A total of 221 interviewees made the correct judgment. However, 31, 33, and 36 interviewees still judged A, C, and D as "original works" (Table 7). Using the analysis of variance, it can be seen that there is no significant difference in the degree of familiarity with the works among the interviewees who judge different works as "original". However, the confidence of interviewees who judged "B" as the original work is higher than those who judged A and C as the original work at a significant level ($F = 2.64, p < .05$). Besides, interviewees from different regions, different genders and education levels, there is no significant difference between their familiarity with different works and their confidence in judging which is the original work.

Regarding the question: "Which of the following elements are you judging which one is the original? (Multiple answers are allowed)", because multiple selections are allowed, there will be multiple combinations of options. Among them, the number of interviewees who make judgments based on "intuition" is relatively high in the ranking of all option combinations. The number of people who chose "intuition" and other options at the same time accounted for the majority. Taking P3 as an example, the number of interviewees (24/7.48%) who make judgments based only on "intuition" is the second largest (the black bar in Fig. 4), and the most combination of options also includes "intuition" (the dark gray stripes bar in Fig. 4). It can be inferred from this that "intuition" is still the main basis and reason for the interviewees to judge what is "original work".

Table 7. The difference between the confidence levels of the interviewees in sample P3 who judge different works as "original". (N = 322)

P3-Q2					F	Comparison
	A (N = 31)	B (N = 221)	C (N = 33)	D (N = 36)		
P3-Q3	2.55(0.99)	2.98(1.08)	2.58(0.94)	2.75(1.23)	2.64*	B > A; B > C

Q2: What is your intuition to determine which one is the original painting?, Q3: What is your confidence in the intuition of the above?; *$p < .05$.

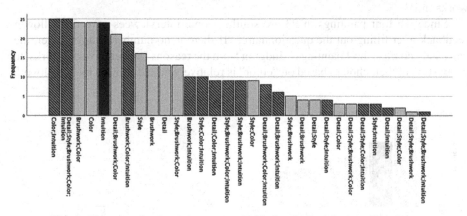

Fig. 4. The votes that interviewees used to judge the "original work" in P3.

Figure 5 shows that the interviewees' perception of the difference between the four paintings in P3. The results show that: (1) When putting "original work" and "imitated work" together, the interviewee thinks that the difference between them was relatively large. (2) When comparing the 3 works of "imitated", the interviewees think the difference between the two is not so obvious.

Comparison of differences between original (B) and imitation works (A, C, and D)

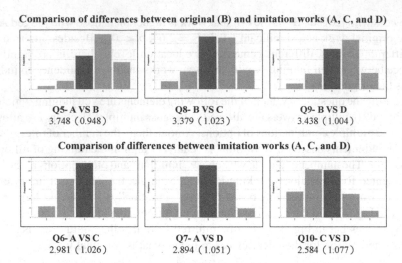

| Q5- A VS B | Q8- B VS C | Q9- B VS D |
| 3.748（0.948） | 3.379（1.023） | 3.438（1.004） |

Comparison of differences between imitation works (A, C, and D)

| Q6- A VS C | Q7- A VS D | Q10- C VS D |
| 2.981（1.026） | 2.894（1.051） | 2.584（1.077） |

Fig. 5. Interviewees' evaluation of the difference between the four paintings in P3.

When the interviewee filled out the questionnaire, they didn't know which one was the original, and the interviewee was more inclined to identify the original by "intuition". Therefore, it can be concluded that the state of the artist's imitating is relatively stable, and he can also grasp the details and effects of the "original works".

In sample P3, more than half of the interviewees (177 people, 55.0%) like "B", and the interviewees who liked "A", "C" and "D" were 38, 38, and 69 respectively. Figure 6 shows the number of votes that the reasons for interviewees to choose their favorite works in P3.

Since the four paintings in P3 are similar, some interviewees gave the following feedback after filling out the questionnaire: "If there is no number as a reminder, they can easily confuse the 4 paintings." Judging from the reasons for their favorite works, the proportion of their choices based on "color" is relatively high, followed by "brushwork"

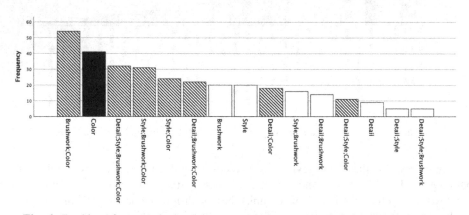

Fig. 6. Ranking of reasons for interviewees when they choose their favorite works in P3.

and "style". Since the four works are similar, there are relatively few interviewees who prefer "details" as the reason for choice. When there is no need to identify which one is the "original" and only choose their favorite work, 45% of the interviewees chose the "imitated work". This can prove once again: the improvement of the artist's imitating skills is proportional to the number of imitating, and it has been continuously improving.

5 Conclusions

This article analyzes an amateur artist who started his painting creation through "imitation". From the results of the interviewees' cognition of his imitating works and the original works, it can be seen that his painting skills have not only improved rapidly with the deepening of copying, but no less than professional painters. However, the interviewee's perception of the work is more dependent on their intuition. As mentioned at the beginning of this article: "Aesthetic sense is innate, but we have specialized and gifted it, thinking that this talent is exclusive to a specific few artist, but this does not mean that we have to give up our intuitive sense of beauty." The conclusions are as follows:

(1) Although this amateur artist didn't start learning painting until he was 70, he has quickly mastered the expression skills of painting through imitation. So that part of his work can even surpass the original.
(2) The interviewees' understanding of the "painting" does not affect their confidence and reason for judging the "original". They rely more on their intuition to make judgments.
(3) Whether the interviewees like the "original works" has little relevance to the attributes they judge they are "original works". Especially when encountering repeated imitating works like P3, the interviewees relied on "color" as the main basis for choosing their favorite work, and "color" can also be regarded as another "intuition".

Science, mathematics, and engineering sound sternly, but they can also be very artistic and beautiful. Many classic forms in artistic creation (such as Fibonacci Numbers and Golden Ratio) are analyzed using mathematical and other scientific methods [18]. A rational and rigorous attitude not only brings order and norms, but also forms a unique sense of beauty. This is exactly the "perceptual and free expression" required for artistic creation. Since design technology must be integrated into humanities and art after all [13], it is not impossible for humanities and art to do the opposite. From the perspective of science and technology, "decoding" and "recoding" art to bring about artistic creation. More possibilities and unexpected beauty.

There are many motivations for amateurs to actively devote themselves to artistic creation. They may be used to pass their leisure time, maybe a whim or they may be just curious. However, this has the effect of improving the aesthetics and humanities of the whole society. Therefore, as a viewer, we should give every amateur artist full encouragement. For amateur artists, the expression methods and techniques of artistic creation can be solved through training, but they are not the only element for creation. Unlike professional artists, they have no fixed mindset and are not restricted by any so-called academic norms, which is their greatest advantage. The concept and conception of the creator derived from life is the soul of the work. However, these concepts and ideas may not be too complicated. The reason is simple, because "Less is more".

As the beginning of a series of studies on amateur art, this study shows that the artist has fully mastered the painting skills and means of expression through copying. Follow-up research will further focus on the creation of this amateur artist in addition to copying and analyze the value and inspiration of "imitating" for creation.

Acknowledgement. Thanks to this amateur artist for authorizing the use of his drawings for this study. His experience and thoughts on the imitating process have also inspired the author. The author would also like to thank the interviewees who participated in the questionnaire. Their active participation made this research go smoothly.

References

1. Barthes, R.: Elements of Semiology (A. Lavers & C. Smith, Trans.). Jonathan Cape, London (1967)
2. Benedetti, J.M.: Folk art terminology revisited: why it (still) matters. In: Roberto, K.R. (ed.) Radical Cataloging: Essays at the Front, p. 113. McFarland & Company, Jefferson (2008)
3. Chen, S., Yen, H., Sandy, L., Lin, C.: Applying design thinking in curating model: a case study of the exhibition of turning poetry into painting. J. Des. **21**(4), 1–24 (2016). (in Chinese)
4. Connnolly, J.: Great Artists Steal! https://www.creativethinkinghub.com/creative-thinking-and-stealing-like-an-artist/, Accessed 04 Nov 2020
5. Davies, D.: On the very idea of 'outsider art.' Brit. J. Aesthetics **49**(1), 25–41 (2009)
6. Dernbach, C.: Dieter rams talks about design at apple. https://www.mac-history.net/apple-history-tv/video-gallery/2012-05-10/dieter-rams-talks-about-design-at-apple, Accessed 04 Nov 2020
7. Fine, G.A.: Everyday Genius: Self-taught Art and the Culture of Authenticity. University of Chicago Press, Chicago (2004)
8. Fiske, J.: Introduction to Communication Studies. Routledge, London (1990)
9. Gao, Ya-Juan., Chen, Li.-Yu., Lee, S., Lin, R., Jin, Y.: A study of communication in turning "poetry" into "painting." In: Rau, P.L.P. (ed.) CCD 2017. LNCS, vol. 10281, pp. 37–48. Springer, Cham (2017). https://doi.org/10.1007/978-3-319-57931-3_4
10. Jones, S.H.: Creative selves, creative cultures, creative futures. In: Jones, S.H., Pruyn, M. (eds.) Creative Selves/Creative Cultures: Critical Autoethnography, Performance, and Pedagogy, pp. 247–249. Palgrave Macmillan, London (2018)
11. Lin, C., Chen, J., Chen, S., Lin, R.: The cognition of turning poetry into painting. US-China Educ. Rev. B **5**(8), 471–487 (2015)
12. Lin, R.: Outsider art and national aesthetics: enrich life after retirement with art. Humanit. Social Sci. Newsl. Q. **18**(3), 81–87 (2017). (in Chinese)
13. Lin, R., Kreifeldt, J.G.: Do Not Touch: Dialogue between "Design and Technology" and "Humanities and Arts." National Taiwan University of Arts, New Taipei (2014). (in Chinese)
14. Lin, R., Lee, S.: Turning "Poetry" Into "Painting": The Sharing of Creative Experience. National Taiwan University of Arts, New Taipei (2015).(in Chinese)
15. Maizels, J.: Raw Creation: Outsider Art & Beyond. Phaidon, London (2000)
16. Maslow, A.H.: A theory of human motivation. Psychol. Rev. **50**(4), 370–396 (1943)
17. Peter, L.J.: Peter's Quotations: Ideas for Our Time, p. 25. Bantam Books, New York (1997)
18. Williams, C.: Origins of Form: The Shape of Natural and Man-made Things. Taylor Trade Publishing, Plymouth (2013)

A Study on the Cognitive Differences of *Incomplete Beauty* in Sculptures Among Audiences

Yuheng Tao[1]([⊠]), Hong Qian Zheng[1], Jing Cao[2], and Po-Hsien Lin[1]

[1] Graduate School of Creative Industry Design, National Taiwan University of Arts, New Taipei City, Taiwan
t0131@mail.ntua.edu.tw
[2] School of Media and Design,
Hangzhou Dianzi University, Hangzhou, People's Republic of China

Abstract. Many sculptures home and abroad in both ancient and modern times have the presentation mode of *incomplete beauty*. Apart from its aesthetic ideology and enjoyment, it can further initiate abstract and deep thoughts of the audiences. The researchers notice that during the artistic creation, the work with *incomplete beauty* will interest audiences more. At the same time, in the world of art, it is mostly the artists themselves or the art critics are discussing about whether the using method of *incomplete beauty* is proper and whether the presenting effect of *incomplete beauty* is good, without a measuring standard. Therefore, this research mainly focuses on the cognitive differences and preference degree in different types of *incomplete beauty* among audiences. This research-based study takes nine sculptures with *incomplete beauty* as experimental samples, and conducts cognitive preference investigations among randomly selected audiences. The research results show that: (1) Although the works' degree of *incomplete beauty* does not dominate the audiences' preference degree, it could estimate the audiences' preference towards the artistic works to a great extent. The higher the *incomplete beauty* degree is, the more audiences like the work. (2) The audiences have a wide acceptable range of the *incomplete beauty* in sculptures, not limited to certain features, while the rational conciseness and direct intensity attract the audiences more easily. (3) The works with vivid style and strong feelings are more easily be interpreted, so it is easier for the audiences to like these works.

Keywords: Incomplete beauty · Cognition of incomplete beauty · Cognition trend

1 Introduction

As early as the 19th century, Rodin, the French sculpture artist, consciously applied ugliness into the artistic works, and clearly proposed the theoretical concepts such as ugly beauty, incomplete beauty, contradictory beauty, which broke the simple aesthetics' research and evaluation mode of beauty in harmony and unity, and ugliness being

P.-L. P. Rau (Ed.): HCII 2021, LNCS 12772, pp. 53–64, 2021.
https://doi.org/10.1007/978-3-030-77077-8_5

incomplete and malformed which have been popular since ancient Greek. Until the early 1980s, the concept of incomplete beauty has been introduced in the oriental academic world. After a long time of research and practice, incomplete beauty has successfully evolved into a new aesthetic category in the aesthetic research, creation and appreciation, and it is accepted by the audiences [9]. Therefore, although the research of incomplete beauty is not the mainstream of aesthetic research, it is of long history and worthy of discussion.

Incomplete beauty is an old topic, and many scholars from different research fields have expressed their opinions about it. However, as to the questions of whether incomplete beauty really exists, and what the nature and scope of incomplete beauty really are, there has not been a rough agreement. In the artistic world, it is mostly the artists themselves or the art critics are justifying themselves about whether the using method of incomplete beauty is proper and whether the presenting effect of incomplete beauty is good, without a measuring standards. Therefore, this research mainly focuses on the cognitive differences and preference degree in different types of incomplete beauty among audiences.

The incompleteness includes artificial incompleteness and natural incompleteness. [3] The natural incompleteness is the mutual compatibility between the entirety and the incompleteness which then reaches harmony and unify. It is a product of the nature. While the artificial incompleteness is usually caused by artists to damage the shape of artistic work so as to obtain spiritual fantasy. At the same time, the subjects and scope of incomplete beauty is quite wide. Apart from the artistic field, it also involves fields such as psychology and philosophy. In order to increase the research accuracy, it is necessary to choose sculpture works as research objects, which is the area of expertise. It is hoped that this research could provide some reference information to artists and designers during their creation, so the artistic works with incomplete beauty discussed in this paper will be limited within the scope of sculpture works with artificial in completeness.

In order to avoid the vicious circle of justifying oneself about the incomplete beauty, this paper will switch into the audiences' perspective from the artists' perspective to conduct relatively objective research analysis. When audiences are appreciating the work, they will subconsciously project their own feelings onto the artistic work to have mutual sympathy. It is difficult to analyze and understand in the scientific perspective about the aesthetic way the audiences feel about the work. Although many western philosophers of generations objected to discussing aesthetic appreciation in cognitive method, the estrangement between audiences and the works will always be there if the issue is not studied by the cognitive theories. Therefore, this research attempts to discuss the difference on preference cognition and aesthetics feelings about sculptures with different kinds of incomplete beauty among audiences.

2   Literature Review

2.1   The Cognition of Incomplete Beauty

The incompleteness could provide opportunities for unique aesthetics. Its exiting way is complex, changeable and unnatural. The incompleteness itself possesses the elements of beauty, and when audiences face this incomplete beauty, with the help of aesthetic imagination involvement and aesthetic thinking transcendence, the audiences can obtain the best aesthetic experience. Rudolf Arnheim, the famous American Gestalt aesthetic psychology, said that, visual image is never the mechanical copy of the perceptual materials, but the innovative mastery of the reality. The image it mastered is the aesthetic image with rich imagination, creativity and sensitivity [6].

Yan Yungui claimed from the perspective of aesthetic psychology that, incomplete beauty is not a objective existence, but an existence of people. It shows the unique relationships between people and objectives, and expresses distinct spiritual value due to difference in time, place and people. It is produced by certain inner spiritual demands of incomplete objects and people fitting together [9]. Yu An'an thought in the perspective of aesthetics that incompleteness is a relative concept, which corresponds to completeness and integrity. It is partial blankness and absence, and the unfinished or lost status of the completeness; while incomplete beauty takes incompleteness as the survey object, which is experiencing the beauty appreciation of incompleteness from the perspective of aesthetic perception [12]. When the audiences are watching the incompleteness, there will emerge some particular graphics psychologically or in their minds. These particular graphics will arouse the related graphical forms in the memory, which, in other words, will arouse the existing visual image and conduct imagination. Therefore, when the audiences see the sculptures with incomplete beauty, firstly they will complete the work by intuition imagination in terms of the missing appearance of the sculpture, and then they will have psychological perception evaluation and meaning interpretation towards the work.

2.2 Kansei Engineering

People's perception is a consecutive process of "consciousness - perception - evaluation", and these three stages are all overlapping with each other [8]. They are all based on visual perception, then interpret and summarize by information processing, and at last evaluate the results of the first two stages. However, during the process of evaluation, people's kansei reactions are more involved [7]. Kansei means the feeling or image people have towards objects, which is the psychologically expected feeling towards objects. Kansei engineering is converting people's expectation of emotion and image into technologies with detailed design by physical design elements [1, 2]. It can be seen that people generate image recognition and evaluation feeling towards the visible objects through intuition experience based on previous environment and configuration. Therefore, in order to use kansei method to evaluate people's sensibility, Nagamachi Mituo [1] has put forward following steps for kansei engineering:

1. Extract image adjectives.
2. The concept space of image adjectives.
3. Extract and decide design elements.
4. Combine kansei and design elements.
5. Build kansei experts system.
6. Implement kansei experts system.

According to the above premise, Huang Chongbin and Harada Akira [4] further integrated the steps 1–6, explaining that it is possible to use semantic differential method raised by Osgood in steps 1 and 2 to extract perceptual elements, so as to measure the emotional tools; as to steps 3 and 4, it is possible to establish the relationship between kansei (image) vocabulary adjectives and design (style) elements by experiment design or market survey; for step 5, it is possible to establish systematic model or construction of kansei engineering via computer technology; for step 6, it is necessary to irregularly update or correct data in kansei engineering system based on the up-to-date kansei trend [5]. This research intends to adopt kansei steps 1–4 based on the research purpose to explore the audiences' perception of incomplete beauty in sculptures.

2.3 Related Researches of Image

Among the many researches of audiences' image perception survey, it is discovered that the researches of many scholars are based on the semantic differential method (SD) raised by Osgood, to conduct researches towards influential elements of image perception of products. There are two collecting methods about obtaining the image vocabulary adjectives: (1) imagination method: as to the proposed concepts, to collect vocabulary of first impression from most of the experimental subjects; (2) literature survey method: to extract appropriate vocabulary from dictionaries or related literature [11]. Therefore, this paper uses semantic differential method to survey common perceptual image of the experimental subjects, so as to understand the cognitive differences of incomplete beauty in experimental subjects psychologically.

3 Research Method

This research conducts surveys of audiences' aesthetic cognition and preferences based on nine sculpture works with incomplete beauty.

The research is divided into three stages: in the first stage, the selection and classification of sculptures are conducted by experts method; in the second stage, the experts are asked to select image vocabulary based on semantic differential method, and then the audiences' cognitive common sense towards incomplete beauty are discussed; in the third stage, the research result is analyzed. The detailed research method and steps are as follows:

3.1 Selection and Limitation of Sculptures

First, world famous sculpture works with incomplete beauty are randomly provided by graduate students in sculpture majors, with a total number of 20 pieces. Then, the sculptures are selected for a second time by the expert team, and after discussion the works selected possess the following different features: some sculptures give up part of the shape, based on maintaining the sculpture's basic form and proportion structure, to express special artistic idea. The audiences could compensate the missing shape by fuzzy thinking, so as to reach a new harmonious relationship; some sculptures imitate the natural incompleteness, trying to add a sense of history by methods of corrosion, cracking or resolving, so as to endow the work with special vitality; other sculptures break the completeness of the sculptures by simplification or transformation on the basic of realism, to create a unique spiritual appeal. Finally, nine experimental samples are appraised and selected based on experts' consensus.

3.2 Questionnaire Survey - Semantic Differential, SD

(I)   In this stage, experimental objects' semantic evaluation of certain objects or concepts are learned by semantic differential method. During the experiment, the experimental objects evaluate certain objective or concept based on measurements constituted by pairs of adjectives with opposite images, so as to understand the meaning and measurements of this objective or concept and its related aspects [10], which is a research method belonging to common sense.

(II) Experts, professors, lecturers, and teachers with artistic and design background and currently working in the education field are asked to interpret and choose the adjectives appeared most frequently and suitable for evaluate the incomplete elements. Finally, nine groups of adjectives with opposite image are selected based on modelling layer, symbolic layer and effect layer, which are also the image vocabulary evaluation measurements of this research (Table 1).

Table 1. Nine groups of sample representative image vocabulary in this research

Level	Sample representative image vocabulary		
Technology	Rigid - vivid	Complex - concise	Specific - abstract
Symbolic layer	Direct - metaphorical	Static - dynamic	Rational - perceptual
Effect layer	Conflicting - harmonious	Restrictive - relaxed	Strong - soft

(III) Set of Measurement: the measurement of evaluating image vocabulary adjectives adopts semantic measurement, with the two corresponding adjectives set respectively at the two ends of the measurements. The scores are from 1 to 5 increasing from left to right, checking 1 and 5 meaning "obvious", clicking 2 and 4 meaning "not bad", clicking 3 meaning "average". For example: conservative 1 2 3 4 5 innovative (Table 2). The experimental objectives could choose the measurement number by his own judgement

(IV) Designation of research tools: this research chooses nine experimental samples, which are appraised and selected based on experts' consensus. In order to avoid the distraction in interpretation of characters and other unrelated image symbols, and further leads to influence judgement, the researchers used graphic software to remove the unrelated symbols outside the image. The pictures after modification are shown in below table (Table 3).

Table 2. Image vocabulary checking and score statistic method

sample	image vocabulary checking							
		obvious	not bad	average	not bad	obvious		
		1	2	3	4	5		
	conflicting					☑		harmonious

(V) Sampling objectives: the research objectives of this research are of different ages with different educational degrees or majors. Before evaluating the visual image, researchers randomly invited 50 audiences to conduct trial questionnaire answering, so as to understand the compatibility of the selected artistic works and visual image vocabulary, and modified again according to the audiences' general knowledge of image vocabulary. During the formal research stage, the survey randomly took examples of total 53 audiences including 17 males and 36 females.

(VI) Research tools: the questionnaire is divided into three parts. The first part is filling in the basic data; the second part is the survey of preference degree of visual image vocabulary and incomplete beauty (with the total of 9 pictures, 9 image vocabulary, 2 cognition items, and 9 image vocabulary and 2 cognition should be filled in for each image); the third part is selecting the best three artistic works with more incomplete beauty and with highest preference degree out of 9 works.

3.3 Stage Three, Analysis of Research Result

Sample summary and arrangement: the number of questionnaire experimental subjects is 53, without any invalid questionnaire. Therefore, the number of actual effective questionnaire is 53 sheets, including 17 from males and 36 from females.

Result analysis: the original data of the questionnaires are analyzed by data coding and then by SPSS statistic software, so as to analyze the aesthetic cognitive difference and preference of sculptures with different incomplete beauty among audiences.

Table 3. Nine Research Tools

artistic works	Image number	Rank of incomplete	Rank of preference
	P1	3	7
	P2	2	4
	P3	4	5
	P4	8	8
	P5	1	1
	P6	6	2
	P7	7	9
	P8	3	1
	P9	9	6

4   Result and Discussion

This research collected the total number of 53 sheets of effective questionnaires, which are evaluated under nine categories, with two dimensions of incomplete beauty and preference degree. Firstly, in terms of the overall testing of validity and reliability among all observation dimensions, Cronbachα value is .838 of the overall reliability performance in the questionnaire. The reliability performance after deletion is between .812–.835, with the average lower than .835, so it is not suitable to delete, showing the good reliability of this questionnaire.

4.1   The Analysis of Incomplete Beauty and Preference Degree

Table 4. The statistic table for audiences to choose incomplete beauty and preference degree in the questionnaire of this research

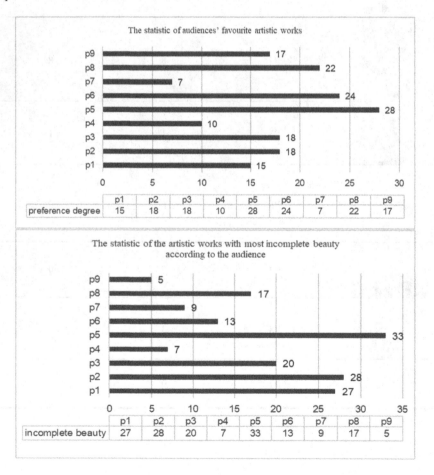

The statistic of audiences' favourite artistic works

	p1	p2	p3	p4	p5	p6	p7	p8	p9
preference degree	15	18	18	10	28	24	7	22	17

The statistic of the artistic works with most incomplete beauty according to the audience

	p1	p2	p3	p4	p5	p6	p7	p8	p9
incomplete beauty	27	28	20	7	33	13	9	17	5

According to the questionnaire, the audiences think that the top three artistic works with the most incomplete beauty is p1, p2 and p5; the top three of audiences' favourite artistic works are p5, p6 and p8; the overlapping top of the two ranking is p5, which is the artistic work with most incomplete beauty according to the audiences, and also the audiences' favourite artistic work. However, apart from the top work, the second and third work are not the same in the two rankings, so the researchers analyze the correlation coefficients between of the incomplete beauty evaluation and preference degree evaluation of the 9 artistic works respectively, as shown in Table 5.

Table 5. Correlation Coefficients between incomplete beauty and preference degree

Artistic works	Correlation coefficients between incomplete beauty and preference degree
P1	.68***
P2	.49***
P3	.50***
P4	.52***
P5	.78*
P6	.63***
P7	.61***
P8	.52***
P9	.40**

*p < .05. **p < .01. ***p < .001.

By analyzing the correlation coefficients between incomplete beauty evaluation and preference degree evaluation of the 9 artistic works, it can be seen that the audiences' sensitivity of works with incomplete beauty and their preference degree towards the works are positively related. To sum up, although the degree of incomplete beauty of artistic works does not dominate audiences' preference degree, it could estimate the audiences' preference towards the artistic works to a great extent. The higher the degree of incomplete beauty is, the higher the audiences' preference degree is.

4.2 The Analysis of Nature of Incomplete Beauty

In the cognitive space analysis of incomplete beauty based on multidimensional scaling (MDS) analysis result relying on the nine tested artistic works and nine images, the pressure index and determination coefficient are Kruskal's Stress = .10052, RSQ = .95572 respectively, showing the two dimensions suitable for describing the space relationship between the nine works and nine images in this research. The research shows that the two dimensional axis of the nine artistic works are as depicted in Fig. 1. According to the research result: p9 is the representative work of the images of abstract, metaphorical and harmonious. P5 is the representative work of the images of vivid and dynamic. P3 is the representative work of the images of complex and strong. P1 is the representative work of the images of rational and restrictive. The top three artistic works with the most incomplete beauty according to the audiences are p1, p2 and p5. It can be seen from Fig. 1 that these three works are not in the same series group, so incomplete beauty is not limited to only one form according to the audiences, and it can be presented with more openness and possibility. The audiences' favourite top three artistic works are p5, p6 and p8, which have relatively higher attribute value of vivid, strong, direct and detailed. Therefore, it can be seen that the works with vivid appearance, causing strong feelings and be easily interpreted, will more likely attract the audiences.

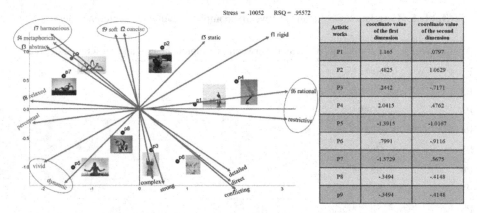

Artistic works	coordinate value of the first dimension	coordinate value of the second dimension
P1	1.165	.0797
P2	.4825	1.0629
P3	.2442	-.7171
P4	2.0415	.4762
P5	-1.3915	-1.0167
P6	.7991	-.9116
P7	-1.3729	.5675
P8	-.3494	-.4148
p9	-.3494	-.4148

Fig. 1. Artistic works and nine images in the research

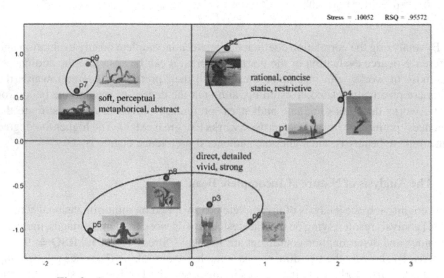

Fig. 2. Group space chart with new categories for the nine sculptures

According to the sample in Fig. 1, the works are grouped and combined with the adjusted space by classification group analysis method, and three groups are obtained in the research: the first group of p7 and p9, the second group of p1, p2 and p4, and the third group of p3, p5, p6 and p8, as shown in Fig. 2, and the groups could be renamed according to the stylized nature distribution and semantics of Fig. 2: metaphorical and abstract, rational and concise, direct and strong. Upon observing Table 4, it can be seen that the top 4 of audiences' favourite works all belong to the group of direct and strong, the tops of works with most incomplete beauty all evenly distributed in the two groups of rational and concise, direct and strong, whereas p7 and p9 in group of metaphorical and abstract both have low rankings in the list of incomplete beauty and preference degree. This proves that the works with detailed appearance and causing direct strong feelings could be more easily understood and liked by the audiences.

5 Conclusion

The reason why incomplete object could cause many mental activities of people and generate aesthetic perception is profound and complex. The completeness is only for an instant, while incompleteness is normal. This is also true for human and the nature. People are always in pursuit of perfectness, but the process of life is always accompanied with incompleteness and repairing incompleteness. After experiencing the incompleteness, the wisest way is to learn to appreciate the beauty of incompleteness. This paper concisely summarizes the understanding of incomplete beauty from the perspective of psychology and aesthetics, and extends and summarizes three groups of artificial incompleteness beauty in sculptures, which are "metaphorical and abstract", "rational and concise" and "direct and strong".

This paper discusses the cognitive differences and preference degree of different kinds of incompleteness among audiences, so the research perspective is switched from the artists to the audiences to conduct a relatively objective research analysis. When the audiences see the sculpture with incomplete beauty, the first thing is to imagine based on intuition and complete the missing appearance of the work, and then psychologically evaluate and interpret the meaning of the work. Therefore, this paper, based on semantic differential method, investigate the common perceptual image of the experimental subjects, so as to understand the cognitive differences of incomplete beauty of the experimental subjects. Finally, it is hoped that the data obtained in this research could provide certain references for the artists and designers during creation, and make humble efforts to the cognitive research on incomplete beauty in the academic world. The detailed conclusions are as follows:

1. Although the degree of incomplete beauty of artistic works cannot dominate the audiences' preference degree, it can estimate audiences' preference towards the work to a great extent. The higher the degree of incomplete beauty is, the higher audiences' preference degree is.
2. Audiences have a wide acceptable range of incomplete beauty in sculptures, not limited in one certain features, and the groups with the features of rational and concise, direct and strong can be more easily accepted by audiences.

3. The audiences' favourite artistic works have the image features of vivid, strong, direct and detailed. The works with vivid appearance and causing strong feelings could be more easily interpreted by the audiences, and will be more easily liked by the audiences.

References

1. Mituo, N.: Kansei Engineering. Kaibundo Publishing Corporation, Tokyo, Japan (1989)
2. Daifen, H., Zhigao, N.: Evaluation and research of Kansei image vocabulary in commercial appearance - a discussion on relevance between styling features and images. J. Archit. **84**, 55–75 (2013)
3. He, Z.:The Aesthetic Value of Incompleteness in Visual Art. Doctoral Dissertation, Sichuan Normal University (2010)
4. Huang, C., Harada, A.: The development status of Japanese Kansei Engineering and the Possibility of Applying to Remote Control Interface. The Published Thesis of Sino-Japan Seminar on Design Education in 1998, Department of Industrial Design, National Yunlin University of Science and Technology (1998)
5. Donglong, L., Jiafang, Y.: The discussion of symbol image on product appearance - an example of Italian design style. J. Cult. Soc. Sci. **1**(1), 19–27 (2005)
6. Arnheim, R.: Art and Visual Consciousness. China Social Sciences Press, China (1984)
7. Miyazaki, K., Matsubara, Y., Nagamachi, M.: A modeling of a design recognition in Kansei engineering. Japan. J. Ergonomics **29**, 196–197 (1993)
8. Papoport, A.: Human Aspects of Urban Form: Towards A Man-environment Approach to Urban Form and Design. Pergamon, Oxford, England (1977)
9. Yungui, Y.: The research on motivation in aesthetic activities of incomplete beauty – from the perspective of aesthetic psychology. J. Guangxi Normal Univ., J. Phil. Soc. Sci. **5**(2), 81–85 (2014)
10. Yang, G.: Social and Behavioral Science Research (Part II). Donghua, Taipei (1992)
11. Qingtian, Y.: The research on preference degree of packaging container. J. Art **69**, 1–14 (2001)
12. Yu, A.: The aesthetic analysis and cultural origin exploration of incomplete beauty. Chin. Cult. Forum **1**, 82–87 (2015)

A Study of Applying Bauhaus Design Idea into the Reproduction of the Triadic Ballet

Yi-Wen Ting[✉], Po-Hsien Lin, and Rungtai Lin

Graduate School of Creative Industry Design, National Taiwan University of Arts,
New Taipei City, Taiwan
t0131@ntua.edu.tw, rtlin@mail.ntua.edu.tw

Abstract. After the Bauhaus was founded, Walter Gropius, the principle of the Bauhaus, requested artist Oskar Schlemmer to design a drama lesson in order to encourage students' cross-field studying, which lead to the 'golden era' of the Bauhaus Theater between 1923 and 1929. Oskar Schlemmer's most straightforward conclusion was: 'human bodies are mobile architecture.' However, compared to architecture and product design, studies and discussions of the Bauhaus Theater are relatively few despite 'Triadic Ballet' providing a pioneer experiment which has sufficient influence over the development and merging of cross- field performance art.

Work began on the 'Triadic Ballet' in 1912 and, led by Schlemmer, and was a collaboration between him and the students, as an experiment which lasted for another ten years. Schlemmer used dancing and machines as implications and tried to expand the potential of Theater performance. This programmed performance has become the standard method of understanding the transformation of modern art and the Bauhaus Theater. This research used qualitative research methods to analyse the 'Triadic Ballet'. In addition, we proposed an aesthetic aspect, 'human bodies in the space' and used it as the main theory to construct a new 'Triadic Ballet'. A quantitative research questionnaire was also used to explore the audiences' understanding of aesthetic experience after watching this whole new 'Triadic Ballet'.

This research emphasizes cross-field collaboration between design and performance art, and used both qualitative and quantities research methods, hoping to once again present the great 'Triadic Ballet' and the Bauhaus spirit.

Keywords: The Bauhaus Theater · Triadic Ballet · Aesthetic experience

1 Introduction

The Bauhaus, a school of architecture and design founded by Walter Gropius (1883–1969) in Weimar, Germany, in 1919, features a rationality-based design combining craftsmanship and industrial technology that provided a new direction in contemporary design. This design concept facilitated the cosmopolitan modern design movement and led to the modernization of design fields in the 20th century. In 2019, which marked the centennial of the Bauhaus, a widespread Bauhaus movement was observed worldwide [30].

© Springer Nature Switzerland AG 2021
P.-L. P. Rau (Ed.): HCII 2021, LNCS 12772, pp. 65–83, 2021.
https://doi.org/10.1007/978-3-030-77077-8_6

Compared with studies related to Bauhaus architecture and design, studies on Bauhaus theater have been relatively few. This study employed the concept of Bauhaus design in theater to explore the influence of the Bauhaus on performing arts in addition to design and architecture. This study also aimed to clarify the importance of Bauhaus design in modern dance, postmodern dance, and the German Tanztheater (dance theater).

This study implemented the Bauhaus concept to explore the Triadic Ballet, which was developed by Oskar Schlemmer and stresses the interdisciplinary integration of design and performance. The Bauhaus concept was used to examine the development of Bauhaus theater and its application in the performing arts. In addition, a concrete quantitative survey on the artistic aesthetic experience in the reproduction and presentation of the Triadic Ballet was conducted to understand audiences' aesthetic experience in Bauhaus theater, thereby clarifying audiences' aesthetic value as well as the cultural value of Bauhaus theater.

This study strived to enhance research on Bauhaus theater by using an interdisciplinary breakthrough in design and performing arts research and a reflection on the centennial of the Bauhaus. This study also aimed to clarify the aesthetic understanding and cognition of the Triadic Ballet's audience from the perspective of the dissemination model of dance arts. The goals of this study are as follows: 1. Analyze the implementation of the Bauhaus concept in the Triadic Ballet and reproduce the ballet. 2. Integrate the creative model of the Triadic Ballet and construct a matrix for evaluating the aesthetic experience of its audience.

2   Literature Review

2.1   The Triadic Ballet of the Theater of the Bauhaus

The experimental theater of the Bauhaus has influenced modern dance and theater [30]. Bauhaus theater courses were opened during the early years of the Bauhaus's establishment in the 1920s and an exclusive theater was built when the school moved to Dessau in 1926. During this period, the courses were led by the painter Oscar Schlemmer (1888–1943) with the aim of enabling students to understand the relationship between the human body and space through theater courses. Furthermore, the course objective was to cultivate students' creative thinking through creative displays of performing arts. The Bauhaus Dances Organization (bauhausdance.org) in the United States suggested that, "Oskar Schlemmer's theater concepts have influenced the performance theory of modern and postmodern dancers such as Merce Cunningham, Alwin Nikolais, and Robert Wilson" [3].

Research on the Bauhaus has mainly focused on design and architecture, and research on the theater of the Bauhaus is relatively scant. In 1925, a book titled *Die Bühne im Bauhaus* was published in the Bauhaus book series, and was translated into English and published as *The Theater of the Bauhaus* in 1961. The English version included an introduction to Walter Gropius and four essays, namely *Humans and Artistic Shapes* and *Theater* by Schlemmer; *Theatre, Circus, Variety* by Laszlo Moholy Nagy; and *U-Shape Theater* by Farkas Molnár. The shock caused by *The Theater of the Bauhaus* was because of its deconstruction of the traditional concept of theater from two aspects, namely theater space and the human body in space. The concept of theater is related to the building of the theater itself; specifically, it involves the great potential of the building to actualize performances. The concept of the human body in space involves the perfection of performance art, which is particularly true for the four laws of the human body in space proposed by Schlemmer. Under the four laws, the traditional narrative form of dance is abandoned, and dance art creation no longer exists to serve characters but returns to the creation of art itself. Additionally, Schlemmer demonstrated the purity and abstractness of art in modernism through bold experiments.

In the posthumously published book *The Letters and Diaries of Oscar Schlemmer*, Schlemmer wrote that, "Human organism, stands in the cubic and abstract space of the stage; humans and space each have different laws, who will become dominant? In one situation, abstract space changes itself to face and adapt to differences of natural people. In another situation, natural people reshape their image to adapt to abstract space." Furthermore, he asserted that, "Those who are involved in these laws are 'individuals as dancers' who follow the laws of the body and also the laws of space. Whether in an abstract movement, a symbolic dance show, or an empty stage… these dancers are all a medium for transitioning to the great world of theater" [29].

The Triadic Ballet started to be appreciated by dancers in workshops as early as 1912. Part of the ballet's content was published in 1915, it premiered in Stuttgart in 1922, and it was performed in the Deutsche National theater Weimar in 1923. For a decade-long experiment of this ballet, Schlemmer used the metaphorical approach of dance and machines to explore the potential of theaters. This ballet, which is least similar to traditional ballet, has become a crucial text for understanding the changes in modern art and the stage ideas of the Bauhaus [30]. Three different methods exist for translating the Triadic Ballet and they were all developed based on three acts and three dancers. German dance critic Ilona Landgraf (2019) explained that the word "Triadic" in "The Triadic Ballet" originated from a Greek word that implied three acts and three dancers. The performance of the ballet consisted of three styles, namely solo dance, duo dance, and trio dance. A total of 12 dance poses including circles, triangles, and squares and 18 sets of costumes were also divided into three series [13]. The whole show consisted of three series in yellow, rose, and black and was performed by two male dancers and one female dancer. The dancers changed into 18 sets of costumes and performed 12 sessions of dances, as indicated in the manuscript of the Triadic Ballet by Oskar Schlemmer in Fig. 1.

2.2 Aesthetic Experience of the Audience

Art involves cognitive functions, which partially determine individuals' aesthetic values [39]. Visualization and mental imagery, which are regarded as the image forms of cognitive states, reflect different states of audiences' aesthetic activities [34]. Goldman argued that evaluating a work of art requires in-depth understanding of the modes of communication between artists and audiences [8], which is attributable to the demands of contemporary social backgrounds and understanding the emotional cognitive experience between the creator and the audience. Studies have incorporated communication theory and theories related to semantic cognition in mental models in exploring topics related to art dissemination [16–18]. According to the school of programming in dissemination theory, successful dissemination must fulfill technical, semantic, and effectual

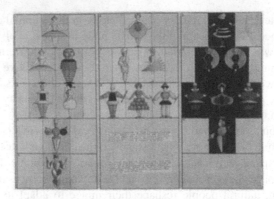

Fig. 1. Manuscript of the Triadic Ballet by Oskar Schlemmer [28]

levels [38]. Specifically, the audience must see the art; that is, they must form sensory impressions involving the perception of appearances. Second, they must understand the art; that is, they must engage in the mode of thinking that involves meaning cognition. Finally, they must be moved by the art; that is, they must engage in psychological activities involving intrinsic feelings. These three levels of artistic creation constitute technical appearance characterization, semantic connotation, and effectual emotional connection as perceived by the audience [18] (Fig. 2 and 3).

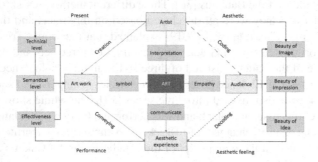

Fig. 2. The cognitive model of dance aesthetics experience [18]

On the basis of these findings, Fang et al. devised an evaluation matrix on the cognitive experience of general audiences regarding dance aesthetics [18], arguing that artists employ the technical, semantic, and effectual levels of their performance to achieve the process of aesthetic cognition, whereas audiences achieve the same process through the beauty of images, constructs, and ideas.

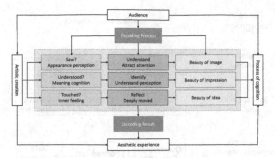

Fig. 3. Evaluation matrix of audiences regarding dance aesthetics [18]

3 Research Design and Method

3.1 Research Process and Framework

This study incorporated five primary steps, namely the collection of literary, audio, and video data, analysis of the Bauhaus theater concept, the practical verification of works, a survey on audience experience, and recording of image data, as Fig. 4:

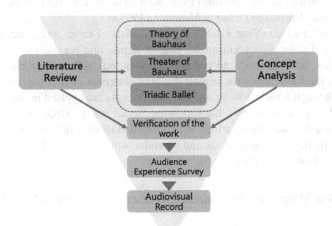

Fig. 4. Research process

Textual, audio, and video data related to the Bauhaus were collected to provide a basis for examining the concept of Bauhaus theater. The *Triadic Ballet* was the focus in this study to clarify the application of the Bauhaus concept in the performing arts. The case analysis results were then implemented in the actual reproduction and presentation of the *Triadic Ballet* for verification; that is, the reproduction was arranged in accordance with the findings in this study and presented for a quantitative study of the audience's experience. Finally, digital audio and video data on the works of Bauhaus theater were recorded. The Fig. 5 presents the framework of this study:

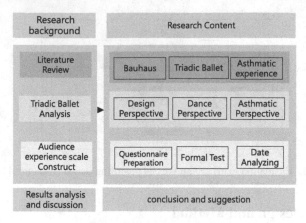

Fig. 5. Research framework

3.2   Core Concepts of Triadic Ballet

The core creative concepts of the *Triadic Ballet* were analyzed according to the description of the Bauhaus concept in dance arts by Schlemmer in the chapter "Man and Art Figure" in *The Theater of the Bauhaus* (1930) as well as the creative processes recorded in *The Letters and Diaries of Oskar Schlemmer* (1958).

The creative structure of the *Triadic Ballet* consists of three core concepts, namely space, shape, and color. Space comprises height, depth, and breadth; shape comprises circles, triangles, and squares; and color comprises red, yellow, and blue. Thus, the entire work of the ballet revolves around the core concepts of the major triad and the minor triad. Through artistic coding, these core concepts are applied in the movements, costumes, and stage designs. See the following figure for the structure of the *Triadic Ballet* as analyzed in this study, which was published in HCI International 2020. This structure was the basis of the analysis and reproduction of the *Triadic Ballet* as well as the audience evaluation matrix (Fig. 6).

3.3   Evaluation Matrix for the Audience Aesthetic Experience of the Triadic Ballet

The evaluation matrix for the aesthetic experience of the *Triadic Ballet*, constructed on the basis of the core concepts of the *Triadic Ballet*, consists of horizontal and vertical dimensions (Table 1). The coding process by the artist and the decoding process by the audience were clarified to analyze the creative model of the *Triadic Ballet* and its audience's aesthetic understanding.

The horizontal dimension consists of the core concepts of the *Triadic Ballet*, namely shape, color, and space; the vertical dimension consists of the three expressive forms of the *Triadic Ballet*, namely movement, costumes, and stage design. Thus, the evaluation matrix provides the theoretical basis for reproducing the Bauhaus concept in the *Triadic Ballet*. The context was established through the sequential relationships between the two dimensions to analyze the relationship between the coding process of the artist and the decoding process of the audience.

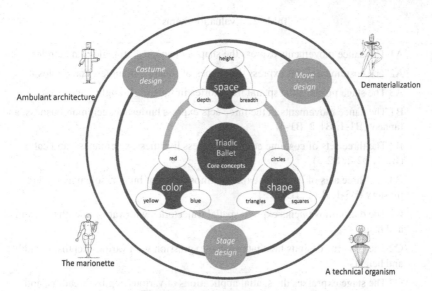

Fig. 6. Triadic ballet framework

On the basis of the matrix, 17 evaluation items were developed, and the participants answered these items on a 5-point Likert scale according to their feelings after viewing the reproduced *Triadic Ballet* (Table 2).

Table 1. Evaluation matrix of the aesthetic experience of the audience of the *Triadic Ballet*

		Move design (1)	Costume design (2)	Stage Design (3)
Shape (A)	Squares	A1 Movement shape	A2 Costume shape	A3 Spatial trajectory of the stage
	Triangles			
	Circles			
Color (B)	Yellow	B1 Meaning of movement	B2 Meaning of costume color	B3 Spatial atmosphere
	Red			
	Blue			
Space (C)	Depth	C1 Trajectory of movement	C2 Overall form	C3 Overall stage space
	Breadth			
	Height			

Table 2. Evaluation items

Shape	A1 The dance movements express the shapes of squares, triangles, and circles
	A2 The costume designs express the shapes of squares, triangles, and circles
	A3 The stage presents the spatial trajectories in squares, triangles, and circles
Color	B1 The dance movements in the three acts express burlesque, ceremoniousness, and fantasy (B1-1, B1-2, B1-3)
	B2 The three sets of costume coloring express liveliness, solemnness, and calm (B2-1, B2-2, B2-3)
	B3 The three acts of the ballet express atmospheres of humor, solemnness, and mystery (B3-1, B3-2, B3-3)
Space	C1 The dance movements express spatial trajectories with various depths, breadths, and heights
	C2 The costume designs facilitate spatial expression with various depths, breadths, and heights
	C3 The stage expresses the spatial applications of various depths, breadths, and heights
Overall	D1 The overall creative expression of the work
	D2 Your overall fondness of the work

4 Discussion

4.1 Applying the Bauhaus Concept in the Reproduction of the *Triadic Ballet*

The analyzed structure of the *Triadic Ballet* was applied in its reproduction, which consisted of three components, namely movement, costume, and stage designs. In continuation of the performance of the rose-colored act II at HCI International 2020, the first sections of act I (yellow-colored) and act III (black colored) were selected for reproduction, resulting in a selection of works that covered all three acts of the ballet.

Movement Design. In act I, to express the humorous atmosphere in accordance with the choreography by Schlemmer, mechanical and angular arm movements were prioritized, and leg movements were designed to form straight lines in accordance with the spatial trajectory, thus presenting a square-shaped dance trajectory (Fig. 7). In act III, to express the mysterious atmosphere, spinning movements were prioritized, and the dancer's rotational trajectory and the space's revolution were designed in coordination with the spatial atmosphere (Fig. 8).

Costume Design. The costumes were redesigned in accordance with those by Schlemmer to emphasize circles; the flat circle skirt design in act I (Fig. 9) and spiral circle skirt design in act III (Fig. 10) presented a flat circle, a vertical circle, and a spiral circle.

Fig. 7. Movement design: act1 (yellow) (Color figure online)

Fig. 8. Movement design: act3 (black)

Fig. 9. Custumes reproduction: act1 (yellow). (Color figure online)

Stage Design. According to illustrations by Schlemmer and records in *The Theater of the Bauhaus* (1930), the movements were rehearsed and recorded in a virtual studio, and yellow (Fig. 11) and black (Fig. 12) stage effects were created postproduction.

Fig. 10. Custumes reproducton: act3 (black)

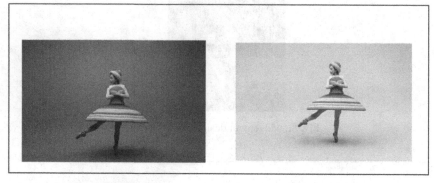

Fig. 11. Stage production: act1 (yellow). (Color figure online)

Fig. 12. Stage production: act3 (black)

4.2 Analysis of the Questionnaire for Evaluating the Aesthetic Experience of the Audience

Evaluation Matrix Analysis of the Aesthetic Experience of the Audience.
The matrix constructed according to the structure of this study was used to evaluate the Triadic Ballet viewing experience. The matrix has two constructs with 17 questions in total. Construct 1 comprises three dimensions centered on core concepts, namely shape, color, and space. Construct 2, which focuses on forms of artistic expression, also comprises three dimensions: choreography, costume design, and stage design. A total of 42 valid questionnaires were retrieved.

Reliability Analysis. As mentioned, 42 valid questionnaires were retrieved. On the basis of the evaluation matrix, the reliability of the questionnaire was determined (Cronbach $\alpha = .899$). As for the two constructs and their three dimensions, the Cronbach α ranged from .730 and .897. Overall, the results were indicative of favorable reliability (Table 3).

Table 3. Reliability analysis

Construct 1	Factor	Conbach α	Conbach α
Shape (A)	A1	.872	.899
	A2		
	A3		
Color (B)	B1	.897	
	B2		
	B3		
Space (C)	C1	.865	
	C2		
	C3		
Construct 2	Factor	Conbach α	Conbach α
Move design (1)	A1	.730	.899
	B1		
	C1		
Costume design (2)	A2	.748	
	B2		
	C2		
Stage design (3)	A3	.747	
	B3		
	C3		

Validity Analysis. Factor analysis was performed to determine the validity of the evaluation matrix. As mentioned, the matrix was divided into two constructs, and the aspect 1 dimensions were shape, color, and space. (1) Space: Between the A1, A2, and A3 factors, one factor, consisting of three questions, was selected after factor analysis. The eigenvalue of 2.390 explained 79.682% of the variation. The factor loadings were between .842 and .900. (2) Color: Between the B1, B2, and B3 factors, one factor, consisting of three questions, was selected after factor analysis. The eigenvalue of 2.486 explained 82.869% of the variation. The factor loadings were between .899 and .926. (3) Space: Between the C1, C2, and C3 factors, one factor, consisting of three questions, was selected after factor analysis. The eigenvalue of 2.365 explained 78.837% of the variation. The factor loadings were between .854 and .907 (Table 4).

Table 4. Validity analysis

Dimensions	Factors	Factor loadings	Communalities	Eigen values	Total variance explained
Shape (A)	A1	.934	.872	2.390	79.682%
	A2	.842	.709		
	A3	.900	.809		
Color (B)	B1	.899	.809	2.486	82.869%
	B2	.905	.820		
	B3	.926	.858		
Space (C)	C1	.902	.814	2.365	78.837%
	C2	.854	.730		
	C3	.907	.822		

As mentioned, construct 2 comprised three dimensions: choreography, costume design, and stage design. (1) Choreography: Between the A1, B1, and C1 factors, one factor, consisting of three questions, was selected after factor analysis. The eigenvalue of 1.953 explained 65.113% of the variation. The factor loadings were between .746 and .869. (2) Costume design: Between the A2, B2, and C2 factors, one factor, consisting of three questions, was selected after factor analysis. The eigenvalue of 1.998 explained 66.603% of the variation of the human factor. The factor loadings were between .756 and .851. (3) Stage design: Between the A3, B3, and C3 factors, one factor, consisting of three questions, was selected after factor analysis. The eigenvalue of 1.994 explained 66.468% of the variation. The factor loadings were between .854 and .907. Overall, the results are indicative of favorable validity with regard to the two constructs and their respective three factors (Table 5).

Key Factor Analysis of Aesthetic Experience of the Audience

Audience Preference Analysis. The coefficients of the correlation between the nine predictor variables and audience preference, namely .381, .308, .294, .367, .445, .461, .523,

Table 5. Factors analysis

Dimensions	Factors	Factor loadings	Communalities	Eigen values	Total variance explained
Move design (1)	A1	.869	.755	1.953	65.113
	B1	.746	.557		
	C1	.801	.641		
Costume design (2)	A2	.837	.701	1.998	66.603
	B2	.851	.725		
	C2	.756	.572		
Stage design (3)	A3	.773	.598	1.994	66,468
	B3	.812	.659		
	C3	.858	.737		

.381, and .510, were all significant. The results from the multiple regression analysis presented in the following table show that the correlation coefficient R of the predictor variables and the dependent variable was .662. The explained variation of the nine factors for audience preference was 38.7%. The F value of 2.24 was significant ($p < .045$). The most significant predictor variable was C1, and its β value was .429, followed by of B2 (.222) and B3 (.181). C1, B2, B3 were all significant ($p < .000, .002,$ and $.001$, respectively). Overall, all nine factors were significantly correlated with audience preference, indicating that they were suitable for explaining and predicting audience preference. The most significant factor was C1, followed by B2 and C3 (movement trajectory, meaning of stage colors, and the overall stage space (Table 6).

Table 6. Audience preference analysis

Factors	Correlation	B	β	T	p
A1	.381	.147	.187	.677	.006
A2	.308	−.011	−.017	−.074	.024
A3	.294	−.155	−.273	−1.018	.029
B1	.367	−.104	−.117	−.431	.008
B2	.445	.233	.222	.849	.002
B3	.461	.158	.181	.672	.001
C1	.523	.296	.429	1.720	.000
C2	.381	−.052	−.076	−.338	.006
C3	.510	.096	.130	.506	.000

1. R = .622 Rsq = .387 F = 2.244 Sig = .045

Analysis of Audience Perception of Creativity. Multiple regression analysis revealed no significant correlations between the nine factors and audience perception of creativity (Table 7).

Table 7. Analysis of audience perception of creativity

Factors	Correlation	B	β	T	p
A1	.345	−.078	−.067	−.227	.822
A2	.319	−.008	−.008	−.033	.974
A3	.400	.277	.331	1.150	.259
B1	.162	.075	.058	.199	.844
B2	.322	.535	.348	1.238	.225
B3	.173	−.263	−.206	−.711	.482
C1	.334	.285	.281	1.053	.300
C2	.334	.213	.210	.879	.386
C3	.150	−.440	−.405	−1.474	.150

$R = .544$ $Rsq = .296$ $F = 1.495$ $Sig = .192$

Relationship Between Respondent Background and the Aesthetic Experience

Sex. The study sample consisted of 11 men and 31 women. The independent samples t test revealed that sex was not significantly correlated with the nine factors, audience preference, and audience perception of creativity. Overall, audience preference and audience perception of creativity were higher among the women than the men (Table 8).

Age Of the 42 respondents, 3, 9, 15, 12, and 3 were aged under 20 years, between 21 and 30 years, between 31 and 40 years, between 41 and 50 years, and over 51 years, respectively. One-way analysis of variance revealed a significant difference for B3 (ambience creation). The Scheffé post hoc comparison showed that the respondents aged under 20 years related poorly to the ambience creation of the performance. Audience preference and audience perception of creativity were the lowest among the respondents aged over 51 years (Table 9).

Differences in Background Domain. Regarding the background domain of the respondents, 16, 11, 6, 2, 3, and 3 were in design, performance, humanities, communications, art, and other fields, respectively. One-way analysis of variance revealed significant differences for A1, expression of movement ($5 < 1 < 3 < 6 < 4 < 2$). Significant differences were also observed for A3, stage design trajectory ($5 < 3 < 1 < 6 < 2 < 4$); B2, symbolism of costume colors ($5 < 4 < 1 < 3 < 2 < 6$); C2, overall expression of design ($5 < 4 < 1 < 2 < 3 < 6$); and C3, overall stage space ($5 < 4 < 1 < 3 < 2 < 6$). Overall, four of the nine factors received lower scores from the respondents with art backgrounds, suggesting that they had stricter standards with regard to the aesthetic evaluation of the *Triadic Ballet*. However, this did not affect their preference with the performance (mean 4.00) (Table 10).

Table 8. Sex

Factor	Sex	Member	M	SD	Sig.	t.
A1	1	11	3.82	.751	.987	−2.857
	2	31	4.52	.677		
A2	1	11	3.55	1.036	.370	−2.406
	2	31	4.29	.824		
A3	1	11	3.82	.982	.670	−.934
	2	31	4.16	1.068		
B1	1	11	3.75	.883	.177	−1.913
	2	31	4.19	.549		
B2	1	11	3.69	.690	.225	−2.212
	2	31	4.11	.483		
B3	1	11	3.72	.866	.477	−1.473
	2	31	4.07	.594		
C1	1	11	4.09	.701	.161	−.441
	2	31	4.23	.920		
C2	1	11	3.82	.751	.543	−1.705
	2	31	4.32	.871		
C3	1	11	3.91	.831	.460	−1.366
	2	31	4.29	.783		
D1	1	11	4.09	.539	.164	−2.883
	2	31	4.65	.551		
D2	1	11	3.91	1.044	.238	−1.935
	2	31	4.48	.769		

Table 9. Age

	Factor	SS	DF	MS	F	Sig.	N	M	SD	Scheffe'
	between groups	4.307	4	1.077			1=3	4.555	.769	
							2=9	3.518	.835	
B3	within group	14.793	37	.400	2.693	.046	3=15	3.888	.599	1<4<5<3<2
							4=12	4.305	.521	
	Total	19.101	41				5=3	4.000	.000	
							All=42	3.984	.682	

Previous Knowledge of the Bauhaus. Among the respondents, 26 and 16 individuals had and did not have previous knowledge of the Bauhaus, respectively. The independent samples t test revealed no significant difference. In other words, previous knowledge of the Bauhaus did not significantly affect the aesthetic experience of the audience.

Table 10. Differences in background domain

		SS	DF	MS	F	Sig.	N	M	SD	Scheffe,
A1	between groups	10.197	5	2.039			1=16	4.25	.775	
							2=11	4.82	.405	
	within group	13.136	36	.365	5.589	.001 *	3=6	4.33	.516	5<1<3<
							4=2	4.50	.707	6<4<2
	Total	23.333	41				5=4	3.00	.000	
							6=3	4.67	.577	
A3	between groups	17.212	5	3.442			1=16	3.94	1.181	
							2=11	4.82	.405	
	within group	27.574	36	.766	4.494	.003 *	3=6	3.83	.753	5<3<1<
							4=2	4.50	.707	6<2<4
	Total	44.786	41				5=4	2.50	.577	
							6=3	4.33	.577	
B2	between groups	3.511	5	.702			1=16	4.0	.486	
							2=11	4.12	.522	
	within group	9.709	36	.270	2.604	.041 *	3=6	4.05	.611	5<4<1<
							4=2	3.66	.000	3<2<6
	Total	13.220	41				5=4	3.33	.666	
							6=3	4.66	.333	
C2	between groups	9.274	5	1.855			1=16	4.06	.854	
							2=11	4.27	.786	
	within group	21.203	36	.589	3.149	.019 *	3=6	4.83	.408	5<4<1<
							4=2	3.50	.707	2<3<6
	Total	30.476	41				5=4	3.25	.957	
							6=3	5.00	.000	
C3	between groups	12.077	5	2.415			1=16	4.06	.680	
							2=11	4.64	.505	
	within group	14.400	36	.400	6.038	.000 **	3=6	4.50	.548	5<4<1<
							4=2	4.00	.000	3<2<6
	Total	26.476	41				5=4	2.75	957	
							6=3	4.67	.577	

5 Conclusion and Recommendations

The present results are discussed in three passages on the basis of the analysis and the construction of the model. The first passage concerns the three parts selected from the reproduction of Oskar Schlemmer's *Triadic Ballet*, which was originally conceived in 1912 (see the production: https://youtu.be/Vd-XXKzd4ZI). The second passage concerns the construction of the evaluation matrix. The third passage concerns a preliminary survey on the aesthetic experience of the audience.

The present findings demonstrate that practicability of applying the core concepts of shape, color, and space and the forms of artistic expression of choreography, costume design, and stage design to the reproduction of the *Triadic Ballet*. The survey results demonstrated that both audience preference () and audience perception of creativity were high (M = 4.3), indicating that modern audiences still have a certain level of appreciation for this work, despite the fact that it came into being more than a century ago, and that they were able to acknowledge the expression of creativity in the performance. The video recording of the performance can be found on this website:.

As mentioned, two constructs of the aesthetic experience of the audience were examined according to the analysis of the *Triadic Ballet*. Construct 1 comprised shape, color, and space, and Construct 2 comprised choreography, costume design, and stage design. Nine factors were identified from these constructs to form the evaluation matrix of aesthetic experience. Both the reliability and factor analyses revealed favorable results, indicating that the matrix can serve as a reference for future studies on audience experience.

The results from the preliminary survey reveal significant differences in the aesthetic experience of audience members of different backgrounds. Notably, the respondents with art backgrounds had stricter standards with regard to the performance expression. However, neither background domain nor previous knowledge of the Bauhaus affected the audience preference or audience perception of creativity. These results demonstrate that the *Triadic Ballet* remains highly accepted by modern audiences.

Historical records indicate that the Bauhaus dances did not necessarily inspire the development of modern Western dance. Moreover, the Bauhaus dances gradually declined in importance after the death of Oskar Schlemmer. However, Schlemmer's life-long exploration of "figure and space delineation" and of "man and art figure" is fully manifested in his experimental works of shape, color, and space. Despite their purity and simplicity, these works were realized through the expression of logical creativity, encapsulating the less-is-more spirit of modernism of the Bauhaus. In conclusion, the reproduction of the *Triadic Ballet* was examined in the present study to rethink how Schlemmer constructed an organic piece of metaphysical art in an abstract form through the use of rational numbers and human sensitivity. This reimagining also captures the transition of colors and forms from a two-dimensional space to the three-dimensional space of the stage.

Acknowledgment. This study was partly sponsored with a grant, MOST 109-2221-E-144-002, from the Ministry of Science and Technology, Taiwan.

References

1. Baumgarten, A.G.: Aesthetics. Culture and Art Publishing House, Beijing (1987). Translated by Wang Xuxiao
2. Banes, S.: Writing Dancing in the Age of Postmodernism. University Press of New England, Hanover (1994)
3. Bauhaus dance. https://bauhausdances.org/. Accessed 25 Nov 2019
4. Chen, S., Yen, H., Lee, S., Lin, C.: Applying design thinking in curating model - a case study of the exhibition of turning poetry into painting. J. Des. **21**(4), 1–24 (2016)
5. Fang, W., Gao, Y., Zeng, Z., Lin, B.: A study on audience perception of aesthetic experience in dance performance. J. Des. **23**(3), 23–46 (2018)
6. Lin, B., Xu, M.: A basic study on triadic ballet. J. Inner Mongolia Arts Univ. **1**, 117–120 (2016)
7. Goldman, A.: Evaluating art. In: Kivy, Peter (ed.) The Blackwell Guide to Aesthetics: Kivy/The Blackwell, pp. 93–108. Blackwell Publishing Ltd., Oxford, UK (2004)
8. Hall, S.: Encoding/decoding. In: Hall, S., et al. (eds.) Culture, Media, Language, pp. 117–127. Hutchinson, London (1980)

9. Jakobson, R.: Language in Literature. Harvard University Press, Cambridge, MA (1987)
10. Ou, J.: History of World Art Dance Volume. Oriental, Beijing (2003)
11. Martin, J.: Introduction to the Dance. Culture and Art Publishing House, Beijing (1994). Translated by Ou Jianping
12. Kant, M.: Oscar Schlemmer's Triadic Ballet (Paris, 1932) and dance discourse in Germany. Three letters with annotation and a commentary. Dance Res. **33**(1), 16–30 (2015)
13. Landgraf on dance. https://www.ilonalandgraf.com/2014/06/patience-pays/. Accessed 01 Dec 2019
14. Langer, S.K.: Problems of Art. Scribner, New York (1957)
15. Langer, S.K.: Feeling and Form. Scribner, New York (1953)
16. Lin, R.: Designing "emotion" into modern products. In: International Symposium for Emotion and Sensibility, KAIST, Korea, 27–29 June 2008, p. 11 (2008)
17. Lin, R., Cheng, R., Sun, Ming-Xian.: Digital archive database for cultural product design. In: Aykin, N.. (ed.) UI-HCII 2007. LNCS, vol. 4559, pp. 154–163. Springer, Heidelberg (2007). https://doi.org/10.1007/978-3-540-73287-7_20
18. Lin, R., Qian, F., Jun, W., Fang, Wen-Ting., Jin, Y.: A pilot study of communication matrix for evaluating artworks. In: Rau, P.-L.P. (ed.) CCD 2017. LNCS, vol. 10281, pp. 356–368. Springer, Cham (2017). https://doi.org/10.1007/978-3-319-57931-3_29
19. Lin, R.: Service innovation design for cultural and creative industries – a case study of the Cultural and Creative Industry Park at NTUA. In: International Service Innovation Design Conference, Dongseo University, Korea, 20–22 October 2008, pp. 14–25 (2008). (Keynote Speech)
20. Liu, C.: Humanity Dance and Mechanical Principles-From "Tridic Ballet" (2018). https://kkn ews.cc/zhtw/culture/pgkz88j.html. Accessed 10 Dec 2019
21. Lu, C., Lin, R.: The influence of Bauhaus style on Taiwan design education. Art Appreciation **6**(3), 28–43 (2010)
22. Lu, Y.: Dance Aesthetics. Central University for Nationalities, Beijing (2011)
23. Gang, L.: Reading for Cultural Studies. China Social Science Press, Beijing (2000)
24. Ou, J.: Appreciation of Foreign Dance History and Works. Higher Education, Beijing (2008)
25. Ou, J.: Dance Appreciation. Jiangsu Education, Nanjing (2009)
26. Liu, Q.: Anthology of Liu Qingyi's Anthology 1-Body Language Study of Modern Dance. Shanghai Music, Shanghai (2013)
27. Liu, Q.: Outline of History of Modern Western Dance. Shanghai Music, Shanghai (2014)
28. Schlemmer, O.: Man and art figure. In: Gropius, W., Wensinger, A.S. (eds). The Theater of the Bauhaus. Wesleyan University Press, Middletown, CT (1961)
29. Schlemmer, O.: The Letters and Diaries of Oskar Schlemmer. Northwestern University Press, Evanston, IL (1990)
30. Smock, W.: The Bauhaus Ideal Then and Now: An Illustrated Guide to Modernist Design. Academy Chicago Publishers, Chicago, IL (2004)
31. Sun, Y., Lin, S., Sun, M.: The evaluation of the classic design in contemporary perspective: reflection on Bauhaus hundred years of prosperity. J. Des. **24**(3), 49–72 (2019)
32. Lu, Qichang., Lin, Rongtai.: The influence of Bauhaus style on Taiwan design education. In: Proceedings of the 2009 Process Design Symposium: 90 Years of Bauhaus Review and Prospect, Department of Craft Design, National Taiwan University of Arts, pp. 30–41 (2009)
33. Triadic Ballet. https://www.youtube.com/watch?v=rlIiT80dqHE. Accessed 25 Nov 2019
34. Zeimbekis, J.: Why digital pictures are not notational representations. J. Aesthetics Art Criticism **73**(4), 449–453 (2015)
35. Zhang, Y.: Western Dance Art from the Perspective of Cultural History Guangxi. Normal University Press (2016)

36. Zhu, L.: The language of dance. Anthology of Modern Western Art Aesthetics Dance Aesthetics Vol. Liaoning Education Press (1990). Original by M. Wigman. Chunfeng Literature and Art Publishing House, Shenyang, 2016/11/21
37. Craig, R.T.: Communication theory as a field. Commun. Theor. **9**(2), 119–161 (1999)
38. Fiske, J.: Introduction to Communication Studies. Routledge, London (2010)
39. Baumberger, C.: Art and understanding. In: Greenlee, M., et al. (eds.) Defence of Aesthetic Cognitivism. Bilder sehen. Perspektiven der Bildwissenschaft, pp. 41–67. Schnell + Steiner, Regensburg (2013)

Discussing the Aesthetic Emotion of Artworks by AI and Human Artists with the Mediating Variable of Aesthetic Fluency

Rui Xu[1,2]([✉])

[1] The Graduate Institute of Design Science, Tatung University, Taipei 104, Taiwan
[2] School of Art and Design, Fuzhou University of International Studies and Trade, Fuzhou 350202, China

Abstract. At the current stage, there is almost no aesthetic emotion research that directly explores the relationship between artistic creation and expertise in AI. Therefore, this study attempts to fill this gap and uses the Aesthetic Fluency Scale compiled by (Smith Empirical Stud. Arts 24(2)229–242, 2006) and the Geneva Emotion Wheel (3.0) created by the Swiss Centre for Affective Sciences to confirm that viewers with richer artistic expertise (the tested expert group, higher levels of aesthetic fluency) will be more interested in AI creation, winning more diverse and higher levels of aesthetic emotion. Besides, Viewers with relatively inadequate artistic expertise (tested novice group, lower levels of aesthetic fluency) will feel more confused and less interested in AI creation, winning a relatively homogeneous and lower aesthetic emotion. Though some of the AI artworks involved in the experiments are already of a fairly high technical level and bear a close resemblance to abstract artworks by human artists in appearance, the results of this study confirm the previous conjecture due to the strong aesthetic-emotional connection between the viewer's level of expertise and the artworks. After collecting and analyzing the experimental data with SPSS software, this study has concluded that there are still significant differences in the emotional perception level between artworks created by AI and those by humans based on the different expertise and different aesthetic experience and emotional perception of artworks. Viewers with more expertise (the tested expert group) always have richer and higher levels of emotional perception in face of artworks by AI and human artists than viewers with less expertise (the tested novice group). Also, viewers with a higher level of expertise (the tested expert group) are more likely to give positive emotional evaluations of the AI artworks and are more tolerant of the AI artist's identity than viewers with a lower level of expertise (the tested novice group). This finding has some implications for the study of AI art creation.

Keywords: Artificial intelligence · Aesthetic fluency · Aesthetic emotion

© Springer Nature Switzerland AG 2021
P.-L. P. Rau (Ed.): HCII 2021, LNCS 12772, pp. 84–94, 2021.
https://doi.org/10.1007/978-3-030-77077-8_7

1   Introduction

Along with advances in AI technology in the art field, Convolutional neural network (CNN) (Donahue 2014) Creative Adversarial Networks (CAN) (ELgammal 2017), Generative Adversarial Networks (GAN) (Broeckmann 2019; Schneider et al. 2018; Goodfellow 2014), Artificial Intelligence Creative Adversarial Networks (AICAN 2019) and Deep Learning (Goodfellow 2016) are increasingly using AI artworks with creative, interesting and aesthetic values into the public eye. Technological change will change people's living habits and affect thinking patterns, evaluation patterns, and aesthetic structure. How to appreciate the art creation of AI has gradually become a hot topic of discussion. Since Berlyne proposed a new type of experimental aesthetics (Berlyne 1971), people's emotional response to artworks has become a core issue in art psychology (Shaler 2006). There have been many theories trying to answer people's aesthetic emotional problems. Cognitive evaluation of emotions by many research institutes to discuss the aesthetic feelings of works of art, most of the research focused on the impact of preference stimuli. But in AI and computer art creation, if these stimuli are still feasible is unknown. In addition, another factor that can influence the aesthetic response of the viewer is the level of artistic professionalism (Hekkert and van Wieringen 1996b), i.e. aesthetic fluidity. From a psychological perspective, different degrees of professionalism lead people to make foreign judgments about the same things (Zorry 2018). Research shows a similar interaction between art appreciation and artistic experience (Tinio 2013). What viewers learn from formal or informal art education can significantly impact the aesthetic experience of artistic creation to a large extent (Pablo 2018). Based on the current stage, there is little direct research on the relationship between AI's artistic creation and professional knowledge, aesthetic interest and confusion. So in order to fill the gap in the research mentioned above, this study aims to achieve the following objectives:

Based on literature review and characteristics of AI art creation, this study attempts to evaluate the aesthetic experience of AI art creation on the basis of the Geneva Emotional Wheel and make relevant assumptions based on aesthetic fluency as an intermediary variable:

Hypothesis 1. Viewers with more prosperous artistic expertise (more aesthetic fluency he tested expert group) will be more interested in AI creation.

Hypothesis 2. Viewers with relatively little aesthetic fluency (less aesthetic fluency) (the tested novice group) will be more confused and less interested in creating artificial intelligence. The study used the Aesthetic Fluency Scale, grouped according to the level of expertise available to the observer (Expert group and Novice group) and using the Geneva Emotional Wheel to evaluate the overall effect. The image stimulation, which focuses on abstract works of art created by AI, explores the influence of professional knowledge on aesthetic feelings and emotions and the change of relationship between them on AI art creation. In a recent experiment, the results showed that the tested object were concentrated in confined spaces (classrooms) by researchers to view abstract works of art as slides (Locher et al. 2001). The experimental results are basically the same as the hypothesis. Art experts rate art more diversely, feel richer, be less confused and be more interested in AI works than people in the Novice group.

2 Literature Review

After reviewing the relevant literature, the study's main components are summarized and discussed in the following sections.

2.1 Aesthetic Experience

As people become more interested in expressing emotions in works of art (Fellous 2006; Armstrong and Detweiler-Bedell 2008; Cupchik et al. 2009; Silva 2010) Emotions are becoming the most expressive part of the artwork (Silvia 2005), which is expressed through creation and shared by watching the artwork. In the history of art, the complex emotions of shock, movement, epiphany, emotion and transformation of the viewer because of their encounter with art are collectively referred to as "aesthetic experience" (Proust 1981/1954, p. 48). Shearer (2005) suggests that aesthetic experiences include moving, happiness, infatuation, admiration, sadness, etc., and that pleasant and unpleasant emotions can exist simultaneously. (Scherer 2005) And this feeling is not limited to formalist aesthetic pleasure. When the aesthetic experience is high, the artworks may also trigger physiological reactions such as tears, goose pimples (Scherer 2001). With the gradual and clear division between daily and aesthetic experiences, the psychological theory of aesthetic experience in art has been developed more fully (Gerald 2009).

2.2 Aesthetic Fluency

Fluency in aesthetic fluency can be divided into three main categories, perceptual fluency, retrieval fluency, and conceptual fluency (Reber et al. 2004). They mainly refer to the degree of difficulty that information flows processed in a person's cognitive, perceptive, and conceptual system (Reber et al. 1998). Many studies have shown that when people make decisions and judgments, they use subjective experience to reference smooth processing (Oppenheimer and Frank 2008; Belke et al. 2010; Silvia 2007). When the processing and flow of information are simple and fast, it is considered fluid, i.e., high fluency and relatively familiarity. Conversely, when the processing and flow of information is difficult and slow, it is considered lack of fluency, i.e. low fluency and unfamiliarity.

Fluency can also be applied flexibly in various professions. In the field of aesthetics, it is generally referred to as aesthetic fluency, and its basic meaning is "a person through the formal way (i.e. through professional art training) and the knowledge base about art and art related to daily life experience" (Smith and Smith 2006). Smith and Smith's (2006) Aesthetic Fluency Scale showcases the art history of professional terminology including artists and artistic styles and genres. Among them, the founder of 19th-century experimental psychology, Fechner (1871), has assumed familiarity can provide a certain emotional basis for things. Familiarity or fluency is a psychological variable that establishes the individual value of the work for each viewer. Alternative concepts of familiarity or fluentness are related to the perceived susceptivity of stimulation processing. Some researchers believe that aesthetic pleasure is the product of the perception of the object after processing. In the early stages of aesthetic perception, in terms of visual or perceived fluency, the viewer can evaluate the perceived characteristics of the work more quickly (Leder 2004), better identify and classify the work, etc. Similarly, fluentness contributes to positive emotional states (Schwarz and Winkielman 2004). Numerous studies have shown that the more familiar people are to things, the more fluent they are and that high levels of fluidity breed a conceptually defined pleasant emotional response. For example, when viewers develop familiarity with certain artwork or artist, the study finds that viewers are more likely to like a work they are familiar with (Leder 2001; Zajonc 1968). The effect is even more intense for works of art with a high degree of negative emotion (Leder 2014), where respondents indicate how well they know each art. This scale has some nice features: it emphasizes people's understanding of art (as opposed to how much they like it or how good they are at it), and researchers can appropriately adjust it to other areas by adding items. Besides, people with a higher level of artistic knowledge and experience tend to show a preference for less traditional and less accessible art than those with lower levels of knowledge and experience (Hekkert and van Wieringen 1996; Leder 2012; Rawlings 2003). An example of this kind of art is abstract art. People with a higher level of artistic knowledge and experience finds it less confusing and more interesting (Silvia 2013). Differences in artistic aesthetic experience due to artistic knowledge and expertise may be rooted in differences in neural function and cognitive processing. People with higher artistic knowledge and expertise deal more comprehensively with art, focusing not only on the content of the artwork but also on the structure and other formal artwork elements (Massaro 2012). In comparison, those with lower artistic knowledge and expertise focus more on the objects depicted (e.g., Cupchik and Gebotys 1988; Nodine 1993).

To a certain extent, with the increase in the viewer's professionalism, more aesthetic pleasure will be generated, as well as more positive mood. On the other hand, non-professional viewers rely heavily on their intuition when evaluating art, consistent with the "information-as-feeling" theory and related models. They prefer something that arouses positive emotions. (Reber 2004) For example, in one study, researchers asked participants with different artistic expertise levels how much they liked a group of abstract artworks (Belke and Leder 2006). Nearly half of the experiment's artworks provided relatively complete text information about style and creators, while other artworks did not have any additional text information. And the results showed that participants with a lower level of artistic expertise preferred paintings that provided text information, while participants with higher artistic knowledge showed opposed patterns. Another study explores the impact of art expert groups and novice group on the overall preference of art. Students and art experts with visual arts expertise rated visual works significantly higher than abstract works and prefer color painting. Studies have shown that art is more about the novelty and originality of a work of art when appreciated and evaluated (Hekkert 1996). In addition, there is a study of the emotional responses of art experts and nods (Pihko 2011) that asks participants to assess the emotional quality of art in both positive and negative dimensions. In short, the expert's judgment is aesthetic, while the newcomer's judgment is personal. Hekkert and Wieringen (1996) found support for this approach in the study of experts (curators and critics) and newcomers (experienced amateurs). When judging slides submitted by young artists, experts are more interested and original in novelty than newcomers, so newcomers seem to have more qualities. In addition, originality judgments have a stronger impact on the quality of experts than on newcomers, a finding that suggests that experts together provide a basis for their judgments. However, few studies have explored the emotional response to art, let alone how artistic levels mediate it. Combining the close correlation between emotions and professionalism, a promising new approach can use a knowledge-based approach to assess expertise.

2.3 The Art of AI Creation

Since 2016, AI represented by Alphago has become a hot topic of continuous discussion in academia and industry. Artificial intelligence is not a new topic. This brilliant performance comes from the commercial level breakthrough of convolutional neural network algorithm based on deep learning, which opens up a vast field. This breakthrough is considered a technological revolution level progress because this strategy's success is not limited to the go field. It can achieve the same level of progress in many fields and produce subversive effects. The field of art is also included. Through deep learning convolutional neural network algorithm, most AI systems have received thousands of paintings of different styles created by artists from all over the world in the past few hundred years. AI can use painting language (color selection, form elements, form arrangement on two-dimensional surface) to create images, and place the combination of these elements to the viewer in the way a viewer look at a painting. Moreover, this has the same effects as the abstract works of art discussed by people. Previous studies have used abstract works of art similar to artificial intelligence works of art or similar geometric patterns as stimuli for experiments. In using abstract art as the stimulus, people may accurately predict that a particular color combination (for example, a more harmonious combination of color opponents) may be more arousing/calming or positive/negative, or mapped to a particular emotional category. For example, the appreciator can feel a relatively happy sense of satisfaction and pleasure by recognizing and appreciating the artwork. In contrast, many abstract artists would make a statement of the aim of his/her artwork, which performs as an instruction to evoke the viewer's emotion. From these artistic experiments, it is not difficult to find that abstract works of art are more closely related to emotional expression and aesthetic experience than other works of art. However, some people point out that the creation of artificial intelligence is too abstract and rigid, and there are many traces of imitation, which makes it difficult for viewers to have a positive aesthetic experience when watching. However, we can still assume that artworks created by artificial intelligence have the same emotional arousal effect.

In addition, in the field of artificial intelligence creation, we also need to pay attention to the fact that the aesthetic experience is likely to be affected not only by the artwork itself but also by the viewer's aesthetic fluency. The level of aesthetic fluency is likely to affect the aesthetic experience of the viewer. Previous studies have shown that people with a higher level of artistic knowledge and experience tend to show a preference for less traditional and inaccessible art, compared with people with a lower level of knowledge and experience. An example of this kind of art is abstract art. The former finds it less confusing and more interesting. The differences in artistic aesthetic experience caused by artistic knowledge and professional knowledge may be fundamentally rooted in the differences in neural function and cognitive processing. People with higher art knowledge and professional knowledge will deal with artwork more comprehensively, focusing not only on the content of artworks but also on the structure and other formal artwork elements. Leder and his colleagues (Leder 2004; Cupchik and Laszlo 1992) argue that experts and non-specialists have different views on art, evaluate creation and experience. These factors usually affect the aesthetic experience, especially the observer's emotional response. The emotional response is an independent model, in which the experts who frequently come into contact with the art may react more slowly to the direct emotional price of the artworks. In the meantime, the expertise will weaken the direct feeling of the art of the expert or the more professional viewer, which may lead to the expert's preference to denying art, preferring to evaluate artworks through a variety of different perspectives such as style, form and the historical context of the art (Leder 2004). Reber et al. (2004) think that the perceiver's cognitive processing greatly influences the aesthetic, arguing that "the more fluent the perceiver can process the aesthetic object, the more positive their aesthetic response will be." For example, if the viewer can obtain detailed descriptions or background information related to the painting when viewing a painting, their feedback on the painting will be more positive.

In contrast, people with lower art knowledge and professional knowledge will focus more on the objects depicted. Besides, the differences between art knowledge and professional knowledge will also impact emotional response, which is likely due to the differences in evaluation models caused by the corresponding differences in art knowledge. For example, Silvia (2006) studied the tested people's interest in abstract art. According to the evaluation method, interest is an emotion produced by two kinds of evaluation: coping potential, or the degree to which people can understand (or deal with) the object or event. And novelty, complexity, or novelty. Complexity is an object or an event. Silvia found that people with more knowledge of art find complex art easier to understand and more interesting. In this case, art knowledge can deepen the understanding of art, which is an example of the direct relationship between emotion and cognition.

2.4 The Geneva Emotion Wheel

It has been a long-term challenge for emotional researchers in different disciplines of social and behavioral sciences to distinguish it from other emotional states or traits and to measure it in a comprehensive and meaningful way. There are a variety of experience testing tools that allow users to discuss and self-report emotional experiences. Geneva emotional wheel (GEW) was founded by Swiss emotional Science Research Center (Scherer 2005; Scherer et al. 2013). The theory is based on the theory of emotion evaluation. Geneva emotional wheel (GEW) is a theoretical derivation and empirical testing tool to measure emotional responses to objects, events, and situations. There are two main evaluation dimensions: control (low to high) and pleasure (negative to positive). Moreover, GEW provides participants with the ability to choose from 20 emotion types (e.g., participation interest, enjoyment-pleasure, sadness-despair, disgust-disgust, stimulation-anger), and the opportunity to rate each emotion type according to five intensity levels, and measure each emotion with a piece of art. The reason why we choose Geneva emotion wheel to evaluate the artworks of AI is: Firstly, the emotion family in GEW covers almost all emotions, representing different valence and control weight, which is relatively comprehensive for the tested and researchers. Second, participants do not need to recall any words to describe their emotional experience. They just need an identification experience or imagine various emotions. (Feiran Zhang 2019). Thirdly, the design of GEW has an element of free-response format, a discrete emotional response format, and an emotional dimension method. Let the interviewees have more freedom to express themselves. Dimension method is reflected in the potency and control dimension.

This process is in sharp contrast to being asked about one's emotional experience or being forced to recall one's feelings, and describing them to researchers, which would make some participants feel uncomfortable. In addition, compared with limited attention to happiness and interest, having a readily visible "emotional field" can provide more comprehensive and detailed emotional reports, and happiness and interest are traditional emotional measurement methods that can be traced back to Berlin's psychobiological methods (Berlin 1971). Therefore, in addition to the "no emotion" and "other emotion" response options, by providing 20 types of emotion, the current method is an improvement on the methodology of the previous research on artistic emotional response (for example, Scherer 2005). Once visitors agree to participate in the study, GEW is first managed as it provides the study's main interest data set. Participants were instructed to observe the work of art and select the main emotion types that best matched the emotions they experienced in the exhibition. They were then instructed to indicate how strong or intense the emotion they experienced by examining the emotion type of one of the circles. And the larger the circle, the closer it was to the edge of the emotion, and the stronger their emotional experience will be. They were told that although they were free to choose other emotions, we would like them to point out the primary emotions generated by their reaction to the exhibition. Half of the participants were instructed to view the emotion types on the GEW in a clockwise fashion, while the other half were instructed to view them in a counterclockwise fashion. This is aimed to eliminate the influence of left to right and top to bottom (or clockwise).

3 Research Methodology

3.1 Stimulus

This study will use abstract artworks as an experimental stimulation to discuss the relationship between AI artworks and aesthetic feeling with aesthetic fluency as an intermediary variable. From previous artistic experiments and tests, it is not difficult to find that abstract artworks have a closer relationship with emotional expression and aesthetic experience than other artworks (Tinio 2018). There have been many studies that have experimented with abstract artworks or similar geometric patterns as stimuli, in which case people are more likely to predict a particular combination of colors accurately, lines, shapes, which may cause or be positive or negative, or map to a specific emotional category of aesthetic feelings. For example, tested people can identify the subject of negative emotions of a painting of Picasso's Blue Period. They can also feel a sense of satisfaction and pleasure in relative happiness by identifying and appreciating the artwork (Silvia 2005; Silvia 2010). The AI artworks used in this study are mainly taken from books, literary journals, and the Internet. For each tested person, the images were printed in the same order in the experimental use packets. Given the discussion of aesthetic fluency in this study, the 10 most well-known works of Google search were selected. Among the packages are: [()] + [(− (()))], Portrait of Edmond de Belamy by Obvious Art's, 79530 Self-Portrait, 2018 by Mario Klingeman, False Teeth (Corpus: Interpretations of Dreams) ©Trevor Paglen and courtesy of Metro Pictures by Trevor Paglen, Seamless (2017) by Theo Triantafyllidis, Deep Dream, Pindar Van Arman, Girl Bing created by AI artists AI-D.

3.2 Procedures

Before the experiment, the tested people were asked to fill out an online consent form and related personal basic information materials (including age, education, and whether or not to receive professional art training, etc.) Because the test sample involves color, the test also needs to confirm that the colorless blindness, vision or corrective vision is normal to ensure the effectiveness of random sampling and the test results' credibility. The viewer will then be concentrated in a large space with a projector (a university classroom in Fuzhou). In the course of the experiment, to exclude the indoor environment, the effects of other interference factors, such as light, on the measured group will be observed in the same classroom over the same period, according to the group's classification. Each image lasts approximately 30 s, and all images and videos observed in the experiment are displayed via a computer to the tested people (brand: Apple Model: Mac Book Pro (Retina, 15-inch, Mid 2014, resolution 2880 × 1880) and projected onto a large screen (projector brand EPSON, model EB-c2040XN, size 1024 × 768) screen brightness. Contrast and resolution are adjusted to ensure that all start-up stimuli are in a uniform optimal state. The experiment organized 50 people to be tested, 22 men, 28 women, aged 18–30 years old. Through the aesthetic fluency measurement scale test, The Aesthetic Fluency Scale (Smith and Smith 2006) asked participants to rate their knowledge (using a five-point scale) of the following 10 art concepts and artists: Mary Cassatt, Isamu Noguchi, John Singer Sargent, Alessandro Botticelli, Gian Lorenzo Bernini, Fauvism, Funerary Stelae, Impressionism, Chinese Scrolls, and Abstract Expressionism. Participants were asked to rate the following 10 art concepts and artist's knowledge (on a 5-point scale): tested people are to answer each item on a scale of 0–4 (0 = I have never heard of the artist or his term of office; 1 = I have heard about it, but I know nothing about it; 3 = I know the artist or idea in the discussion; 4 = I can talk about the artist or idea intelligently in art). After test, they are divided into novice group and expert group, and every group has 25 people. Given that the "sensory component" of emotions is inherently subjective, emotions can only be evaluated by self-reporting methods, such as the Geneva Emotional Wheel (GEW; Scherer 2005). This study uses the third edition of the Geneva Emotional Wheel (GEW) (3.0). The study aims to figure out how AI's artistic creation is felt under the influence of aesthetic fluency. Before the experiment began, the tested people will be told that they were free to select the most important emotions among the 20 emotional groups after viewing the sample. The researchers wanted to measure tested people's main emotions generated by their reactions to the sample.

4   Result Analysis

Theoretically, it is not rigorous enough to analyze emotional types and their correspond-ing emotional intensity individually, because these two concepts are easily confused (Scherer 2005). As a result, the Geneva Emotional Wheel (GEW) offers two different types of options for each participant: the main emotional types experienced during obser-vation of AI creations and works of art created by human artists and the corresponding emotional type intensity. Through data collation and analysis, the data is visualized to build an emotional heat map, which is very similar to heat maps. The latter is used to present eye gaze data in eye tracking studies, with hotter chunks indicating more eye gaze in specific parts of the image. In this study, the more obvious spots represent the feelings and consistency of the observer's emotional response to AI or works created by human artists. Overlaying GEW color spots represents the emotions and intensity of emotions reported by visitors of the type (see, for example, Fig. 1). Larger and significant spots (red, yellow) indicate that more observers choose this particular type of emotion as the primary experience of emotion.

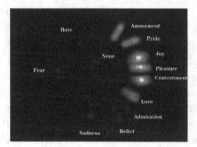

Fig. 1. Novice group (Color figure online)   **Fig. 2.** Expert group

5   Discussion

According to the emotional heat map, the main emotional responses of the Novice group when watching works by AI artists (Fig. 1) were: higher levels of Pleasure, Admiration and Joy, moderate Interest, Disappointment, Guilt, Fear, Shame, Contentment and low level of Hate, Disgust. Emotions such as Anger, Compassion and Pride were not chosen. By contrast, the expert team looking at the AI creations (time Fig. 2) showed higher levels of Pride, Joy, Pleasure, Love, and Amusement, as well as a moderate level of Sadness, Relief, Admiration. In addition to showing subtle emotional differences in the face of AI artworks for people with less related knowledge, it also showed that the expert group was measured to give AI creation a stronger degree of positive emotions. In contrast, the Novice group showed a strong degree of positive emotions than negative emotions. In contrast, the low-to-medium level of positive emotions and negative emotions are more evenly distributed. By comparing the two, we can draw the conclusion that the mood of the expert group is richer and more diverse in the face of the creation of AI, showing a more positive mood and more interest in works in unknown territory, i.e., hypothesis one and hypothesis two are true. Based on the different aesthetic experiences and emotional perception of art, aesthetic fluency does affect the aesthetic feelings and emotions of the tested people, especially in the negative parts of the artworks created by relatively unfamiliar AI. Although the AI artists considered here have a fairly high level of technology, and their works are almost similar in appearance to abstract artworks by human artists, these are not enough. This study also shows that more tested non-specialists believe that the art of AI creation is not enough to evoke their aesthetic experience to give them a richer and higher level of emotional feeling about artworks.

References

Elgammal, A., Liu, B., Elhoseiny, M., Mazzone, M.: CAN: creative adversarial net- works, generating "Art" by learning about styles and deviating from style norms. arXiv preprint. arXiv: 1706.07068 (2017)

Broeckmann, A.: The machine as artist as myth. Arts **8**(1), 25 (2019). https://doi.org/10.3390/art s8010025

Boden, M., Edmonds, E.: What is generative art? Digit. Creativity **20**(1–2), 21–46 (2009)

Boden, M.A.: The Turing test and artistic creativity. Kybernetes **39**(3), 409–413 (2010)

Baenziger, T., Tran, V., Scherer, K.R.: The emotion wheel. a tool for the verbal report of emotional reactions. In: Poster Presented at the Conference of the International Society of Research on Emotion, Bari, Italy (2005)

Melcher, D.: Perception of emotion in abstract artworks: a multidisciplinary approach. Prog. Brain Res. **204**, 191–216 (2013). https://doi.org/10.1016/B978-0-444-63287 6.00010-5

Fellous, J.-M.: A mechanistic view of the expression and experience of emotion in the arts. Am. J. Psychol. **119**(4), 668–674 (2006)

Goodfellow, I.J., et al.: Generative adversarial nets. In: Paper Presented at the Advances in Neural Information Processing Systems, Montreal, QC, Canada, 8–13 December (2014)

Hong, J.-W., Curran, N.M.: Artificial intelligence, artists, and art: attitudes toward artwork produced by humans vs. artificial intelligence. ACM Trans. Multimedia Comput. Commun. Appl. **15**, 16 (2019). 2s, Article 58

van Paasschen, J., Bacci, F., Melcher, D.: The influence of art expertise and training on emotion and preference ratings for representational and abstract artworks. PLOS ONE **10**(8), e0134241 (2015). https://doi.org/10.1371/journal.pone.0134241

Coeckelbergh, M.: Can machines create art? Philos. Technol. **30**(3), 285–303 (2016). https://doi. org/10.1007/s13347-016-0231-5

Mazzone, M., Elgammal, A.: Art, creativity, and the potential of artificial intelligence. Arts **8**(1), 26 (2019). https://doi.org/10.3390/arts8010026

Badea, M., Florea, C., Florea, L., Vertan, C.: Can we teach computers to understand art? Domain adaptation for enhancing deep networks capacity to de-abstract art. Image Vis. Comput. **77**, 21–32 (2018). https://doi.org/10.1016/j.imavis.2018.06.009

Tinio, P.P.L., Gartus, A.: Characterizing the emotional response to art beyond pleasure: correspondence between the emotional characteristics of artworks and viewers' emotional responses. Prog. Brain Res. **237**, 319–342 (2018). https://doi.org/10.1016/bs.pbr.2018.03.005. ISSN 0079-6123

Chamberlain, R.: Putting the art in artificial: aesthetic responses to computer-generated art article. Psychol. Aesthetics Creativity Arts **12**, 177–192 (2017)

Schneider, T., Rea, N.: Has artificial intelligence given us the next great art movement? Experts say slow down, the 'field is in its infancy'. Artnetnews, 25 September 2018. https://news.art net.com/art-world/ai-art-comes-to-market-is-it-worth-the-hype-1352011 (2019)

Audry, S., Ippolito, J.: Can artificial intelligence make art without artists? Ask the viewer. Arts **8**, 35 (2019)

Silvia, P.J.: Emotional responses to art: from collation and arousal to cognition and emotion. Rev. Gen. Psychol. **9**(4), 342–357 (2005)

Silva, P.J.: What is interesting? Exploring the appraisal structure of interest. Emotion **5**(1), 89–102 (2005)

Silva, P.J.: Aetistic training and interest in visual art: applying the appraisal model of aesthetic emotions. Empirical Stud. Arts **24**(2), 139–161 (2006)

Silvia, P.: Interest—the curious emotion. Curr. Dir. Psychol. Sci. **17**(1), 57–60 (2008)

Silva, P.J.: Looking past pleasure : anger, confusion, disgust, pride, surprise, and other unusual aesthetic emotions. Psychol. Aesthet. Creat. Arts **3**(1), 48–51 (2009)

Silva, P.J.: Confusion and interest: the role of knowledge emotions in aesthetic experience. Psychol. Aesthet. Creat. Arts **4**(2), 75–80 (2010)

Smith, L.F.: Effects of time and information on perception of art. Empirical Stud. Arts **24**(2), 229–242 (2006)

Tan, E.S.: Emotion, art, and the humanities. In: Lewis, M., Haviland-Jones, J.M. (eds.) Handbook of Emotions, 2nd edn., pp. 116–134. Guilford, New York (2000)

A Study of Chinese Audience Preferences for Mythological Film and Television Works

Sheng Ye(✉) 🆔

Fuzhou University of International Studies and Trade, 28, Yuhuan Road, Shouzhan New District, Changle District, Fuzhou 350202, Fujian, China

Abstract. In the context of globalization, mythological film and television works of various countries, as mass communication media and ideological carriers, are facing challenges and impacts from various aspects in cross-cultural communication. In the future development of film and television industry, how to respond to the competition with more active and effective creation of film and television works containing regional cultural characteristics and how to win a place in the cross-cultural communication in the world are important issues that will be faced in the development of film and television works containing regional cultural characteristics. This study is an attempt to analyze the preferences of Chinese audiences for mythological works in the cross-cultural communication environment, and to give some opinions to help mythological works be more easily recognized and liked by the public in their creation, and to provide reference for the cross-cultural communication of mythological works with regional cultural characteristics.

Keywords: Mythology · Preferences · Cross-cultural communication

1 First Section

The concept of "intercultural film and television productions" has recently begun to be used more frequently by scholars in different academic fields. Most notably, scholars in film and television studies and intercultural communication studies have found the application of an intercultural perspective in their analysis of film and television productions. The use of this perspective can be understood as expressing a critical awareness of film and television depictions of cultural encounters, transnational migration, and cultural differences in contemporary multicultural societies, as well as the need for illustrative audiovisual representations of intercultural communication. socially and culturally, globalization has changed the perception of what a community is, redefined the meaning of cultural identity and civic society, and demanded a new way of intercultural interaction. Overall, the concept of intercultural film and television productions implies a perspective in which scholars use the support of a range of audiovisual literature to clarify cross-cultural differences at different levels of analysis. Interculturality has been adopted by a number of different academic subjects and is used differently by different scholars. The analysis focuses on film as a representation or illustration of cross-cultural communication, cultural or linguistic misunderstandings, or culture shock experiences.

P.-L. P. Rau (Ed.): HCII 2021, LNCS 12772, pp. 95–106, 2021.
https://doi.org/10.1007/978-3-030-77077-8_8

This study was conducted to summarize the preferences of mythological film and television works in the cross-cultural communication environment among Chinese audiences, in order to help mythological film and television works to be more easily recognized and enjoyed by the public when they are created. The study was conducted with the case studies of Japanese and European mythological films and videos, and the questionnaire survey was conducted with Chinese audiences of all ages, starting from the preferences of mythological films and videos, the perception of the background of mythological stories, and the evaluation of mythological films and videos.

2 Intercultural Communication

Intercultural communication refers to communication activities between speakers of one national language and speakers of another national language. At the same time, intercultural communication also includes communication activities between people who have different cultural concepts and cultural backgrounds. In short, it refers to how to properly communicate with non-native speakers, to avoid communication barriers due to cultural differences, and to understand the cultural background of non-native speakers and pay attention to what topics to avoid when communicating. In cross-cultural studies, "culture" is mainly defined as the part of social life that binds people together and is closely related to national culture, ethnic culture, or so-called subcultures that exist within national borders.

With the development of the times, the communication between the people of the world is becoming closer and more frequent, therefore, in this case, the cultural differences caused by different cultural backgrounds and different ideologies bring certain obstacles to the language communication between people of different countries, and these obstacles will undoubtedly affect the harmonious communication between people, therefore, it is important to study cross-cultural communication and propose the necessary measures and Therefore, it is important to study intercultural communication and propose necessary measures and methods to solve the barriers caused by different cultural backgrounds.

3 Data Collection and Analysis for Chinese Audiences

The questionnaire surveyed users of different age groups on their preferences for Japanese mythology films and TV series (TV series, movies, animations) and European mythology films and TV series (TV series, movies, animations), as well as their knowledge of Japanese mythology stories and European mythology works.

Figure 1 shows the age frequency and percentage distribution of the respondents. It is clear that the majority of respondents were young and middle-aged, with 74 (37%) aged 10–25. 57 (28%) aged 26–40, 51 (26%) aged 41–55, and 18 (9%) aged 56 or older.

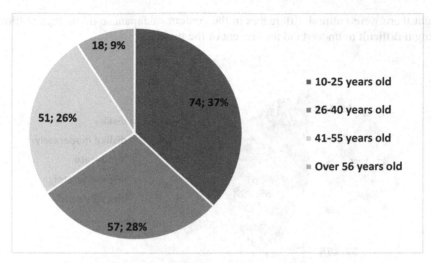

Fig. 1. Age group distribution

3.1 Analysis of Chinese Audiences' Preference for Japanese Mythological Film and Television Works

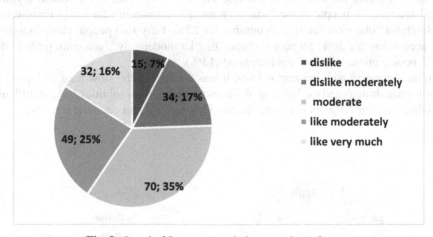

Fig. 2. Level of Japanese mythology movie preference

First of all, we analyzed Chinese audiences' preference for Japanese mythological movies. Figure 2 shows that among the 200 questionnaires collected, 32 people chose "like very much", accounting for 32%. Forty-nine people chose "like moderately", accounting for 24.5%. Seventy people chose "moderate" (35%), 34 people chose "dislike moderately" (17%), and 15 people chose "dislike" (7.5%) not interested, accounting for 7.5%.

The survey found that Japanese mythological films are relatively well made, such as Ashura-jô no hitomi, but most of the respondents chose "moderate" because they thought there were cultural differences in the content of Japanese mythological films, making it difficult to understand the content of the myths.

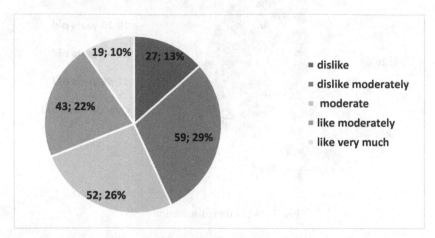

Fig. 3. Level of Japanese mythology TV series preference

Figure 3 shows the analysis of Chinese viewers' preference for Japanese mythological dramas, 19 people chose "like very much", accounting for 10%. Forty-three people chose "like moderately", accounting for 22%. Fifty-two people chose "moderate", accounting for 26%, 59 people chose "dislike moderately", accounting for 29%, and 27 people chose "dislike" not interested (13%).

In the interview with the respondents, it was found that the slow pace of Japanese mythological dramas and the language differences that require subtitles make it difficult for audiences over 40 years old to quickly develop interest and continue watching.

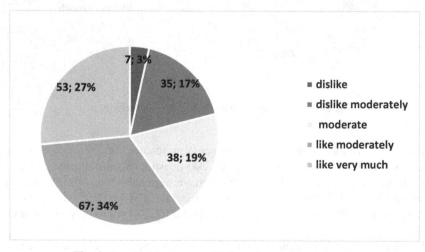

Fig. 4. Level of Japanese mythology Animation preference

Figure 4 shows the analysis of Chinese audience's preference for Japanese mythological animation, 53 people chose "like very much", accounting for 27%. Sixty-seven people chose "like moderately", accounting for 34%. Thirty-eight people chose "moderate", accounting for 19%, 35 people chose "dislike moderately", accounting for 17.5%, and 7 people chose "dislike" not interested, accounting for 3.5%.

In terms of the evaluation of Japanese mythological anime, most of the 10–40 year olds gave it a good rating, with 79% of them giving it a moderate to high rating. In the interview with the respondents, we know that the mythological animation works generally summarize some characteristics or character traits of the mythological characters in the mythological stories for secondary creation, and the story rhythm of the animation works is also more acceptable to the audience (Table 1).

Following the one-way ANOVA method and procedure, the hypothesis test H0 was proposed: there is no significant difference in the respondents' knowledge of Japanese mythological stories and their evaluation of Japanese mythological film and television works. Alternative hypothesis H1: There is a significant difference between the respondents' knowledge of Japanese mythology and their evaluation of Japanese mythology films and TV works.

The results of the one-way independent sample ANOVA were used to analyze the effect of respondents' knowledge of Japanese mythology on the evaluation of Japanese mythological movies. The results showed that there was a significant difference between the respondents' knowledge of Japanese mythology and their preference for Japanese mythological movies, $F = 40.46$, $p = 0$. There was a significant difference between the respondents' knowledge of Japanese mythology and their preference for Japanese mythology animation, $F = 32.962$, $p = 0$. There was a significant difference between the respondents' knowledge of Japanese mythology and their preference for Japanese mythological dramas, $F = 58.553$, $p = 0$.

According to the principle of one-way ANOVA, the hypothesis test H0 should be rejected and the alternative hypothesis H1 should be accepted, that is, there is a significant difference between the respondents' knowledge of Japanese mythology and their evaluation of Japanese mythological movies and TV series.

3.2 Analysis of Chinese Audiences' Preference for European Mythology Film and Television Works

Figure 5 shows the analysis of Chinese audiences' preference for European mythology movies. 22 people chose "like very much", accounting for 11%. Fifty-three people chose "like moderately", accounting for 27%. Seventy-one people chose "moderate" (35%), 40 people chose "dislike moderately" (20%), and 14 people chose "dislike" (3.5%) not interested (7%).

The number of people who rated European mythology films as moderate to high reached 73%. In the interview with the respondents, most of them had heard of European mythology, such as Pandora's box and the sword of Damocles. European mythology film works are full of mystery and the special effects are well produced and loved by most audiences.

Table 1. Comparative analysis of respondents' evaluation of Japanese mythological films and TV works (grouped by level of knowledge of Japanese mythology).

Descriptives

		N	mean	Std.Deviation	Std.Error	95% Confidence Interval for Mean Lower Bound	Upper Bound
Level of Japanese movie preference	No knowledge	26	2.42	.758	.149	2.12	2.73
	General	77	2.66	.954	.109	2.45	2.88
	Understand	71	3.73	.910	.108	3.52	3.95
	Very well	26	4.46	.859	.169	4.11	4.81
	Total	200	3.25	1.141	.081	3.09	3.40
Level of Japanese Animation preference	No knowledge	26	2.81	.939	.184	2.43	3.19
	General	77	3.09	.934	.106	2.88	3.30
	Understand	71	4.06	1.040	.123	3.81	4.30
	Very well	26	4.81	.694	.136	4.53	5.09
	Total	200	3.62	1.154	.082	3.46	3.78
Level of Japanese TV series preference	No knowledge	26	1.88	.711	.140	1.60	2.17
	General	77	2.18	.839	.096	1.99	2.37
	Understand	71	3.37	.945	.112	3.14	3.59
	Very well	26	4.31	.884	.173	3.95	4.66
	Total	200	2.84	1.188	.084	2.67	3.01

ANOVA

		Sun of squares	df	Mean Square	F	Sig.
Level of Japanese movie preference	Between Groups	99.051	3	33.017	40.460	.000
	Within Groups	159.944	196	.816		
	Total	258.995	199			
Level of Japanese Animation preference	Between Groups	88.905	3	29.635	32.962	.000
	Within Groups	176.215	196	.899		
	Total	265.120	199			
Level of Japanese TV series preference	Between Groups	132.754	3	44.251	58.553	.000
	Within Groups	148.126	196	.756		
	Total	280.880	199			

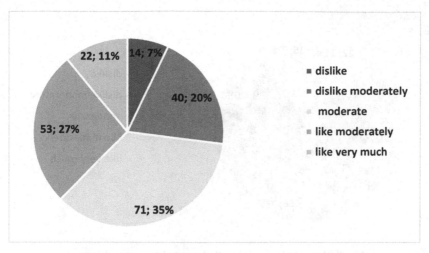

Fig. 5. Level of European mythology movie preference

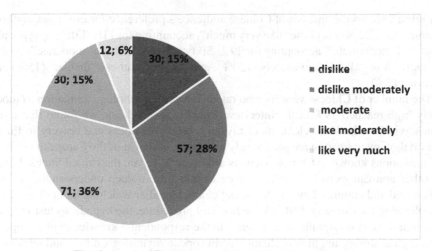

Fig. 6. Level of European mythology TV series preference

Figure 6 shows the analysis of Chinese viewers' preference for European mythological dramas, 12 people chose "like very much", accounting for 6%. Thirty people chose "like moderately", accounting for 15%. Seventy-one people chose "moderate", accounting for 36%, 57 people chose "dislike moderately", accounting for 28%, and 30 people chose "dislike" not interested (15%).

In the interviews with the respondents, it was found that European mythological dramas have the same problems as Japanese mythological dramas, such as slow pacing, large language differences and the need for subtitles. Most audiences watch European mythology dramas in order to learn English.

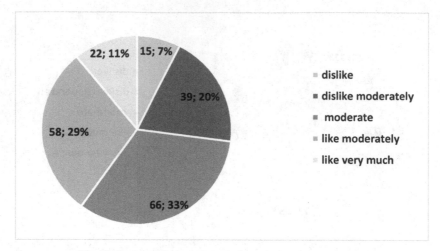

Fig. 7. Level of European mythology Animation preference

Figure 7 shows the analysis of Chinese audience's preference for European mythology animation, 22 people chose "like very much", accounting for 11%. Fifty-eight people chose "like moderately", accounting for 29%. Sixty-six people chose "moderate" (33%), 39 people chose "dislike moderately" (20%), and 15 people chose "dislike" (15%) not interested (7%).

The number of Chinese viewers who rated European mythology animation as moderately high reached 79%.In the interview with the respondents, we found that most Chinese viewers think the elements of mystery, bloodthirstiness and bravery in European mythology animation are particularly attractive, but most of the European mythology animations known to Chinese viewers are made in Japan, the United States, Korea and other non-European countries, so they cannot have a deep understanding of the background and culture of the mythological characters after watching them (Table 2).

Following the one-way ANOVA method and procedure, the hypothesis test H0 was proposed: there is no significant difference in the respondents' knowledge of European mythological stories and their evaluation of European mythological film and television works. Alternative hypothesis H1: There is a significant difference between the respondents' knowledge of European mythology and their evaluation of European mythology films and TV works.

The results of the one-way independent sample ANOVA were used to analyze the effect of respondents' knowledge of European mythology on the evaluation of European mythological movies. The results showed that there was a significant difference between the respondents' knowledge of European mythology and their preference for European mythological movies, $F = 49.837$, $p = 0$. There was a significant difference between the respondents' knowledge of European mythology and their preference for European mythology animation, $F = 47.395$, $p = 0$. There was a significant difference between the respondents' knowledge of European mythology and their preference for European mythological dramas, $F = 43.751$, $p = 0$.

Table 2. Comparative analysis of respondents' evaluation of European mythological films and TV works (grouped by level of knowledge of European mythology).

Descriptives

		N	mean	Std.De-viation	Std.Er-ror	95% Confidence Interval for Mean	
						Lower Bound	Upper Bound
Level of Eu-	No knowledge	34	2.15	.784	.134	1.87	2.42
ropean	General	85	2.80	.799	.087	2.63	2.97
movie pref-	Understand	68	3.79	.856	.104	3.59	4.00
erence	Very well	13	4.62	.870	.241	4.09	5.14
	Total	200	3.15	1.082	.076	2.99	3.30
Level of Eu-	No knowledge	34	1.94	.694	.119	1.70	2.18
ropean Ani-	General	85	2.22	.905	.098	2.03	2.42
mation pref-	Understand	68	3.32	.818	.099	3.13	3.52
erence	Very well	13	4.31	.751	.208	3.85	4.76
	Total	200	2.69	1.087	.077	2.53	2.84
Level of Eu-	No knowledge	34	2.06	.952	.163	1.73	2.39
ropean TV	General	85	2.94	.917	.100	2.74	3.14
series pref-	Understand	68	3.71	.754	.091	3.52	3.89
erence	Very well	13	4.69	.630	.175	4.31	5.07
	Total	200	3.17	1.097	.078	3.01	3.32

ANOVA

		Sun of squares	df	Mean Square	F	Sig.
Level of European	Between Groups	100.736	3	33.579	49.837	.000
movie preference	Within Groups	132.059	196	.674		
	Total	232.795	199			
Level of European	Between Groups	98.868	3	32.956	47.395	.000
Animation prefer-	Within Groups	136.287	196	.695		
ence	Total	235.155	199			
Level of European	Between Groups	96.080	3	32.027	43.751	.000
TV series prefer-	Within Groups	143.475	196	.732		
ence	Total	239.555	199			

According to the principle of one-way ANOVA, the hypothesis test H0 should be rejected and the alternative hypothesis H1 should be accepted, that is, there is a significant difference between the respondents' knowledge of European mythology and their evaluation of European mythological movies and TV series.

4 Summary

The analysis of the collected questionnaires shows that the audience of European and Japanese mythology films and videos in China is mainly aged 10–40. Chinese audiences mainly know Japanese mythology in the form of mythological animation works, but most of the mythological characters and storylines in the animation works have been recreated, and they only have a one-sided understanding of the background and worldview of the mythological stories. Because of the many exchanges between China and Japan in history, there are many similarities between Japanese mythology and Chinese mythology, such as "the creation of heaven and earth" and "the five elements of yin and yang", so Chinese audiences are more able to understand and accept Japanese mythology stories. Chinese audiences mainly understand European mythology films and TV series in the form of mythology movies and mythology TV series. Most of the European mythology films and TV series can truly restore the characters' characters and related stories in the mythology stories, so Chinese audiences can have a certain understanding of the background and world view of European mythology. However, because the cultural connotation and values of European mythology differ greatly from those of China, the understanding and acceptance of character and story plots are generally low.

Therefore, in order to improve the dissemination effect of mythological films and videos, the content of the films and videos created should be popularized to fit the audience's knowledge base, social interaction, outlook on life and value orientation. European mythology can make it easier for Chinese viewers to understand the mythology itself and restore the character of each character in the mythology in the work.

There are cross-cultural differences between Chinese and Japanese mythology and European mythology, and the cultures of the world are so different that different cultural phenomena are presented in the film and television works of different countries, conveying different cultural characteristics and values. When creating mythological film and television works, the creators usually construct the perspective and theme of the mythological story according to the local culture and value system, and also follow the local logic of thinking to narrate and express emotions. On the other hand, when audiences from different regions appreciate and understand cross-cultural film and television works, they tend to deconstruct and reconstruct them according to their own culture's customary cultural values, which inevitably leads to misinterpretation. Therefore, cultural differences will inevitably cause certain barriers to understanding, making it difficult to achieve effective and accurate transmission of information across cultures. For Japanese and European mythological works, the differences in the cultural values conveyed in them are mainly reflected in the following aspects.

1. Chinese and Japanese mythology pursue harmony between man and nature, and between man and self, while European mythology emphasizes the transformation of nature and the conquest of nature.

2. Chinese and Japanese myths focus more on the whole, advocate cooperation and emphasize collective power, while European myths focus on the individual, promote individual heroism, emphasize individuality and pursue freedom and equality.
3. In the face of conflict, Chinese and Japanese mythology places more emphasis on peaceful resolution, turning conflict into peace, while European mythology advocates competition and conquering rivals.

These Asian and European mythological biases obviously have different, or even diametrically opposed, cultural values, which are more or less reflected in film and television works. Audiences from different cultural backgrounds may also experience barriers to understanding or biases when interpreting the same film or television work. Therefore, in the creation of film and television scripts, it is necessary to produce works according to different audience groups, not only to take care of the mainstream aesthetics of the road public, but also to maintain the character traits of the characters in the mythological stories, in order to help the audience to understand the characters and backstories of the mythological stories while accepting the mythological film and television works better.

The shortcomings of this study are that the number of data samples collected is not large enough and there may be some errors. Also, the audience group collected is Chinese audience, so the conclusion may not have the same effect in different countries.

References

1. Chen, G.M., Zhang, K.: New media and cultural identity in the global society. In: Taiwo, R. (ed.) Handbook of Research on Discourse Behavior and Digital Communication: Language Structures and Social Interaction, pp. 801–815 (2010)
2. Piller, I.: Intercultural Communication: A Critical Introduction. Edinburgh University Press, Edinburgh (2011)
3. Stier, J.K.: En introduktion till interkulturella studier. Lund: Studentlitteratur (2009)
4. Marks, L.U., Polan, D.: The Skin of the Film: Intercultural Cinema, Embodiment, and the Senses. Duke University Press (2000)
5. Condon, J.: Exploring intercultural communication through literature and film. World Engl. 5(2–3), 153–161 (1986)
6. Jacobsson, A.: Intercultural film: Fiction film as audio-visual documents of interculturality. J. Intercultural Stud. 38(1), 54–69 (2017)
7. Shao, P., Pan, X.: Discuss to intercultural communication strategy of Chinese film under the context of globalization. J. Zhejiang Univ. (Humanit. Soc. Sci.) 1, 65–73 (2006)
8. Petro, P.: Mass culture and the feminine: the "place" of television in film studies. Cinema J. 25(3), 5–21 (1986)
9. Wang, C., Wen, Y.: on the differences between chinese and western cultures from the perspective of the movie GuaSha treatment. In: Proceedings of the 2nd International Conference on Literature, Art and Human Development, ICLAHD 2020. Atlantis Press (2020)
10. Jacobsson, A.: Intercultural film: fiction film as audio-visual documents of interculturality. J. Intercult. Stud. 38(1), 54–69 (2017)
11. Chen, G.M.: The impact of new media on intercultural communication in global context (2012)
12. Liebes, T.: Cultural differences in the retelling of television fiction. Crit. Stud. Media Commun. 5(4), 277–292 (1988)

13. Wierzbicka, A.: Cultural scripts: a new approach to the study of cross-cultural communication. In: Pütz, M.. (ed.) Language Contact and Language Conflict, pp. 69–87. John Benjamins Publishing Company, Amsterdam (1994)

14. Mead, R., Jones, C.J.: Cross-cultural communication. In: The Blackwell Handbook of Cross-Cultural Management, pp. 283–291 (2017)

15. Frye, N., Macpherson, J.: Biblical and Classical Myths: The Mythological Framework of Western Culture. University of Toronto Press (2004)

16. Patel, R.: Understanding the culture through mythological stories. Am. J. Psychoanal. **20**(1), 83–85 (1960)

17. Nan, Z.: The mythological residue in culture. J. Sichuan Int. Stud. Univ. **5**, 100–102 (2001)

18. Wang, J.: Consideration to the Chinese mythological culture of the goddess mending the sky. J. Gansu Educ. Coll. (Soc. Sci.) **2**, 40–44 (2000)

19. Arvidsson, S.: Aryan Idols: Indo-European Mythology as Ideology and Science. University of Chicago Press (2006)

20. Yoshida, A.: Japanese mythology and the Indo-European trifunctional system. Diogenes **25**(98), 93–116 (1977)

21. Bengtson, J.D.: Iarl and Iormun-; Arya-and Aryaman-: a study in Indo-European comparative mythology. Comp. Mythol. **2**, 33–67 (2016)

22. Allen, N.J.: The Indo-European background to Greek Mythology. In: Dowden, K., Livingstone, N. (eds.) A Companion to Greek Mythology, Blackwell Companions to the Ancient World, pp. 341–356. Malden, Oxford (2011)

23. Lofstedt, T.M.G.: Russian Legends About Forest Spirits in the Context of Northern European Mythology, p. 3841 (1994)

24. Gadeleva, E.: Susanoo: one of the central gods in Japanese mythology. Nichibunken Jpn. Rev. **12**, 165–203 (2000)

25. Sever, M.: Japanese mythology and nationalism: myths of genesis, Japanese identity, and familism. In: The International Conference on Japan & Japan Studies 2016: Official Conference Proceedings (2016)

26. Shuxian, Y.: A new interpretation on the Chinese mythology. Acad. J. Grad. Sch. Chin. Acad. Soc. Sci. **5**, 71–77 (2005)

27. Liu, Y.: A new model in the study of Chinese mythology. J. Chin. Humanit. **3**(1), 1–22 (2017)

Discussing How the Viewer, the Author, and the Work See and Be Seen in the Photography Works of "Farewell to the Island"

Hong Qian Zheng(✉), Yuheng Tao(✉), Rungtai Lin, and Po-Hsien Lin

Graduate School of Creative Industry Design, National Taiwan University of Arts,
New Taipei City, Taiwan
{rtlin,t0131}@mail.ntua.edu.tw

Abstract. Through the creation of the video editing work "Farewell to the Island", the use of photographic creation, the arrangement of images with a sense of painting, and the series of seemingly honest photos, make them a way of viewing memories. The photograph captures not reality, but gives a viewing angle and location, which is processed through subjective thinking to tell the memory of wandering between the real and the virtual. The memory should be inspired by dots, and the hands of the author will give viewers more imagination and viewing angles. I printed most of the photos, and I was alone with them in the space, letting the tide of memory take me to put them in the right place, and no longer limited to the rigorous screening of whether the graphics on the screen were rigorous, and found the freedom of painting through editing them. In the arrangement of the image exhibition, hundreds of photos are connected in one space through three arrangement methods: concrete image extension, element extension, and image extension. After several private choreography, the author and the work looked at each other before going to a public exhibition. The audience sees the work in the space, the audience sees the author through the work, and the author sees the audience through the work. The author's creative meaning becomes a physical work through coding, and the audience decodes the author's creative process through the work. The accuracy and gap between these transfers is an interesting study.

Keywords: Island · Memory · Relationship · Photography · Viewing

1 Introduction

I used the term 'ephemera' to describe myself. Taipei was the fifth city I had lived in. I never felt like staying thousands of miles away from home. "Therefore" in the dictionary has the past tense, dead meaning, hometown, perhaps refers to the past tense place, after leaving that place in the passage of time, constantly like these two directions can not turn back forward. I know very well that I can never really go back to that hometown again. For me, going home on New Year's Day and festivals has only become a ceremony to

P.-L. P. Rau (Ed.): HCII 2021, LNCS 12772, pp. 107–115, 2021.
https://doi.org/10.1007/978-3-030-77077-8_9

commemorate my hometown. "No man ever steps in the same river twice" quoted from Heraclitus. I can never go back to that hometown.

I can trace back and understand my world in the past, but my (this branch) future consists of multiple worlds. Taking painting as the starting point of vector, try various possibilities of being watched, and present the memory of a person, a place, or a relationship.

In early 2019, I realized that I was about to leave Taiwan, the island where I had lived for more than 1,800 days. A strong voice in my heart told me to seriously say goodbye to the island as a non-tourist.

Farewell to the Island is a rite of passage for your time in Taiwan. The journey lasted more than 500 h, starting and ending in Taipei, the city where I live, taking a local bus from the east coast all the way south and from the west coast up north. Taiwan, which is connected by nearly 164 local bus stops, uses a roll of the dice to determine the next destination to visit, using photography as the medium, and negatives as the medium to search for proof of my presence on the island.

Just like the shoreline that artist Zhang Xiao walked along, Alec Soth followed the Mississippi River. Their journey was long without a strong purpose of travel, and they used photos to tell the things they saw around them. Otherwise, we create new nodes for the detections and connect them with existing nodes.

Since my graduation, I have been constantly reviewing the works I have made in the past few years, the things I have focused on, and the past life track. I have tried several different creative media and themes, the connection between them, the connection between them and me realized at the beginning of the year that I was leaving this summer. I had planned to go to the places I had been to after the end of the semester to say goodbye to Taiwan. But one night before I went to bed thinking about it, I said to myself, "Why don't I just do it?".

So came this trip around the island, which I call "The Island Say Goodbye." I picked it up on a journey that seemed like it was time to say goodbye, leave a school, leave a city, leave an island, leave school.

I used the term 'ephemera' to describe myself. Taipei was the fifth city I had lived in. I don't remember how strongly I felt about home and belonging. Never thought of using any form of record, the memory stored in the carrier constantly flip through the proof of their existence, in an attempt to have a moment can go back to the past days. Force yourself to be the person who never misses the past, forever yearning for the tomorrow that has not yet begun. Every time I leave, I can only choose the most necessary and light items to pack into my luggage and go to the next station with me.

This strange state ceased to exist at the beginning of the institute's creation process. Looking back at my work in Taiwan, I find that the core of all my works revolves around the memory of the past. Taking painting as the starting point of vector, try various possibilities of being watched, and present the memory of a person, a place, or a relationship.

In early 2019, I realized that I was about to leave Taiwan, the island where I had lived for more than 1,800 days. A strong voice in my heart told me to seriously say goodbye to the island as a non-tourist. After leaving, I will return here as a short-term visitor with only half a month to stay in China. Taiwan may no longer be Taiwan and I may no longer be me.

Farewell to the Island is a rite of passage for your time in Taiwan. The journey lasted more than 500 h, starting and ending in Taipei, the city where I live, taking a local bus from the east coast all the way south and from the west coast up north. Taiwan, which is connected by nearly 164 local bus stops, uses a roll of the dice to determine the next destination to visit, using photography as the medium, and negatives as the medium to search for proof of my presence on the island.

I have been to many places in Taiwan, and the beginning of this journey is to think that I might go to the places I have been to and have a look at them again, and maybe to cherish the traces of my past existence. At the same time, I am also greedy to go to different places to see, which is why I choose to use the number of dice to decide the destination.

Depart from Taipei at 20:12 pm on March 23, 2019. Roll the 20-sided dice. The first stop is Ruifang Station. The number I get is the number of stops in the interval. A person with a suitcase and camera, just like this road. On the way, I took pictures of all the people I spoke to, the animals that responded to me, and looked at me in silence. To be carried by dice to stop after stop to familiar or unfamiliar places.

It's a romantic journey, where you will go next, what you will see on the way, and who you will say goodbye to in the future.

Luggage: 50 rolls of film, film camera, printed short sleeves, new white shoes, toiletry bag, dice.

The reason why I choose the form of film shooting is that I know I can't watch the image I record at the moment. After the trip around the island is completely finished, I will take all the negatives and sweep them, so as to obtain the result images, negatives and shells that must be physically present in electronic files. The purpose of the trip was not to capture amazing photos, but to look back at what had happened in the past as I organized the photos, photographing every island I thought of in the present.

2   Literature Review

Alec Soth, who is good at executing narrative shooting projects, travels all over the world to record stories. The works often take ordinary social conditions as the theme, with people as the connection, deriving a melancholy, sensitive and nostalgic mood.

His experiences along the Mississippi River road took three years to compile into a series of works called Sleeping by the Mississippi, about time, about wandering, about escaping. Capturing the reality of marginalization, it presents people, landscapes and the landscape of their homes. These trivial images are left behind in the seemingly plain picture. Alec Soth takes pictures with a large-format camera, strings these independent images together, and finally constructs a new world. The uniqueness of his works leads the viewer into an atmosphere of solitude [1].

In a sense, I followed the same path as Alec Soth along the Mississippi River. Alec Soth of on the way to the next destination is with a person to get along with the process of clues to be his next destination, he didn't decided to good before we start the journey of each station, Alec Soth travel the way of the middle and lower a destination with randomness, the scenery near the Mississippi River grand surprise also is no reason for his trip photos, his photo description about time, about roaming, about to flee.

He defines Sleeping by the Mississippi as a poetic encounter between past and future worlds, and the title of his project, Sleeping by the Mississippi, is more of a metaphor for paranoid travel.

When it comes to photography, this big topic, Alec Soth gives the experience summed up as follows: "I am the incredible images and iconic moments are not interested in more and more, they do sometimes, sometimes not. Anyone can make a good photo, but important for me to do, is to edit photos and then put them together, that kind of choice behavior, and try to make them mutual echo. This should be the ultimate task. The only is the overall image is only let me be more interested in [1]."

After I took a series of photos around the island, I was faced with 1194 photos and I didn't know how to organize and present them. I was inspired by Alec Soth's summary of photography. Editing and sorting is a process of selection, which can make photos respond to each other across time and space. The focus in organizing the images, from selecting the best images to finding the connections between the images, should be more important to editing the image as a whole.

The shoreline photographed by Zhang Xiao is essentially a record of the wandering and lonely souls who have left their hometown for construction. Because of my home-town and background, I am deeply impressed by the works taken by Zhang Xiao. People who have left their hometowns, people who have lost their sense of belonging. People in China have all kinds of reasons to leave their hometowns and their familiar living environment. As a city living on the coast of China, I am one of them [2]. China has a vast landscape, which is different from Taiwan, and there may be a huge difference when arriving in another province or city. For example, when I was in junior high school, I left the small town where I was born and grew up and went to study in a municipal middle school. Geographically, these two places belong to the same city, but I still felt a strong sense of exclusion. After I chose Shanghai, or came to Taiwan, these cities made me feel that I am an outsider, here is not my hometown. After a few years of living, I have got used to the living habits of this city or island. However, the household registration and foreigners' stay, as well as the inconveniences caused by people who are not in the city, constantly remind me that I do not belong here.

Long time away from home, let me return to their own legal homeland, the rhythm of life, rhythm and so on have become very strange to me. I know very well that I can no longer really go to that hometown, and for me, returning home every New Year and holidays has only become a ceremony to commemorate my hometown.

Feldmann's approach to art is to collect, sequence and reproduce in order to use everyday images to create ingenious installations.

Feldmann's most famous works include black-and-white photographs of a woman's clothes, her unmade bed, her own shoes, etc. And cashed in his Hugo Boss prize in $1 bills plastered all over the walls of the Guggenheim. Feldmann always draws inspiration from images of everyday life and forms installation works after careful thinking. "Art is a process, an impression, a feeling, but never a real object," he said.

At the same time, he is collecting old paintings. Feldmann used these landscapes as a topographic study: a particular kind of sky that depicted nature in a certain way. 11

Horizon is a collection of eleven oil paintings, created by different artists at different times. Although they vary in size, they are aligned on the visible horizon to draw a continuous line between different images, thus creating an uninterrupted panorama of the negative line. Feldmann poetically fuses all these places, real and fictional, to immerse the observer in a new landscape.

Just like Feldmann's usual creation method, I was deeply attracted by his works which were classified into the arrangement. The arrangement method of subsequent attempts brought me a lot of inspiration. For example, "11 Horizon" connects landscapes of different times and space through the horizon of each picture to create a sense of spatial flow, and the picture is no longer confined to a rectangular canvas [5]. The collocations in Photographs Taken From Hotel Room Windows While Traveling are full of white space between photos and are not edited in such a way that images are collaged with spatial clues, but the white space outside the photos and the montage of screen transformations form a tight viewing logic [4]. In my subsequent editing attempts, I also arranged the photos I took with different reading logic.

In the second part of John Berger's book About Looking, Chap. 4, The Use of Photography, I read about the relationship between painting and photography, as well as between photography and memory.

"Before the invention of the camera, what kind of thing had the function of a photograph? The usual answers are prints, drawings or paintings. But the more revelatory answer is probably: memory. Before the invention of photography, the way for people to record the world was painting. Although painting must be the image described after people's memory is internalized, before the invention of photography, painting also tried to be close to photography in a certain period and fixed the image as much as possible in some way. Such as using the pinhole imaging principle to actually project the world into a dark room and depict it as accurately as possible" [3].

3 Research Method

3.1 Experiment 1: Morphological Analysis of the Photos

After sweeping through all the negatives, I had 1,194 pictures. In the process of organizing the photos, I tried several ways to organize them.

"Morphological analysis is based on morphological methods to analyze things. Its characteristic is, the problem of the research object, or is divided into some basic components, and then to a fundamental part of a separate processing. Provide all kinds of solutions to the problem or solution, respectively, and finally form the total solution to solve the problem of the whole. At this time there will be a number of total solutions, because it is through different combination relations and getting a different solution. Each of all the total packages is workable, must use mathematical morphology methods that are analyzed."

field domain	come across	weather and time	color
water	male	sunny	cool tone
load	female	cloudy	warm tone
land	animal	rainy	light tone
sky	plant	daytime	dark tone
city	abiotic	night	wight
room			

When performing morphological analysis, it is very rational to list some of the conditions that will be photographed around the island. Several combinations are listed randomly by rolling dice.

The discovery of the accident, I thought that these basic conditions can choose a lot of consistent photos, in the way of looking for photos even having the impression that I have photographed. But there are two conditions that can be rolled and nothing can be done. In some cases, only one photo can be selected. With the proof of the photos, I found that my memory has changed into something else after time and internalization of my brain. Is my memory real? At that moment, the photos began to look strange and distant.

3.2 Experiment 2: Vector Classification

After the computer previews and small images, print out all the photos for the next editing attempt. When the pictures materially appeared in front of me in large numbers, they seemed to be coming towards me.

The classification was inspired by Hans-Peter Feldman's creative approach, which uses sorting and reproduction after collection and shooting. Start with one image and extend around its boundaries to the next image.

Experiment 2: In the initial experiment, different photos were briefly connected by colors and object boundaries, so that the rectangular picture was no longer confined to a single narrative, and thus a sense of flow was generated between them.

When you look at the photos, you will also find some places you never thought you could see. I thought blue and people were the most common images of the trip. In the classification process of using color as a clue, I unexpectedly found that there was a lot of green in the pictures I shot, and green was hidden in the pictures in different objects and forms. The green elements make up the largest number of images on the record.

I never thought green was my favorite color, but unconsciously, I was constantly attracted to green and took pictures of all kinds of green. In the picture with green as the clue, I gradually found that my mood in this journey was mostly lonely and dull. The roll of the dice didn't always carry me to places I used to know. It took me to islands I'd never been to before, and perhaps the trip found that thinking I knew enough about this tiny island I'd lived on for five years was an illusion. These pictures also tell me that I may never know about this island.

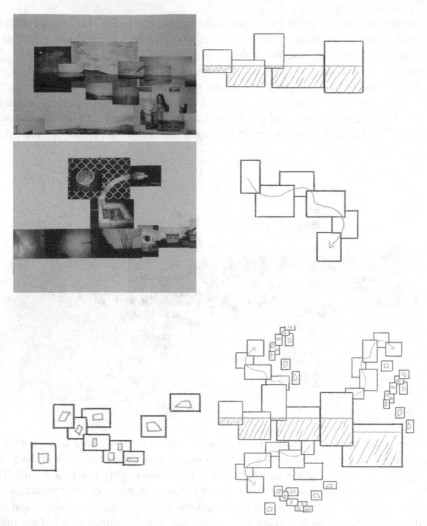

These photos are pasted in the living space as if to create another extension of time and space for the room. I live with these photos day by day, arranging where I will appear in the next one, and the picture grows gradually in this space. It's not so much that I can decide whether or not to use the image as the next destination, it's rather that the image decides the next destination itself, and like a roll of the dice, I'm taken there.

Continuing the editing style based on space, "Island Farewell" has different ways of arranging and reading in different exhibition spaces. Like memories, they will spread through space in a very different manner depending on the type of field being viewed.

4 Conclusion

Most people think that photographs capture reality, but painters don't. Drawing ability means the ability to place objects in a believable space, something that people who can't draw can't do. The eye is a part of the mind, and what is seen is influenced by the subjective mind. Images travel through your body in a mental way, into your brain, into your memory, where they stay and are transmitted by your hands. Painters imagined the world more humanely, they talked about the relationship between objects [6].

Photographs are all about seeing everything at the same time, in the blink of a camera, but we don't. We need time to see. That's why space was created.

Using photography to create, using painting consciousness to arrange images, connecting seemingly honest photos, making them a way of seeing memories. Photos do not capture reality, but give a viewing of Angle and place. Through subjective thinking processing, they tell the memory wandering between the real and the virtual.

From the moment you receive the scanned negatives, viewing more than a thousand pictures on the screen is not much at all. A typical three-hour shoot can be of the same order of magnitude. But when it was all printed and spread out in space, I realized how massive it was, and it was all coming at me. In the process of editing them on the wall, we found the problem we once encountered in painting: whole and detail.

Edited for a holistic view, the memory seems too dispassionate. I had little idea of what the Polish situation, the uncontrolled emotions, looked like, as I usually did. Some people say that the photos I take, I see the distance, the bland, the loneliness.

Memory should be inspired by the spread of points, and my hands bring more imagination space and viewing Angle to the audience. I printed most of the photos, stayed alone with them in space, let the wave of memory carry me to put them in the right place, no longer rigidly screening whether the pictures and graphics are rigorous, through editing them to find a sense of freedom in painting.

Links are the boundaries of one photo and serve as the starting point for a sequence to the next. From the most magnificent Cote d 'Azur, to the green environment where I grew up and lived day by day, to the city full of people, to the small and safe private space.

References

1. Soth, A.: Sleeping by the Mississippi, MACK, America (2017)
2. Xiao, Z.: Coastline, Fake Magazine, China (2004)
3. Berger, J.: About Looking.Translated by Liu Huiyuan, Wheat Field Publishing House (2017)
4. Berger, J.: Taken From Hotel Room Windows. https://www.303gallery.com/gallery-exhibitions/hans-peter-feldmann4?view=slider#2 (2010)
5. 11 Horizon. https://www.artbasel.com/catalog/artwork/31506/Hans-Peter-Feldmann-11-Horizons
6. Gayford, M.: A Bigger Message: Conversations with David Hockney. Thames & Hudson, England (2011)
7. Gayford, M.: A Bigger Message: Conversations with David Hockney. Thames & Hudson, England (2011)

Culture, Learning and Well-being

ISDT Case Study of We'll App for Postpartum Depression Women

Wen-Ko Chiou[1]([✉]), Szu-Erh Hsu[1], Yu-Chao Liang[1], Tai-He Hong[2], Liang-Ming Lo[2], Hao Chen[3], and Chao Liu[3]

[1] Department of Industrial Design, Chang Gung University, Taoyuan City, Taiwan
wkchiu@mail.cgu.edu.tw
[2] Department of Obstetrics and Gynecology,
Chang Gung Memorial Hospital at Taipei, Taipei City, Taiwan
{thh20,lmlo}@cgmh.org.tw
[3] Graduate Institute of Business and Management,
Chang Gung University, Taoyuan City, Taiwan

Abstract. Objective: Following the concept I-Sustainability Design Thinking (ISDT), this study will design and develop a mobile application to relieve postpartum depression in pregnant women. Background: Depression has become one of the common diseases of affluence; however, the pregnant women are mainly affected by hormonal changes and other factors, influenced by emotional disorder in particular, thus causing the commits of suicide. To reduce the emotional issues of expectant and lying-in women, the study attempted the product conception and design adopting design approach under ISDT principle. Methods: The process of the ISDT method is divided into macro and micro forces. The macro forces are based on the Socio-Economic and Technology as regime, with resource conditions favorable for business operations, in line with sustainable development goals. Micro-forces, in micro-user orientations, through approaches of scenario story, character mapping, and scenario sketch brainstorming, the products designed may meet the needs of users and become more creative. Results: After macro and micro force analyses, the value proposition of the product with maximum values by satisfying needs by product and service audiences is provided, and the product design concept and prototype are developed. Conclusions: The APP takes the promotion of social support and self-efficacy as the core and transforms it into a game interaction method to achieve the goal of sustainability is more valuable than the value opportunity analysis of existing products. It is expected that ISDT can be used in product design, service design, graphic design, and designers in related design fields can also value and attempt to adopt ISDT's new design thinking to achieve the sustainable development goals and mutual prosperity of human beings.

Keywords: I-Sustainability Design Thinking · Postpartum depression · Mobile application development

© Springer Nature Switzerland AG 2021
P.-L. P. Rau (Ed.): HCII 2021, LNCS 12772, pp. 119–137, 2021.
https://doi.org/10.1007/978-3-030-77077-8_10

1 Introduction

With the changes of the times, depression has become one of the common diseases of affluence; however, the pregnant women are mainly affected by hormonal changes and other factors, influenced by emotional disorder in particular, thus causing the commits of suicide.

The Remote Assessment of Disease and Relapse device selection framework provides a structured yet flexible approach to device selection for health care programs and can be used to systematically approach complex decisions that require teams to consider patient experiences alongside scientific priorities and logistical, technical, or regulatory constraints [1]. The co-designed women's health screening tool is a first step towards addressing screening barriers from both primary care provider's and community women's perspectives. Future research will explore the facilitators of and barriers to implementing the tools in different primary care settings. Future work should also more systematically examine whether and how screening processes may reinforce or contribute to women's feelings of being stereotyped, and how screening processes can be designed to avoid stereotype threat, which has the potential to reduce the effectiveness of screenings intended to promote women's health [2].

There is a need for development of theoretical insights and practical approaches to align design for sustainability practices taking place at micro- and meso-levels of socio-technical systems. The conceptual framework is developed by integrating theories from sustainability science, system innovations and transitions theories and design perspective on system innovations [3]. The concept of design thinking (DT) with its five key principles (i.e., problem framing, user focus, diversity, visualization, experimentation and iteration) is presented. Buhl et al. [4] developed a research framework with four propositions that demonstrate the suitability of DT's key principles for meeting the identified sustainability-oriented innovation challenges. Finally, boundary conditions, practical implications and opportunities for further research are pointed out. Maher et al. (2018) provided an overview of Research through Design methodology then examined a case study of its application. It involved five stages, each including: framing the problem/opportunities, designing possible solutions, testing them collaboratively and reflecting critically. They concluded the case study by providing an overview of MetaMAP—a graphical tool for collaborating to understand social–ecological systems holistically and design well-integrated sustainability initiatives. Reflecting on that case study, it presented some fundamental design principles which were demonstrated through the research through design case study and their value for achieving Sustainable Development Goals (SDGs).

To reduce the emotional issues of expectant and lying-in women, the study attempted the product conception and design adopting design approach under I-Sustainability Design Thinking (ISDT), expecting the offering of better living environment and well-being to human beings through new design thinking model. This study attempts to, based on social, economic, technical, commercial resources and sustainable development factors, find out factors that may solve the emotional barriers of postpartum as well as improving social support and self-efficacy as a priority consideration and evaluation standard for design, and, through wisdom of human beings, to adopt and adapt the beings and sustainability of the world, paying constant attention to innovation and designs, and considering the sustainability of the earth and the human beings on the earth.

2 Literature Review

2.1 Postpartum Depression

Women suffer from depression twice as much as men [5–8]. Among types of female depression, postpartum affective disorder during pregnancy and lying-in has the most serious impact, which in severe cases the expectant women may commit suicide with their newborns, causing serious social issues. The main pathogenesis is the rapid postpartum hormone changes, with minor factors including medical history of depression (including prenatal depression), low social support, major life events and stress during pregnancy, gestational diabetes, etc. [9, 10]. Such depression can further be, by severity, divided into postpartum blues (maternity blues or baby blues), postpartum depression (PPD) and postpartum psychosis [10].

The prevalence rate of postpartum blue is 40%–80% [11], featuring a transient state of depression beginning at 2 to 3 days after delivery [12], which contains psychological and emotional manifestations such as anxiety, emotional ups and downs, bad temper, tiredness, easy tear shedding, insomnia, headaches, and excessive sensitivity to things; physical symptoms such as insomnia, headaches, nightmares, etc., recurring for no more than 2 weeks. As such transient symptoms do not require medical intervention [13, 14], the postpartum women still need more care and support from family and friends for recovery. Mothers often neglect their mental health status, and the risk of postpartum depression can be developed in severe cases eck [15].

Postpartum depression is one of non-psychotic major depression, with a prevalence rate of 10–15% [16–19]; it usually occurs to women from 2 to 4 weeks postpartum to 1 year postpartum. Symptoms include depression, low mood, bad temper, tiredness, and insomnia; constant sense of guilt or worthlessness; eating disorder, easy tear shedding, inability to concentrate, loss of interest in the surrounding life and favorite things or often feeling of inability to cope with life; lack of parental self-efficacy. These symptoms last for 2 weeks to several months, and severe cases may have suicidal ideation and cause danger to the newborn. About 20% of mothers end their lives by suicide [20], thus, such demographics require medical assistance and care.

2.2 I Social-Support and Self-efficacy

Social support is broadly defined as members or experts in social networks providing support and assistance through material, cognition and emotion [21, 22]. Social network members include family members, intimate partners, friends, and peers, among which partners, mothers, and sisters are most frequently contacted [23]. It is extremely important for a lying-in mother to receive substantial assistance from her partner and mother [24], especially as the lying-in woman's childcare self-efficacy can be improved through the receipt of Parenting experience sharing and verbal encouragement; hence, there is a significant correlation between appraisal support and self-confidence of the lying-in woman [25]. Most lying-in women are highly satisfied with the experience of peer support and exchange of experiences between peers providing emotional, information and appraisal support. Maternal satisfaction is related to the number of peers and duration of their contacts [26]. In addition to physical care in the early postpartum period, women after birth giving are required to take care of the newborn, which would reduce the chance of going out and socializing. Through the Internet, the mothers can connect to the world outside the living environment, and surfing the internet may help reduce loneliness and depression, improving social support and self-esteem [27]. Social media is a modern tool widely used to convey information, on which people enter virtual communities and network platforms to create, share, and exchange opinions, perspectives and experiences. Among the platforms, the non-public groups on Facebook are usually used as forums where users seek and share suggestions as well as social support with or without involvement of professionals [28, 29].

2.3 E-Mental Health

As the population suffering from depression is increase day by day, there are studies proposing the provision of treatment services for mental conditions through the internet model i.e. patients with depression can more easily obtain treatment services through mobile APP on their smartphones or mobile devices, therefore enabling the unleash from the conventional and restrained psychological counseling and popularization of screening and treatment services.

In the literature review of Dol et al. [30], there are sufficient evidence that mHealth intervention for the postpartum period can improve the sense of social support during this period. In addition, compared with lack of intervention, it was found that mHealth intervention for mental health can reduce postpartum depression. The study of Baumel et al. [31] also indicated the feasibility and acceptability of accessing the digital platform 7Cups by women with postpartum depression symptoms as an interventional measure for mHealth, with practical results clinically obtained. Since smartphones and the internet are currently the most widely used technology network, different types of applications have also flourished in response to various needs and fields. Among them, applications related to medicine and healthcare including chronic disease auxiliary management, disease self-diagnosis, general physical and mental health, and fitness attain growth by 25% annually. Therefore, provision of treatment and services through mobile APP has become the current trend.

2.4 I-Sustainability Design Thinking (ISDT)

The two hexagrams of the universe as well as the major and minor transitions of the yang and yin phases also suggest the procedural method of ISDT applying human wisdom to factor and adapt to things in the world and changes, constantly focusing on innovation and design of things while considering the sustainable development of Earth and human beings on Earth as needed [32].

Relevant studies by the European Union indicate that about 80% of the environmental impact factors of products are determined in the creative and design stages. Therefore, a systematic and perfect sustainable design appraisal system is an important basis for its development. In addition to green products, the focus of ISDT should also contribute more focus on its extension such as the design at aspect of human and spiritual needs, allowing consumers to experience the product itself while also feeling the psychological and spiritual care brought by the diversified services of product [33].

3 Materials and Methods

3.1 Case Study

In terms of case study, Eisenhardt [34] considered the case study method to be focusing on study on dynamic state under a single background, which is especially suitable for new study topics. Eisenhardt also formulated the eight steps of the case study method: (1) defining research question; (2) selecting cases; (3) collecting data; (4) entering the field; (5) analyzing data; (6) cross-case pattern search; (7) shaping hypotheses; (8) enfolding literature. He believed that the case study method is derived from the connection, comparison, and induction of multiple databases whose data sources were combined with practices, and their hypotheses and theories deduced from it had higher feasibility. However, due to the complexity of these data, the inferred theory may have shortcomings that were not easy to understand.

Yin [35] believed that the definition of case study "is an empirical inquiry that investigates a contemporary phenomenon within its real-life context, especially when the boundaries between phenomenon and context are not clearly evident…[and] relies on multiple sources of evidence practical method of investigation. When the boundary between the researched phenomenon and real life is not clear, the situation is investigated through evidence from multiple sources." Yin [35] also believed that case studies must follow three principles: (1) multiple sources of evidence; (2) a case study database; and (3) chains of evidence.

Combining the viewpoints of scholars aforementioned, the case study method is suitable for exploratory research which no scholars have ever conducted. In order to guarantee the integrity of the hypothesis and proposition, the source of case data should be obtained from multiple sources of data collection, and the proposition or hypothesis is proposed upon closure as subsequent study reference.

3.2 ISDT Process

The process of the ISDT method is divided into macro and micro forces. The macro forces are based on the socio-economic scenery, taking core technology as regime, with resource conditions favorable for business operations (business resources), in line with SDGs. Micro-forces, in micro-user orientations, highlight the key needs and creative ideas in the application context of product (object) based on who, what, when, and where the product is applied. Through approaches of scenario story, character mapping, and scenario sketch brainstorming, the products designed may meet the needs of users and become more creative. After macro and micro force analyses, the value proposition of the product with maximum values by satisfying needs by product and service audiences is provided, and the product design concept and prototype are developed. Then, through the comparison between the designed product and the existing products, the product value opportunities are proposed to analyze the opportunities based on eight aspects for enhancing the product values, which are divided into eight categories, namely: flow, mindfulness, sustainable development, aesthetics, human factors and ergonomics, health, quality and core technology i.e. the core values of ISDT. After establishing the value and advantages of product design, the business model is planned as final step.

A product is valuable if it's useful, easy to use, and attractive. Value can be disintegrated into various and concrete product attributes that can support product usability, ease of use, and desirability that are the exact attributes connecting the product's functional features and value. As the product creates a certain experience for the user, the better the experience, the higher the value of the product to users [36].

4 Results

4.1 Mandalas Drawing Orientation

Design is a creative activity and a life philosophy that explores communication from individuals to groups. The Mandala orientation aims to combine Western psychology and Oriental meditation activity flow theory, combined with Mihaly's flow and Jung's psychological analysis and the concept of Mandala, educating designers through the study of the collective unconsciousness of specific groups and age groups. Taking the cooperative mandala as the work camp orientation warm-up activity, through the cooperative painted mandala activities, designers can not only meet their own expression needs, but also position themselves in a safe space for their spirits, while developing empathy and revealing oneself and furthermore exchanging with others. The meditation effect of Mandala is equivalent to the mindfulness meditation practice method used in brain neuroscience research. In Jung's "Psychoanalysis", he also made an important disclosure on the inner spiritual perfection of Mandala, and various studies on Mandala have indicated its significant impact on the promotion of creativity and empathy [37] (Fig. 1).

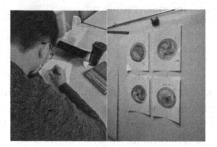

Fig. 1. Mandalas drawing orientation

4.2 Macro Forces

Macro Socio-Economic (SE) as Scenery, Core Technology (T) as Regime, and the resource conditions favorable for business operations (business resources), in line with the SDGs for generating value propositions for innovative products and services [38].

Economic and Technology Forces Divergent. The discussion is performed in form of brainstorming and co-creation by cross-sector team members and through the use of yellow post-it notes. Based on the aforementioned SE. and T., more than 50 influencing forces are diverged and then arranged by grouping and in order (Ranking). At this stage, the teams start with the socio-economic and technological background, and diverge as much as possible with yellow post-it notes to find potential chains, as shown in Fig. 2.

Fig. 2. Social economic (SE) scenery divergent and technology (T) divergent

Social Economic Convergent TOP10. More than 10 important influencing forces (TOP10 Forces) are listed, and names of the forces of each group are posted in pink post-it notes, as shown in Fig. 3.

Fig. 3. Social economic (SE) convergent

Business Resources and Sustainable Development Goals.
Business Resources Divergent and Convergent
    The discussion is performed in form of brainstorming and co-creation by cross-sector team members and through the use of yellow post-it notes. In response to the

aforementioned Business Resources, the influencing forces are diverged respectively, and then arranged in the order of grouping and ranking. The important influencing factors of Business Resources are selected, and items of the important influencing factors of each group are posted in pink post-it notes. In this section, through divergence and convergence through the currently existing resource items, four major business resource items are obtained (Fig. 4).

Fig. 4. Business resources divergence and convergence

Sustainable Development Goals Relevant Items
According to the UN's seventeen goals for sustainable development, three major items and their sub-items are selected to identify sustainable development issues that can be designed (Fig. 5) (Table 1).

Fig. 5. SDGs relevant items, with relevant item picked based on selected topics.

SE.T.B.S Potential Opportunity Gap (POG) Synthesis and Product Ideas Generation. From the ranking of top 10 forces for the aforementioned SE., T & BS Potential Opportunity Gaps (POG) each, the forces, the relevance of the opportunity gaps are referenced and synthesized into 3–4 items each for supporting background of the Product Ideas (Fig. 6).

Table 1. Through 17 Goals of SDGs, three major items and their sub-items are selected.

Relevant item picked based on selected topics		
Mother and baby healthcare are base of sustainable development of human beings	Good health and social welfare	Ending hunger, realizing food safety, improving nutritional condition and promoting sustainable agriculture
Development of pregnant and lying-in women and child rearing service industries	Industry, innovation and infrastructure	Promoting a durable, inclusive and sustainable economic growth, promoting a sufficient productivity employment and employment for everyone
Innovation and value-adding for digital technology	Industry, innovation and infrastructure	

Fig. 6. SE., T. & B.S. Forces integration, generation of innovative product ideas generation and proposal screening, and SE., T. & B.S backgrounds

Product Idea and Potential Opportunity Gap Statement. The aforementioned integrated SE., T & B.S. Potential Opportunity Gaps are compiled and turned into Fig. 7 below.

Under the context of the socio-economy, it is known that the current lifestyle, life of compact family, work pressure, and maternal emotional disorders need to be valued. Depression has become one of the common diseases of affluence, and, at present, through artificial intelligence, rapid transmission, E-mental health technology, technologies will help human beings achieve a better quality of life. The combination of existing business resources, including online-to-offline (O2O) services, medical care, food delivery, etc., are there for better welfare. In the sustainable development goals, good health and social welfare, industrial innovation, food safety and nutritional status are all issues that need to be addressed at the status quo. Combining the above, the study team has found potential

Fig. 7. Potential opportunity gap

opportunities for current products at a macro perspective. The team takes the postpartum physical and mental health platform as the starting point of topic, and then develops the product from a micro perspective.

4.3 Micro Forces

Micro-forces, in micro-user orientations, highlight the key needs and creative ideas in the application context of product based on who, what, when, and where the product is applied.

Scenario Story Approach. In view of the product opportunity gaps and product ideas generated from the aforementioned macro forces, a typical user representative is set, and the scenario story for such representative is used to describe the requirements and forces to be met in the context of product use. From the above macro forces, we have found the gap of potential opportunities, hence, the study, based on the lying-in women as target audience, set the potential product application context in terms of timing and location to develop and narrate the scenario story, as shown in Fig. 8.

Character Mapping. In view of the above-mentioned macro product conception direction and background, attributes of the target audience of the product and the range of each attribute (range) are set. And, within the defined range, representatives with different attributes are selected. In general experience, 6–10 differentiated representatives and the story scenarios (scene) of the occasion are selected. The user characteristics discussed in the role mapping stage can be used as a reference when anticipating user scenarios [39], which helped the design team to organize the discussed user characteristics from a large number of different scenarios. In addition, when anticipating user characteristics, the user's personality, interest, and psychological characteristics are added to provide aides to the team in explore users' needs from their psychological level.

The research team select different representatives according to different attributes and different age groups, as shown in Fig. 8.

Fig. 8. Scenario story approach & character mapping

Scenario Sketch Brainstorming Development. Conceptual development of situational story sketches: Team members select different user representative roles, with each member concepting and drawing the scenarios concerning when the product is needed or applied by users in different scenarios, followed by introduction of the critical issues and key ideas in the scene to the group members. Members from the same team then concept with empathy, brainstorming and converging pictures specific to the scenario, radiating more needs and creative contents, and then post the contents recorded on yellow post-it notes between the pictures (Fig. 9).

Fig. 9. Scenario sketch brainstorming development

Top 10 Themes Converged After Diverging Critical Issues and Key Ideas. Contents of the Critical Issues and Key Ideas obtained by diverging the yellow post-it notes are arranged in order of grouping and importance (ranking), and then summarized into the innovative proposal-the 10 important topics that must be achieved (Top10 Themes) (Fig. 10) (Table 2).

Fig. 10. Critical issue divergence, creative conception and convergence

Value Proposition. The value proposition refers to the characteristics provided for the needs of products and service objects. By combining on the Top10 Themes above, the team comes up with a solution and put forward the value proposition of this research. The final objective of this research team is to establish a postpartum physical and mental health management service platform, and the details of which are valuable and can be used as follow-up prototype development (Table 3).

Prototyping. Based on application scenarios of user to products, models are used to simulate use process and method to verify the appropriateness of product under different use scenarios. Through value proposition, two items are selected for modeling and simulation and verification, followed by product proposals with greater simulation value selected (Fig. 11).

Prototype Simulation and Evaluation. Based on the Postpartum Affective Disorder Assistance System, an APP is built for verification (Fig. 12).

Value Opportunity Analysis. Value opportunity analysis can be applied to tangible product, service and product-service system. All value opportunity categories can be applied to services, which some keywords can become more relevant to product and service design terminology directly (Fig. 13).

From the comparison between the existing affective APP and the postpartum affective disorder APP, it can be seen that shows that the APP designed through ISDT contains more valuable.

Table 2. Top10 key themes

THEMES					
URBAN-RURAL GAP (LIFESTYLE)	Lack of Childrearing Knowledge and Guidance as the Mother and Mother-in-Law live in different locations	Individual Compact Families having Urban Life			
LACK OF PARENTING EXPERIENCE AND KNOWLEDGE	Unfamiliarity of Childcare Knowledge	Parenting Knowledge Platform (O2O)	Reliability of Internet Information	Parenting Knowledge Platform	
LACK OF POST-PARTUM DIETARY AND NUTRITIONAL KNOWLEDGE	Worry on Postpartum Nutrition of Lying-In Women	Insufficient Dietary and Nutritional Knowledge after Delivery	Food Formula Delivery Issue	Various Limits Imposed by "Sitting the Month"	
FEAR FOR UNAFFORDABILITY OF ECONOMY POST-PARTUM	Economic Burden to Core Families	Worry about Baby Growth Burden	Mental Burden Caused by Inability to Tend After Work	Worrying about Transition to Work after Maternity Leave	Emotion Monitoring
PSYSIOLOGICAL INFLUENCE FORCES	Long-Term Fatigue due to Insufficient Sleep	Insecurity as Expectant Women	Emotion Influenced by Hormone	Stress Unable to Vent	
INTERPERSONAL RELATIONSHOP STRESS	Worry about Deformed Body Shape	Worry about Affairs of Husband	Lack of Entertainment after Birth giving	Loss of Social Activities with Families and Friends	Fitness
CHILDCARE STRESS INFLUENCING EMOTION	Feeling Restless when Tending After Baby's Defecation, Urination, Wailing	Psychological Instinct to Baby Crying	Anger by Husband's Reluctance in Caretaking	Insufficient Sleep due to Worry about Baby	Lack of Stress Relief via Entertainment
AI BABY PHYSIOLOGICAL AND ACTIVITIES MONITORING	Worry about Baby Safety, Danger and Discomfort	Nighttime Baby Wailing Monitoring Alter	Neighbor Disturbed by Baby Crying at Nighttime	AI Monitoring Technology	Provision of Psychological Consulting
LACK OF COMMEN SENSE FOR PARENTING MEDICINE	Inconvenience in Seeking Physician Advice	Currently lacking Professional Knowing Platforms			

Table 3. Value proposition

VALUE PROPOSITION
POSTPARTUM PHYSICAL AND MENTAL HEALTH MANAGEMENT SERVICE PLATFORMS
Parenting Knowledge Service Platform
Baby Physiology Control and Monitoring
Lying-In Women Dietary and Nutritional Knowledge Service Platform
MOTHER AND BABY MEDICAL KNOWLEDGE SERVICE PLATFORM
Pregnant and Lying-In Women Emotional Disorder Guidance Platform
Pregnant and Lying-In Women Formula and Health Service Platform
Postpartum Affective Disorder Assistance APP

Prototype1. Pregnant and Lying-In   Prototype2. Postpartum Affective Disorder
       Knowledge Sharing Platform   Assistance System

Fig. 11. Prototype

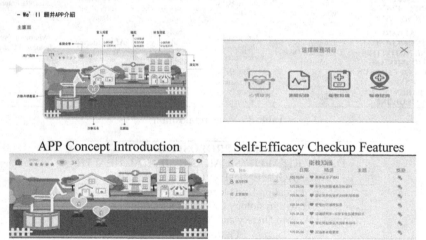

APP Concept Introduction   Self-Efficacy Checkup Features

Interactive Wishmaking Game-   Healthcare Education Interaction
Social Support Feature   Feature

Fig. 12. Prototype simulation and evaluation

Business Model Generation. Business model planning: Based on the nine important factors of product planning strategy, yellow post-it notes and enterprise product development cross-field professional teams, and brainstorming divergence and convergence

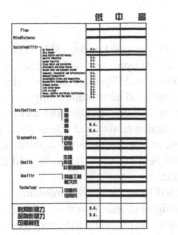
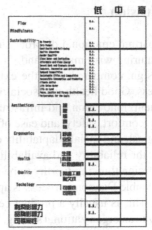

Postpartum Affective Disorder APP   **Existing Affection APP**

Fig. 13. Value opportunity analysis

methods are adopted to generate business models and main content that meet business conditions (Fig. 14).

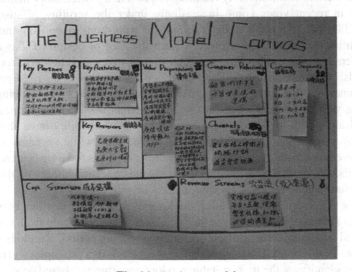

Fig. 14. Business model

5 Discussion

The postpartum emotional disorder support APP designed under ISDT, via interactive games featuring wish making and through social support and self-efficacy as the core of the design, compared with the existing affective APP, has a higher value in flow, mindfulness, Good health and social welfare item and entrepreneurship in sustainable development, innovation and infrastructure items, visual, audible and tactile senses in aesthetics, comfort, safety, and ease of use for human factors and ergonomics, physical, psychological, and social adaptability of health, craftsmanship and durability of quality, as well as the reliability and availability of core technologies. It can be said that ISDT is a new design thinking worthy to be promoted.

The Double Diamond process is appropriated from the design problem solving process [40]. This is usually a product centric design process, however, is applied in that case study to an organizational setting. The Double Diamond method provides a problem solving process for organizations to develop sustainability strategies based on objective science to significantly reduce environmental impacts. The questioning within the Double Diamond process enables clear contributions from specific disciplines to contribute to a holistic plan. The Double Diamond method of life cycle and design thinking provides a process to identify practices that can be targeted with the highest impact, based on objective science. It uses design thinking to develop strategies to respond to the environmental crisis in significantly reducing impacts in a participatory manner [41].

DT has in recent years come increasingly under the scrutiny of sustainability researchers [42–44], as a method and a format for workshops taken from the business field (which itself in turn had borrowed it from the field of design). DT is a human-centered, iterative problem-solving approach that involves stakeholders from various backgrounds. In contrast to linear innovation approaches, DT is no rigid process but rather a framework that integrates creative and analytic modes of reasoning, certain mindsets, as well as various hands-on tools and techniques [45]. DT's specific limitations in dealing with the super-wicked problem of sustainability have already been suggested by some researchers: Fischer [46] argued that, while sustainability issues focus on present *and* future generations, the framing of DT is too user-centered and too focused on the needs of individuals. Instead, it should concentrate more on the needs of current and future generations.

This new systematic product design thinking by ISDT analyzes that theory product designers should carefully analyze the social, economic, technological, commercial resources and sustainable development factors in a specific period, abandons the previous single pre-design analysis theory, and proposes new design principles and evaluation standards for identifying the most suitable product opportunities based on the analyses. It is found that the conventional preliminary analysis methods and theories of product design contain defects and deficiencies. Hence, the postpartum emotional disorder assistance APP designed by the research team through ISDT is more market competitive and more valuable, thus making it a thinking worthy to be valued by design industry.

6 Conclusion

The ISDT framework provides a structured yet flexible prescriptive process where multidisciplinary teams take a user-oriented approach to come up with relevant solutions to complex or 'wicked' problems. Also, the presented ISDT provides a means to integrate I Ching into a creative problem solving process to inform strategic decision-making prospectively within business that may well help contribute to curtailing environmental impacts.

For the postpartum emotional disorder assistance APP designed by ISDT design thinking used for the case, the APP finds the appropriate product opportunity value according to the needs of the times. The APP takes the promotion of social support and self-efficacy as the core and transforms it into a game interaction method to achieve the goal of sustainability is more valuable than the value opportunity analysis of existing products. Design approaches to achieving SDGs can be advanced by (1) collaborating and learning from those experienced in creative design methods; (2) expanding opportunities for publishing creative explorations and visioning; and (3) applying design methods to SDGs and sharing the results and process.

It is expected that ISDT can be used in product design, service design, graphic design, etc., and designers in related design fields can also value and attempt to adopt ISDT's new design thinking to achieve the goal Earth sustainability and mutual prosperity of human beings.

References

1. Polhemus, A.M., et al.: Human-centered design strategies for device selection in mHealth programs: development of a novel framework and case study. JMIR Mhealth Uhealth 8(5), e16043 (2020)
2. Foley, K.A., et al.: Primary care women's health screening: a case study of a community engaged human centered design approach to enhancing the screening process. Matern. Child Health J. 23(11), 1446–1458 (2019)
3. Gaziulusoy, A.I., Brezet, H.: Design for system innovations and transitions: a conceptual framework integrating insights from sustainability science and theories of system innovations and transitions. J. Cleaner Prod. 108, 558–568 (2015)
4. Buhl, A., et al.: Design thinking for sustainability: why and how design thinking can foster sustainability-oriented innovation development. J. Cleaner Prod. 231, 1248–1257 (2019)
5. Andrade, L., et al.: The epidemiology of major depressive episodes: results from the international consortium of psychiatric epidemiology (ICPE) surveys. Int. J. Meth. Psychiatr. Res. 12(1), 3–21 (2003)
6. Burt, V.K., Stein, K.: Epidemiology of depression throughout the female life cycle. J. Clin. Psychiatry 63(suppl 7), 9–15 (2002)
7. Gutiérrez-Lobos, K., Scherer, M., Anderer, P., Katschnig, H.: The influence of age on the female/male ratio of treated incidence rates in depression. BMC Psychiatry 2(1), 1–8 (2002)
8. Kessler, R.C., et al.: The epidemiology of major depressive disorder: results from the national comorbidity survey replication (NCS-R). JAMA 289(23), 3095–3105 (2003)
9. Milgrom, J., et al.: Antenatal risk factors for postnatal depression: a large prospective study. J. Affect. Disord. 108(1–2), 147–157 (2008)
10. Robertson, E., Grace, S., Wallington, T., Stewart, D.E.: Antenatal risk factors for postpartum depression: a synthesis of recent literature. Gen. Hosp. Psychiatry 26(4), 289–295 (2004)

11. O'hara, M.W., Swain, A.M.: Ratesand risk of postpartum depression—ameta- analysis. Int. Rev. Psychiatry **8**(1), 37–54 (1996)
12. Henshaw, C.: Mood disturbance in the early puerperium: a review. Arch. Women'S Mental Health **6**(2), s33–s42 (2003)
13. Kennerley, H., Gath, D.: Maternity blues: I. detection and measurement by questionnaire. Brit. J. Psychiatry **155**(3), 356–362 (1989).https://doi.org/10.1007/978-1-349-09789-0_9
14. Pitt, B.: Maternity blues. Brit. J. Psychiatry **122**(569), 431–433 (1973)
15. Beck, C.T., Reynolds, M.A., Rutowski, P.: Maternity blues and postpartum depression. J. Obstetric, Gynecologic, Neonatal Nursing **21**(4), 287–293 (1992)
16. Darcy, J.M., Grzywacz, J.G., Stephens, R.L., Leng, I., Clinch, C.R., Arcury, T.A.: Maternal depressive symptomatology: 16-month follow-up of infant and maternal health-related quality of life. J. Am. Board Family Med. **24**(3), 249–257 (2011)
17. Gavin, N.I., Gaynes, B.N., Lohr, K.N., Meltzer-Brody, S., Gartlehner, G., Swinson, T.: Perinatal depression: a systematic review of prevalence and incidence. Obstet. Gynecol. **106**(5 Part 1), 1071–1083 (2005)
18. Vesga-Lopez, O., Blanco, C., Keyes, K., Olfson, M., Grant, B.F., Hasin, D.S.: Psychiatric disorders in pregnant and postpartum women in the United States. Arch. Gen. Psychiatry **65**(7), 805–815 (2008)
19. Dorn, A., Mautner, C.: Der Gynäkologe **51**(2), 94–101 (2018). https://doi.org/10.1007/s00 129-017-4183-3
20. Lindahl, V., Pearson, J.L., Colpe, L.: Prevalence of suicidality during pregnancy and the postpartum. Arch. Women's Mental Health **8**(2), 77–87 (2005)
21. Gottlieb, B.H., Bergen, A.E.: Social support concepts and measures. J. Psychosom. Res. **69**(5), 511–520 (2010)
22. Thoits, P.A.: Mechanisms linking social ties and support to physical and mental health. J. Health Soc. Behav. **52**(2), 145–161 (2011)
23. Leahy-Warren, P., McCarthy, G., Corcoran, P.: First-time mothers: social support, maternal parental self-efficacy and postnatal depression. J. Clin. Nurs. **21**(3–4), 388–397 (2012)
24. Häggman-Laitila, A.: Early support needs of Finnish families with small children. J. Adv. Nurs. **41**(6), 595–606 (2003)
25. Leahy Warren, P.: First-time mothers: social support and confidence in infant care. J. Adv. Nurs. **50**(5), 479–488 (2005)
26. Dennis, C.-L.: Postpartum depression peer support: maternal perceptions from a randomized controlled trial. Int. J. Nurs. Stud. **47**(5), 560–568 (2010)
27. Shaw, L.H., Gant, L.M.: In defense of the Internet: the relationship between internet communication and depression, loneliness, self-esteem, and perceived social support. Eur. J. Mark. **54**(7) (2004)
28. Cavallo, D.N., Tate, D.F., Ries, A.V., Brown, J.D., DeVellis, R.F., Ammerman, A.S.: A social media–based physical activity intervention: a randomized controlled trial. Am. J. Prev. Med. **43**(5), 527–532 (2012)
29. Herring, S.J., Cruice, J.F., Bennett, G.G., Davey, A., Foster, G.D.: Using technology to promote postpartum weight loss in urban, low-income mothers: a pilot randomized controlled trial. J. Nutr. Educ. Behav. **46**(6), 610–615 (2014)
30. Dol, J., Richardson, B., Murphy, G.T., Aston, M., McMillan, D., Campbell-Yeo, M.: Impact of mobile health (mHealth) interventions during the perinatal period for mothers in low-and middle-income countries: A systematic review. JBI Evid. Synth. **17**(8), 1634–1667 (2019)
31. Baumel, A., Tinkelman, A., Mathur, N., Kane, J.M.: Digital peer-support platform (7Cups) as an adjunct treatment for women with postpartum depression: feasibility, acceptability, and preliminary efficacy study. JMIR mHealth uHealth **6**(2), e38 (2018)
32. Lui, I.: The Taoist I Ching: Shambhala Publications (2005)

33. TenHouten, W.D., Wang, W.: The eight trigrams of the Chinese I Ching and the eight primary emotions. Asian J. Soc. Psychol. **4**(3), 185–199 (2001)
34. Eisenhardt, K.M.: Building theories from case study research. Acad. Manage. Rev. **14**(4), 532–550 (1989)
35. Yin, R.K.: Discovering the future of the case study. Method in evaluation research. Eval. Pract. **15**(3), 283–290 (1994)
36. Vechakul, J., Shrimali, B.P., Sandhu, J.S.: Human-centered design as an approach for place-based innovation in public health: a case study from Oakland California. Matern. Child Health J. **19**(12), 2552–2559 (2015)
37. Liu, C., Chen, H., Liu, C.-Y., Lin, R.-T., Chiou, W.-K.: Cooperative and individual mandala drawing have different effects on mindfulness, spirituality, and subjective well-being. Frontiers Psychol. **11**, 2629 (2020)
38. Cagan, J., Cagan, J.M., Vogel, C.M.: Creating Breakthrough Products: Innovation from Product Planning to Program Approval. Ft Press, Upper Saddle River (2002)
39. Verplank, B., Fulton, J., Black, A., Moggridge, B.: Observation and Invention: The Use of Scenarios in Interactive Design. Tutorial notes from INTERCHI 1993 (1993)
40. UK Design Council: The Design Process. UK design Council, London (2005)
41. Clune, S.J., Lockrey, S.: Developing environmental sustainability strategies, the Double Diamond method of LCA and design thinking: a case study from aged care. J. Cleaner Prod. **85**, 67–82 (2014)
42. Carlsson, A., et al.: Sustainability Jam Sessions for vision creation and problem solving. J. Cleaner Prod. **98**, 29–35 (2014)
43. Fischer, M.: Design it! solving sustainability problems by applying design thinking. GAIA Ecol. Perspect. Sci. Soc. **24**(3), 174–178 (2015)
44. Maher, R., Maher, M., Mann, S., McAlpine, C.A.: Integrating design thinking with sustainability science: a research through design approach. Sustain. Sci. **13**, 1565–1587 (2018)
45. Liedtka, J.: Perspective linking design thinking with innovation outcomes through cognitive bias reduction. J. Product Innov. Manage. **32**, 925–938 (2015)
46. Fischer, M.: Design it! Solving sustainability problems by applying design thinking. GAIA-Ecol. Perspect. Sci. Soc. **24**(3), 174–178 (2015)

A Study on User Experience of COVID-19 Emergency Communication Platform from Cross-cultural Perspective of View

Ting Gao⑩, Shipei Xue(✉)⑩, Yuqi Zeng⑩, Jiayao Xu⑩, and Xiuyuan Guo⑩

Hunan University, Changsha 410082, China

Abstract. From certain point of view, the emergency communication platform plays an important role in fighting against COVID-19. This research aims to explore the user experience of the COVID-19 emergency communication platform in a cross-cultural background, with the purpose of relevant information promoting strategy under different culture recognition. This study takes China's Tencent health platform and the UK's NHS COVID-19 APP as the research objects. We built a user experience model first, then obtained user experience data by collecting 172 valid questionnaires and conducting interviews with 17 users. This research explores the current situation of users' experience on two different national platforms, compares and analyzes the feedback, found the differences between Chinese and British emergency communication platforms based on cultural theory. Our research shows that the different cultural characteristics of China and Britain make the two platforms variance in terms of sensory, interactive and satisfaction experience.

Keywords: Emergency communication · User experience · Cross-cultural

1 Introduction

In public emergencies, emergency communication is an essential element in communicating key information, transmitting emergency measures, and pacify emotion. It is well known that the media plays a critical role in emergency communications in most emergency situations. However, for the COVID-19, the single information dissemination function of the media can no longer meet people's needs. In order to solve this, many countries have developed emergency communication platforms which have played a multi-faceted role in assisting to fight against the epidemic, such as epidemic reporting, tracking, risk inquiry, online medical services, etc.

As a human-computer interaction platform, the user experience needs to be paid attention. What we have to realize is that user experience is an intuitive reflection of whether the product meets the user's habits, while the quality of the experience affects people's willingness to use the platform. Thus, a good user experience is a foundation for smooth operation and working effect in that and it is necessary to explore the elements which affect the user experience Different cultures will raise different user requirements

© Springer Nature Switzerland AG 2021
P.-L. P. Rau (Ed.): HCII 2021, LNCS 12772, pp. 138–149, 2021.
https://doi.org/10.1007/978-3-030-77077-8_11

and evaluation criteria, and cause different social patterns that would affect people's psychological complexity, such as perception, memory and comprehension. According to related research, the design of the user experience for the Internet platform should consider the influence of cultural factors. It is because users from different cultural backgrounds have completely different understanding about the same design. The influence of cultural factors on user experience should not be underestimated. This study will conduct cross-cultural user experience research by comparing China's Tencent Health platform with the UK's NHS COVID-19 platform. This will not only explore the current status of user experience on Chinese and English platforms but also compare the differences in user experience between these two countries under different cultures.

2 Literature Review

2.1 User Experience of Emergency Communication Platform

The construction of an emergency communication platform is an integral part of emergency management. Generally speaking, user experience often affects the effectiveness of emergency communications. In order to optimize the design of the emergency communication platform, people have conducted a lot of research that mainly analyzes user experience and put forward many constructive opinions based on such analysis. The platform objects selected for these studies usually include apps, websites, and social media accounts that are championed by emergency management sponsored by government departments [1], as well as emergency popular science websites or accounts established by certain companies [2]. It is worth noting that there is almost no research on specialized emergency communication platforms.

2.2 User Experience of Emergency Communication Platform from a Cross-cultural Perspective

Past cross-cultural studies have shown the differences in user experience will exist due to the different cultural backgrounds [3], and this difference is reflected in aesthetic preferences [3], risk perception [4], decision-making tendency and many other aspects [5] etc. However, in fact, in the field of emergency management, the research direction of user experience mainly focuses on system quality, page design, usability and other indicators, while ignoring the influence of the user's social and cultural environment to a certain extent. With the continuous development of globalization, the global nature of risks has become a consensus [6]. Many people think that emergency management is a social issue that must be paid attention to, which causes that more attention to the impact of different cultures on emergency management is crucial. Therefore, it is necessary to introduce a cross-cultural perspective when studying the user experience of emergency communication platforms.

2.3 The Emergency Communication Platform in the Context of the Covid-19 Pandemic

In the covid-19 pandemic, the emergency communication platform played an active role in assisting to fight against the epidemic. To conduct research on this, some researchers chose a typical analysis platform, such as Hallam Stevens, etc., and discussed the impact of the Trace together application released by the Singapore government during the epidemic on civil society behaviour [7]. At the same time, some other researchers also noticed the differences in emergency communication platforms brought about by different countries and conducted the comparative analysis. For example, by comparing Australia's Covid Safe and New Zealand's NZ Covid Tracer, they pointed out that Bluetooth-based Covid Safe will be more conducive to the realization of a contact tracking system [8]. These studies mainly study the effectiveness of the platform and its social impact, while few studies start from the user experience and aim to optimize the platform design.

3 Theoretical Basis and Related Model

3.1 Theoretical Basis

The Embodied Theory
The embodied cognition theory proposes that human cognition is based on the body and the interaction between the body and the environment [9, 10]. According to this theory, we can conclude that the direct interaction between people and products directly affects the user's sensory experience when using the product and this sensory experience directly affects the user's perception and evaluation for that. Scholars such as Sung Yeun Kim also found that the level of user embodiment improves user experience [11]. In addition, experience also has situational characteristics [12]. In the process of product use, user experience not only comes from the interaction process between the user and the product but also takes into account the user's use environment, including the real and the virtual environment. In other words, current customer usage and long-term social and cultural environment need to be taken into consideration.

Cultural Dimension Theory
Hodstein demonstrates that cultural differences between different countries do have a huge impact on people in terms of values, morals and aesthetic concepts. Here, he proposed the five dimensions of culture, namely power distance, individualism and socialism. Collectivism, masculinity and femininity, avoid uncertainty and long-term orientation [13]. According to Hofstede's cultural dimension theory, China belongs to the collectivist culture, which is a long-term orientation cultural dimension, while the United Kingdom belongs to the individualistic culture, which is a short-term orientation cultural dimension. In 1998, Barber and other scholars proposed the concept of cultural usability to deal with the impact of cultural differences on website interfaces. Scholars believe that cultural markers can directly impact user performance, which shows that culture and usability are already interacting [14].

3.2 Model

Since the introduction of user experience, scholars have proposed user experience elements from different aspects and constructed various user experience models. In The

Elements of User Experience, Jesse James Garrett proposes a model to design the user experience which divide user experience into five levels of elements: strategy, scope, structure, skeleton, and surface [15]. Fan Xiuchen et al. propose a three-dimension model of service experience, including functional experience, affection experience and social intercourse experience [16].

This article integrates the dimensions of user experience, combined with the particularity of the epidemic emergency communication platform and constructs the user experience element model of the epidemic emergency communication platform in terms of sensory experience, interactive experience and efficacy experience respectively. To further demonstrate the three dimensions mentioned above, Sensory experience includes visual experience elements such as information presentation and interface design. Interactive experience consists of the nature of navigation, fluency and usability. Lastly, efficacy experience involves information timeliness and service efficiency (Fig. 1).

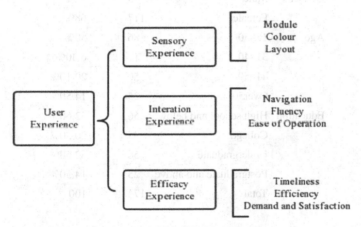

Fig. 1. A user experience evaluation model for COVID-19 emergency communication platform.

4   Research Methodology

4.1   Survey Instrument

This Research was based on the feedback of local users from the Tencent Health platform in China and the NHS COVID-19 platform in the UK. For the Chinese platform, the study uses the questionnaire survey method. Among questionnaires, 283 of them are collected online. However, 172 questionnaires are finally retained after eliminating invalid ones. For the UK platform, the study used a method called semi-structured interviews. 17 UK users of the NHS COVID-19 platform are communicated through the Hello Talk international language learning platform. The interview outline is the English version that corresponds to the questionnaire.

4.2 User Experience Analysis of the China and UK Platforms

Descriptive Analysis of the Questionnaire Sample. This Research was based on the feedback of local users from the Tencent. Based on the sample, the majority of the interviewee are female whose percentage is 68%. For the age distribution, the proportion of young people aged from 18 to 30 is 50%, followed by middle-aged people aged 41–50, accounting for 29.10%. Finally, high school education and bachelor's degree are the critical components in terms of the distribution of education which are both about 32.60%. As shown in Table 1.

Table 1. Descriptive analysis of the sample (N = 172).

		Frequency	Rate
Gender	Male	55	32%
	Female	117	68%
Age	18–30	86	50%
	31–40	11	6.40%
	41–50	50	29.10%
	Over50	25	14.50%
Education	High school and below	56	32.60%
	College	35	20.30%
	Undergraduate	56	32.60%
	Postgraduate and above	25	14.50%
	Total	172	100

Sensory Experience on China and UK Platforms. The sensory experience includes module design, color, and interface layout.

From the data, only 50% of Chinese users could clearly recognize that the platform is divided into 4 modules, while 14.50% of Chinese users think they are not clear, which means the module design needs to be adjusted. 61.60% of users prefer the color design of the platform, while only 1.20% of users take opposite view on this, which shows the platform has good color matching. For the interface layout, the user experience is better than the previous two aspects, 64.53% of users think the interface layout is clear and orderly. As shown in the Table 2.

Based on interviews with users of the UK NHS COVID-19 platform, the sensory experience of UK platform users is better. UK users hold the opinions that they could clearly recognize the module division of the platform, e.g. User H: "The app is very clear and well structured for children and adults to use." Most users are satisfied with the color scheme of the platform, e.g. User K: "yes I like the color assortment which supports the NHS logo." The layout is clear and clean for most of users, but some users feel it is too simple cause they would like to see more interactive options from the layout,

Table 2. The sensory experience of Chinese users.

	Item	Rate
Do you have a clear idea that the platform is divided into four modules?	Clear	50.00%
	Ordinary	35.50%
	Not clear	14.50%
	Total	100
Do you like the color scheme of the platform?	Like	61.60%
	Ordinary	37.20%
	Dislike	1.20%
	Total	100
How does the platform interface layout feel to you?	Clear and orderly	64.53%
	Ordinary	33.14%
	Messy	2.33%
	Total	100

e.g. User H: "It's ordinary and easy to navigate.", User F: "The layout is clear however I don't like that the main pages are quite modular since there are little options".

Interactive Experience on China and UK Platforms. The interactive experience includes navigation, fluency, and ease of operation.

From the data, 72.67% of Chinese users consider that they could find the expected functions quickly, which means the navigation of the platform is perfect. In addition, 58.14% of Chinese users consider the platform provide a smooth and fast experience, while 39.53% of users think that the response speed of the platform would sometimes remain smooth but sometimes lag, which indicates the response speed of this platform should be improved. When it comes to operational issues, almost half of users show that they have encountered operational obstacles, which indicates that the convenience of operations needs to be improved. As shown in Table 3.

According to interviews with NHS COVID-19 users in the UK, the platform is very suitable for providing users with network navigation, because user F said: "I could find quickly the information which I am looking for cause the app could provide good guidance." Some users interviewed think that the platform runs smoothly, while some show that it occasionally gets stuck, e.g., user K: "It's smooth and fast." User C: "Sometimes it's smooth, but sometimes it's stuck. " Regarding the problem of operational obstacles, half of the users consider that they had never encountered operational obstacles, but half of the respondents say that they did encounter operational obstacles before, such as user H: "Few glitches from time to time".

From the above analysis, it can be concluded that British users have similar experience to the smoothness and ease of use of the platform as Chinese users.

Table 3. Interaction experience for Chinese users.

	Item	Rate
Can you find the desired function quickly?	Yes, I can	72.67%
	Ordinary	23.26%
	No, I Can not	4.07%
	Total	100
How do you feel when using the platform and jumping from one page to another?	Smooth and fast	58.14%
	Sometimes smooth and sometimes stuck	39.53%
	Stuck	2.33%
	Total	100
Have you ever encountered the problems that do not know how to operate?	Yes, I have	49.40%
	Never	50.60%
	Total	100

Efficacy Experience on China and UK Platforms. The efficacy experience includes the timeliness of information, efficiency of functions and demand satisfaction.

It can be seen from the data that 69.20% of Chinese users consider that the information on the platform is updated in a timely manner, indicating that the information on the platform is very timely. Excluding 33.70% of users who have not used online medical services, 48.80% think that the functions of the platform are convenient and fast, which indicates that the operation of this platform is highly efficient. Regarding demand satisfaction, 47.10% of users believe that the existing functions of the platform have not yet met all their needs during the epidemic. As shown in Table 4.

Table 4. Efficacy experience for Chinese users.

	Item	Rate
What do you think of the information provided by the app?	It is updated timely	69.20%
	Ordinary	25.60%
	It is lagging	0
	Never viewed it	5.20%
	Total	100
How do you feel about the functions of the online medical services provided by the app?	Convenient	48.80%
	Ordinary	16.30%
	Troublesome	1.20%
	Never used	33.70%
	Total	100
Have you ever found any information and functions that you want but the app does not provide?	Yes	47.10%
	No	52.90%
	Total	100

According to the interviews with UK users, the information of the platform is updated timely, such as User K: "The information is accurate and is updated fast." Half of the interviewees consider that the efficiency of use is not satisfied, indicating that the efficiency of the platform features needs to be updated. When answering the question "Have you ever been unable to find the information and functions which you looked for on this program?", most users deny that, which means that the current functional design of the UK platform basically suits the needs of users.

5 A Comparative Analysis of the China and UK Platforms

In this section, the user experience of Chinese and UK emergency communication platforms is compared by considering various factors, including observations of the platforms, questionnaire data from China and interview results from the UK.

5.1 Comparative Analysis of Sensory Experience

According to the observation of the interface layout of the two platforms, it shows that the interface of the Chinese platform has more content and is more complicated compared to the interface of the UK platform.

The data indicates that 64.53% of Chinese users agree the interface layout of Chinese platform is clear and neat. However, the interviewees in the UK users also hold the same opinion for the layout of the British platform. In other words, the users of the two platforms each prefer the design style of their own platform respectively, which reflects the difference opinions in user experience between these two counties.

The cross-cultural study written by Zhou Xu points out that for Chinese users, a large amount of information in the interface means more choices and full consideration for users. By contrast, less content represents visual lackness and inadequate delivery of information. However, for British users, the large information content of the interface represents cumbersome, intrusive and inefficient and less content represents efficient [17]. This study also fits the conclusion of the previous paper, which reflect the impact of cultural differences on user experience (Fig. 2).

5.2 Comparative Analysis of Interaction Experience

The levels settlement in Chinese platform are excessive, with some functions requiring six levels of accomplishment. The number of interaction buttons on the platform's homepage is high, while the UK platform is on the low side.

The data shows that 72.67% of Chinese users can find the expected function quickly. 58.14% of Chinese users think the platform is smooth and efficient, while British users hold the same view for the NHS COVID-19 platform. Even though there is exceptionally different interaction design between China and the UK, users' perceptions of the platform related to easy usage and fluency in both countries are similar, reflecting the differences in user experience between China and the UK.

According to the cultural theory proposed by Hodstede, China is a long-term oriented country, where people can accept delayed satisfaction of needs and pay attention to performance and details. Hence, the many levels pattern in platform do not make a bad experience for the users, due to Chinese users adapted to the multi-level and multi-interaction button design. Since The UK is a short-term oriented country, people expect their requirements to be satisfied as soon as possible, they pursue direct and fast. The design of the UK platform also represents that. The different cultural characteristics of China and Britain lead to the difference in user experience between China and Britain, as shown in the Table 5.

Table 5. Observations on the interactive experience of platform

	Tencent Health	NHS COVID-19
Number of interactive page switches	1–6	1–3
Number of home page interaction buttons	>20	6

Fig. 2. Main interface of the China Tencent Health platform (left) and the UK NHS COVID-19 platform (right).

5.3 Comparative Analysis of Efficacy Experience

After observation, there are significant differences in functional design between the Chinese and British emergency communication platforms, and we mainly compare the functional requirements of the platforms in terms of effectiveness experience.

Both platforms have the function of epidemic risk inquiry, but the Chinese platform is more comprehensive and also involves online medical services, epidemic science and reporting services, while the UK platform is dedicated to the individual risk inquiry and tracking only. For comparison purposes, we classified the functions provided by the platforms. As shown in Table 6.

Table 6. Observations on the function design of platform

Tencent Health	NHS COVID-19
Risk enquiry	Risk enquiry
Electronic health code	Check-in
Epidemic news report	Close contact tracing alert
Epidemic knowledge dissemination	Symptom self-test and disease prediction
Online medical service	Vaccination advice

From the data, the top 3 functions used by users of China Tencent Health Platform are Electronic Health Card, Epidemic News Report, and Epidemic knowledge Dissemination As shown in Table 7.

Table 7. Functional usage of the China platform.

Item	Number of response	Rate
Electronic health code	148	33.90%
Epidemic news report	102	23.40%
Epidemic knowledge dissemination	58	13.30%
Risk enquiry	53	12.20%
Online medical service	42	9.60%
Others	33	7.60%
Total	436	100.00

The users are asked which functions people would like to be added to the NHS COVID-19 platform, using the functions offered by the Chinese platform as options which are approved by many interviewees. e.g. User K: "A dynamic map sounds like a good idea, as well as Being able to book covid tests, vaccine appointments on the app would be great too."

The most frequently selected function is detailed risk query, following online medical service. Detailed risk query means that the platform does not only providing information about the risk level of the region where it is located, but also can check the number of cases around them and the distance between cases and enter the flight number to find out if there are any cases on your train or plane. It shows that the UK users are more focus on personal risk. On the other hand, the Chinese users are more concerned about the overall epidemic situation in the country.

Based on the cultural dimension theory proposed by Hodstede, China is a collectivist culture country, and the UK is an individualist culture country. In a collectivist culture country, people regard the achievement of collective as a more important goal. Since, in countries with individualistic culture, mainstream concepts emphasize more on individuality independence, individual rights and interests. The functional design and user demands of both Chinese and British platforms reflect their own different cultural characteristics.

6 Conclusion

This paper divides the user experience of the epidemic communication platform into three dimensions. Firstly, the research explores the current situation of the user experience of the epidemic communication platform in China and the UK and then analyze the cross-cultural differences in the user experience of them. The study indicates that the overall user experience of China Tencent Health platform is great, but the interface module design, interaction fluency and easy operational usage need to be improved. For the NHS COVID-19 platform of the UK, it has a satisfied user sensory experience, but interaction fluency and functional efficiency need to be improved. The study also finds that the different cultural characteristics of China and the UK have led to differences in user experience between the Chinese and UK platforms. Furthermore, the differences in sensory experience are specifically manifested in the Chinese users' preference for a sufficient information interface style, where rich content means enthusiastic and full consideration, while the UK users prefer a simple interface style, where less content means simplicity and efficiency. The difference of interaction experience is that Chinese users are accustomed to multi-level, multi-interaction button interaction design and prefer to have more options, while British users prefer less level, direct and efficient navigation interaction design. Finally, the difference in effectiveness experience is that Chinese users require the big picture of dynamic changes of epidemic, However, the priority consideration of British users is personal risks information.

References

1. Lin, H., Jun, X., Mengdi, W.: The disposal function realization and effect promotion for public opinion of government wechat based on user requirements. Inf. Sci. **37**(06), P101–107 (2019)
2. Li, N.: Research on the Satisfaction of Health Wechat Public Number Users——Taking "Clove Doctor"as an example. Hubei: South-Central University for Nationalities (2019)
3. Xie, A., Rau, P.L.P., Tseng, Y., Su, H., Zhao, C.: Cross-cultural influence on communication effectiveness and user interface design. Int. J. Intercult. Relat. **33**(1) (2008)
4. Rosillo-Díaz, E., Blanco-Encomienda, F.J., Crespo-Almendros, E.: A cross-cultural analysis of perceived product quality, perceived risk and purchase intention in e-commerce platforms. J. Enterprise Inf. Manage. **33**(1) (2019)
5. Li, C., Wang, W., Guo, H., Dietrich, A.: Cross-cultural analysis of young drivers' preferences for in-vehicle systems and behavioral effects caused by secondary tasks, **10**(11) (2018)
6. Yang, D.: Globalization, Risk Society and Complex Governance Marxism & Reality, 4, P61–77(2004)
7. Stevens, H.: Monamie bhadra haine: trace together: pandemic response, democracy, and technology. East Asian Sci. Technol. Soc. **14**(3), 523–532 (2020)
8. A Tale of Two Contact-Tracing Apps–Comparing Australia's COVIDSafe and New Zealand's NZ COVID Tracer
9. Barsalou, L.W.: Perceptual symbol systems. Behav. Brain Sci. **22**(4), 577–660 (1999)

10. Thelen, E., Schoner, G., Scheier, C., Smith, L.B.: The dynamics of embodiment: a field theory of infant perseverative reaching. Behav. B rain Sci. 24(1), 1–86 (2001)
11. Yeun, S., Prestopnik, N., Biocca, F.: Body in the interactive game: how interface embodiment affects physical activity and health behavior change. Comput. Hum. Behav. **36**, 376–384 (2014)
12. Li, H., Sheng, X.: Embodiment of cognition. Stud. Sci. Sci. **2,** 184 (2006)
13. Wenjuan, L.: Hofstede's culture dimensions and intercultural studies. J. Soc. Sci. **12** (2009)
14. Barber, W., Badre, A.: Culturability: The merging of culture and usability. In: Proceedings of the 4th Conference on Human Factors and the Web, Basking Ridge, New Jersy (1998)
15. Garrett, J.J.: The Elements of User Experience: User-Centered Design for the Web. New Riders publishing, pp. 13–20 (2003)
16. Fan, X.: An empirical research on three dimension service experiences. Tourism Sci. **2,** 54–59 (2006)
17. Zou, X.: A Cross-Cultural Comparative Research of User Experience for Mobile Applications: Based on the Explanation of Semiotics. Beijing Foreign Studies University (2017)

Study on the Effect of Art Training on Proportion Control

Yang Gao[1(✉)], Jianping Huang[1], Jun Wu[2], and Rungtai Lin[1]

[1] Graduate School of Creative Industry Design, National Taiwan University of Arts,
New Taipei City, Taiwan
rtlin@mail.ntua.edu.tw
[2] School of Journalism and Communication, Anhui Normal University,
Wuhu, People's Republic of China

Abstract. Art training could improve our ability to discover and express beauty, yet we don't know much about the effect of art training. With rectangle as the research object, this study evaluates the influence of art training on proportion control of rectangles via experiments and using of Bloom classification theory, so as to understand the effect of art training and the differences existing in proportion preference of contemporary audiences. According to the research: 1. Art training could effectively improve the subjects' ability of cognitive judgement towards proportion, as well as creativity. 2. Education level has positive influence on overall proportion control. 3. The most popular rectangle proportion is 1: 1.618, followed by 1:1 and 1:2.

Keywords: Art training · Proportion · Rectangle

1 Introduction

In daily life process, people accumulated abundant aesthetic experience, which is not limited in art school and art field, but in any places [1]. These abundant experience converge into expertise, which in turn could guide us to make daily judgement. The research shows that related training of professional knowledge could improve aesthetic ability [2]. Therefore, we believe that artists and designers with professional training have more abundant aesthetic expertise than common people, so that they could better discover and express beauty.

What kinds of effect does art training possess? This is the question that interests the author. Bloom and other scholars conducted classification of education training purposes in 1956 [3]. (The latest revised edition was published in 2001 [4], which is one of the most widely used learning outcome classifications at present [5]). It is also an evaluation framework of training effects. This classification divides the education purposes into three fields, which are cognitive field, affective field and psychomotor field [3]. This classification covers the whole process of training, from the cognitive understanding at the beginning, to affective judgement and the final technical expression. We could understand the training outcome by evaluating these three fields. Kobayashi Katsuhiro

© Springer Nature Switzerland AG 2021
P.-L. P. Rau (Ed.): HCII 2021, LNCS 12772, pp. 150–161, 2021.
https://doi.org/10.1007/978-3-030-77077-8_12

believes that proportion is the main factor of generating beauty [6], which is also the important concept of classical aesthetics [7]. In the field of art and design, proportion is also one of the artistic research themes. Reviewing the related researches, we found that many important researches are related to the visual superiority that approved golden ratio, and usually take rectangle as research objects [8–11]. These researches provide experimental samples for this paper. Based on above content, this research takes rectangle as its research object, and evaluates the influence of art training towards proportion control of rectangles via experiments and using of Bloom classification theory. The research purposes of this paper is as below:

Study the effects of training towards cognition, estimation and drawing techniques of rectangle proportion.

Discuss the proportion preference of contemporary audiences.

2 Literature Review

2.1 Art Training

.Richard Jung once described the function of art training with one sentence, "In general, the significance and beauty of art are only apparent to those who can see and are trained in viewing [12]." It can be seen that training is crucial to art appreciation. It is widely believed by artists and art teachers that aesthetic quality of visual works can be discovered by training the eyes, while this aspect of art training could directly affect the well-trained audience's emotional analysis and appreciation of visual works [13], and consequently affect their emotional responses to art [14]. Related researches show that: the abstraction level of paintings can lower layman's evaluation of aesthetic judgement and emotional appraise, but will not affect experts' opinions [15]. It can be seen that training can expand audiences' aesthetic object forms, helping them to be able to appreciate the abstract paintings with the same aesthetic ability of concrete paintings. Another research shows that: training can turn the preference towards relatively complicated arts [14, 16, 17]. The explanation of this result points to the content level of paintings. Some of the researchers believe that people with art training find complex pictures more interesting, and they appraised them as easier to understand [13, 18–20]. Well trained audiences can unify the pictures into coherent images with narrative sentences by using symmetry, while the audiences without training could never do it [13]. Other researches also prove that experts' positive experience of art was accompanied by feeling able to understand the art [21]. This shows that art training has positive effect towards more complex forms and content understanding with more profound meanings.

2.2 Researches on Proportions

From ancient Greece until today, proportion has always been the research topic in fields like philosophy, mathematics, construction and art. Kobayashi Katsuhiro divided proportion into two types: One can be directly grasped; the other is based on number ratio. He believes that although the latter one is more precise, the former one is more flexible and effective [6]. Le Corbusier (1887–1965) also believes that: the strength of direct proportion is stronger than the proportion with precise number ratio relationship [7]. "Golden Ratio" was almost the whole content of proportion research, which was raised as a mathematical concept. During the Renaissance, due to the introduction of "Divine Ratio" concept [22], and the universal recognition of mathematics and perspective, some artists began to widely use science based methods in their works, especially the "Golden Ratio". Of all the times, as an important formal beauty principle, Golden Ratio is considered as an aesthetic classical rule passing on from generation to generation. Currently, "Golden Ratio" has become one of the requisite textbook content in many art or design courses [23–25].

2.3 Rectangle Aesthetic Cognition

Goldenberg and Cuoco (1998) believed that geometric figure was a powerful medium in establishing mental habits [26]. While among all the geometric figures, many researchers declared that the golden rectangle was the most beautiful in all kinds of rectangles. The attraction of rectangles in different proportions was the concern object of many scholars. Livio elaborately sorted out these researches in his book *The Golden Ratio* [27], and this paper will briefly describe this content.

Many researchers declared that the golden rectangle was the most beautiful in all kinds of rectangles. Adolph Zeising believed that: the Golden Ratio offered the key to the understanding of all proportions in "the most refined forms of nature and art." [28] Later, Fechner proved this statement by experiments [8]. The experiment showed that the golden rectangle was the most popular, with the ratio of width to height of 1: 1.6180. However, not all of Fechner's participants had preferred the golden section, a minority instead preferring the square. McManus also proved the result that golden ratio is the most popular via experiments [9]. It summarized as below: There is therefore a very nonlinear relationship in the meanings attached to rectangles [9]. Analysis suggests that there are two major, broad groups of preferences, one based around the square, and the other based broadly although not precisely at about the golden section [9, 10].

Many researchers had different findings. Some found that the instructions and the direction and size of the paper may affect the aesthetic judgment of the respondents [29–32]. The experimental result of Davies showed that the most popular rectangle proportion was 1: 2 [11]. L. A. Stone and L. G. Collins suggested that the preference for the rectangle was related to people's field of view, witha length-to-width ratio of about 1.5 [27]. The experiments of Schiffman and Bobka approved this conjecture, but it revised the average visual field to 1: 1.9 [33].

3 Design of Experiment

In order to understand the training's influence on cognitive, affective and technical field, this research designs an experiment based on rectangle cognition and reappearance. The experiment is divided into two stages: Stage one is the proactive test, during which expert team draw the rectangle proportion, providing tested sample of the formal test in stage two. Stage two is constituted by five steps: a. free drawing, b. choosing, c. imitation, d. draw from memory, e. estimation, wherein steps a and b are affective training, step d being technical training, step e being cognitive training, and step c being overall evaluation. There are total 174 volunteers participating in the experiment.

3.1 Proactive Test

73 students with specialty of fine arts are requested to draw rectangles with best proportions freely. These rectangles are grouped (with grouping unit of 0.1) according to proportion values (width/height), and the results of top 6 groups are selected and recorded (5 groups in horizontal, and 1 group in vertical). The average of rectangle proportion in each group is calculated, and finally 6 different rectangle proportions are obtained (Table 1), which are taken as the option sample of the formal test.

Table 1. The rectangle data summary of proactive test

Rectangle proportion	0.7–0.8	1.3–1.4	1.4–1.5	1.5–1.6	1.6–1.7	1.7–1.8
Number of rectangles	5	8	9	7	12	7
Average value	0.75	1.36	1.45	1.56	1.65	1.75

3.2 Formal Test

There are total 101 participants, wherein 61 major in art and design, 40 major in other subjects; there are 51 females and 50 males; 75 are in college or below level, 26 in graduate school or above; 20 are in age of 19 or below, 37 in the age of 20–29, 33 in the age of 30–39, and 11 in the age of 40 or above. There are five steps in the test:

Step one (free drawing): Subjects are requested to draw the rectangle with best proportion in a horizontal frame of 900*500 px.

Step two (choosing rectangle): Subjects are requested to choose the rectangle with the best proportion among 7 rectangles with different proportions (1 of the 7 rectangles coming from step one, and the other 6 coming from proactive test), and the 7 rectangles are arranged randomly.

Step three (estimation of proportion): Subjects are requested to estimate the ratio of width to height of the rectangle chose in step two (the picture can be seen).

Step four (imitation of rectangle): Subjects are requested to draw the rectangle chose in step two (the picture can be seen).

Step five (drawing rectangle from memory): Subjects are requested to draw the rectangle chose in step two (the picture cannot be seen).

In order to reduce the impact of environment, and get subjects ready for aesthetic experience, the experiments are requested to be taken on computers (using mouse and keyboard), and the subjects are explicitly informed that they are having experiments related to aesthetic and artistic experience.

4   Analysis and Discussion of Results

4.1   The Affect of Art Training

Overall Evaluation: The proportional differences between the rectangles drew by participants in step four and original rectangles (the ones chose in step two) in professional group and non-professional group are calculated respectively, and the average value and standard deviation is also calculated (Fig. 1). The result shows that the average value of error and standard deviation between rectangles drew by professional team and the original picture are respectively: 0.123 and 0.187. The average value of error and standard deviation of the non-professional team are respectively 0.101 and 0.114. Comparing with the professional team, the non-professional team has lower proportion error rate in imitation.

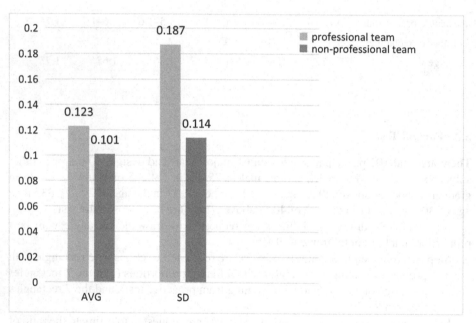

Fig. 1. Comparison of proportion error in imitation

Affective: The rectangle chose by subjects in step two is compared with the rectangle freely drew in step one, and results with proportion (width/height) error less than 0.1 in professional team and non-professional team are respectively selected and recorded (Fig. 2). The result shows that the proportion of the results with low error in professional team is about 24.6%, while that in non-professional team is 40%. Comparing with the professional team, the non-professional team has lower error ratio.

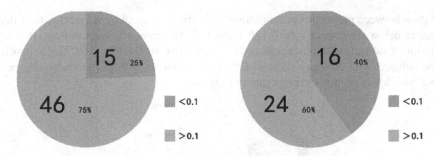

Fig. 2. Related data of drawing and choosing rectangles

Cognitive: The proportion error between the rectangles drew by subjects in step five and the original rectangles (chose in step two) in professional team and non-professional team is calculated, and the average value and standard deviation are also calculated (Fig. 3). The result shows that the error average value and standard deviation between proportion estimated by professional team and the proportion of original picture are respectively: 0.174 and 0.136. The error average value and standard deviation of non-professional team are respectively 0.334 and 0.701. Comparing to the non-professional team, the professional team has lower error rate in estimated proportion.

Psychomotor: The proportion error between estimation made in step three and original picture in the two teams is calculated, and the average number and standard deviation are also calculated (Fig. 3). The result shows that, the error average value and standard deviation between proportion in drawing by memory and original picture in professional team are respectively: 0.134 and 0.194. The error average value and standard deviation in non-professional team are 0.108 and 0.117. Comparing to professional team, the non-professional team has lower proportion error rate in drawing by memory.

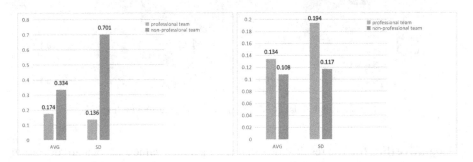

Fig. 3. Estimation error and error in drawing by memory

4.2 Influence of Educational Background on Proportion

The influence of background training is analyzed using the method same as above. **Overall evaluation** (Fig. 4): The result shows that the error average value and standard deviation between proportions of imitation and original picture by subjects with college degree or below are respectively: 0.126 and 0.181. The error average value and standard deviation of subjects with postgraduate degree or above are 0.080 and 0.077. Comparing to the subjects with college degree or below, the subjects with postgraduate degree or above have lower proportion error rate in imitation.

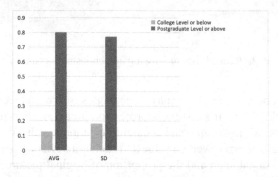

Fig. 4. Comparison of proportion error in imitation.

Affective (Fig. 5): The result shows that the proportion of results with low error (<0.1) of subjects with college degree or below is about 29.3%, while that of subjects with postgraduate degree or above is 26.9%. Comparing to the subjects with college degree or below, the subjects with postgraduate degree or above have lower error proportions.

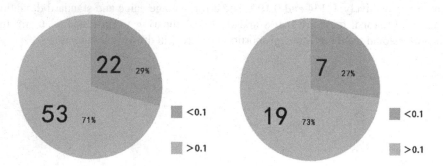

Fig. 5. Related data of drawing and choosing rectangles

Cognitive (Fig. 6): The result shows that error average value and standard deviation of estimated proportions and original picture of subjects with college degree and below are respectively: 0.262 and 0.524. The error average value and standard deviation of estimation of subjects with postgraduate degree and above are 0.166 and 0.125. Comparing to the subjects with college degree or below, the subjects with postgraduate degree or above have lower proportion error rate in estimation.

Psychomotor (Fig. 6): The error average value and standard deviation of proportions between drawing by memory and original pictures of subjects with college degree or below are respectively: 0.139 and 0.186. The error average value and standard deviation of subjects with postgraduate degree or above are 0.081 and 0.085. Comparing to the subjects with college degree or below, the subjects with postgraduate degree or above have lower proportion error rate in drawing by memory.

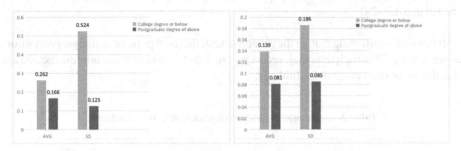

Fig. 6. Estimation error and error in drawing by memory

4.3 Cognitive Analysis of Subjects' Preferences

The rectangles drew in step one are grouped (with unit of 0.1) according to proportions (width/height), and the results of top three groups with the most members in professional team, non-professional team and both teams (with revised numbers) are selected and recorded respectively (Table 2). The result shows that the results of professional team and both teams are similar, while the results of non-professional team and both teams are not completely consistent.

Table 2. Rectangle proportion distribution

Proportion ranges	Professional team	Non-professional team	Both teams (with revised numbers)
1-1.1	7	3	.190
1.1-1.2	7	1	.140
1.5-1.6	8	0	.131
1.6-1.7	7	5	.240
1.7-1.8	6	9	.323
1.9-2.0	4	5	.191

(Revised number=the number in the range of non-professional team/the total number of non-professional team+ the number in the range of professional team/the total number of professional team)

All subjects: The most popular rectangle proportion ranges are respectively: 1–1.1 and 1.6–1.8.
Professional team: The most popular rectangle proportion ranges are respectively: 1–1.2 and 1.5–1.7;
Non-professional team: The most popular rectangle proportion ranges are respectively: 1.6–1.8 and 1.9–2.0.

It is worth mentioning that, in the proactive test, the most popular rectangle proportion ranges among 73 participants majored in art are 1.6–1.7, where there are few rectangles with the proportion close to 1 (Table 3).

Table 3. Rectangle proportion distribution in proactive test

Proportion ranges	0.8-0.9	0.9-1.0	1-1.1	1.6-1.7
Number	2	0	2	12
Proportion	2.7%	0	2.7%	16.4%

The rectangles chose in step two are grouped (with unit of 0.1) according to proportion (width/height), and the results of the top one group with most members of professional team, non-professional team and both teams (with revised numbers) are selected and recorded respectively (Table 4). The result shows that the results of professional team and both teams are similar, while the results of non-professional team and both teams are not consistent.

All subjects: The most popular rectangle proportion ranges are: 1.6–1.7.
Professional team: The most popular rectangle proportion ranges are: 1.6–1.7.
Non-professional team: The most popular rectangle proportion ranges are: 1.3–1.5.

The rectangles freely drew by two teams of subjects in step one are divided into two groups of horizontal and vertical, and the proportion and numbers are calculated (Fig. 7). The result shows that about 16.4% subjects in professional team drew vertical rectangles, while only 2.4% subjects in non-professional team drew vertical rectangles.

Table 4. The distribution of subjects' preferable rectangles

Proportion ranges	Professional team	Non-professional team	Both teams (with revised numbers)
1.3-1.4	11	7	0.355
1.4-1.5	5	7	0.257
1.5-1.6	11	6	0.330
1.6-1.7	16	5	0.387

(Revised number = the number in the range of non-professional team/the total number of non-professional team + the number in the range of professional team/the total number of professional team).

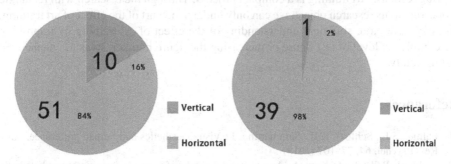

Fig. 7. The calculation of rectangles in horizontal and vertical drew by subjects

5 Conclusion and Suggestion

After integration and analysis of the research result, we come to the below conclusion:

1. Professional background has influence on audiences' judgement towards rectangle proportion. In the stage of proportion estimation capability (**Cognitive**), professional team performs better than non-professional team, which shows that art training could effectively improve the cognitive judgement ability of subjects towards proportion; in the stages of proportion imitation (overall), drawing by memory (**Psychomotor**) and stability of choosing (**Affective**), non-professional team performs better than professional team, which shows that art training could not improve these three kinds of abilities. When speculating extremely simple geometric figures, the degree of emphasis of professional team may be reduced; in terms of rectangle directions, the number of vertical rectangles drew by professional team is much higher than that of non-professional team, which shows that the art training could effectively

improve subjects' creativity, helping subjects to break through the interference factor of horizontal computer screen and conduct free drawing, choosing and judgement.

2. Education degree has influence on audiences' judgement towards rectangle proportion. Comparing to the subjects with college degree or below, the subjects with postgraduate degree or above have better abilities in proportion judgement (**Cognitive**), imitation (**overall**) and drawing by memory (**Psychomotor**), while in terms of choosing stability (**Affective**), the experimental results of two teams are similar. It shows that education degree has positive correlation with judgement on rectangle proportion, and education level has positive influence on overall grasp of proportion.

3. In terms of contemporary audiences' preference analysis on rectangle proportion, the experiment shows that the most popular rectangle proportion at present is close to 1:1.618, followed by 1:1 and 1:2. This result is similar with the research result of Fecbner (1876), Davies (1933) and Schiffman (1978). It shows that the preference cognition of contemporary audiences' rectangle proportion doesn't change significantly in the past two centuries.

Suggestions: Art training is a complex process. Through the research with rectangle proportion as its research object, we can only understand part of the effect of art training. We may have more sufficient understanding of the effect of art training by improving the complexity level of test figure or increasing the figure number, so as to enhance the test difficulty.

References

1. Palmer, S.E., Schloss, K.B., Sammartino, J.: Visual aesthetics and human preference. Ann. Rev. Psychol. **64**, 77–107 (2013)
2. Leder, H., Belke, B., Oeberst, A., Augustin, D.: A model of aesthetic appreciation and aesthetic judgments. Brit. J. Psychol. **95**(4), 489–508 (2004)
3. Bloom, B.S., Englehart, M.D., Furst, E.J., Hill, W.H., Krathwohl, D.R. (eds.): Taxonomy of Educational Objectives. HANDBOOK I: Cognitive Domain, pp. 4–5. David McKay, New York (1956)
4. Anderson, L.W., Krathwohl, D.R. (eds.): A Taxonomy for Learning, Teaching and Assessing: A Revision of Bloom's Taxonomy of Educational Objectives. Complete edition. Longman, New York (2001)
5. Rutkowski, J., Moscinska, K., Jantos, P.: Application of Blooms taxonomy for increasing teaching efficiency–case study. In: International Conference on Engineering Education ICEE-2010 (2010)
6. Katsuhiro, K., Chen, Z.: Building Form Means. China Building Industry Press, Beijing (2003)
7. Ji, T., Yi, Q.: Return of the orde: comment on katsuhiro kobayashi' s work "building form means". Comments Forum, 35–37 (2011)
8. Fecbner, G.T.: Vorschule der Aesthetik [Prolegomenon to Aesthetics]. Breitkopf & Haertel, Leipzig (1876)
9. McManus, I.C.: Tbe aestbetics of sitnple figures. Brit. J. Psychol. **71**, 505–524 (1980)
10. McManus, I.C., Cook, R., Hunt, A.: Beyond tbe golden section and normative aesthetics: why do individuals differ so much in tbeir aestbetic preferences for rectangles? Psychol. Aesthetics Creativity Arts **4**, 113–126 (2010)
11. Davis, F.C.: Aesthetic proportion. Am. J. Psychol, **45**, 298–302 (1933)

12. Jung, R.: Art and visual abstraction. In: Gregory, R.L. (ed.) The Oxford Companion to the Mind, p. 46. Oxford Univ. Press, New York (1987)
13. Nodine, C.F., Locher, P.J., Krupinski, E.A.: The role of formal art training on perception and aesthetic judgment of art compositions. Leonardo 26(3), 219–227 (1993)
14. Walker, E.L.: Psychological Complexity and Preference: A Hedgehog Theory of Behavior. Brooks-Cole, New York (1980)
15. Pihko, E., et al.: Experiencing art: the influence of expertise and painting abstraction level. Front. Human Neurosci. 5, 94 (2011)
16. Bragg, B.W.E., Crozier, J.B.: The development with age of verbal and exploratory responses to sound sequences varying in uncertainty level. In: Berlyne, D.E. (ed.) Studies in the New Experimental Aesthetics, pp. 91–108. Hemisphere, Washington (1974)
17. Francès, R.: Comparative effects of six collative variables on interest and preference in adults of different educational levels. J. Pers. Social Psychol. 33, 62–79 (1976)
18. Silvia, P.J.: Artistic training and interest in visual art: applying the appraisal model of aesthetic emotions. Empir. Stud. Arts 24(2), 139–161 (2006)
19. Crozier, J.B.: Verbal and exploratory responses to sound sequences varying in uncertainty level. In: Berlyne, D.E. (ed.) Studies in the New Experimental Aesthetics, pp. 27–90. Hemisphere, Washington (1974)
20. Locher, P.J., Smith, J.K., Smith, L.F.: The influence of presentation format and viewer training in the visual arts on the perception of pictorial and aesthetic qualities of paintings. Perception 30, 449–465 (2001)
21. Millis, K.: Making meaning brings pleasure: the influence of titles on aesthetic experience. Emotion 1, 320–329 (2001)
22. Huntley, E.H.: The Divine Proportion. Dover, New York (1970)
23. Berlyne, D.E.: Aesthetics and Psychobiology. Appleton-Century-Crofts, New York (1971)
24. Ching, F.D.K.: Architecture: Form, Space, and Order. Van Nostrand Reinhold, New York (1979)
25. Enjafield, J., Pomeroy, E., Saunders, M.: The golden section and the accuracy with which proportions are drawn. Canad. J. Psychol. 34, 253–256 (1976)
26. Goldenberg, E.P., Cuoco, A.A.: What is dynamic geometry? In: Lehrer, R., Chazan, D. (eds.) Designing Learning Environments for Developing Understanding of Geometry and Space, pp. 351–367. Erlbaum, Mahwah (1998)
27. Livio, M.: The golden ratio: the story of phi, the world's most astonishing number. Crown, 178–183 (2008)
28. Zeising, A.: Der goldne Schnitt. Druck von E. Blochmann & Son in Dresden, Halle (1884)
29. Hekkert, P., Peper, C.L.E., Van Wieringen, P.C.: The effect of verbal instruction and artistic background on the aesthetic judgment of rectangles. Empir. Stud. Arts 12(2), 185–203 (1994)
30. Höge, H.: Fechner's experimental aesthetics and the golden section hypothesis today. Empir. Stud. Arts 13(2), 131–148 (1995)
31. Höge, H.: The golden section hypothesis—a funeral, but not the last one. Visual Arts Res. 22, 79–89 (1996)
32. Russell, P.A.: The aesthetics of rectangle proportion: effects of judgment scale and context. Am. J. Psychol. 113(1), 27–42 (2000)
33. Schiffman, H.R., Bobka, D.: Preference in linear partitioning: the golden section reexamined. Percept. Psychophys. 24, 102–103 (1978)

The Effect of We'll *App* on Social-Support, Self-efficacy, and EPDS for PPD

Szu-Erh Hsu[1], Hao Chen[2], Chao Liu[2], Ding-Hau Huang[3], Liang-Ming Lo[4], Tai-He Hong[4], and Wen-Ko Chiou[1(✉)]

[1] Department of Industrial Design, Chang Gung University, Taoyuan City, Taiwan
wkchiu@mail.cgu.edu.tw
[2] Graduate Institute of Business and Management, Chang Gung University,
Taoyuan City, Taiwan
[3] Institute of Creative Design and Management, National Taipei University of Business,
Taoyuan City, Taiwan
[4] Department of Obstetrics and Gynecology, Chang Gung Memorial Hospital at Taipei,
Taipei City, Taiwan
{lmlo,thh20}@cgmh.org.tw

Abstract. Postpartum depression (PPD) is a common disease in the world, which often results in many social problems. In recent years, many studies have mentioned that social support enhancement can reduce PPD. According to the etiology and treatment methods of postpartum depression and non-clinical intervention, the importance of psychosocial factors is emphasized. Social support is generally considered as an important factor to effectively prevent and reduce postpartum depression. According to the theoretical framework of social support constructed by Leahi-Warren et al. [1], social support is one of the influencing factors that help predict and reduce the risk of postpartum depression. Social support can also indirectly improve maternal parental self-efficiency and effectively reduce the risk of postpartum depression. E-Mental Health (EMH) system is one of the modern effective solutions to psychological problems. It has become a modern social trend to apply electronic mental health service systems to enhance social support. In the past research, Chiou et al. [2] designed a We'll App through the application of EMH to enhance social support, and then enhance maternal self-efficacy, so as to reduce or solve PPD and postpartum depression. This study will continue to carry out clinical trials through We'llAPP, and EPDS, social-support, self-efficiency questionnaires are used to understand the status of maternal emotional disorders, social support and self-efficacy, and conduct clinical research analysis.

Keywords: Postpartum depression · Mobile application development · Social-support · Self-efficacy · EPDS

1 Introduction

1.1 Postpartum Depression

Depression is one of the common diseases in the 21st century. According to the statistics of English literatures, the prevalence rate in the world is 5–8%, about 15% of people have

© Springer Nature Switzerland AG 2021
P.-L. P. Rau (Ed.): HCII 2021, LNCS 12772, pp. 162–171, 2021.
https://doi.org/10.1007/978-3-030-77077-8_13

suffered from or still suffer from depression, and it is even as high as 25% in females [3]. However, female suffer from depression twice as much as male [4–7]. Postpartum affective disorders during pregnancy and childbirth are the most severe among female depression. Maternity and motherhood are necessary stages in the process of human development. Past studies have shown that many postpartum women suffer from postpartum mood disorder. The psychological state of postpartum mood disorder is studied from "postpartum blues" to "postpartum psychosis". Postpartum depression belongs to a mild depression with a prevalence rate of 50–80%. It occurs within 10 days after delivery [8]. Symptoms include sadness, irritability, uneasiness, anxiety and insomnia. Generally, it does not need special medication or treatment. With adequate nutrition, rest and psychological support, it will gradually improve within about 2 weeks. However, if the depressed mood lasts for more than two weeks and becomes more and more serious, the patients should seek medical treatment as soon as possible. Although transient symptoms do not require medical intervention [9, 10], the patients still need more care and support from family and friends to recover. Maternity often neglects mental health status, and severe cases may increase the risk of postpartum depression [11].

O'Hara and Swain [12] combined 59 studies and found that the prevalence of PPD was 13%. In addition, Meta-analysis of [13] found that psychosocial factors were important predictors: prenatal depression, self-esteem, child care stress, prenatal anxiety, life stress events, social support, marital relationship, history of depression, infant temperament, postpartum depression, marital status, socio-economic status and unplanned pregnancy. Nearly half of PPD women have not been diagnosed, because their symptoms are similar to postpartum physiological changes such as weight loss and fatigue, so they are not easy to be confirmed. Moreover, many postpartum women are reluctant to discuss melancholy with others because the general social perception believes that having children is a happy event, so they are often ashamed to speak or afraid of being stigmatized as melancholy [14]. The Edinburgh Postnatal Depression Scale (EPDS), most commonly used clinically, is a popular tool that can quickly assess the mental status of pregnant and lying-in women.

1.2 Social-Support and Self-efficacy

According to the social exchange theory [15, 16] and Bandura self-efficacy theory [17] construct the theoretical framework of social support. Social support is directly related to parenting self-efficacy and postpartum depression, which is helpful to predict and reduce the risk of postpartum depression. One of the influencing factors [13, 18], parenting self-efficacy has a direct negative correlation with postpartum depression. Social support is broadly defined as the material, cognitive and emotional support and assistance given by members or experts in social networks [19, 20]. Members of social networks include family members, intimate partners, friends and peers, with partners, mothers and sisters most frequently contacted [1]. However, it is extremely important for the parturient to obtain substantial assistance from the partner and the mother of the parturient [21], especially the mother of the parturient. Through sharing parenting experience and verbal encouragement, the parenting self-efficacy of parturients can be improved, so evaluative support has a significant correlation with the self-confidence of parturient [22]. However, most parturients are very satisfied with the experience of peer support. Peer exchange of experience provides emotional, information and evaluation support. Maternal satisfaction is related to the number and duration of peer contact [23]. At present, the social support and parenting self-efficacy of parturients can be detected by the scale. This study used the Multidimensional Scale of Perceived Social Support (MSPSS) created by Zimet et al. [24] to test the function and role of social support.

The perceived material parenting self-efficacy (PMP S-E) tool was used to measure the self-confidence of parturients in various tasks of parenting. The content included 20 questions, which were established from four aspects: infant care style, arousal behavior, perceived behavior or signs, and situational thinking. The score of each question ranged from 1 point (very disagree) to 4 points (very agree), and the internal consistency Cronbach's α was 0.89.

1.3 E-mental Health

E-mental health (EMH) is a modern trend, providing professional functions to solve mental health problems. It provides four service functions through social media, chat rooms, forums, electronic bulletin boards and blogs through the Internet, including (1) information provision [25, 26]; (2) Screening, evaluation and monitoring [27–33]; (3) Medical intervention [34, 35]; (4) Social support (Scharer, 2005).

The popularity of smart phones has transformed EMH into a service mode of mobile medical APP. According to the results of WHO survey on existing mobile medical APPs, depression ranks second only to diabetes [37].

1.4 Purpose of Research

Currently, there are few studies on the application of EMH to PDD in Taiwan. The purpose of this study is as follows: (1) To investigate the PPD situation in Taiwan and try to understand the needs of parturients; (2) To investigate the social support status of postpartum women in Taiwan and analyze their social relations. (3) To investigate the self-efficacy of postpartum women in Taiwan (4) To use We'll app as a solution to PPD in Taiwan, and analyze whether there is any difference before and after use.

2 Method

The research site was located in Taipei Chang Gung Obstetrics and Gynecology, 60 subjects were openly recruited from the physician clinic and divided into two groups, with 30 cases who agreed to use APP intervention in pregnant and lying-in women experimental group, and 30 cases who did not use APP in control group. The study participants will conduct user clinical trials to test the clinical effectiveness of APP and questionnaire survey after delivery. The content does not affect the health of pregnant and lying-in women and fetuses. The questionnaire consists of four parts: (1) demographic data (2) Edinburgh Postnatal Depression Scale-Taiwan version (EPDS-T) (3) Multidimensional Scale of Perceived Social Support (MSPSS) (4) Maternal Self-efficacy Scale.

At the early stage of this study, the design, development and testing of APP have been completed, and clinical implementation and evaluation will be carried out. At this stage, non-invasive clinical trials will be conducted, and the steps are as follows:

The experimental group brought APP into real life for 6 to 8 weeks, filled in 3 scales (Edinburgh Postnatal Depression Scale 10 questions, Maternal Self-efficacy Scale 12 questions, Social Support Scale 20 questions) for 10 to 20 min at the outpatient clinic 36 to 40 weeks before delivery, started the use of APP immediately after delivery, and filled in 4 experimental questionnaires for 10 to 20 min four weeks after delivery. (Edinburgh Postnatal Depression Scale 10 questions, Maternal Self-efficacy Scale 12 questions, Social Support Scale 20 questions and Usage Assessment Scale 10 questions).

The control group filled in three scales for 10–20 min (Edinburgh Postnatal Depression Scale 10 questions, Maternal Self-efficacy Scale 12 questions, Social Support Scale 20 questions) at the outpatient clinic 36–40 weeks before delivery, and followed the normal life after delivery. Work and rest, and fill in three experimental questionnaires for 10–20 min four weeks and eight weeks after postpartum use. (Edinburgh Postnatal Depression Scale 10 questions, Maternal Self-efficacy Scale 12 questions, Social Support Scale 20 questions). Through this study, the data can be obtained, including maternal user needs, EPDS depression test results, social support status, parenting self-efficacy status, and APP usage status.

The statistical software SPSS 20.0.0 was used for analysis, the confidence interval was set at 95%. Descriptive statistics were used to analyze the basic statistical data, so as to understand the distribution of the basic data of the subjects, and the differences before and after using APP were compared by ANOVA.

3 Result

Three 2 (Group Type: APP, Control) × 2(Time: Pre, Post) ANOVA with repeated measures (Fig. 1) was conducted on the Postpartum Depression (EPDS), Parenting self-efficacy (PMPSE), Social Support (MSPSS).

For Postpartum Depression, there was a significant main effect of Time: $F(1,58) = 6.726$, $p = 0.012$, $\eta^2_p = 0.104$; and there was a significant interaction between Time and Group Type: $F(1,58) = 11.251$, $p = 0.001$, $\eta^2_p = 0.162$; but there was also no significant main effect of Group Type: $F(1,58) = 0.285$, $p = 0.595$.

For Parenting self-efficacy, there was a significant main effect of Time: $F(1,58) = 4.143$, $p = 0.046$, $\eta^2_p = 0.067$; but there was also no significant main effect of Group Type: $F(1,58) = 0.135$, $p = 0.715$; and there was no significant interaction between Time and Group Type: $F(1,58) = 3.126$, $p = 0.082$.

For Social Support, there was no significant main effect of Time: $F(1,58) = 0.186$, $p = 0.668$; and there was also no significant main effect of Group Type: $F(1,58) = 0.333$, $p = 0.566$; and there was no significant interaction between Time and Group Type: $F(1,58) = 0.360$, $p = 0.551$. Although the results of Social Support were not significant, it could be seen that there was a slight increase in the post-test data of the APP use group compared to the pre-test, while there was a slight decrease in the post-test data of the control group compared to the pre-test (Table 1).

Table 1. Means and standard deviations

Group	Measures	Mean (SD)	
		Pre	Post
APP	EPDS	1.977(0.389)	1.690(0.298)
	PMPSE	2.087(0.496)	2.395(0.597)
	MSPSS	5.827(0.745)	5.944 (0.682)
Control	EPDS	1.763(0.485)	1.800(0.475)
	PMPSE	2.282(0.617)	2.303(0.773)
	MSPSS	5.980(0.653)	5.961 (0.770)

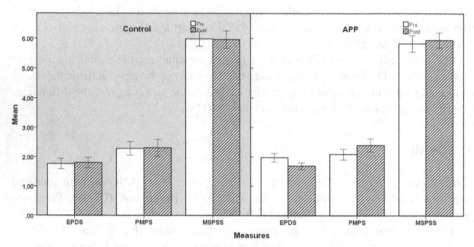

Fig. 1. Results of ANOVA

4 Discussion

The results of this study suggest that the use of MBI We'll App can effectively decrease their postpartum depression. These findings may be relevant to lifestyle changes in women following pregnancy. Mindfulness therapy can reduce impulsivity in various ways to increase awareness of one's own experience and thus increase control of impulsivity. This allows women to adjust their behavior to the greatest extent possible and reduce the internal anxiety and discomfort associated with role change. MBI We'll App training does not view life's stresses as difficulties or disasters, but as an adjustable way to relieve stress. Through mindfulness training, the emotional information of postpartum depression patients is offset, so that the negative memory is occupied by positive emotions such as mindfulness, love, compassion, etc., get rid of the accustomed uncomfortable thinking mode, and promote the postpartum women to adapt to the new life and new role as soon as possible [39]. Long-term mindfulness training can lead to a decrease in the density of gray matter in the amygdala, which is the brain tissue that produces, recognizes and regulates emotions, suggesting that mindfulness training can effectively regulate emotions [40]. Mindfulness practice alone has been shown to have positive health effects, improving chronic pain, reducing perceived stress and depressive symptoms during pregnancy, and promoting mental health. After the improvement of the level of mindfulness, the pregnant women are abler to deal with their negative emotions in an open, accepting, non-judgmental and non-reactive manner in the face of labor induction events, and focus on the present body, mind and activities, so as to reduce the symptoms of anxiety and depression. Mindfulness emphasizes awareness of one's own feelings, thoughts, and judgments, thereby automating and reducing redundant thoughts, negative thoughts, and avoidance behaviors. After the improvement of the level of mindfulness, the puerpera have rich psychological resources in the face of stressful environment, will view the personal stress response from a positive perspective, and show good adaptation results, which is completely consistent with the effect of mindfulness coping. When women engage in cognitive integration, they take their thoughts as reality, such as the belief that they are stupid and incapable of raising children, which can lead to anxiety and depression. When women become aware of the present and live in the here and now, they activate their self-management system and promote inner harmony, which can reduce depression [42].

The improvement of maternal Parenting self-efficacy is mainly because the physiological state of the puerpera has been changed by the MBI We'll App, and the negative emotional state of the puerpera, such as anxiety, tension and fatigue, has been relieved after the application of the APP. In the face of stressful events, women often judge self-efficacy based on their heart rate, blood pressure, breathing and other physiological arousal levels. Different physical reaction state will affect the achievement level of the activity, the calm reaction makes people calm, confident, and then to behavioral response indicators to confirm or achieve the confidence before the activity, so improve the maternal self-efficacy. Individuals with postpartum depression are often affected by the experience of failure. Once faced with negative life events such as bringing up children, they will think that they will repeat the mistake of failure, so they will have discomfort feelings such as tension and anxiety. Scholars call this phenomenon as negative stimulation and excessive connection between emotion and self. This is when an individual is overly immersed in his or her previous experience and future imagination associated with current events, and this association is usually negative or threatening, so repeatedly, if this phenomenon occurs, over time, forming a habit or automated way of thinking, when individuals once encountered with children, would have a failure of automation beliefs, anxiety, namely individual effectively cope with the negative emotions, self-efficacy is low, so we will adopt the way of escape from the test to cope with depression, although escape way can temporarily alleviate depression, but at the same time also strengthened the escape behavior, depression cannot get effective treatment. The power of mindfulness is to automate and change the way people think. First, the belief that an individual has failed to cope with negative emotions does not immediately go into automation; Secondly, to change the individual's thinking mode, prompting individuals to no longer avoid the way, but to regard depression as an object existence, do not bring in too much subjective evaluation, and then effectively deal with depression.

With the increase of individuals' experience in effectively dealing with negative emotions, the corresponding sense of self-efficacy will also be improved. After all, individual successful experience is one of the most important information sources of self-efficacy. MBI We'll App training improves maternal self-efficacy, thus improving individual physiology, maintaining physical and mental stability, enhancing self-confidence, helping patients adopt positive coping styles and promoting positive health behaviors. The higher the self-efficacy, the better the level of self-management. For patients with high level of mindfulness, they are abler to focus on the present emotional experience, more likely to show confidence in the acceptance and management of the disease, promote the improvement of their internal self-efficacy level, and the projected external performance is the improvement of the patient's self-management level of the disease [43, 44].

The increase in maternal social support is not significant after MBI We'll App training. The more aware they are of themselves and their surroundings, the more aware they are of the present, and the abler they are to accept things in the present without judgment. This awareness and acceptance of the present can minimize maternal emotional distress. In other words, the higher the maternal level of mindfulness, the less social support needed. The state of mindfulness requires that the maternal psychology is always in the attention of what is happening in front of her, but also experience the state of their own feelings, so that the psychological state is in the state of mindfulness, can pull people out from the painful thinking and emotions, reduce the damage caused by the symptoms, known as the decentralized process. These mechanisms can free consciousness from rigid frameworks about itself and the world. When a mindful state of consciousness can be established, the mother can reorient her environment and develop mental resilience. MBI We'll App training can make the maternal consciousness function become stronger, such as stable attention, clear awareness, can accept and bear pain, resolve the conflict and transcend the soft mentality of obstacles, so that the thinking from the conflict and obstacles free. "Attention" is the directed attention to this consciousness, "awareness" is the awareness of oneself and the external environment, through the directed awareness individuals can fully understand the internal and external world rather than being limited to a certain mind.

5 Conclusion

This study will continue to carry out clinical trials through We'll APP, EPDS, social-support, and self-efficiency questionnaires are used to understand the status of maternal emotional disorders, social support and self-efficacy, and conduct clinical research analysis. Future research with the newly developed We'll APP tools and processes will explore the facilitators of and barriers to its implementation in different primary care settings. Future work should also more systematically examine whether and how intervention processes may reinforce or contribute to pregnant women's feelings of being stereotyped, and how intervention processes can be designed to avoid stereotype threat, which has the potential to reduce the effectiveness of interventions intended to promote pregnant women's health.

Our empirical research did not end with that conclusion: We engaged in a transdisciplinary follow-up project aiming to further articulate our suggested improving design

We'll APP, with concrete elements. However, the insights from this next stage in our research would go beyond the scope of this article, and will follow in a future publication.

References

1. Leahy-Warren, P., McCarthy, G., Corcoran, P.: First-time mothers: social support, maternal parental self-efficacy and postnatal depression. J Clin Nurs **21**(3–4), 388–397 (2012). https://doi.org/10.1111/j.1365-2702.2011.03701.x
2. Chiou, W.-K., Kao, C.-Y., Lo, L.-M., Huang, D.-H., Wang, M.-H., Chen, B.-H.: Feasibility of utilizing E-mental health with mobile app interface for social support enhencement: A conceptional solution for postpartum depression in Taiwan. In: Marcus, A., Wang, W. (eds.) Design, User Experience, and Usability: Designing Pleasurable Experiences, pp. 198–207. Springer International Publishing, Cham (2017). https://doi.org/10.1007/978-3-319-58637-3_15
3. Kessler, R., et al.: Lifetime and 12-month prevalence of DSM-III-R psychiatric disorders in the united states: results from the national comorbidity survey. Arch. Gen. Psychiatr. **51**(1), 8 (1994). https://doi.org/10.1001/archpsyc.1994.03950010008002
4. Andrade, L., et al.: The epidemiology of major depressive episodes: results from the international consortium of psychiatric epidemiology (ICPE) surveys. Int. J. Methods Psychiatr. Res. **12**(1), 3–21 (2003). https://doi.org/10.1002/mpr.138
5. Burt, V.K., Stein, K.: Epidemiology of depression throughout the female life cycle. J. Clin. Psychiatr. **63**(suppl 7), 9–15 (2002). https://www.ncbi.nlm.nih.gov/pubmed/11995779
6. Gualtieri, C.T.: An Internet-based symptom questionnaire that is reliable, valid, and available to psychiatrists, neurologists, and psychologists. Medscape Gen. Med. **9**(4), 3 (2007)
7. Kessler, R.C., et al.: Screening for serious mental illness in the general population. Arch. Gen. Psychiatr. **60**(2), 184–189 (2003). https://doi.org/10.1001/archpsyc.60.2.184
8. Evins, G.G., Theofrastous, J.P.: Postpartum depression: a review of postpartum screening. Prim. Care Update Ob/Gyns **4**(6), 241–246 (1997)
9. Kennerley, H., Gath, D.: Maternity blues. I. detection and measurement by questionnaire. Br. J. Psychiatry **155**(3), 356–362 (1989). https://www.ncbi.nlm.nih.gov/pubmed/2611547
10. Pitt, B.: Maternity blues. Br. J. Psychiatr. **122**(569), 431–433 (1973). https://doi.org/10.1192/bjp.122.4.431
11. Beck, C.T., Reynolds, M.A., Rutowski, P.: Maternity blues and postpartum depression. J. Obstet. Gynecol. Neonatal. Nurs. **21**(4), 287–293 (1992). https://doi.org/10.1111/j.1552-6909.1992.tb01739.x
12. O'hara, M.W., Swain, A.M.: Rates and risk of postpartum depression—a meta-analysis. Int. Rev. Psychiatr. **8**(1), 37–54 (1996)
13. Beck, C.T.: Predictors of postpartum depression: an update. Nurs. Res. **50**(5), 275–285 (2001). https://doi.org/10.1097/00006199-200109000-00004
14. Heneghan, A.M., Mercer, M., DeLeone, N.L.: Will mothers discuss parenting stress and depressive symptoms with their child's pediatrician? Pediatrics **113**(3), 460–467 (2004)
15. Blau, P.M.: Social exchange theory. **3**(2007), 62 (1964)
16. Homans, G.C.: The humanities and the social sciences. Am. Behav. Sci. **4**(8), 3–6 (1961)
17. Bandura, A.: The anatomy of stages of change. Am. J. Health Promot. AJHP **12**(1), 8–10 (1997)
18. Robertson, E., Grace, S., Wallington, T., Stewart, D.E.: Antenatal risk factors for postpartum depression: a synthesis of recent literature. Gen. Hosp. Psychiatr. **26**(4), 289–295 (2004). https://doi.org/10.1016/j.genhosppsych.2004.02.006

19. Gottlieb, B.H., Bergen, A.E.: Social support concepts and measures. J. Psychosom. Res. **69**(5), 511–520 (2010). https://doi.org/10.1016/j.jpsychores.2009.10.001
20. Thoits, P.A.: Perceived social support and the voluntary, mixed, or pressured use of mental health services. Soc. Mental Health **1**(1), 4–19 (2011)
21. Haggman-Laitila, A.: Early support needs of Finnish families with small children. J. Adv. Nurs. **41**(6), 595–606 (2003). https://doi.org/10.1046/j.1365-2648.2003.02571.x
22. Leahy Warren, P.: First-time mothers: social support and confidence in infant care. J. Adv. Nurs. **50**(5), 479–488 (2005). https://doi.org/10.1111/j.1365-2648.2005.03425.x
23. Dennis, C.L.: Postpartum depression peer support: maternal perceptions from a randomized controlled trial. Int. J. Nurs. Stud. **47**(5), 560–568 (2010). https://doi.org/10.1016/j.ijnurstu. 2009.10.015
24. Zimet, G.D., Dahlem, N.W., Zimet, S.G., Farley, G.K.: The multidimensional scale of perceived social support. J. Pers. Assess. **52**(1), 30–41 (1988)
25. Lambousis, E., Politis, A., Markidis, M., Christodoulou, G.N.: Development and use of online mental health services in Greece. J. Telemed. Telecare **8**(2_suppl), 51–52 (2002)
26. Santor, D.A., Poulin, C., Le, B.J., Kusumakar, V.: Online health promotion, early identification of difficulties, and help seeking in young people. J. Am. Acad. Child Adolesc. Psychiatry **46**(1), 50–59 (2007). https://doi.org/10.1097/01.chi.0000242247.45915.ee
27. Becker, J., et al.: Functioning and validity of a computerized adaptive test to measure anxiety (A-CAT). Depress. Anxiety **25**(12), E182-194 (2008). https://doi.org/10.1002/da.20482
28. Chinman, M., Hassell, J., Magnabosco, J., Nowlin-Finch, N., Marusak, S., Young, A.S.: The feasibility of computerized patient self-assessment at mental health clinics. Adm. Policy Mental Health Mental Health Serv. Res. **34**(4), 401–409 (2007)
29. Diamond, G., et al.: Development, validation, and utility of internet-based, behavioral health screen for adolescents. Pediatrics **126**(1), e163-170 (2010). https://doi.org/10.1542/peds. 2009-3272
30. Donker, T., van Straten, A., Marks, I., Cuijpers, P.: A brief Web-based screening questionnaire for common mental disorders: development and validation. J. Med. Internet Res. **11**(3), e19 (2009). https://doi.org/10.2196/jmir.1134
31. Gringras, P., Santosh, P., Baird, G.: Development of an Internet-based real-time system for monitoring pharmacological interventions in children with neurodevelopmental and neuropsychiatric disorders. Child. Care Health Dev **32**(5), 591–600 (2006). https://doi.org/10. 1111/j.1365-2214.2006.00653.x
32. Heron, K.E., Smyth, J.M.: Ecological momentary interventions: incorporating mobile technology into psychosocial and health behaviour treatments. Brit. J. Health Psychol. **15**(1), 1–39 (2010)
33. Khazaal, Y., et al.: Brief DISCERN, six questions for the evaluation of evidence-based content of health-related websites. Patient Educ. Couns. **77**(1), 33–37 (2009). https://doi.org/10.1016/ j.pec.2009.02.016
34. Bergstrom, J., et al.: Internet-versus group-administered cognitive behaviour therapy for panic disorder in a psychiatric setting: a randomised trial. BMC Psychiatry **10**(1), 54 (2010). https:// doi.org/10.1186/1471-244X-10-54
35. Khanna, M.S., Kendall, P.C.: Computer-assisted cognitive behavioral therapy for child anxiety: results of a randomized clinical trial. J. Consult. Clin. Psychol. **78**(5), 737–745 (2010). https://doi.org/10.1037/a0019739
36. Scharer, K.: Internet social support for parents: the state of science. J. Child. Adolesc. Psychiatry Nurs. **18**(1), 26–35 (2005). https://doi.org/10.1111/j.1744-6171.2005.00007.x
37. Martínez-Pérez, B., De La Torre-Díez, I., López-Coronado, M.: Mobile health applications for the most prevalent conditions by the World Health Organization: review and analysis. J. Med. Internet Res. **15**(6), e120 (2013)

38. Shulman, B., Dueck, R., Ryan, D., Breau, G., Sadowski, I., Misri, S.: Feasibility of a mindfulness-based cognitive therapy group intervention as an adjunctive treatment for postpartum depression and anxiety. J. Affect. Disord. **235**, 61–67 (2018)
39. Solhaug, I., et al.: Long-term mental health effects of mindfulness training: a 4-year follow-up study. Mindfulness **10**(8), 1661–1672 (2019)
40. Spek, V., Nyklicek, I., Cuijpers, P., Pop, V.: Predictors of outcome of group and internet-based cognitive behavior therapy. J. Affect. Disord. **105**(1–3), 137–145 (2008). https://doi.org/10.1016/j.jad.2007.05.001
41. Guardino, C.M., Dunkel Schetter, C., Bower, J.E., Lu, M.C., Smalley, S.L.: Randomised controlled pilot trial of mindfulness training for stress reduction during pregnancy. Psychol. Health **29**(3), 334–349 (2014)
42. Pedrini, L., Ferrari, C., Ghilardi, A.: Psychometric properties of the Italian perceived maternal parenting self-efficacy (PMP SE). J. Clin. Psychol. Med. Settings **26**(2), 173–182 (2019)
43. Vargas-Porras, C., et al.: Psychometric properties of the spanish version of the perceived maternal parenting self-efficacy (PMP SE) tool for primiparous women. Matern. Child Health J. **24**, 1–9 (2020)

Description of Role Orientation of College Teachers in Online Education Under Epidemic Emergency

Zhengliang Li[1]([⊠]) [iD] and Miaoqi Tian[2] [iD]

[1] Hunan University, Changsha 410000, Hunan, China
[2] Chaohu University, Hefei 230000, Anhui, China

Abstract. Since COVID-19 suddenly broke out in 2020, the model of teaching in universities has changed completely. In order to improve the unsatisfied experience of online education under the epidemic situation and to meet the teaching needs of college teachers in the emergency situation, and on the basis of the online teaching practice of the Advertising Creativity course in Hunan University, the roles of online education college teachers can be divided into four major categories: learning experience designer, learning process guider, new knowledge production cooperator and learning ecosystem constructor.

Keywords: Epidemic emergency · Online education · College teachers · Role definition

1   Introduction

To accelerate the development, application and popularization of online education under the background of sudden COVID-19 outbreak in 2020, higher education needs to adapt to the changes of the times, while college teachers should take the initiative to create their own roles, take advantage of the new conditions, practice new ideas, see new changes and meet new challenges in the face of the emergency.

2   The Challenge and Call of College Teacher Roles in Online Education in the Case of Epidemic Emergency

2.1   New Changes of Teaching Situation in Colleges and Universities Under Epidemic Emergency

Weight of New Technologies in the Teaching Theme. Internet technology has become a part of social life. People often use information technology in their life and work, and mastering Internet technology has become one of the necessary life skills for modern people. For college teachers who nurture and promote civilization in the new era, understanding and mastering Internet technology is an important part of their teaching work. More importantly, mastering and using Internet technology has become one

P.-L. P. Rau (Ed.): HCII 2021, LNCS 12772, pp. 172–182, 2021.
https://doi.org/10.1007/978-3-030-77077-8_14

of the important factors that determine whether we can find a job we love and even whether we can realize the value of our life. The development of Internet technology has brought about many new educational technologies. Besides, online education has also been profoundly affecting the reform of the teaching theme in colleges and universities. For example, in 2017, China released the *New-Generation Artificial Intelligence Development Plan* which proposed to actively develop intelligent education and popularize artificial intelligence teaching.

At the same time, under the situation of sudden epidemic, whether teachers and students can master and use Internet technology is directly related to the successful implementation of teaching activities, and also directly affects the teaching quality. Thus it can be seen that Internet technology has become a crucial subject of modern higher education in the case of emergency situation, which puts forward new requirements for higher education and higher educators.

UGC and OGC Mode of Teaching Content. In the Internet era, the continuous advancement of information technology and the continuous development of information value have brought about massive data. In higher education, new disciplines constantly emerge and traditional ideas and knowledge are constantly updated and substituted with ever-increasing speed. Therefore, the teaching content must also be adapted to the update information. New research and development results must be integrated into the teaching content so that students can receive the most cutting-edge knowledge. In the case of emergencies, the output and teaching of this kind of cutting-edge content is no longer a simple occupationally-generated content (OGC) mode, but a combination of the OGC mode with the user-generated content (UGC) mode. Hence, the content of teaching is not only the professional and specialized knowledge output of teachers, but more a representation of knowledge guided by teachers and participated by students. It is more in line with the development of "Internet + education" and the requirements of the emergency situation.

The Trend of Individualization of the Teaching Form. In the information society, the requirements for employees are also changing, including diverse professional skills and increasingly higher requirements for knowledge. Therefore, in order to adapt to these changes, the form of teaching needs to fully arouse the enthusiasm of each student, adopt a teaching system that varies from person to person, and prepare humanized education and training classes, progress and teaching materials. Meanwhile, the fast-developing online education in the case of epidemic emergency has transformed the organizational mode of higher education from a certain fixed time and fixed area within a university to without age limit, without fixed teaching time, and without a unified teaching area. Under this premise, the "1vn" form of higher education depending only on the traditional classroom teaching can no longer meet the different study time, region and occupational needs of students, and the "1v1" or even "nv1" teaching form has become the new expectation of college teaching.

Furthermore, the teaching method is transforming from the merely traditional knowledge transfer to the individual and interactive method of teaching. In 2016, Tsinghua University integrated "mobile terminal" into "rain classroom" teaching. Ever since that, the form of mobile learning has been gradually accepted by the public, and "interaction" and "individual" have gradually become the key points to control a classroom. The diversified, interactive and individualized teaching method is a teaching reform in the development of online education, which is also the evolution and innovation of higher education in emergency situations.

Comprehensive Demands of Teaching Goals. The goal of higher education should not only emphasize the science and technology that students have created by inheriting the cultural wealth of human civilization and human history, but also pay attention to cultivating students' willingness to continue learning and the ability of lifelong learning. In the face of unexpected circumstances, when offline education is unavailable, students must rely on the mastered Internet technological skills to adapt to the constantly changing teaching environment and to further achieve self-improvement and self-development. In April 2018, China issued the *Education Informatization Action Plan 2.0* which proposed to "build a national credit bank and lifelong e-learning archives" [1], to provide more guarantee for lifelong learning. Besides, how to help students acquire the skills and means of sustainable learning is also an important issue that college teachers need to contemplate in order to realize the sustainable teaching goal.

In addition, students' mental health education and emotional counseling have become one of the main demands of college education in the emergency situation. The negative changes of social environment caused by the outbreak of the epidemic have seriously affected the daily life, work and emotion of every citizen. The condition of having to stay at home for a long time often leads to the increasing antagonism among students. In this period, higher educators need to pay more attention to the emotional demands and psychological instruction of students. Therefore, the teaching objectives of online education in the case of epidemic emergency are more diversified and comprehensive.

The Strengthening of the "Reverse" of the Teaching Subject. Online education in emergency situation relies on a teaching mode that is different from the traditional "teacher-centered" or "teacher-led" teaching mode. Instead, it emphasizes "student-orientation", highlights the dominant role of students in teaching, and strengthens the real "reserve" classroom. In the Internet age, students are the subject of learning. Only by helping students master the dominant power of learning, can college teachers truly achieve the goal of higher education. In this way, learners are no longer the objects of knowledge transmission. They have become the core subjects of educational activities. The whole process of teaching is advanced around students, and every teaching step, including setting the teaching objectives, designing the teaching process, selecting teaching resources, and developing teaching activities, must have the learners as the core. Because students can find whatever information they need on the Internet, what colleges teachers really need to think about is "what can I teach" based on "what students need to learn".

The Connotation Extension of Teaching Space. In the traditional sense, the so-called teaching space is limited to the scope of school. As recorded in *The Book of Rites • The Note of Learning*, "ancient teachers had their own schools, some families had their private schools, towns and cities provided public schools, and the country had the Imperial College". School teaching relies on teaching space. In different periods of Chinese history, teaching space has different physical carriers, but it often changes in the context of physical space. Under the circumstances of emergencies, the development of online education has accelerated worldwide. The traditional physical teaching space has been unable to adapt to the abrupt changes of the social environment. Students cannot participate in the regular teaching activities. In order to conduct continuous teaching activities, people are constantly exploring the use of technologies to broaden the concept of school, build new teaching space based on technical means, such as artificial intelligence, big data, and Internet plus, which, to a large extent, have accelerated the transfer of physical teaching space to cyberspace, and begin to examine the possibility of integrating physical space and cyberspace for college teaching in the post epidemic era. Hence, the connotation of teaching space in college teaching is constantly deepening and extending.

3   Pain Points of Online Education for College Teachers in the Case of Epidemic Emergency

Compared with the traditional classroom teaching in colleges and universities, online education under the situation of epidemic emergency has great differences in many aspects, such as the teaching content, form, methods, means, and techniques. College teachers are also experiencing diversified pain points in the process of online education. The major pain points can be roughly divided into four aspects, that are, teaching resources, teaching platform, teaching evaluation and teaching support, for further analysis.

3.1   Insufficient Appropriateness of Teaching Resources

Statistics show that, during the COVID-19 epidemic, more than 950,000 teachers in China opened 942,000 online courses or 7.133,000 online courses/time, among which 5000 were new courses [2]. On the one hand, such a large scale of curriculum resources provided a solid guarantee for online teaching during the epidemic period, greatly alleviated the conflicts between teaching resource supply and demand under the emergency situation, and increased the possibility to start school online in the spring semester. However, on the other hand, there was an obvious problem of whether the focus of the teaching resources matched the learning needs of students. The lack of appropriateness of teaching resources has become a major disadvantage of many college teachers in online education.

First of all, a large number of high-quality online course resources were launched during the epidemic period. But due to the urgency of time, the time for planning and designing teaching resources was shortened or even skipped. As a result, a lot of redundant teaching resources were released. There were abundant public courses, junior-grade courses and theoretical courses but few professional training courses. In particular, there was a great shortage for professional curriculum resources for senior-grade students. Secondly, it was difficult to guarantee the substantial equivalence of curriculum resources. Most online courses were not synchronous with students' actual learning process. It was difficult to fully access students' learning demands and learning effects before courses were launched and during the courses. Consequently, there was a time gap between course teaching and students' learning, which made it difficult to fit the real-time and individualized needs of online learning students into the online courses. Finally, using the author's college online education practice as an example, most teachers in the author's college hadn't made any emergency psychological preparation or curriculum resource preparation for the sudden outbreak of the epidemic. Therefore, more than half of them chose to use the existing or free open course resources, which resulted in more serious separation of curriculum teaching. Because of the lack of appropriateness of curriculum resources and even the use of free open curriculum resources, teachers could not access students' learning conditions in time. They cannot grasp or acquire students' learning effect just from homework. Therefore, it was difficult for them to carry out targeted online teaching.

3.2 Lack of Cooperativity Among Teaching Platforms

The teaching platform is a major tool of online education in the case of epidemic emergencies, and the quality of teaching platforms is directly related to the effect of online education. Under the emergency situation of COVID-19, the Ministry of Education of China organized 37 online course platforms and technology platforms to take the lead in opening online courses free of charge to colleges and universities across the country, followed by the active participation of more than 110 social and university platforms [3]. Then a series of online teaching platforms were launched one after another to provide guarantee for online education under the emergency situation. While using such teaching platforms, college teachers experienced not only the advantages of teaching convenience and rapidity brought by the platforms, but also some disadvantages, among which the most prominent one was the lack of cooperativity among the teaching platforms.

The collaborative problem of online teaching platforms is generally manifested in the following three aspects: First, the collaborative problem of platform content: Each university may have a different positioning. Junior colleges, application-oriented universities and academic universities have different requirements on curriculum resources, curriculum setting and supporting services. However, the existing online teaching platforms have not been able to develop the content with different characteristics and complementary advantages for these different universities. Second, the collaborative problem of platform operation: At present, a majority of the online teaching platforms are running their own businesses without any optimized or integrated system. In the online teaching of the college where the author works, students in the same class may use 1–5 or even more different learning platforms for different courses, which invisibly consumes a lot of their time and energy in the process of platform cognition and proficiency. Third, the collaborative problem of platform functions. In online education during the epidemic period, some teaching platforms often had excessive visits and they needed to upgrade and improve their systems in a short period of time to adapt to the excessive visits. As a result, they had no time to develop and adjust other functions. For example, the MOOC platform "Love Course" has advantageous curriculum resources but lacks interactive functions. Teachers often need to use other platforms, such as QQ group, Dingding, and Tencent conference to make deep interaction with their students.

3.3 Dull and Fixed Teaching Evaluation

The teaching modes, methods, resources, tools and other teaching elements of online education are quite different from those in traditional offline teaching. The diversified and personalized learning methods also need multi-dimensional teaching evaluation. However, from the online education practices under the emergency situation of COVID-19, most teachers were still using the traditional offline assessment methods, such as organizing online final examination at the end of the semester, scoring students' learning effects by marking papers, in the process of teaching evaluation due to the lack of scientific planning and guidance. Some universities even organized unified offline exams in the beginning of the second semester just because of archiving problems of students' exam papers. Such rigid and dull teaching evaluation not only failed to give full play to the advantages of online education, but also increased the burden of teachers and students, causing an imbalance of the learning focus in the learning process. In the teaching evaluation of online education in the university where the author works, the university required the teachers to include the daily performance of students in the assessment. The daily performance may include online homework, video learning, online interaction, and online discussion. The relevant data can be obtained from the activity sections, such as sign-in, answering questions, discussion, questioning, vote, and topic discussion provided by the teaching platform. Such teaching evaluation, to a certain extent, covers the assessment of students' learning process and breaks through the traditional test system; but it pays more attention to the quantitative data in students' learning process. As for the qualitative assessment (such as accessing the cultivation of learning habits, the improvement of learning ability, the mastery of learning skills, etc.), this evaluation mode is still insufficient. In short, there is still a lack of individualized and procedural teaching evaluation.

3.4 Lagging of Teaching Support Services

An important difference between online education under the epidemic emergency and regular online education lies in the organization disorder caused by the urgency of time, which leads to the incompleteness of online teaching support systems and the lagging of support services. From the perspective of teachers' online teaching support services, the online education support systems need to resolve some core issues, such as how to provide feasible and convenient online teaching platforms and operation manuals for teachers in the shortest time and how to help teachers develop online course implementation plans, course interaction plans, and project implementation plans. However, from the online education practices in the college where the author works, there were only a small number of college teachers who can master online teaching skills, especially older college teachers. However, the online training or lecture sharing organized by schools or online education platform still cannot fully satisfy the actual needs of college teachers. There were few targeted assistance and guidance activities, and the teachers' online education cooperation community has not really formed yet. From the perspective of students' online learning support services, more efforts need to be made on the support services in improving the effectiveness of students' online learning and personalized development. The learning requirements of all-round student development require the teachers to pay attention not only to students' mastery of knowledge, but also to the improvement of their comprehensive abilities in cognition, skills, and way of thinking etc. For this reason, in addition to course teaching, the support systems also should focus more on students' mental health education in home-based learning and help students achieve the ultimate goal of healthy, happy, autonomous and effective learning.

4   A Glimpse of the Roles of College Teachers in the Epidemic Emergency of COVID-19

To better meet the challenge of role orientation in the face of teaching situation reform under the emergency situation of the epidemic situation, college teachers must update the traditional concept of role orientation, turn the table, and adapt their roles in line with the needs of the times. On the basis of the relationship between teachers and students in colleges and universities, the roles of teachers in colleges and universities can be divided into four aspects: learning experience designer, learning process guider, new knowledge production partner, and learning ecosystem constructor.

4.1   Online Education Learning Experience Designer

In the context of online education, college teachers should provide students with more targeted, interactive and individualized learning experience services. Under the epidemic emergency, college teachers, as the online education learning experience designer, should implement clear control over the online learning characteristics of students and make scientific teaching strategies during the epidemic situation to achieve the goal of online teaching. College teachers are gathered to serve as professional curriculum online education learning experience designers so that they "can not only make full use of a certain course, but also find and resolve the problems in the process of course design" [4].

Then, what aspects should a course designer focus on? Firstly, a course designer needs to make full use of the "Network gatekeeper" role of teachers. In the process of learning experience design, the identification, screening and processing of information is the key premise of learning experience design. Secondly, an online course designer needs to examine the needs of students on deep and systematic learning. In an era where fragmented learning is prevalent, college teachers also need to study how to integrate students' fragmented knowledge and how to develop curriculum projects to help students carry out holistic, systematic and continuous thinking. Thirdly, in the process of information integration and processing, college teachers should be capable of clearly grasping the relationship between information and providing students with matching online courses. At the same time, the online course design in the epidemic emergency should also have the courses updated and improved in time based on the rapid change of social environment and the update speed of information knowledge to ensure that students can have access to the latest information knowledge so as to meet the talent cultivation needs of social development in emergency situations. Finally, at the same time of online course design, college teachers should also consider the integration and interconnection of different disciplines. College teachers of different disciplines, different schools, and different regions can continuously evaluate and improve the designed multi-disciplinary classroom system in the form of online cooperative teaching. For example, in 2017, China launched the first batch of 490 national quality online open courses, which is an embodiment of the role orientation of learning experience designers and developers created by college teachers under the background of online education.

4.2 Online Learning Process Guider

In the face of epidemic emergency, teachers play a more prominent role in guiding students' online learning. Through online education, teachers can grasp students' learning dynamics and psychological changes through curriculum data and other information, and implement targeted strategies to guide the all-round development of students' comprehensive quality.

"Under the traditional teaching mode, college teachers are more inclined to impart knowledge to students than to cultivate their abilities" [5]. A college teacher in the dominant position usually forces his/her students into a passive position, which greatly restricts the students' subjective initiative in learning, and is eventually not conducive to the students' sustainable learning and comprehensive improvement of quality. Teaching practices at home and abroad have clearly proved this conclusion: Only when students are in an active position in the classroom can they give full play to their learning potential. With the continuous development of online education, students have transformed the higher education mode in the process of actively exploring professional knowledge and solving doubts into an interactive process of equal dialogues between teachers and students. Teachers' knowledge transfer is no longer the only way for students to rely on in the process of online learning. Students can actively access new information, address doubts by themselves, and have fun from the high-level research-based learning. They can personally verify the research ideas and methods and develop their own information research skills and abilities.

The role orientation of college teachers in online education requires them to walk out of the traditional dominant and authoritative position and have equal dialogues with their students. As online learning process guiders in higher education, college teachers should attach importance to the following seven aspects: first, guide students to develop appropriate and exclusive learning objectives; second, guide students in the roadmap and methods on how to research and verify problems; third, guide the development of scientific learning strategies; fourth, guide information collection, screening, judgment and assessment; fifth, guide the development of individual advantages and personality characteristics; sixth, guide the acquisition of communication and cooperation in different situations; and seventh, guide innovation and creation based on actual conditions.

Under the epidemic emergency situation, teachers, as the online learning process guiders, should also play an important role in emotional counseling. The sudden change of the learning environment often gets some students into a state of confusion or disorder. Besides, long-term home staying will also result in psychological problems. Therefore, teachers should give full play to their role of mental health counselors and the role of emotion tutors in the process of online education and guide students to have a correct view of social development and their own studies so that the students can take part in online learning with a positive and optimistic attitude.

4.3 New Knowledge Production Cooperator

From the perspective of the current higher education curriculum, In the process of online learning, the role of college teachers has gradually shifted from a dominator to a learner. Through online learning, the interactive, sharing and open characteristics of information have enabled teachers and students to have efficient and effective communication dialogues, so as to achieve cooperation and mutual assistance. In this online learning process, college teachers are not to tell students what to do but to participate in students' learning process as a learner, participate in topic discussion and knowledge sharing, and provide constructive and valuable opinions for students, so as to ultimately promote the output of new knowledge and new results.

Firstly, from the perspective of students, online cooperative learning with teachers can better organize students to carry out in-depth contemplation on a specific issue. Meanwhile, the suggestions, evaluation, feedback and encouragement made by college teachers in online cooperative learning are important factors that affect the quality of students' learning outcomes, and can serve as the technical support, research experience guidance and clues for resolving doubts. Secondly, from the perspective of college teachers themselves, the development of online education requires teachers to stay as learners all the time. In the process of knowledge production, teachers should not only improve their ability by self-learning, but also learn to cooperate with and learn from students. American scholar Margaret Mead once proposed that prefigurative culture is closer to the cultural transmission mode of the current network era, which indicated that the older generation has to learn from the younger generation the type of culture they have never experienced before [6]. The students growing up with the Internet are often more capable of grasping the cutting-edge culture of the times. Therefore, under the background of online education, creating the role of cooperator in the production of new knowledge is also an inevitable choice for college teachers to improve themselves.

Using MOOC teaching as an example, the setting and arrangement of online curriculums is no longer the traditional "teaching-learning" relationship, and the most valuable learning outcomes are often presented jointly by teachers and students through cooperation and mutual assistance. For instance, in the MOOC teaching of *The Power of Design*, professor He Renke from Hunan University cooperated with students to produce new knowledge, such as the "world design map". For another example, in the MOOC teaching of *Advertising Creativity* during the epidemic emergency period, the author of this paper helped students to carry out innovative and entrepreneurial activities and create exclusive design brands through online cooperative learning with students. In the production of new knowledge, not only the students can make progress, but also the college teachers, as the cooperators, can improve a lot so as to better adapt to the development needs of the times.

4.4 Online Learning Ecosystem Constructor

The quality of students' online learning activities is not determined by a single factor, and whether the online learning ecosystem is perfect or not directly determines whether students can achieve the ideal learning effect. Therefore, the role creation of college teachers should not only consider a certain aspect or a single link, but should establish a global view and make college teachers the constructor of the online learning ecosystem of higher education. The online learning ecosystem can also be called "whole learning" ecosystem which points to the ultimate goal of students' lifelong and autonomous learning. The construction of a learning ecosystem by college teachers refers to the overall construction of scientific balance of space, environment, resources, technology and culture.

The construction of an online learning ecosystem means the proper connection of the input and output systems through the Internet platform, with its harmonious, stable and sustainable operation guaranteed. The input system includes college teachers, students, experts, enterprises, knowledge, information and resource database, test system, rich media resources etc. The input system should meet the physiological and psychological needs of students in terms of study and life as much as possible, and suit the students' practical online learning progress and actual situation. With the assistance of "Internet plus", the technologies, such as multimedia, VR, AR, and holographic projection, have enabled the constructed input system to be able to meet the learning needs of students in various forms, to provide access for students to acquire the information they need in an open space outside the classroom and seek professional answers. The output system includes knowledge, ability, sharing, entrepreneurship, employment, new knowledge production and even happy life. Therefore, a course of higher education is not just an online course, and the output of a course is not just the academic performance of students. The function of it is more poly-functional and targeted.

The author's MOOC teaching of *Advertising Creativity* suggested that the teaching process is also a process of exploring the construction of multi-functional online learning ecosystem. In this ecosystem, the online course starting point is the needs of students, and the end point is the growth of students. It is a multi-functional online learning ecosystem with advertising creativity as the theme, QR code as the contact node, "love course" as the basic platform, sharing, cooperation and growth as the principle, and teachers, students, experts and advertising enterprises as the participants. To meet the challenge of online education, it is necessary and conditional for college teachers to create the role of learning ecosystem constructor.

Someone held that "the role of teachers will eventually withdraw from the stage of history, and will be completely replaced by online teaching". However, the value of college teachers should be determined by the quality and ability of the college teachers themselves. Facing the impact and challenge brought by online education under the emergency situation of epidemic situation, college teachers must actively adapt to their own roles, adjust their relationship with students, and adapt to the new demands of the new era.

References

1. Ministry of Education of the People's Republic of China. "Ministry of Education on Printing and Issuing Education Informatization Action Plan 2.0" [DB/OL]. http://www.moe.edu.cn/src site/A16/s3342/201804/t20180425_334188.html,2018-4-13
2. Wu, Y.: Coping with Crises, Seeking Opportunities form Crises, and Doing a Good Job in the Construction of an International Online Teaching Platform and Course Resources [EB/OL] [2020-05-12]. https://baijiahao.baidu.com/s?id=1665543572921255251&wfr=spider&for=pc

3. Zhang, S.: Analysis of Teachers' Roles in SPOC. China Education Info, vol. 6 (2016)
4. Li, G., Liu, Y., Wang, L.: University Teacher Role Orientation and Classroom Innovation in the Reverse Classroom Teaching Mode. China University Teaching, vol. 05 (2018)
5. Liu, Z., Wang, W.: Analysis of the Roles of University Teachers in the Ecological Environment of Smart Education. Fujian Forum (Humanities and Social Sciences Edition), vol. 05 (2017)

Taking Micro-breaks at Work: Effects of Watching Funny Short-Form Videos on Subjective Experience, Physiological Stress, and Task Performance

Yang Liu, Qin Gao[✉], and Liang Ma

Department of Industrial Engineering, Tsinghua University, Beijing, People's Republic of China
gaoqin@tsinghua.edu.cn

Abstract. As short-form video applications have become popular recently, watching short-form videos as micro-breaks is common during leisure time at work. Short-form comedies are the most popular category of short-form video. This study conducted a laboratory study to examine the effects of watching funny short-form videos during micro-breaks at work participants' subjective experience (i.e., self-reported mood and task engagement willingness), physiological stress (indexed by heart rate and heart rate variability), and task performance. For comparison, another two kinds of micro-break activity (i.e., listening to music and watching a documentary clip) were introduced. The results revealed that watching short-form videos significantly improved participants' mood and task engagement willingness, relieved physiological stress, and maintained task performance. Among the three kinds of micro-break activity, watching short-form videos was found to be the most effective in relieving physiological stress. We also discussed the implications of the role of watching short-form videos in work-related wellbeing.

Keywords: Short-form video · Micro-break · Stress

1 Introduction

Short-form video applications, such as Snapchat, Vine, TikTok, and Snack Video, have skyrocketed in popularity globally in the last few years. Short-form video applications are a new entertaining media form that enable users to watch, comment on, create, and share entertaining videos that last from seconds to a few minutes in areas such as short-form comedy, food, dancing, and traveling. Compared with traditional videos on TV and computers, the lengths of these videos are usually measured by seconds. The most popular content is short-form comedies, and these videos are the most shared by short-form video users (Fang et al. 2019; Vandersmissen et al. 2014). The entertainment orientation and length of short-form videos satisfy the fragmented entertainment needs of the public, which makes it possible for users to view them in micro-breaks at work (Yang et al. 2019).

© Springer Nature Switzerland AG 2021
P.-L. P. Rau (Ed.): HCII 2021, LNCS 12772, pp. 183–200, 2021.
https://doi.org/10.1007/978-3-030-77077-8_15

Compared to off-the-job recovery activities (e.g., vacation), relatively few studies have paid attention to micro-breaks at work (Kim et al. 2017). Micro-breaks refer to short recovery activities on the job instead of recovery activities off the job (Kim et al. 2017; Trougakos and Hideg 2009). Micro-break activities take various forms, including relaxing activities such as walking around and daydreaming, nutrition-intake activities such as snacking, social activities such as chatting with coworkers, and cognitive activities such as watching videos and reading books (Kim et al. 2018). Given that individuals have engaged in more mental work and cognitive resources are limited and deplete under continuous use (Halbesleben et al. 2014), some researchers have argued that employees need micro-breaks at work to detach themselves from long and continuous work to replenish cognitive resources, improve their wellbeing, and sustain work performance (Bosch and Sonnentag 2019; Trougakos et al. 2008; Zacher et al. 2014).

The effects of micro-breaks on work performance and employees' wellbeing observed in previous research are controversial. On the one hand, according to the effort recovery model (Meijman et al. 1998) and conservation of resources theory (Hobfoll 1989), taking micro-breaks helps to recover the self-regulatory resources necessary to address work demands and diminish the cumulative negative effects of prolonged work. Indeed, some studies have found that taking micro-breaks fosters work engagement, improves productivity, and reduces physical pain, fatigue, and negative emotions (Abdelall et al. 2018; Hunter and Wu 2016; Kühnel et al. 2017; Zacher et al. 2014). On the other hand, Scholz et al. (2018) examined the effects of three kinds of micro-break (i.e., boxing, deep relaxation, and usual breaks) in a stressful working environment and found no significant difference in mood change and cognitive performance between these micro-breaks and no break. Some researchers have found that micro-breaks for nutrition intake have no significant effects, unlike some socialization and relaxation activities (Kim et al. 2017; S. Kim et al. 2018). These studies indicate that the effects of micro-breaks hinge on the activities people undertake. Studies have found that of the various micro-break activities, less effortful and more enjoyable ones provide better recovery effects (Hunter and Wu 2016; Trougakos et al. 2008). The broaden-and-build theory posits that positive events induce positive emotions that can improve performance with increased ability (Fredrickson 1998, 2001).

As a new entertaining media form, the effects of watching short-form videos in micro-breaks remain to be investigated. Entertainment media use, or personal internet use at work, has mostly been labelled with negative connotations (Richards 2012), such as cyberloafing (Andel et al. 2019) and internet abuse (Chen et al. 2008). Ferreira and Du Plessis (2009) have suggested that personal use of social media at work introduces a risk of distracting employees and decreasing work performance. Ali-Hassan et al. (2015) have also found that employees tend to have lower performance if they use social media for passing the time and entertainment at work. However, Ivarsson and Larsson (2011) have argued that personal internet use at work, including using entertainment media, is a natural response to stressful work. According to mood management theory (Zillmann and Bryant 1985), the use of entertainment media is driven by people's desire to minimize negative mood or maximize positive mood. Indeed, previous research has found that using media as recovery activities (i.e., off-the-job activities and micro-break activities) benefits psychological wellbeing. Reinecke found that employees experienced subjective recovery and job satisfaction from using video games at work and when off work (Reinecke 2009a, 2009b). Besides subjective wellbeing, some researchers have found objective recovery outcomes including improved cognitive performance, productivity, and creativity (Coker 2011; Reinecke et al. 2011; Rieger et al. 2014; Vitak et al. 2011).

Watching short-form videos in micro-breaks may produce different experiences than using other entertaining media, such as music, TV shows, and full-length feature films. First, short-form videos have to grab users' attention faster and immerse users in the content for most of or the total watching duration, because their lengths are measured in seconds. Previous psychological research has suggested that short-form videos whose content is attention-grabbing and elicits high-arousal emotions are more likely to be popular (Nelson-Field et al. 2013; Qiu et al. 2015). Second, individuals are frequently switching among videos with different content when watching short-form videos due to the short length. Thus, they are continuously receiving fresh stimuli and may produce high-arousal emotions. Thus, users' arousal level when watching short-form videos may be different from that when taking some commonly used relaxing activities such as listening to gentle music or walking around, which are often characterized by a low arousal level (McManus et al. 2018; Russell and Carroll 1999). Zillmann (1991) demonstrated that attention-grabbing media message provided relief from stress by intervening in negative cognitions and ruminations. Short-form videos eliciting high-arousal emotions and producing an attention-grabbing media environment may foster psychological detachment from work stress, but may also prevent individuals from focusing back on their work immediately after the micro-break.

Research focusing on the effect of watching short-form videos in micro-breaks is very limited because short-form video applications are just emerging in recent years. Bennett (2015) found that watching several minutes of a funny video increased self-reported attention and reduced self-reported fatigue among university students after finishing a ten-minute task. Furthermore, some researchers have compared the effects of watching different kinds of videos after work. Janicke et al. (2018) found that funny videos were better at eliciting psychological detachment, whereas meaningful videos were better at eliciting mastery recovery experiences. Janicke-Bowles et al. (2019) found that participants reported less stress after watching any kind of video (i.e., elevation inducing videos, gratitude inducing videos, funny videos, and a nonentertaining control video), but reported the highest level of energy after watching an elevating inducing video. Existing research on short-form videos has several limitations. First, no studies have compared the effects of watching short-form videos with those of using other entertaining media in micro-breaks. Second, the effect on work performance of watching short-form videos remains to be investigated. Third, little research has used physiological measures to objectively assess the effects on psychological wellbeing of watching short-form videos or using other entertaining media in micro-breaks.

In this study, we conducted a laboratory study to explore the effects of watching short-form videos as micro-breaks at work using subjective, physiological, and performance measures. Considering that comedies are the most popular category on short-form video platforms and eliciting high-arousal emotions is an important characteristic of popular short-form videos, we selected funny and high-arousal short-form videos as the most representative type as experiment materials. We also compared the effects of watching short-form videos and using two traditional entertainment media (i.e., listening to gentle music and watching a documentary clip). Given that repetitive or physical work has been greatly reduced in modern society, for ecological validity, we chose English proofreading requiring reading comprehension and deeper linguistic processing as experiment tasks.

The research questions of this study are as follows:

1. What is the effect of watching funny short-form videos on mood, task engagement willingness, physiological stress, and task performance?
2. What is the difference between watching funny short-form videos and using other entertaining media as micro-break activities in terms of effect on mood, task engagement willingness, and task performance?

2   Materials and Methods

2.1   Pretest: Selecting Short-Form Videos, Music, and a Documentary Clip

Besides watching short-form videos, we also selected listening to music and watching a documentary clip for comparison, considering that listening to music is a commonly used relaxation activity and documentaries are a traditional video format. Previous studies have suggested that activities inducing positive emotions can lead to a good recovery experience (Fredrickson 1998; 2001). Besides, short comedies and eliciting higher-arousal emotions are outstanding features of popular short-form videos distinguishing them from gentle music and documentary. Therefore, we planned to select funny short-form videos eliciting more positive and higher-arousal emotions as experiment material. For the theme of short-form videos, given that both men and women watched a lot of animal/pet videos (Kogan et al. 2018), we chose six short-form videos of funny moments featuring pandas from the TikTok account of Chengdu Research Base of Giant Panda Breeding for the formal experiment. For example, a short-form video recorded the moment that two pandas were climbing and chasing on a thin trunk. Then the trunk was broken because they were too heavy. The total length of these short-form videos was about three minutes. Gentle music has been proved to be relaxing (Baird and Sands 2004; Knight and Rickard 2001); therefore, for music material, we chose a three-minute piece of gentle music named "Peace Remembered". To avoid interference caused by theme differences, we selected a three-minute clip from a panda documentary for documentary material.

To validate that the material selected can induce positive emotions and the selected funny short-form videos elicit more positive and higher-arousal emotions, we surveyed the evoked emotions. These were measured by the valence and arousal subscale of self-assessment-Manikin (Hodes et al. 1985), which are two pictorial nine-point scales. We recruited twenty participants (11 males and 9 females) aged from 21 to 33 (M = 24.15, SD = 2.63). The material and questionnaire were sent to the participants by e-mail and they completed the questionnaire after listening to or watching each three minutes of material on their mobile phone or computer.

For the valence dimension, only after listening to the music, two participants reported negative emotions (less than five points). To examine the difference in the valence and arousal of emotions elicited by the three materials, we conducted Friedman tests and Wilcoxon signed-rank tests for post hoc tests. A significant difference was observed in both valence (χ^2 (2) = 23.79, p < .001) and arousal (χ^2 (2) = 24.11, p < .001) elicited by the three materials. The results of post hoc tests revealed that the valence and arousal level of emotions elicited by watching the short-form videos (valence: M = 8.20, SD = 1.15; arousal: M = 5.35, SD = 1.76) were higher than those elicited by watching the documentary clip (valence: M = 6.80, SD = 1.32; arousal: M = 3.15, SD = 1.60) and listening to the music (valence: M = 6.25, SD = 1.37; arousal: M = 2.25, SD = 1.25). We found no significant difference between listening to the music and watching the documentary clip at a 5% significance level. The results indicated that emotions evoked by the three materials were all positive in general and the short-form videos elicited more positive and higher-arousal emotions.

2.2 Participants and Tasks

To understand the effects of watching short-form videos in micro-breaks, we conducted a laboratory experiment. We recruited 30 Chinese students (16 males and 14 females). They were aged from 19 to 30 years (M = 23.10, SD = 2.12) with no hearing impairment and no neurological or mental disorders.

Given that people are engaged in lots of mental work nowadays, we selected proof-reading tasks to simulate working conditions. As a kind of cognitive task, proofreading tasks have been used to induce mental fatigue in previous studies (Laumann et al. 2003; Li and Sullivan 2016; Park et al. 2019; Raanaas et al. 2011). To increase the difficulty of proofreading tasks, we selected English documents rather than Chinese documents and set grammatical errors requiring reading comprehension and integration of information across multiple words, instead of spelling errors. Besides, we did not provide reference documents. Considering that the proofreading tasks in our study are more cognitively demanding, each proofreading task lasted for 10 min in our study instead of 15 min in some previous studies (Laumann et al. 2003; Park et al. 2019). In each proofreading task, participants were asked to proofread two English documents randomly chosen from eight English documents. Besides, another English document was prepared for practice. The nine English documents were excerpted from the Journal of Teaching Language Skills. Each document included about 1100 words and sixteen grammatical errors. Both formal and practice tasks were conducted using Microsoft Word 2010 on the computer provided by the experimenter.

2.3 Measures

Subjective Experience. Three kinds of subjective experience were measured in this study: mood, task engagement willingness, and willingness to relax. The mood of participants was measured by the 24-item Profile of Mood States (POMS) developed by Terry et al. (1999). The POMS is a five-point adjective rating scale on six mood dimensions: anger, confusion, depression, fatigue, tension, and vigor. Each dimension of mood is calculated by totalling the scores of the four items in that dimension, and a total mood disturbance score is calculated by totalling the scores of the six mood dimensions, with vigor items scored negatively.

Participants' task engagement willingness before and after each micro-break was measured by the pre-task version of the task engagement subscale of the 30-item Dundee Stress State Questionnaire (Matthews et al. 2013).

Previous studies have suggested that if breaks are not taken voluntarily, they can be experienced as work interruptions and cause distractions, backlogs, and frustrations (Jett and George 2003; Kim et al. 2017). We measured participants' willingness to relax using a five-point Likert item ("I want to have a rest for a few minutes") when they finished each task. We used this scale not as a survey instrument for statistical analysis, but solely as a manipulation check to ensure that the micro-breaks were not experienced as interruptions by participants.

Physiological Stress. A majority of research has found that higher heart rate (HR) and lower HR variability (HRV) indicate higher mental stress (Chandola et al. 2010; Dijkstra et al. 2009; Taelman et al. 2009). More and more research has suggested that HRV can be extracted from photoplethysmogram (PPG) signals as well as the traditionally used electrocardiogram (ECG) signals (Lu et al. 2008; Peng et al. 2015). In this study, we used the root mean square of successive differences (RMSSD) of adjacent peak to peak intervals to index HRV. Previous studies have found that decreased RMSSD effectively indicating higher mental stress (Grantcharov et al. 2019; Orsila et al. 2008). Both HR and HRV were extracted from PPG. The signals were recorded at 2000 Hz with the Biopac MP150 data acquisition system. We resampled the raw signals to 250 Hz and applied a 0.87–2 Hz band-pass filter using AcqKnowledge 4.4.

Task Performance. The number of accurate corrections in each task was counted.

2.4 Procedure

After arriving at the laboratory, participants received instructions for the experiment task. They were told that they were participating in an English test and their rewards were positively related to the number of accurate corrections of grammatical errors. As shown in Fig. 1, before formal tasks, participants undertook a five-minute practice of English document proofreading. Once they had completed each ten-minute formal task, they filled the POMS questionnaire and engagement willingness questionnaire. The willingness to relax was also measured. Then they experienced a three-minute micro-break in which they watched short-form videos, listened to music, or watched a documentary clip using their mobile phone. The duration of each micro-break was determined based on the following reasons. (1) Micro-breaks are short, often lasting for a few seconds to a few minutes (Cheng 2019). (2) A three-minute break produces recovery effects as well as a 10-min break (Tyler and Burns 2008). (3). A three-minute break was preferred over 30-s breaks from computer work (Henning et al. 1997). (4) The duration of each formal task (i.e., ten minutes) is not long in our study. Therefore, we set a three-minute micro-break between tasks consistent with previous studies (Ito and Takahashi 2020; Mouw, 2015; Nakphet et al. 2014). To balance the influence of the experimental sequence, the sequence of the three micro-break activities was balanced. After each micro-break, the participants filled the POMS questionnaire and task engagement willingness questionnaire (pre-task version). We recorded the PPG signals when the participants were performing the proofreading tasks and taking micro-breaks.

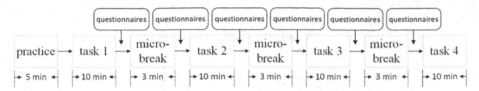

Fig. 1. The experiment procedure.

3 Results

3.1 Subjective Experience

Mood. To compare the mood of participants before and after taking a micro-break, we conducted Wilcoxon signed-rank tests for POMS items. We excluded one participant from the mood change analysis after watching the documentary clip because he forgot to finish the POMS questionnaire. The Wilcoxon signed-rank tests (see Table 1) for POMS items showed significant differences before and after listening to the music in total mood disturbance score and six mood dimensions. However, before and after watching the documentary clip, no significant difference was observed in vigor. Furthermore, the test results showed no significant difference in fatigue and vigor before and after watching the short-form videos.

To compare the mood of participants before and after taking a micro-break, we conducted Wilcoxon signed-rank tests for POMS items. We excluded one participant from the mood change analysis after watching the documentary clip because he forgot to finish the POMS questionnaire. The Wilcoxon signed-rank tests (see Table 1) for POMS items showed significant differences before and after listening to the music in total mood disturbance score and six mood dimensions. However, before and after watching the documentary clip, no significant difference was observed in vigor. Furthermore, the test results showed no significant difference in fatigue and vigor before and after watching the short-form videos.

Task Engagement Willingness. To examine whether there was a significant change in participants' task engagement willingness after taking a micro-break, we conducted Wilcoxon signed-rank tests. The test results showed that task engagement willingness after listening to the music (M = 19.30, SD = 5.84) and watching the short-form videos (M = 18.87, SD = 5.23) was significantly higher than that before listening to the music (M = 16.73, SD = 5.66, P < .001) and watching the short-form videos (M = 17.07, SD = 6.55, P = .003). No significant difference was observed in task engagement willingness before (M = 18.60, SD = 5.85) and after watching the documentary clip (M = 18.97, SD = 5.77, P = .406).

To compare the task engagement willingness of participants before taking different kinds of micro-break, we carried out Friedman tests. A marginally significant difference was found in the task engagement willingness of participants before taking different kinds of micro-break (χ^2 (2) = 5.73, p = .057). Participants had the highest task engagement willingness before watching the documentary clip. We also compared participants'

Table 1. Mean values, standard deviations, and results of statistical tests for HR and HRV.

	Watch the short-form videos			Listen to the music			Watch the documentary clip		
	Pre-break	Post-break	p	Pre-break	Post-break	p	Pre-break	Post-break	p
Anger	1.93 (2.84)	0.80(1.70)	.002*	1.57(2.53)	0.47(1.15)	.004*	1.97(2.87)	0.55(1.35)	.001*
Confusion	6.20 (4.53)	3.37(2.77)	<.001**	5.70(3.68)	2.83(2.38)	<.001**	5.97(4.31)	3.03(2.72)	<.001**
Depression	4.57 (4.36)	1.43(2.04)	<.001**	4.26(3.48)	1.73(2.28)	<.001**	4.03(3.94)	1.55(2.43)	<.001**
Fatigue	5.43 (3.77)	4.43(3.31)	.050	6.17(4.03)	4.40(3.49)	<.001**	5.23(2.65)	3.97 (2.66)	.007*
Tension	4.33 (4.31)	2.13(2.14)	<.001**	3.87(3.15)	1.87(1.98)	<.001**	3.77(4.05)	2.00(2.24)	.005*
Vigor	5.63 (3.52)	5.93(3.21)	.201	5.20(3.39)	5.97(3.34)	.026*	6.43(3.53)	6.20(3.12)	.719
Total	16.83(17.52)	6.23(9.93)	<.001**	16.37(13.76)	5.33(9.85)	<.001**	14.53(16.85)	4.73(10.05)	<.001**

** p < .001; *p < .05

task engagement willingness after taking different kinds of micro-break and found no significant difference (χ^2 (2) = 0.72, p = .697).

Willingness to Relax. We excluded one participant from the descriptive statistical analysis of willingness to relax after watching the documentary clip, because he for-got to finish the questionnaire after watching the documentary clip. The average score of the participants' willingness to relax before listening to the music (M = 3.17, SD = 1.27), watching the documentary clip (M = 3.00, SD = 1.03), or watching the short-form videos (M = 3.43, SD = 1.15) were all no less than three on a five-point scale. This indicates that the participants did not resist taking a micro-break on the whole.

3.2 Physiological Stress

Table 2 presents the means and standard deviations of HR (measured as beats per minute) and HRV (indexed by RMSSD) of participants during each kind of micro-break and the task before it. To compare the HR and HRV of participants before and after taking a micro-break, we conducted paired t-tests. As shown in Fig. 2 and Fig. 3, the results showed a significant decline in HR and a significant increase in HRV after each kind of micro-break at a 5% significance level.

Table 2. Mean values, standard deviations, and results of statistical tests for HR and HRV.

	HR (beats/minute)		HRV (ms)	
	Task	Micro-break	Task	Micro-break
Listen to the music	75.25 (11.99)	72.54 (12.80)	36.15 (14.58)	40.73 (14.)
Watch the documentary clip	74.28 (11.30)	70.30 (11.96)	37.51 (15.70)	45.04 (16.36)
Watch the short-form videos	74.69 (12.48)	69.84 (11.80)	34.19 (14.29)	45.10 (16.62)

To compare the HR and HRV of participants in task phases, we conducted repeated measures ANOVAs. As shown in Fig. 2 and Fig. 3, the results revealed no significant difference in both HR (F (2, 58) = 1.60, p = .212) and HRV (F (2, 58) = 2.59, p = .084).

To compare the HR and HRV of participants during taking different kinds of micro-breaks, we conducted repeated measures ANOVAs. For HR data, Mauchly's test indicated that the assumption of sphericity was violated (W = 0.706, p = .008). Therefore, Greenhouse-Geisser corrected tests were reported. As shown in Fig. 2, the results revealed a significant difference in participants' HR after taking the three kinds of micro-breaks (F (2, 58) = 5.67, p = .010). Bonferroni post hoc tests showed that participants' HR after watching the short-form videos (M = 69.84, SD = 11.80) was significantly lower than that after listening to the music (M = 72.54, SD = 12.80, p = .008). There was no significant difference between the participants' HR after watching the documentary

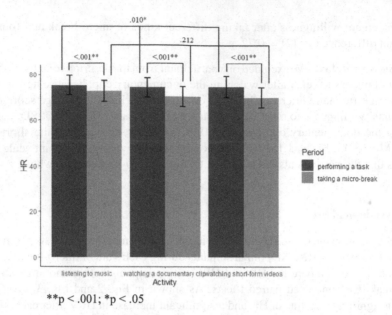

**p < .001; *p < .05

Fig. 2. Means, 95% confidence interval (error bars), and P values of the statistical tests on HR data.

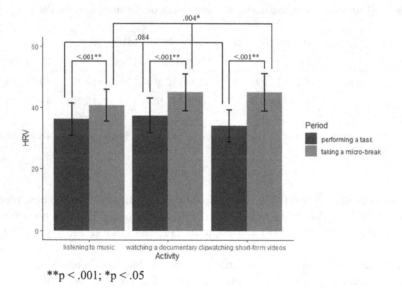

**p < .001; *p < .05

Fig. 3. Means, 95% confidence interval (error bars), and P values of the statistical tests on HRV data.

clip (M = 70.30, SD = 11.96) and taking the other two kinds of micro-breaks at a 5% significance level. For the ANOVA on HRV, as shown in Fig. 3, the effect of micro-break types was significant (F (2, 58) = 7.85, p = .004). Bonferroni post hoc tests revealed that participants' HRV after watching the short-form videos (M = 45.10, SD = 16.62) and watching the documentary clip (M = 45.04, SD = 16.36) was significantly greater than that after listening to the music (M = 40.73, SD = 14.33) at a 5% significance level.

3.3 Task Performance

Table 3 shows the means and standard deviations of accurate corrections in the four proofreading tasks. We conducted a Friedman test to compare the number of accurate corrections in the four proofreading tasks. The results showed no significant difference among the four tasks (F (3, 116) = 0.43, p = .730).

Table 3. Mean values, standard deviations, and results of statistical tests for HR and HRV.

	M	SD
Task 1	4.26	2.00
Task after listening to the music	4.63	1.94
Task after watching the documentary clip	4.73	2.26
Task after watching the documentary clip	4.53	2.87

4 Discussion

4.1 Effects of Watching Short-Form Videos and Using Other Media

We found that all three kinds of micro-break could improve participants' self-reported mood. Before watching short-form videos and watching a documentary clip, participants' self-reported vigor was already at a relatively high level, similar to that after listening to music. Therefore, participants reported significantly greater vigor only after listening to music. In the other five mood dimensions and the total mood disturbance measured by POMS, all three kinds of micro-break caused significant improvement. Furthermore, participants reported moods of no significant difference in six mood dimensions and the total mood disturbance after taking different kinds of micro-break. This indicates that taking different kinds of micro-break at work had similar effects in improving self-reported mood.

In terms of task engagement willingness, participants reported significantly higher task engagement willingness only after watching short-form videos and listening to music. We found that participants' task engagement willingness was at a relatively high level before watching a documentary clip. This could be why the increase in task engagement willingness after watching a documentary was not significant. Besides, participants showed no significant difference in task engagement willingness after taking different kinds of micro-break. This indicates that all three kinds of micro-break activity can improve or maintain participants' task engagement willingness at a relatively high level.

Participants showed significant differences in HR and HRV after they took different kinds of micro-breaks. The results suggested that watching funny short-form videos led to lower HR and higher HRV than listening to music. Although neither participants' HR nor HRV was significantly different after watching funny short-form videos and watching a documentary clip, watching a documentary clip did not show a better effect in decreasing HR than listening to music. Therefore, watching funny short-form videos seemed to be the most effective among the three kinds of micro-break in relieving physiological stress. This is different from the results of subjective measures, in which participants reported no significant difference in tension after taking different kinds of micro-break. Previous research indicates that people are not always conscious of emotions, feelings, and moods that demonstrably occur (Berridge and Winkielman 2003). In this case, it is difficult to use subjective measures to recognize unconscious states because they rely on participants' self-report, whereas physiological measures capturing physiological responses are still effective. Our results also indicated that physiological measures were more sensitive than subjective measures in terms of identifying variation in work-related stress.

There was no significant difference in performance among the four proofreading tasks. This indicates that participants maintained their task performance after taking any kind of micro-break. This is different from the conclusion in the study of Ali-Hassan et al. (2015), that hedonic use of social media, including watching entertainment videos, harmed routine job performance. In their study, the hedonic use of social media was recorded rather than being controlled. Employees have less time to perform their work tasks when they spend more time on the hedonic use of social media (Teigland and Wasko 2009). In this study, watching short-form videos occurred in micro-breaks and we controlled the length of watching social short-form videos. Therefore, time-wasting caused by the hedonic use of social media did not exist in our study. This suggests that the duration of media use plays an important role in how media use affects job performance.

4.2 Implications and Design Insights

Our study sheds some light on how to choose micro-break activities. Sandstrom and Russo (2010) found that low-arousal music was more effective than high-arousal music in recovery from stress. Their results indicated that stimuli eliciting lower-arousal emotions generate a better recovery experience. However, we found that funny short-form videos eliciting higher-arousal emotions were more effective in reducing physiological stress. Reinecke (2009a) argued that increased arousal level and recovery experience were not contradictory. Recovery effects for arousing activities including doing sports and playing computer games have been observed in previous research (Byrne and Byrne 1993; Childs and de Wit 2014; Reinecke and Trepte 2008). Previous studies consistently reveal that doing sports is effective in relieving stress (Byrne and Byrne 1993; Childs and de Wit 2014; Currie 2004). Reinecke and Trepte (2008) found that participants' who played a computer game after a text correction task performed better in a subsequent concentration test. Therefore, activities eliciting low-arousal emotions, such as listening to gentle music and closing one's eyes for a rest, are not the only option for a micro-break. Proper use of entertainment media such as short-form videos that elicit high-arousal activities can detach employees from work stress and improve their cognitive performance.

Our results also suggest that media content eliciting positive emotions generates a recovery experience. The short-form videos, music, and documentary clip used in this study were found to elicit positive emotions in the pretest. Tsutsumi et al. (2017) also found that watching a preferred sea or forest video improved mood. Videos that fail to elicit positive emotions may also fail to generate a recovery experience. Steinberg et al. (1997) found that watching a monotonous documentary about rock formations in the English Lake District decreased positive mood in participants. These provide evidence for the broaden-and-build theory (Fredrickson 1998; 2001). Therefore, if users watch videos in micro-breaks during work or study, they should choose videos that elicit positive emotions to generate a better recovery experience.

The positive effects on moods, task engagement willingness, and physiological stress of short-form videos were observed when controlling the length of watching. Short-form video addiction is a potential problem affecting its ability to play a positive role in daily work. About 22 percent of TikTok (a short-form video application) users use it for more than one hour a day (Penguin Intelligence 2018). Previous studies suggest that excessive use of short-form video applications may lead to negative consequences such as distraction and poor time management (Hong et al. 2014). Besides, users may experience guilt if they immerse themselves in the entertainment media without self-control, which in turn reduces psychological wellbeing (Reinecke et al. 2014). If the use of short-form video applications is at the expense of users' job goals and responsibilities, the positive effects observed in this study may disappear. We recommend that people should control the time spent watching short-form videos or using other entertainment media at work by setting an alarm clock or with the help of a time management application, especially for people with low self-control.

Furthermore, designers of short-form video applications can improve the design to better meet users' need to watch short-form videos in micro-breaks. They can develop a 'work' mode and advise users to use this mode in micro-breaks at work. In this mode, funny and relaxing short-form videos are recommended to users to elicit positive emotions. This benefits users' psychological wellbeing and helps to maintain work performance. Also, in the work mode, the duration of use is controlled or promoted by the application. This prevents users from wasting a lot of time watching videos and experiencing a feeling of guilt.

4.3 Limitations and Further Study

This study has several limitations. Firstly, although the experimental materials were found to elicit positive emotions in the pilot study, they were selected by the experimenter rather than the participants, which is different from how people choose what to watch or listen to in micro-breaks in most real-life situations. Secondly, the scope of selected short-form videos is limited to the funny animal theme. Thirdly, watching short-form videos is only one kind of behavior in the use of short-form video applications. To acquire more insights into the effect of using short-form video applications in micro-breaks, other user behaviors such as searching, sharing, and commenting need to be studied in future research.

5 Conclusions

This study conducted a laboratory study to examine the effects of watching funny short-form videos in micro-breaks at work compared with listening to music and watching a documentary. All kinds of micro-break activities were found to improve participants' self-reported mood and task engagement willingness, reduce their physiological stress, and maintain task performance, but watching funny short-form videos was the most effective in reducing physiological stress. Our findings suggest that watching funny short-form videos is a good micro-break activity at work when done in moderation, which provides guidance for employees and students to choose proper micro-break activities to improve their psychological wellbeing and maintain work performance.

References

Abdelall, E.S., Lowndes, B.R., Abdelrahman, A.M., Hawthorne, H.J., Hallbeck, M.S.: Mini breaks, many benefits: Development and pilot testing of an intraoperative microbreak stretch web-application for surgeons. In: Proceedings of the Human Factors and Ergonomics Society Annual Meeting, vol. 62, No. 1, pp. 1042–1046. SAGE Publications, Sage CA, September 2018. https://doi.org/10.1177/1541931218621240.

Ali-Hassan, H., Nevo, D., Wade, M.: Linking dimensions of social media use to job performance: the role of social capital. J. Strat. Inf. Syst. 24(2), 65–89 (2015). https://doi.org/10.1016/j.jsis.2015.03.001

Andel, S.A., Kessler, S.R., Pindek, S., Kleinman, G., Spector, P.E.: Is cyberloafing more complex than we originally thought? cyberloafing as a coping response to workplace aggression exposure. Comput. Hum. Behav. 101, 124–130 (2019). https://doi.org/10.1016/j.chb.2019.07.013

Baird, C.L., Sands, L.: A pilot study of the effectiveness of guided imagery with progressive muscle relaxation to reduce chronic pain and mobility difficulties of osteoarthritis. Pain Manage. Nursing 5(3), 97–104 (2004). https://doi.org/10.1016/j.pmn.2004.01.003

Bennett, A.: Take five? Examining the impact of microbreak duration, activities, and appraisals on human energy and performance. Ph.D. thesis, Department of Business, Virginia Commonwealth University (2015)

Berridge, K., Winkielman, P.: What is an unconscious emotion? (The case for unconscious "liking"). Cognition Emotion 17(2), 181–211 (2003). https://doi.org/10.1080/02699930302289

Bosch, C., Sonnentag, S.: Should I take a break? a daily reconstruction study on predicting microbreaks at work. Int. J. Stress Manage. 26(4), 378 (2019). https://doi.org/10.1037/str0000117

Byrne, A., Byrne, D.G.: The effect of exercise on depression, anxiety and other mood states: a review. J. Psychosomatic Res. 37(6), 565–574 (1993). https://doi.org/10.1016/0022-3999(93)90050-P

Chandola, T., Heraclides, A., Kumari, M.: Psychophysiological biomarkers of workplace stressors. Neurosci. Biobehav. Rev. 35(1), 51–57 (2010). https://doi.org/10.1016/j.neubiorev.2009.11.005

Chen, J.V., Chen, C.C., Yang, H.H.: An empirical evaluation of key factors contributing to internet abuse in the workplace. Ind. Manage. Data Syst. 1, 87–106 (2008). https://doi.org/10.1108/02635570810844106

Cheng, Y.S.: Are social media bad for your employees? Effects of at-work break activities on recovery experiences, job satisfaction, and life satisfaction. Ph.D. Thesis, Department of Hospitality Management, University of Missouri-Columbia (2019)

Childs, E., de Wit, H.: Regular exercise is associated with emotional resilience to acute stress in healthy adults. Front. Physiol. 5, 161 (2014). https://doi.org/10.3389/fphys.2014.00161

Coker, B.L.: Freedom to surf: the positive effects of workplace Internet leisure browsing. New Technol. Work Employ. **26**(3), 238–247 (2011). https://doi.org/10.1111/j.1468-005X.2011.002 72.x

Currie, J.: Motherhood, stress and the exercise experience: freedom or constraint? Leisure Stud. **23**(3), 225–242 (2004). https://doi.org/10.1080/0261436042000251987

Dijkstra, K., Charness, N., Yordon, R., Fox, M.: Changes in physiological stress and self-reported mood in younger and older adults after exposure to a stressful task. Aging, Neuropsychol. Cogn. **16**(3), 338–356 (2009). https://doi.org/10.1080/13825580902773859

Fang, J., Wang, Z., Hao, B.: Analysis of "Anesthesia" Mechanism in Mobile Short Video Applications. In: The First International Symposium on Management and Social Sciences (ISMSS 2019). Atlantis Press, April 2019. https://doi.org/https://doi.org/10.2991/ismss-19.2019.75.

Ferreira, A., Du Plessis, T.: Effect of online social networking on employee productivity. South African J. Inf. Manag. **11**(1), 1–11 (2009). https://doi.org/10.4102/sajim.v11i1.397

Fredrickson, B.L.: What good are positive emotions? Rev. General Psychol. **2**(3), 300–319 (1998). https://doi.org/10.1037/1089-2680.2.3.300

Fredrickson, B.L.: The role of positive emotions in positive psychology: The broaden-and-build theory of positive emotions. Am. Psychol. **56**(3), 218 (2001). https://doi.org/10.1037/0003-066X.56.3.218

Grantcharov, P.D., Boillat, T., Elkabany, S., Wac, K., Rivas, H.: Acute mental stress and surgical performance. BJS Open **3**(1), 119–125 (2019). https://doi.org/10.1002/bjs5.104

Halbesleben, J.R., Neveu, J.P., Paustian-Underdahl, S.C., Westman, M.: Getting to the "COR" understanding the role of resources in conservation of resources theory. J. Manage. **40**(5), 1334–1364 (2014). https://doi.org/10.1177/0149206314527130

Henning, R.A., Jacques, P., Kissel, G.V., Sullivan, A.B., Alteras-Webb, S.M.: Frequent short rest breaks from computer work: effects on productivity and well-being at two field sites. Ergonomics **40**(1), 78–91 (1997). https://doi.org/10.1080/001401397188396

Hobfoll, S.E.: Conservation of resources: a new attempt at conceptualizing stress. Am. Psychol. **44**(3), 513 (1989). https://doi.org/10.1037/0003-066X.44.3.513

Hodes, R.L., Cook, E.W., III., Lang, P.J.: Individual differences in autonomic response: conditioned association or conditioned fear? Psychophysiology **22**(5), 545–560 (1985). https://doi.org/10.1111/j.1469-8986.1985.tb01649.x

Hong, F.Y., Huang, D.H., Lin, H.Y., Chiu, S.L.: Analysis of the psychological traits, Facebook usage, and Facebook addiction model of Taiwanese university students. Telemat. Inform. **31**(4), 597–606 (2014). https://doi.org/10.1016/j.tele.2014.01.001

Hunter, E.M., Wu, C.: Give me a better break: choosing workday break activities to maximize resource recovery. J. Appl. Psychol. **101**(2), 302 (2016). https://doi.org/10.1037/apl0000045

Ito, T., Takahashi, K.: Effects of various behaviours in the break times between learning. Information **11**(9), 407 (2020). https://doi.org/10.3390/info11090407

Ivarsson, L., Larsson, P.: Personal Internet usage at work: a source of recovery. J. Workplace Rights **16**(1) (2011). https://doi.org/https://doi.org/10.2190/WR.16.1.e.

Janicke, S.H., Rieger, D., Reinecke, L., Connor, W.: Watching online videos at work: the role of positive and meaningful affect for recovery experiences and well-being at the workplace. Mass Commun. Soc. **21**(3), 345–367 (2018). https://doi.org/10.1080/15205436.2017.1381264

Janicke-Bowles, S., Rieger, D., Connor, W.: Finding meaning at work: the role of inspiring and funny YouTube videos on work-related well-being. J. Happiness Stud. **20**(2), 619–640 (2018). https://doi.org/10.1007/s10902-018-9959-1

Jett, Q.R., George, J.M.: Work interrupted: a closer look at the role of interruptions in organizational life. Acad. Manage. Rev. **28**(3), 494–507 (2003). https://doi.org/10.5465/amr.2003.10196791

Kim, S., Park, Y., Headrick, L.: Daily micro-breaks and job performance: general work engagement as a cross-level moderator. J. Appl. Psychol. **103**(7), 772 (2018). https://doi.org/10.1037/apl0000308

Kim, S., Park, Y., Niu, Q.: Micro-break activities at work to recover from daily work demands. J. Organ. Behav. **38**(1), 28–44 (2017). https://doi.org/10.1002/job.2109

Knight, W.E., Rickard, N.S.: Relaxing music prevents stress-induced increases in subjective anxiety, systolic blood pressure, and heart rate in healthy males and females. J. Music Therapy **38**(4), 254–272 (2001). https://doi.org/10.1093/jmt/38.4.254

Kogan, L.R., Hellyer, P.W., Clapp, T.R., Suchman, E., McLean, J., Schoenfeld-Tacher, R.: Use of short animal-themed videos to enhance veterinary students' mood, attention, and understanding of pharmacology lectures. J. Vet. Med. Educ. **45**(2), 188–194 (2018). https://doi.org/10.3138/jvme.1016-162r

Kühnel, J., Zacher, H., De Bloom, J., Bledow, R.: Take a break! Benefits of sleep and short breaks for daily work engagement. Eur. J. Work Organ. Psychol. **26**(4), 481–491 (2017). https://doi.org/10.1080/1359432X.2016.1269750

Laumann, K., Gärling, T., Stormark, K.M.: Selective attention and heart rate responses to natural and urban environments. J. Environ. Psychol. **23**(2), 125–134 (2003). https://doi.org/10.1016/S0272-4944(02)00110-X

Li, D., Sullivan, W.C.: Impact of views to school landscapes on recovery from stress and mental fatigue. Landscape Urban Plann. **148**, 149–158 (2016). https://doi.org/10.1016/j.landurbplan.2015.12.015

Lu, S., et al.: Can photoplethysmography variability serve as an alternative approach to obtain heart rate variability information? J. Clin. Monit. Comput. **22**(1), 23–29 (2008). https://doi.org/10.1007/s10877-007-9103-y

Matthews, G., Szalma, J., Panganiban, A.R., Neubauer, C., Warm, J.S.: Profiling task stress with the dundee stress state questionnaire. Psychol. Stress: New Res. **1**, 49–91 (2013)

McManus, M., Siegel, J., Nakamura, J.: The predictive power of low-arousal positive affect. Motivation and Emotion **43**(1), 130–144 (2018). https://doi.org/10.1007/s11031-018-9719-x

Meijman, T.F., Mulder, G., Drenth, P., Thierry, H.: Psychological aspects of workload. In: Drenth, P.J.D., Thierry, H. (eds.) Handbook of Work and Organizational Psychology, vol. 2: Work psychology, pp. 5–33. Psychology Press, Hove (1998)

Mouw, L.: Physical activity and time-on-task. Master of Education Program Theses, Dordt College (2015). https://digitalcollections.dord.edu/med_theses/84

Nakphet, N., Chaikumarn, M., Janwantanakul, P.: Effect of different types of rest-break interventions on neck and shoulder muscle activity, perceived discomfort and productivity in symptomatic VDU operators: a randomized controlled trial. Int. J. Occup. Saf. Ergon. **20**(2), 339–353 (2014). https://doi.org/10.1080/10803548.2014.11077048

Nelson-Field, K., Riebe, E., Newstead, K.: The emotions that drive viral video. Australasian Mark. J. (AMJ) **21**(4), 205–211 (2013). https://doi.org/10.1016/j.ausmj.2013.07.003

Orsila, R., et al.: Perceived mental stress and reactions in heart rate variability—a pilot study among employees of an electronics company. Int. J. Occup. Saf. Ergon. **14**(3), 275–283 (2008). https://doi.org/10.1080/10803548.2008.11076767

Park, S., et al.: Effects of display curvature and task duration on proofreading performance, visual discomfort, visual fatigue, mental workload, and user satisfaction. Appl. Ergon. **78**, 26–36 (2019). https://doi.org/10.1016/j.apergo.2019.01.014

Peng, R.C., Zhou, X.L., Lin, W.H., Zhang, Y.T.: Extraction of heart rate variability from smartphone photoplethysmograms. Computational and mathematical methods in medicine, 1–11 (2015). https://doi.org/10.1155/2015/516826

Penguin Intelligence, 2018. Exploring the bonus of billions of new users: Douyin and Kuaishou user research report. https://tech.qq.com/a/20180409/002763.htm. Accessed 23 Nov 2020

Qiu, L., Tang, Q., Whinston, A.B.: Two formulas for success in social media: Learning and network effects. J. Manage. Inform. Syst. **32**(4), 78–108 (2015). https://doi.org/10.1080/07421222.2015.1138368

Raanaas, R.K., Evensen, K.H., Rich, D., Sjøstrøm, G., Patil, G.: Benefits of indoor plants on attention capacity in an office setting. J. Environ. Psychol. **31**(1), 99–105 (2011). https://doi.org/10.1016/j.jenvp.2010.11.005

Reinecke, L.: Games and recovery: the use of video and computer games to recuperate from stress and strain. J. Media Psychol. **21**(3), 126–142 (2009). https://doi.org/10.1027/1864-1105.21.3.126

Reinecke, L.: Games at work: The recreational use of computer games during working hours. CyberPsychol. Behav. **12**(4), 461–465 (2009). https://doi.org/10.1089/cpb.2009.0010

Reinecke, L., Hartmann, T., Eden, A.: The guilty couch potato: the role of ego depletion in reducing recovery through media use. J. Commun. **64**(4), 569–589 (2014). https://doi.org/10.1111/jcom.12107

Reinecke, L., Klatt, J., Krämer, N.C.: Entertaining media use and the satisfaction of recovery needs: recovery outcomes associated with the use of interactive and noninteractive entertaining media. Media Psychol. **14**(2), 192–215 (2011). https://doi.org/10.1080/15213269.2011.573466

Reinecke, L., Trepte, S.: In a working mood? the effects of mood management processes on subsequent cognitive performance. J. Media Psychol. **20**(1), 3–14 (2008). https://doi.org/10.1027/1864-1105.20.1.3

Richards, J.: What has the internet ever done for employees? A review, map and research agenda. Employee Relations **34**(1), 22–43 (2012). https://doi.org/10.1108/01425451211183246

Rieger, D., Reinecke, L., Frischlich, L., Bente, G.: Media entertainment and well-being—Linking hedonic and eudaimonic entertainment experience to media-induced recovery and vitality. J. Commun. **64**(3), 456–478 (2014). https://doi.org/10.1111/jcom.12097

Russell, J.A., Carroll, J.M.: On the bipolarity of positive and negative affect. Psychol. Bull. **125**(1), 3–30 (1999). https://doi.org/10.1037/0033-2909.125.1.3

Sandstrom, G.M., Russo, F.A.: Music hath charms: the effects of valence and arousal on recovery following an acute stressor. Music Med. **2**(3), 137–143 (2010). https://doi.org/10.1177/1943862110371486

Scholz, A., Ghadiri, A., Singh, U., Wendsche, J., Peters, T., Schneider, S.: Functional work breaks in a high-demanding work environment: an experimental field study. Ergonomics **61**(2), 255–264 (2018). https://doi.org/10.1080/00140139.2017.1349938

Steinberg, H., Sykes, E.A., Moss, T., Lowery, S., LeBoutillier, N., Dewey, A.: Exercise enhances creativity independently of mood. British J. Sports Med. **31**(3), 240–245 (1997). https://doi.org/10.1136/bjsm.31.3.240

Taelman, J., Vandeput, S., Spaepen, A., Van Huffel, S.: Influence of mental stress on heart rate and heart rate variability. In 4th European conference of the international federation for medical and biological engineering, pp. 1366–1369. Springer, Berlin, Heidelberg (2009). https://doi.org/https://doi.org/10.1007/978-3-540-89208-3_324.

Teigland, R., Wasko, M.: Knowledge transfer in MNCs: examining how intrinsic motivations and knowledge sourcing impact individual centrality and performance. J. Int. Manage. **15**(1), 15–31 (2009). https://doi.org/10.1016/j.intman.2008.02.001

Terry, P.C., Lane, A.M., Lane, H.J., Keohane, L.: Development and validation of a mood measure for adolescents. J. Sports Sci. **17**(11), 861–872 (1999). https://doi.org/10.1080/026404199365425

Trougakos, J.P., Beal, D.J., Green, S.G., Weiss, H.M.: Making the break count: an episodic examination of recovery activities, emotional experiences, and positive affective displays. Acad. Manage. J. **51**(1), 131–146 (2008). https://doi.org/10.5465/amj.2008.30764063

Trougakos, J.P., Hideg, I.: Momentary work recovery: The role of within-day work breaks. In Research in Occupational Stress and Well-being, Sabine Sonnentag, Pamela L. Perrewé and Daniel C. Ganster (eds.) Emerald Group Publishing Limited, pp. 37–84 (2009). https://doi.org/10.1108/S1479-3555(2009)0000007005.

Tsutsumi, M., Nogaki, H., Shimizu, Y., Stone, T.E., Kobayashi, T.: Individual reactions to viewing preferred video representations of the natural environment: a comparison of mental and physical reactions. Japan J. Nursing Sci. **14**(1), 3–12 (2017). https://doi.org/10.1111/jjns.12131

Tyler, J.M., Burns, K.C.: After depletion: the replenishment of the self's regulatory resources. Self Identity **7**(3), 305–321 (2008). https://doi.org/10.1080/15298860701799997

Vandersmissen, B., Godin, F., Tomar, A., De Neve, W., Van de Walle, R.: The rise of mobile and social short-form video: an in-depth measurement study of vine. In: Workshop on Social Multimedia and Storytelling, vol. 1198, pp. 1–10 (2014)

Vitak, J., Crouse, J., LaRose, R.: Personal Internet use at work: understanding cyberslacking. Comput. Hum. Behav. **27**(5), 1751–1759 (2011). https://doi.org/10.1016/j.chb.2011.03.002

Yang, S., Zhao, Y., Ma, Y.: Analysis of the reasons and development of short video application— taking Tik Tok as an example. In: Proceedings of the 2019 9th International Conference on Information and Social Science (ICISS 2019), Manila, Philippines, pp. 12–14, July 2019. https://doi.org/10.25236/iciss.2019.062

Zacher, H., Brailsford, H.A., Parker, S.L.: Micro-breaks matter: a diary study on the effects of energy management strategies on occupational well-being. J. Vocat. Behav. **85**(3), 287–297 (2014). https://doi.org/10.1016/j.jvb.2014.08.005

Zillmann, D., Bryant, J.: Affect, mood, and emotion as determinants of selective exposure. In: Zillmann, D., Bryant, J. (eds.) Selective exposure to communication, pp. 157–190. Lawrence Erlbaum Associates, Hillsdale, NJ (1985)

ISDT Case Study of Loving Kindness Meditation for Flight Attendants

Chao Liu[1]([⊠]), Hao Chen[1]([⊠]), Yu-Chao Liang[2]([⊠]), Rungtai Lin[3]([⊠]),
and Wen-Ko Chiou[2]([⊠])

[1] Graduate Institute of Business and Management, Chang Gung University,
Taoyuan City, Taiwan
[2] Department of Industrial Design, Chang Gung University, Taoyuan City, Taiwan
wkchiu@mail.cgu.edu.tw
[3] Graduate School of Creative Industry Design, National Taiwan University of Arts,
New Taipei City, Taiwan
rtlin@mail.ntua.edu.tw

Abstract. Objective: Following the concept of I-Sustainability Design Thinking (ISDT), we will design and develop an APP with the theme of loving kindness meditation to help cultivate and enhance the mindfulness, spirituality and service quality of flight attendants in civil aviation industry. Background: Due to the job nature of flight attendants and the particularity of the work environment, it is determined that their psychology is always in the state of negative psychology. The main responsibility of a flight attendants is to ensure the safety and comfort of passengers on the flight. The positive psychology of a flight attendants is very important for the safety and service quality of civil aviation. Loving kindness meditation is a practice that allows practitioners to wish themselves and others happiness and maintain this emotional state anytime and anywhere. Loving kindness refers to giving happiness to oneself and other beings, which is not only a happy mood and a peaceful state of mind, but also a sound personality. Methods: Based on the current research status of sustainable design and related research results of service design, this study analyzes and studies the work and life of flight attendants, and extracts ISDT method for the "product design process" that affects the sustainable development of research and development activities, and use design practice cases as empirical evidence. Results: According to the concept and principle of ISDT, we developed an APP that integrates design thinking development model and mind mapping framework. It is used to guide the development process of loving kindness meditation APP. Conclusions: ISDT is a sustainable design method with the significance of moral positive energy. With the advantages of scientific and commercial design process, it guides design to be more inclusive and realizes the design vision of "design for positivity".

Keywords: I-Sustainability design thinking · Loving kindness meditation · Service quality · Flight attendants

© Springer Nature Switzerland AG 2021
P.-L. P. Rau (Ed.): HCII 2021, LNCS 12772, pp. 201–216, 2021.
https://doi.org/10.1007/978-3-030-77077-8_16

1 Introduction

With the growth of China's economy and the development of the civil aviation industry, the types of passengers present diversified trends such as business, travel, personal travel, family travel and study, and the number of passengers also shows a multiple growth year by year. It is estimated that by the end of 2034, the fleet size of Chinese airlines will reach 6,360, and China will also become the fastest growing country in the world's civil air transport market (Song et al. 2018). In 2018, the number of air passengers in China was 610 million, including 550 million on domestic routes and 60 million on international routes. These data indicate that the number of passengers in China's air transport industry is in a period of rapid growth. In 2019, China's civil aviation handled 660 million passenger trips, up 7.9% year on year (Su et al. 2019). Although the number of passengers has increased, with the opening of the market, the world's top airlines have entered the Chinese market one after another, making the competition among airlines in the medium and long distance international route market increasingly fierce. And with the rapid development of China' high-speed rail system, more travel options are available, and the transportation time advantage that airlines have is slowly being lost, especially on short-haul routes of less than two hours (Li et al. 2018). Therefore, after several rounds of competition in the ticket price and routes, airlines can no longer meet the needs of passengers by relying on a single advantage such as low ticket price or wide distribution of routes. Compared with the competitive conditions of low prices, more and more passengers pay more attention to the high level of service quality, satisfaction and comfort perception during the flight. Therefore, airlines need to pay attention to the problem of improving service value and management, reposition their service advantages, promote service innovation, and provide quality service is of great significance for the survival and development of airline enterprises (Ho and Wu 2019).

The cabin service process from boarding to deplaning is the service content that passengers have the longest contact with and the most intuitive feeling. Besides the main purpose of transport service from A to B, it is the main service content for airlines to participate in the competition. Cabin service mainly consists of software services such as the image and demeanor of the cabin crew, service attitude, service efficiency, service language ability, problem-solving skills and scientific rationalization design of service process (Sezgen et al. 2019); At present, the cabin service of Chinese airlines generally lacks the company's own characteristics, and there is widespread homogenization in many aspects, such as service consciousness, service process design, service technology, new employee training, service facilities and service quality evaluation system. There is no obvious difference between the cabin service provided by different airlines. To a certain extent, the most important evaluation criterion for passengers' satisfaction with the overall service effect of an airline company comes from the satisfaction with the flight attendants' service (Jiang and Zhang 2016).

The job of flight attendants can be viewed from the perspective of "emotional labor". In this process, the face and body of flight attendants such as smile, beauty, charm and vitality become a commodity form of airlines. Emotional labor requires flight attendants to induce or suppress their emotions in order to maintain an image that both empathizes and pleases customers. Emotional labor is the effort to understand others, to empathize with their situation, to feel what they feel as part of one's own (Hochschild 2012). In the airline service industry, the sustained happy facial expression of the flight attendants is a necessary condition for building a friendly passenger relationship. A happy face reflects the service quality of the airline. A deadpan face can mean unfriendly behavior for passengers, and SWB can maintain the happy facial expressions of flight attendants at work (Whitelegg 2007). The loving-kindness meditation (LKM) helps to open one's heart, to experience and perceive the feelings of others and oneself in a loving, kind, peaceful and considerate way, and to generate and cultivate qualities and emotions such as acceptance and care (Lutz et al. 2008). Through the perception and awareness of negative emotions, LKM has a regulating effect by directly transforming negative emotions into positive ones (Lutz et al. 2009). Due to the nature of work, flight attendants generally have the need to actively regulate their emotions. In the selection of specific emotional regulation strategies, they tend to avoid using those that consume physical and cognitive resources (Tungtakanpoung and Wyatt 2013). LKM converts emotions directly without the need for an intermediate cognitive reevaluation process, and the practice content and method of LKM are easy to understand and operate, which are consistent with the characteristics of flight attendants (Graser and Stangier 2018). Therefore, LKM may be an effective way to help flight attendants regulate and improve their emotions.

1.1 Loving-Kindness Meditation

LKM has been practiced by Buddhists for more than 2500 years (Bodhi 2012), but its usefulness as a psychological intervention has only recently been explored (Hofmann et al. 2011). LKM is about caring for all living beings besides oneself, the purpose of which is to cultivate feelings of unconditional love, kindness, and acceptance (Bodhi 2012). When practicing LKM, the practitioner directs loving-kindness, in a stepwise fashion, toward themselves, loved ones, acquaintances, strangers, and finally, all sentient beings (Zeng et al. 2015). LKM is versatile, it can be practiced at any time and in a variety of postures such as lying down, sitting, walking (Hofmann et al. 2011). Compared to traditional meditation methods, LKM is a simpler and easier way, less susceptible to the constraints of space and time, and can be performed at any time and place (Hofmann et al. 2011). Therefore, LKM is more suitable for the nature of flight attendants and will not affect or interfere with their work. When they encounter a sudden situation, they can also use LKM to calm their emotions and resolve conflicts in a timely manner. Therefore, this study chooses LKM as the intervention method for flight attendants (Liu et al. 2020).

1.2 Airline Service and Transition Design

Researchers from the 80 s began to focus on service innovation, the research of service innovation in the past 30 years is in constant progress, because the tangible service products must cover the content of technological innovation in service innovation, the research of service innovation are in a period of a simple understanding to the study of technological innovation. Desmarchelier et al. discussed how to classify the departments that introduce advanced technology. He identified the service sector as a sector dominated by the product provider (Desmarchelier et al. 2020). Barras's research also embodies the

service enterprise or service related departments in self-improvement should be dominated by products provider, thought innovation law of service enterprises and relevant
departments should first of all, from the manufacturing sector achieved new technology,
then began to promote product innovation, thus radiation for different operation stages of
product suppliers. During this period of research, researchers encountered a fundamental conceptual question: "What is the essential meaning of producing a service?" The
reasonable interpretation of this concept will directly influence the research direction of
service innovation (Barras 1990). Gallouj et al. proposed that every production of itself
is a service in order to solve a problem, service production is not a physical product,
the service is to combine many different ability, produce to the customer demand and
the solutions to problems of enterprise internal management, the solution accuracy of
a wide range of changes will happen. The core idea of this definition is that, in addition to technological innovation, service providers' understanding of customer needs,
coordination of human resources and internal comprehensive management capabilities
are equally important to production and service delivery. The definition also states the
need to make a clear distinction between highly standardized tangible service products
and customer-dominated intangible service products. Different from tangible products,
in products with strong customer dominance, the cooperation between customers and
service providers becomes the most critical factor in the process of production and service (Gallouj et al. 2018). With the deepening of the research, the research field of
service innovation is also gradually expanding, and there are two viewpoints which are
recognized by scholars and of great significance. First of all, the innovation of many
service enterprises is not generated by external factors such as technology promotion.
Service enterprises can generate a considerable amount of innovation through internal
resource integration, which is called non-technical factors by the academic circle. Non-
technical factors are very important in intangible service innovation. It is one-sided to
think that service innovation is dominated by product suppliers. Secondly, in addition to
the technology innovation method, it is also very important to form a research method for
the innovation of intangible services based on the characteristics of intangible services,
which can reduce the dependence of service innovation researchers on the technology
innovation research method (Anders Gustafsson et al. 2020).

After the concept of experience economy was put forward, more and more experience
processes and richer experience forms have been integrated into various consumer categories, and the market and enterprises also promote the design to respond to this. Terry
Irwin focused on the social role of design in the process of transition from traditional
society to sustainable future. She proposed transition design as a new design orientation
and method from a broad vision and perspective. Transition design fully considers the
customer-oriented nature of intangible service products in service innovation and the
overlapping characteristics of production and consumption process, and emphasizes the
important role of the collaboration between customers and the staff and managers of
service enterprises in the generation and implementation of new product concepts. It
is a design theory suitable for the characteristics of intangible service products (Irwin
2018). Transition design is a design approach that proposes a design-led transformation
of society to achieve a more sustainable future. Transition design uses the power of interdependence and symbiosis to aim at changing lifestyles, making these more enjoyable

and participatory, and harmonizing them with the natural environment. It emphasizes the time element of all design methods – how they relate to past traditions and indigenous cultures, and how they unfold, develop and connect over short, medium and long periods of time. Transitional design aims to intervene in social, economic, political, and technological systems to help people meet their needs and establish mutually beneficial relationships between people, the natural environment, and the built and designed world (Irwin 2015). This process is particularly inspired by the theory of living systems, which uses concepts such as self-organization, interdependence, emergence, global structure, and phase transition. It involves changing the way people make a living, changing the organizational structure of business, manufacturing, agriculture, finance, health care, education and tourism. Transition design aims to foster lifestyles and everyday living styles that meet basic needs in an integrated, location-based way and encourage symbiotic relationships between communities and between communities and their ecosystems (Irwin et al. 2015).

The products of the service industry are different from those of the manufacturing industry. The products of the manufacturing industry are visible both in the production process and in the product itself, while the products of the service industry are mostly intangible and perishable, and the production process and consumption process usually overlap (Cheng and Krumwiede 2017). For example, in some service industries, smile is a kind of service product. Service personnel produce a smile service product to customers, and customers consume it when the service personnel produce a smile. The whole production process and consumption process occur simultaneously and are invisible. Due to the characteristics of this kind of intangible service products, the general presentation of their service innovation is the new service concept or service method to solve the problems encountered in the service, that is to say, the service innovation of this kind of service products is usually the innovation of the service concept without physical objects (Ding and Keh 2017). Moreover, the definition of new service concept is also very broad. It can be a conceptual innovation from scratch, or a concept that has been recognized by consumers in some products and markets. However, in other products and markets where the concept has never been applied, the application of the concept itself is also a kind of innovation (Milanova and Maas 2017).

Therefore, the application of transition design theory to service innovation does not mean that a new service concept must be developed from scratch. It is also possible to introduce a service concept that is not available in the industry from other industries or markets. And according to the intangible characteristics of some service products, the service innovation of developing new service concepts is often the most suitable way for these service enterprises (Truong et al. 2020). But before that can happen, service companies need to figure out what they want in order to retain existing customers and attract new ones, and whether the products of their major competitors have the same characteristics. Then, through the cooperation of multiple departments within the enterprise, the information is integrated to extract the new service concept from it, and at the same time, the method of delivering the new service concept to existing customers and potential customers is developed. The new service concept formed from this is customer-oriented (Babaei and Aghdassi). Service enterprises find innovation inspiration through research and analysis of market demand. The formation of the new concept of services required by the service enterprise must fully understand the existing services and upcoming new services, as well as the existing services provided by the main competitors and upcoming new services, to clear its own innovative features, and as a fulcrum constantly according to the change of market environment, changes in consumer demand and changes of rival products continue to develop new service concept, and form a benign competition of the market. Therefore, the new service concept itself and the process of its generation can also be called the business intelligence of the intangible product service enterprise, which is applicable to the study of aviation service (Gustafsson et al. 2020).

1.3 I-Sustainability Design Thinking

A changing world: The book of I Ching records the earth's rotation and revolution around the sun in the universe, as well as the eternal rule changes in the four seasons of the year, spring, summer, autumn and winter, which constitute the birth and growth of all things on the earth. As the wisest of all creatures, human beings should take the mindfulness and rationality of the unity of "heaven, earth and man" in product design, coexist with nature in time, and take sustainable development as the goal. This is the best way for human beings to coexist with each other on earth (Wilhelm et al. 1967)!

In the first two hexagrams in the book of I Ching, the "Qian Diagram" represents the rotation and revolution of the earth around the great sun, which represents the positivity of the heavenly movement and the phenomenon of endless circulation. It metaphors all living things in the world, from birth, growth, prosperity, decline, and subsequent regeneration, endless circulation and sustainable development. In the process of "I-sustainability design", it represents the innovative design and development of products and services. From creativity to commercial feasibility, it can be transformed into "dragons" through the process of rigorous divergence, convergence of qualitative research, qualitative research and experimental verification. We should be alert to our "highlight dragon's shame" and plan for the second generation of products as soon as possible, continuing the ancestral line, inheriting and developing forever. Finally, "no leader in a host of dragons" appears to caution us in the "I-sustainability design" group when it comes to the importance of group collaboration without a leader (Lu 2008)!

"Kun Diagram", terrain Kun, virtue carrying things, represents the earth like a mother, with the maternal nature of "kindness" and "Virtue", nurturing the growth of all things on the earth. In the universe, the coincidence between the sun and the earth, the distance between the sun and the earth, the inclination of the earth's axis and the common rotation axis, making it 365 days a year, just forming the earth of spring, summer, autumn and winter, which is suitable for nourishing all things (Cheng 1988). The combination of yin and Yang of heaven and earth can be introduced into the I-sustainability design. The "Qian Diagram" is a metaphor for the firmness and perseverance of the heaven, the practice and positivity of the innovative design. While the "Kun Diagram" is also a metaphor for the mindfulness that designers must have to serve human beings and design to improve human life and living environment. In addition, "Qian Diagram" and "Kun Diagram" supplement each other, and the earth can nourish the growth of all things by absorbing the energy of the sun (Ma 2005)!

In the two Diagram of Qian and Kun, the dominant and subordinate changes of the Yang and Yin also imply the "orientation" and "qualitative" of the main changes in the first part of the "double diamond" method of "I-sustainability design", and the "position" and "qualitative" of the latter part (Clune and Lockrey 2014).

In the center of the eight Diagram, the Taiji image of balance of Yin and Yang is a symbol of the eternal movement and sustainable balance of the heavenly movement. It is also a metaphor for the "I-sustainability design". With human wisdom, it is necessary to consider the sustainable development of the earth and the human beings on the earth in terms of innovation and design (Lui 2005).

In the eight trigrams of Taiji in the book of I Ching, the three trigrams represent the changes and rules of the unity of heaven, earth and man. The eight trigrams represent the heaven, the earth, the thunder, the electricity, the mountains, the rivers, the water and the fire that human beings face. In the natural environment, there are eight main phenomena of natural and physical science, which Human beings live in. How to use human wisdom and I-sustainability design thinking to achieve sustainable development with the earth is the purpose and goal of "I-sustainability design" (TenHouten and Wang 2001).

2   The ISDT Process

The steps of the ISDT design method are shown in Table 1. First, use the cooperative mandala coloring based on the philosophy of I Ching as the guide program before starting. Secondly, analyze the driving factors in the field of socio-economic and technological (S.E.T.) from a macro perspective, and draw potential opportunity gap (POG). Then analyze the user's usage scenarios from a micro perspective, so as to get the key themes and value propositions to be solved. Finally, comprehensively propose the prototype concept and business model canvas of the product.

Table 1. ISDT process

I Ching orientation	1. Cooperative mandala drawing
Macro factors analysis	2. Macro S.E.T. forces brainstorming
	3. S.E.T. top10 forces converging
	4. Business resources and sustainable development goals
	5. Product ideas and POG statement
Micro factors analysis	6. Scenario brainstorming sketch
	7. Character map
	8. Top10 key themes converging
Prototype development	9. Value proposition and opportunity analysis
	10. Prototype simulation and evaluation
	11. Business model generation

3   Materials and Methods

3.1   Case Study

This study takes the design and development of a mobile application platform as a case study, which aims to improve the service quality of flight attendants by using LKM as a guide. The case study took the form of a workshop in which 30 flight attendants were recruited to discuss the core issues of the product under the guidance of ISDT theory and to develop the product prototype concept.

3.2   ISDT Process

Cooperative Mandala Drawing
The practice of cooperative mandala drawing (Fig. 1), through the collaborative creation of two or more people, allows participants not only to express their inner selves but also to present the spiritual reality of creating a mandala process with others, helping them to generate positive psychology, and also to symphony with the group, and to experience the beauty of unity (Liu et al. 2020).

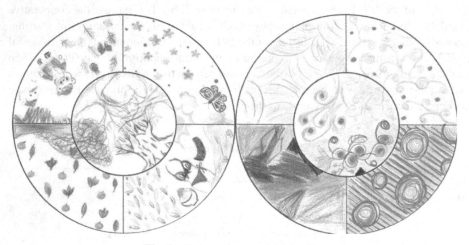

Fig. 1.   Cooperative mandala drawing

Macro Factors Analysis
The POG of innovative products and services is generated by taking the background factor of Social economy (SE), the Core Technology (T) as the dominant factor, and the favorable Business resources of enterprise operation in line with the goal of sustainable development. Using yellow 3M sticky notes, cross-field team members brainstorm to create together. According to the above mentioned SET, more than 50 influencing factors are divergent respectively, and then they are ranked in order of group and importance.

Fig. 2. Macro S.E.T. top10 forces

Select more than 10 Top10 Forces, and list the project names of the important influencing factors of each group with purple sticky notes (Fig. 2).

In the same way, analyze and summarize the business resources (Fig. 3) of the design team.

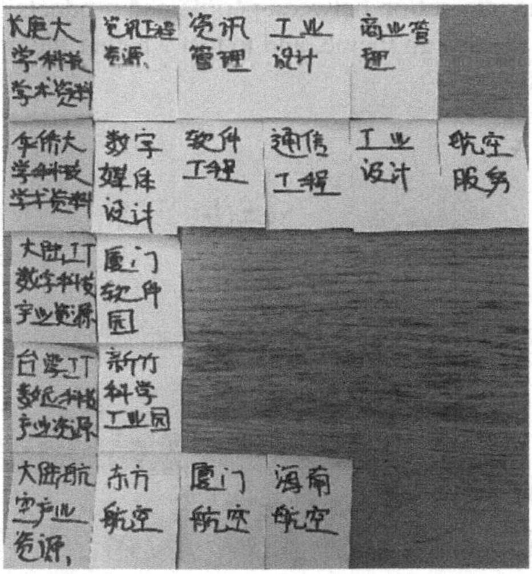

Fig. 3. Business resources

According to the 17 sustainable development goals (SDGs) set by the United Nations, the sustainable goals (Fig. 4) to be achieved by this research are determined.

Micro Factors Analysis

Scenario story principle is to simulate the use of future products through an imaginary story in the process of product design and development. In the simulation process, the relationship between the typical user's characteristics (Fig. 5), events, products and the

Fig. 4. SDGs of United Nations and goals of this case study

environment are considered, and the personnel involved in the design and development are continuously guided in a visual and practical way to explore the idea of the product from the perspective of the user. Through the use of scenario story simulation (Fig. 6), to explore and analyze the interaction between people and products, to judge whether the concept is in line with the design theme, and to test whether the product concept meets the potential needs of users.

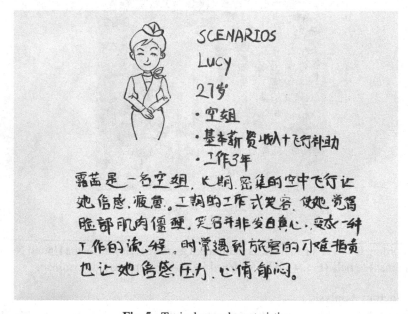

Fig. 5. Typical user characteristics

Fig. 6. Scenario story simulation

4   Results

4.1   P.O.G. Statement

Starting from the macroscopic analysis of social economy, the important phenomenon, obvious trend and the driving force behind it are obtained. Then analyze the possibility

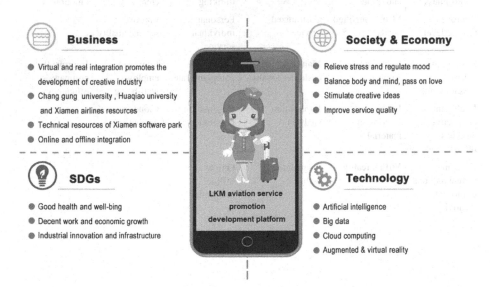

Fig. 7. Product ideas and POG statement

of solving these problems under the existing technology conditions, resulting in POG statements (Fig. 7). Combined with the business resources we have and the sustainable development goals we want to achieve, we have a clearer concept and thinking about the products to be designed.

4.2 Top10 Themes

Combining the results of micro-scenario analysis with the S.E.T. top 10 driving forces of macro analysis, we finally obtained the top 10 key themes (Table 2) to be solved by the product.

Table 2. Top10 key themes

High working pressure	Long working hours	Heavy task	Frequent overtime	Squeezing into leisure time	Difficulty in maintaining balance
Negative emotions are hard to relieve	Negative emotions at work	Negative emotions in life	Lack of relief to vent emotions	Anxiety and depression	
Affect the quality of service	Job burnout	Cold service	Mechanized service	Perfunctory	Complete the task mentality
Used to mobile phones	Time fragmentation	Phubber	Information anxiety	Mobile app is widely used	
Pass on love	Improve empathy	Transpositional consideration	Compassion and empathy	Pass on warmth	
Improve mindfulness	Balance body and mind	Relieve pressure	Activate thinking	Stimulate creativity	Regulating emotion
Improve service level	Meet diversified needs	Customized service	Personalized individual service	Improve service quality	
Promoting aviation development	Enhance brand value	Maintain customer loyalty	Reduce the complaint rate	Improve employee well-being	Improve the company's efficiency
Intelligent connectivity enriches information	Intelligent filtering of material	Information analysis	Information integration	Cloud database	
Combine virtual and real to promote creativity	Virtual reality	Augmented reality	Online and offline integration		

4.3 Value Analysis

Through value analysis, we further clarify what the designed product is, what its main functions are, what needs are met, and what value proposition (Table 3) was put forward.

Table 3. Value proposition

Creative development platform based on transcendental meditation
LKM guidance platform
Mindfulness promotion platform
Body and mind balance emotional regulation platform
Aviation service quality improvement platform
Online and offline intelligent interconnection platform
Love service promotion platform

4.4 Business Model

Based on the above, the business model canvas of the product is put forward and the prototype concept of the product is formed (Table 4).

Table 4. Business model canvas

Key Partners	Key Activities	Value Proposition	Customer Relationship	Customer Segments
• Chang Gung University • Huaqiao University • Xiamen Software Park • LKM Meditation Center • Mindfulness Training institutions • Xiamen airlines	• LKM Training • Mindfulness training • Emotion regulation • Service quality improvement • Send care send warmth	• LKM guidance platform • Mindfulness promotion platform • Body and mind balance emotional regulation platform • Aviation service quality improvement platform • Online and offline intelligent interconnection platform • Love service promotion platform	• Customer problem information feedback system • Customer maintenance management system	• The flight attendants • Other service industry employees
	Key Resources		**Channels**	
	• Chang Gung University • Huaqiao University • Xiamen Software Park • LKM Meditation Center • Mindfulness Training institutions • Xiamen airlines		• App store platform promotion • WeChat, Weibo, Facebook, Twitter and other social platforms promotion • TikTok and other short video platform promotion • Professional Community Promotion • Online and offline integration and promotion	

Cost Structure	Revenue Stream
• Mobile application development • Product iterative upgrade and maintenance • Intelligent platform system construction • Customer maintenance management system construction • Database construction • Promotion and marketing cost • Cost of online and offline activities	• Revenue from fee-paying members • Advertising revenue • Revenue from sales of information materials • Training benefits

5 Discussion

The LKM APP designed by the "ISDT method" takes the approach of LKM, through mindfulness and flow as the core of the design. When value opportunity analysis, compared with the existing APP in mind flow, mindfulness meditation, the sustainable development of good health and social welfare projects and entrepreneurship, innovation and infrastructure projects, the aesthetics of the vision, hearing and touch, comfortable, safe and easy to use for engineering, healthy physical, psychological and social adaptability, the quality of the manufacturing process and the durability, the core technology of reliability and availability are more highly value, can say ISDT is straight the praise highly of the new design thinking.

Today, the concept of sustainable development has gone beyond the simple understanding of the form and local ecological improvement, and the vision of sustainable development has expanded to the global ecological environment, social and cultural life, life values and other aspects. Sustainable development requires consideration of social and environmental factors as well as economic ones, of the base of living and non-living resources, and of the strengths and weaknesses of long-term and short-term alternatives. Its development has pointed out the direction for the design technology and made the modern design have more work emphasis. More importantly, it arouses the designer a sense of morality and responsibility, and makes people realize that design has more important goals than the market and consumers, and more important pursuits than commercial value. A new task for designers is to "design what can and must be done is to point out a new way of life that can be adapted to the environment of daily living, family living, global living and working". With its huge cultural field and design effectiveness, the concept of ISDT, which fully integrates into people's life and improves people's life style, is the inevitable trend of future design development.

Easy to design the new product design thinking, analysis of the theory of product designer should be careful analysis of the specific period of society, economy, technology, business resources and sustainable development factors, give up the previous single pre-design analysis theory, and put forward the new design principles and evaluation criteria, based on the analysis to determine the most suitable products. The traditional preliminary analysis method and theory of product design have some defects and deficiencies. Therefore, the postpartum LKM APP designed by this research team through the design thinking of ISDT is more competitive in the market, and also more valuable, which is worthy of attention by the design industry.

6 Conclusion

Use ISDT design thinking for case designed by LKM APP, the APP through the demand of The Times, to find the right product opportunity value, APP in order to enhance are mindful flow as the core, into the airline quality service, to achieve the goal of sustainable, compare the value opportunity analysis of existing products, and more valuable. In the future, ISDT designers in product design, graphic design and other related design fields are expected to attach importance to and try to apply ISDT's new design thinking, so as to achieve the goal of sustainable earth and common good for mankind.

References

Babaei, M., Aghdassi, M.: Measuring the dimensions of quality in service innovation: a dynamic capability and organisational competency perspective. Total Quality Management & Business Excellence. https://doi.org/10.1080/14783363.2020.1861933

Barras, R.: Interactive innovation in financial and business services: the vanguard of the service revolution. Res. Policy 19(3), 215–237 (1990)

Bodhi, B.: Comprehensive Manual of Abhidhamma: The Abhidhammattha Sangaha. Pariyatti Publishing, Onalaska (2012)

Cheng, C.-Y.: On harmony as transformation: paradigms from the I Ching. Harmony and Strife: Contemporary Perspectives, East & West, pp. 225–248 (1988)

Cheng, C.C., Krumwiede, D.: What makes a manufacturing firm effective for service innovation? the role of intangible capital under strategic and environmental conditions. Int. J. Prod. Econ. 193, 113–122 (2017)

Clune, S.J., Lockrey, S.: Developing environmental sustainability strategies, the Double Diamond method of LCA and design thinking: a case study from aged care. J. Clean. Prod. 85, 67–82 (2014)

Desmarchelier, B., Djellal, F., Gallouj, F.: Towards a servitization of innovation networks: a mapping. Publ. Manag. Rev. 22(9), 1368–1397 (2020)

Ding, Y., Keh, H.T.: Consumer reliance on intangible versus tangible attributes in service evaluation: the role of construal level. J. Acad. Mark. Sci. 45(6), 848–865 (2017)

Gallouj, F., Rubalcaba, L., Toivonen, M., Windrum, P.: Understanding social innovation in services industries. Ind. Innov. 25(6), 551–569 (2018)

Graser, J., Stangier, U.: Compassion and loving-kindness meditation: an overview and prospects for the application in clinical samples. Harvard Rev. Psychiatry 26(4), 201–215 (2018)

Gustafsson, A., Snyder, H., Witell, L.: Service innovation: a new conceptualization and path forward. J. Serv. Res. 23(2), 111–115 (2020)

Ho, C.-W., Wu, C.-C.: Using job design to motivate employees to improve high-quality service in the airline industry. J. Air Transp. Manag. 77, 17–23 (2019)

Hochschild, A.R.: The Managed Heart: Commercialization of Human Feeling. Univ of California Press, Oakland (2012)

Hofmann, S.G., Grossman, P., Hinton, D.E.: Loving-kindness and LKM: potential for psychological interventions. Clin. Psychol. Rev. 31(7), 1126–1132 (2011)

Irwin, T.: Transition design: a proposal for a new area of design practice, study, and research. Des. Cult. 7(2), 229–246 (2015)

Irwin, T.: The emerging transition design approach (2018)

Irwin, T., Tonkinwise, C., Kossoff, G.: Transition design: an educational framework for advancing the study and design of sustainable transitions. Cuad. del Centro de Estud. en Diseño y Comun. 23(105), 31–65 (2015)

Jiang, H., Zhang, Y.: An investigation of service quality, customer satisfaction and loyalty in China's airline market. J. Air Transp. Manag. 57, 80–88 (2016)

Li, X., Jiang, C., Wang, K., Ma, J.: Determinants of partnership levels in air-rail cooperation. J. Air Transp. Manag. 71, 88–96 (2018)

Liu, C., Chen, H., Liu, C.-Y., Lin, R.-T., Chiou, W.-K.: The effect of loving-kindness meditation on flight attendants' spirituality, mindfulness and subjective well-being. Healthcare 8, 174 (2020a)

Liu, C., Chen, H., Liu, C.-Y., Lin, R.-T., Chiou, W.-K.: Cooperative and individual mandala drawing have different effects on mindfulness, spirituality, and subjcetive well-being. Front. Psychol. 11, 2629 (2020b)

Lu, S.: I Ching and the origin of the Chinese semiotic tradition. Semiotica 2008(170), 169–185 (2008)

Lui, I.: The Taoist I Ching. Shambhala Publications, Boulder (2005)

Lutz, A., Brefczynski-Lewis, J., Johnstone, T., Davidson, R.J.: Regulation of the neural circuitry of emotion by LKM: effects of meditative expertise. Plos One **3**(3), e1897 (2008)

Lutz, A., Greischar, L.L., Perlman, D.M., Davidson, R.J.: BOLD signal in insula is differentially related to cardiac function during LKM in experts vs. novices. Neuroimage **47**(3), 1038–1046 (2009)

Ma, S.S.: The I Ching and the psyche-body connection. J. Anal. Psychol. **50**(2), 237–250 (2005)

Milanova, V., Maas, P.: Sharing intangibles: uncovering individual motives for engagement in a sharing service setting. J. Bus. Res. **75**, 159–171 (2017)

Sezgen, E., Mason, K.J., Mayer, R.: Voice of airline passenger: a text mining approach to understand customer satisfaction. J. Air Transp. Manag. **77**, 65–74 (2019)

Song, F., Hess, S., Dekker, T.: Accounting for the impact of variety-seeking: theory and application to HSR-air intermodality in China. J. Air Transp. Manag. **69**, 99–111 (2018)

Su, M., Luan, W., Sun, T.: Effect of high-speed rail competition on airlines' intertemporal price strategies. J. Air Transp. Manag. **80**, 101694 (2019)

TenHouten, W.D., Wang, W.: The eight trigrams of the Chinese I Ching and the eight primary emotions. Asian J. Soc. Psychol. **4**(3), 185–199 (2001)

Truong, N.T., Dang-Pham, D., McClelland, R.J., Nkhoma, M.: Service innovation, customer satisfaction and behavioural intentions: a conceptual framework. J. Hospitality Tourism Technol. **11**(3), 529–542 (2020). https://doi.org/10.1108/jhtt-02-2019-0030

Tungtakanpoung, M., Wyatt, M.: Spirituality and cultural values in the reported cognitions of female cabin attendants on Thai Airways. J. Air Transp. Manag. **27**, 15–19 (2013)

Whitelegg, D.: Working the Skies: The Fast-paced, Disorienting World of the Flight Attendant. NYU Press, Manhattan (2007)

Wilhelm, R., Baynes, C.F., Jung, C.G.: The I Ching: Or, Book of Changes, Princeton University Press Princeton, NJ (1967)

Zeng, X.L., Chiu, C.P.K., Wang, R., Oei, T.P.S., Leung, F.Y.K.: The effect of loving-kindness meditation on positive emotions: a meta-analytic review. Front. Psychol. **6**, 1693 (2015). https://doi.org/10.3389/fpsyg.2015.01693

Study on Creative Learning Strategies of Gender Grouping in Collaborative Learning of Graduation Project

Hung-Chug Ou[1,2]([✉]) [iD] and Yen Hsu[1] [iD]

[1] The Graduate Institute of Design Science, Tatung University, No. 40, Sec. 3, Zhongshan N. Rd., Zhongshan Dist., Taipei City 10452, Taiwan (Republic of China)
[2] Department of Environmental Design, Fuzhou University of International Studies and Trade, NJ 10452, No. 28, Yuhuan Road, Shouzhan New District, Changle District, Fuzhou City 350202, Fujian, China

Abstract. This study is an exploratory study to explore the best creative learning strategies in graduation project after comparing learning choices between different groups through "collaborative guidance" and "mentor guidance". The main study methods are multi-factor experimental design, among which, the main variables are gender grouping, and the dependent variables are "mentor guidance" and "collaborative guidance". The collaborative guidance means that four main orientations of "base investigation", "design transformation", "design expression" and "paper writing" in the graduation project process are explained by four graduation project mentors in the way of network lectures in the mid-semester. The participants were fourth-graders in the Department of Environmental Design at a university. In order to understand and clarify whether gender grouping can enhance learning creativity through collaborative guidance in graduation project, the study divided it into experimental group and control group to compare and analyze data. The "experimental group" is composed of the students who completed the graduation project of the whole semester through the collaborative guidance of computer-supported collaborative learning between gender groupings. The "control group" is composed of the students learning under the traditional graduation project teaching style. In addition to identifying whether gender groupings in graduation project can enhance learning creativity through computer-supported collaborative learning "collaborative guidance", the strategies of teaching method in future graduation project are also discussed in this study.

Keywords: Collaborative guidance · Mentor guidance · Creative learning strategy · Computer-supported collaborative learning · Teaching method

1 Introduction

With In the era of information society, technology has become a tool for complementary learning, expanding the possibility of exploring innovative learning patterns (Kirschner 2002). Learning through the Internet is no longer just a one-way learning of the computer or the Internet for individuals, but rather a learning activity that can interact with

P.-L. P. Rau (Ed.): HCII 2021, LNCS 12772, pp. 217–229, 2021.
https://doi.org/10.1007/978-3-030-77077-8_17

members of the community. Computer-supported collaborative learning (CSCL) is the new learning paradigm and area of learning (Koschmann 1996; Stahl et al. 2006) in this information age. With the support of CSCL learning platform, students can engage in the cooperative learning activities such as group discussion, practice and topic without restriction of time and space, so that students can combine knowledge closely. Even people of different ages, times and places can study cooperatively. This kind of learning activity is in accordance with the relationship level of "learning with computer" (Jonassen 2000) in the relationship between computer and learning, and it is also the relationship level of today's social use of computer, not learning computer knowledge, but enhancing the learners' social interaction and promoting learning through the support of information technology, and gradually forming a sense of consensus in the interaction process.

In the computer-supported collaborative learning process, each of two or more students has a certain level of thinking, feeling and behavior. How to work together to solve the same problem. Group members may have different views and understandings on the same issue, so by constantly discussing and debating, a group cognition (Stahl 2006) is finally established, which is the construction of knowledge. In the era of information network, a lot of different learning patterns are created using the combination of science and technology and education, and it also makes the original education mode have more possibilities. But this situation causes the educators to begin to think, we should assist the students to cultivate the more mature knowledge viewpoint and to achieve the efficient study, rather than the traditional teaching at the knowledge receiving mode which makes the students' thought is rigid and restricted by authority. In view of this, the author holds that cooperative learners can learn more diversely through computer-supported collaborative learning, and enhance their learning effectiveness in this way. In the study of traditional graduation project, teacher-apprentice learning model is not helpful for students' creative learning and thinking. Therefore, the author also thinks that two or more graduation project mentors cam lead the students to carry out the graduation project with the creative teaching method of reciprocal teaching, thus the students' learning effectiveness and creativity can be strengthened by the combination of their own ideas or teaching methods and the new ideas and ideas of other mentors. This study focuses on the study of creative learning strategies, and tries to improve students' creativity with the combination of collaborative teaching method and computer-supported collaborative learning.

This study is an exploratory study to explore the best creative learning strategies in graduation project after comparing learning choices between different groups through "collaborative guidance" and "mentor guidance". Specifically, this study will attempt to answer the following questions: (1) What are the differences of learning choices between gender grouping students in the design process under "mentor guidance" and "collaborative guidance"? (2) What are the differences of learning choices between "experimental group" and "control group" students in the design process under "mentor guidance" and "col-laborative guidance"? (3) Are there differences in learning choices between boys and girls in different gender learning groups?

2   Literature Review

The main literature discussed in this study includes three aspects: "creative teaching", "computer-supported collaborative learning" and "cooperative learning", which are as follows:

2.1   Creative Teaching

Mayer (1999), in reviewing the study findings and future directions of creativity over the past 50 years, took the definition of creativity by scholars in the Handbook of Creativity (compiled by Sternberg (1999)) as an example, and argued that each scholar may use a different language to describe creativity, but most of the definitions of creativity are "originality" and "usefulness." Zhan Zhiyu (2002), from the perspective of knowledge evolution, believed that creation is the process of variation and selection, and that variation is the source of originality. The selection is to make the most useful variation remain through selection pressure, so "selection" is also the source of "usefulness". If we look at creative teaching in terms of "novelty" and "value", it means that teacher's teaching must be novel and valuable.

From the perspective of novelty, the teaching methods, contents, strategies and orientations used by teachers must be novel. If we explore the meaning of the so-called "teaching is novel" from a relative point of view, it may be easier to understand:

(1)   For tradition, novelty must be something that has not been adopted by tradition or that tradition doesn't have, that is, it must not follow the teaching methods, contents, behaviors and so on used in the past.
(2)   Compared with invariance, novelty represents changeability and pluralism, which is not only single, but also that teacher's teaching is pluralistic, changeful and not invariable.
(3)   Novelty also represents the behavior or activity of teaching is original, created by the teachers and others have not used it.

2.2   Computer-Supported Collaborative Learning

Computer-supported collaborative learning (CSCL) is a growing branch of learning. Many critics will see it as a boring and anti-social act, a safe haven for computer players, and a mechanical, inhuman form of training. (Stahl et al. 2006). In fact, CSCL is based on the exactly opposite vision, which advocates the development of new software and applications to facilitate "co-learning" and to provide creative activities for mental exploration, as well as social interaction. CSCL was developed in the 1990s in response to software that forced students to learn in isolation. The amazing potential of the Internet to link people together in innovative ways has inspired CSCL research; with the development of CSCL, the emergence of more and more unexpected obstacles in the design, dissemination, and effective use of innovative educational software, people need to change the concept of learning, including significant changes in schools, teaching, and student.

CSCL emphasizes collaboration between students, who are not only isolated from those online textbooks, but learning happens mainly through interaction between students. Students learn in the process of expressing problems, exploring together, teaching each other, and looking at how others learn. The main way of learning E-learning is to carry out such collaborative learning. It is not easy to stimulate and maintain high student interaction. It requires ingenious planning, as well as coordination and implementation between curriculum, pedagogy and science and technology. In addition, CSCL is concerned about face-to-face collaboration. Computer-supported learning is more than just an online medium of communication. Computer support, for example, may involve computer simulation of a scientific model, or a shared interactive representation, in which collaboration focuses on the construction and exploration of simulations or representations. In addition, a group of students may use a computer to browse information on the Internet, and discuss, argue, assemble, and display the results of their collaborative learning.

2.3 Cooperative Learning

The cooperative learning is a learning method by which students work together to achieve their learning goals (Lefrancois 1997), that is to say, the cooperative learning is a structured and systematic learning strategy in which teachers assign students to groups and encourage them to help each other based on their abilities, gender, ethnicity, etc. so as to improve the learning effect of individuals and achieve the goals of the group (Lin Peixuan 1992; Chen Shuji 1995). According to such a statement, it can be seen that cooperative learning is a kind of teaching concept which is different from the traditional goal of competition and ranking. This teaching method means that students work together to achieve common goals. It is not like competition, but rather a learning process. Therefore, cooperative learning is a kind of teaching design which combines pedagogy, social psychology, group dynamics and so on. It mainly makes use of the division of labor among the group members and the mutual support to carry on learning activities, and uses the group-based evaluation and the social psychological atmosphere of the inter-group competition to improve the learning effect (Liu Xiuman 1998).

And when it comes to the above-mentioned literature, many studies show that there are still some unclarified parts. Therefore, the aim of this study is to improve students' learning effectiveness and creativity with gender grouping by combining collaborative teaching method and computer-supported collaborative learning based on graduation project.

3 Study Methods

3.1 Study Process

The study process is divided into four stages: The first stage is related literature discussion; the second stage is the questionnaire design, and the scale dimensions and each question item are established through the relevant study analysis and expert interview; the third stage is the study object selecting and test, and in this stage, the students are taken as the study sample for the questionnaire test; the fourth stage is the study result and the discussion, and it carries on the analysis of the valid questionnaires for the study hypothesis verification later, and in the end, the conclusion and suggestion are put forward.

3.2 Study Questions and Hypotheses

This study is an exploratory study to explore the best creative learning strategies in graduation project after comparing learning choices between different groups through "collaborative guidance" and "mentor guidance". Specifically, this study will attempt to answer the following questions:

(1) What are the differences of learning choices between gender grouping students in the design process under "mentor guidance" and "collaborative guidance"?
(2) What are the differences of learning choices between "experimental group" and "control group" students in the design process under "mentor guidance" and "collaborative guidance"?
(3) Are there differences in learning choices between boys and girls in different gender learning groups?

Three hypotheses were put forward according to the study questions: The first hypothesis was that the 2 M (two male) group of the single gender had better collaborative guidance preference than the 2F (two female) group of the single gender. This is because boys have better digital knowledge than girls, which can be responded in computer-supported collaborative learning (CSCL) correspondingly. The second hypothesis was that 2F (2 female students) in the gender equilibrium group preferred mentor guidance. Because many studies show that the majority of female students are less accustomed to computer collaborative learning, this may also lead to the impact of female students learning style. The third hypothesis was that there was no significant difference in learning choice between gender unequilibrium group 1M1F (1 male and 1 female) group and the gender equilibrium group.

3.3 Selection and Testing of Study Objects

Participants are fourth-graders in the Department of Environmental Design at a university who studied Sketch up and 3D max computer software in the second and third grades. The study objects are the fourth grade graduation project group students, altogether 197 students and they are guided by 18 graduation project mentors altogether. The grouping situation is that: three study objects in one group, a total of 15 objects in 5 groups, and two study objects in one group, a total of 156 objects in 78 groups. One object in one group, a total of 26 objects in 26 groups. The main objects of this study are (2 M, 2F, 1M1F) groups, and the valid sample is 156 objects, after the total number of 41 persons in three-person group and one-person group are deducted. The study is divided into two groups, namely, experimental group and control group. The "experimental group" is composed of the students who completed the graduation project of the whole semester through the collaborative guidance of computer-supported collaborative learning between gender groupings. While the "control group" is composed of the students learning under the traditional graduation project teaching style.

3.4 Study Tools

The study is conducted by questionnaire through network and mobile phone. The questionnaire is divided into four dimensions according to the process of graduation project. The order of the questionnaire design is base investigation, design transformation, design expression and paper writing. The explanation is given as follows: 1. Base investigation: It refers to the "base investigation and case analysis" of the students in the initial stage of graduation project, whether the guidance of tutors themselves or collaborative teaching has any substantial help for students in creative design ideas. 2. Design transformation: Design transformation refers to the effect of this part's process of graduation project on gender grouping learning by means of collaborative teaching. 3. Design expression: Design expression means the expression of the whole vision in the graduation project, whether the mentor guidance or collaborative teaching can influence the student's study. 4. Paper writing: The influence of collaborative teaching method on students' learning performance in design report writing skills. Questionnaire is divided into two dimensions: mentor guidance and collaborative guidance. There are 4 dimensions, all of which there are 16 items.

3.5 Experimental Design

This course of "graduation project topic" is the last required course of a series of core design courses in our department from the lower grades. After four years of space design education, the course mainly enables the students of Department of Environmental Design to integrate all their professional knowledge, thinking logic, humanistic viewpoint, aesthetic ability and creative ideas, and finally put forward their own views on space design. The department is mainly divided into two main design directions of "interior design" and "landscape design". In the process of graduation project, it is necessary to put forward a complete topic direction, observation and analysis, design strategy and different development design plan and design report according to the prescribed time schedule. Finally, it presents the design proposal of professional education level in the "defense of graduation project". It includes oral communication, graphic and model results, which can only be passed after the full-time teacher's joint review.

The main study method is multi-factor experimental design, giving priority to 3×2 experimental design. Three of the explanatory variables are gender grouping, and the target variables are "mentor guidance" and "collaborative guidance". The collaborative guidance means that four main orientations of "base investigation", "design transformation", "design expression" and "paper writing" in the graduation project process are explained by four graduation project mentors (each mentor is responsible for one of the orientations) in the way of network lectures and the method of computer-supported collaborative learning in the last semester. The graduation project starts from the base investigation and ends at the last semester, the time spent by each group on it is about 4–5 months. The time of the questionnaire is one week before the end of last semester. The investigation tool is conducted on a computer or mobile phone in the form of a network. The questionnaire is designed with Likert-type 5-point scale, one point represents for "very disagreed", two points for "disagreed", three points for "uncertainty", four points for "agreed", and five points for "very agreed". Different grades of scores are given according to the propensity of the statement. The questionnaire is divided into four dimensions: "base investigation", "design transformation", "design expression" and "paper writing". There were 156 students in five classes with Cronbach's α coefficient of 898 for all the 16 items, which showed that this scale had good reliability.

4 Results and Discussion

In order to understand and clarify whether gender grouping can enhance learning creativity through collaborative guidance in graduation project, the study divided it into experimental group and control group to compare and analyze data. Questionnaire design is divided into four dimensions: "base investigation", "design transformation", "design expression" and "paper writing". The independent sample t-test is used to examine and analyze the learning choices among the gender grouping in the design of the experiment. The mean analysis and multi-factor variance analysis are used to examine the differences between the hypotheses.

4.1 The Study Hypothesis in Independent Sample T-Test Data Analysis

The independent sample t-test in this study is used to investigate the hypothesis problem in two directions: the difference of learning choice between genders, and the contrast analysis between groups. In the independent t-sample, there was no significant difference in all items of four dimensions between gender and grouping in the learning choices between "mentor guidance" and "collaborative guidance". The results overturned all the study hypotheses. And this also seems to mean that boys and girls have uncertainty about the learning of "collaborative teaching", and therefore are more accustomed to the traditional graduation project teaching style. In the experimental group and the control group, the results of t-test analysis are as follows (Table 1). The results showed that there are significant differences between the two groups in four dimensions of mentor guidance (for example, Q2) and [$t(154) = -2.72$, $p = .02$, $d = 0.28$]. This shows that students in the experimental group are slightly influenced by "onsite learning" in the collaborative learning process because they joined in the collaborative guidance. As a result, the score of the dimension of mentor guidance is relatively lower in the questionnaire survey. The students in the control group were more trusting of their mentors because they were not under collaborative guidance. Therefore, it is common to show high marks in mentor guidance. From the survey data, we can know that collaborative learning can be properly added to the process of graduation project learning, but how to master the teaching style needs to be studied further.

Table 1. Data analysis results of independent sample t test between experimental group and control group

Type	Item	Experimental group (78 people) Mean	Control group (78 people) Mean	Assume that the variance is equal significance (double tail)	Do not assume that the variance is equal significance (double tail)
Mentor guidance	1	4.18	4.41	.053	.053
	2	4.09	4.37	.024*	.025*
	3	4.14	4.41	.033*	.033*
	4	4.15	4.44	.027*	.027*
	5	4.14	4.42	.023*	.023*
	6	4.21	4.49	.020*	.020*
	7	4.17	4.58	.000*	.001*
	8	4.19	4.49	.012*	.012*
Collaborative guidance	1	4.09	4.15	.676	.676
	2	4.14	4.10	.788	.788
	3	3.99	4.12	.423	.423
	4	4.01	4.05	.810	.810
	5	4.00	4.05	.747	.747
	6	4.05	4.09	.808	.808
	7	4.03	4.12	.568	.568
	8	3.97	3.97	1.000	1.000

4.2   The Study Hypothesis in Statistical Analysis of Single-Factor Variance

(1) In the statistical analysis of single-factor variance, two hypothetical problems are mainly discussed, one is the learning choice difference between gender groupings, and the other is the statistical analysis results of the experimental group and the control group. The results of data analysis showed that there was no significant difference in the design process of gender grouping "mentor guidance" and "collaborative guidance". This is not consistent with the first hypothesis that the single gender (2 M) group is superior to the single gender (2F) group in collaborative guidance. The second hypothesis is that students in the gender equilibrium (2F) group are more likely to be directed by their own mentors, and the results are inconsistent. Compared with the third hypothesis, there is no significant difference in learning choice between gender unequilibrium (1M1F) group and gender equilibrium group.

(2) In the single-factor variance analysis between experimental group and the control group, there are 7 different items in the dimension of mentor guidance. The results are as follows (Table 2). Take the mentor question Q2 "communicate with group members frequently" of "base investigation" as an example, $[F(1,154) = 5.160, p =$

.024] has a significant difference. This shows that the students also discuss closely after school besides the discussion and communication with the mentors, shown in the part of base investigation. For two items about the internalized application of knowledge in the part of the design transformation, the analysis statistics are [F $(1,154) = 4.616$, p $= .033$], [F $(1,154) = 5.012$, p $= .027$], respectively. This shows that the part of design transformation is usually complicated and difficult in the process of students' graduation project operation, which requires careful guidance from the tutor and intensive discussion. Therefore, the students showed a desire to design knowledge, and both the experimental group and the control group showed positive attitude towards collaborative guidance.

(3)   In the design expression part of the mentor guidance, the analysis statistics of two items of case teaching are [F $(1,154) = 5.280$, p $= .023$] and [F $(1,154) = 5.543$, p $= .023$], respectively. This showed that both boys and girls in the gender grouping wanted to demonstrate with cases in the part of design presentation; the experimental group showed better learning effectiveness than collaborative guidance in the onsite guidance by mentor. The students in the control group hold reservations for the teaching effect of collaborative learning (CSCL). In the part of the paper guidance, the analysis statistics are [F $(1,154) = 12.656$, p $= .000$], [F $(1,154) = 6.400$, p $= .012$]. Because paper writing usually encounters problems that arise outside of

Table 2. Results of single-factor variance analysis of the experimental group and the control group in the dimension of "mentor guidance"

Item	Category III sum of squares	Degree of freedom df	Mean sum of squares	F	Significance
Q1	2.077	1	2.077	3.791	.053
Error	84.359	154	.548		
Q2	3.103	1	3.103	5.160	.024*
Error	92.590	154	.601		
Q3	2.827	1	2.827	4.616	.033*
Error	94.321	154	.612		
Q4	3.103	1	3.103	5.012	.027*
Error	95.333	154	.619		
Q5	3.103	1	3.103	5.280	.023*
Error	90.487	154	.588		
Q6	3.103	1	3.103	5.543	.020*
Error	86.205	154	.560		
Q7	6.564	1	6.564	12.656	.000*
Error	79.872	154	.519		
Q8	3.391	1	3.391	6.400	.012*
Error	81.603	154	.530		

writing, it takes more time for mentors to guide. Therefore, both the experimental group and the control group hope that the mentor can guide on the spot, and students hold wait-and-see attitude towards the computer-supported collaborative learning teaching style.

4.3 The Study Hypothesis in Statistical Analysis of Multi-factor Variance

In the statistical analysis of multi-factor variance, two hypothetical problems are mainly discussed, one is the learning choice difference between gender groupings, and the other is the statistical analysis results of the experimental group and the control group. It can be seen from (Table 3) that there is no significant difference in gender grouping between the experimental group and the control group under the "collaborative guidance" multi-factor variance analysis statistics. This shows that although students have a fresh feeling and stimulation about the collaborative learning method used for graduation project in the process of learning, both the experimental group and the control group hold a wait-and-see attitude. However, the satisfaction of the 2 M group in the gender grouping is obviously low in the design transformation and the paper writing in the collaborative guidance dimension, which showed that the female students are uncertain and are not adapt to the computer-supported collaborative teaching. In the design transformation and expression of collaborative guidance in 1M1F group, the paper writing also shows a situation that the degree of satisfaction is slightly lower than other items, which also shows that the female students are more accustomed to mentor's onsite guidance of graduate project, and are full of doubts about the collaborative teaching and learning.

4.4 The Study Hypothesis in Statistical Analysis of Mean and Standard Deviation

In this study, three hypotheses are proposed based on the previous hypotheses: The first hypothesis was that the 2 M (two male) group of the single gender had better collaborative guidance preference than the 2F (two female) group of the single gender. The second hypothesis was that 2F (2 female students) in the gender equilibrium group preferred mentor guidance. The third hypothesis was that there was no significant difference in learning choice between gender unequilibrium group and the gender equilibrium group. From the data, it can be concluded that both male and female students have the same satisfaction degree in the mentor guidance, which shows that both the gender grouping and the students are fond of onsite guidance by mentor. They feel uncertain about collaborative guidance. In contrast to the collaborative guidance, the analysis of the data from (Table 4) shows that female students are less satisfied with the items 3 to 6 of collaborative guidance. Since these four questions are related to the dimension of design transformation and design expression, this may explain the understanding of knowledge-level transformation through internalization then coming the design products, especially that it needs the teaching by mentor personally. Not only that, it also needs to be explained through the design case. This also validates previous hypotheses, because many studies show that the majority of female students are less accustomed to computer collaborative learning, this may also lead to the impact of female students learning style.

Table 3. Results of multi-factor variance analysis of gender grouping of the experimental group and the control group in the dimension of "collaborative guidance"

Item	Category III sum of squares	Degree of freedom df	Mean sum of squares	F	Significance
Q1	.425	2	.213	.228	.796
Error	139.943	150	.933		
Q2	.190	2	.095	.117	.890
Error	122.036	150	.814		
Q3	.134	2	.067	.067	.936
Error	150.573	150	1.004		
Q4	.036	2	.018	.018	.982
Error	150.966	150	1.006		
Q5	.373	2	.186	.187	.829
Error	149.307	150	.995		
Q6	.234	2	.117	.118	.889
Error	149.148	150	.994		
Q7	.054	2	.027	.028	.973
Error	146.679	150	.978		
Q8	.430	2	.215	.176	.838
Error	182.626	150	1.218		

Table 4. Analysis results of gender in mean and standard deviation

Gender	Data	Q1	Q2	Q3	Q4	Q5	Q6	Q7	Q8
Male	Average value	4.19	4.15	4.13	4.15	4.13	4.16	4.13	4.07
	N	85	85	85	85	85	85	85	85
	Standard deviation	.906	.893	.923	.906	.897	.924	.973	1.078
Female	Average value	4.04	4.08	3.96*	3.89*	3.90*	3.96*	4.00	3.86
	N	71	71	71	71	71	71	71	71
	Standard deviation	1.006	.890	1.075	1.076	1.084	1.048	.986	1.112

5 Conclusions and Suggestions

In the era of information society and the advent of innovative learning model, learning through the Internet is no longer just a one-way learning of the computer or the Internet for individuals, but rather a learning activity that can interact with members of the community. Therefore, the "collaborative learning" teaching style is bound to form a trend. In this study, according to the related literature, theoretical construction and analysis, the author explores the best creative learning strategy in graduation project after comparing the differences of learning choice between gender groupings through "collaborative guidance" and "mentor guidance". The results of this study can be used as a reference for future teaching patterns in collaborative learning. The conclusions are as follows:

(1) This study investigated whether the gender grouping of graduation project can improve students' learning creativity through collaborative guidance by "mentor guidance" and "collaborative guidance" in the form of questionnaire survey. It found that male students were interested in this learning style, and female students were still used to traditional teaching. And this is quite consistent with a lot of research, because male students are more acceptable to network information products, while female students are the opposite. As a result, new strategies have emerged for gender grouping teaching styles, and in the group with more male students, we can consider implanting "collaborative learning" teaching patterns to promote their interest in learning. In the group with more female students, web-based learning can be used as an aid in teaching.

(2) On the other hand, the author thinks in his own teaching experience that there are individual differences in students' knowledge, quality and attitude in terms of enhancing students' creativity, so it is very difficult to make strategies. Teaching itself is teaching according to individual student's personality, quality and attitude, and the student's self-study attitude will be related to the teacher's teaching. In the network information age, how to use this tool to make the best learning effect of students while teachers, teaching materials and learners can achieve the best interaction should be the goal that teachers must strive for in the future.

As like the expected contribution of this study, one is to clarify whether gender grouping can enhance students' learning creativity through collaborative guidance of collaborative learning in graduation project. This study attempts to explore the parts that have not been studied in computer-supported collaborative learning, focusing on gender-specific learning differences, and trying to explore ways to enhance learning creativity. The second is the study of teaching methods in graduation project. Currently, the topics of university graduation project give priority to the group cooperation design, and there are differences in learning styles in the gender. In the network information age, we need to think about how to use this tool to create the best learning environment, so that students can acquire the knowledge and then obtain creativity. The follow-up study can expand the investigation of students' personality traits and make further research and discussion on the learning software and hardware of the Department of Environmental Design.

Acknowledgement. This study was funded by the Phase Results Fund of Fashion Industrial Design in Fuzhou University of International Studies and Trade (Fashion Industrial Design Element No.: 2018 KYTD-07), and thanks to all the participants who participated in this study.

References

Chen, S.: A practical study on "guidance - cooperative learning" teaching strategies to improve reading comprehension of elementary school children. Ph. D. thesis, Institute of Educational Psychology and Counseling, National Taiwan Normal University (1995)

Fuller, R.G., Bail, J.: Team teaching in the online graduate environment: collaborative instruction. Int. J. Inform. Commun. Technol. Educ. **7**(4), 72–83 (2011)

Huang, B., Lin, S.: A study on the effect of cooperative learning on learning effect: an integrated analysis. J. Educ. Psychol. **34**(1), 21–42 (2002)

Jonassen, D.H.: Computers as Mindtools for Schools: Engaging Critical Thinking, 2nd edn. Merrill, Upper Saddle River (2000)

Kirschner, P.A.: Can we support CSCL? educational, social and technological affordances for learning. In: Kirschner, P.A. (Ed) Three worlds of CSCL. Can we support CSCL, pp. 61–91. Heerlen, Open Universiteit Nederland (2002)

Koschmann, T.: Computer Supported Collaborative Learning: Theory and Practice of an Emerging Paradigm. Laurence Erlbaum, New Jersey (1996)

Lin, P.: Experimental study on cooperative learning's teaching method in senior vocational schools in Taiwan. Master thesis, Institute of Education, National Taiwan Normal University (1992)

Lin, W.: Creativity teaching and creativity cultivation—a case of [Design Thinking]. Educ. Mater. Res. Bimonthly **100**, 53–57 (2011)

Xiuman, L.: Teaching strategies for cooperative learning. J. Citizensh. Training **7**, 285–294 (1998)

Lefrancois, G.R.: Psychology for teaching. Wadsworth (1997)

Mayer, R.E.: Fifty years of creativity research. In: Sternberg, R.J. (Ed.) Handbook of Creativity, pp. 449–460. New York, Cambridge (1999)

Rubin, B., Fernandes, R.: Measuring the community of online classes. J. Asyn-chronous Learn. Netw. **17**(3), 1–21 (2013)

Stahl, G., Koschmann, T., Suthers, D.: Computer-supported collaborative learning: an historical perspective. In: Sawyer, R.K. (Ed.) Cambridge Handbook of the Learning Sciences, pp. 409–425. Cambridge University Press, Cambridge, UK (2006)

Sternberg, R.J.: Handbook of Creativity. Cambridge University Press, New York (1999)

Stahl, G., Koschmann, T., Suthers, D.: Computer-supported collaborative learning: an historical perspective. In: Sawyer, R.K. (Ed.) Cambridge Handbook of the Learning Sciences, pp. 409–426 (2006)

Walters, K., Misra, J.: Bringing collaborative teaching into doctoral programs: faculty and graduate student co-teaching as experiential training. Am. Sociologist **44**(3), 292–301 (2013)

Zhan, Z., et al.: Effects of gender grouping on students' group performance, individual achievements and attitudes in computer-supported collaborative learning. Comput. Hum. Behav. **48**, 587–596 (2015)

Zhiyu, Z.: The definition of creativity and the development of creativity—will children create? Educ. Res. Mon. **100**, 117–124 (2002)

Shihui, Z.: Inquiry into creative teaching, learning and evaluation. Educ. Mater. Res. Bimonthly **100**, 1–21 (2011)

Work-Life Imbalance, Health and Wellbeing of Older Workers: A Meta-analysis

Kapo Wong[1]([✉])[iD], Pei-Lee Teh[2,3][iD], and Tsz Wang Au[1]

[1] Department of Systems Engineering and Engineering Management, City University of Hong Kong, Kowloon, Hong Kong
`{kpwong42-c,tszwangau2-c}@my.cityu.edu.hk`
[2] School of Business, Monash University Malaysia, Bandar Sunway, Selangor Darul Ehsan, Malaysia
`teh.pei.lee@monash.edu`
[3] Gerontechnology Laboratory, Global Asia in the 21st Century (GA21) Platform, Monash University Malaysia, Bandar Sunway, Malaysia

Abstract. This paper aims to provide a meta-analytic examination of the relationship between work-life imbalance and health and wellbeing of older workers. Five hundred forty-four records were extracted from the databases. It was found that the overall odds ratio (OR) between work-life imbalance and the health of older workers was 1.369. Five types of health-related conditions were identified, namely burnout, mental health, physical health, self-rated health and social wellbeing. The category of burnout had the highest effect size and followed by self-rated health, mental health and physical health. The category with the lowest effect size was social wellbeing. The potential moderators in the relationship between work-life imbalance and the health of older workers included gender, region, decade of publication, working class and factors of work-life imbalance. The findings of this study suggest that work-life imbalance has an impact on health and wellbeing of older workers. Policy makers and organizational stakeholders should promote sustainable human resource practices so that staff development and employee wellbeing are targeted at all age groups including older workers. Older workers should have equal access to employability enhancing practices. Older workers and supervisors should be engaged in social dialogue to foster conversations on older workers' needs and expectations regarding work, non-work and personal fulfillment.

Keywords: Older workers · Work-life imbalance · Health · Burnout · Meta-analysis

1 Introduction

With the improvement of medical science and living standards, life expectancy in many countries is increasing, leading older workers to remain in the workforce longer. Post retirement employment is widely seen as an important part of the solution to aging population. However, employers are slow in retaining their older workers to tackle this

© Springer Nature Switzerland AG 2021
P.-L. P. Rau (Ed.): HCII 2021, LNCS 12772, pp. 230–240, 2021.
https://doi.org/10.1007/978-3-030-77077-8_18

societal challenge [1]. Much prior research on older workers has examined the individual-and organizational-factors that influence the work motivation and exit behavior [2–4]. However, recent studies have suggested that work-life balance that is largely focused on younger workers and workers with young children, may be an important factor in employment decisions and job performance of older workers [5, 6]. Therefore, there is a need for management scholars to understand the role of work-life balance (imbalance) on health and wellbeing of older workers.

Work-life balance refers to the ability to meet commitment at paid work and the rest of life outside work [5, 7]. At the individual level, work-life balance is the capability of joining work with other aspects of life [6]. Being able to maintain the balance between work and personal life can improve the health, work performance and life satisfaction of an individual [7]. Nonetheless, there are variations of the meaning of balance within individuals. For example, older workers may prefer healthcare benefits to childcare support in order to seek a balance between work and other aspects of their lives. In comparison with younger workers, older workers did not have the equal opportunity to attain work-life balance in the organizations [8]. In the workplace, placing skilled older workers in training and mentoring roles would add value to the organization [2]. However, organizations that do not reinvent their human resource practices in the support of work-life balance for older workers may have negative impact on the health and wellbeing of older workers. Numerous studies have found that the lack of work-life balance resulted in poor physical health and self-assessed health [8, 9]. Thus, the organizations should take seriously the issue of work-life imbalance in the workplace if they wish to maintain highly involved and productive older workers. To this end, we answer Angrisani et al. [5] call for research to examine the relationship between work-life balance (imbalance) and older worker's behavior. This line of research is particularly timely as the workforce ages.

This study departs from the common scholarly practice of studying work-life balance through survey method, and investigate the relationship between work-life imbalance and the health and wellbeing of older workers by using meta-analysis which synthesizes the results from multiple studies to generate a weighted average effect size [10]. To our knowledge, no prior research has conducted to examine these relationships.

2 Theoretical Background and Hypotheses

The term "older worker" has been used to refer to workers aged 50 or 55 and above [2]. Recently, North [11] has supplemented the definition of older workers with the concepts of Generation, Age, Tenure, and Experience (GATE) to address the overreliance on chronological age as the definition of older worker. Generation older workers are classified based on birth-cohort and their formative experiences [11]. Age-based workers exist at a certain chronological point in the lifespan [3]. Older workers who are employed in the organization for a certain period are known as the "old guard" by organizational tenure [11]. North [11] equate experience older workers with seasoned older workers who acquired knowledge and skillset over time. To this point, we use the GATE conceptualization of age in our study.

We draw on socioemotional selectivity theory [12], developed by Laura L. Carstensen and her collaborators to propose our hypothesis. Socioemotional selectivity theory suggests that motivation and life goal change as people grow older [12]. These changes in perspective lead older workers to navigate their environment in order to achieve work-life balance. Adopting the socioemotional selectivity theory, we argue that when older workers perceive time horizons are constrained, they prioritize meaningful goals by seeking a balance between work and outside work activities such as family care and community work. Therefore, it is expected that work-life imbalance will negatively affect the health and wellbeing of older workers. Furthermore, the meta-analysis conducted by Pinquart and Sörensen [13] reported that a strong quality of social networks had a positive effect on the wellbeing amongst older adults. From this, we postulate that a balance between work and nonwork life will positively affect the wellbeing of older workers. This backdrop led us to hypothesize:

H1: Work-life imbalance has a negative impact on the health and wellbeing of older workers.

3   Research Methods

3.1   Literature Search and Selection

The studies selected for conducting the meta-analysis were acquired from several databases, including Medline (PubMed), PsycINFO and Google Scholar. The keyworks used for searching the studies (work-life imbalance OR work-life balance) AND (health OR burnout OR mental health OR physical health OR self-rated health OR social wellbeing). The abstracts of each extracted article were screened, and duplications were removed. Article extraction was performed from 5th January to 15th March 2020. One thousand five hundred forty-three articles were extracted in the initial stage. One hundred fifty-six articles were identified for review based on the criteria for conducting the meta-analysis. First, only English publication were included. Second, the articles should provide the values of odds ratios and 95% confidence interval or sufficient data for computing the odds ratios. Third, the articles comprising sample of mature-age or older workers were included. In other words, articles with sample of retirees (i.e. unemployed samples in the studies) were excluded. Therefore, the cut-off age in this meta-analysis was 50 or above. Fourth, the studies investigating the relationships between work-life imbalance and health of older workers using organizational-level variables were excluded. Ultimately, twenty articles were selected and analyzed. These 20 articles used self-report method to collect data. Figure 1 shows the flow diagram of the extraction process of articles.

3.2   Coding for Studies

Authors, year of publication, gender, working class and factors of work-life imbalance were extracted from the studies. Gender was categorised into both male and female. Year of publication was grouped into three decades including 1990s, 2000s and 2010s. Given that there is a transformation change to the workplace in each decade, we coded the

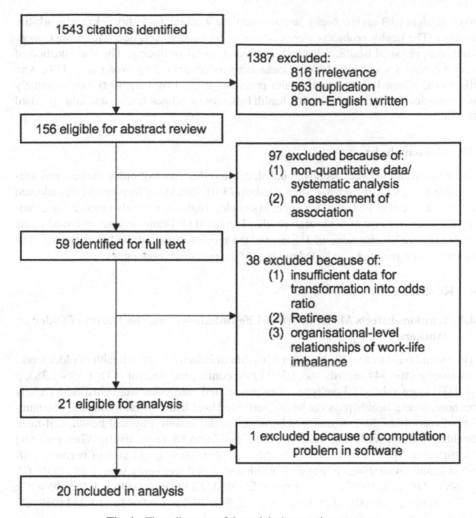

Fig. 1. Flow diagram of the articles' extraction process

studies into these three decades to make a comparison. Working class was classified into blue-collar occupations, cross-occupations, gold-collar occupations, pink-collar occupations and white-collar occupations. Blue-collar occupations were workers performing manual jobs, for example, construction, manufacturing and maintenance. Gold-collar occupations refer to the workers participating in problem solving and high knowledge work. Pink-collar occupations were the labours engaging in service industry. White-collar occupations generally refer to the management and office workers. Factors of work-life imbalance, which were the factors threatening the harmony between work and personal life, were identified from the studies. The factors of work-life imbalance were heavy workload, high job strain, high time pressure, lack of rest between work days, lack of rest between work periods, no work time flexibility, overtime working (41–55 h/week), work at night (>3 nights/week), serious overtime working (>55 h/week) and work-life conflict. The health problems were coded into five categories, namely, burnout, mental health, physical health, self-rated health and social wellbeing. The classification of health categories was based on the meta-analysis conducted by Wong et al. [14], who illustrated a broad spectrum of health problems caused by long work hours, namely physiological health, mental health, health behaviours, related health, and non-specified health.

3.3 Meta-analysis

The relationship between work-life imbalance and the health of older workers was analyzed by using Comprehensive Meta-Analysis (3.0). Random effects model was adopted to estimate the effects sizes as variances in samples, regions and study methods. To examine the heterogeneity of the overall results, I-squared (I^2) statistic was computed in the study. The higher the value of I^2 statistic, the more substantial the heterogeneity. The subgroup analysis was conducted to identify the potential moderators.

4 Result

4.1 Random-Effects Model of Work-Life Imbalance and the Health of Older Workers

The overall odds ratio (OR) between work-life imbalance and the health of older workers amongst the 544 records was 1.369 (95% confidence interval (CI): 1.356–1.383, p < 0.001) (see Table 1). Five types of health-related categories were classified, namely burnout, mental health, physical health, self-rated health and social wellbeing. The number of records in the subgroups of burnout, mental health, physical health, self-rated health and social wellbeing were 24, 109, 276, 77 and 58, respectively. When grouping by different types of outcomes of health, the aggregated effect size of burnout, self-rated health, mental health, physical health and social wellbeing were 2.189 (95% CI: 1.988–2.410, p < 0.001), 2.048 (95% CI: 1.980–2.118, p < 0.001), 1.408 (95% CI: 1.376–1.440, p < 0.001), 1.293 (95% CI: 1.278–1.309, p < 0.001) and 1.234 (95% CI: 1.175–1.297, p < 0.001).

Table 1. Random effects meta-analysis of relationship between work-life imbalance and the health of older workers.

Health category	Number of records	Effect size and 95% interval			Heterogeneity	
		Overall OR	95% lower	95% upper	P-value	I-squared
Overall	544	1.369	1.356	1.383	0.000	88.491

Q and I^2 statistic are capable to examine the heterogeneity of the overall effects size. Q statistic is sensitive to the number of records, while I^2 statistic is not dependent with the number of records and estimated effect size [15]. The I^2 value of the overall effect size is 88.491% which indicated a considerable heterogeneity.

4.2 Publication Bias

Trim-and-fill analysis was adopted to evaluate the existence of publication bias [16]. Figure 2a demonstrated the meta-analysis performing for 544 records without adjustment. To adjust the bias effect size, 155 new data were added to the left of the mean of the funnel plot (see Fig. 2b) and the new effect size was 1.206 (95% CI: 1.196–1.21714).

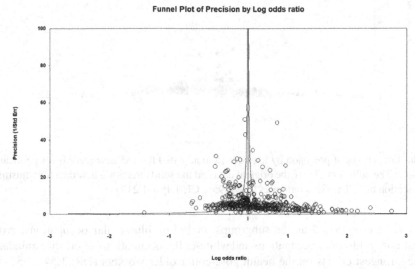

Fig. 2a. Funnel plot of precision by log odds ratio for publication bias. Note: The hollow circle are the original data. The odds ratio was 1.369 (95% CI: 1.356–1.383).

4.3 Moderator Analysis

Moderator analysis was used to examine the potential sources of the heterogeneity. The potential moderators were gender, region, decade of publication, working class and factors of work-life imbalance. It was found that these five sources were the moderators of the relationship between work-life imbalance and the health of older workers ($p <$ 0.000) (see Table 2). For gender, the impacts of work-life imbalance on the health of female older workers (OR: 1.409, 95% CI: 1.380–1.438) were stronger than the male older workers (OR: 1.229, 95% CI: 1.202–1.256). For region, there were three types of subgroups, namely, Asian countries, European countries and North America. North America (OR: 1.529, 95% CI: 1.498–1.561) exerts the most significant effects on the relationship between work-life imbalance and the health of older workers compared by Asian countries (OR: 1.198, 95% CI: 1.178–1.219) and European countries (OR: 1.430, 95% CI: 1.409–1.451). For the decade of publication, 1990s (OR: 2.129, 95% CI: 1.943–2.334) has the greatest influence on the association between work-life imbalance and the health of older workers compared by 2000s (OR: 1.394, 95% CI: 1.371–1.417) and 2010s (OR: 1.346, 95% CI: 1.330–1.363). For working class, four types of working

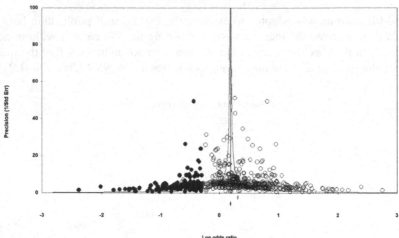

Fig. 2b. Funnel plot of precision by log odds ratio adjusted for 155 new records for publication bias. Note: The hollow circle are the original data and the solid circles are new data for adjustment of publication bias. The odds ratio was 1.206 (95% CI: 1.196–1.217).

classes were categorised as the subgroups, including blue-collar occupations, cross-occupations, gold-collar occupations and white-collar occupations. Work-life imbalance has the strongest effects on the health gold-collar older workers (OR: 1.540, 95% CI: 1.434–1.653). For factors of work-life balance, there were 10 subgroups, namely, heavy workload, high job strain, high time pressure, lack of rest between work days, lack of rest between work periods, no work time flexibility, overtime working (41–51 h/week), work at night (>3 nights/week), serious overtime working (>55 h/week) and work-life conflict. Lack of rest between workdays has the highest value of odds ratio which is 3.173 (95% CI: 2.357–4.271).

Table 2. The relationship of work-life imbalance and the health of older workers in relation to gender, region, decade of publication, working class and factors of work-life imbalance.

Moderator	Effect size and 95% interval			Test of null		Test to model	
	Overall OR	95% lower	95% upper	p-value	I-squared	$df(Q)$	Meta-regression p-value
Gender						175	0.000
Female	1.409	1.380	1.438	0.000	94.332		
Male	1.229	1.202	1.256	0.000	90.102		
Region						543	0.000

(continued)

Table 2. (*continued*)

Moderator	Effect size and 95% interval			Test of null		Test to model	
	Overall OR	95% lower	95% upper	*p*-value	*I*-squared	*df (Q)*	Meta-regression *p*-value
Asian countries	1.198	1.178	1.219	0.000	97.438		
European countries	1.430	1.409	1.451	0.000	79.892		
North America	1.529	1.498	1.561	0.000	92.671		
Decade of publication						543	0.000
1990s	2.129	1.943	2.334	0.000	64.212		
2000s	1.394	1.371	1.417	0.000	78.649		
2010s	1.346	1.330	1.363	0.000	93.623		
Working class						543	0.000
Blue-collar	1.120	1.089	1.152	0.000	85.410		
Cross section	1.421	1.406	1.436	0.000	88.130		
Gold-collar	1.540	1.434	1.653	0.000	63.546		
White-collar	1.170	1.114	1.228	0.000	96.6992		
Factors of work-life imbalance						543	0.000
Heavy workload	1.040	0.873	1.239	0.000	85.599		
High job strain	1.312	1.233	1.396	0.000	73.261		
High time pressure	1.345	1.122	1.612	0.000	68.653		
Lack of rest between work days	3.173	2.357	4.271	0.297	18.461		
Lack of rest between work periods	1.393	1.205	1.610	0.001	72.812		
No work time flexibility	0.989	0.822	1.189	0.582	0.000		
Overtime working (41–55 h/week)	1.298	1.265	1.331	0.000	79.297		

(*continued*)

Table 2. (*continued*)

Moderator	Effect size and 95% interval			Test of null		Test to model	
	Overall OR	95% lower	95% upper	*p*-value	*I*-squared	*df* (*Q*)	Meta-regression *p*-value
Work at night (>3 nights/week)	1.640	1.411	1.906	0.151	43.381		
Serious overtime working (>55 h/week)	2.005	1.910	2.105	0.000	76.024		
Work-life conflict	1.354	1.339	1.370	0.000	91.883		

5   Discussion and Conclusion

The purpose of this study is to examine the association of work-life imbalance and the health and wellbeing of older workers through a meta-analysis approach. Five hundred forty-four records were extracted from 20 articles were used to investigate the relationship. The results show that work-life imbalance would increase the likelihood of older workers suffering from health problems. Five types of health-related problems were identified from the records. Burnout was found to be the most serious health problem confronted by the older workers under work-life imbalance.

The findings of this study are aligned with previous research. Older workforce literature found that older workers without benefiting from flexibility might suffer from physical and mental health problems [8]. It was also found that an unsustainable workplace environment, for example, no protection and rights at work, which was adversely affected the health of the older workers [17]. From these, different types of policies and working cultures might greatly influence the work-life balance of employees. There were various factors contributing to work-life imbalance, for instance, overtime working, lack of rest and no flexibility. These factors were found to be negatively correlated with the health of older workers [18, 19]. The results of this study confirm the association between different factors of work-life imbalance and the health of older workers. Lack of rest between workday was found to be the strongest effect on the health and wellbeing of older workers. This result suggests that it is important to take break between work to maintain and improve the employee wellbeing.

Furthermore, gender, region, decade of publication and working class were assessed as the significant moderators in the relationship between work-life imbalance and the health of older workers. The female older workers had a stronger odds ratio than the male older workers may be due to the combination of paid and nonpaid work at home amongst female older workers [17]. Interestingly, we found that North America and European countries constituted stronger significant effects on the relationship between work-life imbalance and the health of older workers compared by Asian countries. The working hours in western countries are usually longer than Asian countries [20] and thus this finding is needed to be further investigated. For the decade of publication, Barber et al. [21] found that the implementation of work-life initiatives amongst organisations improves the work-life balance of workers. For working class, gold-collar workers had the strongest effects size compared by blue- and white-collar workers. A possible explanation for this result may be high dedication in the careers and jobs amongst gold-collar workers. Further study is required to evaluate this phenomenon.

From a practical point of view, the findings of this study have several important implications for future practice. Understanding the detrimental effect brought by work-life imbalance to the health and wellbeing of older workers, reforming the health services to meet the needs of older workers, improving the management and adjusting the attitude towards older workforce are the effective ways to alleviate the problems [22]. All these reforming and improvement are the new challenges to many organizations. However, managerial policies and practices should be revisited to hire or retain older workers to accommodate a rapidly older workforce. Older workforce has numerous constructive attributes to the organisations, for instances, loyalty, high engagement and low turnover rate [23]. Organizations should treat older workers with respect and dignity and develop effective strategies to promote work-life balance among older workers.

This study is not without limitations. First, the study is dependent on the data from published articles. Many articles did not classify the types of occupations of the participants. As a result, the findings of this study do not provide insights into the effects of occupation types on the relationship between work-life imbalance and the health and wellbeing of older workers. Second, some articles in our analysis did not provide the percentage of the male and female. It would be valuable to have future empirical studies to report the sample's gender profile. Third, this meta-analysis only included the articles published in English. Future research could include other languages in their meta-analysis study.

References

1. Kulik, C.T., Perera, S., Cregan, C.: Engage me: the mature-age worker and stereotype threat. Acad. Manage. J. **59**(6), 2132–2156 (2016)
2. Kooij, D., de Lange, A., Jansen, P., Dikkers, J.: Older workers' motivation to continue to work: five meanings of age. J. Manag. Psychol. **23**(4), 364–394 (2008)
3. Manzi, C., Coen, S., Crapolicchio, E., Medina, L., Paderi, F.: The right place for me: a moderated mediation model to explain the involvement of employees aged over 50 years. J. Appl. Soc. Psychol. **51**(1), 42–52 (2020)
4. Shacklock, K., Fulop, L., Hort, L.: Managing older worker exit and re-entry practices: a "revolving door"? Asia Pac. J. Hum. Resour. **45**, 151–167 (2007)
5. Angrisani, M., Casanova, M., Meijer, E.: Work-life balance and labor force attachment at older ages. J. Labor Res. **41**(1), 34–68 (2020)
6. Gardiner, J., Stuart, M., Forde, C., Greenwood, I., MacKenzie, R., Perrett, R.: Work–life balance and older workers: employees' perspectives on retirement transitions following redundancy. Int. J. Hum. Resour. Manag. **18**(3), 476–489 (2007)
7. Guest, D.E.: Perspectives on the study of work-life balance. Soc. Sci. Inf. **41**(2), 255–279 (2002)

8. Richert-Kaźmierska, A., Stankiewicz, K.: Work–life balance: does age matter? Work **55**(3), 679–688 (2016). https://doi.org/10.3233/wor-162435

9. Wainwright, D., et al.: Extending working life and the management of change. Is the workplace ready for the ageing worker? Ageing Soc. **39**(11), 1–23 (2018)

10. Sutton, A.J., Abrams, K.R., Jones, D.R., Sheldon, T.A., Song, F.: Methods for Meta-Analysis in Medical Research. Wiley, Chichester (2000)

11. North, M.S.: A GATE to understanding "older" workers: generation, age, tenure, experience. Acad. Manag. Ann. **13**(2), 414–443 (2019)

12. Charles, S.T., Carstensen, L.L.: Social and emotional aging. Ann. Rev. Psychol. **61**, 383–409 (2010)

13. Pinquart, M., Sörensen, S.: Influences of socioeconomic status, social network, and competence on subjective well-being in later life: a meta-analysis. Psychol. Aging **15**(2), 187–224 (2000)

14. Wong, K., Chan, A.H.S., Ngan, S.C.: The effect of long working hours and overtime on occupational health: a meta-analysis of evidence from 1998 to 2018. Int. J. Environ. Res. Publ. Health **16**(12), 2102 (2019)

15. Higgins, J., Thompson, S.G.: Quantifying heterogeneity in a meta-analysis. Stat. Med. **21**(11), 1539–1558 (2002)

16. Duval, S., Tweedie, R.: Trim and fill: a simple funnel-plot–based method of testing and adjusting for publication bias in meta-analysis. Biometrics **56**(2), 455–463 (2000)

17. Vives, A., Gray, N., González, F., Molina, A.: Gender and ageing at work in Chile: employment, working conditions, work–life balance and health of men and women in an ageing workforce. Ann. Work Expo. Health **62**(4), 475–489 (2018)

18. Chandra, V.: Work–life balance: eastern and western perspectives. Int. J. Hum. Resour. Manag. **23**(5), 1040–1056 (2012)

19. Barber, L.K., Grawitch, M.J., Maloney, P.W.: Work-life balance: contemporary perspectives. In: Grawitch, M.J., Ballard, D.W. (Eds.) The Psychologically Healthy Workplace: Building a Win-Win Environment for Organizations and Employees, pp. 111–133. American Psychological Association (2016). https://doi.org/10.1037/14731-006

20. Choi, E., Kim, J.: The association between work–life balance and health status among Korean workers. Work **58**(4), 509–517 (2017). https://doi.org/10.3233/wor-172641

21. Mensah, A., Adjei, N.K.: Work-life balance and self-reported health among working adults in Europe: a gender and welfare state regime comparative analysis. BMC Publ. Health **20**(1), 1–14 (2020). https://doi.org/10.1186/s12889-020-09139-w

22. Ilmarinen, J.: The ageing workforce—challenges for occupational health. Occup. Med. **56**(6), 362–364 (2006). https://doi.org/10.1093/occmed/kql046

23. Loretto, W., White, P.: Employers' attitudes, practices and policies towards older workers. Hum. Resour. Manag. J. **16**(3), 313–330 (2006). https://doi.org/10.1111/j.1748-8583.2006.00013.x

Cross-Cultural Education: The Effects of AR Technology and Learning Styles on Learning Achievements of Sculpture Course

Weilong Wu[ID], Yen Hsu[✉][ID], Xin Cao, and Jiangjie Chen

The Graduate Institute of Design Science, Tatung University, No. 40, Sec. 3, Zhongshan N. Road, Taipei City 10461, Taiwan, China

Abstract. Objectives: In the wake of the COVID-19 epidemic, more and more schools are opting for online learning, and the integration of AR or VR technology into learning is becoming a trend that is gaining popularity. For learners from different cultures around the world, cross-cultural AR technology may help them improve their learning effectiveness.

With the development of technology, it has become common to integrate technology in teaching and learning. There is a growing debate about the way teachers teach in the school classroom, and there is a general desire for teachers to be the leaders of students, helping them to think and solve learning problems. Such a situation forces teachers to be constantly receptive to new knowledge, to improve themselves, and to better guide their students through flexible and varied teaching styles. Therefore, the use of appropriate technology in the classroom will improve the quality of teaching and the learning experience of students, and the development of augmented reality (AR) technology has brought a great change to the learning in the classroom.

AR technology supports interaction between real and virtual environments, allowing users to manipulate the application interface of AR software. AR technology offers many benefits to the education sector, as it has the potential to engage students in more effective learning than traditional methods. It allows students to participate in real-life 3D environment simulations, increase their attention span, and engage in interactive learning through virtual manipulation.

At the same time, in the learning process, students from different cultural backgrounds will follow their own preferred learning styles to conduct learning activities. Students perform tasks and learning activities in the learning process in accordance with their preferred learning styles. The study of learning styles has been of great value to the field of education, and therefore has received a lot of attention and input from educational researchers, gradually evolving into a separate field of study.

The Sculpture Course is a required course for product design majors and is taught in a way that the instructor demonstrates to students the techniques of making relief clay sculptures. Since no previous research has applied AR technology to the teaching of relief sculpture, this study attempts to investigate the effect of AR teaching style on learning effectiveness when applied to Sculpture Course by using teaching style and learning style as independent variables, and then analyze the difference in learning effectiveness between students with different learning styles in traditional teaching and AR teaching style.

© Springer Nature Switzerland AG 2021
P.-L. P. Rau (Ed.): HCII 2021, LNCS 12772, pp. 241–250, 2021.
https://doi.org/10.1007/978-3-030-77077-8_19

Since no previous research has applied AR technology to the teaching of relief sculpture, this study attempts to apply the unique interactive function of AR technology to the relief sculpture course, allowing students to use AR technology to make relief clay models in the relief sculpture course. Therefore, this study attempts to investigate the effect of AR teaching style on learning effectiveness when applied to relief courses by using teaching style and learning style as independent variables, and then analyze the difference in learning effectiveness between students with different learning styles in traditional teaching and AR teaching style.

Methods: In this study, 39 students from the product design department of a university in China, who were basically from different regions and had different cultural backgrounds, were selected for the experimental design. The students in the experimental group practiced relief sculpture in the AR teaching method, while the students in the control group studied in the traditional teaching method. They were given a pre-test of VAK (Visual, Auditory, and Kinesthetic Learning Styles) learning styles to distinguish which learning style type they were.

In the pre-test portion, the subjects are first asked to fill out the VAK learning style scale to classify those with different learning styles. After the pre-test, students were informed of the grouping requirements and provided with the same instructional materials and resources (i.e., picture study sheets and AR tools) before proceeding to the experimental design, with the difference being that the control group used the picture study sheets to learn to make the relief clay sculptures, while the experimental group used the picture study sheets and AR tools to learn.

The experiment was conducted in a professional sculpture classroom, and the control group and the experimental group were in two different classrooms for the experiment. At the end of the relief sculpture course, the teacher will score the students' works and the scores of the works will be analyzed as the learning effectiveness of the study.

Results: The results of the experiment showed that the AR teaching method significantly improved students' learning outcomes compared to traditional teaching, and that the visual and kinesthetic students performed better than the auditory students in the different learning styles. Auditory students did not differ significantly between the traditional and AR teaching styles.

Conclusions: The results of the study also showed that the AR teaching method has significant differences for different learning styles in cross-cultural contexts, and has a certain enhancement effect for students who are good at learning with their hands. The AR teaching method does have a substantial effect on the Sculpture Course, and will also provide beneficial help in product design education research in the future.

Keywords: AR technology · Learning styles · Design education · Cross-cultural education

1 Introduction

In the wake of the COVID-19 epidemic, more and more schools are opting for online learning, and the integration of AR or VR technology into learning is becoming a trend that is gaining popularity [19]. For learners from different cultures around the world, cross-cultural AR technology may help them improve their learning effectiveness. With the development of technology, it has become common to integrate technology in teaching and learning [20]. There is a growing debate about the way teachers teach in the school classroom, and there is a general desire for teachers to be the leaders of students, helping them to think and solve learning problems [29]. Such a situation forces teachers to be constantly receptive to new knowledge, to improve themselves, and to better guide their students through flexible and varied teaching styles [21, 30]. Therefore, the use of appropriate technology in the classroom will improve the quality of teaching and the learning experience of students, and the development of augmented reality (AR) technology has brought a great change to the learning in the classroom [20].

AR technology supports interaction between real and virtual environments, allowing users to manipulate the application interface of AR software [22]. AR technology offers many benefits to the education sector, as it has the potential to engage students in more effective learning than traditional methods. It allows students to participate in real-life 3D environment simulations, increase their attention span, and engage in interactive learning through virtual manipulation [23]. At the same time, in the learning process, students from different cultural backgrounds will follow their own preferred learning styles to conduct learning activities. Students perform tasks and learning activities in the learning process in accordance with their preferred learning styles [24]. The study of learning styles has been of great value to the field of education, and therefore has received a lot of attention and input from educational researchers, gradually evolving into a separate field of study [25]. The learning styles of students in cross-cultural contexts are individually different, and it would be more helpful for students' learning effectiveness if teachers could improve their teaching styles to meet the individual differences of students from different cultural backgrounds [24].

The Sculpture Course course is a required course for product design majors and is taught in a way that the instructor demonstrates to students the techniques of making relief clay sculptures [12]. During the course, students begin to apply and master the basics of relief sculpture creation through the study of relief making techniques [26]. As a common art form in students' daily lives, relief sculpture may not be noticed, so students may feel unfamiliar and lack interest in learning how to make relief models at the beginning [27].

Since no previous research has applied AR technology to the teaching of relief sculpture, this study attempts to apply the unique interactive function of AR technology to the relief sculpture course, allowing students to use AR technology to make relief clay models in the relief sculpture course.

Therefore, this study attempts to investigate the effect of AR teaching style on learning effectiveness when applied to sculpture course by using teaching style and learning style as independent variables, and then analyze the difference in learning effectiveness between students with different learning styles in traditional teaching and AR teaching style.

2 Literature Review

2.1 Learning Styles

Since the 1970s, research on the learning style has gradually begun. Rita Dunn, Kenneth Dunn and David Kolb were the first scholars to study learning styles [8]. Regarding the definition of learning style, Dunn (1984) pointed out that learning style is a method or skill for learners to absorb and memorize information [6]. No matter how to deal with information, there is a significant difference between each learner. Dunn & Griggs (1988) further suggested that students' learning outcomes will be affected by different time and feelings in different places; and the students' attitude towards learning will also affect their learning outcomes [7]. Garger & Guild (1984) also proposed that learning style is the characteristic that individual students show when they are learning. It is the interaction between their learning behavior and personality traits [10]. There are many classifications and studies on learning styles. For example, famous experts Kolb (1985) classify learning styles into two major facets based on the perception and processing of information, and then further summarize the learning theories according to the learners' experience: Diverger, Accommodator, Convergers and Assimilators are four different learning styles [14]. Gregorc (1985) is a collection of four classification modes: Concrete-Sequential, Abstract-Sequential, Concrete-Random, and Abstract-Random [11]. In addition, Felder & Silverman (1988) developed a learning style scale based on years of research, and divided the learning style into four major facets, each of which is divided into two types, totaling eight types of learning styles [9, 15].

The learning style selected in this study is divided by Bandler, Grinder, & O'Stevens (1979) according to the human senses. By analyzing the learner's past preferences, the learner's learning style is divided into visual and auditory and kinesthetic, namely VAK (Visual, Auditory, and Kinesthetic Learning Styles) learning style [5, 10]. Different from the learning style proposed by Kolb or Felder-Silverman et al., the VAK learning style proposed by Bandler & Grinder is classified by the sense of human intuition. The application of the maturity in selecting subjects is broader and more suitable. Applied to all ages [1]. This classification model considers the way in which learning messages are absorbed and better considers the preferences of learners or teachers [17, 18]. Sharp, Bowker, & Byrne (2008) also pointed out that in the learning style teaching strategies developed by British teachers, more teachers chose VAK learning style theory to carry out teaching because of "simple and fast" [16]. Since the research object of this research is students of art design, they will be more intense in sensory experience than other students, and this study is the application of AR in the Clay Sculpture course [4]. Vision is a very important reference factor in research. Therefore, it was decided to use the VAK learning style theory proposed by Bandler & Grinder as the basis for the research tool scale.

2.2 Augmented Reality Technology

Augmented Reality (AR) uses the real environment and virtual environment as the two ends of the system in the real-virtual continuity system [22]. The continuous interval in the center is mixed reality, in which Augmented Virtuality is called augmented reality

(AR), which is close to the real environment, to establish a virtual environment to provide the transmission of interactive messages [23]. Berryman, (2012) pointed out that AR can enable users to integrate virtual objects into the real environment in the real world by image overlay to increase the user experience [2].

In teaching process, AR tools provide students with immediate and relevant information, such as videos and 3D images, to help them analyze and solve problems and improve their motivation and understanding [28]. Guan, J. Q., et al. indicates that in the experiential learning using AR tools, children can be in an interactive environment between learning materials and participate in virtual operations while being associated with the real environment to attract their space [28]. Therefore, it can be found that the advantage of AR application is that the teaching materials are presented in a rich and diverse manner, allowing the user to directly interact with the teaching materials and immersed in the AR teaching mode [23]. However, whether the AR teaching method plays its due role in the teaching time than the traditional teaching method, Rau et al., (2018) pointed out that in the Chinese reading speed, the students want to compare with the desktop display device by using VR and AR. It was found that students chose about 10% more time on VR and AR [3].

3 Experiment Design

3.1 Participant

In order to improve the effectiveness of the research, this study combines the syllabus of the sculpture course of higher education to enable the subjects to learn related embossed content. The subjects were 39 first-year freshmen from the sculpture department of a university in southern China. They were divided into a control group and an experimental group. The control group consisted of 19 people and the experimental group was 20.

3.2 Measuring Tools

This study explores the differences in learning achievements between students with different teaching styles and different learning styles. Therefore, a scale and a transcript are used, respectively, for the VAK Learning Style Scale and academic scores. The VAK Learning Style Scale divides the learning style into visual, auditory and kinesthetic. There are 15 items. According to the proportion of each item in 15 items, the type of student's learning style is determined. In terms of reliability, the visual reliability is .86, the auditory reliability is .80, and the kinesthetic reliability is .75. Finally, the transcripts of the Clay Sculpture Courses, the syllabus requirements of the embossed course of this study, score the scores of the Clay Sculpture Courses produced by the students, with a total score of 100 points. The three teachers who teach at the College of Art and Design of the University will be graded, then the expert validity will be evaluated, and the average score of the total score will be obtained as the basis for the evaluation of the learning outcome after the experiment. In developing software, 3D modeling development software uses Zbrush, while virtual buttons use Unity 3D and Voforia Augmented Reality Suite. The App software mainly uses the "Lion Head" as the material space model as a textbook for students to produce embossed clay sculptures. The APP software applications are applicable to smart phones of IOS and Android systems respectively.

3.3 Experimental Process

The relief course is a compulsory course for the first-year university students. The course lasts for 5 weeks and 80 h. The main purpose of this study is to explore the impact of different teaching methods on learning style and learning outcomes. Therefore, in the pre-testing part, the subjects will first fill in the VAK learning style scale to classify different learning styles. After the pre-test, students will be informed of the grouping requirements and provide the same teaching materials and resources (ie, picture learning sheets and AR tools) before the experiment is designed. The difference is that the control group uses the picture learning list to learn to make the embossed clay sculpture. The experimental group used picture learning sheets and AR tools to learn. The experimental site was in a professional sculpture classroom, and the control group and the experimental group students were experimented in two different classrooms. After the embossing course is over, the teacher will score based on the work produced by the student, and the score of the work will be analyzed as the learning outcome of the study.

In this study, 39 students from the product design department of a university in China, who were basically from different regions and had different cultural backgrounds, were selected for the experimental design. The students in the experimental group practiced relief sculpture in the AR teaching method, while the students in the control group studied in the traditional teaching method. They were given a pre-test of VAK (Visual, Auditory, and Kinesthetic Learning Styles) learning styles to distinguish which learning style type they were. Just shown in the Fig. 1.

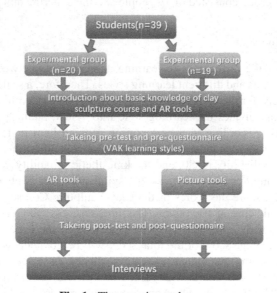

Fig. 1. The experimental process

In the pre-test portion, the subjects are first asked to fill out the VAK learning style scale to classify those with different learning styles. After the pre-test, students were informed of the grouping requirements and provided with the same instructional materials and resources (i.e., picture study sheets and AR tools) before proceeding to the experimental design, with the difference being that the control group used the picture study sheets to learn to make the relief clay sculptures, while the experimental group used the picture study sheets and AR tools to learn.

The experiment was conducted in a professional sculpture classroom, and the control group and the experimental group were in two different classrooms for the experiment. At the end of the relief sculpture course, the teacher will score the students' works and the scores of the works will be analyzed as the learning effectiveness of the study.

4 Experimental Results

4.1 Explore the Impact of Different Teaching Methods on Students' Learning Effectiveness

As can be seen from Table 1, the independent sample t-test analysis is used to study the differences between traditional teaching and AR teaching on learning effectiveness. It can be seen from the table that different teaching methods all show significant effects on learning effectiveness ($P < 0.05$), which means that different teaching methods have differences in learning effectiveness. Specific analysis shows that different teaching methods have a significant level of 0.05 in learning effectiveness ($t = -2.49$, $P = 0.02$), and the specific comparison shows that the average value of traditional teaching (78.74) will be significantly lower than the average of AR teaching Value (82.70). Therefore, the results show that different teaching methods all show significant differences in learning effectiveness.

Table 1. Learning achievements

Learning achievements	Group	N	Average	SD	t	p
Sculpture course	Traditional	19	78.74	4.68	2.49	.017*
	AR	20	82.70	5.21		

$*p < .05$ $**p < .01$

4.2 Explore the Differences in Learning Effectiveness of Different Teaching Styles

It can be known from Table 2 that a paired t-test is used to analyze the differences in experimental design. From the table, it can be seen that there are 3 pairs of data, which are visual, auditory, and kinesthetic. Among them, there are differences in visual and kinesthetic paired data (P < 0.05). The specific analysis shows that the visual students of traditional teaching and the visual students of AR teaching have a significant level of 0.01 (t = −3.19, P = 0.01), and the specific comparison shows that the visual students of traditional teaching The average (79.17) will be significantly lower than the average (82.67) of visual students in AR teaching. There is a significant level of 0.05 (t = −7.00, P = 0.02) between the kinesthetic students of traditional teaching and the kinesthetic students of AR teaching, and the specific comparison shows that the average of kinesthetic students of traditional teaching is The value (78.00) will be significantly lower than the average value of kinesthetic students in AR teaching (85.00). Therefore, among the three pairs of data, there are differences between the visual and kinesthetic students in their learning effectiveness.

Table 2. Learning styles

VAK	Learning styles	Average	SD	MD	Standard error	t	p
Visual	Traditional	79.17	5.39	−3.5	3.802	−3.19	.009**
	AR	82.67	5.99				
Auditory	Traditional	78.00	4.24	−2.75	3.754	−1.99	.14
	AR	80.75	5.38				
Kinesthetic	Traditional	78.00	2.65	−7	1.732	−7	.02*
	AR	85.00	1.00				

$*p < .05 **p < .01$

5   Discussion and Conclusions

The purpose of this study is to explore the influence of different teaching methods on learners' learning effectiveness and the differences between different teaching methods and different learning styles. In the teaching of sculpture course, compared with the traditional teaching method, the teaching method of AR significantly improves the learning effect of students. In addition, visual and kinesthetic students have better learning performance than auditory students in different learning styles. There is no significant difference between the traditional teaching method and AR teaching method for auditory students. Visual students for AR learning will have good interest in learning the way of teaching, the research results also show that AR teaching methods are obviously different for students with different learning styles, and have certain enhancement effect for students who are good at learning with hands-on ability [13]. Therefore, AR teaching way in the sculpture course does have the significant effect, will be back in the visual art education research provided the beneficial help. The results of the study also showed that the AR teaching method has significant differences for different learning styles in cross-cultural contexts, and has a certain enhancement effect for students who are good at learning with their hands. The AR teaching method does have a substantial effect on the sculpture course, and will also provide beneficial help in product design education research in the future. According to the research results, there are the following Suggestions for future research. First, the small sample size is a problem. Secondly, the art foundation of the subject can be added into the control variable, because the art foundation is likely to affect the learning effect.

References

1. Cassidy*, S.: Learning styles: an overview of theories, models, and measures. Educ. Psychol. **24**(4), 419–444 (2004)
2. Berryman, D.R.: Augmented reality: a review. Med. Ref. Serv. Q. **31**(2), 212–218 (2012)
3. Rau, P.-L.P., Zheng, J., Guo, Z., Li, J.: Speed reading on virtual reality and augmented reality. Comput. Educ. **125**, 240–245 (2018)
4. Balakrishnan, V., Gan, C.L.: Students' learning styles and their effects on the use of social media technology for learning. Telematics Inform. **33**(3), 808–821 (2016)
5. Sandier, R., Grinder, J.: Frogs Into Princes. Real People Press, Moab (1979)
6. Dunn, R.: Learning style: state of the science. Theor. Pract. **23**(1), 10–19 (1984)
7. Dunn, R., Griggs, S.A.: Learning styles: Quiet revolution in American secondary schools: ERIC (1988)
8. Felder, R.M., Henriques, E.R.: Learning and teaching styles in foreign and second language education. Foreign Lang. Ann. **28**(1), 21–31 (1995)
9. Felder, R.M., Silverman, L.K.: Learning and teaching styles in engineering education. Eng. Educ. **78**(7), 674–681 (1988)
10. Garger, S., Guild, P.: Learning styles: the crucial differences. Curric. Rev. **23**(1), 9–12 (1984)
11. Gregorc, A.F.: Gregorc style delineator: A self-assessment instrument for adults: Gregorc Assoc. (1985)
12. Grigorenko, E.L., Sternberg, R.J.: Thinking styles. International handbook of personality and intelligence, pp. 205–229. Springer, Boston (1995). https://doi.org/10.1007/978-1-4757-5571-8_11
13. Hawk, T.F., Shah, A.J.: Using learning style instruments to enhance student learning. Decis. Sci. J. Innov. Educ. **5**(1), 1–19 (2007)
14. Kolb, D.A.: Learning-Style Inventory: Self-Scoring Inventory and Interpretation Booklet. TRG Hay/McBer (1985)
15. Pritchard, A.: Learning Styles. Ways of Learning: Learning Theories and Learning Styles in the Classroom. Milton Park, Abingdon, Oxon, Routledge, New York (2005)
16. Sharp, J.G., Bowker, R., Byrne, J.: VAK or VAK-uous? Towards the trivialisation of learning and the death of scholarship. Res. Pap. Educ. **23**(3), 293–314 (2008)
17. Vázquez, A.L., Delfin, R.T.: Learning styles in high school mathematics. Am. Sci. Res. J. Eng. Tech. Sci. (ASRJETS) **31**(1), 207–213 (2017)
18. Zacharis, N.Z.: The effect of learning style on preference for web-based courses and learning outcomes. Br. J. Educ. Tech. **42**(5), 790–800 (2011)
19. Khan, S., Mian, A.: Medical education: COVID-19 and surgery. Br. J. Surg. **107**(8), e269 (2020)
20. Iwanaga, J., Loukas, M., Dumont, A.S., Tubbs, R.S.: A review of anatomy education during and after the COVID-19 pandemic: revisiting traditional and modern methods to achieve future innovation. Clin. Anat. **34**(1), 108–114 (2021)
21. Ibáñez, M.B., Portillo, A.U., Cabada, R.Z., Barrón, M.L.: Impact of augmented reality technology on academic achievement and motivation of students from public and private Mexican schools. a case study in a middle-school geometry course. Comput. Educ. **145**, 103734 (2020)

22. Azuma, R.T.: A survey of augmented reality. Presence: Teleoperators Virtual Environ. **6**(4), 355–385 (1997)
23. Billinghurst, M.: Augmented reality in education. New Horiz. Learn. **12**(5), 1–5 (2002)
24. Wang, R., Lowe, R., Newton, S., Kocaturk, T.: Task complexity and learning styles in situated virtual learning environments for construction higher education. Autom. Constr. **113**, 103148 (2020)
25. Khamparia, A., Pandey, B.: Association of learning styles with different e-learning problems: a systematic review and classification. Educ. Inf. Tech. **25**(2), 1303–1331 (2019). https://doi.org/10.1007/s10639-019-10028-y
26. James, P.: The construction of learning and teaching in a sculpture studio class. Stud. Art Educ. **37**(3), 145–159 (1996)
27. Medkova, E.S.: Sculpture in modern environment: educational technology. Int. J. Innov. Tech. Explor. Eng. **8**(10), 2704–2712 (2019)
28. Guan, J.Q., Wang, L.H., Chen, Q., Jin, K., Hwang, G.J.: Effects of a virtual reality-based pottery making approach on junior high school students' creativity and learning engagement. Interact. Learn. Environ. **51**, 1–17 (2021)
29. Wu, W.L., Hsu, Y., Yang, Q.F., Chen, J.J., Jong, M.S.Y.: Effects of the self-regulated strategy within the context of spherical video-based virtual reality on students' learning performances in an art history class. Interact. Learn. Environ., 1–24 (2021). https://doi.org/10.1080/10494820.2021.1878231
30. Wu, W., Yen, H., Chen, J.: The influence of virtual reality learning system on the learning attitudes of design history. In: Shoji, H., et al. (eds.) Proceedings of the 8th International Conference on Kansei Engineering and Emotion Research. KEER 2020. Advances in Intelligent Systems and Computing, vol. 1256, pp. 284–291. Springer, Singapore (2020). https://doi.org/10.1007/978-981-15-7801-4_30

Application of Experience Design in Environmental Education Experience Activities

Cheng Hsiang Yang[✉], Rungtai Lin, and Po-Hsien Lin

Graduate School of Creative Industry Design, National Taiwan University of Arts,
New Taipei City, Taiwan
rtlin@mail.ntua.edu.tw, t0131@ntua.edu.tw

Abstract. Environmental sustainability has been a popular topic across the globe. So far, teachers in school are limited by course time constraints, lack of knowledge, fragmented course content, and inadequate supporting resources, all of which are obstacles in implementing environmental education courses. Relevant research has shown that excessive dependence on environmental education-related knowledge provided in school yields unsatisfactory effects. the present study indicated that environmental education issues must be incorporated with local issues through actual experience scenarios to enhance the participants' interest and enthusiasm. Through holding environmental education experience camps, this study invited approximately 100 families (comprising parents and children) to participate in relevant experience activities. Parents collaborated with their children as a team to experience the activities in a venue of nature. After the event ended, we asked the participants to complete questionnaires. A total of 89 responses were collected. Subsequently, this study explored the effects of the topic, venue, and interaction on environmental education learning effectiveness. The results revealed that the topic, venue, and interaction significantly affected environmental education effectiveness with interaction having the greatest influence, followed by the venue and the topic.

Keywords: Experience design · Environmental education · Activities

1 Introduction

Environmental sustainability has become a serious international issue in recent years. A Swedish student named Greta Thunberg initiated a school strike for climate called "Fridays for Future" to protest the inaction of governments and companies worldwide with regard to climate change. People from more than 150 countries worldwide followed suit [1]. Environmental education is an education-based approach to solve environmental issues fundamentally and thus to promote environmental sustainability. Environmental issues traverse national borders and must be faced together by all countries worldwide. Therefore, various countries are committed to promoting the concepts and principles of environmental education. Despite gaining great support from government agencies and the public, the promotion of environmental education has encountered numerous

© Springer Nature Switzerland AG 2021
P.-L. P. Rau (Ed.): HCII 2021, LNCS 12772, pp. 251–264, 2021.
https://doi.org/10.1007/978-3-030-77077-8_20

difficulties. First, most environmental education in campuses has been ineffective. Many students obtain information on environmental education concepts from informal media. Most of the environmental education knowledge of students in Malaysia and Singapore comes from television, not textbooks. Television becomes one of the few media of environmental education, which indicates that environmental education outside the campus has become a crucial source of knowledge for students [2, 3]. Second, the development of most environmental education has stopped at the stage of knowledge transfer and hence has been unable to result in pro-environmental attitudes and behaviors. Because considerable environmental education knowledge is obtained from nonformal education outside the classroom and knowledge-based teaching lacks a sense of mission and empowering content, students lack the motivation and ability to take action [4]. Third, environmental education is currently mainly taught through regular campus courses. However, teachers are restricted by the burden of limited course time, lack of related knowledge, fragmented course content, and insufficient supporting resources, which hinder course implementation [5]. Excessive reliance on the provision of environmental education on the campus results in unsatisfactory learning outcome of students according to international research. Moreover, studies have indicated that a long time is required to change student behavior. Such changes cannot be achieved through a single course, unit, or annual project. Fourth, the campus curriculum is confined by the campus space, in which students find it impossible to experience environmental changes. Because most children grow up in urban areas and are far away from the natural environment for a long time, they have relatively few opportunities to practice the concepts learned in environmental education. Environmental education courses can enhance students' environmental awareness but are ineffective in changing their actions and behaviors [3]. Stern (2000) suggested that unalterable behavior may be attributable to environmental constraints, technologies, laws, social policies, social values, and social norms. Therefore, such education should focus on learners' participation in action. Due to the aforementioned factors, the outreach of most environmental education is limited to people's awareness level and fails to change their behaviors. Thus, environmental education should be focused on instilling a sense of mission and empowerment in people to inspire their environmental actions [6].

Numerous studies have provided different suggestions on how to improve the learning outcomes of environmental education. (1) Contextual experience as a nonformal education medium: Environmental sensitivity is established through one's long-term exposure to a deteriorating living environment, and such an exposure can be created through environmental experience in nonformal education. Environmental education requires joint promotion from formal and nonformal education. Cross-grade cooperation and integrating nonformal education with local regional education resources have a relatively high probability of causing changes in students' behaviors because students exhibit high environmental participation behaviors outside school [4]. (2) Usefulness of real-world environments for understanding and practicing environmental education concepts: By participating in real-world situations, students can observe and imitate expert experience and behavior in real time. This may stimulate students' interest in learning about the environment, ignite their enthusiasm for learning, and help them acquire new knowledge and skills [7]. Learning outside the classroom is essential for improving environmental awareness. Contextual learning activities should also be included in the design of on-campus environmental education activities [2]. (3) Combining exhibitions and nonformal education: Students' eagerness can be prompted by posting the question "What can I do?" to them in exhibitions; thus, exhibitions must be used as a starting point rather than an ending point of environmental education. In addition, exhibitions are a beneficial tool for increasing students' concerns on global issues. (4) High resonance of issues related to oneself among students: The issues of concern in a particular region depend on the characteristics of the region. For example, British students care about crime and congestion, American students care about pollution and crime, and Australian students care about pollution and transportation [2]. (5) Children being the bridge between environmental education and the family: Environmental education is the responsibility of all human beings. In addition to changing personal behavior, environmental education influences others through value development. Children, who act as a bridge of environmental education between the campus and the family, can strengthen the communication between family generations through environmental education [8].

The experience economy regards experience as a type of economic output. Goods have the highest economic value, followed by commodities, services, and experience. Thus, experience is a new type of economic output. In particular, excellent outcomes have been achieved when using experience in teaching. Kao (2020) conducted an investigation on food and agriculture education and discovered that experience improved the performance of students with relatively low learning outcomes in formal education to a greater extent than that of students with relatively high learning outcomes in formal education. The results of Kao's study revealed that students with low learning outcomes preferred experience-based learning, which promoted their willingness to interact with others, motivated them to understand the meaning of education, and enhanced their willingness to apply what they had learned in daily life. In addition, experience can improve the effect of environmental education [9]. A study focusing on American middle school students found that in the experience of the natural environment, novelty, beauty, and naturalness can enhance the positive learning effect. In summary, the literature indicates that the learning outcomes of environmental education are limited by campus education, and students cannot experience environmental changes personally [10]. Moreover, most assessment of learning outcomes was limited to the theoretical knowledge of students but failed to reflect their action and practice. In addition, the learning themes lacked a connection with real local issues and resonance with the students. Although experience can improve students' learning in environmental education, design thinking has been rarely applied to the research on environmental education activities. Therefore, this study applied experience to the planning of environmental education activities through design thinking for understanding the effects of experience on the learners' satisfaction with and learning outcomes of environmental education activities.

2 Literature Review

2.1 Learning Outcomes of Environmental Education

The five goals of environmental education and learning are developing environmental awareness and sensitivity, obtaining knowledge of environmental concepts, establishing environmental values and attitudes, obtaining skills related to environmental actions, and obtaining environmental action experience. The five goals constitute a progressive learning process from being aware of the environment to really taking action [5]. Under climate change and demands for sustainable development, the promotion of environmental education has become increasingly essential. However, the current promotion of environmental education is limited to the understanding level and cannot result in the effective development of attitudes and triggering actions. The main reason for the aforementioned fact is that the people who receive environmental education lack a sense of mission and empowerment. Although environmental education improves learners' knowledge, changing behavior patterns through environmental education is difficult because these changes only occur after continuous communication for a long time, not merely through a single activity or within a short time. How to promote knowledge dissemination to the action level has become the aim of promoting environmental education.

Some researchers have proposed possible solutions. (1) Strengthening cooperation with educational units outside the school: Changes in students' environmental education behaviors must be developed by combining formal and nonformal education. Extracurricular activities can directly or indirectly enhance students' learning outcomes by enhancing their learning interest and self-concept, and students may exhibit a high frequency of environmental participation behaviors outside school [4]. (2) Learning through real-world experience: Because experience gained in activities situate people in real situations, they can observe and imitate expert experience and behaviors in real time and understand the real-world manifestation of environmental knowledge. In the activities, interest is stimulated, enthusiasm for learning is ignited, and finally new knowledge and skills are acquired. [7] (3) Localizing learning themes: Relevant studies have indicated that British students are concerned about congestion and crime, American students are concerned about pollution and public security, and Australian students are concerned about pollution and traffic [2]. These findings signify that environmental education issues must be contextualized to the local environment to attract public attention. (4) Taking children as a starting point for the family: Children act as a bridge between the campus and the family for environmental education and can strengthen the communication between family generations. Thus, bringing environmental education into family life through children allows for the implementation of environmental education in daily life and for influence on family members through children. According to the aforementioned literature, the activity design focuses of this study were as follows: (1) families with young children were selected as the participants, with additional focus on the children; (2) the activity design emphasized the processes from knowledge learning to hands-on practice; (3) the theme setting was based on local issues; and (4) experience contexts were created to simulate real-world environments.

2.2 Experience Design

Norman (2004) analyzed product design using a holistic method in the book titled Emotional Design. According to Norman, work creation comprises three levels, namely the visceral, behavioral, and reflective levels. The visceral level comprises the first effect that originates from senses such as vision, smell, and hearing. This level involves immediate and distinct responses. A high-quality design can often arouse positive emotions from users. The behavioral level focuses on the overall experience of a product. The function of a product is crucial—a product must be easy to identify and use. Finally, the reflective level comprises the feelings after an event, according to which users generate a sense of identification [11]. Lin (2014) proposed a sensory experience model for the creative industry by using a story as the center to convey ideas through settings, experiences, and products [12]. In addition, Chang (2011) proposed four experience media for the art and cultural industry: products, services, activities, and spaces [13]. Lin (2011) proposed four similar media for tourism parks: products, services, activities, and settings [14]. In summary, all the aforementioned papers have mentioned the product, activity, and setting attributes of design and some papers have mentioned the service attribute.

This study believes that environmental education activities generally have educational significance, and the story attribute depends on the perspective of cultural product design. Considering that the theme setting was the basis of environmental education activities, the story attribute was replaced with a theme. In addition, setting and activity are crucial attributes for environmental education; therefore, these attributes were also included in this study. However, environmental education activities are usually short-term activities, most of which involve the purchase of ready-made products as souvenirs or prizes, and activity-exclusive products are rarely produced; therefore, the product attribute were not included in this study. Finally, both services and activities represent interpersonal interactions and are prone to overlap; thus, these attributes were combined into the activity attribute. In summary, in this paper, theme is the core text of environmental education activities; setting is a comprehensive manifestation of tangible hardware and the intangible atmosphere; and activity represents the interaction between all people. Therefore, the experience design of this study used themes, settings, and activities as the evaluation indicators.

3   Methodology

The independent variables of the research framework were experience design and activity satisfaction, and the dependent variable was learning outcomes. Experience design comprised the factors of content localization, setting authenticity, and activity interaction; satisfaction comprised hardware, software, and personnel; and learning outcomes comprised knowledge, attitude, and behavior. This study aimed to understand the effect of experience design and satisfaction on learning outcomes. The research framework is displayed in Fig. 1.

3.1   Framework of the Evaluation Criteria

This study considered experience design to be the communication medium between planners and participants. The planners conveyed the meaning of environmental education to the participants through themes, fields, and activities in the coding process so that the participants could experience the text, space, and interaction of environmental education. The planner began with concrete ideas and then moved to more abstract ideas only later in the learning activities—in the order of the layers of technology, semantics, and effect—the participants could grasp the planner's ideas gradually through the stages of

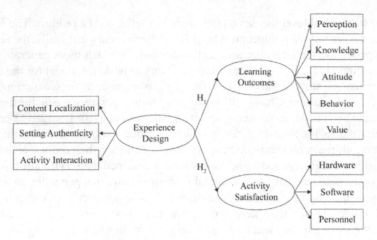

Fig. 1. The conceptual framework

attention and perception, understanding and feeling, and finally feeling deeply touched. This study used experience design as the horizontal axis and communication level as the vertical axis to draft an environmental education experience design model. Experience design was divided into content localization, setting authenticity, and activity interaction. First, in terms of content localization, participants could experience environmental changes in the natural ecosystem by paying attention to the local natural ecosystem, which allowed them to recognize the coexistence of people and the environment. Second, in terms of the setting authenticity, the outdoor environment allowed the participants to be exposed to nature, to really see the problems in the natural environment, and to feel a sense of responsibility for environmental conservation. Finally, in terms of activity interaction, family members could participate together in parent–child activities that allowed them to understand that environmental conservation requires the cooperative efforts of all people. The join participation of children and their parents could facilitate mutual growth between them. The research Framework of the Evaluation Criteria is displayed in Table 1.

Table 1. Framework of the evaluation criteria

Communication level	Content localization	Setting authenticity	Activity interaction
Technical level	Natural ecosystem	Outdoor environment	Family together
Semantic level	Environmental changes	Immersive nature	Cooperative effort
Effective level	Coexistence with nature	Environmental conservation	Mutual growth

3.2 Activity Description

This study was conducted on the basis of the concepts of local theme, setting authenticity, and parent–children co-learning. The local theme allowed the participants to connect themselves with the environmental changes. Therefore, themes with local characteristics were used to form the environmental education content. The setting authenticity linked real-world settings with environmental education and led participants to feel the environmental changes themselves. Parent–child co-learning aimed to better engage the children's family and relatives in practicing environmental education in daily life. The activity process was designed according to the principles of cooperation and co-learning. The activities were held during the summer vacation in the Environmental Education Park. The participants were mainly families with young children. The activities were conducted in two rounds, with a total of 112 participants. Considering social distancing requirements and indoor gathering size restrictions under the pandemic, each round of the activities accommodated approximately 60 participants, who were divided into four groups of approximately 15 people each.

This study planned five themes according to environmental education trends: understanding marine pollution, carbon footprint, food miles, ecological adventure, and understanding the pond. For the first theme, understanding marine pollution, the localized content concerned marine debris along the local coast, specifically the effect of marine debris on marine wildlife and discussion on the concept of plastic soup. The setting authenticity was manifested through the on-site display of marine debris to show that marine debris is never limited by national borders. In addition, the activity interaction involved seeking solutions to marine pollution and learning to sort and recycle plastic products through cooperation. In the second theme, the discovery of carbon footprint, the local content comprised the practice of energy saving and carbon reduction under in response to climate change as the theme. The setting authenticity involved presenting the participants with the excessive use of disposable products in daily life and introducing them to a lifestyle of reusable items. Moreover, the activity interaction comprised a parent–child activity that required the participants to use natural materials to make reusable beeswax wrap. The third theme was food miles, and the local content was related to cherishing food. The local content explained the concept of using ugly and local ingredients wisely in the daily diet. The setting authenticity allowed the participants to use real ingredients, understand the edible value of ugly ingredients, and learn about the delicious and inexpensive local ingredients. The fourth theme was ecological adventure. The local content was related to the use of water resources. This content informs the public of the responsibility of maintaining clean water resources under the threat of water pollution. For setting authenticity, participants were brought to an actual aquatic plant pond, where they learned about the symbiosis between water resources and aquatic plants. Furthermore, the activity interaction involved parent–child cooperation for completing challenges related to the climate and water resources. Finally, in the fifth theme, understanding the pond, the local content allowed the public to understand the local landforms and hydrological characteristics through learning about the irrigation function and ecosystem conservation of the pond culture. The pond also revealed the history of agricultural development. The activity interaction involved the participants understanding the significance of the pond for agriculture and ecology by observing and recording the characteristics and ecosystem of the pond. The research of theme activities is displayed in Table 2.

Table 2. Theme activities

Activities	Content localization	Setting authenticity	Activity interaction
Understanding marine pollution	Plastic soup	Marine debris	Plastic sorting and recycling methods
Discovery of the carbon footprint	Climate change	Disposable products	Homemade reusable beeswax cloth
Food miles	Food appreciation	Ugly local ingredients	Making energy-conserving food
Ecological adventure	Water resources	Aquatic plant pond	Team activity
Understanding the aquatic plant pond	Local ecology	Natural pond	Pond ecosystem observation

3.3 Questionnaire Design

The research questionnaire comprised three items on the participants' background (i.e., place of residence, age, and information source), three items about activity preferences (i.e., factors influencing their choice, favorite activities, and learning themes), nine items about content localization (cronbach's $\alpha = .947$, KMO $= .779$), five items on the learning outcomes of environmental education (cronbach's $\alpha = .977$, KMO $= .856$), and three items on activity satisfaction (cronbach's $\alpha = .980$, KMO $= .783$). The participants filled in the questionnaire through a QR code after the activity and were provided gifts after completing the questionnaire as an incentive for participation in the survey. The participants who were in the first grade of elementary school or lower were assisted by their parents or the researchers in filling the questionnaire. The questionnaire test was conducted in two rounds. Through a dual mechanism of network setting and manual review, we optimized the valid response rate of the questionnaire survey. A total of 112 individuals participated in the activities, and 89 valid responses were returned.

4 Results and Discussion

4.1 Descriptive Statistics

Most of the participants were local residents (73%), and some of the participants were from neighboring counties (16.9%) and distant counties (10.1%). Approximately one quarter of the participants were from other counties and cities. Because the conducted activities required a long time, involved high transportation costs, and required registration beforehand, the participants showed high commitment to the activities. The fact that these activities attracted participants from different counties and cities showed that these activities had a cross-regional attraction. All the participants demonstrated moderately high learning needs for environmental education. In addition, approximately 40% of the participants were in elementary school or lower; therefore, most of these children adopted the family-centered model. This is contrary to families with children studying in junior high school or higher, where the children would have a certain degree of autonomy and may be inclined to use the peer model.

The content localization, setting authenticity, activity interaction, environmental education learning outcomes, and activity satisfaction were measured using a 5-point Likert scale. Higher scores indicated higher levels of agreement or satisfaction. The mean total scores for content localization, setting authenticity, activity interaction, environmental education learning outcomes, and activity satisfaction were 4.89, 4.86, 4.87, 4.87, and 4.88, respectively. The mean total scores of the content localization, setting authenticity, and activity interaction were similar, indicating that participants considered the arrangement of these three aspects to be balanced in the activities. In addition, the participants had a high degree of agreement in terms of the knowledge and attitude aspects of the environmental education learning outcomes but exhibited a low level of agreement regarding the action aspect of knowledge sharing. This is possibly because environmental education involves the interpersonal communication of personal values, lifestyles, and relevant information, making some people selective in the things they share with another person according to how the person may disagree with them. In terms of activity satisfaction, most of the participants expressed a high level of satisfaction with the theme design, services, and hardware equipment.

4.2 Analysis of Variance

4.2.1 Place of Residence

Because local individuals accounted for 73% of the research participants, the place of residence was divided into two categories: local and nonlocal. Nonlocal participants scored significantly higher than local residents in terms of setting authenticity ($t = -2.387*$), activity interaction ($t = -2.532*$), and activity satisfaction ($t = -2.237*$). However, the two groups of participants differed non-significantly in content localization and learning outcomes of environmental education. The activity venue was a location where environmental education camps had always been held and where agricultural expositions had been held by the local government over the past few years. Some of the local participants may have participated in activities in the venue; thus, they may have had a relatively low sense of novelty toward the venue environment. In addition, the local participants had participated in related activities held by the study and were familiar with the design of the activity interaction; thus, they felt less strongly about the activity interaction.

4.2.2 Age

This study also analyzed the variances in content localization, setting authenticity, activity interaction, the learning outcomes of environmental education, and activity satisfaction in relation to age. The results of one-way analysis of variance suggested that age differences did not significantly affect the perception evaluation of the aforementioned variables.

4.3 Regression Analysis

4.3.1 Effect of Experience Design on the Learning Outcomes of Environmental Education

In the stepwise regression analysis for the learning outcomes of environmental education, activity interaction was the first variable to be added to the equation, with an explanatory power of 90% and an F value of 788.906 and was the most predictive variable. Setting authenticity was the second one, with an explanatory power of 3.5% and an F value of 635.575, amounting to a joint variance explained of 93.5%. Then, content localization was added to the equation, with an explanatory power of 0.7% and an F value of 468.597, which amounted to a joint variance explained of 94.1%.

The results of multiple regression analysis for the effects of different variables on the learning outcomes of environmental education were as follows: activity interaction: $\beta = .507$, $t = 8.163$, and $p < .001$; setting authenticity: $\beta = .396$, $t = 6.822$, and $p < .001$; and content localization: $\beta = .186$, $t = 3.077$, and $p < .01$. These results indicate that the aforementioned three variables had significant predictive power for the learning outcomes of environmental education. In addition, the unstandardized coefficients (β) of the activity interaction ($\beta = .507$), setting authenticity ($\beta = .396$), and content localization ($\beta = .186$) were used to obtain the following regression equation: learning outcomes of environmental education $= 0.507 \times$ activity interaction $+ 0.396 \times$ setting authenticity $+ 0.186 \times$ content localization. The regression analysis in learning outcome is displayed in Table 3.

Table 3. Regression analysis in learning outcome

Model		Unstandardized B	Std. error	β	t
1	Activity interaction	.507	.062	.504	8.163^{***}
2	Setting authenticity	.396	.058	.403	6.822^{***}
3	Content localization	.186	.060	.116	3.077^{**}
$R_2 = 94.1\%$ $F = 468.597^{***}$					

$N = 89$, $**p < .01$, $***p < .001$

4.3.2 Effect of Experience Design on Activity Satisfaction

In the stepwise regression analysis for activity satisfaction, activity interaction was first added to the equation; it had an explanatory power of 86.7% for activity satisfaction and an F value of 572.646 and was the most predictive variable. Setting authenticity was the second variable to be added to the equation, with an explanatory power of 1.4% and an F value of 327.609, amounting to a joint variance explained of 88.1%. According to the results of multiple regression analysis for the effects of different variables on activity satisfaction, activity interaction ($\beta = .690$, t $= 8.155$, p $< .001$) and setting authenticity ($\beta = .284$, t $= 3.429$, p $< .01$) had significant predictive power for satisfaction. Furthermore, the unstandardized coefficients (β) of activity interaction ($\beta = .690$) and setting authenticity ($\beta = .284$) were used to obtain the following regression analysis equation: satisfaction $= 0.690 \times$ activity interaction $+ 0.284 \times$ setting authenticity. The regression analysis in activity satisfaction is displayed in Table 4.

Table 4. Regression analysis in activity satisfaction

Model		Unstandardized B	Std. error	β	t
1	Activity interaction	.690	.085	.677	8.155***
2	Setting authenticity	.284	.083	.285	3.429***
$R_2 = 88.1\%$ F $= 327.609$***					

N $= 89$, **p $< .01$, ***p $< .001$

The results of this study suggest that the activity interaction can affect the learning outcomes of environmental education and activity satisfaction. By engaging participants better in the activities through hands-on activities, the setting authenticity enhanced the learning out-comes of environmental education and activity satisfaction. In addition, situating participants in the natural environment contextualized the education content for them. Although content localization also exhibited a significant effect on the learning outcome, the effect is weaker than those of the activity interaction and setting authenticity. The results indicate that in addition to focusing activity content on the themes, interactive communication methods, and contextual experience at the venue should be considered in the design of similar activities in the future.

5 Conclusion and Suggestion

5.1 Conclusion

5.1.1 Nonlocal Participants Felt More Strongly About the Setting Authenticity, Activity Interaction, and Activity Satisfaction

In this study, nonlocal participants felt more strongly about the setting and activities. According to Dale et al. (2020), the novelty, beauty, and naturalness of the natural environment affects one's enthusiasm for learning, which indicates that the perceived novelty of the natural environment can affect the experience of individuals. In this study, most of the local participants had participated in various similar activities held in the same venue, which made them less curious about the setting than the nonlocal participants were. In addition, because the activities conducted by the study had been held annually and most local participants signed up through social media platforms, which indicated that many local participants were regular participants of these activities. Therefore, the local participants may have been more familiar with the activity interaction design and satisfaction than the nonlocal participants were, which may be why the local participants identified less with the activities than did their nonlocal counterparts.

5.1.2 Experience Design Significantly Affected on the Learning Outcomes of Environmental Education, with Activity Interaction Showing the Strongest Effect

This study examined the effect of experience design on learning outcomes. The findings revealed that activity interaction, setting authenticity, and content localization all had significant effects on learning outcomes, with activity interaction having the strongest effect. In addition, parent–child cooperation and competitiveness were the most popular modes of activity among the participants, showing that the activities enhanced the participants' family communication. This result is similar to that of Blanche-Cohen and Reilly (2017) [8].

5.1.3 Experience Design Significantly Affected Activity Satisfaction, with Activity Interaction Showing the Strongest Effect

This study explored the effect of experience design on activity satisfaction and found that Activity Interaction and setting authenticity had significant effects on activity satisfaction; however, the content localization showed a nonsignificant effect. This result was obtained probably because the Participant's main motivation is a family activity on holiday, to activity content doesn't the most important; The results indicate that activity interaction and setting authenticity both significantly increased the activity satisfaction of the participants and increased their identification with the activity interaction through the activity with competitive and cooperative. Moreover, the real-world setting deepened the participants' learning through immersion.

5.2 Recommendations

5.2.1 Incorporation of Familiarity as a Variable

In this study, the local participants felt less strongly about the activity satisfaction, setting authenticity, and activity interaction than did the nonlocal participants. This result was obtained possibly because the local participants had more experience than the nonlocal participants did in participating in related activities. Studies have indicated that novelty can affect learning motivation. Therefore, the local participants may have had reduced curiosity because they had participated in related activities many times. However, this study did not include the frequency of participation into the research questionnaire; thus, further verification could not be conducted. Consequently, future researchers are recommended to explore how participants' familiarity with activities, settings, and content affect the effect of experience design.

5.2.2 Use of Experience Design to Enhance Learning Outcomes Through Parent–Child Interaction

Environmental education is a professional education field, and the topics covered in this field include climate change, resource repurposing, and environmental pollution. Promoting pro-environmental understanding and then behaviors among school-age children is an essential goal of environmental education. In this study, parent–child interaction and teamwork elements were used to enable relatives and friends to complete the activities of different environmental education themes through cooperation and to avoid the situation of children completing the activities alone. Moreover, the participants must complete the challenges of various themes through exploratory activities and answering questions. These activities overturned the conventional one-way oral lecturing and achieved high parent–child colearning.

References

1. Vox. https://www.vox.com/2019/9/17/20864740/greta-thunberg-youth-climate-strike-fri days-future. Accessed 8 Feb 2021
2. Ivy, T.G.C., Road, K.S., Lee, C.K.E., Chuan, G.K.: A survey of environmental knowledge, attitudes and behaviour of students in Singapore. Int. Res. Geogr. Environ. Educ. 7(3), 181–202 (1998). https://doi.org/10.1080/10382049808667574
3. Said, A.M., Yahaya, N., Ahmadun, F.L.R.: Environmental comprehension and participation of Malaysian secondary school students. Environ. Educ. Res. 13(1), 17–31 (2007). https://doi.org/10.1080/13504620601122616
4. Hungerford, H.R., Volk, T.L.: Changing learner behavior through environmental education. J. Environ. Educ. 21(3), 8–21 (1990). https://doi.org/10.1080/00958964.1990.10753743
5. Yang, L.C., Kao, T.S.: Review and foresight for the curriculum integration of environmental education. J. Educ. Res. Dev. 15(2), 1–25 (2019). https://doi.org/10.3966/181665042019061 502001
6. Stren, P.C.: Toward a coherent theory of environmentally significant behaviour. J. Soc. Issues 56(3), 407–424 (2000). https://doi.org/10.1111/0022-4537.00175
7. Kalogiannakis, M., Papadakis, S.: Combining mobile technologies in environmental education: a Greek case study. Int. J. Mob. Learn. Organ. 11(2), 108–130 (2017). https://doi.org/10.1504/IJMLO.2017.084272
8. Blanchet-Cohen, N., Reilly, R.C.: Immigrant children promoting environmental care: enhancing learning, agency and integration through culturally-responsive environmental education. Environ. Educ. Res. 23(4), 553–572 (2017). https://doi.org/10.1080/13504622.2016.1153046
9. Kuo, T.C., Chin, K.Y.: Study on exploring the influence of the food and agriculture education experience course on the self-efficacy of middle school students. J. Lib. Arts Soc. Sci. 16(2), 157–181 (2020). https://ir.lib.ntust.edu.tw/handle/987654321/80928
10. Dale, R.G., Powell, R.B., Stern, M.J., Garst, B.A.: Influence of the natural setting on environmental education outcomes. Environ. Educ. Res. 26(5), 613–631 (2020). https://doi.org/10.1080/13504622.2020.1738346
11. Norman, D.: Emotional Design: Why We Love (or Hate) Everyday Things, 1st edn. Basic Books, New York (2004)
12. Lin, R.T.: Culture and creativity, 1st edn. National Taiwan University of Arts, New Taipei City (2014)

13. Chang, S.H.: The exploring of customer experience design in creative life industries-a case study of "dragonfly beads art studio." J. Nat. Taiwan Coll. Arts **89**, 151–174 (2011). https://doi.org/10.6793/JNTCA.201110.0160

14. Lin, R.T.: From service innovation to qualia product design. J. Des. Sci. **14**(S), 13–31 (2011). https://doi.org/10.30105/JDS.201106.0002

What Do Young Adults Like About E-planting? A Questionnaire Survey

Runting Zhong[1](✉) (iD), Hongyi Fang[1], Jiahui Rao[1], Yue Sun[2], Ji Xu[1], and Xing Peng[2]

[1] School of Business, Jiangnan University, Wuxi 214122, China
zhongrt@jiangnan.edu.cn
[2] School of Internet of Things Engineering, Jiangnan University, Wuxi 214122, China

Abstract. E-planting is a new agricultural product promotion platform and pan-entertainment products based on Internet + agriculture. The objective of this study is to understand the preferences of users on an e-planting App for agricultural crop types and planting methods. An online questionnaire was designed. After one month's investigation, we received a total of 201 valid questionnaires. We analyzed users' requirements, attitudes, and expectations towards the e-planting App and the results indicated that participants were basically positive. The most preferred function of users was to plant and communicate about crops on the platform. Based on user requirements, we designed prototypes of an e-planting App for young adults. The main functions included 'My farm', 'Community', 'Shop', and 'Me'. The results of this study will help designers to understand young adults' preferences for e-planting.

Keywords: Agriculture · E-Planting · Prototype · Questionnaire · User market analysis

1 Introduction

China is a big agricultural country [1]. Under the environment of the Internet +, agriculture is also an important part. Based on the online and offline equivalence of production and marketing information, this project designs an e-planting App through the new model of production and marketing of agricultural products on the Internet. The App would allow people living in the city to enjoy the rural atmosphere at a fast pace, and at the same time farmers to increase their income.

The objective of this study is to investigate the user requirements of younger Chinese adults for e-planting. This study then proposes prototypes of an e-planting App based on these requirements. The results will help designers to understand young adults' preferences for e-planting.

2 Literature Review

2.1 E-planting Around the World

Japan. Japan uses land trusts to make savings of scale in land use. At the same time, the efficient use of the Internet in the process of land trust is further improving the production

© Springer Nature Switzerland AG 2021
P.-L. P. Rau (Ed.): HCII 2021, LNCS 12772, pp. 265–274, 2021.
https://doi.org/10.1007/978-3-030-77077-8_21

efficiency of agriculture and bringing about a green digital revolution in agriculture. Fresh O2O (online to offline), B2B (business-to-business), B2C (business-to-consumer) and other forms deserve our consideration [2].

America. Commerce in the agricultural sector of the United States adopts a combination of B2B and B2C modes. It will fully adopt the B2B mode to connect agricultural enterprises with planting and breeding subjects. E-commerce of agricultural products adopts a mixed mode combining B2B and B2C to connect planting and breeding subjects with downstream processors and consumers [3].

Bangladesh. An App called *AgriTouch* was developed to allow users to grow crops on rooftops. The software platform provides a range of services, including information and initial steps for beginners to plant, design and safely use a roof, expert advice, and agricultural tracking and weather alerts [4].

China. A Chinese company is taking the production and brand marketing of organic agricultural products as its core, taking the high-end consumption areas of Beijing, Shanghai, and other cities as the market orientation, and setting up organic vegetable planting and industrial research and development projects according to the growth rules of plants. It is committed to creating a "new industrial chain of organic ecological agriculture" [5].

Germany. Urban food production is currently experiencing a renaissance, with urban gardening becoming a global trend. On every continent, more and more people are starting to garden in cities. The motivation for this development is manifold and varies from urban garden to urban garden and from region to region [6]. In the states of southern Germany, urban gardening is often driven by the basic human needs of food consumption, with poorer people in particular gardening in order to become food secure [7].

2.2 Market Analysis of E-planting Apps

The existing e-planting Apps are unable to meet the diverse requirements of users. Take the *Yungeng Yunmu* App as an example. *Yungeng Yunmu* provides an online shopping mall to display the interface of online digital virtual pasture and crop purchasing. This app is similar to the ordinary fresh purchase App *AgriTouch*, which encourages users to grow crops on their roofs. The platform provides beginners with information and initial steps on planting, design, safe roof use, expert advice, agricultural tracking, and weather warnings [3]. *Ant Forest* is a public welfare action designed by Alipay for promoting green behaviors. Users can reduce their carbon emissions by walking, subway travel, online payment of water, electricity and gas bills, online payment of traffic tickets, online registration, online ticket purchase and other behaviors, which could be used to raise a virtual tree in Alipay. The virtual tree planted online will be converted to a physical tree planted in a certain area in reality [8].

The operation modes of the three Apps are different. *Yungeng Yunmu*'s mode is similar to an ordinary take-out software. Users can quickly obtain fresh products by placing orders. *AgriTouch* mainly improves the urban greenspace, guiding agricultural planting as the core, helps ordinary citizens with roof planting, and serves as a guaranteed platform for users to trade crops. *Ant Forest* can increase user engagement and make great contributions to public welfare through gamification.

All three Apps have drawbacks. *Yungeng Yunmu*, it is more like a fresh purchase App, and its scale is small. It can only set up production bases around some big cities or in remote areas, which means it is difficult to meet the consumer demand of a wider market. For *AgriTouch*, each user grows on their own roof, which is a decentralized, small scale production model. The quality of the crops grown cannot be effectively monitored. For *Ant Forest*, users do not feel the payoff of planting a tree.

After understanding some advantages and disadvantages of such Apps in the market, we believe that the design of an App should be closer to the needs of users. Therefore, in order to understand the main role of the users of e-planting Apps and their actual demand for the e-planting industry, we conducted the following research through a questionnaire survey.

3   Methods

3.1   Questionnaire Design

In this study, questionnaires were used to investigate the demands of students, white-collar workers, and elderly people for e-planting. There are 19 questions in the questionnaire, including 18 objective questions and one subjective question. It covers such aspects as gender, age, residence, attitude towards Internet planting and functions that the user would hope to have on such Apps. The questionnaire design is presented in Table 1.

Table 1. Questionnaire design for e-planting.

Items	Questions
Q1	Gender
Q2	Age group
Q3	Education
Q4	Monthly income
Q5	Residence
Q6	Do you have any interest in Internet agriculture?
Q7	How much do you know about agriculture?
Q8	Have you ever planted any plant yourself?
Q9	How long is your planting experience?
Q10	Do you wish to eat vegetables planted by yourself?
Q11	Have you ever used the following e-planting apps? (Multiple choices)
Q12	Are you willing to spend time and energy on online e-planting?
Q13	Do you have any expectations for e-planting to provide functions such as tourism and agricultural poverty alleviation?

(continued)

Table 1. (*continued*)

Items	Questions
Q14	If it is possible to buy and sell vegetables online, are you willing to use them?
Q15	Are you willing to supervise the planting process and operate remotely in person?
Q16	Are you willing to make social contact and share planting with your friends on the e-planting App?
Q17	Are you willing to accept the experience feedback survey of the primary interface of the e-planting App?
Q18	Are you willing to use the e-planting App?

Note: Q7, Q13, Q14, Q15, Q16, Q18 were measured on a scale from 0 to 10, where 0 means the least willingness and 10 means the most willingness.

3.2 Data Collection

In order to understand young adults' requirements and preferences towards e-planting, we designed our questionnaire using the Questionnaire Star (https://www.wjx.cn/). Participants were recruited using WeChat. The survey period lasted for 2 weeks between December 13, 2020 and December 27, 2020. Finally, a total of 201 valid questionnaires were collected.

3.3 Data Analysis

Data were analyzed using descriptive analysis of frequency and percentage. For categorical variables, frequency and percentage were summarized. For continuous variables, mean and standard deviation were calculated.

4 Results

4.1 Sample

Table 2 presents an overview of the participants' profiles. The sample involved 201 participants, with 118 men and 83 women. Participants were mostly in the 18–24 years group.

The 201 participants came from 15 provinces and cities in China, covering East, South, Central, North, Northwest and Southwest China. Most of them were young and middle-aged people with a bachelor degree or above (91.0%). 87.6% of them had a monthly income of 4000 yuan or less.

4.2 Planting Experience

More than half of the participants (66.17%) are interested in Internet agriculture, and 76.12% have grown plants by hand, and 84.58% hope to eat green vegetables grown by hand, which indicates the broad prospect of the e-planting App market.

Table 2. Participants' profiles ($N = 201$)

Variables	Frequency	Percentage (100%)
Gender		
Male	118	58.7
Female	83	41.3
Age		
Under 18	7	3.5
18–24	173	86.1
24–50	19	9.5
Over 50	2	1.0
Education		
Senior high school and below	18	9.0
Undergraduate	175	87.0
Master and above	8	4.0
Monthly income		
4000 CNY and below	176	87.6
4000–8000 CNY	9	4.5
8000–20000 CNY	12	6.0
20000 CNY and above	4	2.0
Residence		
City	121	60.2
Countryside	80	39.8

Regarding participants' planting experience, 74.63% have planting experience of less than a year. Regarding their agricultural knowledge, only 25.38% have some understanding of agriculture, and some (10.45%) said they do not have any knowledge of agriculture. This indicated that in the modern age, people generally lack agricultural knowledge. Therefore, it is necessary to popularize agricultural knowledge in the App.

Most of the participants (78.61%) expressed some understanding of the e-planting App, and nearly half of the participants (68.17%) expressed their willingness to buy and sell vegetables online. However, a considerable number of participants (31.83%) expressed their reluctance to use such an App, and the reasons for their reluctance should be followed up in the future. At the same time, the majority of participants (84.58%) expressed their desire to eat hand-grown green vegetables, which also proved the demand and feasibility of users' participation in the agricultural planting market [9].

For e-planting Apps in the market, 81.59% of the participants have used *Ant Forest*. 78.61% have used *QQ Farm* and 54.2% have ever used *QQ Ranch*. About one third of the participants have used *Pinduoduo Orchard* (33.3%) and *Taobao Baba Farm* (34.3%).

Only a small proportion (4.0%) have ever used *Yungeng Muyuan*. Detailed statistics can be found in Table 3.

Table 3. Participants' planting experience ($N = 201$)

Variables	Frequency	Percentage (100%)
Have you ever planted any plant yourself?		
Yes	153	76.1
No	48	23.9
How long is your planting experience?		
Less than 1 year	150	74.6
1–3 years	24	11.9
3–5 years	17	8.5
5–8 years	2	1.0
8 years and above	8	4.0
Have you ever used the following e-planting apps?		
QQ Farm	158	78.6
QQ Ranch	109	54.2
Ant Forest	164	81.6
Yungeng Muyuan	8	4.0
Pinduoduo Orchard	67	33.3
Taobao Baba Farm	70	34.8

4.3 Attitude Towards the E-planting App

Table 4 presents the participants' rating on their attitude towards different functions of the e-planting App. The mean and standard deviation of each item was calculated. It was found that the most preferred function was to buy and sell vegetables online ($M = 6.7$, $SD = 2.5$), followed by supervising the planting process ($M = 6.3$, $SD = 2.7$), tourism and poverty alleviation ($M = 6.2$, $SD = 2.7$), and socializing with friends ($M = 6.1$, $SD = 2.7$).

4.4 Expectations for the App Functions

Information monitoring

Some participants provided suggestions for the App. Comments included "*I want real-time feedback on planting*". "*Strengthen the monitoring of e-planting.*" More than half of our participants (63.67%) want to supervise the planting process and operate remotely in person. Therefore, we hope to add the function of information monitoring in our App.

Table 4. Participants' rating of the questions ($N = 201$)

Items	M	SD
Q7. How much do you know about agriculture?	5.1	2.4
Q12. Are you willing to spend time and energy on e-planting?	5.4	2.8
Q13. Do you have any expectations for e-planting to provide functions such as tourism and agricultural poverty alleviation?	6.2	2.7
Q14. If it is possible to buy and sell vegetables online, are you willing to use them?	6.7	2.5
Q15. Are you willing to supervise the planting process and operate remotely in person?	6.3	2.7
Q16. Are you willing to make social contact and share planting with your friends on the e-planting App?	6.1	2.7
Q18. Are you willing to use the e-planting app?	6.3	2.6

Note: M = Mean, *SD* = Standard deviation. The items were measured on a scale from 0 to 10, where 0 means the least willingness, and 10 means the most willingness.

In order to capture the data of plants and present it to our users, we may need to use all kinds of sensors, such as temperature, optical, and humidity sensors. In order to give users a more intuitive monitoring effect, we will also use the monitoring camera that allows users to observe their own plants directly.

Plant for Poverty alleviation
As for the design of tourism and agricultural poverty alleviation in the e-planting App, most participants (67.65%) expressed their expectations for such services. They hoped to provide farmers with help within their capacity by purchasing unmarketable agricultural products, which fully affirmed the value of the e-planting App.

Crop trading
Others offered suggestions on what features they would like the e-planting App to offer. Most participants (70.6%) are willing to buy and sell crops online. Some participants mentioned they would like to exchange their own crops with others, which also provides a new idea for the design of our App.

At the same time, some people mentioned a "planting forum". In this survey, most people (61.79%) are willing to make social contact with friends and share planting with friends in the e-planting App, which indicates the necessity of increasing communication channels between users. Whether we can combine the idea of a "planting forum" with the idea of "exchanging with other people" is also a point we need to discuss in depth in the future.

5 Discussion

5.1 Design Implications

According to the above survey, we believe that the e-planting App needs at least four main modules. The prototype design of the e-planting App is presented in Fig. 1.

My farm

This is the most important functional area of the e-planting App. Its interface is like QQ Farm. On this page, the user needs to select the location of the real planting farm, then purchase the land and seeds, click to plant, and check the real-time status of the plant.

Community

This page is designed as a planting forum, where users can discuss the growth of plants and promote their own agricultural products. There are also key points of crop conservation and the popularization of agricultural knowledge.

Shop

On the one hand, users can buy and sell their own crops to each other. Besides, they can also buy agricultural products from farmers, to help farmers reduce losses. Furthermore, users can also contact farmers here to learn about their crop growth, choose and buy their favorite crops, and help to sell farmers' crops through their own actions. This is the design of transaction and poverty alleviation in our App.

Me

The 'Me' interface includes my order, my address, contact customer service, my red envelope, invite friends and other functions.

Fig. 1. Prototype design of e-planting.

5.2 Participants' Attitude Towards the App

Basically, the surveyed users have a positive attitude towards the e-planting we investigated. Users are interested in our project. Most users (77.94%) are attracted by the content and characteristics of the project and only a small number (22.06%) of them are not interested [8]. This also requires us to further expand the market and improve the popularity in the following project promotion process.

In addition, we also found in our survey that young adults in China are more willing to plant crops that are in line with young people's preferences, such as fruits and flowers, which are more social [9].

5.3 Limitations and Future Studies

This study is not without limitations. First, the sample size is relatively small ($N =$ 201). The sample of this study are mostly students. The results may vary by age and occupation. Future study should be expanded to include a larger sample of older adults and urban white-collar workers. Second, we used descriptive analysis in this study. Future study may explore in-depth data analysis such as cluster analysis to identify typical user profiles. Third, user evaluation of the prototype could be conducted to improve the user experience.

6 Conclusion

This study helped to understand young adults' requirements and preferences for e-planting. Through a questionnaire survey among 201 young adults, this study highlights the design implications for an e-planting App among young adults, namely, 'My farm', 'Community', 'Shop', and 'Me'. This study proposed a prototype design of e-planting for young adults.

Acknowledgement. This study is supported by Innovation and Entrepreneurship Training Program for College Students of Jiangsu Province 202010295111Y and Philosophy and Social Science Projects in Universities of Jiangsu Province 2020SJA0861.

References

1. Wu, J., Ge, Z., Han, S., Xing, L., Liu, J.: Impacts of agricultural industrial agglomeration on China's agricultural energy efficiency: a spatial econometrics analysis. J. Clean. Prod. **260**, 121011 (2020)
2. Guan, Y.F., Dai, S.: Land trust in Japan to promote the development of green agriculture under the background of Internet +. J. Jilin Ind. Commer. Univ. **34**(148), 35–39 (2018) [in Chinese]
3. Li, G.: The development space and trend of agricultural information under the background of the internet-learning from the experience of the United States. World Agric. (10), 15–20 (2015) [in Chinese]
4. Islam, M., Shahriar, F.: Agritouch-an efficient smartphone based approach for rooftop gardening. Recent Res. Sci. Technol. **12**, 19–23 (2020)

5. Wang, Y., Liu, X., Zhang, F.: Research on the marketing mode of modern agriculture under the background of internet +. Bus. Econ. (1), 139–140+168 (2020) [in Chinese]
6. Kalantari, F., Mohd Tahir, O., Akbari Joni, R., Fatemi, E.: Opportunities and challenges in sustainability of vertical farming: a review. J. Landscape Ecol. **11**(1), 35–60 (2017)
7. Nicole, R., Insa, T., Carola, S.: social sustainability through social interaction—a national survey on community gardens in Germany. Sustainability 10, 1085 (2018)
8. Mi, L., et al.: Playing ant forest to promote online green behavior: a new perspective on uses and gratifications. J. Environ. Manage. 278, 111544 (2021)
9. E-planting Market Survey. https://www.wjx.cn/report/97263765.aspx

Social Change and Social Development

Exploring the Applicability of User-Centred Design Practices in Rural Yemen

Abdulwahed Bin Mothana$^{(\boxtimes)}$ and Anke Dittmar$^{(\boxtimes)}$

University of Rostock, Albert-Einstein-Straße 22, 18059 Rostock, Germany
{abdulwahed.motahna,anke.dittmar}@uni-rostock.de

Abstract. User-centred design methodologies are employed in many developing world design initiatives to pay more attention to and involve end-users in the design process. However, studies have shown that they need to be appropriated to the specific contexts. The paper presents an early design study that was conducted to investigate the applicability of user-centred design in the context of Yemeni culture at the example of a management system for a school in a rural area. Applied methods include rapid ethnography, focus group, interview, sketching techniques, paper prototyping, and high-fidelity prototyping. In contrast to the results of previous studies which indicate that users often do not see sufficient value in the design process itself, participants in this study found the process meaningful (although they were not fully engaged in each design activity). Some of the reasons may be in the nature of the design task and in the role of the researcher/designer and the schoolmaster who can be considered as key individuals. The present study contributes to the growing body of design-oriented field studies in the area of Human-Computer Interaction for Development.

Keywords: User-Centred Design (UCD) · Information and communication technologies for development (ICT4D) · Human-Computer Interaction for Development (HCI4D)

1 Introduction

Recent years have seen a rapid proliferation of information and communication technologies (ICTs) throughout developing regions. Information and communication technologies for development (ICT4D) concerns the design and deployment of computer based solutions for developing countries [1]. It is of a particular importance to investigate how ICTs can be properly designed to meet the specific user and infrastructure requirements that the designer face in such cross-cultural environments [2]. The area of Human-Computer Interaction for Development (HCI4Dev) emerged as "a subfield of ICT4D that focuses on understanding how people and computers interact in developing regions, and on designing systems and products specifically for these contexts" [2]. HCI4Dev "is concerned specifically with the relationship between humans and technology in the context of international development, ranging from lower-level interface design issues to higher-level social interactions" [3].

© Springer Nature Switzerland AG 2021
P.-L. P. Rau (Ed.): HCII 2021, LNCS 12772, pp. 277–288, 2021.
https://doi.org/10.1007/978-3-030-77077-8_22

It is fair to assume that a significant part of HCI4D research is distinguished by the introduction of new technologies to developing regions. In this context, user-centred design (UCD) methods have been employed in many design initiatives to pay more attention to and involve end-users in the design process. However, studies such as [4–7] show that they need to be appropriated to the specific contexts (cultural settings, existing technological infrastructure etc.). The paper presents an early design study that was conducted to investigate the applicability of user-centred design in the context of Yemeni culture at the example of a management system for a primary school in the Al-Dhale rural area in the south of the country. Nine of the thirteen teachers and the schoolmaster participated in a first UCD cycle which were initiated and guided by first author. To our knowledge, this is the first study on UCD practices in Yemen. Applied methods included rapid ethnography, contextual inquiry and modeling, focus group, sketching techniques, paper prototyping, general computer training, introduction of the software prototype and training, and in situ test.

In contrast to the results of previous studies which indicate that users often do not see sufficient value in the design process itself, participants in this study found the process meaningful although they were not fully engaged in each design activity. Some of the reasons may be in the nature of the design task and in the role of the researcher/designer and the schoolmaster during the design process. They can be considered as key individuals who use their experience from elsewhere to introduce new technology into their community to find local solutions [8]. The paper also questions the term HCI4D and related vocabulary such as "developing world users". Based solely on a categorization of "developed" and "developing" countries or regions, design situations can easily be lumped together in a useless or even harmful way.

The rest of the paper is structured as follows. Section 2 gives a background in its description of design-oriented field studies in the area of HCI4D and their challenges. The details of the study are presented in Sect. 3. The paper closes with a discussion of the results and conclusions in Sects. 4 and 5.

2 Background and Related Work

UCD is an approach to designing interactive systems that focuses on the users and their tasks and aims to actively involve them in the design process. It emerged in the 1980ies as a response to the dominance of technology-centred software development approaches. Other principles that guide user-centred design processes include iterative and incremental systems development with explicit and conscious design activities, the use of simple design representations which can be easily understood by users and other stakeholders and the use of prototypes (ranging from paper prototypes to advanced software prototypes) [9]. A variety of methods, techniques and design representations has been developed or adopted from other fields to support the main UCD activities mentioned in ISO 13407 (understanding and specifying context of use, specifying user requirements, producing design solutions, evaluation) [10, 11].

Maunders et al. [4] point out that some of the assumptions traditionally made in UCD are not valid in a HCI4D context to produce locally acceptable technologies. The authors call for an overarching approach or framework for the implementation of UCD within

4Dev design initiatives [4]. In the following, we discuss some of the design-oriented field studies in the area of HCI4D which can contribute to such a framework in terms of design tasks, users and contextual aspects, experiences with applied UCD methods and challenges. A complete overview is beyond the scope of the present paper.

Parikh et al. [5] describe their user-centred design of the user interface for an information system for managing grassroots micro-finance operations as a success story. The system was intended to be used by members of village-based self-help groups in India which form larger organizational networks. The design challenge was to develop an accessible interface for illiterate users because most members were women with low literacy and educational levels but with a basic understanding of calculations. The researchers used rapid ethnography and contextual techniques and, based on that, they created a paper prototype and several versions of a software prototype which they tested over a period of six weeks. Parikh and colleagues [5] saw themselves as being outside the culture and environment they were designing for and they emphasize: "Staying in the local area and doing design work in the field was a very important part of our design process. By spending over two months there we were able to imbibe local culture, and understand to some degree the pace of life and perspectives of the user community. The users got to know us better, and were not afraid to give pointed feedback and criticisms about our designs." Another success factor was the use of physical models and tangible prototypes which the participants could handle and touch [5].

Ramachandran et al. [6] utilized technology artifacts in three early stage co-design studies to observe participants in their community settings for gathering information for system design. The first study involved participants from an agricultural village in India who were asked to use a handheld, battery-powered communication device during short-term group sessions. The researchers observed their interactions with the aim to better understand existing and possible communication patterns between participants. In the second study, conducted in Uganda in the domain of microfinance, an off-the-shelf point-of-sales technology was used to stimulate the participants' discussion about its effectiveness and possible future applications. In the third study, rural school children were given a digital camera to take pictures of their daily lives. Ramachandran et al. [6] conclude that people in developing regions who, in most cases, have in common low exposure to technology and strong sense for community (as the participants in the studies) can be engaged in early stage co-design activities by the use of technological artifacts or prompts in community events. What is missing in the paper is a differentiated discussion of the (active) role of the users and the different roles of the researchers in the three studies (e.g., their role of third-party evaluator in the second study).

A more critical account of methodological and practical challenges of HCI4D research is provided by Chetty et al. [1]. The authors conducted a user-centred design study to improve the communication between the nurse in the clinic and the doctor at the hospital of two villages in the Eastern Cape province in South Africa. Based on interviews, questionnaires, brainstorming, paper prototyping, focus groups, software prototyping and testing they developed a multi-modal telemedicine intercommunicator. Chetty et al. [1] discuss ethical aspects (managing the expectations of the stakeholders), planning issues (e.g., lack of infrastructure, lack of computing familiarity, physical safety threats for researchers), and technical issues concerning UCD practices. They mention, for example, that the participants' lack of experience with computers made it difficult for them to co-design interfaces. Another challenge is related to the participants' attitude towards criticizing a user interface (they would view it as impolite). Generally, the researchers found it difficult to understand the sources of some of the cultural differences they experienced and how they would interact with the design and use of their systems. They suggest to use anthropological fieldwork in such cases.

Many of the above points are also echoed in the overview report by Anokwa et al. [3]. The authors identify five relevant themes in HCI4D fieldwork: studying users, choosing users, managing expectations, developing content, and deploying technology. Recommendations include the use of a local facilitator in certain contexts (e.g., during interviews of female users in some cultures), reflecting on the position and the responsibilities of the researcher and forms of participation, developing a flexible attitude about interruptions (e.g. due to power outages), and planning for adoption, ownership and long-term use of the proposed solution.

Based on their studies in rural communities in South Africa, Maunder et al. [4] point out that existing UCD methods and techniques for the analysis phase are useful in a HCI4D context as well. However, they often fail to recognize wider environmental and socio-cultural factors, "to address these deeply rooted and intricate socio-cultural issue, leaving seemingly appropriate, useful and usable technology designs at risk of being 'unsuccessful'" [4]. Furthermore, problems can arise when it comes to the translation of the analysis findings into requirements. Maunder et al. [4] are more critical of UCD prototyping methods than other authors. They argue that some of the underlying assumptions are not valid in a HCI4D context (e.g., users understand how technology might aid their work or daily lives; users are able to grasp abstract design concepts). As a consequence, developing world users typically have difficulties seeing the benefit of the design process itself. The authors suggest that "before any design prototype is presented to the user for evaluation, the user and the supportive environment must be developed to a level suitable for the current design phase" [4].

The study that is presented in the following section contributes to the growing body of design-oriented field studies in the area of HCI4D. The discussion of the results of the study in Sect. 4 is informed by themes outlined above.

3 The Study

The present design study was conducted in a primary school for about 300 boys in the Al-Dhale rural area in the south of Yemen. Nine of the thirteen teachers and the schoolmaster participated over a period of 4 months (March to June 2019) in a first UCD cycle for a school management system (SMS). The objectives of the study are to investigate the applicability of user-centred design in the context of Yemeni culture and, of course, to achieve the design goal described below.

3.1 Setting, Participants and Researcher, Design Goal

Yemen is situated in the Middle East between Saudi Arabia and Oman, at the southern tip of the Arabian Peninsula. According to the United Nations, Yemen is currently the country with the most people in need of Humanitarian aid (due to inner conflicts and military interventions from outside since 2015). There is generally a digital divide between rural and urban areas in the country. But additionally, the crisis has also a devastating impact on the education system by damaging infrastructure, reducing school spending, and shortage of teachers' salaries. The Al-Farouq school in the study (see Fig. 1) connects various villages. Many students and half of the teachers have to walk long distances to come to school. The school has one personal computer and printer which, before the war, were used by the schoolmaster to write reports. There was intermittent electricity but it is completely cut off due to the war. There are no fixed telephone lines and lacking mobile network coverage in the school building, lack of water supply and flush toilets.

Ten of the fourteen staff members of the school participated in the study. All of them were male and between 32 and 52 years old (41 years on average). The schoolmaster (47) and two of the teachers had higher education and computer skills, three teachers had little and four others no experiences with computers. The first author of this paper conducted the design-oriented field study. He was born and grew up in the Al-Dhale area. His family still lives there and he is in regular contact with some of the community members.

The design goal in the present study was to transform the existing paper-based administration of the school into a digital format that would fit into the working practices at the school. The design vision emerged from previous conversations between the researcher and the schoolmaster who had seen during a school visit in Aden (an urban area in Yemen) that they printed students' certificates electronically. In the study, the schoolmaster with his significant knowledge about the local school had not only the role of a key informant [12], he also assisted in setting up the research relationship.

3.2 UCD Methods and Data Collection

We performed one UCD cycle by applying the following methods.

– *Understanding and specifying context of use:* running rapid ethnography [13] and contextual inquiry in parallel [14], questionnaire, construction of contextual models [15],
– *Specifying user and organizational requirements:* focus group, scenarios,
– *Producing design solutions:* user interface sketching, paper prototyping; software prototype of the SMS,
– *Evaluating the design:* deployment and testing of the SMS prototype, interviews.

Data were collected for two purposes: 1) to inform the design of the SMS in the project, 2) to reflect upon the applicability of UCD methods. Collected data include paper artifacts currently used for administrative purposes (e.g., examples of certificates and school reports), survey forms, interview material, pictures, work models, recording of the focus group, user interface sketches, material of the paper prototype, training material, and the personal diary about the design process.

3.3 Results

We structure the presentation of the results along the core UCD activities [11] and describe design activities, aspects of participation, and intermediate outcomes.

3.3.1 Understanding and Specifying Context of Use

Over a period of one month, we focused during frequent field trips on developing an understanding of the way staff members work and collaborate et al.-Farouq school. The school entirely relied on paper documents to record students' grades and prepare reports for the Department of Education. In particular, we wanted to prove whether an integrated school management system is actually needed and would be an appropriate solution. We started by observing school workflows and communication patterns between teachers, class leaders, and the schoolmaster. After establishing a degree of familiarity and confidence, we conducted individual interviews at the participants' workplaces to monitor their activities step by step and to understand their strategy and motivation (see Fig. 1). The findings were finally captured in a series of contextual models (physical model, sequence model and flow model).

Fig. 1. The Al-Farouq school (in the center of the left picture), current use of paper artifacts (right picture).

The schoolmaster and the teachers were always willing to answer questions concerning their tasks and practices. But many of them hesitated to describe their computer skills and felt more comfortable with filling out a brief questionnaire concerning those questions. Only two teachers owned a computer because it is too expensive. Many participants also expressed that they find it difficult to understand modern technology. The schoolmaster was immediately interested in the project due to his working tasks and his basic IT knowledge (e.g., in using Excel). He proved invaluable for building rapport and was a key informant.

In parallel to the contextual inquiry, we have maintained the computer (including the installation of Windows 10). Due to power outage, we borrowed an electric motor during the maintenance period. At this phase we made checkups for all computer components and the printer where we also replaced the ink cartridge. After completing the maintenance, we connected the computer with cheaper solar energy (see the equipment in Fig. 4). A small workshop was organized to find out more about the participants' computer skills and to provide the opportunity to practice using Windows 10 and basic applications (Microsoft Office Word, Paint). The workshop also increased our understanding of user requirements.

Fig. 2. During the focus group discussion.

3.3.2 Specifying User and Organizational Requirements

After having understood the context of use, the next step is to translate the results into requirements of the SMS. We created scenarios of the administration work in the school which informed a focus group discussion (e.g., the teacher reviews and collects the subject grades at the end of the semester and provide them to the class leader). The organization of the focus group (Fig. 2) was guided by Krueger's [16] recommendations. Group members were welcomed, an overview of the topic was given and the ground rules were described. Open-ended questions concerned, e.g., the recording of student grades, what is problematic in this context and what the participants would like to see in the SMS. Everyone could express his opinion and write down information. In the subsequent reflection phase, participants were asked to write down their needs. After selecting the most relevant items, some participants sketched ideas for a user interface. They had visited a school in Aden city which used a digital administration system. The participants were very collaborative and excited about the focus group session.

Initial functional requirements of the SMS included data management of students, course registrations, documenting exams and grading, and tracking student attendance.

3.3.3 Producing Design Solutions

The input from the focus group was used by the researcher to create user interface sketches, and based of them, a paper prototype of the SMS (see Fig. 3). We conducted a paper prototyping session with the schoolmaster and the two teachers with more computer skills to introduce the SMS concept early on in the design process and to capture their reactions, feedback and comments. The session started with an inspection of the final user interface sketches. We then explored the design concepts by navigating through "the system". But as the session progressed, the participants looked annoyed about "these cards, these kid's games". The session failed to extract any important feedback on the SMS design. It was clear that the participants did not appreciate the usefulness of the paper version of the system.

Fig. 3. Some final sketches and paper prototyping.

We retained the ideas of the paper prototype and developed a high fidelity prototype (implemented in C# and with a SQL database). Our goal was to provide an artifact to the users that had the final product look and feel, in an effort to remove any abstractions that may have caused confusion.

3.3.4 Evaluating the Software Prototype

We first conducted a small training program at school to teach the participants the necessary skills for interacting with the software prototype (uploading a photo for the student, enter student data, print the report etc.). The teachers worked together on the school computer and sometimes on the researcher's laptop. Other devices were not available.

In the subsequent in situ test, the same three participants were involved like in the paper prototyping. The test showed that participants were able to engage with the researcher in a technology-related conversation. They grasped the core concepts behind the technology and the application and linked information to the previous paper-based system. For example, the schoolmaster asked for facilitating reporting, he and another participant requested to add the teachers' data to the system. One teacher proudly entered his son's name, information and photo, the other went to take a photo of his son by cell phone. The participants in the in situ test perceived the provided application as being valuable and decided to use it. However, their feedback also highlighted the fact that the overall usability of the SMS depends in part on the usability and the availability of the computer itself. The only school computer was a desktop device that difficult to take it home.

3.3.5 Participation and Roles

The researcher not only shared the same language and culture with the participants, he grew up in the same village and is still in contact with some people there. The community

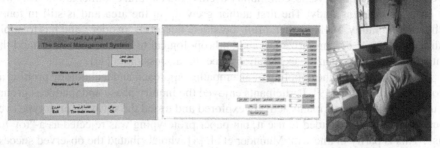

Fig. 4. The SMS prototype in the testing phase (electricity is provided by a set of solar panels that charge the battery pack in the schoolmaster's office).

of the village welcomed him and this had a positive effect on participation. Especially the schoolmaster was enthusiastic about the project. He was not only a key informant but actively promoted the design initiative. He and two of the teachers acted as co-designers.

For half of the teachers, participation was not only more difficult due to limited or no computer skills, but it was hampered by the fact that they live in distant villages. Only four participants could attend the many informal afternoon meetings at the researcher's home where they also tested the system on his laptop. In addition, the older teachers had few interest in learning to use new technology. These participants acted in the role of informants.

The research relationship is kept alive through the communication with the schoolmaster via Whatsapp and Facebook. Although the school was closed for longer periods of time, he has ideas for additional features.

4 Discussion

The study confirms other studies (see Sect. 2) showing that user-centred design approaches are generally applicable in HCI4D design, but that they need to be adopted to the specific social and economic contexts. In the following, we discuss the results of the present study in more detail and refer to similarities and differences with related studies.

Ramachandran et al. [6] characterize people "in the greater developing regions realm" as having low exposure to technology and strong sense for community. Many studies in the rural developing world emphasize that one has to consider the limited education levels of the participants, underemployment, and lack of disposable income [5, 17, 18]. The participants in our study form a heterogeneous group although they all suffer from war and poor economic conditions. Three of the ten participants had higher education, no one was illiterate, there were differences in computer skills, some participants lived near the school, others spent long hours every day to walk to school. The participants' specific situations influenced their degree of participation in the design initiative.

A design challenge that is often discussed in literature concerns the position of the researcher. In most studies, the researchers come from "outside the culture and environment" [3–6, 17, 18] and need to build trust and relationships with the participants, for example, by frequent visits, community events, and cultural commentators. This was not so in the present study. The first author grew up in the area and is still in touch with the community. He is neither a full 'outsider' nor a full 'insider', and has to apply both techniques of defamiliarization and anthropological techniques to understand the context of use and to manage expectations (see the discussion in [1]).

The results support the coupling of an empathic approach and technology probing as recommended, e.g., in [19]. Participants enjoyed the inquiry phase and the focus group. A sub-group of the participants actively explored and tested the software prototype over a period of time and decided to use it, but paper prototyping was rejected as a "toy for kids". This is partly in line with Maunder et al. [4] who attributed the observed success of empathic approaches and the failure of using abstract design representations to the fact that, in empathic approaches, "there is no dependence on the users understanding or knowledge of a technology, choosing between technological alternatives or a technology assessment of any sorts". However, some participants in our study contributed design ideas in the form of user interface sketches. Reasons for their rejection of paper prototyping may not only be a lack of grasping abstract design concepts (as reported in the literature) but an awareness of their lack of technological equipment and infrastructure. An important initial step in the design process was to maintain the only existing computer and ensure power supply and to provide some initial training for increasing computer skills in general.

Given the current situation in the region, the SMS has to be a desktop application. It is designed for local use. Participants regularly met each other, informally and in formal sessions. UCD methods such as personas aiming at increasing the developers' understanding of the users of their (generic) applications are less necessary in such contexts.

Maunders et al. [4] noted that "developing world users have difficulties seeing the benefit of the design process itself". This could not be confirmed in the present study. Not all participants engaged in each single design activity but they found the general process meaningful. One reason may be the nature of the design task. Perhaps in contrast to some other HCI4D projects, many participants could understand quite early how the SMS might aid their daily work as it could replace paper work. Another reason may be the role of the schoolmaster and the researcher who can be considered as key individuals [8]. From the beginning, the schoolmaster was enthusiastic about the project and could see the advantages of using the envisaged application. He promoted a participatory design process. The researcher acted in the role of designer who acquired knowledge and skills abroad. Key individuals who use their experience from elsewhere to introduce new technology into their community to find local solutions are important not only in HCI4D design contexts. This is shown, for instance, by Bødker et al. [8] in their study on digital artifact use in a volunteer-based community in Denmark. Above points also contribute to a questioning of the term HCI4D (and related vocabulary such as "developing world users"). Based solely on a categorization of "developed" and "developing" countries or regions, design situations can easily be lumped together in a useless or even harmful way.

5 Conclusions

The general applicability of user-centred design methods in the context of Yemeni culture was shown at the example of a local school management system. Although all participants in the study were male teachers they formed a heterogeneous group due to differences in education level, computer skills and other constraints. This leads to different degrees of participation and the paper suggests the importance of key individuals in such design processes. The current economic and political crisis in the region badly affects the life of the people and also limits their possibilities of technology use. The results of the study and future work on the sustained maintenance of the SMS have to be understood in this wider context.

Acknowledgement. The authors thank the participants in the design-oriented field study.

References

1. Chetty, M., Grinter, R.E.: HCI4D: HCI challenges in the global south. In: CHI'07 Extended Abstracts on Human Factors in Computing Systems, pp. 2327–2332 (2007)
2. Ho, M.R., Smyth, T.N., Kam, M., Dearden, A.: Human-computer interaction for development: the past, present, and future. Inf. Technol. Int. Dev. **5**(4), 1 (2009)
3. Anokwa, Y., et al.: Stories from the field: reflections on HCI4D experiences. Inf. Technol. Int. Dev. **5**(4), 101–116 (2009)
4. Maunder, A., Marsden, G., Gruijters, D., Blake, E.: Designing interactive systems for the developing world-reflections on user-centred design. In: International Conference on Information and Communication Technologies and Development, 2007. ICTD 2007, pp. 1–8 (2007)
5. Parikh, T., Ghosh, K., Chavan, A.: Design studies for a financial management system for micro-credit groups in rural India. ACM Sigcaph Comput. Phys. Handicap. (2002)
6. Ramachandran, D., Kam, M., Chiu, J., Canny, J., Frankel, J.F.: Social dynamics of early stage co-design in developing regions. In: Proceedings of the SIGCHI Conference on Human Factors in Computing Systems, New York, NY, USA, pp. 1087–1096 (2007)
7. Teka, D., Dittrich, Y., Kifle, M.: Contextualizing user centered design with agile methods in Ethiopia. In: 2017 IEEE AFRICON, Cape Town, pp. 911–916 (2017)
8. Bødker, S., Korsgaard, H., Saad-Sulonen, J.: A farmer, a place and at least 20 members' the development of artifact ecologies in volunteer-based communities. In: Proceedings of Computer-Supported Cooperative Work & Social Computing (CSCW 2016), pp. 1142–1156. ACM (2016)
9. Gulliksen, J., Göransson, B., Boivie, I., Blomkvist, S., Cajander, Å.: Key principles for user centred systems design. Behav. Inf. Technol. **22**(6), 397–409 (2003)
10. Maguire, M.: Methods to support human-centred design. Int. J. Hum.-Comput. Stud. **55**(4), 587–634 (2001)
11. Jokela, T., Iivari, N., Matero, J., Karukka, M.: The standard of user-centered design and the standard definition of usability: analyzing ISO 13407 against ISO 9241-11. In: Proceedings of the Latin American Conference on Human-Computer Interaction (CLIHC 2003), pp. 53–60. ACM (2003)
12. Lavrakas, P.J.: Encyclopedia of Survey Research Methods (2008)

13. Millen, D.R.: Rapid ethnography: time deepening strategies for HCI field research. In: Proceedings of the 3rd Conference on Designing Interactive Systems: Processes, Practices, Methods, and Techniques, pp. 280–286. ACM (2000)
14. Simonsen, J., Kensing, F.: Using ethnography in contextual design. Commun. ACM **40**, 82–88 (1997)
15. Beyer, H., Holtzblatt, K.: Contextual Design - Designing Customer-Centered Systems. Morgan Kaufmann (1998)
16. Krueger, R.A.: Focus groups: a practical guide for applied research. Sage publications (2014)
17. Medhi, I., Sagar, A., Toyama, K.: Text-free user interfaces for illiterate and semi-literate users. In: Proceedings of International Conference on Information and Communication Technologies and Development, pp. 72–82. ACM (2006)
18. Parikh, T.S., Lazowska, E.D.: Designing an architecture for delivering mobile information services to the rural developing world. In: Proceedings of the 15th International Conference on World Wide Web (WWW 2006), pp. 791–800 (2006)
19. Millen, D.R.: Rapid ethnography: time deepening strategies for HCI field research. In: Proceedings of the 3rd Conference on Designing Interactive Systems: Processes, Practices, Methods, and Techniques, pp. 280–286. ACM (2000)

Redesign, Transformation and Reflection of Local Marriage Custom Articles: A Case Study of "Ten-Mile Red Dowry"

Jing Cao[1,2]([⊠]), Wai Kit Ng[1], Yuheng Tao[1], and Po-Hsien Lin[1]

[1] Graduate School of Creative Industry Design, National Taiwan University of Arts,
New Taipei City, Taiwan
t0131@ntua.edu.tw

[2] School of Media and Design, Hangzhou Dianzi University, Hangzhou, P.R. China

Abstract. Traditional marriage custom articles are practical objects which are full of "stories" and "ritual sense" and formed from the combination of life experience, cultural customs and traditional skills of ancient laboring people. As an important carrier of traditional culture, they contain positive value orientation and spiritual pursuit in people's life. In this study, the marriage custom "ten-mile red dowry" in Zhejiang Province is selected as the research object, and it is divided into three stages. In stage 1, through literature discussion, it proposes to redesign use object, use field, cultural story and vessel shape characteristics of marriage custom articles from technical, semantic and effect levels and establishes an evaluation architecture. In stage 2, according to the evaluation architecture, the redesign pattern of marriage products in "ten-mile red dowry" is proposed by using the cultural product design pattern, and the feasibility of using the design architecture in the redesign of marriage custom products is investigated and analyzed by questionnaire method. In stage 3, the evaluation results are evaluated, and the design reflection of this study and suggestions for further optimization are proposed.

Keywords: Ten-mile red dowry · Design transformation · Design quaila

1 Introduction

Zhejiang Province is located in the south of the Yangtze River, China, boasting a long history and profound human resources. From the Southern Song Dynasty to the Republic of China, "red dowry" was popularly used in Ninghai and Shaoxing of Zhejiang Province. Here, "red dowry" means "dowry". When some rich families married off their daughters, the bridal procession was extravagant and luxurious. These bridal processions carry red dowry extended several miles, so it was called "ten-mile red dowry". This kind of grand occasion of marrying off daughters began to decline gradually until the middle of the 20th century. "Ten-mile red dowry" is a typical representative of Chinese traditional marriage culture. It is a kind of "ceremony", which includes folk marriage customs and a large number of traditional red dowry articles. In 2008, this marriage custom was included in the national intangible cultural heritage list of China. Chinese marriage culture runs

© Springer Nature Switzerland AG 2021
P.-L. P. Rau (Ed.): HCII 2021, LNCS 12772, pp. 289–302, 2021.
https://doi.org/10.1007/978-3-030-77077-8_23

a long history and is closely related to our life. It is a symbol of culture. Although the marriage etiquettes have been simplified with the change of times, the Chinese culture is a developing and historical category, which is inclusive and sustainable [10]. "Ten-mile red dowry" has produced a profound influence on the marriage ceremony and customs of contemporary Chinese people. The psychology and desire of the marriageable men and women to have a harmonious marriage for a hundred year and good luck have never ever changed.

Traditional red dowry marriage procedures used a large number of marriage articles, most of which are almost no longer suitable for modern life. Inheriting China's cultural heritage is not to accept the ancient culture indiscriminately but to inherit its fine traditions and discard its dross [10]. To apply the original meaning and image of folk culture characteristics and use new production technologies and design thinking to transform them into modern products that meet the demands of the contemporary consumer market is the way out for folk culture products to return to the contemporary era. At present, theories and practices of transforming traditional folk culture and folk products into modern design symbols emerge in endlessly, but there is a problem of cognitive one-sidedness in the combination of theory and practice. This study aims to explore the manufacturing process of traditional marriage custom products and their performance in traditional aesthetics of creation by taking the theme of "ten-mile red dowry" as an epitome and make the traditional marriage custom cultural products closer to the lifestyle and consumption psychology of modern ordinary people while reserving the traditions.

2   Literature Discussion

2.1   Relevant Research on the Marriage Custom of "Ten-Mile Red Dowry"

The research on the culture and utensils of red dowry in China were begun in the 1980s. He Xiaodao from Ninghai Dongyuan Yaji compiled Daughter's Dream in Ten-mile Red Dowry and Red Dowry strengthened people's understanding on traditional red dowry culture in eastern Zhejiang [5]. In his books, he gave a detailed explanation on the main production techniques of red dowry products, gold-painted lacquerware and gold paint woodcarving as well as the applications of various red dowry products. Ms. Fan Peiling, a scholar of Zhejiang Provincial Museum, pushed the research of "ten-mile red dowry" to a more academic and systematic level. Ten-Mile Red Dowry-Dowry Furniture in Ningbo-Shaoxing Region compiled by her further described the rise and decline of "ten-mile red dowry", conducted a detailed study on the cultural implication of "ten-mile red dowry" and proposed that red dowry articles were divided into outer room articles and inner room articles [3]. "Ten-mile red dowry" is not only a kind of marriage "ceremony" but also a variety of dowries. It uses different "forms" to show the traditional marriage ceremony, which is a cultural symbol. It paves the way for other scholars to conduct the follow-up studies on red dowry culture and red dowry products.

2.2   Marriage Culture Products and Design Pattern

"Culture" is a kind of lifestyle, which was formed from "life proposition (creativity)" proposed by a group of people under the cultural development at that time. It is a kind of "life taste (form)" created by the products in daily life, which is recognized by more and more people and forms a fashionable "lifestyle (ceremony)" [7]. "Ten-mile red dowry" was the carrier of social marriage ceremony and utensils at that time on the premise of meeting the use functions. Ancient Chinese arts and crafts creation ideas emphasized on benefiting people for practical purposes, making utensils according to the situation, making proper arrangement, gentleness, containing thoughts in techniques and creating works with skills [4]. It includes individual subject, human and nature, Taoism and utensils, life needs, function of things, function and decoration, which coincides with Maslow's hierarchy of needs theory [9] and emphasizes the relationship among "things", "human" and "material culture". In addition to following the ancient Chinese arts and crafts creation ideas, traditional marriage culture products should be characterized by mass production, market orientation and practical priority and attach importance to the interaction and communication between products and people so as to realize the transformation from function to feeling.

Gombrich said that once human beings opened their eyes, they could "see" things, but they needed to learn how to select what they wanted to see from all the things they saw, and after selecting it, they had to learn how to "see" what they saw [9]. Therefore, the key factors in the design of marriage culture products are to let the audience firstly experience the ritual sense and story of red dowry marriage custom, learn about the symbolic way of communication, understand the marriage culture products and finally get moved. The introduction of mass communication theory, the combination of products, designers and users and the simulation of the interaction between them as the process of meaning expression and information transmission will help designers to reexamine their design processes and study the essence of red dowry marriage culture products.

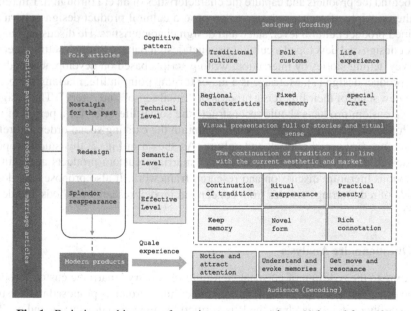

Fig. 1. Redesign architecture of marriage custom products (Adopted from [8])

The process school of communication theory holds that successful communication needs to meet three levels: technical level, semantic level and effect level [6]. In the process of transforming the marriage custom of "ten-mile red dowry" into modern marriage custom cultural products, the relationship among designers, audiences and products can be understood as the one between decoding and encoding in product modeling design methods [8]. Designer is the creator of product forms and the coder of information. Whether the products can be seen, understood and moved by audiences is guided by the inner subjective process, and this is the decoder of the product. According to the three levels of design meaning (technical level of appearance perception, semantic level of cultural connotation and effect level of inner feeling), this study takes the case study of "ten-mile red dowry" as an example, proposes an architecture of marriage custom product redesign in Fig. 1 through literature discussion and verifies the validity of the study by evaluating the recipient's messages.

3 Research Methods

3.1 Design Pattern of "Ten-Mile Red Dowry" Marriage Products

According to the literature discussion, the starting point of the study on the marriage custom of "ten-mile red dowry" is the study on material and material culture. With the historical development, marriage utensils highlight the characteristics of social culture and reflect the social lifestyle of an era. In the design of marriage custom culture products, products are the carrier of environment and culture. The key point of the design of modern marriage custom culture products to combine products with life, touch the mind behind the products and capture the characteristics of an era through it. Lin (2007) used the principle of scenario design to propose a cultural product design pattern that combined product cultural level, stage and design characteristics. He discussed cultural product design and developed a cultural product design pattern through setting scenario by survey, telling stories by interaction, writing scripts based on development and executing product design [7]. Marriage is a major turning point in life, marking the parties enter a new stage of their life. It is a process of "ritual sense" and "story". The design of marriage custom products should reconstruct "the social lifestyle" for a period of time through the reappearance of the scenario, maintain the existing social order and reflect the contemporary social outlook and culture. As shown in Fig. 2, this study proposes the redesign pattern of "ten-mile red dowry" marriage custom products according to the previous literature discussion and research framework. It also proposes the design methods of red marriage articles from conceptual model, research methods and design process.

3.2 Questionnaire Analysis

According to the redesign of personal "ten-mile red dowry" marriage custom products and the design architecture of marriage custom cultural products proposed in this study, the feasibility of the research methods is verified by questionnaire survey and attribute evaluation. In this study, 75 respondents at the marriageable age of above 20 years

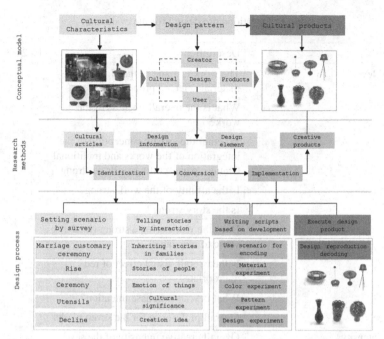

Fig. 2. Design pattern of "ten-mile red dowry" marriage products (Adopted from [8])

were randomly selected to participate in the questionnaire survey. The questionnaire structure was divided into four parts (introduction, basic data, specific cognition and overall evaluation), covering a total of 9 questions. Questions 1–6 were about basic data. Question 7 was divided into technical, effect and semantic levels, including 8 questions and 2 overall evaluation questions. Question 8 was the single choice in which the respondent could select the favorite work. Question 9 was the multiple choice in which the respondents could select the words that could most accurately summarize the characteristics of the works. The questionnaire was designed with a total of seven works as the whole unit, and the respondents were invited to answer the questions in the form of Likert five-point scale. The respondents were divided into 3 groups with different backgrounds, including 40 respondents from design-related backgrounds, 4 respondents from art-related backgrounds and 31 respondents from other backgrounds.

The data were collected from the questionnaires and analyzed by the SPSS software: in the first stage, reliability analysis was used to test the reliability of the questionnaire; in the second stage, independent sample T-test and analysis of variance (ANOVA) were used to test the evaluation of each dimension of the works by the respondents with different backgrounds; in the third stage, multiple regression analysis was used to test the influence of technical, semantic and effect levels on purchase intention, preference and creative intensity; in the fourth stage, Chi-square test was used to test whether there were any differences in the work preferences of the respondents with different backgrounds. Finally, the characteristic words were generalized and summarized (Table 1).

Table 1. Questionnaire design for the evaluation

Questions	Description	1	2	3	4	5
Technical level	The work is made of metal. Is the material selected properly?					
	What is the overall fineness of the work?					
	Whether the artistic conception of the integration of the works and traditional Chinese paper cutting skills us strong?					
Semantic level	Is the affinity of the work strong?					
	Is the story strong?					
	Does the work bring a strong ritual sense to marriage?					
Effect level	Is the overall visual effect of red appropriate?					
	What is your purchase intention?					
Preference	Overall preference for the seven works					
Creative intensity	Overall creative intensity of the seven works					

Which of these seven works do you like the best?

Pease select the words that you think can most accurately summarize the characteristics of these seven works?

4   Research Results and Discussion

The purpose of the reliability analysis of the questionnaire is to discuss the internal consistency of each dimension of the scale and the reduction of Cronbach α coefficient of each dimension after the deletion of a single question, which can be used as a reference standard for the selection of questions and evaluate the reliability advantages and disadvantages of the scale. It was found after questionnaire analysis that Cronbach α coefficient was .896. The corrected total correlation of each dimension and single question ranged between .379–.795. After "the α coefficient was deleted", it ranged between .876–.898. It could be seen that the internal consistency among the selected questions was relatively high and set reasonably, and the questionnaire was of good reliability. This research scale was reviewed and revised by experts and scholars, featuring expert content validity.

4.1   Cognitive Analysis of the Works by the Respondents with Different Backgrounds

The evaluation of the individual design cases for the redesign architecture transformation of marriage custom products was set in technical level, effect level and semantic level, covering a total of 8 elements and 2 overall evaluations and testing the respondents' cognition for the redesign creation of "ten-mile red dowry" marriage custom articles.

(1) Cognitive differences among the respondents with different genders, marital statuses and educational backgrounds

Gender, marital status and educational background in the basic personal data of the respondents were taken as independent variables, and 8 elements and 2 overall evaluations of the works were taken as dependent variables. The independent sample T-test showed that there was no significant difference in the evaluation of each dimension of the works by the respondents with different genders, marital statuses and educational backgrounds.

(2) Cognitive differences among the respondents of different ages

The age in the personal basic data of the respondents was taken as an independent variable, and 8 elements and 2 overall evaluations of the works were taken as dependent variables. Tests were conducted according to each dimension, and the one-way analysis of variance (ANOVA) was used to test whether different ages had a significant influence on the evaluation of work characteristics. The test results showed that there were no significant differences in other factors except "metal material", "affinity", "ritual sense" and "creative intensity", as shown in Table 2. It could be seen from the results that there were significant differences in the technical level of the works and "metal material". After comparison, it could be seen that the scores of the respondents aged 50 and above were significantly higher than those of other age groups. After comparison, their average numbers were ranked as 50 years old and above > 30–39 years old > below 29 years old > 40–49 years old. There was a significant difference in the "affinity" element of the effect level. After comparison, the scores of the respondents aged 50 and above were significantly higher than those of other age groups. After comparison, their average numbers were ranked as 50 years old and above > 30–39 years old > 40–49 years old > below 29 years old. The "ritual sense" at semantic level was analyzed by SPSS Chi-square test, showing a strongly significant difference. After comparison, it could be seen that the scores of the respondents aged 50 and above were significantly higher than those of other age groups. After comparison, their average numbers were ranked as 50 years old and above> 30–39 years old > 40–49 years old > below 29 years old. The "creative intensity" in the overall evaluation showed a significant difference. After comparison, it could be seen that the scores of the respondents aged 50 and above were significantly higher than those of other age groups. After comparison, their average numbers were ranked as 50 years old and above > 40–49 years old > 30–39 years old > below 29 years old. There were significant differences in "metal material", "affinity", "ritual sense" and "creative intensity" due to age difference. The scores of the respondents aged 50 and above were significantly higher than those of other age groups. It indicated that the above factors of the works showed a strong contrast in the degree of identification among the older audiences and were accepted and favored by the group aged above 50. However, they did not get a sense of identification among the younger audiences.

(3) Cognitive differences among the respondents from different occupations

The occupation in the respondent's personal basic data was taken as an independent variable, and 8 elements and 2 overall evaluations of the works were taken as dependent variables. Tests were conducted according to each dimension, and the one-way analysis

Table 2. ANOVA analysis of the respondents of different ages and the elements of the work

Variables	Works	F	M	Scheffe's post hoc
Metal material	Below 29	4.042*	3.17	4 > 1
	30–39 years old		3.54	
	40–49 years old		3.14	
	Above 50 years old		4.05	
Affinity	Below 29	3.278*	3.35	4 > 1
	30–39 years old		3.69	
	40–49 years old		3.43	
	Above 50 years old		4.11	
Ritual sense	Below 29	5.288**	3.74	4 > 1
	30–39 years old		4.15	
	40–49 years old		4.14	
	Above 50 years old		4.63	
Creative intensity	Below 29	3.119*	3.52	4 > 1
	30–39 years old		3.77	
	40–49 years old		3.86	
	Above 50 years old		4.32	

$^{*}p < .05$, $^{**}p < .01$

of variance (ANOVA) was used to test whether the evaluation of work characteristics was significant at different ages. The test results were shown in Table 3. The results showed that there was no significant difference in the technical level and the elements of the works. After comparison, it could be seen that the scores of the respondents from art-related occupations were significantly higher than those from other occupations. After comparison, their average numbers were ranked as art-related occupations > other occupations > design-related occupations. There was a significant difference in the elements of "ritual sense" of the semantic level. After comparison, it could be seen that the scores of the respondents from other occupations were significantly higher than those from design-related and art-related occupations. After comparison, their average numbers were ranked as other occupations > art-related occupations > design-related occupations. After comparison, it could be seen that the scores of the respondents from other occupations were significantly higher than those of other age groups. After comparison, their average numbers were ranked as other occupations > art-related occupations > design-related occupations. There were many significant differences among the factors of "affinity", "ritual sense" and "creative intensity" due to occupation differences. The respondents from design-related occupations had the lowest identification for the above factors. The above three factors were at the semantic level and under overall evaluation. The respondents from design-related occupations had higher interpretation and judgment abilities in these two aspects. It could be considered that there was still room for improvement in the semantic level expression and the overall creative intensity of the works in the cognition of professionals.

Table 3. ANOVA analysis of the respondents of different ages and the elements of the work

Variables	Works	F	M	Scheffe's post hoc
Affinity	Design-related	3.794*	3.43	3 > 1
	Art-related		4.00	
	Other		3.94	
Ritual sense	Design-related	3.781*	3.93	3 > 1
	Art-related		4.25	
	Other		4.42	
Creative intensity	Design-related	4.234*	3.58	3 > 1
	Art-related		4.00	
	Other		4.16	

*$p < .05$, **$p < .01$

4.2 Regression Analysis of Different Element, Preference and Creativity Intensity

In order to discuss the influence of each variable on preference and creative intensity, this study divided the questionnaire into technical level, semantic level and effect level, covering a total of 8 factors. Multiple regression analysis was conducted to examine the correlation of these three levels on the respondents' preference and creative intensity.

4.2.1 Preference

In order to discuss the influence of each variable on preference, preference was taken as a dependent variable and the three levels of the work were taken as independent variables to examine which attributes were related to the preference of the respondents. It could be seen from the results in Table 4 that the F value of the overall regression model was 26.556, which reached the strongly significant level ($p < 0.001$). It showed that taking 9 items such as metal material as independent variables could predict the score of overall evaluation appropriately. The multiple correlation coefficient was $R = .797a$, and the determination coefficient was $R2 = .529$. Among the standardized regression coefficients of 9 independent variables, the β value of the effect level was ($t = 4.337$, $p < 0.001$), which reached a significant level. It could be seen that the effect of the work was the most important factor affecting the respondents' preference for the design of the work.

Creative Intensity. In order to discuss the influence of each variable on creative intensity, creative intensity was taken as a dependent variable and the three levels of the work were taken as independent variables to examine which attributes were related to

Table 4. Multiple regression analysis of three levels and work preference

Independent variable	Predictor variable	B	r	β	t
Preference	Technical level	.289	.584***	.206	1.891
	Semantic level	.080	.524***	.062	.562
	Effect level	.497	.707***	.532	4.337***
	R = .797	$R^2 = .529$		F = 26.556***	

*p < 0.05 **p < 0.01 ***p < 0.001

the creative intensity of the respondents. It could be seen from the results in Table 5 that the F value of the overall regression model was 35.475, which reached the strongly significant level ($p < 0.001$). It showed that taking technical, semantic and effect levels as independent variables could predict the score of creative intensity appropriately. The multiple correlation coefficient was R = .774a, and the determination coefficient was R2 = .600. Among the standardized regression coefficients of the three levels, the β value of the effect level was (t = 4.062, p < 0.001), which reached a strong significant level; the β value of the semantic level was (t = 2.437, p < 0.01), which reached a significant level. It could be seen that the effect and semantic levels of the work were the most important factors for the respondents to judge the creative intensity of the work design.

Table 5. Multiple regression analysis of three levels and work perference

Independent variable	Predictor variable	B	r	β	t
Creative intensity	Technical level	.251	.602***	.171	1.707
	Semantic level	.335	.643***	.248	2.437**
	Effect level	.448	.734***	.459	4.062***
	R = .774		$R^2 = .600$	F = 35.475***	

*p < 0.05 **p < 0.01 ***p < 0.001

4.3 Validation of the Preference of the Respondents

As for whether there were any differences in the selection of the favorite works by the respondents with different genders, ages, occupations, marital statuses and educational backgrounds, the analysis results showed that there were no significant differences in genders, ages, occupations, marital statuses and educational backgrounds. However, there was a significant difference in the selection of the respondents with different educational backgrounds. It could be seen from Table 6 that the respondents with bachelor's degree or below preferred No. 4, those with master's degree also preferred No. 4, and those with doctor's degree and above preferred No. 7. According to the correspondence analysis in Fig. 3, No. 5, No. 6 and No. 1 were the most favorite works of the respondents with bachelor's degree and below, and No. 4, No. 7 and No. 3 were the most favorite works of the respondents with higher degrees. It could be seen that educational background had a great influence on the work preference than other factors.

Table 6. Chi-square test of the preferences of the respondents with educational backgrounds

Independent variable	Items							X^2(df)
		1	3	4	5	6	7	
Bachelor's degree and below	f	6	6	13	8	8	6	**18.490* (10)**
	%	12.8%	12.8%	27.7%	17%	17%	12.8%	
Master's degree	f	0	2	9	0	1	3	
	%	0.0%	13.3%	60.0%	0.0%	6.7%	20.0%	
Doctor's degree and above	f	1	0	4	0	2	6	
	%	7.7%	0.0%	30.8%	0.0%	15.4%	46.2%	
Total	f	7	8	26	8	11	15	75
	%	9.3%	10.7%	34.7%	10.7%	14.7%	20%	100.0%

*$p < .05$

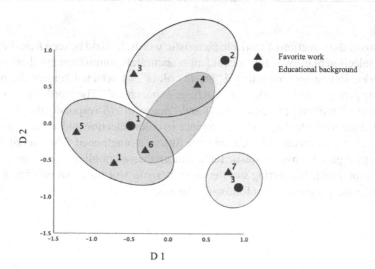

Fig. 3. Correspondence analysis of the preferences of the respondents with educational

4.4   Analysis of Respondents' Preferences and Characteristics of Design Transformation

The respondents were required to select their favorite works in terms of the redesign of modern products transformed from "ten-mile red dowry". According to the statistical analysis, the proportion of No. 4 selected by the respondents was the highest, reaching 34.7%, and it was followed by No. 7, reaching 20% and No. 6, reaching 14.7%. It was worth noting that the proportions of No. 3 and No. 5 were both 10.7%. The number of the respondents selecting No. 2 was 0, indicating that No. 2 was the least popular among the audiences. There was room for improvement in the overall design. The preference ranking is shown in Table 7.

Table 7. Ranking table of the respondents' preference for the works

	No. 4 >	No.7 >	No.6 >	No.3 =	No.5 >	No.1 >	No.2
Preference ranking							
Preference proportion ranking	34.7%	20%	14.7%	10.7%	10.7%	9.3%	0%

In terms of the selection of work characteristic words, it could be seen from Fig. 4 that as for the selection of the words that could most accurately summarize the characteristics of the works, 45 respondents selected "bright colors", 41 selected "inherit the past and develop the present" and 34 selected "marriage expectation". The words that were least selected were "implicit" (5 respondents) and "practical" (8 respondents). The results showed that the works had a good performance in color selection and artistic conception expression, but their practicality needed to be further strengthened. The overall effect of the works gave people an enthusiastic feeling more than an implicit effect, and the effect was very prominent. By sorting out the characteristic words, it can provide a certain reference for the progress of the follow-up studies.

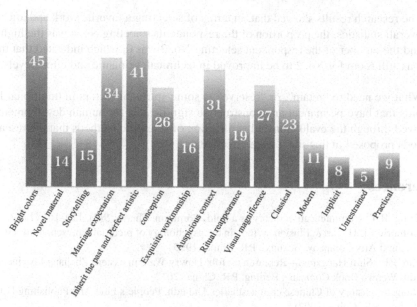

Fig. 4. Selection proportion of characteristic words of the work

5 Research Conclusions and Suggestions

It is hoped in this study that ordinary people can feel the warmth and connotation of traditional marriage culture and marriage utensils in modern products through design, arouse emotional resonance and relink the products and culture that seem to have gradually disappeared from the public vision with ordinary people's life. It also provides a valuable reference for designers to create textured marriage culture products. Based on the previous studies and analysis, relevant research suggestions are given as follows:

1) The research results showed that there were no significant differences in tech nical, semantic and effect levels and overall evaluation of the works among the respond ents of different genders and marital statuses. There were significant differences in the cognition of the respondents of different ages in the material of technical level, the ritual sense and affinity of semantic level and the overall creative intensity. The recognition of the respondents aged 50 years old and above was higher than that of other age groups. The overall recognition of the works by the nonprofessional audiences was higher than that of the professionals. It could be seen that there was still room for optimization of design creativity.

2) The research results showed that purchase intention and creative intensity were the most important factors affecting the design preference of the respondents. Color, story and preference were the important factors affecting the respondents' judgment of the creative intensity of the works. Affinity and preference were the influencing factors of purchase intention of the respondents. Thus, it could be seen that preference was the standard to measure the public's comprehensive evaluation of the works.

3) The research results showed that, in terms of selecting a favorite work and after the overall statistics, the proportion of the respondents selecting No. 4 was the highest, and the number of the respondent selecting No. 2 was 0, which indicated that there was still room for No. 2 to be improved in technical, semantic and effect levels.

What we need to "retain", or "reserve" is some spirits or factors in traditional folk customs that have permanent and constructive significance for human development. It is proved through the evaluation and verification of scientific methods that the research methods proposed in this study were effective.

References

1. Craig, R.T.: Communication theory as a field. Common. Theory. 9(2), 119–161 (1999)
2. Gombrich, E.H.: Art & Illusion: a study in the psychology of pictorial representation, 1st edn. Guangxi Arts Company, Guangxi, P.R. China (1999)
3. Fan, P.L.: Shili Hangzhou—Research on folk Dowry Ware in eastern Zhejiang Province. 1st edn. Wenwu Book Company, Beijing, P.R. China (2012)
4. Hang. J.: History of Chinese craft aesthetics.1nd edn. People's Fine Arts Publishing House, Beijing, P.R. China (2007)
5. He, X.D.: Shili Hangzhou Daughter dream,1st edn. Zhonghua Book Company, Beijing, P.R. China (2008).
6. Lin, H.M.: The coding and decoding of shape in product design. J. Des. 6(2), 39–52 (2001)
7. Lin, R, Lin, P.H.: Analysis mode of "form" and "ceremony" in cultural innovation design. unpublished paper (2018)
8. Lin, R.: Transforming Taiwan aboriginal cultural features into modern product design: a case study of a cross-cultural product design model. Int. J. Des. 1(2), 45–53 (2007)
9. Van Nostrand Maslow, A.H.: Toward a psychology of being, pp. 75–85. Simon and Schuster (2013)
10. Zhu, X.X.: Ancient Chinese Etiquette System, 1st edn., pp. 24–36. The commercial press, Taiwan (1995)

Speculative Scenarios: The Exhibition as a New Space of Thinking

Yu Chen[1] and Zhiyong Fu[2(✉)]

[1] Central Academy of Fine Arts, Beijing 100102, China
[2] Tsinghua University, Beijing 100084, China
fuzhiyong@tsinghua.edu.cn

Abstract. In this paper, curating exhibition is used as a tool to show future scenes from the perspective of speculative design. Speculative scenarios are used to provide a platform for researchers to show and transmit information. Through the tools of design fiction and prototype design, we can deduce, design and foresight the possible development of future scenarios. Audiences conduct nonlinear exploration and interactive experience in the process of exhibition, and get reflection in the speculative scenarios. The purpose of this paper is to improve our ability of constructing futures thinking and design prototypes. This paper will discuss three levels: diegetic prototype, discursive space and social engagement. This paper analyzes the diegetic logic and curatorial methods of speculative scenarios, discusses the role relationship among curators, audiences and works. And explores the audience's behavior changes and speculative feedback in the speculative scenarios. Through the speculative scenarios in the exhibition, this research aims to show the future possibilities of technology and humanity through the speculative scenarios in an exhibition hall, encourage people to imagine freely, and trigger new thinking of the future. The research intuitively shows the theoretical thinking of enterprises and institutions on the future through speculative scenarios, so as to pursue a more desirable future.

Keywords: Speculative scenarios · Speculative design · Curating exhibition · Design fiction · Futures thinking

1 Introduction

Exhibition, as the main form of display function in design language, plays a very important role in contemporary design education. The term exhibition was originated in the late Enlightenment [1] Movement in the 17th century. With the development of the navigation industry, Europeans set off a collection fashion, and invented the term "Cabinet of curiosities" [2], which literally translating as art- or wonder-room. It was the prototype of exhibition. The role of curators is caretakers of treasures. Just like the original name of curators, the Latin "curatus", means "take care of". Curator was once regarded as the administrator of the collection, until 1987, when Paul O 'Neill [3] published *The Culture of Curating and the Curating of Culture(s)* [4]. The concept of curation was redefined.

© Springer Nature Switzerland AG 2021
P.-L. P. Rau (Ed.): HCII 2021, LNCS 12772, pp. 303–317, 2021.
https://doi.org/10.1007/978-3-030-77077-8_24

Curator practice has gradually become a creative activity. In the past twenty-five years, a large number of excellent exhibitions and international biennale activities have appeared in the public eye. And curation has gradually become a mainstream activity. The curator has changed from behind-the-scenes organizer and chooser to visible and important cultural producer. In the book *The Curator's Handbook——Museums, Commercial Galleries, Independent Space* [5] the author Andrian George, he emphasizes the identity of the curator and their creative duties. From concept to contact, fund-raising, exhibition album, interpretation of media materials, to exhibition space design, cooperation with artists and creditors, organization concept opening and other activities, the curator has become the connector of communication between works and the public.

As a research method, curating exhibition can flexibly observe, sort out and analyze social phenomena, and provide audiences with a new perspective to interpret and think. As curator Hans Ulrich Obrist said, "The function of curating exhibition is to help artists and audiences connect the distance between ideal and reality, which is to present the unrealized plans in their minds. And curators need a clearer plan to form a new reading perception to the public." [6].

In recent years, there have been many science and technology exhibitions discussing the topic of "technology" and "future". New media exhibition and immersive exhibition have become popular cultural consumption methods. Ethics of Technology, Beijing Media Art Biennale [7] in 2016, Post-Life, the 2nd Beijing Media Art Biennale [8] in 2018, Nine cities, Millions of futures, Bi-City Biennale of Urbanism\Architecture (Shenzhen) [9], 40 Years of Humanizing Technology - Art, Technology and Society, Ars Electronica [10] in 2019 and Foresight · Visible—International Exhibition on Design Futures [11] in 2020.

The exhibition of science and technology have the characteristics of entertainment, immersion and topic. That has become both academic and commercial. The technical problems discussed can help many organizations and people in the industry to have a new thinking on the relationship between technology and society. In the face of the current situation of science and technology exhibitions, curator Zhang Ga [12] said "thinking about the direction of science and technology is people's daily life, and design researchers need to use their imagination and innovative vocabulary to interpret and express." By visiting the immersive exhibition, the curator makes the audience get closer to the works, leaving the audience with a space for rational thinking, thus making the audience aware of the relationship between the works of art and the social background. Whether the exhibition can bring public thinking, and whether it has historical sense, documentary and academic value has become the cultural responsibility of the curator.

2   Speculation and Practice

This study explores the application value of speculative design and exhibition practice from the theoretical characteristics and practical methods of speculative design works. The purpose of speculative design is to let the audience think about problems and design presentation methods for specific topics. Under the cultivation of interdisciplinary, design researchers use product prototypes, interactive devices, photographic works, digital images, graphic works, performance art, research reports and other forms to show the future of design. The audiences criticize and discuss the speculative works, thus helping to think about the new future possibilities.

2.1 Speculative Technology and Future

Speculative design was put forward by British designers Anthony Dunne and Fiona Raby. The literature *Speculative Everything: Design, Fiction, and Social Dreaming* [13] clearly defines speculative design as a design method. Speculative design is a research method that considers the possibility of future design. It considers the application possibility of technology in future life and how it will affect the development track of society. The purpose of speculative design is to break away from the shackles of inherent ideas and present the multiple possibilities of future development. The models and scenes constructed by speculative design can effectively stimulate discussion and reflection on ethics, social environment and history and culture. In this way, we can reflect on the problems of today's society for transcendental innovation or checking erroneous ideas at the outset. The direction of speculative design also focuses on the future, expressing through design, thinking figuratively, and using the interactive, experiential and enlightening characteristics of design to lead the audiences to "understand" and think about the future.

When everyone participates in thinking and discussion, and forms subjective thoughts, society is more likely to avoid the shackles of future development due to commercial profit-seeking, and develop in a desirable direction. As Anthony Dunn and Fiona Rebby mentioned in their book. "Speculative design is not an imaginary future, but a design to explore all possibilities with controversial value, and to define a common and desirable future for the most specific majority of people: from enterprise to city to society. Instead of defining the future for everyone, design researchers should cooperate with ethicists, political scientists, economists and other professionals to produce a future that people really need".

Fig. 1. Matthieu Cherubini, Ethical Autonomous Vehicles, 2014, touchscreen. Screenshots from https://mchrbn.net/ethical-autonomous-vehicles/

There are numerous technical ethics issues in future technology development. These tangible futures enable us to understand the public's thinking mode and expectation for the future. For example, the Ethical Autonomous Vehicles [14] developed by Matthieu Cherubini is a speculative design work that leads the audience to reflect on autonomous driving (see Fig. 1). The work is based on the premise that autonomous driving technology will gradually mature in 2025, and autonomous driving cars will replace traditional cars. In the future, people just like choosing the color of a car, ethics can become a commodified feature in autonomous vehicles that one can buy, change, and repurchase, depending on personal taste.The designers developed a series of hypotheses to create three different algorithms -each adhering to a specific ethical principle/behaviour set-up – and embedded into driverless virtual cars that are operating in a simulated environment. The audience can choose a vehicle from the works for simulation experiment, and observe the choice of the car in the face of moral dilemma.

Fig. 2. Foresight: An Interesting World, artist Fei Jun, online work in 2021, Screenshots from: forecastingworlds.invisibledust.com

Speculative design works rely on the imagination of design researchers about the future and technology. From the perspective of research, it is a long-term, considerable and sustainable research tool. Forecasting: Interesting Worlds [15] by artist Fei Jun is a global speculative investigation tool (see Fig. 2). The artist triggers audience reflection: "What do you think is the interesting world?" On this online platform, the artist invites audiences from the world to participate in and build their own ideal worlds, and discusses on the platform. This work collects and observes people's complex and diverse world views on the "uncertain future". The artist mentioned that the core strategy to deal with the uncertain future is flexible and innovative ways of working and thinking, and activism and participation are more important than ever. Design researchers expect to use situational space to stimulate and encourage people to imagine freely, let the audience participate in reflection, and gain ability to understand things.

2.2 Speculation in the Exhibition Hall

In today's society, with rapid and diversified media, exhibition is no longer just a way to serve creative works with artistic beauty, but a way to spread the views of artists and design researchers. From the creation of Fountain [16] by Marcel Duchamp in art history to Droog Design [17] in the Netherlands, which criticized and reflected on culture and life in design history. Artists, designers, and theorists use exhibitions as a means of communication. Therefore, exhibition halls which are convenient for the public to appreciate the works appeared. The appearance of exhibition hall enables researchers to present the contentsin books and conferences through offline forms, and speculative works also need to be displayed. Exhibition hall, as a presentation tool, has played a great role in the ideological trend of speculative design, which started from the computer-related design direction of Royal College of Art in London in the 1990s. Speculative design is based on critical theory, which is different from commercial design, that is, blindly accepting the commodity design with sales demand in the market, but a non-commercial concept and behavior design, trying to make people realize the harm of commercial design. Nowadays, speculative design is based on science (such as biotechnology, robotics and nanotechnology, etc.), which explores the impact of science and technology on the current society, and makes it possible to see the future through negation and speculation.

Fig. 3. United Micro Kingdoms, Anthony Dunne and Fiona Raby. 2012/13. Pictures from https://unitedmicrokingdoms.org/

The exhibition hall is the medium of speculative design display, and the curators also use exhibition practice to arouse the audience's reflection and speculation on specific topics. The United Micro Kingdoms [18] (see Fig. 3) is the research of Dunne and Raby with design fiction as tool of design. The exhibition allows audiences to see the potential future of society, and designers and audiences can discuss their ideality in one space. In the micro-kingdom, the curator provided multi-angle speculation on the future of the country, designed the speculative scenario between reality and fiction, and speculated the potential possibility of the future. The purpose of this exhibition is to show the audience the future model with thinking value, competition awareness and technological and economic development.

Fig. 4. Design and the Elastic Mind, Museum of Modern Art, 2008. Pictures from https://www. moma.org/calendar/exhibitions/58

The exhibition space curated from speculative perspective is no longer authoritative, class-specific and orderly, but an open, avant-garde and critical speculative scenario. It spreads in one direction, audiences have also become the object of "investigation". Timely feedback makes the design and research content better promoted. For example, the exhibition Design and the Elastic Mind [19] (see Fig. 4) displayed in Museum of Modern Art in 2008. It shows the embodiment of scientific and technological progress in art design in the past ten years, and brings people indescribable visual pleasure. The exhibition brings together the cutting-edge creation and critical thinking of designers, scientists, architects and engineers all over the world, using hybrid varieties of bioengineering, robots with emotional fluctuations, sperm carrying secret information… From nanotechnology to organic design, interactive design to perceptual design. The purpose of speculative exhibition is to better show and interpret the contents and meanings of exhibits, and guide the audience to think about the future from multiple levels and angles, and discuss the possibility of the future.

3   Frame and Structure of Speculative Scenarios

This study analyzes the research methods of speculative scenarios, which is the integration of speculative design and curating exhibition. Speculative design focuses on the thinking level, while curating exhibition is implemented in practice, which can refer to the research model of speculative scenarios (see Fig. 5). Design researchers show their theories in a visual way, and the presentation of future scenarios opens up a new space for the audience to think. This method can help design researchers and audience to imagine and communicate together. Using exhibition space and speculative props, the vision of future life can be displayed intuitively. It initiates the audience's discussion on this possible future scene in an open way, and collects the audience's thoughts again by interviewing or recording information at the exhibition, thus deepening the research.

The curator Paola Antonelli mentioned in *States of Design 04: Critical Design* [20], the most important thing of speculative design is not to produce useful products immediately, but to provide a constructive direction for a better future. Speculative scenarios

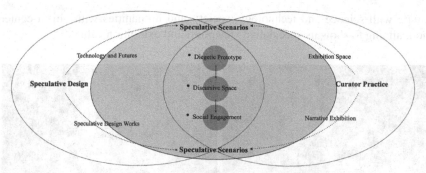

Fig. 5. Research model of speculative scenarios. Speculative scenarios are displayed in combination with curating exhibition on the premise of speculative discussion of future and technology and speculative design works. Speculative scenarios will have the characteristics of diegetic prototype, discursive space and social engagement.

provide audiences with a variety of considerable futures. When constructing speculative scenario, design researchers and audiences will learn how to keep a speculative attitude towards problems in the future. The construction of speculative scenarios helps us to imagine the future life and technology, so as to prepare for the possible future. The display of speculative scenarios opens a window for us to visualize the future, through which we look forward to the possible impacts, opportunities, risks and potential possibilities of the current world due to technology, politics, society, culture and the environment. Through rational research and thinking, we can plan a more ideal future direction.

This study analyzes and summarizes the model, space and experience of speculative scenarios, taking several cases of speculative scenarios as research objects, and concludes that the objects in speculative scenarios are diegetic, the space is conversational, and the experience is reflective. The paper discusses the core value and application direction of speculative scenarios, and deeply discusses the implicit and explicit practice ways of speculative scenarios in space, as well as the interaction and experience between audience and works in space.

3.1 Diegetic Prototype

Speculative design and design fiction can be understood as a discipline and a method. Bruce Sterling, an American science fiction writer, put forward the concept of "design fiction [21]" for the first time in *Shaping Things* [22] published in 2005, thinking that fantasy should be used to inspire future-oriented technical product design. He believes that design fiction can make people give up their doubts about change through conscious use of diegetic prototype. Under the background of fictional design, diegetic prototype can be understood as a speculative scenario in the fictional world seen by users. There are many ways to show its practice, from tradition to cutting-edge design and art forms. It also shows that speculative design has various media attributes. The objects in the diegetic prototype are presented as the most important content in the curatorial speculative scenario, and the curator carries out curating exhibition and diegetic experience on the objects in the exhibition hall. As a kind of public media, curation combines diegetic prototype with science and technology, society and humanities with object-centered method, aiming to show its speculative viewpoint and exhibition value.

Fig. 6. 3D Printing of the Unknown Cities, by Yan Wu, Yufan Xie and Chen Yu, 2019. Exhibited in Nine cities, Millions of futures, Bi-City Biennale of Urbanism\Architecture (Shenzhen).

The Unknown Cities [23] (see Fig. 6) is a series of diegetic prototype works jointly created by Yan Wu, Yufan Xie and me. That is a collaboration of three identities: science fiction writer, architect and artist. The work is based on the short science fiction *Thousands of Cities, Millions of Futures* [24], which launches the speculative imagination of the future city by Cixin Liu and Yan Wu. The book describes the future city with the high development of space-time science and technology. Inspired by the novel, artists show four groups of future cities and discuss the relationship between cities and people again. As the sea level rises, people move to the undersea cities where deep sea coexists with giant creatures, and there are also pipeline cities which are ready to leave the ship to find new homes due to the thinning of the atmosphere and the harsh living environment. The Unknown Cities generates the city form in real time through the algorithm, and displays it visually in front of the audience by means of digital images and 3D printing, which triggers a new round of public reflection and speculation. The exhibition composed of speculative scenarios is consisted of several diegetic archetypes, or several speculative objects to discuss futures thinking.

3.2 Discursive Space

The speculative scenarios in the exhibition hall is not a subjective display, it is more like an experiment and an open discussion space. Exhibition space has become an important space for spreading ideas, knowledge, information, values and emotions, and a shared space for democratizing knowledge and art. The audience gives everyone the same opportunity to read, acquire and experience in the exhibition space. The space in the speculative scenario is the field of "Conversation" between audiences and the curator. A speculative exhibition is an exchange process of emotions and thoughts that can not only stimulate the audience's interest, but also explain the meaning of resources. In other words, it is necessary to make the audience understand and find it interesting, so as to sublimate to a kind of thinking. Therefore, the realization of this kind of "Discursive space" is undoubtedly the most important need of museum owners, curators and designers in the original intention of building and exhibition.

The mobility in the exhibition hall space is reflected in the behavior change of the audience during the exhibition. Reasonable arrangement of space, proper organization of exhibition route, rich layout of works and diegetic clues, and active organization of space props and lighting settings will help the audience to obtain information and social engagement in the exhibition. Space design in speculative scenarios is the most complex design part in curating exhibition. Objectively, it extends action from concept and integrates design factors such as two-dimensional, three-dimensional and four-dimensional. Subjectively, it is the planning and implementation of information and its specific space-time relationship.

Fig. 7. Asia digital art exhibition, 2019.

Asia Digital Art Exhibition [25] is a theme exhibition project that uses space to give the audience association. The use of "space" language in the exhibition shows the blending of Asia in the context of geography and globalization, which seems to be complicated and wrong behind different digital art features. The exhibition builds a discursive platform between art and science and technology in the live space, and uses digital media to show cross-disciplinary cultural innovation facing the future. The exhibition tries to build a new discursive platform, in which the audience experiences and interacts in the exhibition hall space according to the exhibition line it shows. There is a clever layout in the exhibition hall, so that space can be reserved between works and diegetic logic can be formed. The art work "Archive Dreaming [26]" by artist Refik Anadol, with machine learning as the driving force behind it, the installation seeks to present viewers with comparisons and similarities between SALT's database of almost two million documents ranging from antique photos to centuries-old written works. In the exhibit is an immersive digital exhibition hall (see Fig. 7) which contains limited number of audiences. The use of space in the exhibition hall allows the audience to watch another artist's long scroll while waiting and queuing outside the work space.

Reasonable layout allows the works in the exhibition hall to be viewed and interpreted to a greater extent.

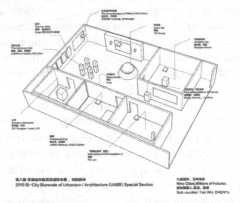

Fig. 8. Nine Cities, Millions of Futures, Bi-City Biennale of Urbanism\Architecture (Shenzhen), 2019. Space design of exhibition.

Fig. 9. Nine Cities, Millions of Futures, Bi-City Biennale of Urbanism\Architecture (Shenzhen), 2019

In curation practice, curators use various speculative props to narrate and use diverse media languages to show different speculative scenarios. The audience explores, participates and experiences nonlinearly in the exhibition hall, which creates a conversation. The exhibition Nine Cities, Millions of Futures is also a sci-fi curatorial exhibition that arouses the audience's thinking, sensory experience and dissemination through speculative scenarios. The whole exhibition area (see Fig. 8) is like a science fiction novel being unfolded, the audience walks into every page of the novel like a reader. The audience can flow freely in the exhibition hall, thinking about the future possibilities of future cities, architecture and technology in speculative props and diegetic prototypes. On the wall of the exhibition hall, there are paragraphs extracted from the science fiction *Nine Cities, Millions of Futures* [27], in which the audience can read and reflect. The exhibition expects the audience to enter the speculative space with curiosity and reflect on the future of the city with enthusiasm (see Fig. 9). During the exhibition, the audience's feedback on the application of speculative scenarios was collected through interviews and investigations, and it was found that the application of speculative scenarios was helpful for the audience to interpret and feel the works in the exhibition hall. Most audiences said that the speculative scenario is a more friendly speculative space, which well presents the speculative prototype and the researcher's thinking direction.

3.3 Social Engagement

Live experience is the most important part of speculative scenarios. The purpose of the speculative scenario is to invite the audience to make nonlinear exploration and interactive experience in the process of appreciating the works, so as to get independent reflection on the subject object in the speculative scenario. The audience will appreciate, learn and feel the visual and auditory experience brought by the speculative scenario in the exhibition hall. During the exhibition, audiences reflect and explore the themes and speculative viewpoints discussed in the works in the exhibition. The audience's experience of speculative scenarios is characterized by exploration, participation, experience and reflection. The curator organizes the distribution of speculative scenarios in the exhibition according to the theme. The speculative scenarios will have the curatorial characteristics of diegetic, spatial, speculative and communicative.

Fig. 10. Post-life, Beijing Media Art Biennale Art Museum, 2018.

Eilean Hooper-Greenhill, who is a museology expert, put forward the concept of "Post-Museum" in *Museums and the Interpretation of Visual Culture* [28] (2000), emphasizing that the interaction of exhibition participants in the museum can form the construction and dissemination of social significance. The proposal of post-museum is in line with the speculation and consideration of the subject construction of different identities in anthropological research. In 2018, in the Post-life Beijing Media Art Biennale (see Fig. 10) releases the expression forms of various arts in the exhibition through the participation of the audience. Immersive Experience teamlab, feast of sound and vision, cross-media interaction and artistic processing of information, overlapping of virtual and reality, interaction between man and machine, and different kinds of new media works of art bring new exhibition experience to the audience and enlighten people to think about existence and future. Today's curators are also users of science and technology, and researchers try to present the availability of technology in speculative scenarios for the audience to experience. Just like novelists and journalists, they know the world in an interlocking way. Researchers build imaginative connections outward and dig more hidden topics inward until the future of science and technology becomes possible again.

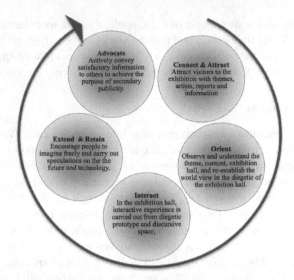

Fig. 11. Experience cycle of the audiences in the exhibition

With the emergence of new media technology, the ways of participating in the experience are constantly enriched. The cross integration of interactive design and exhibition provides technical support for the audience to experience interaction. The emergence of new media technology subverts the traditional way of exhibition. Different types of exhibits have a more diversified way of expression, and at the same time, the audience also has social engagement in the exhibition. The experience cycle of the audiences in watching the exhibition is shown in the figure (see Fig. 11). 1) Connect and attract: First, the visitors will be invited or attracted from the theme of the exhibition, artists, reports and the information of the exhibition. The audience will be interested at the beginning of the experience; 2) Orient: observe and understand the theme, content, exhibition hall and significance of the work during the exhibition, and re-establish the world view in the diegetic of the exhibition hall; 3) Interact: in the exhibition hall, interactive experience is carried out from diegetic prototype and discursive space; 4) Extend and retain: encourage people to imagine freely and carry out speculations on the the future and technology. 5) Advocate: Actively convey satisfactory information to others to achieve the purpose of secondary publicity.

4 Discussion

4.1 How to Design Speculative Scenarios

As a display tool of speculative design, creating speculative scenarios guided by future technologies and trends are conducive to making long-term future plans. The design principles of speculative scenario(see Fig. 12) have the following four aspects:1) Speculative scenario will be discussed around the exhibition theme, and context will be built technological, social and cultural environment in the future, in which the audience can

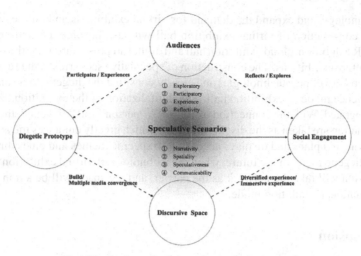

Fig. 12. Design principles of speculative scenario

participate and feel; 2) Speculative scenarios discuss various future, and develop break-through prototype design with futures thinking; 3) The exhibition hall is composed of prototype scenes, and the space is characterized by narrativity spatiality speculativeness and communicability, which better helps the audience to participate in the exhibition hall for exploratory, participatory, experience and reflectivity; 4) Collecting audience feedback in the form communication of speculative props is an important part of speculative scenario, which helps to deepen the research again.

The author thinks that the exhibition space presented by speculative scenarios consists of two parts, one is the curatorial theme, the theoretical basis, speculative topic, research direction and research process of the art works themselves; The other part is the exhibition itself "as a specific medium and form". As an artistic practice and a cultural production activity of joint creation, curation needs to be studied and practiced at the conceptual and methodological levels. Interlacing the two parts is the realistic embodiment of promoting the exhibition concept. Speculative scenarios focus on future and technical topics, and speculate on future trends and development directions.

4.2 Futures Research of Speculative Scenarios

In curator Paul O'Neill's *The Curatorial Conundrum: What to Study? What to Research? What to Practice?* [29], Paul discusses the future direction of curating exhibition, and curatorial needs to establish a "new world" that works, artists, curators and audiences express together - a speculative scenario that shows social topics at all times. Speculative scenarios will become the necessary application direction in public education, science and technology enterprises, research institutions and art space display in the future.

While discussing the future value of speculative scenarios, it is also necessary to further discuss the application possibility of speculative scenarios in the post-epidemic era. The global outbreak of Covid-19 severely impacted the museums and art institutions in various countries. Therefore, we need to promote the application of Internet and media technology, and expand the demand for virtual exhibitions and online exhibition halls. The construction of virtual exhibition hall will also become a brand-new topic, VR/AR/XR exhibition, cloud exhibition hall and digital art presentation are the inevitable trends of future exhibitions. The construction of speculative scenarios in the future needs to make good use of new technologies and clearly construct the diegetic logic and brand-new experience mode of exhibition hall. The digitalization of the exhibition hall is also greatly integrated, With the connection of "object", "person" and "diegetic", the exhibits and information are taken as the display contents, which greatly enhances the audience's participation, and plans and displays according to specific themes and clues through the curator's diegetic logic. In the future, when the technology of virtual exhibition matures, the exhibition will take the network as the carrier, and the space will be a non-physical and informational exhibition mode.

5   Conclusion

This paper discusses speculative scenario as a necessary exhibition tool in speculative design from the perspective of research. Speculative scenarios are important part in the discussion of technology and speculation, and it is also one of the common display means. How to make better use of speculative scenarios is a necessary study area for designers and researchers. Speculative scenarios can intuitively show researchers' thinking about the future, and also help people to better judge the future.

This paper hopes to help people better imagine the future through the research and interpretation of speculative scenarios, better predict the future development and deployment through speculative design and exhibition practice, examine the current application direction and pursue a desirable future. If speculation is the necessary way forward, then speculative scenarios are the windows open to the future, where we can look forward to the future, and we have the best chance to see the future.

Acknowledgements. This article specially thanks should be given to Professor Wu Yan, co-curator of Nine Cities, Millions of Futures, for inviting me to plan the 8th Shenzhen-Hong Kong Urban Architecture Biennale. I would also like to thank Professor Fei Jun and Professor Xiaowen Chen from the Art and Science Department of the CAFA for their guidance and opportunity of curating the Beijing Media Art Biennale.This paper is supported by Tsinghua University Teaching Reform Project (2021 autumn DX05_01 Creativity, innovation and entrepreneurship education).

References

1. The Enlightenment. https://www.britannica.com/event/Enlightenment-European-history
2. Cabinet of curiosities. https://en.wikipedia.org/wiki/Cabinet_of_curiosities
3. Paul O'Neill. https://curatorsintl.org/collaborators/paul-oneill
4. O'Neill, P.: The Culture of Curating and the Curating of Culture(s). MIT Press, Cambridge (2012)
5. George, A.: The Curator's Handbook——Museums, Commercial Galleries. Thames & Hudson, Independent Space (2015)

6. Obrist, H.U.: A Brief History of Curating, JRP|Ringier & Les Presses Du Réel, Zurich (2010). https://www.gsd.harvard.edu/event/hans-ulrich-obrist/
7. Ethics of Technology, Beijing Media Art Biennale (2016). https://www.cafamuseum.org/en/exhibit/detail/544
8. Post-Life, the 2nd Beijing Media Art Biennale (2018). https://www.cafa.com.cn/en/news/details/8325652
9. Nine cities, Millions of futures, Bi-City Biennale of Urbanism\Architecture (Shenzhen) (2019). https://www.szhkbiennale.org.cn/En
10. Years of Humanizing Technology – Art, Technology, Society, Ars Electronica (2019). https://ars.electronica.art/press/en/2019/10/28/shenzhen2019/
11. Foresight · Visible—International Exhibition on Design Futures. https://www.xiaobaijidi.com/t/32539
12. Ga, Z.: https://www.infoartdesign.org/teacherdetail?id=d754219e-e626-4a7a-903f-2107d309d377
13. Dunne, A., Raby, F.: Speculative Everything: Design, Fiction, and Social Dreaming, MIT Press (2013)
14. Ethical Autonomous Vehicles. https://mchrbn.net/ethical-autonomous-vehicles/
15. Forecasting: Interesting Worlds. https://forecastingworlds.invisibledust.com/zh/about/
16. Fountain. https://en.wikipedia.org/wiki/Fountain_(Duchamp)
17. Droog Design. https://www.droog.com/
18. United Micro Kingdoms. https://unitedmicrokingdoms.org/
19. Design and the Elastic Mind. https://www.moma.org/calendar/exhibitions/58
20. Antonelli, P.: States of Design 04: Critical Design, Domusweb.it. N.p., n.d. Web, 12 December 2016
21. Design fiction. https://en.wikipcdia.org/wiki/Design_fiction
22. Bruce Sterling. Shaping Things. MIT Press (2005)
23. The Unknown Cities. https://uvnlab.com/zh/the-unknown-city/
24. Liu, C., Yan, W.: Thousands of cities, Millions of futures, China Development Press (2019)
25. Asia Digital Art Exhibition. https://www.xinhuanet.com/english/2019-05/17/c_138064829.htm
26. Archive Dreaming. https://refikanadol.com/works/archive-dreaming/
27. Nine cities, Millions of futures. https://www.szhkbiennale.org.cn/News/Details.aspx?id=10003325
28. Eilean Hooper-Greenhill, Museums and the Interpretation of Visual Culture, Routledge (2000)
29. O'Neill, P.: The Curatorial Conundrum: What to Study? What to Research? What to Practice? MIT Press, USA (2016)

Innovation Geometry Model as a Way to Explore Future Innovative Opportunities

Shuxin Cheng[✉]

Central Academy of Fine Arts, Beijing 100102, China
shuxincheng@cafa.edu.cn

Abstract. Trans-disciplinary innovative methods enable designers to collaborate with people from different industries, unleashing a higher level of creativity and exploring future innovation opportunities. The Innovation Geometry model redefines the category and evaluation criteria of innovation, which was originally established by the author to guide the R&D innovation of enterprises. Based on the author's teaching practice in China, this paper discusses the application of Innovation Geometry model in design education, especially to guide how to design future opportunities. Innovation Geometry model borrows the spatial dimensions of Geometry and integrates the six core elements that drive innovation: market, technology, product, people, aesthetics and trend, which upgrades the two-dimensional innovation model that focused on technology-driven innovation and market-driven innovation to the spatial dimension Innovation Design, and introduces the fourth dimension time. This research analyses the author's teaching practices of Innovation Design undergraduate program at the Central Academy of Fine Arts in Beijing and aims to summarize the methods of applying Innovation Geometry model to explore future innovative opportunities in design education.

Keywords: Design for social change in global markets · Innovation design · Innovative tools · Design education · Trans-disciplinary design

1 Introduction

As competition intensifies, corporations in industry face increasing pressure to identify the next big opportunity as early as possible. However, trend forecasting organizations tend to create technology-led insights prediction for the future and fail to imagine creative possibilities beyond this. This fixation on technological thinking has also bled into daily life through the seamless integration of modern technologies into a myriad of consumer sectors. The disruption and backlash this is causing can be partially attributed to the contrasting speeds of technological development compared with policy making, but issues such as concern over privacy have been increasingly in the limelight as their effects are realized by society. Many critical humanist questions are raised as awareness grows, and now is the time to begin integrating these considerations into design education.

In the past few decades, some cutting-edge interdisciplinary design teaching modes have been formed. Design engineering, interdisciplinary design, trans-disciplinary innovation, design thinking methodologies have been growing and spreading from the academic world into commercial practice. Postgraduate programs like MA/MSc Innovation

P.-L. P. Rau (Ed.): HCII 2021, LNCS 12772, pp. 318–329, 2021.
https://doi.org/10.1007/978-3-030-77077-8_25

Design Engineering and Global Innovation Design from Royal College of Art and Imperial College; Dyson School of Design Engineering; Shenkar College of Engineering, Design and Art; Stanford d.school; Master in Design Engineering from Harvard Graduate School of Design; and MIT Media Lab have been exploring the tools, environments and new models of innovation.

The traditional design engineering approach focuses on technology feasibility and engineering techniques, which educate the next generation of product design engineers to solve technical problems in developing a physical product. Solving problems without having an assumption of the output format is crucial for creating innovative solutions. The humanist perspective might help to create the next model for innovation. An understanding of human behaviors, mindsets, rational analysis, critical thinking, awareness of the environment and sustainability provides valuable perspectives for innovators.

Globalization and cultural exchanges have also been influencing human behaviors, giving rise to new models of economy, tangible and intangible innovations, a new form of collaborations and conflicts have been created. China as an important player in the global context, providing the experimental ground and insights for developing the new model of innovative education and practices. This paper analyzes the application of Innovation Geometry model, established by the author and its application in the design education practice of the Innovation Design program of the School of Design at Central Academy of Fine Arts in China, in an attempt to explore the methods and possibilities of creating innovative opportunities in the future.

2 Innovation Geometry Model

2.1 Definition of Innovation Geometry Model

Innovation Geometry is a set of trans-disciplinary innovation model. On the basis of the two-dimensional indicators of innovation containing technology and market, comprehensively integrating people, product, aesthetics and trend to construct the spacial model of Innovation Design. It also introduces the fourth dimension of time, to create a dynamic model that could change during the time. Innovation Geometry model was originally created for corporations to conduct organizational diagnosis, research and development innovation and reference for future strategy [1]. This paper studies the application of Innovation

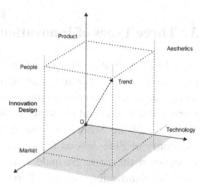

Fig. 1. Innovation Geometry model

Geometry model in design education, especially in exploring future opportunities (Fig. 1).

2.2 Six Elements of Innovation Geometry Model

There are six elements in the Innovation Geometry model that need to be considered and studied during the teaching process of exploring future innovative opportunities.

The first step to construct the possibility of future innovation is to establish a topic worth researching. "People" represents the insight into the fundamental needs of human, not only implies to solve the problems and improve the user experience, but also to explore the potential needs. In combination with extensive observation, visit and preliminary research of people, it is more important to find a valuable research question than to find a right answer.

"Product" does not emphasize the direct satisfaction of user needs, but lies in the development of new and valuable product categories. Its form does not necessarily refer to physical output, but may also be a virtual service process. During the exploration of futures, products of future could not be imagined based on current situation, but a deep analysis of all the forces related to a certain industry, functions and product groups can be helpful. "Aesthetics" refers to artistic expression, concept, taste or modeling, etc., which covers the appearance of physical results to the virtual pleasure and satisfaction. "Trend" refers to the research and forward-looking prediction of future lifestyles. Through the study of changes and developments in sociology, psychology, anthropology, economics and culture, we are able to predict the potential trends of people's prospective lifestyle, which offers a guidance to form an innovative projection to adapt for the future.

"Market" refers to the business situation and the change of market demand to promote innovation. "Technology" means the new ability brought by scientific research and technological inventions that can be provided for future innovative outcomes. Market-driven innovation, technology-driven innovation and design-driven innovation have been widely discussed in the past. Innovation Geometry model aims to integrate, rather than isolate the factors that drive innovation. The above elements do not have a linear sequence, and dynamically coexist in the three-dimensional model.

3   Three Types of Innovation Design

Based on the spatial changes of the Innovation Geometry model, innovation can be divided into three categories: incremental innovation, revolutionary innovation and strategic innovation. The author takes the School of Design, the Central Academy of Fine Arts as the experimental site to develop the undergraduate teaching framework of Innovation Design. Through Innovation Design students apply designerly, scientific, and ultimately humanist processes to explore the complex needs of our current society into the future and sustainable innovative solutions. It includes three parts: Innovative Methods, Design Engineering and Trends Design.

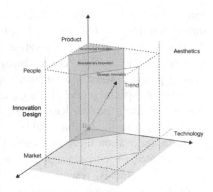

Fig. 2. Innovation Geometry model - three types of innovation

Insights are drawn equally from the humanities as from science and technology and interpreted using interdisciplinary innovation techniques. The aim is to cultivate innovative talents with international vision, cross-domain design process, trans-cultural understanding, critical thinking, and social insight.

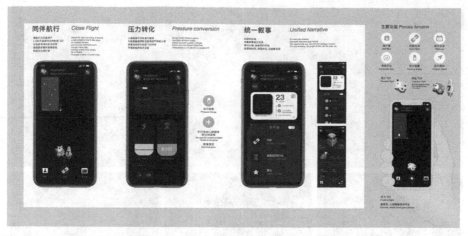

Fig. 3. Pressure Flight, designed by Xiang Qi at Healthcare Innovation Design course, taught by Shuxin Cheng in 2020, School of Design, Central Academy of Fine Arts.

A useful way Innovation Design distinguishes between innovations is via the fourth dimension time of the Innovation Geometry model: the 1–3 year near future targeting "incremental innovation design", the 3–5 year mid-term future focused on "revolutionary innovation", and the 5 + year future discussion of "strategic design" (Fig. 2).

3.1 Incremental Innovation

Incremental innovation refers to innovation results that are based on the iteration and improvement of existing technologies and existing markets. This category of results often does not require new technology development, or exploration of a new market, which is equivalent to continuous small changes, resulting in a low-risk success rate. Design thinking method is often used for this category in design education and introduced into business school. Its human-centered concept, capturing on empathy and double-diamond work flow often bring effective results for the formation of incremental innovation.

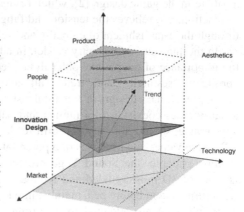

Fig. 4. Innovation Geometry model of Pressure Flight

Pressure Flight is a projected created by Xiang Qi, a third year student of Innovation Design, School of Design, Central Academy of Fine Arts at the author's Comprehensive Healthcare Innovation Design course in 2020. Pressure Flight is a psychological narrative game, which help the user to shift their stress subconsciously during the virtual flying experience on this mobile app. In this game, the user starts to fly freely in the space when he turn on the game. Based on the data changes from skin detection and screen usage time, he can match his partner to fly together. Without competition and pressure, they

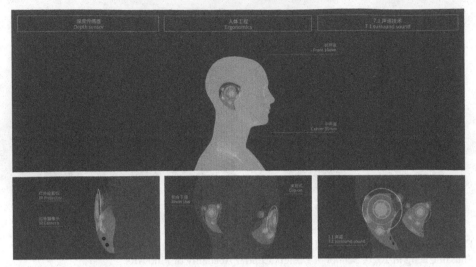

Fig. 5. Sound Yoga, designed by Chen Li at Healthcare Innovation Design course, taught by Shuxin Cheng in 2020, School of Design, Central Academy of Fine Arts.

move forward together in the virtual space, forming a sense of mutual companionship. Through a clever way, the project intervenes from the opposite angle of the competitive attribute in the game design [2], which brings a peaceful sense of company in the form of inaction, and relieves the tension and fatigue brought by mobile phones in daily life through the establishment of empathy and substitution (Figs. 3 and 4).

In the Innovation Geometry model, in addition to design thinking that emphasizes the importance of people, the other three elements in the innovative design dimension "product", "aesthetics" and "trend", all have a guiding role in innovation research and development. The design of the future should shift from a human-centered state to a harmonious coexistence of human and nature. The output in the basis of the good appearance, should not only conform to the trend of future development, but also to reflect the values and lifestyles of a potential future.

For example, the Sound Yoga project is a set of 3D music-guided and feedback relaxation system before bed, mainly aimed at people who are addicted to electronic screens (Fig. 5).

It was created by Chen Li at the author's Comprehensive Healthcare Innovation Design course in 2020. Based on the lifestyle change at home after the epidemic, the project creates a system that the hardware and software complement each other, and can be easily customized by users' exercise habits. It constructs the sound creation ecosystem to provide future opportunity for creators and users (Fig. 6).

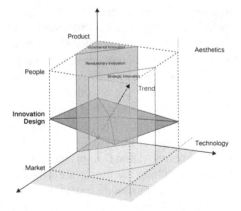

Fig. 6. Innovation Geometry model of Sound Yoga

As this project can be realized in recent years, the technology, market are relatively mature, from the people, product and aesthetics angle, which proposed scenario is relatively niche and potential, it could be seen as incremental innovation.

3.2 Revolutionary Innovation

Revolutionary innovation refers to groundbreaking innovation results. Driven from the technological dimension which often called "radical innovation", and driven by the market is defined as "disruptive innovation" [3]. The revolutionary innovation based on the definition of the Innovation Geometry model is derived from the new scientific technology, market or business model, user groups, product category, such as trends or aesthetic point of view, is not limited to scientific and technological innovations. When upgrading from market-driven and technology-driven, two-dimensional to Innovation Geometry three-dimensional evaluation, the success rate of a revolutionary achievements is easier to increase. Revolutionary innovation often sees its revolutionary breakthrough in a certain field after a lapse of many years.

Fig. 7. Digital Embryo Framework, created by Zixiong Wei, ©SCRY

Although the research and development of this category of innovation results has a long cycle and difficult, the value it brings is incomparable. It also gives small start-ups the chance to create breakthrough companies. Projects that often do not come directly from the industry itself can help create revolutionary innovations.

Zixiong Wei's SCRY is a great example for revolutionary breakthrough to the traditional footwear industry. He takes shoes as the research object and conducts cross-boundary research through different innovative means. He created the Digital Embryo framework, which studies the intersection of digital design, materials science, and future needs, with the aim of exploring new models for design and manufacturing. Digital Embryo aims to construct an underlying framework for fully digital footwear design and manufacture. It is not targeted at a particular pair of shoes, but a common underlying system architecture, a system architecture with ultra-high customization capability, rapid design iteration capability, and high design freedom [4] (Fig. 7).

During the innovation journey, he started off his research two years ago by exploring a more sustainable way to design and manufacture in the footwear industry. Traditional shoes were assembled and glued by different parts, which slows down the pathway for recycling [5].

In one of his early sustainable innovation project Form Board, he used virtual dismantle method to analyze the entire life cycle of footwear from the raw materials to the final stage of usage and created the Form Board project. This project offers users a template, which can be downloaded from the Internet, that can be made from discarded clothing to create an upper that can be worn over a sole that is no longer worn. Instead of traditional product development and production, the project combines co-creation open source templates to build a new possible category (Fig. 8).

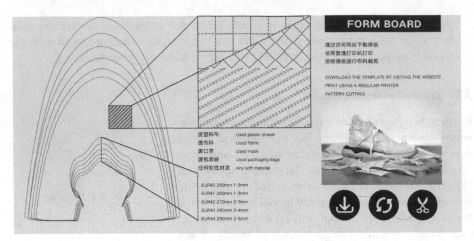

Fig. 8. Form Board, designed by Zixiong Wei at Sustainable Innovative Engineering course, taught by Shuxin Cheng in 2018, School of Design, Central Academy of Fine Arts.

In the Footwear-GAN project, Zixiong aims to use generative adversarial networks to achieve design empowerment and promote designers' progress, taking shoe design as a sample. The basic idea of generating antagonistic network (GAN) is derived from the two-person zero-sum game in game theory, which consists of a generator and a discriminator, and is trained by the way of antagonistic learning. In the conception, the design tool of future confrontation production network will constantly summarize the existing design patterns and styles, summarize and cluster them, and quickly learn the design language and style of modeling, so as to promote the progress of designers (Figs. 9 and 10).

Different forces to his innovation have contributed to his revolutionary project SCRY Shuttle, which is the world's first pair of integrated additive manufacturing footwear that is actually wearable [6].

Technology certainly plays an important role in it, but indicators such as trends market, users, products, aesthetics all play an important role in this project.

In this case, Zixiong's design needs for SCRY promoted the research and development of technologies from his collaborator PollyPolymer, which pushed the boundary of their material research and technical development. In this way, technology, market, user, product, aesthetics and trend jointly promoted the birth of a brand new category in the footwear industry (Figs. 11 and 12).

3.3 Strategic Innovation

Strategic innovation refers to results that have forward-looking significance and trend guidance. The outcomes are often not directly put into the market, but can be understood as conceptual works. After their release, they will have a subtle impact on the industry and promote the production of revolutionary results.

Different from social art and science fiction, forward-looking innovative design is built on the possibility of a certain topic in the future, combined with a large number of

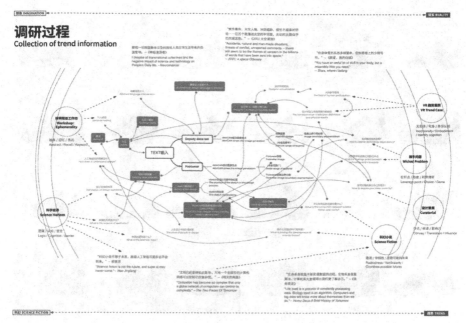

Fig. 9. Process of Footwear-GAN, designed by Zixiong Wei at Trend Design - reality and imagination in science fiction course, taught by Shuxin Cheng in 2019, School of Design, Central Academy of Fine Arts.

research and testing, through a certain provocative creation to stimulate people's nerves. It forms a subtle influence on the future and breaking through the tradition of linear thinking about the future.

Qi Xiang's Memory issuance created an innovative proposal of future service - insurance of memory that driven from the send of smell. Based on some hints in science research, he created this service to keep the smell of children at their 1–5 years old. As there might be significance to awaken and strengthen the deep memory, and five years respectively preserved lineal consanguinity, preferences, living environment, toys, smell the smell of pets through the device of the molecular structure of amplification odor molecules enhance memory and emotions to ease, social sharing, relative succeed, such as medical service to smell for the innovation of the medium service experience (Fig. 13).

Le Zhang's Virtual brain project is a creative thinking management software that records collective wisdom for large innovative enterprises. The virtual creative resource incarnation is formed through the virtual record of thinking in the program. The efficient management of data can effectively collect and organize a large number of creative connection information, resulting in the emergence of creativity. The will links of thousands of employees will be connected to the virtual brain in an organic form and become the core think tank of the enterprise. After the foundation is built, members can call the information base by searching or AR scanning, or supplement and delete (Figs. 14 and 15).

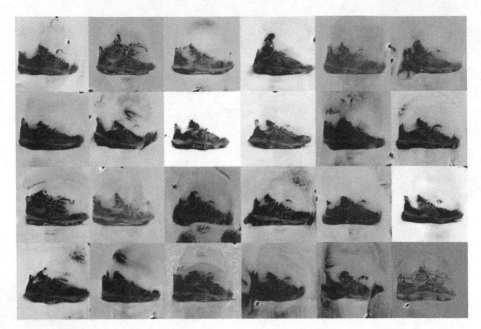

Fig. 10. Experiments of Footwear-GAN, designed by Zixiong Wei, 2019

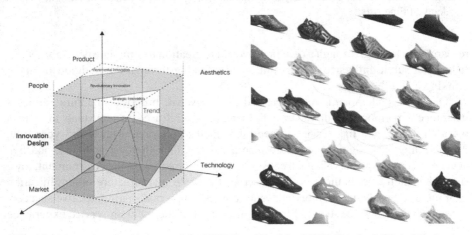

Fig. 11. Innovation Geometry model of SCRY   **Fig. 12.** SCRY Shuttle & Digital Embryo

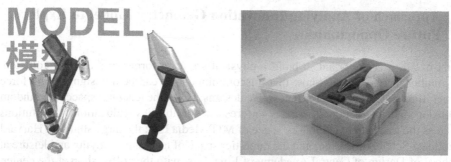

Fig. 13. Memory Insurance, designed by Xiang Qi at Trend Design - reality and imagination in science fiction course, taught by Shuxin Cheng in 2019, School of Design, Central Academy of Fine Arts.

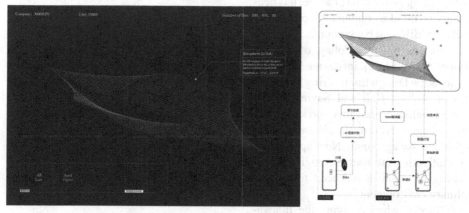

Fig. 14. Virtual Brain, designed by Le Zhang in 2020, annual solo project supervised by Shuxin Cheng, School of Design, Central Academy of Fine Arts.

"You get paid for the insights about possible futures you produce, the understanding of consumer reaction to your artefacts—not for new solutions to create and sell." Clive van Heerden, visiting professor of Central Academy of Fine Arts and co-founder of vHM Design Futures created Non-linear prediction methods to probe the future, which emphasize the important of thinking outside of the linear projection of the future [7, 8].

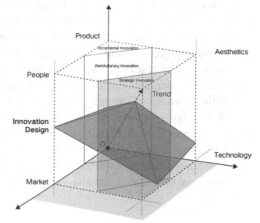

Fig. 15. Innovation Geometry model of Virtual Brian

4   Approach of Applying Innovation Geometry Model to Explore Future Opportunities

First of all, it is important to build a physical space to form cross domain collision. A number of case studies show that miscommunication can be a design driving force generating multiple routes for innovative designs. [9] In the teaching space, the random collision and interaction stimulates unforeseen possibilities. Educational institutions such as the transparent laboratory space of MIT Media Lab; the large studio of Harvard Graduate School of Design; and the three-tier space of teaching, studying and leisure at School of Design of Central Academy of Fine Arts, with the coffee shop at the center, students, teachers and visitors meet and talk much more than the traditional office hour teaching mode (Fig. 16).

Secondly, when implementing innovative design education practice, it is necessary to build a combination of personnel from different backgrounds and abilities, such as the Royal College of Arts and Imperial College's joint degree MA/MSc Innovation Design Engineering [10]. Professor Ashley Hall and Savina Torrisi have developed innovative curriculum for the dynamic crew from different countries and backgrounds. New approaches in cultivating innovative designer, facilitating to create a balanced transdisciplinary environment.

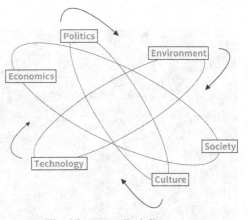

Fig. 16. Trans-disciplinary area

Thirdly, when applying the Innovation Geometry model, we need to choose a topic worthy of study from the fundamental needs of people, conduct research from the current market situation and technical means, carry out the process from design to experiment, think about solutions or potential innovation opportunities based on the dimension of the product, also maintain the design aesthetic attribute of the results from the aesthetic dimension, and analyze its trend level in the design process. During the design process, the evaluation and test are repeated continuously, and test the prototype in the real environment. All six elements do not have a linear order, and they can be applied based on different situations.

Lastly, Innovation Geometry integrates and optimizes innovative tools and methods for different types of innovation goals. Incremental innovation is the most widely produced. Combining market feedback for business analysis, technology optimization and the application of design thinking tools can all iteratively improve products; revolutionary innovation often comes from experimental innovation. It require time to test and prove the final outcome. It can also expand from designer's own creation to co-creation with user.

5 Conclusion

The aim of this paper is to make a contribution to discuss the application of Innovation Geometry model in design education to explore future innovative opportunities. When talking about the future and designing the future lifestyle, it's important to keep an eye for far out and sideways at the same time. Propose a valuable question is more important than creating a solution. With the cases from Innovation Design program that analyzed in this paper, it shows the guidance of innovative creation. People, product, aesthetics, trend, market and technology are six important elements of Innovation Geometry model cohesively contribute to an innovative outcome. With the change of time, the relevant information is constantly updated for the final formation of a more breakthrough innovation.

References

1. Cheng, S.: Innovation Geometry – transdisciplinary multidimensional innovation, enhance innovation integration capability of enterprise. Tsinghua Bus. Rev. **84**(9), 58–64 (2020)
2. Schell, J.: The Art of Game Design: A Book of Lenses. 2nd edn. A K Peters/CRC Press, United States (2014)
3. Christensen, C.M.: The Innovator's Dilemma: When New Technologies Cause Great Firms to Fail, Harvard Business School Press, Boston (1997)
4. SCRY Digital Embryo section page. https://scccccry.com/digitalembryo. Accessed 11 Feb 2021
5. Brain, E.: Emerging Sneaker Brands Are Taking on the Big Boys, One Step at a Time -Keep notwoways, Virón, SCRY™ Lab, Good News and Roscomar on your radar. Hypebeast. https://hypebeast.com/2021/1/emerging-sneaker-brands-notwoways-ros comar-scry-lab-viron-good-news. Accessed 11 Feb 2021
6. SCRY Homepage. https://scccccry.com. Accessed 10 Feb 2021
7. Tharp, B., Tharp, S: Discursive Design: Critical, Speculative, and Alternative Things. The MIT Press, United States (2019)
8. vHM Design Futures x Speculative Futures LDN 004. https://medium.com/@speculati vefutureslondon/speculative-futures-ldn-x-vhm-design-futures-1227da1d2c4e. Accessed 11 Feb 2021
9. Torrisi, S., Hall, A.: Missing miscommunications in interdisciplinary design practice. In: International Conference on Engineering and Product Design Education 5&6 September 2013, Dublin Institute of Technology, Dublin, Ireland
10. Hall, A.: Experimental design: design experimentation. Des. Issues **27**(2), 17–26 (2011)

A Case Study of Social Innovation Based on Ten Years' Practice-Taking the Project of "Design for Country" in Shanghai as an Example

Wei Ding, Xiaolin Li, Junnan Ye$^{(\boxtimes)}$, Xinyao Huang, and Qianyu Zhang

School of Art Design and Media ECUST, Shanghai 200030, China

Abstract. In the current competitive environment, design no longer serves scale competition, but serves innovation competition. If a city wants to build an innovative city, it must carry out industrial transformation. in the past, a large number of Chinese manufacturing industries have been pursuing scale competition in a rough way, which can not adapt to the current competition environment. Especially in some regions that rely on traditional manufacturing industries to develop their economy. The project of "Design for Country" is a social innovation plan with the goal of promoting the transformation and upgrading of regional economy, which is driven by the government and led by enterprises and universities. This paper introduces the guiding ideology of "Design for Country" in different stages in the ten-year practice process, explains the theoretical evolution reason of the project in the process of exploring the economic transformation and upgrading scheme in underdeveloped areas with cases study.

Keywords: Design for Country · Social innovation design · Creative industry

1 Background

Since the reform and opening up, China has experienced the largest and fastest process of urban development in the world, and has made achievements that have attracted worldwide attention. Looking at the world, design, as an innovative resource, is playing a more and more important role in urban competition and even national competition. After 40 years of development, the value of design is reflected in more and more fields. Design and its related industries will play an important role in the process of China's economic structural reform, industrial upgrading and urbanization. In the era of global economic development driven by innovation, innovative design will play a more and more prominent role in the process of enhancing the core competitiveness of countries and cities and building an innovative country [1].

1.1 The Change of the Role of Design

As an important center of design activities, with the deepening of the study of social form and design practice, the object of industrial design is also extending: from symbols

© Springer Nature Switzerland AG 2021
P.-L. P. Rau (Ed.): HCII 2021, LNCS 12772, pp. 330–343, 2021.
https://doi.org/10.1007/978-3-030-77077-8_26

to objects, to activities, to relationships, services and processes. All the way to systems, environments and mechanisms (such as financial and social systems). With the transformation of the global industrial structure from "industrial economy" to "industrial economy", the design has changed from the design in the industrial economy era to the design in the service economy era, and the design is developing in depth. On a global scale, with the deterioration of the global environment and the increasingly complex problems faced by human beings, design is being regarded by more and more people as the key to solve the crisis, and design has been given a new historical mission. Professor Ezio Manzini of the Polytechnic University of Milan has been committed to design and promote social innovation. "We define social innovation as new ideas about products, services and models that meet social needs and create new social relationships or models of cooperation. In other words, these innovations are not only beneficial to society, but also increase the driving force for social change" [2]. Professor Manzini defines social innovation in this way in his book: Social innovation is a new means to solve complex and dangerous problems, by combining social roles in different fields, creating social relations that are different from traditional ones, and making use of new technologies to re-plan, integrate and utilize social resources. in order to achieve social sustainable development [3]. The connotation of social innovation design is to think about what design (product or process) should have, why and how to design, in order to quickly meet the needs of a changing society [4].

Under the background of the current industrial and economic development stage, design has participated in the work of social governance, the goal of design has changed from "product-oriented" to "value-oriented". The role of design has changed from "design products" to "organizing social participation", and the management mode of design has changed from "process management" to "ecological management". Through reasonable organization and innovation, Envision and realize sustainable visions and programs.

1.2 Plan "Design for Country"

"Design for Country" is a social innovation plan led by enterprises and designers and cooperating with local government [5]. The program was jointly launched by East China University and Technology (ECUST) and Shanghai MOMA Design Company (MOMA) in 2011 and is now in its tenth year. This paper hopes to introduce the practical experience and phased theoretical iteration of the design county in the past ten years, so as to provide reference for the research of social innovation design.

2 The Origin of the Plan

In 2010, the United Nations Educational, Scientific and Cultural Organization (UNESCO) officially announced that it would award Shanghai the title of "City of Design". From building Shanghai's "design capital" and promoting "design-led transformation" to the establishment of Shanghai free trade zone and adopting the mechanism of "opening up to form reverse pressure", its core is to change the mode of economic development and adjust the macro-industrial structure to achieve sustainable economic development. In the face of the unbalanced development of regional design industry, the introduction of Shanghai design power to underdeveloped areas can not only solve this problem, but also help Shanghai design power to find new demand and growth points, and realize the sustainable development of Shanghai economy.

2.1 Original Thought

In 2011, MOMA and the School of Art Design and Media (ADM) of ECUST jointly set up a design team to conduct research in Baoying, Jiangsu Province. to help the four traditional local industries--crystal, glass, random stitch embroidery, stationery and Cultural and educational toys--carry out product design, enhance the comprehensive competitiveness of their products and enterprises, and finally achieve the goal of promoting the transformation and upgrading of the county economy. Gradually form the planning model of "designing a county." (Cheng Jianxin, 2011) [6] The original intention of the concept of "Design for Country" is to promote the transformation and upgrading of the regional economy by building a creative ecology and using the power of design. One of the core contents of the construction of the plan is to narrow the gap between the design and the enterprise as soon as possible, and to change the mismatch between the talent training of design education and the demand of the industry. Therefore, the initial foothold of the project is to serve the traditional manufacturing enterprises in Yangtze River Delta with the help of Shanghai design resources and design think tanks.

2.2 Look Back from Now

Since 2007, when China proposed to attach great importance to the development of industrial design, the State Council and various ministries and commissions have launched policies to support the development of industrial design, and local governments and relevant departments have also launched corresponding design policies in line with the pace of the country. Zhejiang, Guangdong and Shandong provinces have promulgated a large number of policies to support the development of the design industry. Beijing, Shanghai and Shenzhen, as design capitals, have also invested a lot of money to promote the development of design creative industries. However, with the same trend of economic development, the development of the design industry has also appeared the problem of uneven development between regions.

Since 2013, the Ministry of Industry and Information Technology has started the biannual certification of national industrial design centers (including Company's Design Center and Industrial Design Company), and by 2020 it has certified four batches. From the regional distribution data certified by national industrial design centers, it can be seen that China's design industry is mainly concentrated in the eastern provinces, the central and western regions are relatively weak, and there is also an imbalance between regions, most of which are concentrated in the central cities. (see Fig. 1) therefore, in the current wave of development of the design industry, it has become an important issue to solve the shortage of design resources in underdeveloped areas through social innovation.

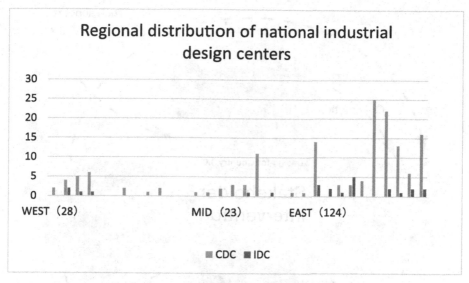

Fig. 1. Regional distribution of national industrial design centers in China

3 The Evolution of the Plan

3.1 Stage 1: Using the Power of Design to Drive the Transformation and Development of Traditional Enterprises

The design work of this stage focuses on the individual enterprise, that is, the stage of design service for the enterprise, and the strategic goal is to drive the transformation and development of traditional industries through the design force. In this stage, the role of design is the service provider, the enterprise is the service object, and the social value created is limited, so it is an unsustainable model. The stakeholders in this stage are shown in Fig. 2.

In the traditional manufacturing enterprises, especially in the cluster areas where small and medium-sized enterprises gather, it is difficult for enterprises to automatically achieve transformation and upgrading, and they urgently need the promotion of external forces. To this end, the team grafted local enterprises with external design forces, established a cooperative relationship with enterprises from project cooperation to strategic cooperation, helped enterprises to improve their product innovation ability, grafted good external resources, and finally established enterprise brands. get out of the predicament of "small profit" of the enterprise. However, cooperation at the project level can not improve the current situation of local talent introduction, nor can it continuously upgrade the industry in a region.

3.2 Stage 2: Establish a Regional Industrial Design Center

Based on the Introspection of the first stage, we reflect and sum up the experience and lessons, short-term design services can not continuously enhance the design competitiveness of enterprises, and the promotion of product competitiveness of individual

Fig. 2. Stakeholder intervention of stage 1

enterprises can not change the difficult situation of regional industrial transformation. Therefore, we put forward the strategic goal of the second stage: to establish a regional industrial design center-to establish a local design center with the support of the local government and local representative enterprises, and to cooperate with local universities to complement each other's advantages. the university provides talents for the design center, and the design center provides a good practice environment for university students (see Fig. 3).

At this stage, the practical nature of the project is more like establishing a commercialized design organization in an area with high demand for design resources but insufficient capacity, cleverly, in the process of project promotion, the service provider with rich design resources acts as the organizer, the government and local enterprises provide support (which may be financial or policy), and establish a cooperative relationship with the university. The core is the follow-up practice of the creative base model, and on the basis of the establishment of an industrial design center, to help the local

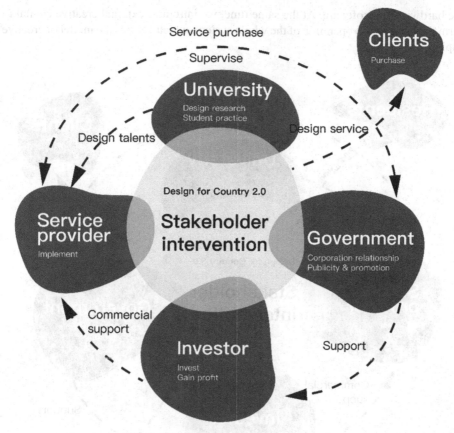

Fig. 3. Stakeholder intervention of stage 2

design competitiveness. This stage is more like a problem-solving idea of social innovative design, in which the design service provider, as the organizer, leads the stakeholders to co-create.

3.3 Stage 3: Create a Gathering Spot of Urban Innovation

The third stage is the iterative version of the second stage, which changes from the construction of "design center" to gathering spot and innovation cluster. Through the construction of urban innovation complex, to provide comprehensive services for urban heritage, pillar industries, innovation and entrepreneurship, design education, through the design power to drive the common development of industry, entrepreneurship and urban innovation.

At the same time, take the gathering spot as the core, attract a large number of innovative enterprises to settle in, at the same time introduce innovative talents, gradually form innovative clusters, and stimulate greater market vitality. At this stage, we put a lot of energy into the early system construction process, fully communicate with stakeholders, make the top-level strategy for the whole plan, and integrate the design management into the hardware and software. At the same time, we introduce external creative capital to form the closed-loop operation of the whole system, which verifies the model of creative capital.

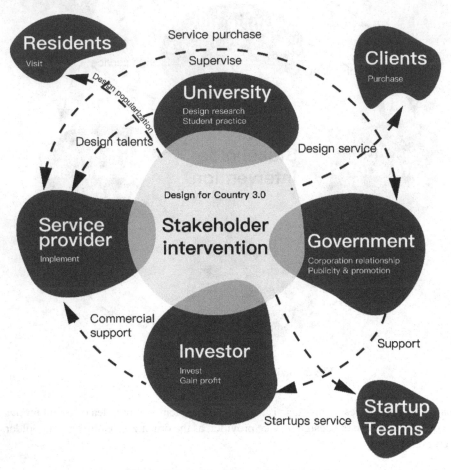

Fig. 4. Stakeholder intervention of stage 3

Compared with stage 2, the advantage of this stage is that it can attract more innovative companies and teams to join the local innovation cluster. at the same time, the gathering spot produced at this stage has stronger commercial attributes. it is accompanied by a number of business forms that provide services for resident enterprises. (see Fig. 4).

3.4 Stage 3: Promote the Integrated Development of Primary, Secondary and Tertiary Industries

The urban design management system in the fourth stage is committed to introducing design concepts for the primary industry, creating peasant culture, developing experiential agricultural economy, promoting agricultural revitalization, providing systematic design services for the secondary industry, applying vertical innovation to the traditional manufacturing industry, creating design exhibition centers, creating space and talent education exchange platforms, etc. Inject the power of design IP into the tertiary industry, create a unique city and historical culture for the city, activate traditional cultural resources, and organically integrate commercial value, design value and service value to form a brand-new service system. (see Fig. 5).

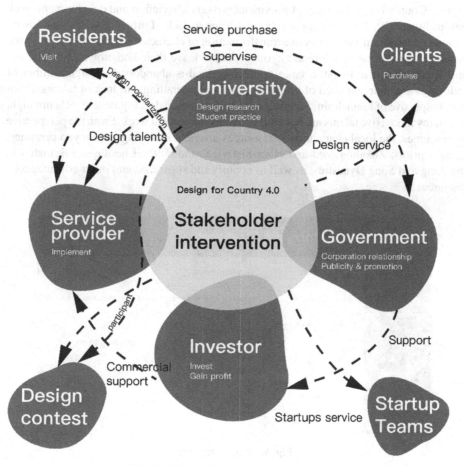

Fig. 5. Stakeholder intervention of stage 4

Under the background that the industrial chain jointly creates value, within and among enterprises, realize vertical innovation and integration, extend the industrial chain, extend upstream to the improvement of agricultural products, and extend downstream to the deep processing of agricultural products, brand construction of agricultural products, market sales and after-sales service, etc., through the co-creation of the whole industrial chain to achieve competitive advantage in the market. This model is conducive to the integration of agricultural and other industrial resources, information and technology, reduce costs, and build brands with strong competitive advantages, so as to enlarge the value of agricultural resources, change the mode of agricultural development, and promote the integrated development of the primary, secondary and tertiary industries.

4 Typical Cases

4.1 Stage 1: Songxi County of Fujian Province

Songxi County is a key county of provincial poverty alleviation and development work before June 2019. There are some problems, such as lack of urban development power, serious talents drain and ineffective transformation of characteristic resources. From the perspective of urban development, young people leave their hometown, only the old and small are left at home, a large number of land is abandoned; a large number of industries are in urgent need of transformation and upgrading, but lack of talents. From the perspective of brain drain, Songxi's regional economic development level is not high, and many innovative talents are not willing to stay in the local work. From the perspective of resources, the local characteristic resources are rich, including jiulongyao ceramics, Songxi prints, Zhanlu sword and other historical and cultural heritages originated in the Tang and Song Dynasties, as well as century old sugarcane and other advantageous resources.

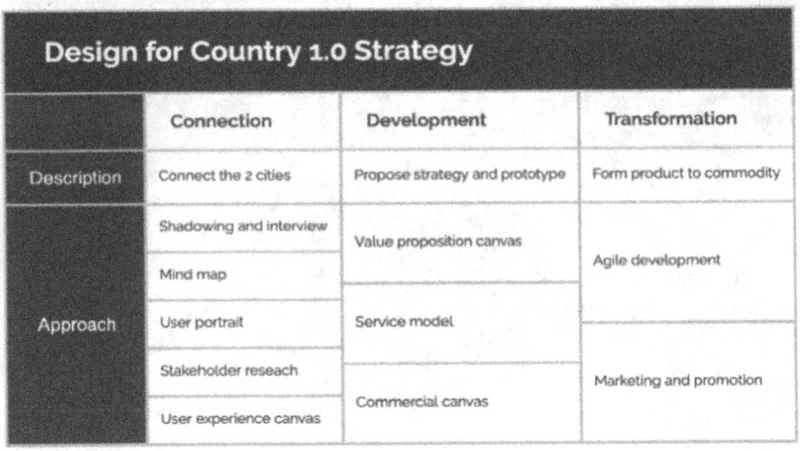

Design for Country 1.0 Strategy			
	Connection	Development	Transformation
Description	Connect the 2 cities	Propose strategy and prototype	Form product to commodity
Approach	Shadowing and interview	Value proposition canvas	Agile development
	Mind map		
	User portrait	Service model	
	Stakeholder reseach	Commercial canvas	Marketing and promotion
	User experience canvas		

Fig. 6. Stage 1 strategy

At the beginning of the project, the design county team went to Songxi to communicate and share ideas with the local government, enterprises, farmers and other participants, in order to establish a link between the two places and different departments.

(see Fig. 6) On this basis, we put forward the brand slogan of "Millennium Songxi, hundred years of Sugarcane", using century-old sugarcane to represent Songxi regional brand, by connecting the resources of urban designers, to inject vitality into Songxi's specialty and realize the virtuous circle of designing county model. Based on this, we have launched local social innovation activities, including forums, design competitions and local projects led by service design. In the end, the project also produced a number of agricultural products and cultural and creative products, which were warmly welcomed in the market.

After these things have been done, we have seen some results. Over the past year, selling sales of tea and brown sugar from Songxi specialty have increased by about 20%. After more than 60 media publicity, more than 300 news reports, more than one million network dissemination, and combined with the promotion of the local tourism festival, the number of tourists in Songxi's century-old hometown of sugarcane has doubled. Songxi County officially took off the hat of a poor county in June 2019 [7].

4.2 Stage 2: Maanshan of Anhui Province

In 2014, four companies, including MOMA, signed a contract to jointly fund the establishment of Maanshan Industrial Design Center. Maanshan Design Center includes four platforms: industrial product display, industrial design service, industry-university-research cooperation and network information. MOMA provides third-party design services (see Fig. 7).

Fig. 7. Maanshan design center

The logic of this model lies in that in order to solve the problems such as the difficulty of gathering innovative talents and innovative forces in relatively backward areas, the project helps to establish a "design center" and links with Shanghai design resources. to solve the problem of gathering design talents and creative talents. Through the purchase of services by the government, inject innovative power into enterprises and better promote the transformation and upgrading of the manufacturing industry. At this stage, a group of design talents who travel back and forth between Shanghai and the regional design center are trained to carry out design work in Shanghai and the regional design center respectively, which not only strengthens their own learning, but also contributes a lot to the construction of the regional design center.

4.3 Stage 3: Rizhao of Shandong Province

Rizhao Gathering Spot mainly includes functional modules such as design center, design exhibition hall, art gallery, creator's office, creator coffee, creative design store, etc., with industrial design as the core, the spot provides services for urban construction, six major industries, innovation and entrepreneurship. The establishment of the Spot builds an important platform for industrial transformation and upgrading. It connects the government, enterprises, design institutions, and colleges and universities. Through a mature operation mechanism, it grafts rich external resources to help enterprises enhance their innovation ability, complete product upgrading, and help the government complete the incubation of creative talents and industrial transformation and upgrading (see Fig. 8).

Fig. 8. Rizhao gathering spot

The advantage of this stage is that it enriches the functions of the design center and expands the scope of the local capacity of the design. However, the practice at this stage is still concentrated in the service industry and manufacturing field. Compared with the miniaturization practice in the first stage, it belongs to the top-down practice. In addition to being able to visit the design exhibition, the public has a weak sense of participation.

4.4 Stage 4: Handan of Hebei Province

Establish an Industrial Design Institute. Handan Industrial Design Institute ((HIDI)) is a municipal industrial design institute jointly established by two companies, including MOMA, according to several policies and measures to support the development of industrial design by the governments of Hebei Province and Handan City. Together with government service center, financial innovation and service center, wave big data center and convention and exhibition center, one-stop enterprise ecological chain service pattern is composed of "one base, six centers" (see Fig. 9).

Fig. 9. Handan design center

HIDI is positioned as a comprehensive operation service provider for the design of the whole industrial chain, with the promotion of industrial design and industrial integration as the starting point, the industrial transformation and upgrading of the service city as the foothold, and the construction of public service system and the introduction of excellent design institutions as the supporting point. Form and promote the concept of industrial design innovation, link design upstream and downstream resources, enable the development of enterprises, promote industrial integration and upgrading, promote industry exchange of industrial design innovation service platform.

Agricultural Product Design Service. Qimei is a local agricultural company in Handan, focusing on the field of organic food and has formed a certain influence in the industry. After the product quality has reached a relatively high standard, the brand of Qimei urgently needs to expand its communication and form a greater influence. Through the intermediary role of Handan Industrial Design Center, Qimei established contact with the design team in Shanghai and contributed to this cooperation.

Fig. 10. Qimei food design

Through the research on the positioning of Qimei brand and its brand concept, the design team helped Qimei define the image of "fertile land of vitality" and "infinity", and defined the brand logo of Qimei accordingly. (see Fig. 10) After the upgrading of brand and packaging design, Qimei's products have gained a better image, and the rise in selling sales has led to the development of agricultural products planting industry in Hebei. Therefore, the cooperation case between Hebei Qimei and Shanghai design team through HIDI is a typical representative of promoting the development of primary, secondary and tertiary industries through design.

Hold a Design Competition. Under the background of COVID-19, which has spread since 2019, emergency rescue products have become an important support system for emerging industries to maintain social stability, ensure economic development and improve people's quality of life. Therefore, the HIDI, the School of Art Design and Media of ECUST and the Handan government jointly held the "Congtai Cup" design competition for emergency rescue products. Participants are encouraged to better drive the innovation of emergency rescue products and service models through the discovery and solution of design problems, so as to improve the efficiency and quality of emergency rescue.

5 Conclusions

Based on ten years of practice, we believe that the "Design for Country" project is an effective exploration of the mode of regional enterprise upgrading and industrial transformation and the value of design in the process of China's economic transformation. The project will continue to explore in practice in the future and provide a reference for the research of social innovation design.

References

1. Ning, Z., Kejun, Z., Shouqian, S., Jiang, X.: Research on the evaluation system of urban design competitiveness. Eng. Sci. China **19**(03), 111–116 (2017)
2. Manzini, E.: Design, When Everybody Designs: An Introduction to Design for Social Innovation. MIT Press, New York (2015)
3. Guangxin, J., Tao, B.: On Social Innovation. J. China Univ. Petrol. (Social Science Edition) **26**(3), 43–47 (2010)
4. Stickdorn, M., Schneider, J.: This is service design thinking. China Productivity Center, Taiwan (2019)
5. Wei, D.: Magnified Design. China Construction Industry Press, Beijing (2015)
6. Can small hand-in-hand workshops in Shanghai become a "model"? October 24, 2011 Xu Meng Source: Jiefang Daily
7. Ding, W., Li, X., Ye, J.: Research and practice of brand design method of local specialty products in developing regions under the concept of service design. In: Kantola, J. I., Nazir, S., Salminen, V. (eds.) AHFE 2020. AISC, vol. 1209, pp. 244–250. Springer, Cham (2020). https://doi.org/10.1007/978-3-030-50791-6_31

User Experience: The Motivation and Promotion of Livestreaming Innovation in Chinese Marketing

Lijun Han[✉]

Hunan University, Changsha 410082, People's Republic of China

Abstract. China's e-commerce livestreaming economy was booming under the influence of the COVID-19, and competition for online users has become the main task of online marketing. To explore the relationship between user experience and livestreaming, this paper used document research, sentiment analysis and depth interview. The results showed that the integration of livestreaming and e-commerce enhanced user experience usability: livestreaming extended to social platform to provide users with positive emotional experience of interactive rituals: user value is an important factor in maintaining long-term and intimate relationships. The results of the present work implied that the rise of e-commerce livestreaming benefited from nice user experience in emergency situation, and the key to future development is also to enhance user experience from consumption scenarios, building interaction rituals and co-creating user value with private traffic.

Keywords: User experience · E-commerce livestreaming · Chinese marketing

1 Introduction

1.1 User Experience

User experience (UX) research is to interpret products or services from the perspective of users. Users immerse in tangible products, spaces or intangible interactions and services set by the designer will produce unforgettable emotional expressions and emotional memories. This kind of emotional memory is not useless,but has become an important starting point for companies to connect with users. Joseph Pine predicted in the book "Experience Economy" that future economic development belongs to the era of experience economy [1]. With the upgrading of new technologies and consumption patterns, users' demand for products is no longer limited to functional satisfaction. Enterprises are also beginning to pay more attention to users' psychological needs, devote themselves to the experience economy, pursue to satisfy users' positive self-feeling, and pay attention to users' self-experience in the consumption process [2]. UX was first proposed by Norman and pointed out that a successful UX must first meet the needs of customers without harassing or annoying users; secondly, the products provided should be simple

P.-L. P. Rau (Ed.): HCII 2021, LNCS 12772, pp. 344–361, 2021.
https://doi.org/10.1007/978-3-030-77077-8_27

and elegant, so that customers can use them happily; In addition, it must be able to bring additional surprises to users [3].

UX is an extension of interactive technology, which is to study the quality of interactive technology from the perspective of product structure, product functional quality to user emotional needs and user experience [4]. As UX expands in content and architecture, its meaning is constantly enriched. The existing literature has not yet formed a unified standard for the definition of UX. In terms of the content of UX, the literature generally believes that UX involves three aspects: user, product or service, and interactive environment. The most influential definition of UX is given by ISO 9241-210: all the reactions and results of people for products, systems or services that are used or expected to be used [5]. In addition, the Usability Professional Association (UPA) defines UX as all user perceptions consisting of all aspects of interaction with products, services or enterprises [6]. The definition of UPA is the expansion of traditional human-computer interaction and usability, which includes not only task-related needs, but also user psychological needs, value needs, etc., but for enterprises, it is relatively general, less operational, and unable to meet the requirements of practitioners. The above definition does not give specific elements for evaluating UX. Hassenzahl and Tractinsky define UX as the user's inner condition (tendency, expectation, demand, motivation, mood, etc.) and a system with certain characteristics (complexity, purpose, usability, functionality, etc.) produced in a specific interactive environment Results [7]. In comparison, the definition given by the latter encompasses almost all aspects of UX, and it also has a certain degree of operability. Barjnik believes that UX includes all user satisfaction (an aesthetic experience), the meaning of the product to the user (meaning experience), and the resulting feelings and emotions (emotional experience) [8]. There are also studies that define UX from the time dimension. Forlizzi and Battarbee define UX as an experience with a definite beginning and end time, and all the use experiences that take place during this time are called UX [9].

From the definition of UX, users, products or services, and interactive environment are the three factors that affect UX. In order to evaluate the design, the evaluation of experience can be quantified to a certain extent. Morville divides the UX into seven aspects: usability, usefulness, ease of use, reliability, easy search, desirability, and value to evaluate UX [10]. Park et al. point out that UX includes usability, emotion and user value [11]. Literature research shows that UX research selects the components according to actual research questions. The UX research related to e-commerce livestreaming can be evaluated from three dimensions: usability, emotional experience, and user value. Any online product should meet the most basic requirements of users can using it normally. For example, an e-commerce livestreaming platform can complete the purchase of goods and interact with the anchor. This is also the experience advantage of the livestreaming economy over offline consumption during the special period of the epidemic. As user needs turn to content and emotional, the standard of bringing positive emotional experience to users should be met. For example, the emotional anxiety caused by the epidemic makes users spend more time on entertainment videos and emotional content. On the basis of meeting the immediate needs of users, continuous user relationship operations can generate long-term user value beyond expectations.

1.2 User Experience in China

In a sense, user experience is a relatively broad concept. UX design is a multi-dimensional perception. This multi-dimensional perception concept includes not only the user's perception and manipulation of the product system, but also the user's perception of the product subjective feelings, including design style, design philosophy, and cultural structure [12]. These UX mainly come from the impact of cultural customs on perception. People are constantly exposed to cultural customs every day, but often deliberately cover it up. In fact, they are part of the cultural structure. Therefore, in order to constantly understand and enrich UX and perception, we need to decode cultural customs, which is an intuitive and qualitative process. Due to the diversity of cultural structures, it also brings diversity of UX.

As the global economy is affected by the Covid-19, China has spawned an economic mode different from other countries – e-commerce livestreaming economy. Under the situation that the national offline consumption is restricted by the epidemic, the e-commerce livestreaming market (GMV caliber[1]) will reach 961 billion in 2020. It can be called a marketing "myth". The uniqueness of China's e-commerce livestreaming is due to the Chinese social and economic background. After the outbreak of the epidemic, Chinese government quickly issued a road closure policy for prevention and control safety to restrict people's offline travel, and offline consumption was suspended. On the basis that China's online shopping market has become more mature, users have fully turned to online e-commerce channels for shopping. Driven by 5G and live broadcast technology, e-commerce live broadcasts have opened up offline and online scenarios. With online and offline integration, corporate marketing has also moved from offline physical stores to online live broadcast rooms. Under different cultural and social backgrounds, even in emergencies that are affected by the epidemic globally, users' perceptions of life and consumption habits are different in various places, and companies' responses and marketing methods to improve user experience are also different. Therefore, the original exploration of user experience must be rooted in the perspective of social culture. China is increasingly becoming a market where experience is king. Nowadays, in the self-media era, the characteristics of decentralization are becoming more and more obvious, and the stronger voice of consumers makes the status of products' self-propagation attributes increasingly elevated. Therefore, whether the marketing can be successful, innovative user experience has become a key factor.

2   Livestreaming Marketing

In 2016, e-commerce live-streaming was launched on Taobao live broadcast. After 4 years of growth, it thrived across the board during the 2020 epidemic. User demand drove the popularity of e-commerce livestreaming, and for a while, many platforms deployed e-commerce livestreaming services. Today's e-commerce livestreaming is no longer limited to the functional attributes of e-commerce platforms selling goods. Social content

---

[1] Note: GMV refers to the transaction amount of the website, including payment amount and unpaid amount.

platforms have also entered the field. Traditional e-commerce platforms and content e-commerce platforms have different e-commerce models based on their own scenarios and user attributes. Traditional e-commerce platforms refer to the initial use of real-time broadcasts, short videos, tweets and other content-based methods to recommend to consumers, to cultivate user trust, increase user stickiness and provide users with a better product experience. The core is to increase the conversion rate of commodity purchases through content; the pain point is that it takes time to build their own content platform and cultivate users' content reading habits, such as Taobao Live, JD Live, Suning Live, Pinduoduo Live. Content e-commerce platforms refer to platforms that originally made content such as graphics, videos, and live broadcasts, then use live broadcasts to sell goods to monetize attention flow. The core is to create content that meets the need; the pain point is that it takes time and efforts to build their own e-commerce chain and user consumption habits. Such as Weibo, Douyin, Bilibili and Xiaohongshu, they use content advantages to carry out e-commerce livestreaming and promote social sharing. People are socialized animals, and the sense of identity and interaction that sharing brings to other people will stimulate positive emotions and bring positive emotional experiences to users.

3 Method

In Fig. 1, the first research method is the document research method. With the help of publicly released information and data, analyze the correlation between online and offline economic differences and user experience. The second is text sentiment analysis. Obtain user feedback through online comment mining, and then conduct sentiment analysis on Weibo comments to analyze the user's emotional experience of the livestreaming. Now users can express their views, feelings and opinions about a product through social media such as Weibo. Compared with questionnaire surveys and other methods, using

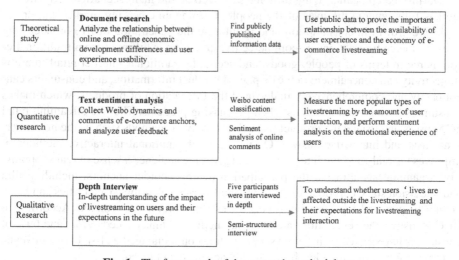

Fig. 1. The framework of the research methodology

social data to obtain users' online reviews of products has the advantage of huge amount of data, strong timeliness, and fast update speed. Due to active sharing from real users, it also avoids the subjectiveness of designer's experience interference. The third is the depth interview method, which conducts comprehensive interviews on user media usage habits outside of the live broadcast scene with five participants,and understands whether there is supplementary media to enhance the user's habit of watching live broadcasts and how users' lives are affected.

3.1 Document Research

IResearch data showed, from March to May 2020, China's online retail sales totaled 2646.40 billion yuan, a year-on-year growth rate of −9.1% compared to the total retail sales of consumer goods, which was 16.4% percentage points higher [13]. It showed that during the epidemic, the stagnation of offline shopping malls caused consumers to shift their shopping behaviors online, and online consumption showed a trend of growth against the trend. IResearch's User Tracker monitoring showed that more than 99% of users believed that e-commerce platforms had played a functional role during the epidemic, and more than 68.5% of users believed that e-commerce platforms had great effects and influence. During the epidemic, users' attitudes towards consumption have changed from panic at the beginning to calm and rational, and online consumption channels have played an important role. Under the orderly organization of online consumption, users quickly regained their confidence in consumer life. More than 50% of users believed that online and offline consumption had resumed, while 34.8% of users said that after the outbreak, their online consumption behaviors were reversed. In contrast, 35.5% of users indicated that their offline consumption has declined compared with before the epidemic. On the whole, the rapid response of online consumption has helped users through the most difficult psychological panic period, and market stability and consumer confidence have improved significantly.

During the epidemic, living at home has become the main scenarios. Livestreaming has fully entered the lives of the people, forming an emerging market that drives explosive growth in consumption, and promoting the penetration of live broadcasting in e-commerce transactions. E-commerce livestreaming is different from traditional e-commerce in terms of people, goods, and scene. In traditional Internet retail, there is subjectivity and concealment in the display of product information, and consumers cannot easily and comprehensively understand the information of products, which makes consumers have certain concerns when purchasing products. The live-streaming retail helps users understand the product through a variety of methods such as the host's personal trial and interactive answer. On the basis of traditional interactive methods, it improves the real-time and interactivity, and gives the audience a sense of real shopping. Livestreaming has attracted the participation of cross-border anchors, including film and television stars, corporate executives, and Internet celebrities. Celebrities can bring greater volume and exposure, improving the effect of product conversion. According to BCG statistics, the penetration rate of social media in China exceeds 97%, and 69% of consumers have shared their online shopping links on social media [14]. In recent years, e-commerce livestreaming has been quickly accepted and loved.

3.2 Text Sentiment Analysis

Select Research Sample

Affected by COVID-19, the number of Taobao live broadcasts in 2020 has exceeded 25.89 million, and the number of products on the shelves for the year has exceeded 50 million. Taobao live broadcast has become a typical representative of China's e-commerce livestreaming market. According to the statistics of Zhigua Data, the number of new anchors exceeded 520,000 [15]. Among them, Li Jiaqi and Viya are the most representative head anchors of Taobao live. According to the list of Taobao Live, during China's Singles' Day shopping carnival in 2020, Li Jiaqi and Viya's Taobao Live Studio have accumulated 150 million and 130 million viewers respectively [16]. The total sales of the livestreaming of Li Jiaqi and Viya on the 20th night were 3.221 billion yuan and 3.327 billion yuan respectively, with the total amount approaching 7 billion yuan. Sina Weibo have become an important platform for obtaining user feedback due to the large number of active users and wide user groups. These two e-commerce anchors have great influence on Weibo. They post live broadcast previews and interact with fans on Weibo. The Weibo platform has become the main platform for maintaining user relationships outside of Taobao Live, and Weibo comments are the main way for fans to interact with the host. Therefore, this research selected Li Jiaqi and Viya's Weibo dynamics as the research object.

Collect Research Data

This research focused on exploring the relationship between livestreaming content and user emotional experience. With the help of octopus collectors, the recent Weibo dynamics of Li Jiaqi and Viya were selected as research samples with the keywords of "live" and "fans" (Jiaqi's fans replaced with "all the girls," Viya's fans replaced with "Viya's women"). We searched through "Live" and "All Girls" in Jiaqi's Weibo and obtained 79 valid data; searched through "Live" and "Viya's Woman" in Viya's Sina Weibo and obtained 87 valid data. Analyzed samples from the two dimensions of review quantity and review quality. In terms of quantity, we counted Weibo publishers, Weibo content, the number of likes, reposts and comments. The data was sorted by the sum of the number of likes, comments, and reposts from large to small, according to the live broadcast format and Weibo Types were classified into the top 10 Weibo posts, and Table 1 and Table 2 are obtained. In terms of quality, this study selects 5 Weibo posts with strong emotional attributes by Li Jiaqi and Viya respectively, and Li Jiaqi's Weibo comments totaled 1522, Viya's Weibo comments totaled 232, excluding duplicate information and meaningless information, and finally got a total of 338 valid samples. Using the ROST Content Mining System[2], sentiment analysis was carried out on the content of comments under Li Jiaqi and Viya's Weibo.

From Table 1, it was found that the most popular Weibo content was the welfare lottery and live broadcast preview; the most popular Weibo content in was fan interaction, followed by live broadcast previews; in terms of livestreaming form, except for the China

---

[2] Shenyang. ROST Content Mining System: software for Content Mining and Analysis. Wuhan University, Hubei, China (2008).

Table 1. Li Jiaqi's Weibo comment

Livestreaming Form	Wb type	Wb text	Reposts	Comments	Like	Sum
Shopping Festival (i.e., 6.18 Mid-Year Promotion)	Welfare lottery	"All girls, don't miss this one! The 618 must-buy hot style list is here!! Pass + transfer, take 1 person to deliver all products, at 0 o 'clock on May 25th! One more person to deliver all the products at 7:00 PM on May 25th! Another 100 people will be randomly sent a product on May 25th"	714287	552581	558291	1825159
Shopping Festival (i.e., Life Festival)	Live preview	"On July 26th at 7:30 PM, the # All Girls' Lives Day is here! Water purifier, washing machine, smart lock and other hot style good things are coming! Click on the picture to view the life festival product notice [attention + comment praise] draw 100 people each to send 726 yuan life festival cash red envelope!! One more Valentino bag!! Draw 100 more life festival canvas bags! # LiJiaQi Live"	135066	370298	210355	715719
Shopping Festival (i.e., Double11 Online Shopping Festival)	Live preview	"Singles Day last carnival!! This time really really really can't miss oh miss is really not so much strength, 10th at 7 PM, 11th at 7 PM, # Li Jiaqi Live # See you! Pass + transfer comments to like, 520 people will be selected as gift bags of famous brands"	5746	208034	438956	652736
Shopping Festival (i.e. Snack Festival)	Fan interaction	"# All the girls! # Come and choose! On July 8th # All Girls Snack Festival, Jia Qi invites all girls to choose food together! Comment section "recommend XXX product + recommended reasons", you recommend your favorite snacks to Jia Qi, this snack festival, you are responsible for recommending delicious, Xiao Li is responsible for talking about the activity # Li Jia Qi Live #"	6626	65958	527983	600567
Festival Gift-Giving Guide	Live preview	"All the boys! All the girls! This video you must not miss, 520 gift guide to come ~ I wish everyone 520 happy holidays Yo, every day happy, sweet ~ follow me + to comment like, draw 60 fans to send gifts in the video (details see comments) ~"	113820	208949	231821	554590
Fans' Day	Welfare lottery	"Thank you to all the girls who have always brought Jiaqi warmth and affection. On the evening of December 22nd, Li Jiaqi and all the girls' warm annual party, the gifts are ready! Everyone must come and play! Get 1000 people to send a gift pack of snacks and another 700 people to send a handmade item to Rachel's grandmother! "	172309	11487	219571	403367
The new show	Live preview	"# Li Jiaqi Live ## Li Jiaqi recently released #+7 new show, big brand Chinese Valentine's Day new collection to come! I wish all the girls happy Chinese Valentine's Day in advance, and I have prepared a gift for you. Please send 1 person a special GG Marmont series small backpack for Chinese Valentine's Day! Double Seventh Festival Valentine special GG Marmont series card bag for 2 people! Details of Austin's Weibo video draw	26435	104881	50009	181325
Celebrity and star	Live preview	"All girls, LVMH Greater China President Andrew Wu is coming for his first live show! At 6:30 PM on August 12th, lock the president's meeting room of Palma Water Tmall studio, "fragrant" about Blue Mediterranean ~ transfer comments, select 10 MM to send Jia Qi with the same Blue Mediterranean California Gui 30ml Li Jia Qi Austin's microblog video	11784	71955	25239	108978
The new show	Live preview	"# Li Jiaqi Live ## Li Jiaqi recently released #+7 new product show, today show big brand makeup new products! Gifts have also been prepared for all of the girls. Check out the comments on Jia-Qi Li Austin's Twitter video for more details of the raffle"	9209	66046	20355	95610
Special performance for brand	Live preview	"7:30 PM on 8th, Tmall International Special Show + NEVA Special Show comes! Take out a random light	22329	997	38692	62018

National Shopping Festival such as Double11 Online Shopping Festival and 6.18 Mid-Year Promotion were themed live broadcasts, and the anchors also revolved around self-made shopping festivals such as Life Festival, Snack Festival, Mother and Baby Festival, Beauty Festival, Fashion Festival, and celebrities entering the live broadcast. In addition, the fan festival held once a year was also widely welcomed. In order to enrich

Table 2. Viya's Weibo comment

Livestreaming Form	Wb type	Wb text	Reposts	Comments	Like	Sum
Public welfare activities	Fan interaction	"I will never forget the people I met on my way to help farmers and alleviate poverty, including every poverty alleviation cadre, enterprises and villagers. Of course, not accompanied by all the women and knights via. It's the end of the year, I hope the New Year will be better for everyone!"	3126	171757	32665	207548
Shopping Festival	Live preview	" On December 17th at 7pm, the Viya Snack Festival will be online again!! Rio, KFC, skim milk... The last shot of 20 years, hurry to stock up on delicious food!! …"	141724	3250	59735	204709
Shopping Festival	Live preview	"Pay attention! The last train for the Spring Festival is on January 9th!! # Viya's must-buy list for Spring Festival # Food, drink and Chinese New Year gifts... Everything imaginable has been arranged for you this time…"	96828	7580	76393	180801
Shopping Festival	Live preview	" November 10 at 7pm cross 0!! Miss a day and wait a year!! Double 11 is really coming!! Tomorrow night!! This time to eat and drink, wear with, makeup skin cares... You have everything you want!..."	88621	588	78431	167640
Special performance for brand	Live preview	"12-12 winter clothes! The new winter products are ready! Bags, accessories, clothes, shoes... 7 o 'clock tonight, lock down the studio..."	48531	3114	75392	127037
Shopping Festival	Welfare lottery	"12-12 carnival 3 days to come!! 7 o 'clock tomorrow night fashion day!! There are explosive day and winter clothing big new, these days set the alarm clock!!..."	71375	2559	53055	126989
Public welfare activities	Fans interaction	"On January 23, Viya's team has prepared 30,000 N95 masks, 10,080 pieces of disinfectant, 100,000 pieces of ready-to-eat food and other supplies with a total value of about 1 million yuan…I hope there will be more women of Viya …"	5592	12595	108542	126729
Shopping Festival	Welfare lottery	Unannounced big bonus is coming!! With the topic # Viya Live Room # post a single! After November 11, we will find 11 women/knights of Viya in the topic page! … Share your hot style list! Thank you for your support, I hope you have a good time!!"	17586	63905	41686	123177
Fans' Day	Fans interaction	"All the way, I really want to thank each and every one of the "Viya woman/knight" behind me! This is a new beginning, "faint mute" will definitely work harder in the future, to bring more good things to everyone! 3000W come on!!	11320	55586	49905	116811
Celebrity and star	Live preview	"Join Lucy Liu, an international movie star who starred in "Lethal Woman," "Charlie's Angels," and "Kill Bill," to share our "healing" story. On August 19th, we will lock the # Viya Live Room	2391	54905	33787	91083

the livestreaming form, Li Jiaqi's live broadcast room added new product shows, and Viya added charity activities.

Sentiment Analysis

The concept of Sentiment Analysis first appeared in the article by Nasukawa et al. [17]. Text sentiment analysis, in simple terms, is the analysis, processing, induction and reasoning of subjective text with emotional color, extracting the emotional polarity (positive, negative, neutral) in the text, and more fine-grained research also extract the emotional target. The initial sentiment analysis originated from the previous analysis of words with emotional color. For example, "good" is a word with a commendatory color, and "ugly" is a word with a derogatory color. With the emergence of a large number of subjective texts with emotional color on the Internet, researchers have gradually transitioned from the analysis and research of simple emotional words to the research of more complex emotional sentences and emotional texts. Based on this, according to the granularity of the processed text, emotional analysis can be divided into several research levels such as word level, phrase level, sentence level, text level and multi-text level. Based on the existing research results, this article summarized sentiment analysis into three progressive research tasks, namely sentiment extraction, sentiment classification and sentiment induction, as shown in Fig. 2.

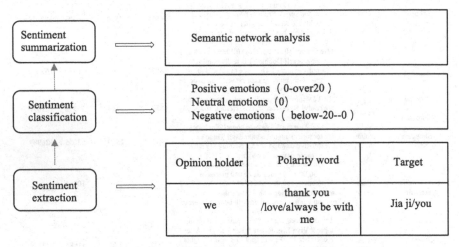

Fig. 2. Research framework of sentiment analysis

Sentiment Extraction

Sentiment extraction was the lowest level task of sentiment analysis. It aimed to extract meaningful information units in sentiment review text. Its purpose was to transform unstructured sentiment text into structured text that was easy to recognize and process by computer, and then provided the upper-level research and application services of sentiment analysis. For example, the sentimental sentence "Thank Jiaqi! We love you, always with you" was transformed into a structured text form as shown in Fig. 2.

Sentiment Classification

Sentiment classification used the results of the underlying emotional information extraction to divide emotional text units into several categories for users to view. The object of this research was Weibo comments, mostly subjective clues. Subjective expressions referred to words or phrases that expressed the subjectivity of emotional text units. In this study, sentiment texts were divided into three categories: positive, neutral, and negative, and were divided into a more detailed level (such as general, moderate, high). The sentiment analysis of the user reviews of Li Jiaqi and Viya Weibo was shown in Table 3.

Table 3. Sentiment analysis statistical results

Analysis results of comments on viya's Sina Weibo		
Positive emotions	23	76.67%
Neutral emotions	3	10.00%
Negative emotions	4	13.33%
Among them, the segmented statistical results of positive emotions are as follows		
General (0 -- 10)	9	30.00%
Moderate (10-20)	7	23.33%
Height (over 20)	7	23.33%
Among them, the segmented statistical results of negative emotions are as follows		
General (-10 -- 0)	3	10.00%
Moderate (-20 -- -10)	1	3.33%
Height (below -20)	0	0.00%
Analysis results of comments on Austin's Sina Weibo		
Positive emotions	127	41.23%
Neutral emotions	168	54.55%
Negative emotions	13	4.22%
Among them, the segmented statistical results of positive emotions are as follows		
General (0 -- 10)	93	30.19%
Moderate (10-20)	23	7.47%
Height (over 20)	11	3.57%
Among them, the segmented statistical results of negative emotions are as follows		
General (-10 -- 0)	9	2.92%
Moderate (-20 -- -10)	2	0.65%
Height (below -20)	0	0.00%

Sentiment Induction

Sentiment analysis was an application-oriented research topic, but the results presented after sentiment classification were not directly usable by users. The summarization of emotional information at the highest level can be regarded as an interface for direct interaction with users, and this level of research was mainly based on the first two tasks for further processing. Summarizing and refining user review information, it was embodied in five key words including companionship, thanks, love, happiness, expectation, and trust, as shown in Table 4.

3.3 Depth Interviews

Depth interviews are qualitative research, a process of social interaction, which is a way for interviewers to obtain information in order to obtain interviewees' motivations, attitudes, behaviors, ideas, needs, etc. Generally speaking, depth interviews are face-to-face communication, but due to the epidemic, face-to-face contact is not convenient. Instead, they are conducted by telephone. Five participants who have the habit of watching live broadcasts were selected for semi-structured interviews. Five participants were selected to have an in-depth understanding of the interviewee's feelings about the live broadcast.

Table 4. Emotional induction of comment text

Emotional induction	The comment text
company	"Thank you for your company." "Thank you Li Jiaqi for accompanying all the girls!" "Thank you for your company." "Sincerely hope to be together until the old! Love jia ji" ...
gratitude	Thank you, "Thanks for your company all year. See you next year." "Thank you Li Jiaqi!! Always by your side." "Thanks for having you." ...
love	"All the girls love you" "Love old man Lee every day!" ... "I really had a good time last night."
happy	"Li is so warm. All love is two-way. I'm glad we are your girls." ...
expectation	"This year, because of your company, every day is worth looking forward to" "If you want the same hat, please send me up so my sister can see." "When to put on some warm tools. It will soon be cold again in the north. " "Ahahah jiaqi I need a snack section of red oil noodles skin snail noodles nanchan mix noodles" ...
trust	"Viya really takes it seriously. She chooses her products carefully." "I chose Viya because of strict selection." "Viya chooses her clothes very carefully and I love the clothes she buys in th studio." "I feel comfortable shopping for clothes in Viya's studio." ...

Conducted a comprehensive interview on user behavior outside the live broadcast scene to understand the impact of the live broadcast on users' consumption habits and lives. Focused on whether users used other private domain media as supplementary information sources outside the live broadcast station. Developed an **Appendix 1: Depth interview outline**.

4   Results

4.1 Usability

"Live + e-commerce" restructure from "people, goods, and scenes" to meet usability requirements. E-commerce livestreaming empowers the role of "people", and anchors have become a strong lead and link between merchants and consumers in new consumption scenarios. The addition of MCN and KOL has enhanced user stickiness. They rely on their professional understanding of products and a very personal style of language to actively recommend the selected products to terminal consumer users. It also interacts with consumers in the live broadcast room to help them make more personalized consumer decisions, shorten the decision-making time, and increase the conversion rate and repurchase rate. Live broadcast e-commerce shortens the propagation path of "goods" from producers to consumers, and speeds up product development, so as to timely match user needs and have the space and ability to customize products. In order to gain the trust of fans, the live broadcast room must strictly control the product selection process, so that all products return to the most essential product competition, the brand effect is relatively weakened, and the door is opened for high-quality emerging products. In addition, by gaining insight into the needs behind user behaviors, live broadcasting continues to expand the boundaries of scene applications. Compared to traditional e-commerce companies that describe products through text and pictures, e-commerce livestreaming more intuitively show the real scene of the product. The anchor interacts with consumers in real time, communicates emotions, and brings consumers a better shopping experience, which makes up for the poor experience of traditional e-commerce information flow to a certain extent.

4.2 Emotional Experience

Weibo has become an important social platform for anchors to interact with users. It maintains the relationship with users by publishing live broadcast previews, welfare draws, and calling for fans to vote for products. The form of live broadcasts is also constantly enriched. In addition to live streaming around the nationwide shopping carnival, themed life shopping festivals have also been created according to user consumption needs. With regular live broadcasts, it can meet users' diverse shopping needs. In order to achieve a closer fit with fans, in addition to Viya and Li Jiaqi, other Taobao anchors also hold fan festivals. It can be seen that fans are the lifeblood of their profession. Whether it was strictly selecting products or enriching the live broadcast format, the most fundamental purpose of the anchor is to serve the fans. Through the analysis of Weibo texts and user comment texts posted by Li Jiaqi and Viya, it is found that when the Weibo content posted by the anchor contained positive emotional words such as "thank you, companionship", fans also respond with positive emotional words, such as "thanks, companionship, love, happiness, expectation, trust". When the anchor is grateful to fans for watching and rewards the fans with lottery and other benefits, the fans also give feedback in the comments to thank the anchors for their company and happily buy good products. The relationship between the host and the user could be summarized as follows: the first step was to establish a trust relationship. Fans purchase goods in the live broadcast room to meet their basic needs; then the host interact with the fans through the social platform to further close the relationship,and continue to enter the fan's life outside the live broadcast room. Daily companionship and social interaction during the special epidemic period have brought positive emotional experiences to users. A virtuous circle of emotions is formed between the anchor and the fans. The two thanked each other for their company, which not only help the anchors continue to provide better goods and services and establish their own strong community activities such as Fan Festival. It also stimulates users to have emotions such as excitement and joy, and subtly cultivates the user's consumption habit of watching while buying, and users invisibly produce perceptual consumption.

Studies have found that live broadcasting can bring people a sense of companionship and other positive emotional experience, but this kind of emotion requires a longer time and more trust from the anchor and the user. It cannot be obtained in a short period of time, and the range of people covered is relatively less. In addition to the sense of companionship, positive emotional experiences also have emotions such as happiness and relaxation. These feelings can be produced through entertainment, variety content and meaningful activities, which are relatively easier to produce, through short video + livestreaming, celebrity + livestreaming, the new show + livestreaming, charity + livestreaming, etc., meet the diverse content needs of live broadcast users, especially during the epidemic to bring comfort to people with emotional anxiety.

4.3 User Value

Appendix 2: Interview Record was obtained after conducting depth interviews with five interviewees. It was found that the main purpose of users watching live broadcasts was to buy discounted products, and they mainly fancy the functional value of live shopping; 3 interviewees would use live broadcasts as a way of entertainment to dispel boredom. To a certain extent, the live broadcast was of entertainment value to them. The interviewee who watched the live broadcast seriously, LJ, said that watching the live broadcast was a kind of companionship, which can resolve a person's emotional loneliness, and the live broadcast bring emotional value to her; respondent CY had a relatively indifferent attitude towards advertising marketing, thinking that advertising cannot affect his shopping decisions, but would generate purchase intentions due to social needs (such as recommendations from acquaintances). All five interviewees said that they would watch the live broadcast link shared by friends. Watching the shared live broadcast would promote common topics among friends. Live broadcast has become a way of social connection and a topic for maintaining relationships between friends, bringing certain benefits to users' social value.

5 Discussion

5.1 Interactive Rituals in Emergency

Analyzing the Weibo texts of anchors during epidemic, it was found that the anchors used social platforms to continuously interact with users, and held ritual interactions such as fan festivals with the theme of overcoming difficulties to maintain fans' emotional. Rituals are a unique social and cultural phenomenon in human society. Interactive rituals originated from the French sociologist Durkheim's discussion of religion [18]. He believed that rituals in religious activities were a means to express and strengthen beliefs. The concept of interactive rituals was put forward by Owen Goffman [19]. From the perspective of micro-sociology, he believed that there were a large number of routine rituals and scenes in daily life. It was in the scenes facing each other that the rituals were created and given the identity of the participant symbol. Collins proposed the concept of interactive ritual chain, the dynamic mechanism of social interaction based on the micro-situational perspective [20]. The interactive ritual chain does not arise out of thin air, but depends on people's emotional connection and sharing in a specific space, forming a common concern and group unity, thereby promoting a larger range of interactive actions. During the epidemic, due to physical separation, although people cannot gather their bodies in the process of home isolation, the live broadcast platform realize that the medium is an extension of the embodiment of people, so that the spatial barriers for individuals to participate in the ceremony are broken. The physical presence is quickly realized during the selling process, and the anchor and users can interact with each other in the same live broadcast room.

From the theoretical perspective of the interactive ritual chain, the formation of interactive rituals requires participants to focus on common objects or activities, so as to know the focus of each other's attention. In general situation, due to the complexity of Internet information, users often have different concerns. However, in the emergency period, the development of the COVID-19 has become a focus of users' attention. The live broadcast platform surpasses time and geographical constraints, maximally meet users' needs for focus, and improve the convenience for both anchors and users to obtain attention. This kind of transcendence attention of "e-commerce + livestreaming" facilitates the ceremony participants to form a common focus of attention and share common emotions and emotional experience with each other while obtaining common group membership. Emotional communities tend to store a huge group of collective power and enhance individual members' sense of dependence on the group. During the epidemic, livestreaming topics such as "Help Hubei" strengthened users' sense of national identity in the process of selling goods and shaped the sense of collective unity to overcome the difficulties together in the special period. While selling goods, the anchor also forms an interactive ritual chain of emotional resonance by passing on spiritual symbols and plays a positive role in guiding emotions [21].

5.2 User Value and Private Traffic

During the epidemic, e-commerce livestreaming became popular, making competition in live broadcast rooms increasingly fierce. In order to retain original users' attention and enhance interaction with fans, many live broadcast rooms have built private traffic channels. Private traffic is a relatively closed and trusted traffic established on the basis of the initial "relationship". This kind of traffic is independently owned by the brand or individual, can be used for free for many times and can reach users directly [22]. E-commerce anchors use the live broadcast room as the traffic entrance and attract users to the self-built private platform through forwarding lottery activities and deepen short-term trading into long-term relationship. Especially in epidemic, users are anxious about the content of public platforms, and the private traffic established based on the trust relationship is conducive to alleviating users' content and emotional anxiety. In emergency situations, the pursuit of a higher level of social value for users is a long-term development direction, which highlights the value of private traffic.

The theory of value points out that the movement and change of any social thing is driven by a certain interest pursuit or value pursuit [23]. Satisfying users' value needs is an important factor in enhancing the relationship between enterprises and users. The value includes functional value, emotional value, entertainment value and social value. First, enhance the functional value of the community to bring users a good sensory experience. Private communities can provide reliable live broadcast previews and welfare lottery and other functional information to reduce the time and opportunity costs. Secondly, emotional value and entertainment value are important motivations for users. Compared with the general situation, users need a positive emotional experience to alleviate pandemic anxiety in emergency situations. The host's personal funny atmosphere and the joyous atmosphere of interacting with stars bring happiness to fans. Enlarging the emotional value can enhance the mood of users and arouse the enthusiasm of community members. Finally, social value can help users realize their self-worth. The process of users participating in the live broadcast is also building themselves, and the derivative activities of the livestreaming provide users with a platform to show themselves. Some people's work has been affected by the epidemic, so they turn to share live broadcast information on social platforms as a part-time job and gained the recognition of the majority of users, which not only realized their own value but also generated social value in helping others.

6 Conclusion

This study uses three methods to analyze the relationship between the components of user experience (availability, emotional experience, user value) and e-commerce live streaming, and proposes that user experience is the motivation and promotion of e-commerce live broadcast innovation in epidemic. It is believed that the key to marketing success is user-centered, especially in emergency situation user experience is of great significance to marketing. User experience is the promotion way of marketing growth. In fact, the epidemic also proved the importance of user experience design in improving marketing effects in crisis situations. Starting from the availability of user experience, when travel is restricted during the epidemic, "livestreaming + e-commerce" realizes the integration of online and offline scenarios. From the previous "people looking for goods" to "goods looking for people", a new form of consumption is reconstructed. In the future, e-commerce livestreaming should focus on personnel management, improve the efficiency of goods, and enhance the interactivity of the scene to bring users better consumer experience. The daily companionship and interactive rituals livestreaming during the epidemic period meet the emotional experience needs of users. For marketers, they should shift from enhancing the functional value to emotional value, using social platforms to publish contents to interact with users, and arouse user emotional resonance. During emergency crisis, seizing the opportunity when users are more willing to participate in in-depth interaction, online marketing should gather core brand users to relatively closed private traffic. Through long-term and stable relationship maintenance, it meets the user's functional value, entertainment value, emotional value and social value needs. Brands and users should form a two-way, high-viscosity cooperation mechanism, and encourage users to create value with the brand, so as to achieve the highest pursuit of user experience that is growing while harvesting.

Acknowledgements. The author would like to thank the interviewees for their participation and all the supporters of the current study and the reviewers for their thoughtful comments. This research was supported by Hunan University and my master tutor.

Appendix 1: Depth Interview Outline

1.   Under what circumstances would you watch the live broadcast?

2. Are there any live broadcast rooms that you often follow?
3. Can you talk about your feelings when watching the live broadcast?
4. What does live broadcast mean to you?
5. Are there other channels to obtain live broadcast information?
6. How does a live streaming shared by friends affect you?
7. Do you want to have more interaction with the anchor?
8. How does joining the fan group affect you?

Appendix 2: Interview Record

Interviewee RF (Girl, Idol)
First watch the live broadcast preview on the Douyin platform. If there is a product that needs to be purchased, she will watch the live broadcast; if there are favorite stars in the live room, she will also watch the live broadcast. The only anchor she pays attention to is Li Jiaqi, because his selection is more tasteful. She liked Li Jiaqi's live broadcast style and thought it was not too boring. She wants to have more interaction with the anchor, and if it can bring the actual value or entertainment value of the discount, she will also consider joining the fan group.

Interviewee WX (Girl, Loves Online Shopping, Value-for-Money)
Watching live broadcasts when she needs to buy things and when she is bored. Live broadcast can sometimes be regarded as an entertainment pastime. She will quit the live broadcast with boring content and is more impatient and doesn't like slow pace. She has been following Li Jiaqi's live broadcast room. The channels for obtaining live broadcast information are the note sharing of Xiaohongshu's preview live broadcast, and the live link shared by friends will also be viewed.

Interviewee CY (Male, Rational and Direct)
When he needs to buy goods, he will use the search function to directly enter the target live broadcast room, and will quickly finish buying things, paying more attention to the actual function value, and not paying too much attention to other emotional expressions of the anchor. The lottery will become a factor that attracts him to participate in the interaction, but it will not be deeply interactive. A relatively indifferent attitude towards advertising will not affect consumption, but will open live links shared by acquaintances, and recommendations from acquaintances will affect consumption decisions.

Interviewee HC (Boy, Likes to Watch Live Matches)
In the evening when he is bored, he will watch livestreaming, which will be used as a pastime entertainment. When he meets something he likes, he will buy it. He watched the live broadcast by randomly choosing a type, or a connection shareed by friends. If there is a lottery and other benefits, he will be willing to join. He did not join the live broadcast community but has a fan group and game community who joined the star. He is in a diving state in the group. The reason for staying in the community is that there will

be match information and a link to watch the match live for free. Bring actual functional value.

Interviewee LJ (Girl, with Live Shopping Habits)
She will watch the live broadcast preview on the anchor's WeChat public account and sharing in Xiaohongshu, watch the live broadcast when she is needed or bored. She often pays attention to Li Jiaqi, and the bloggers she likes; she thinks that live broadcast products are more favorable than normal shopping channels. Shopping through live broadcasts has become a priority shopping habit. When she was alone during the epidemic quarantine, she believed that the live broadcast channel could connect with outside anchors and spend lonely moments as a companion. She believes that the most attractive aspects of live broadcasting are the discounts and lottery benefits. If entertainment games and warm content can be added, it will be more attractive. And she is willing to join the fan group to facilitate access to more preferential information, and on the other hand, she can find more people with common interests to share life with.

References

1. Pine, B.J., Gilmore, J.H.: Experience Economy. China Machine Press, Beijing (2008)
2. Ding, Y., Guo, F., Hu, M., Sun, F.: Summary of research on user experience at home and abroad. Ind. Eng. Manage. **19**(04), 92–97 + 114(2014)
3. Norman, D., Miller, J., Henderson, A.: What you see, some of what's in the future, and how we go about doing it: HI at apple computer. In: Conference Companion on Human Factors in Computing Systems, p. 155. ACM, Massachusetts (1994)
4. Hassenzahl, M.: User Experience (UX): towards an experiential perspective on product quality. In: Proceedings of the 20th International Conference of the Association Francophone d' Interactive Homme-Machine, pp. 11–15. ACM, Matz, New York (2008)
5. ISO 9241-210:2010. Ergonomics of human system interaction - part 210: Human -centered design for interaction systems (formerly known as 13407). pp. 7–9. International organization for Standardization (ISO). Switzerland (2010)
6. UPA (Usability Professionals Association), Usability Body of Knowledge. http://www.usabilitybok.org/glossary Accessed 30 Jan 2021
7. Hassenzahl, M., Tractinsky, N.: User experience a research agenda. Behav. Inf. Technol. **25**(2), 91–97 (2006)
8. Brajnik, G., Giachin, C.: Using sketches and storyboards to assess impact of age difference in user experience. Int. J. Hum Comput Stud. **72**(6), 552–566 (2014)
9. Forlizzi, J., Battarbee, K.: Understanding experience in interactive systems. In: Proceedings of the 5th Conference on Designing Interactive Systems: Process, Practice, Methods, and Techniques, pp. 261–268. ACM, Cambridge, New York (2004)
10. Mervill, P.: User experience design. http://semanticstudios.com/publications/semantics/000029.php Accessed 30 Jan 2021
11. Park, J., Han, S.H., Kim, H.K., et al.: Modeling user experience: a case study on a mobile device. Int. J. Ind. Ergon. **43**, 187–196 (2013)
12. Ouyang, B., He, Y.: User research and user experience design. J. Jiangsu Univ. (S1), 55–57 + 77 (2006) Natural Science Edition
13. IResearch Institute: China Post-epidemic Era Retail Consumption Insight Report 2020. http://report.iresearch.cn/wx/report.aspx?id=3618 Accessed 2 Feb 2021

14. BCG, Tencent TMI, 2020 White Paper on Social Retail in China. http://www.199it.com/arc hives/1003650.html. Accessed 30 Jan 2021
15. Zhigua data: the Taobao 2020 live platform development trend of the whole https://mp.wei xin.qq.com/s/UIwE5VyooMcyZbkMKDpOgA. Accessed 2 Feb 2021
16. Taobao list, Taobao Live: 2020 Taobao Live Double 11 Merchants Live Data Report http:// www.199it.com/archives/1175203.html. Accessed 2 Feb 2021
17. Nasukawa, T., Nasukawa, T., Yi, J.: Sentiment Analysis: Capturing Favorability Using Natural Language Processing. In: International Conference on Knowledge Capture. DBLP (2003)
18. Durkheim, E.: The elementary forms of religious life. Free Press, 56. New York (1965)
19. Goffman, E.: The presentation of self in everyday life, pp. 17–18. Anchor Books, New York (1959)
20. Randall, C.: Interaction ritual chain. In: Lin, J., Wang, P., Ning, L. translated. The Commercial Press, Beijing (2009)
21. Qiang, Y., Sun, Z.: Officials acting as live streaming hosts: from the theoretical paradigm of interactive ritual. J. Chin. Acad. Sci. **10**, 21–26 (2020)
22. Li, Z., Han, L.: From weak relationship to strong relationship: innovation of user relationship construction in private domain traffic. Mod. Advertising **20**, 42–46 (2020)
23. Zhou, Z., Chen, R., Zhang, J., Wang, Q.: The relationship formation mechanism in online brand communities——based on the internet journal of Chery Xinqijun forum. Manage. Case Stud. Rev. **6**, 500–512 (2015)

Industrial Internet Talent Cultivation in China from the Perspective of Undergraduate Majors

Ziyang Li, Zhuoran Li, and Ang Zhang(✉)

China Academy of Industrial Internet, 100102 Beijing, China

Abstract. Industrial Internet is becoming a topic of immense interest in the industrial sector. Talented workers possessing the relevant skills and capacities are the key to the development of Industrial Internet. This study investigated Industrial Internet talent cultivation in China from the perspective of undergraduate majors. Two experiments were conducted to this end. In Experiment 1, industry experts (N = 4) were invited to select Industrial Internet-related majors. In Experiment 2, a questionnaire was designed and distributed to teachers (N = 49) across 38 universities in China. Our results indicated that there was no Industrial Internet major in China, but there existed 43 undergraduate majors that were significantly relevant to this field. The core relevant majors were found to be (1) Internet of Things Engineering, (2) Artificial Intelligence, (3) Data Science and Big Data Technology, (4) Intelligence Science and Technology, and (5) Big Data Management and Application. We also proposed that Industrial Internet talents should master information technology, operation technology, and communication technology with the percentage of technologies required being 41.82%, 32.33%, and 25.86%, respectively. Information-related departments and Industrial Internet-related departments in universities were found to be the most preferred for Industrial Internet talent cultivation. Furthermore, our research revealed that Chinese universities were facing a shortage of textbooks, teachers, practice bases, courses, funds, and equipment for cultivating the necessary Industrial Internet talent and needed to work on these aspects.

Keywords: Industrial Internet · Talent cultivation · Undergraduate majors

1 Introduction

The Industrial Internet describes a large-scale operation in which all industrial processes and elements are interconnected by the Internet. This connectivity facilitates data collection, exchange, and analysis, which in turn helps increase the productivity and efficiency of the industrial processes [1–3]. Industrial Internet of Things (IIoT) and Industry 4.0 are concepts related to the Industrial Internet. The Industrial Internet is essentially the integration of industrialization and information, which extends to diverse industrial sectors such as manufacturing, agriculture, energy, transportation, and mining. The global Industrial Internet market was valued at USD 313.27 billion in 2020 and is expected to reach USD 607.73 billion by 2026 [4].

© Springer Nature Switzerland AG 2021
P.-L. P. Rau (Ed.): HCII 2021, LNCS 12772, pp. 362–373, 2021.
https://doi.org/10.1007/978-3-030-77077-8_28

The rapid development of Industrial Internet (including IIoT and Industry 4.0) needs the involvement of talented people with the relevant skills. To this end, undergraduate education is an important means to cultivate the required professional talent. An undergraduate degree, for example in software engineering, economics, or architecture, reflects the systematic education that a student received and the professional skills that they mastered during the course. In China, the higher education system is dominated by the number of undergraduates. In fact, 3.95 million Chinese students graduated in 2019 [5], of which more than 70% entered the labor market in 2019 (while most of the remaining graduates continued to study) [6]. Young and well-educated undergraduates are the future of the Industrial Internet labor market. To the best of our knowledge, there has been no research conducted that focuses on the cultivation of undergraduate students to support the development of the Industrial Internet. In this study, we investigate this very aspect by analyzing relevant academic majors that can prepare undergraduates for the Industrial Internet and help develop it further. Moreover, our study aims to facilitate higher education systems to create Industrial Internet-related majors.

2 Related Work

2.1 Industrial Internet

The term Industrial Internet was first introduced by General Electric Company (GE) in 2012, which adapted IoT to industries in general (i.e., both manufacturing and non-manufacturing) [2, 7]. Moreover, GE partnered with AT&T, Cisco, Intel, and IBM to form the Industrial Internet Consortium (ICC), which is a nonprofit and open membership organization to accelerate the development and widespread use of Industrial Internet [8]. ICC defined Industrial Internet as an "internet of things, machines, computers, and people enabling intelligent industrial operations using advanced data analytics for transformational business outcomes," and proposed that Industrial Internet would redefine the landscape for businesses and individuals [3, 9].

Many countries are actively promoting the development of Industrial Internet. The German government proposed, as well as accelerated, their "Industrie 4.0" initiative. The United States listed advanced manufacturing systems enabled by Industrial Internet in their 2022 Research and Development Budget Priorities. China proposed the Industrial Internet Development Strategy in November 2017 and incorporated Industrial Internet into the government work reports from 2018 to 2020.

2.2 Industrial Internet Talents

The development of Industrial Internet has brought new requirements and challenges for talent acquisition. Industrial Internet has merged digital technologies and the Internet with conventional technologies [10]. It is enabled by technologies such as IoT, cloud computing, artificial intelligence (AI), cyber-physical systems, blockchain technology, and big data analysis [11]. These technologies are changing the working environment and traditional working methods as conventional educational and technical skills are no longer sufficient. Industrial Internet talents include engineers, knowledge workers, and etc., who need to be educated with the new curricula to cope with the increasing industrial demands of future factories [12]. Moreover, they should be able to manage or control Industrial Internet systems that represent knowledge hidden deep within the product or production process [13]. In this context, an Industrial Internet talent shortage is apparent. In 2020, China experienced a 7.5 million shortfall in the next-generation IT industry talents [14]. Thus, the overall Industrial Internet talent shortage is expected to be even higher than this.

2.3 Undergraduate Talent Cultivation

Higher education is considered vital for talent development to meet labor market demands. At present, higher education fails to respond rapidly to the demands imposed by Industrial Internet causing a disparity between labor supply and demand [15]. Previous studies showed that the creation of suitable academic majors is closely related to meeting the demand for industrial talent. Freeman and Hirsch (2008) [16] analyzed over 26 years' worth of employment data, occupational information, and bachelor degree data in the United States and found that the choice of undergraduate major is responsive to changes in the knowledge content of jobs. Holzer (2012) [17] highlighted that the shortage of students in certain industries was owing to a lack of information about the job market, and that this shortage is likely to affect the well-being of individuals and the quality of the recruited industry workers. Bardhan et al. (2013) [18] found that higher education in the United States was weakly responsive to short-term signals of labor market demands, and hence, they suggested matching degree programs with new occupational requirements. Therefore, the investigation of Industrial Internet-related academic majors is extremely important.

3 Experiment 1

3.1 Method

Design. In Experiment 1, we invited Industrial Internet experts to select the Industrial Internet-related majors among China's undergraduate majors. The Undergraduate Majors Catalog of Higher Education Institutes 2020 (UMCHEI) [19], disclosed by the Ministry of Education of the People's Republic of China, is a guide for universities in mainland China to set-up and create academic majors[1]. UMCHEI contained 703 undergraduate majors, however there was no major named "Industrial Internet." Thus, Experiment 1 adopted an expert evaluation method, where experts were invited to screen the Industrial Internet-related majors from UMCHEI based on the concept, framework, and enabling technologies of the Industrial Internet.

Procedure. Four experts (three male and one female experts) from the China Academy of Industrial Internet were invited for Experiment 1 to select the Industrial Internet-related majors. The average age of the experts was 32.75 years, with a standard deviation (SD) of 5.12 years. All the experts engaged in the cultivation of Industrial Internet talents

---

[1] This study only considered undergraduate majors in mainland China.

and research related to the development of Industrial Internet. Their work experience ranged from 1 to 12 years (mean = 6.50 years, SD = 4.03 years). The experimental procedure adopted was as follows. (1) Three experts were invited to an office and introduced to the purpose of the study, which was to select undergraduate majors related to their understanding of Industrial Internet. (2) Each expert was supplied with a laptop with a PDF version of UMCHEI. The experts were given 40 min to select the Industrial Internet-related majors without any limit on the number of majors. (3) On completing the selection, the experts were invited to participate in a group discussion. They were asked to provide a list of Industrial Internet-related majors that they all agreed upon. The group discussion lasted approximately two hours. (4) Finally, the experts were interviewed about their opinion on the cultivation of Industrial Internet undergraduates.

3.2 Results

Forty-three majors were selected as Industrial Internet-related from 703 undergraduate majors, which accounted for 6.1% of the total. The selected majors belonged to three broad areas (i.e., science, management, and engineering) and 11 directions (e.g., mechanical engineering, computer engineering, automation, and mathematics). The relationships between area, direction, and majors were stipulated in UMCHEI, such that the scope becomes more focused and the concept more specific as one goes from the area to the major (see Table 1 for details). During the interview, the experts pointed out that Industrial Internet is a combination of information technology (IT), operation technology (OT), and communication technology (CT). Hence, they argued that an undergraduate being cultivated for Industrial Internet should be a compound talent possessing a combination of IT, OT, and CT skills. When selecting the related majors, the experts considered both the current concepts and core technologies defining Industrial Internet as well as the compound talent factor in Industrial Internet undergraduate cultivation.

Table 1. Industrial Internet-related undergraduate majors.

Area	Direction	Major
Engineering	Weapon	Intelligent Unmanned Systems Technology
	Electrical	Intelligent Electrical Machinery, Electrical Engineering, and Intelligent Control
	Electronic Information	AI, Electronic Information Engineering, Electronic Science and Technology, Communication Engineering, Information Engineering, Integrated Circuit Design and Integrated System, Telecommunications Engineering and Management, Microelectronics Science and Engineering

(continued)

Table 1. (*continued*)

Area	Direction	Major
	Management Science and Engineering	Big Data Management and Application, Information Management and Information System, Engineering Management
	Machinery	Mechanical Design Engineering and Automation, Process Equipment and Control Engineering, Intelligent Manufacturing Engineering, Mechanical Engineering, Industrial Design, Process Equipment and Control Engineering, Microelectromechanical Systems Engineering
	Computer	Data Science and Big Data Technology, Cyberspace Security, Virtual Reality Technology, Blockchain Engineering, Computer Science and Technology, Software Engineering, Network Engineering, Information Security, IoT Engineering, Intelligence Science and Technology, Electronic and Computer Engineering
	Instrumentation	IntelliSense Engineering
	Automation	Robotics Engineering, Intelligent Equipment and System, Industrial Intelligence, Automation
Science	Mathematics	Data Computing and Application, Information and Computing Science
Management	Industrial Engineering	Industrial Engineering
	Logistics Management and Engineering	Supply Chain Management, Logistics Management, Logistics Engineering

4   Experiment 2

4.1   Method

Design. In Experiment 2, we adopted a questionnaire survey method. Based on the results of Experiment 1, we designed a questionnaire on the cultivation of Industrial Internet undergraduates, which was distributed to teachers from Chinese universities using online platforms. 49 valid responses from 38 universities were collected.

Questionnaire. The questionnaire contained three parts. (1) Participants filled in their demographic information, such as current school, gender, age, and title. (2) Participants compared the relevance of the "selected majors" (i.e., the Industrial Internet-related majors selected in Experiment 1) to Industrial Internet. The corresponding question-naire items were worded as 'How much do you think is this major related to Industrial Internet?''. Participants rated the items on a 7-point Likert scale (from $1 = $ "not at all" to $7 = $ "very much"). They were also invited to write down the relevant majors that were not listed in the questionnaire. (3) Participants described their understanding of the cultivation of Industrial Internet talents. The questions were as follows: "What are the percentages of IT, CT, and OT technologies that Industrial Internet talents should master?" (sum of the three technologies must equal 100%); "Which departments in the universities should mainly cultivate Industrial Internet talents?" (multiple choice question with options: IT-related departments, such as Department of Computer Science and Technology and Department of Software Engineering; machinery-related departments, such as Department of Mechanical Engineering and Department of Automation; a sep-arate department for Industrial Internet; all departments; other); "What problems dose your school encounter when cultivating talent for Industrial Internet?" (multiple choice question with options: cultivation has not started yet; lack of textbooks; lack of courses; lack of teachers; lack of funds; lack of equipment; lack of a practice base; other); and "What is your advice for Industrial Internet talent cultivation?" (open question).

4.2 Results

There were 49 participants from 38 universities across 14 provinces in China includ-ing Tsinghua University, Beijing Jiaotong University, Hebei University of Technology, Harbin Engineering University, Guizhou University of Commerce, Taiyuan University of Technology, Jimei University, and Sichuan Tourism University. Demographic infor-mation of the participants is shown in Table 2. The average age of the participants was 41.53 years (SD $= 8.29$ years). More than half of them (29 out of 49) had a title of Associate Professor or higher. Approximately half of the participants (23 out of 49) had administrative positions. The department names vary across universities in China, and hence, we divided the departments that the participants belonged to into the three aforementioned areas in this study: engineering (e.g., Departments of Information Engi-neering, Transportation, Computer Engineering, Aerospace, and Mechanical Engineer-ing), science (e.g., Departments of Science and Mathematics), and management (e.g., Departments of Economics and Management, Business, Management, and Logistics).

Relevance of Selected Majors to Industrial Internet. The data were not normally distributed, and hence, non-parametric tests were conducted for the analysis. Friedman's test showed a significant difference between the relevance of the selected majors and Industrial Internet ($\chi^2(42) = 282.7$, p < 0.001). The mean and SD of the data are shown in Table 3, where the majors are listed in descending order of the mean. However, post hoc tests showed that there was a significant difference between the data of only a few majors (e.g., the data corresponding to Cyberspace Security was significantly higher than that of Industrial Design and Microelectromechanical Systems Engineering). In fact, no major was significantly more relevant to Industrial Internet than the others. The top five majors with the highest relevance scores (called core relevant majors) were: (1) IoT Engineering, (2) AI, (3) Data Science and Big Data Technology, (4) Intelligence

Table 2. Demographic information of the participants.

Information	Category (number of the participants)
Gender	Male (24), Female (25)
Title	Lecturer (20), Associate professor (21), Professor (8)
Position	Dean (13), Associate Dean (8), Head of the Discipline (2), N/A (26)
Province	Beijing (8), Tianjin (1), Shanxi (9), Jilin (4), Heilongjiang (8), Shanghai (2), Jiangsu (7), Fujian (1), Hubei (2), Hunan (3), Chongqing (1), Sichuan (1), Guizhou (1), Yunnan (1)
Department (Area)	Engineering (12), Science (7), Management (30)

Science and Technology, and (5) Big Data Management and Application. All the core relevant majors had a mean higher than 6.1. These majors belonged to three primary directions of the Engineering area, namely Electronic Information, Management Science and Engineering, and Computer (see Table 1). Thus, the core relevant majors were mainly engineering technologies.

Furthermore, Wilcoxon tests were performed to compare the means of the data against the scale midpoint (i.e., 4). The results showed that all the means were significantly higher than 4. This implies that the participants perceived the selected majors to be relevant to Industrial Internet (i.e., p-values < 0.001). In other words, the participants of Experiment 2 thought that all the selected majors were equally relevant to Industrial Internet.

Most participants (45 out of 49) had no advice regarding the majors not listed and believed that the selected majors were sufficient. Four participants suggested that intelligent building technology (1 out of 49), finance (1 out of 49), materials engineering (1/49), and biology (1 out of 49) could be added (note that each major was mentioned by only one participant). These four majors are driven by the Industrial Internet (i.e., they are direct industrial applications), and hence were not included in the list of related majors.

Percentage of IT, CT, and OT Skills. These data were normally distributed. Repeated Analysis of Variance (ANOVA) tests showed that the percentages of IT, CT, and OT technologies that Industrial Internet talents should master were significantly different from each other ($F_{(2,96)} = 19.80$, p-value < 0.001, $\eta^2 = 0.29$). Holm post hoc tests revealed that the percentage of IT (mean $= 41.82\%$, SD $= 9.54\%$) was significantly higher than that of both OT (mean $= 32.33\%$, SD $= 8.86\%$, $p_{IT\text{-}OT} < 0.001$) and CT (mean $= 25.86\%$, SD $= 12.23\%$, $p_{IT\text{-}CT} < 0.001$). The percentage of OT was significantly higher than that of CT ($p_{IT\text{-}CT} = 0.022$). Thus, provided the sum of the three technologies is 100%, participants perceived that Industrial Internet talents should master IT, OT, and CT technologies in descending order of importance.

Departments for Talent Cultivation. Regarding the departments ideal for Industrial Internet talent cultivation, the options IT-related departments, machinery-related departments, a separate department for Industrial Internet, and all departments, were supported by 16, 7, 13, and 9 participants, respectively. Four participants chose "other." Thus, the

Table 3. Mean and SD of the data corresponding to the relevance of the majors to Industrial Internet.

Ranking	Major	Mean	SD	Ranking	Major	Mean	SD
1	IoT Engineering	6.35	0.90	23	Logistics Engineering	5.67	1.30
2	AI	6.24	0.90	24	Supply Chain Management	5.65	1.20
3	Data Science and Big Data Technology	6.18	0.95	25	IntelliSense Engineering	5.65	1.25
4	Intelligence Science and Technology	6.10	1.10	26	Industrial Engineering	5.63	1.59
5	Big Data Management and Application	6.10	0.82	27	Telecommunications Engineering and Management	5.63	1.22
6	Computer Science and Technology	6.04	1.02	28	Robotics Engineering	5.63	1.22
7	Cyberspace Security	6.02	1.13	29	Information Engineering	5.59	1.27
8	Information Security	6.02	1.18	30	Intelligent Unmanned Systems Technology	5.59	1.24
9	Data Computing and Application	6.00	1.17	31	Automation	5.53	1.36
10	Information and Computing Science	6.00	1.12	32	Intelligent Equipment and System	5.51	1.34
11	Network Engineering	5.96	1.17	33	Logistics Management	5.47	1.32
12	Information Management and Information System	5.96	0.98	34	Engineering Management	5.41	1.24
13	Virtual Reality Technology	5.90	1.12	35	Integrated Circuit Design and Integrated System	5.37	1.27
14	Electronic Information Engineering	5.88	0.99	36	Intelligent Electrical Machinery	5.31	1.36

(continued)

Table 3. (*continued*)

Ranking	Major	Mean	SD	Ranking	Major	Mean	SD
15	Blockchain Engineering	5.86	1.08	37	Process Equipment and Control Engineering	5.29	1.34
16	Software Engineering	5.84	1.11	38	Mechanical Design Engineering and Automation	5.27	1.25
17	Electronics and Computer Engineering	5.82	1.11	39	Microelectronics Engineering	5.22	1.28
18	Industrial Intelligence	5.82	1.24	40	Electrical Engineering and Intelligent Control	5.22	1.33
19	Electronic Information Science and Technology	5.78	1.12	41	Mechanical Engineering	5.10	1.26
20	Communication Engineering	5.73	1.11	42	Microelectromechanical Systems Engineering	5.02	1.20
21	Electronic Science and Technology	5.71	1.10	43	Industrial Design	5.00	1.29
22	Intelligent Manufacturing Engineering	5.69	1.23				

participants preferred information-related departments (16 out of 49) and Industrial Internet-related departments (13 out of 49) for Industrial Internet talent cultivation.

Problems Encountered. More than half of the participants (26 out of 49) reported that their school had not yet launched an Industrial Internet talent cultivation program. A lack of textbooks, teachers, a practice base, courses, funds, and equipment were chosen as the underlying reasons by 19, 19, 18, 15, 15, and 14 participants, respectively. Two participants chose "other." Overall, the universities appeared to lack the required supporting resources for Industrial Internet undergraduate cultivation.

Advice. The participants' advice on Industrial Internet talent cultivation can be classified as strategic or tactical. From a strategic point of view, participants (14 out of 49) mentioned that Industrial Internet was a future trend and that national-level considerations were needed for talent cultivation. From a tactical point of view, participants (17 out of 49) pointed out that universities should cultivate compound talents according to industrial needs by integrating industry and education; participants (19 out of 49) also indicated that universities needed to strengthen their undergraduate major creation programs and provide the required supporting resources.

5 Discussion

In this study, undergraduate majors related to Industrial Internet were selected and verified from both industrial and educational perspectives. 43 Industrial Internet-related majors were selected by four industrial experts in Experiment 1. Furthermore, these majors were perceived as significantly relevant to Industrial Internet by university teachers in Experiment 2. Although currently there was no Industrial Internet major in China, universities offered majors related to the core supporting technologies of Industrial Internet. Students enrolled in these related majors would be the main source of Industrial Internet talent. The core relevant majors were: (1) IoT Engineering, (2) AI, (3) Data Science and Big Data Technology, (4) Intelligence Science and Technology, and (5) Big Data Management and Application. The means of the data corresponding to the relevance of these majors to Industrial Internet were all higher than 6.1. The keywords related to these five majors were IoT, AI, and big data, which are consistent with some of the enabling technologies of Industrial Internet mentioned in previous studies [11, 20]. This further reflects the realization of university teachers that industrial technologies and undergraduate major creation are linked to each other. Our results can provide important directions for undergraduate talent cultivation and recruitment in Industrial Internet.

Industrial Internet undergraduates need to be compound talents who have mastered IT, OT, and CT technologies, and the required proportion of mastering these technologies was found to be 41.82%, 32.33%, and 25.86%, respectively (declining significantly from IT to CT). This also reflects a current trend in Industrial Internet talent cultivation, namely IT being the most desired skill, followed by OT and CT. Similarly, IT-related departments, such as the Department of Computer Science and Technology, were perceived as more suitable for cultivating Industrial Internet undergraduates than machinery-related departments. Besides, establishing a separate department for Industrial Internet was also regarded as a good way for Industrial Internet undergraduate cultivation, which makes the task of talent cultivation more focused. However, the current situation is not very optimistic. Our analysis showed that more than half of the universities have not even started the process of Industrial Internet undergraduate cultivation. Textbooks, teachers, practice bases, courses, funds, and equipment needed for Industrial Internet undergraduate programs are all lacking. Therefore, Industrial Internet undergraduate cultivation is still in its early stages. Fortunately, universities have recognized the importance of Industrial Internet talent cultivation and the need for supporting resources. We believe that the creation of Industrial Internet-related majors could be one of the most important steps for Industrial Internet development.

6 Conclusion

Talented workers possessing the relevant skills and capacities are the key to the development of Industrial Internet. This study analyzed the current status of China's Industrial Internet talent cultivation from the perspective of related undergraduate majors. There was currently no Industrial Internet major in China, however there were 43 undergraduate majors related to the field, such as IoT Engineering, AI, Data Science, and Big Data Technology. Undergraduates from these related majors could facilitate the development of Industrial Internet. Industrial internet undergraduates should master more IT skills (42.81%) compared to OT (32.33%) and CT (25.86%) skills. IT-related departments were perceived to be more suitable for cultivating Industrial Internet talents. Industrial Internet undergraduate cultivation was in a primary stage owing to a shortage of textbooks, teachers, practice bases, courses, funds, and equipment. Universities should strengthen their undergraduate major creation strategies and provide the necessary supporting resources.

References

1. Hoffman, F.: Industrial Internet of Things vulnerabilities and threats: what stakeholders need to consider. Issues Inf. Syst. **20** (2019)
2. Aazam, M., Zeadally, S., Harras, K.A.: Deploying fog computing in industrial internet of things and industry 4.0. IEEE Trans. Ind. Inform. **14**, 4674–4682 (2018)
3. Boyes, H., Hallaq, B., Cunningham, J., Watson, T.: The industrial Internet of Things (IIoT): an analysis framework. Comput. Ind. **101**, 1–12 (2018)
4. ReportLinker: Industrial Internet of Things (IIoT) Market - Growth, Trends, Forecasts (2020 – 2025). http://www.globenewswire.com/news-release/2020/08/27/2084962/0/en/Industrial-Internet-of-Things-IIoT-Market-Growth-Trends-Forecasts-2020-2025.html
5. Ministry of Education of the People's Republic of China: Number of Students of Formal Education by Type and Level. http://www.moe.gov.cn/s78/A03/moe_560/jytjsj_2019/qg/202006/t20200611_464788.html
6. MyCOSInstitute: Chinese 4-year colledge graduates' employment-Annual report (2020)
7. Evans, P.C., Annunziata, M.: Industrial internet: pushing the boundaries of minds and machines (2012). https://www.ge.com/docs/chapters/Industrial_Internet.pdf
8. ICC: Industrial Internet Consortium. https://www.iiconsortium.org/
9. Industrial Internet Consortium: What is the Industrial Internet?. https://www.iiconsortium.org/about-industrial-internet.htm
10. Davies, R.: Industry 4.0 Digitalisation for productivity and growth. Euro. Parliamentary Res. Serv. **1** (2015)
11. Khan, W.Z., Rehman, M.H., Zangoti, H.M., Afzal, M.K., Armi, N., Salah, K.: Industrial internet of things: recent advances, enabling technologies and open challenges. Comput. Electr. Eng. **81**, (2020)
12. Chryssolouris, G., Mavrikios, D., Rentzos, L.: The teaching factory: a manufacturing education paradigm. Procedia Cirp. **57**, 44–48 (2016)
13. Caldarola, E.G., Modoni, G.E., Sacco, M.: A Knowledge-based approach to enhance the work-force skills and competences within the industry 4.0. In: The Tenth International Conference on Information, Process, and Knowledge Management, Rome (2018)
14. Ministry of Education of the People's Republic of China, Ministry of Human Resources and Social Security of the People's Republic of China, Ministry of Industry and Information Technology of the People's Republic of China:《制造业人才发展规划指南》. http://www.gov.cn/xinwen/2017-02/24/content_5170697.htm
15. Flynn, J., Dance, S., Schaefer, D.: Industry 4.0 and its potential impact on employment demographics in the UK. Adv. Transdiscipl. Eng. **6**, 239–244 (2017)
16. Freeman, J.A., Hirsch, B.T.: College majors and the knowledge content of jobs. Econ. Educ. Rev. **27**, 517–535 (2008)
17. Holzer, H.J.: Good workers for good jobs: improving education and workforce systems in the US (2012)
18. Bardhan, A., Hicks, D.L., Jaffee, D.: How responsive is higher education? the linkages between higher education and the labour market. Appl. Econ. **45**, 1239–1256 (2013)

19. Ministry of Education of the People's Republic of China: 教育部关于公布2019年度普通高等学校本科专业备案和审批结果的通知. http://www.moe.gov.cn/srcsite/A08/moe_1034/s4930/202003/t20200303_426853.html

20. Jeschke, S., Brecher, C., Meisen, T., Özdemir, D., Eschert, T.: Industrial Internet of Things and cyber manufacturing systems. In: Jeschke, S., Brecher, C., Song, F., Rawat, D.B. (eds.) Industrial Internet of Things. SSWT, pp. 3–19. Springer, Cham (2017). https://doi.org/10.1007/978-3-319-42559-7_1

A Study of Machine Ethics in Human-Artificial Intelligence Interactions

Haoran Sun, Pei-Luen Patrick Rau$^{(\boxtimes)}$, and Bingcheng Wang

Department of Industrial Engineering, Tsinghua University, Beijing, China
rpl@mail.tsinghua.edu.cn

Abstract. This study evaluates people's attitude and preferences toward human-machine interaction from a machine ethics perspective. An interview was first conducted with 30 participants to gather ideas and concerns about future AI technology. Then a survey was conducted with 103 participants to collect quantitative data, and an in-depth interview held with 30 participants to support and provide insights to the questionnaire results. It revealed that severity, time and relativity have significant impacts on people's choices over automation level, decision-making approach, and responsibility allocation. Either monitored control, consensual control, or both, were the selected as the most preferred automation levels in the different scenarios as opposed to manual control and full automation. The results of this study indicated that AI technology should be adaptively designed to suit specific situations with different combinations of influence factors.

Keywords: Artificial intelligence · Machine ethics · Human-machine interaction

1 Introduction

With the fast development of technologies, artificial intelligence is no longer what only written in the science fictions but is becoming reality and gradually stepping into human society. Deep learning is a technology that allows the machines to learn on its own and make decisions by itself based on big data, complex computations, and the information it retrieves from the outside environment. Ever since the breakthrough on this killer technology in 2006, the speed of commercialization of AI has rapidly increased. In 2015, Microsoft and Google have designed software beats the best human at image recognition for the first time. Baidu also beats humans in recognizing two languages. Moreover, Microsoft and China University of Technology and Science taught a computer network how to take an IQ test, and it scored better than a college postgraduate. And one of the most important media and public hotspots in 2016 is that AlphaGo, a computer program developed by Google DeepMind, beats Lee Sedol in a five-game Go match, the first time a computer Go program has beaten a 9-dan professional without handicaps. Currently, artificial intelligence has already been implemented in many areas including medical imaging, financial services, advertising, energy discovery, autonomous driving, military combat and much more. Due to the reason that machines have many congenital

© Springer Nature Switzerland AG 2021
P.-L. P. Rau (Ed.): HCII 2021, LNCS 12772, pp. 374–395, 2021.
https://doi.org/10.1007/978-3-030-77077-8_29

advantages than humans when doing computations or completing dangerous tasks, the growing involvement of AI in more sectors is definite.

Human is a high intelligent biological specie with feelings and emotions, this grants human the social nature which helps us to survive from the nature and enables us the ability to invent and create new things. However, these biological characteristics also make humans weak compare to machines in certain aspects. When machines are doing work, the chances of error are almost nil and greater precision and accuracy can be achieved. They can replace human beings in many areas of work and free human from laborious tasks. Machines can be employed to do certain dangerous tasks; they can be made to act quickly and unaffected by factors that affect humans. In addition, due to lacking the emotional side, robots can think logically and take the "right" decisions. And most noticeable to normal citizens is that AI powered machines such as autonomous vehicle or smart home appliances can support humans in their daily needs and make their life a lot easier. The issue of how to implement and design an artificial intelligence (AI) moral agent becomes increasingly pressing as AI technology moves ever closer to the goal of producing fully autonomous agents.

If machines have capabilities to do things autonomously and that are useful to humans, they will also have the capacity to do things that can harm humans. It is important to take AI morality into consideration when design new autonomous systems, giving machines ethical principles or a procedure for discovering a way to resolve the ethical dilemmas they might encounter, enabling them to function in an ethically responsible manner through their own ethical decision making. However, there are challenges for developing such artificial moral agents from controversies among ethicists about the moral theory itself and from computational limits to the implementation of such theories.

The adjusted version of the famous trolley problem [1, 2] can be used as an example to illustrate a dilemma that may face by the AI in the future. An autonomous vehicle is driving on the road at a fast speed and suddenly encounters a great danger at the front. If the vehicle does not make a sharp right turn, then the lives of five passengers including a child and a baby would be under serious threat, but if the vehicle does turn, then an innocent man who is crossing the road will be hit and likely be killed. Under this critical situation, any action or inaction is going to kill people. The question is, whom and how many? Should human ever give machine this authority to make life and death decisions for them? If the vehicle must make the decision, what would the passengers want it to be? What about the public? And if in the end, a "wrong" decision has been made, who should we blame? The AI, the designer, or the operator?

This study proposes that automation and decision support systems driven by artificial intelligence should not always guarantee human satisfaction. In this paper, we aim to explore the degree of automation that machines should have when facing with different types of ethical dilemmas from the human comfort perspective. We also want to investigate in the approaches that people want AI to follow when making ethnical decisions and discover whom the public tend to blame when failure or problem occurs. In addition, we want to find out the impact of personal background on people's choices and judgment on AI morality.

2 Background

2.1 Automation and Decision Support Systems

According to Parasuraman, Sheridan, and Wickens [3], automation is defined as the partial or full replacement of a function previously carried out by a human operator. And depending on the nature of the task being performed, it can be selectively automated, with varying degree or level of automated decision aiding. A system that supports managerial and technological decision making by assisting in the organization of knowledge is a decision support system (DSS).

Decision support systems often can offer the advantages of increased efficiency, better data monitoring and analyzing capabilities and higher process speed than human decision makers. Moreover, it offers the potential to enhance diagnostic decision making by circumventing the limited information processing capabilities of human operators [4]. DSSs and automated diagnostic aids often assist human operators in several critical decision-making tasks, however, with little raw data about system states is available to the human. In general, DSSs help supplement or elucidate the information already available to the user by highlighting relevant areas, providing suggestions, recommending courses of action, or even performing the action for the user. The degree of decision aiding may vary with the highest level of fully automation and the lowest level of complete manual control. Moreover, several levels between these two extremes have also been proposed, including the four automation levels used by Rau, Dai, Gong and Cheng in their automatic environment control research [5] and other researches done by Sheridan and Verplank [6–8].

In the ideal state, the combination of human decision maker and automated decision aid should result in a high-performing team that eliminates the errors normally made by the human decision maker alone [4]. However, the actual relationship is complex and often resulting human dissatisfied with the system. Therefore, to make automation and decision aiding systems truly enhance the quality of human-machine joint performance, it is essential that the design of such systems be based on thorough analysis of human cognition and decision-making processes.

2.2 Morality

Machine ethics is the field of research concerned with designing Artificial Moral Agents (AMAs), robots or artificially intelligent computers that behave morally or as though moral [9]. Criteria including transparency, predictability, and responsibility that apply to humans performing social functions should also be considered in an algorithm intended to replace human judgment of social functions [10].

According to Hastie, Tibshirani, and Friedman [11], the transparency of the AI on how it makes its decision is one of the many socially important properties. If the machine learning algorithm is based on a complicated neural network, or a genetic algorithm produced by directed evolution, then it may prove nearly impossible to understand why, or how, the algorithm is making ethical judgements it made. From their study, a machine learner based on decision trees or Bayesian networks is much more transparent to programmer inspection, which may enable an auditor to discover that the AI algorithm uses to address moral dilemmas.

Predictability is another desirable feature of AI based on Bostrom and Yudkowsky's view [10]. One of the most important functions of the legal system is to be predictable, so that, e.g., contracts can be written knowing how they will be executed. The job of the legal system is not necessarily to optimize society, but to provide a predictable environment within which citizens can optimize their own lives. And same thinking can be applied to AI morality.

Another important social criterion for dealing with organizations is being able to find the person responsible for getting something done [10]. It is the question of whom to blame when an AI system fails at its assigned task. Even if an AI system is designed with a user override, one must consider the career incentive of a bureaucrat who will be personally blamed if the override goes wrong, and who would much prefer to blame the AI for any difficult decision with a negative outcome. In these situations, people often come across moral dilemmas.

A moral dilemma is defined as a sophisticated circumstance that often involves an apparent mental interference between moral imperatives, in which to follow one would result in violating another. Terrance McConnell believes there are usually distinctions among different types of dilemmas [12] One of the distinctions is to differentiate onto-logical conflicts from epistemic conflicts. The epistemic conflicts are those between many moral requirements and the subject is confused with the conflicting requirements take precedence under the situation. The ontological conflicts are those between many requirements and neither is overridden. The other important distinction is between the dilemmas that were self-imposed, and dilemmas imposed on a subject by the surrounding. Due to the agent's own wrongdoing, the self-imposed conflicts arise [13]. By contrast, dilemmas imposed on the subject by the surrounding do not arise because of the one's rascality. And finally, there is distinction between prohibition and obligation dilemmas. The obligation dilemmas are circumstances in which more than one viable action is obligatory and the prohibition dilemmas involve circumstances in which all viable actions are forbidden.

Many philosophers and ethicists have suggested at least five different sources of ethical standards we should use when facing ethical dilemmas [14]. These include the utilitarian approach, the rights approach, the fairness or justice approach, the common good approach, and the virtue approach.

2.3 Research Framework

Our research focused on three research questions around the general research of AI morality in human-machine interactions.

RQ1. What level of automation should AI have when it faces moral decisions?

The first one is the level of automation that AI should have when it faces moral decisions. We tend to find out the acceptable and comfortable level of automation that a machine with artificial intelligence should have when facing ethical dilemmas from the users' perspective. Four major levels of automation are shown in Table 1.

Three factors are identified to have potential influences on people's judgement and decision making into the design of ethical dilemma scenarios for this research.

Table 1. Automation level description

Automation level	Description
Manual control	Human must do everything without assistance from automation
Consensual control	Automation offers suggestion and acts only with user consent
Monitored control	Automation executes one of the suggestions if there is no veto from user, and sends notification
Full automation	Automation decides everything without asking user

- Severity (High vs Low): effect of severity on people's reliance on automation; we define high severity scenarios as those have impact on human's life and death, and low severity scenarios as those are in normal circumstances.
- Time (Short vs Long): effect of available time before action on people's reliance on automation; we define short time limit scenarios as those which immediate actions must be taken, and long-time limit scenarios as those participants have long enough time to think before making decisions.
- Relativity (Self vs Others): effect of relativity on people's reliance on automation; we define self-relevant scenarios as those that the decisions participants made will have impacts on himself/herself, and self-irrelevant scenarios as those that the decisions participants made will have impacts only on others.

RQ2. What approach should AI follow when it faces moral dilemmas?

When machines are granted with authority to act on its own, we want to investigate on the appropriate approach that public expect to see machines to follow when making ethnical decisions. Since not every dilemma can be solved based on a single approach, therefore we select two decision making approaches that are commonly encountered and knowledgeable by the public for our research: the emotional/utilitarian approach and the fairness/justice approach. In addition, the factors of relativity and severity are also considered in this part.

RQ3. Who tend to blame when problem or failure caused by AI?

In this question, three stakeholders are identified: the owner or the task appointer of the system, the machine system powered by artificial intelligence that is able to feel "punishments" and the designer of the machine system powered by artificial intelligence. The three factors, severity, time and relativity, are also investigated in this part to find out their impact on people's judgement over responsibility allocation when failure happens involving AI automation.

The research method consists of an interview to assist in the creation of a scenario-based survey and a survey regarding the public's satisfaction rate on the different research focuses discussed in the previous section. The survey will consist of an online questionnaire and an in-depth interview of the survey respondents to gather feedback about the reasons and concerns for their selection in the survey. The Fig. 1 is a representation of the overall organization of this research.

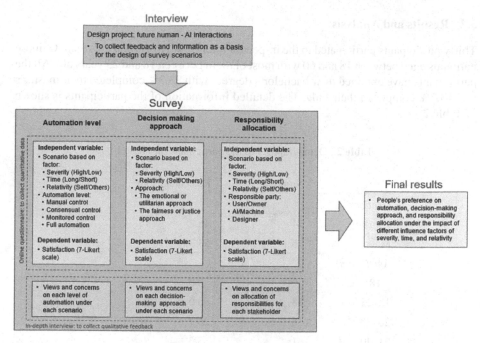

Fig. 1. Research framework

3   Phase I: Preliminary Interview on Public Interests in Future Human-AI Interactions

3.1   Methodology

This part aims to explore people's general ideas, attitudes, and opinions for AI technology. The result of phase I will be served as a basis for the creation of scenarios involving AI in the following studies.

There are two parts in the interview. During the first part of the interview, the participants were asked to imagine the future world where super artificial intelligence exists and picture the interactions between humans and machines. The participants were told to write down or describe their experiences with the AI in their imagination using words in 10 to 15 min' time, with as much detail as possible. This part of the experiment was designed to collect qualitative data on the participant's thoughts and ideas on the topic of the research. This step not only helped the participant to get their mindset into a world involving AI-human interactions, but also provides the basis of the making of ethical dilemma scenarios for the questionnaire. In the second part of the interview, participants were also asked to think about the concerns they have about AI in the future within the scenes they imagined in the first part. The scenes and concerns that were mentioned by the largest number of participants were considered in the making of ethical dilemmas for the survey.

3.2 Results and Analysis

Thirty participants participated in the in-person interview. All participants were Chinese nationals aged between 18 and 60 with most of them between 18 and 25 years old. All the participants have obtained their bachelor's degree, with 33.3% completed their master's and 13.3% completed their PhD. The detailed information of the participants is shown in Table 2.

Table 2. Demographics of the participants in Phase I

	Number		Percentage (%)	
Gender				
Female	14		46.7	
Male	16		53.3	
Age (Years)				
<18	0		0.0	
18–25	18		60.0	
26–30	8		26.7	
31–40	1		3.3	
41–50	1		3.3	
51–60	2		6.6	
>60	0		0.0	
Education				
Elementary and less	0		0.0	
Middle school	0		0.0	
Bachelor's degree	16		53.3	
Master's degree	10		33.3	
PhD and above	4		13.3	
Familiarity with AI (10 points scale)	*Min* 1	*Mean* 6.5	*Median* 7	*Max* 10
Dependency level (10 points scale)	*Min* 2	*Mean* 8.7	*Median* 7	*Max* 10

In the first part of the interview, the participants mentioned various ideas and concepts when asked to describe the different areas of the future involving AI technology and how their lives were impacted by the implementation of AI technology in the future world.

The results from the first part of the interview revealed that although AI could be found in many products and services that people use in their everyday lives, many people are unaware of their dependency on AI. Most people are knowledgeable about the simple concepts of AI, but are not familiar with the actual applications and implementations of AI in the common products and services that they use in their daily lives, not to mention how AI actually works. This was especially prominent in the older participants. In general, AI has had great impacts of the participant's lives even without them knowing it due to the unfamiliarity with AI products and also due to the fact that people have become so used to the assistance of AI in their lives that they did not think more of it. The most popular concepts mentioned by the participants were separated into different categories. The categories are smart homes, autonomous vehicles, AI professionals, military combat, and others.

In the second part, participants were asked to discuss about their concerns with the AI products and services used for the scenes they imagined in the first part. Their concerns were assorted into five categories derived in the first part, as was shown in Table 3. In the category of smart homes, 23 participants were concerned about the degree of control their smart home has on their lives. As for autonomous vehicles, 8 participants were concerned about the complex driving environments that the autonomous vehicle must process. 18 participants concerned about the degree of control the driver should have: should the AI vehicle be allowed to make all the decisions? Or should the driver be in control during difficult situations? For the category of AI professionals, 27 participants raised the concern that AI cannot express the same emotions as humans do, neither can AI feel humans' emotions. 21 participants were concerned with AI making difficult decisions in military combat. In the "other" category, participants were mostly concerned about the ethics and morality of AI. Overall, most of the concerns mentioned were related to ethical and moral problems related to AI, which confirms the purpose of this study. The concerns were also incorporated into the scenario-based survey to study the reaction of the public to those concerns.

Above all, five most popular categories of future AI products and services from the imagination of the interview participants were formed. These categories are: Smart homes, autonomous vehicles, AI professionals, military combat, and others. The ideas mentioned under these five categories were used as a guideline for the creation of the scenarios for the survey. Participants' concerns were also categorized in to those five categories. Many of the concerns mentioned were related to ethical and moral problems related to AI, which confirms the purpose of this study. The concerns were also incorporated into the scenario-based survey to study the reaction of the public to those concerns in phase II and phase III.

4 Phase II: Ethical Dilemma Scenario Online Survey

4.1 Methodology

The online survey aims to get a quantitative evaluation of each automation level, decision-making approach, and responsible stakeholder presented.

The questionnaire consists of two parts. The first part is about demographics of the participants and their familiarity and dependency level toward products or services with

Table 3. Concerns for AI products and services

	Number	Percentage (%)
Smart homes		
Degree of control	23	76.7
Autonomous vehicles		
Complex environment	8	26.7
Degree of control	18	60.0
Morality and ethics	22	73.3
AI professionals		
Human emotions	27	90.0
Human judgement	14	46.7
Responsibility allocation	26	86.7
Military combat		
Difficult decisions	21	70.0
Ethics and morality	26	86.7
Others		
Ethics and morality	19	63.3

AI. The second part is about their responds in different moral dilemma scenarios. There are 8 different moral dilemma scenarios. Each scenario was designed based on unique combination of the three factors: severity, time, and relativity (see Table 4). Under each scenario, each participant was asked to rate his/her satisfaction or agreement degree on each automation level, decision-making approach, and responsible party. The scenarios were designed according to the mostly mentioned future AI technology categories resulted from the interview described in phase I, and we use 7-level Likert scale to measure the people's preference on each of the four automation levels, two decision-making approaches, and responsibility allocation to three parties for each of the eight scenarios.

4.2   Results and Analysis

Participants

We collected a total of 119 answers to the questionnaire, which summed up to 103 questionnaires valid for analyze after discarding the incomplete ones and those considered as randomly filled in. The participants were aged from 18 to 60 years old with majority in the range of 18–25 years old. There were 54 male participants against 49 female participants which make a ratio of 52.4–47.6% sufficiently close to 50–50%. All participants are Chinese, and all are educated (higher than middle school) with most of them have a bachelor's degree (58% of the sample). As for the religious belief, 11 respondents stated they are theists, which corresponding to only about 10.7% of the total sample. The detailed demographics of the participants is shown in Table 5.

Table 4. Factor combination of scenarios

Scenario	Category	Factor combination
S1: The plagiarized report	AI professionals	Low severity/Long time/Self-irrelevant
S2: Healthy life	Smart homes	Low severity/Long time/Self-relevant
S3: Charitable funds	Others	Low severity/Short time/Self-irrelevant
S4: Stock investment	Finance	Low severity/Short time/ Self-relevant
S5: Sick patients	AI professionals	High severity/Long time/Self-irrelevant
S6: The court	A.I professionals	High severity/Long time/Self-relevant
S7: The drone	Military combat	High severity/Short time/Self-irrelevant
S8: Autonomous vehicle	Autonomous vehicles	High severity/Short time/Self-relevant

Automation Preference

To find out whether the decision-making influence factors of severity, time, and relativity have significant impact on people's preference on automation level, repeated measures ANOVA is used. We examine with-in participant effects and check whether the impact of the factor is significant. Table 6 gives the descriptive statistics for ratings of satisfaction for each automation levels in eight scenarios.

We first check the main effect of automation level (corrected with Greenhouse-Geisser). Result revealed that the difference between participants' preferences on automation level is significant, $F(3, 408) = 81.347, p < 0.001, \eta^2 = 0.444$. Post hoc analysis indicates that monitored and consensual control of the automation levels are favored by people during human-machine interactions from the AI morality perspective.

We then examine whether the impact of severity on automation preference is significant. We find that the factor of severity does have a significant impact on people's preference over automation level, $F(3, 408) = 22.122, p < 0.001, \eta^2 = 0.178$. Figure 2(a) shows the statistical interactions between satisfaction from the sample on each of the automation level under circumstances of low severity and high severity. The results show that the sample has slightly higher satisfaction toward full automation, monitored control, and consensual control when the severity level is low than those when severity level is high. However, as for the automation level of manual control, the results delivered that people tend to be more satisfied with manual control with high severity scenarios than low severity scenarios.

We examine the effect of time on people's preference on automation level of human-machine interaction in the decision-making process, and we find that the factor of time does have a significant impact on people's preference over automation level, $F(3, 408) = 65.704, p < 0.001, \eta^2 = 0.392$. Figure 2(b) shows the statistical interactions between satisfaction from the sample on each of the automation level under circumstances of long time and short time available before action. The results show that the sample has a more positive attitude toward full automation when time available for decision-making process is short and immediate action must be taken. The satisfaction level became close to each other with negligible difference when the automation level is monitored control. A big difference lies in the automation level of consensual control,

Table 5. Demographics of the participants in Phase II

	Number	Percentage (%)		
Gender				
Male	54	52.4		
Female	49	47.6		
Age				
<18	2	1.9		
18–25	73	70.9		
26–30	16	15.5		
31–40	4	3.9		
41–50	2	1.9		
51–60	6	5.8		
>60	0	0.0		
Education				
Elementary and less	0	0.0		
Middle school	9	8.7		
Bachelor's degree	60	58.3		
Master's degree	30	29.1		
PhD and above	4	3.9		
Religion				
Atheist	92	89.3		
Theist	11	10.7		
Familiarity with AI (10 points scale)	*Min*	*Mean*	*Median*	*Max*
	1	6.7	7	10
Dependency level (10 points scale)	*Min*	*Mean*	*Median*	*Max*
	2	8.6	7	10

where the sample's satisfaction level from long available decision-making process time is significantly higher than that from short available decision-making process time.

We examine the effect of relativity on people's preference on automation level of human-machine interaction in the decision-making process, and we find that the factor of time does have a significant impact on people's preference over automation level, $F = 8.869, p < 0.001, \eta^2 = 0.08$. Figure 2(c) shows the statistical interactions between satisfaction from the sample on each of the automation level under circumstances of long time and short time available before action. The results show that the sample has a slightly

Table 6. Mean and standard deviation of Automation level under different scenarios

Scenario	Severity	Time	Relativity	Automation level							
				Full auto		Monitored		Consensual		Manual	
				Mean	SD	Mean	SD	Mean	SD	Mean	SD
S1	Low	Long	Irrelevant	3.95	1.32	5.35	1.22	5.91	1.10	3.19	1.46
S2	Low	Long	Relevant	4.76	1.59	5.39	1.29	5.28	1.35	3.69	1.54
S3	Low	Short	Irrelevant	4.81	1.21	5.17	1.40	4.29	1.45	3.50	1.57
S4	Low	Short	Relevant	4.14	1.41	4.99	1.31	4.92	1.37	2.72	1.35
S5	High	Long	Irrelevant	3.60	1.56	4.91	1.46	5.93	0.98	3.51	1.65
S6	High	Long	Relevant	3.76	1.52	5.01	1.43	5.58	1.41	3.93	1.78
S7	High	Short	Irrelevant	4.07	1.55	5.21	1.43	4.57	1.53	4.02	1.70
S8	High	Short	Relevant	4.72	1.50	5.08	1.56	3.50	1.55	4.58	1.95

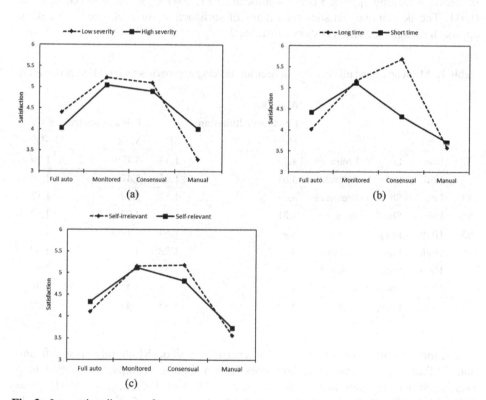

Fig. 2. Interaction diagrams for automation level. (a) severity * automation level interaction diagram; (b) time * automation level interaction diagram; (c) relativity * automation level interaction diagram

more positive attitude toward full automation when facing self-relevant ethical dilemma scenarios. The satisfaction level became close to each other with negligible difference when the automation level is monitored control. As for the automation level of consensual control, results show that people from the sample have a more positive attitude under self-irrelevant circumstance than that under self-relevant circumstance.

Overall, we can conclude that the sample favors monitored and consensual control automation strategies rather than full automation or manual control under self-irrelevant scenarios. Under self-relevant circumstance, monitored control is favored. The manual control which human must do everything without assistance from AI is rated the lowest, which again symbolize people do not want to completely reject technologies from their lives.

Decision-Making Approach

We first check the main effect of decision-making approach (corrected with Greenhouse-Geisser). The result reveals that no significant difference between sample's preferences on decision-making approach is not significant, $F(1, 204) = 3.210, p = 0.076, \eta^2 = 0.031$. The descriptive statistics for ratings of satisfaction for each decision-making approach in eight scenarios is shown in Table 7.

Table 7. Mean and standard deviation of decision-making approaches under different scenarios

				Approach			
				Emotional/Utilitarian		Fairness/Justice	
				Mean	SD	Mean	SD
S1	Low	Long	Irrelevant	4.75	1.33	4.47	1.29
S2	Low	Long	Relevant	3.65	1.65	5.47	1.36
S3	Low	Short	Irrelevant	3.74	1.57	5.79	1.17
S4	Low	Short	Relevant	4.81	1.24	4.75	1.12
S5	High	Long	Irrelevant	3.90	1.64	5.17	1.33
S6	High	Long	Relevant	4.61	1.28	4.20	1.40
S7	High	Short	Irrelevant	4.92	1.52	4.13	1.53
S8	High	Short	Relevant	4.80	1.25	4.43	1.38
S1	Low	Long	Irrelevant	4.75	1.33	4.47	1.29

We then examine whether the impact of severity on approach preference is significant, and we find that the factor of severity does have a significant impact on participants' preference over decision-making approach, $F(1, 204) = 65.476, p < 0.001, \eta^2 = 0.391$. Figure 3(a) shows the statistical interactions between satisfaction from the sample on each of the approach under circumstances of low severity and high severity. The results show that the sample has slightly higher satisfaction toward emotional/utilitarian approach when facing high severity ethical dilemma scenarios.

We examine the impact of relativity on people's preference on decision-making approach from the AI morality standard perspective, and we find that relativity does have a significant impact on people's preference over decision-making approach, $F(1, 204) = 19.141, p < 0.001, \eta^2 = 0.158$. Figure 3(b) shows the statistical interactions between

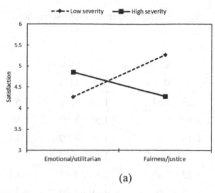
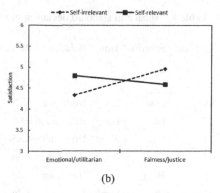

(a)   (b)

Fig. 3. Interaction diagram for decision-making approach: (a) severity × approach interaction diagram; (b) relativity × approach interaction diagram

satisfaction from the sample on each of the approach under self-irrelevant and self-relevant circumstances. The results show that the sample has slightly higher satisfaction toward emotional/utilitarian approach when facing self-relevant ethical dilemma scenarios. In other words, when faces dilemmas which decision AI made has impact on user's own lives, then people's attitude toward emotional/utilitarian approach is higher for high self-relevant scenarios than the self-irrelevant scenarios. In contrast, the sample has higher satisfaction attitude toward fairness/justice approach when facing self-irrelevant scenarios than self-relevant scenarios.

Responsibility Allocation
To find out whether the decision-making influence factors of severity, time, and relativity have significant impact on people's preference on responsibility allocation, repeated measures ANOVA is used. Table 8 gives the descriptive statistics for ratings of satisfaction for each automation levels in eight scenarios.

We check the main effect of responsibility allocation (corrected with Greenhouse-Geisser) which reveals significant difference between participants' preferences on responsibility allocation, $F(2, 306) = 45.888$, $p < 0.001$, $\eta^2 = 0.310$. Post-hoc analysis indicates that that in general circumstance, when incidents happen, the user/owner of the AI system is the responsible stakeholder that people tend to blame from an AI morality perspective. From our results, the difference between level of responsibility of AI/machine and designer is not significant, but AI/machine does appear to be the lowest rating stakeholder in terms of responsibility allocation.

We then examine the impact of severity on people's judgement on allocation of responsibility when incidents happen, and we find that severity does have a significant impact on people's judgement over responsibility allocation, $F(2, 306) = 3.799$, $p = 0.027$, $\eta^2 = 0.036$. Figure 4(a) shows the statistical interactions between responsibility agreement rates from the sample on each of the stakeholder under circumstances of low severity and high severity. The results show that the sample has the same agreement rate to allocate responsibility to user/owner under both circumstances of low and high severity. As for allocate responsibility to AI/machine, the results show that people believe that this stakeholder should take more responsibility under high severity scenarios than

Table 8. Mean and standard deviation of responsibility allocation under different scenarios

Scenario	Severity	Time	Relativity	Responsibility allocation					
				User/owner		AI/machine		Designer	
				Mean	SD	Mean	SD	Mean	SD
S1	Low	Long	Irrelevant	5.22	1.23	4.59	1.76	5.11	1.57
S2	Low	Long	Relevant	6.07	0.95	3.32	1.55	3.50	1.88
S3	Low	Short	Irrelevant	4.85	1.44	4.47	1.56	4.50	1.77
S4	Low	Short	Relevant	5.46	0.99	4.08	1.62	3.97	1.76
S5	High	Long	Irrelevant	5.46	1.22	4.45	1.66	4.35	1.82
S6	High	Long	Relevant	5.46	1.27	4.49	1.69	4.40	1.77
S7	High	Short	Irrelevant	5.52	1.22	4.46	1.70	4.64	1.78
S8	High	Short	Relevant	5.17	1.52	4.34	1.72	4.34	1.83
S1	Low	Long	Irrelevant	5.22	1.23	4.59	1.76	5.11	1.57

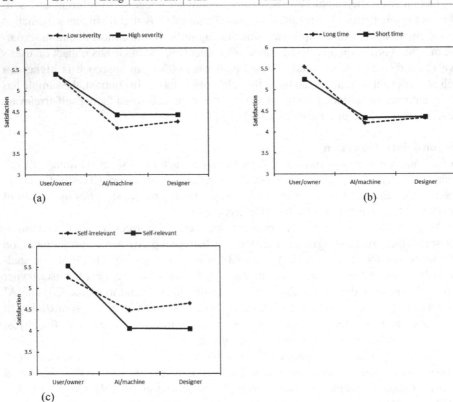

Fig. 4. Interaction diagrams for responsibility allocation (a) severity * responsibility allocation interaction diagram; (b) time * responsibility allocation interaction diagram; (c) relativity * responsibility allocation interaction diagram

low severity scenarios. Similarly, with the designer, results show our sample' attitude for giving responsibility to the AI designer is slightly more positive under high severity than low severity circumstances.

We examine the impact of time on people's judgement on allocation of responsibility when incidents happen, and we find that time does have a significant impact on people's judgement over responsibility allocation, $F(2, 306) = 9.311$, $p < 0.001$, $\eta^2 = 0.084$. Figure 4(b) shows the statistical interactions between responsibility allocation rates from the sample on each of the stakeholder under circumstances of long time and short time available before action. The results show that when incidents happened, people tend to blame on user/owner of the AI system more when there is enough time available for them to make decision than the circumstances when immediate decisions need to be made. As for AI/machine and designer of AI, people's attitude to the level of responsibility they should take is similar, our sample believe that they should take slightly more responsibility when available time is short than when available time is long.

We examine the impact of relativity on people's judgement on allocation of responsibility when incidents happen, and we find that the factor of relativity does have a significant impact on people's judgement over responsibility allocation, $F(2, 306) = 30.810$, $p < 0.001$, $\eta^2 = 0.232$. Figure 4(c) shows the statistical interactions between responsibility agreement rates from the sample on each of the stakeholder under circumstances of self-irrelevant and self-relevant. The results show that the sample tend to allocate a higher level of responsibility to user/owner when faces ethical dilemmas that are self-relevant than that of self-irrelevant. However, as for stakeholders of AI/machine or designer, our sample shows that people tend to apply more responsibility to them when the scenarios are self-irrelevant.

4.3 Summary

Results of repeated measures ANOVA on the survey data showed that all three factors have significant impacts on people's choices over automation level, decision-making approach, and responsibility allocation. The in-depth interview not only explained the reasons behind the questionnaire results, but also explained some unexpected results from the questionnaire.

Monitored control was most satisfied in scenarios that have short available time for decision-making, because participants said that they trusted the highly efficient and accurate analytical skills of AI machines in situations where humans will not be able to make the decision in time. Consensual control was most satisfied in scenarios a where long time was available for decision-making. Users preferred both monitored control and consensual control over manual control and full automation in both low and high severity scenarios, and in scenarios that are self-irrelevant. Questionnaire results showed that people preferred monitored control in situations that are self-relevant, which was unexpected because we thought people would want to make decisions that are self-relevant by themselves. However, during the in-depth interview, it was found that some participants showed diffidence with their own analytical skills and put their confidence in the abilities of the AI. Therefore, it is reasonable for some people to trust issues that are important to them, or such as self-relevant issues, to the more intelligent and reliable machine. It should be noted that under none of the scenarios was full automation chosen as the preferred automation level. This result shows that people does not fully trust AIs.

As of the preference on decision-making approach, the fairness/justice approach was most welcomed in low severity and self-irrelevant scenarios, where the emotional/utilitarian approach was most welcomed in high severity and self-relevant scenarios. This was because they wanted the AI to be able to behave like humans and consider various aspects when making decisions, including emotions.

Finally, results showed that people believe that user/owner of the AI should bear the highest level of responsibility if an incident occurred. Participants thought that the responsibility should be allocated to the humans instead of the machines, and that when a person purchases an AI machine, that person should be responsible for the AI's actions and results of the actions.

5 Phase III: In-Depth Interview

5.1 Methodology

There are several limitations to the phase II online survey. Since the ethical dilemmas were presented to the participants through written paragraph and in a one-way communication, which means they could not ask any questions regarding unclear points. Therefore, it is possible that the participants did not fully understand the scenarios and the answers may not completely represent the values of the participants. In addition, we could not gather the reasoning behind answers, we do not know why the participants made the choice he/she made for each question and their concerns.

Therefore, to make this study complete, we conducted an in-depth interview with a number of online questionnaire participants, which we could two-way communication with the participants to help them better understand the scenarios and collect qualitative feedbacks about the targeted areas of the research.

The third phase of this research involves a qualitative evaluation of a series of scenarios presenting different ethical dilemmas by the participant. We conducted an in-depth interview for 30 university students selected randomly from those who have completed the online questionnaire in phase II. The details of the participants are shown in Table 9.

The scenarios were presented to the participants by discussions with the interviewer and with visual aids for a better understanding. These scenarios were the same ones from the online questionnaire that were designed based on the different combination of decision-making influence factors of severity, time, and relativity. The participants were asked to express their concerns and opinions on each of the scenarios regarding each level of automation, each kind of decision-making approach, and each responsibility party. The responses of the participants were recorded, and trends and similarities of responses between the participants were then concluded as the results.

5.2 Results and Discussion

The results of the in-depth interviews provided some explanations behind the results of the scenario-based questionnaire.

Table 9. Demographics of the participants in Phase III

	Number		Percentage	
Gender				
Female	14		46.7	
Male	16		53.3	
Age (Years)				
<18	0		0.0	
18–25	18		60.0	
26–30	8		26.7	
31–40	1		3.3	
41–50	1		3.3	
51–60	2		6.6	
>60	0		0.0	
Education				
Elementary and less	0		0.0	
Middle school	0		0.0	
Bachelor's degree	16		53.3	
Master's degree	10		33.3	
PhD and above	4		13.3	
Familiarity with AI (10 points scale)	*Min*	*Mean*	*Median*	*Max*
	1	6.5	7	10
Dependency level (10 points scale)	*Min*	*Mean*	*Median*	*Max*
	2	8.7	7	10

In terms of automation level, AI robots or programs were not fully trusted by humans, especially when it comes to high severity situations or situations that are self-relevant, as a participant said: "I don't think I will be comfortable siting in a car which might sacrifice my life for some pedestrian crossing the road while the car was driving, just so the car can follow its ethical standards." In addition, some participants expressed that they tend to want to have control of their own lives, instead of leaving it in the hands of a robot.

For decision-making approach, participants showed a lean towards the emotional or utilitarian approach when facing issues that are self-relevant. This was because they did not want the AI to be overly strict when it comes to problems affecting themselves but wanted the AI to be able to behave like humans and consider various aspects when making decisions, including emotions. For example, a participant said, "I think the AI should consider all aspects of my life and does not give me a 'death sentence' for a little mistake that I made". However, participants were less fond of this approach when the issue was self-irrelevant, as a participant said "If it is only the small problems, yeah, it should be fair. That's the right way...".

In all the scenarios, most participants preferred that the responsibility to be allocated to the user/owner. In some scenarios, some participants said that the responsibility should be the AI/machines. Very few participants allocated the responsibility to the designer. Most participants thought that the user/owner should take the main responsibility when accidents occur. A participant said "...once you buy the machine, it's yours. It's up to you what you want to do with it, or what you want it to do, but at the end of the day, if it does something wrong, you are the one who has to clean up the mess." Some participants thought that AI machines cannot be thought of as the same as humans, so they do not have the power to take responsibility, as a participant said: "If self-driving car accidentally kills my son, would it be enough to put the car in jail for the rest of its 'life'? Or even destroy the car? No. because it is just a machine. Punishing a machine does cannot pay for my son's death". Another participant also gave an example: "Say an AI engineer design a bridge that collapsed and killed 50 people. I don't think the family of those 50 people would be satisfied if the AI was jailed or sentenced to death. They would want a human to take this responsibility, such as the person who put the AI on the job." These results showed that many people still think of AI as machines and tools created by humans. Even if they are intelligent, can talk, or even look like humans, their life is not valued as the same as human life.

Above all, results from the in-depth interview revealed that most participants centered their concerns around the idea that, in their opinion, AI's life does not have the same value as human life, therefore AIs shouldn't have the power make decisions which can impact or even end the life of humans. In addition, some participants still thought of AI as an object created by humans, therefore they would not be able to assume responsibility, and the responsibility should be allocated only to humans.

6   Conclusion

Our study focused on three unique dimensions around the general research of AI morality in human-machine interactions. The first one was to investigate in the preferred automation level of AI when it faces ethical dilemmas from the users' perspective. We considered four levels of automation here: full automation, monitored control, consensual control, and manual control. The second dimension was to find out the decision-making approach that people would like AI to follow when making ethnical decisions. Two general approaches we considered in this case to solve ethical dilemmas are the emotional or utilitarian approach and the fairness or justice approach. The final dimension was to discover people's attitude toward the allocation of responsibilities when failure of incidents involving AI ethics happen. Here, we considered three general stakeholders: the user or owner of the machine, the machine and AI itself, and the designer of the AI. Furthermore, we applied three factors that may have an impact to people's decision-making process based on the previous studies to the research on the three dimensions above. These factors are severity, time, and relativity. Each factor has two levels. Severity has levels of high and low, we defined high severity as those scenarios which may have impact on human's life and low severity as those are in normal circumstances. The length of available time for decision-making process has levels of short and long, we defined short time limit scenarios as those which immediate actions must be taken and long time limit as those which people have long enough time to think before making decisions. Finally, relativity has levels of self-relevant and self-irrelevant, we defined self-relevant scenarios as those that the decisions people made will have impacts on himself/herself and self-irrelevant scenarios as those only will have impacts on others. In this research, we found whether these factors have an impact on people's decisions and attitude over AI morality. We also analyzed the interaction effects of these factors with the main dimensions of study.

To realize the above research objectives, we conducted a research process that consisted of an interview and scenario-based survey. The purpose of the interview was to gather qualitative data on the concerns of the public to make sure that the design of the scenario-based survey fits the interest points and concerns of the public. The survey will consist of an online questionnaire and an in-depth interview of the survey respondents to gather feedback about the reasons and concerns for their selection in the survey.

30 participants were asked to imagine their lives in the future world involving human-AI interactions, and their concerns about the future AI technology. After the interview, five most popular categories of future AI products and services from the imagination of the interview participants were formed. These categories are: Smart homes, autonomous vehicles, AI professionals, military combat, and others. Concerns about AI under these five categories were also described by the participants, which mainly revolved around the distrust that humans have with AI and AI ethical problems. The ideas and concerns mentioned under these five categories were used as a guideline for the creation of the scenarios for the survey.

For the scenario-based survey, first an online questionnaire was conducted and participants' attitude toward each study dimension were measured. The questionnaire included 8 real-life ethical dilemma scenarios that may face by human and AI in the future, created based on the five most mentioned categories about future AI technology from the interview. Each one of these scenarios was designed with a unique combination of the different levels of decision-making factors. Totally, 103 effective responds were collected. Overall results from the survey indicated that monitored and consensual control was both preferred in low and high severity and self-irrelevant scenarios. Consensual control was preferred in scenarios with a long decision time. Monitored control was preferred in situations that are self-relevant, and situations with a short decision time. These preferences were due to the reason that people trusted the highly efficient and accurate analytical skills of AI machines in situations where humans will not be able to make the decision in time, and some people showed diffidence with their own analytical skills, and put their confidence in the abilities of the AI. It should be noted that under none of the scenarios was full automation chosen as the preferred automation level. This result shows that people does not fully trust AIs. As of the preference on decision-making approach, the fairness/justice approach was most welcomed in low severity and self-irrelevant scenarios, where the emotional/utilitarian approach was most welcomed in high severity and self-relevant scenarios. This was because they wanted the AI to be able to behave like humans and consider various aspects when making decisions, including emotions. Finally, results showed that people believe that user/owner of the AI should bear the highest level of responsibility if an incident occurred. Participants thought that when a person purchases an AI machine, that person should be responsible for the AI's actions and results of the actions. Results from the in-depth interview revealed that most participants centered their concerns around the idea that, in their opinion, AI's life does not have the same value as human life, therefore AIs shouldn't have the power make decisions which can impact or even end the life of humans. In addition, people gave the feeling that AI are only machines created by humans and is not able to assume responsibility.

Overall, the results indicated that AI technology should be adaptively designed to suit specific situations with different severity, time limit for decision making process, and relativity of impact on the decision maker.

6.1 Limitations and Future Research

All results from this study can be used as reference or guideline when designing new AI systems, however, limitations do exist in our research. One of them was that our results were only collected from a selected group of people and could only represent opinion of Chinese university students, they cannot represent opinions of the society at large. In addition, there were some limitations in the way the survey was built. The eight scenarios can only simulate few of the mass real-life situations that may encountered by AI in the future and there are much more other factors that may influence people's decision-making process which we did not take into consideration. Therefore, results collected from people may change if more factors and scenarios were added to the research. Another limitation is that the study was conducted in China and the result may be influenced by the culture difference. That being said, future research can focus the views of people with different cultural backgrounds on AI and ethical issues.

References

1. Thomson, J.J.: The trolley problem. Yale Law J. **94**, 1395–1415 (1985). https://doi.org/10/c2rrks
2. Nyholm, S., Smids, J.: The ethics of accident-algorithms for self-driving cars: an applied trolley problem? Ethical Theor. Moral Pract. **19**, 1275–1289 (2016)
3. Parasuraman, R., Sheridan, T.B., Wickens, C.D.: A model for types and levels of human interaction with automation. IEEE Trans. Syst. Man Cybern.-Part A: Syst. Hum. **30**, 286–297 (2000)
4. Mosier, K.L., Skitka, L.J.: Human decision makers and automated decision aids: Made for each other? In: Automation and Human Performance, pp. 201–220. Routledge (2018)
5. Rau, P.-L.P., Gong, Y., Dai, Y.-B., Cheng, C.: Promote energy conservation in automatic environment control: a comfort-energy trade-off perspective. In: Proceedings of the 33rd Annual ACM Conference Extended Abstracts on Human Factors in Computing Systems, pp. 1501–1506 (2015)
6. Sheridan, T.B., Verplank, W.L.: Human and computer control of undersea teleoperators. Massachusetts Inst of Tech Cambridge Man-Machine Systems Lab (1978)

7. Riley, V.: A general model of mixed-initiative human-machine systems. In: Proceedings of the Human Factors Society Annual Meeting, pp. 124–128. SAGE Publications Sage CA, Los Angeles, CA (1989)

8. Endsley, M., Kaber, D.: Level of automation eﬀects on performance, situation awareness and workload in a dynamic control task. Ergonomics **42**, 462–492 (1999). https://doi.org/10/fk54hd

9. Anderson, M., Anderson, S.L.: Machine ethics: Creating an ethical intelligent agent. AI Mag. **28**, 15 (2007)

10. Bostrom, N., Yudkowsky, E.: The ethics of artificial intelligence. Camb. Handb. Artif. Intell. **1**, 316–334 (2014). https://doi.org/10.1017/CBO9781139046855.020

11. Hastie, T., Tibshirani, R., Friedman, J.: The elements of statistical learning: data mining, inference, and prediction. Springer Science & Business Media (2009)

12. McConnell, T.: Moral dilemmas (2002)

13. McConnell, T.C.: Moral dilemmas and consistency in ethics. Can. J. Philos. **8**, 269–287 (1978). https://doi.org/10/ggwxfm

14. Markkula Center for Applied Ethics: A Framework for Ethical Decision Making, https://www.scu.edu/ethics/ethics-resources/ethical-decision-making/a-framework-for-ethical-decision-making/. Accessed 23 May 2020

Design Strategies of Multifunctional Exhibition for Community Regeneration: Two Case Studies in Beijing

Huan Wang[1], Wen Li[2], and Jie Hao[3]([envelope])

[1] Capital Normal University, Beijing 100048, China
whuan@cnu.edu.cn
[2] Maryland Institute College of Art, Baltimore 21217, USA
[3] Beijing Institute of Fashion Technology, Beijing 100029, China

Abstract. The increasing performance of urban regeneration tends to the public sector and local initiatives for general sustainability concerning projects, which introduces the information dissemination media technique into the community-oriented renovation. Derived from the community renewal projects, the subdistrict exhibition space in Beijing establishes a two-way expression vividly for the citizens individually and contributes to public engagement. This paper aims at providing an analysis of the exhibition spaces in the subdistrict area, as well as in processes of urban media design that take place on challenging a requirement of multifunctional community public space in Beijing. To contribute to the various practical situation, this paper presents the design strategies for subdistrict exhibition in the context for urban regeneration; an urban media-supported design approach developed by demand of the multifunctional space accessible. Follow with the approaches, it describes how the design strategies facilitate the interactive exhibition of two subdistrict projects in Xicheng District of Beijing. These projects strengthen the discussion that the role of the multifunctional exhibition can be promoted by dominative interdisciplinary cooperation of design process to further consider urban sustainability.

Keywords: Multifunction · Exhibition design · Urban regeneration · Beijing

1 Introduction

Globally, increasing urbanization is forcing the designer to think creatively about how to rearrange the existing construction efficiency and sustainability, especially for a historical mega-city like Beijing. Instead of destruction and reconstruction, most megalopolises of China have embarked on the change of micro-level urban regeneration. Urban regeneration is acknowledged the initial definition as a "comprehensive and integrated vision and action which seeks to resolve urban problems and bring about a lasting improvement in the economic, physical, social and environmental condition of area" (Granger and Sykes 2016). By the 21st century, urban regeneration went beyond reconstruction, redevelopment, and reintroduction of a site, its emphasis on the private sector and local

P.-L. P. Rau (Ed.): HCII 2021, LNCS 12772, pp. 396–407, 2021.
https://doi.org/10.1007/978-3-030-77077-8_30

initiatives, as well as a generally smaller scale of projects (Pugalis et al. 2013). Within this context, the identification and evaluation of feasible urban regeneration encourage the practical project to verify a timely.

In recent years, positioned at the principal stage, Beijing has focused on improving the comprehensive city-life quality and cultural confidence through urban regeneration projects on the neighborhood scale. It is a generally established achievement that urban space renovation primarily means optimizing the distribution of space. From the year 2017, the government-leading program started by removing the illegal construction and then shifted the focusing work on how to reshape the public are practical and cultural-meaningful on the subdistrict scale level, which is the fundamental governmental management unit in China. The direct attempts enable a creative design of the reutilized space including a resident activity center, community library, neighborhood restaurant, and community supermarket. The pioneering projects originated from functional consideration and actually contribute to more accessible community service; however, their spatial concerns seem not enough for culture succession. From the increasingly urban informatization perspective, the real-time communication of city governance requires a present sense for the delivery of community management and communication on policies. In this instance, those subdistricts that are sensible of the dormant tendency of public space renovation, the purpose of processing space with both culture dissemination and community communication more accurate and personalized.

The tentative application of the exhibition for facilitating communication in Beijing indicates the possibilities for multifunctional exhibition space in the neighborhoods. In 2019, *Regulatory Detailed Planning of the Capital Functional Core Area (Sub-strict Level) (2018–2035) (Draft)* was released to invite the public to contribute their view both online and at the exhibition hall. More than the leading exhibition in Beijing Planning Exhibition Hall, the announcement initiated a "Micro exhibition" primarily, which works as a specific temporary exhibition space that sited in thirty-two subdistrict stations of Beijing and enables a citizen participatory for regulation and policy reviewing process at the neighborhood. The action indicates a willingness that the government swiftly communicating leadings to a public dimensionality from the citizens' perspective. Meanwhile, it activated a concern on exhibition for subdistrict with a multifunctional medium on culture demonstrating, regulation communicating, and neighborhood activities. As of the middle of 2020, of the fifteen subdistricts of Xicheng district in Beijing, there are nice subdistrict exhibition halls built and opened (Data Resource: https://www.ccgp-bei jing.gov.cn). Among the rest of the unbuilt ones, four subdistricts have already finished the design and bidding process (Fig. 1).

The increasing number shows a typical practice exploited: subdistrict exhibition hall. The exhibition aims to a distinct cultural expression and community harmony promotion supported by the government and subdistrict offices. Despite the tendency of the subdistrict exhibition hall is unnoticeable, the design approach of this specific public space for the community needs a systematic consideration of both theoretical and technique. For Beijing's context, it receives obviously strength from the support of governmental urban regeneration regulation, the rich historical and cultural resources, and modern digital media for exhibition expression. For example, the Tianqiao subdistrict exhibition adopts a sliding screen to elaborate the history sites instead of a paper board

Fig. 1. Map of the subdistrict exhibition halls in Beijing. (By Huan Wang)

exhibition stand, which increases the extent of interactivity by touching and selecting from the audience. Simultaneously, a digital platform that displays the historical site is hang up on the wall with a digital subdistrict map interface.

However, the exhibition design finds insufficient methods and practices supportively facing the comprehensive site situation and multifunctional requirement. Firstly, the inexperienced design may cause a display in the form beautiful and the content void, the costly and type redundant. The works should be set apart by a strong focus on local history and culture. Secondly, the traditional display has already been challenging to meet contemporary visitors' demand in a new way to perceive. It drives the designer to introduce a combination of art and technology through a new dimension. Otherwise, we have to talk about the importance of sustainable operation of an exhibition with a potential capability of a real-time community status platform or disseminated information across all platforms, from traditional radio and television to digital, mobile, and social networks (Figs. 2 and 3).

Given that, our research group has been working on this typical urban public exhibition space since 2018. This paper discusses a multifunctional and interactive subdistrict exhibition hall deployed to support urban regeneration and a sense of community in a historical and cultural city, such as Beijing. In particular, the discussion will focus on the design phase of alternative exhibition strategies for the renovated space of public ownership with a sustainable exhibition plan. Following two practical projects for Taoranting Subdistrict and Xinjiekou Subdistrict in Beijing advanced exhibition spatial design for Taoranting Subdistrict and Xinjiekou Subdistrict in Beijing, the last section of this paper intense to the further discussion and consideration.

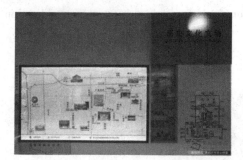 

Fig. 2. A photo of Tianqiao subdistrict exhibition center (Resources: https://interview. qianlong.com/2018/0419/2527638.shtml)

Fig. 3. A photo of Dshiliar living experience center (By Huan Wang)

2 Strategies

2.1 What is Supposed to Be Present?

Design and planning of what to exhibit are the challenging beginning when creating an interactive urban public space. The traditional exhibition works in a one-way direction of the information transfer model with the form of posters, paper broads, and show stands. The demonstration results to unattractive and only contain the general culture of the subdistrict. It is unavoidable to keep a distance from the viewer through they are inhabitant themselves. The urban regeneration-oriented exhibition presents an integrated context including history and culture, subdistrict and governance, and residents and living.

Exhibition for history and culture needs progressive expression. To create an attractive and interactive display, one needs to reduce the solidified graphics and literature narration, to turn a large part of vivid practicality and stories into the exhibition state. The interactive development is also defined as a process that suggests the comparative appeal of scenes, that acts as a meeting atmosphere through time and space also bridges the local culture confidence and variability in the contemporary city today poses. It sometimes requires an imaginative plan to construct a new program of media technology.

Subdistrict governance is frequently developed improperly in front of the citizens. An exaggerated show can easily lead to praise, while a moderate present sets a barrier to an entire understanding. There is a potential demand for the transition process to convert the professional conception, regulation, and definition into a visual language from the residents' perspective. The H5, motion graphics, and videos are more perceivable and tangible than the regulation words.

Residents and living is a specific exhibition object as for a performance in an activity area. From the architectural dimension perspective, the room is arranged for the citizens with furniture, teapot, magazines, and tools for daily convenience, which is a welcome to have a seat and communicate among the neighbors. On the display surface dimension, a user-friendly operation platform with a service of providing local news, weather forecasts, and traffic notices can be inserted in a regular section. Another necessity is a particular section that coordinated with subdistrict management to exhibit achievement and collect the opinions through mobile terminals for giving rise to the consideration and discussion for the community (Fig. 4).

Fig. 4. The three exhibition dimensions for subdistrict. (By Huan Wang)

2.2 How to Exhibit?

As a specific public space for residents, the exhibition presents a two-way information delivery instead of a single one-way display direction. It emphasizes two procedures in the exhibition hall plan section, those are the show interface stage and the show operation stage. Show interface stage is facing the audience, by promoting pictorial, animate, and interactive objects for exhibition, it nurtures the sense of the community engagement of individuals. Show operation stage is essential for a long-term support planning appears in a real-time update information system that is applicable in revealing policy and working schedule timely. It devises a function that converts the community data into a visualized display language intensely. That requires a beneficial introduction of information technology for the subdistrict exhibition. To break through the limitation of stable display installation and senses, the way of demonstration can insert media terminals to extend spatial dimensions that structure a time-space convergence (Fig. 5).

2.3 How to Operate Sustainably?

Hence, how to promote sustainable urban regeneration projects? Changing approaches to urban exhibition hall affects the roles of the factors developing involved. It is generally acknowledged that the sustainability of the exhibition hall sort into content and space in sustainable planning.

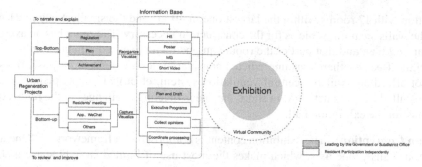

Fig. 5. The exhibition operation model. (By Huan Wang)

Our research insists that a multi-information transmission system is feasible in bottom-up and top-down information cycle updating reality. The top-down information from the subdistrict office and urban regeneration department can be classified into regulation, plan, and achievement. As opposed to just spreading guidelines from the management offices, the instruction fosters practical and scientific developmental actions of communities in China. For instance, the National People's Congress means a followed extensive learning in the scale of a whole society, integrated with an announcement of regeneration measures promising. The bottom-up relies on citizens and the community workers of every subdistrict. In recent years, it is an increasing promotion of individuals' community engagement through resident council meetings, which activates the residents to contribute suggestions and ideas for the neighborhood. Also, on the mobile terminals, such as Wechat, Shequ Tong App, and Wechat official account, where the collected reflection can be integrated into a workable solution resource are the fundamental communicating platform.

The urban regeneration-oriented exhibition also indicates that the single-space making needs to be supported by an understanding of the potential of a multifunctional requirement. The specific exhibition profile that along with digital techniques and other drivers, shapes the bottom-supported fixed installation, decorative physical board into a virtual surface, associated with a minimized space occupation. It's a truth universally acknowledged that the interactive digital board and projector are rewarding in expanding the viewing screen but only find slightly spatial usage. Besides, the magic wall, sliding screen, and glass screen are outstandingly facilitated in an exhibition for the advantages of operation interactivity, updating feasibility, and space-saving efficiency.

3 Project Description in Beijing

3.1 Taoranting Subdistrict Exhibition Hall

Site Description: The project locates in Building 8 of Nanhua West in Taoranting Subdistrict. The site is on the underground floor of a residential building. It used to be an aggregative renting apartment and was redecorated for community public space in 2016. The next plan is to set a long-term exhibition for urban regeneration. Through the site with a large floor area of more than 750 m^2, it is divided into a fragmentary situation with 17 rooms within the largest one in 40 m^2 and the smallest one in 21 m^2. All the walls are unmovable as for the construction necessary. The room has an average height of 2.6 m, and that part of the room equipped with exposed pipelines only 2.2 m in height. Because there was unpredicted consideration on extensive purpose, the site cannot afford an available central ventilation system, electrical circuit planning, and pre-installed wireless network. In short, the site is meeting challenges in the renovation process for the exhibition hall.

Design Conception: The exhibition content is composed of a framework of "One axis and four halls". One axis, which makes the most use of limited straight space among rooms, develops an exhibition wall that presents history storytelling of the Taoranting area. Taking the unchangeable factors into consideration, designers segregate rooms into four main sections where it restarts the independent rooms according to the tangible objects immersively. The four halls are plan to be developed into secondary themes series, which are: 1) Impression of Taoran (A)——A general introduction of the Taoranting subdistrict. 2) Co-construction of Taoran (B)——A vivid and comprehensive storytelling of the urban regeneration achievement in the Taoranting subdistrict. 3) Highlights of Taoran (C)——Show the notably natural, cultural, and historical characters of the area. 4) Neighborhood of Taoran (D)——A homelike space for local inhabitants' activities (Figs. 6, 7 and 8).

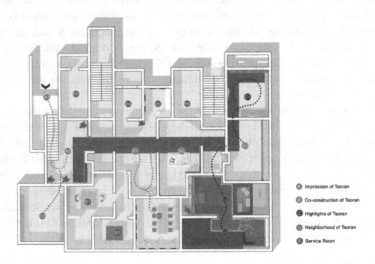

Fig. 6. The layout of Taoranting subdistrict exhibition hall. (By Huan Wang)

3.2 Xinjiekou Subdistrict Exhibition Center

Site Description: The project is also in the Xicheng District of Beijing, and locating at No. 42 of Zhaodengyu Road in Xinjiekou Subdistrict. The site is a single-story brick-concrete flat roof building with Zhaodengyu Road on the west side and Hutong area

Fig. 7. The interactive digital sandbox of co-construction of Taoran in Taoranting subdistrict exhibition hall (By Wen Li)

Fig. 8. The cultural and historical items of highlights of Taoran in Taoranting subdistrict exhibition hall. (By Wen Li)

on the south side. The surrounding area is mainly residential. In the urban regeneration management and renovation process, it has been returned to an activity center for the neighborhood from a restaurant and decorated in a pleasant public space, were not only for the inhabitants as well for the whole district area. The site has a total floor area of 284 m^2 with six rooms, which are the entrance hall for the reception in 33 m^2, the main hall in 111 m^2 for the organized activities of the Xinjiekou subdistrict office and residents' group, two meeting rooms are 40 m^2 and 18 m^2 in area respectively, and a function-undecided greenhouse, however, most of the places is vacant.

Compared with the Taoranting subdistrict exhibition hall, Xinjiekou has site characters of both negativity and positivity. The dominant position is noticeable. Along with the main road, the site owns a territory of more than half of the subdistrict available to come on foot and confirms the need to service inclusively. The last revocation project supported a modern-style interior space and traditional facade to appropriate the street background with an equipped water and electricity system. On the contrary, the inferior position resulting from an unworkable functional definition. The primary function is a single activity room without extensive concern in popular science propaganda and characteristics exhibition, which leads to a content deficiency of the physical space. It was inescapable to encounter a situation that the site that is limited to local usage. The subdistrict office of Xinjiekou makes requirements on activating the potential opportunity of history and culture capability, urban regeneration process, and welcoming the visitors in terms of retaining the activity function. For a long-lasting willingness, the redesigned exhibition center works as a popular place that attracts young people and representative a multifunctional practice for the future public space renovation project (Fig. 9).

Design Conception: The new exhibition center re-creates four pillars involved three spatial parts and one virtual part that explores a connection between the real-world and social community. The description of three physical pillars focuses on the universal materials on the history, neighborhood culture, and renovative project for urban regeneration to make "crossed the boundaries of the space" feasible. We resort to the interactive ground sand table (A) and touchable screen as the exhibition surface instead of the board filled with graphics and literature. A new exhibition like an interactive playground is being installed in the main hall by installation a sliding screen (B-1), holographic electric

Fig. 9. Photos of the site context (By Wen Li)

fan (B-2), and a magic wall (B-3). The middle of the hall's structural column supports a sliding screen that can narrate stories by switching the position. For re-presenting the inexistent objects in a vivid reflection, we insert holographic electric fans into the bookshelves and hide the switches between the books. When the audience moves the specific book, the relevant holographic electric fans begin to produce a virtual object. The magic wall is for the whole subdistrict renovation project exhibition by touch the activating-point on the board, then the board starts a show correspondingly. The activity room (C-1) and meeting room (C-2) are retained and redecorated with movable furniture and whiteboard for a digital pre-function consideration, as well as the greenroom where are prepared with tables, chairs, teapot, and fridge for daily service (Figs. 10 and 11).

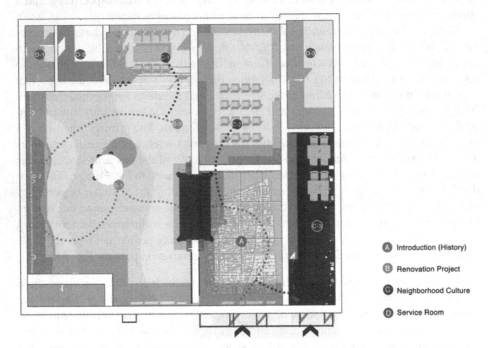

Ⓐ Introduction (History)

Ⓑ Renovation Project

Ⓒ Neighborhood Culture

Ⓓ Service Room

Fig. 10. The layout of Xinjiekou subdistrict exhibition center. (By Huan Wang)

Our creation of this exhibition in a public place and aims to be a scenic spots in Xicheng District, so the virtual part is planned extensively in urban media, such as TikTok, Weibo, and WeChat. Along with the design stage, a local IP developing program

Fig. 11. The photos of Xinjiekou subdistrict exhibition center. (By Huan Wang)

plan for the physical place is launched as well. To connect with the virtual society and sustain the center's engagement, the subdistrict office encourages submitted a draft of the cultural and creative products proposal with the design of the logo, T-shirt, and stationery in the first version. It was re-organizing a public exhibition of symbolic objects and texts that were new and experimental for The Xinjiekou subdistrict within the urban regeneration process exhibition plan (Fig. 12).

Fig. 12. The ID of Xinjiekou subdistrict exhibition center. (By Wen Li)

4 Discussion

The Possibility of the Multifunctional Exhibition Space

It is universally acknowledged that the exhibition hall is an independent design that departs from the function for activity-oriented space temporary and exclusive, without reference to the specific subject or the community regeneration. On the contrary, the public space for the subdistrict underlines a citizens-centered design sustainably and inclusively. Even though the exhibition hall should not be blended into neighborhoods, the pioneering performance shows a positive experience that can be extended. On one side, linked with the multifunctional design concept, the display imports the visualized street-scale information and interacts with the subdistrict real-timely, which achieves the visitors' enjoyment immersive. On the other side, by re-organizing the local history and culture, the exhibition broadens a humanistic dimension to the cultural experience for youngers of the city accessible.

There is obviously a tendency of city diversified within multifunctional neighborhoods supported by the exhibition, however, an inevitable challenge of this rising practical projects is that how to re-narrate the stories of urban regenerated construction projects and managerial promoting in a reader-inclusive way as well as a rational sense of community-harmonious engagement. The interdisciplinary design cooperation for modern cities leads to a general acceptance that the urban designer takes the responsibility of community renovation. If the information designer, urban media planner, artist, and graphics designer are involved in the flexible design process, the multifunctional exhibition plan can be activated in a cross-border combination sustainably. In a word, conversely, the crucial concerns shown by communities' multifunctional exhibitions in response to urban regeneration are related to an urban renovation project that is attributed by the urban government department, planner, designer, artist, engineers, and the residence themselves.

The Role of the Exhibition in a Virtual Community

A "Deep Involvement" of city life in the network shows an increasing fact, especially when the human beings encountered the Covid-19 pandemic in 2020, which motivates a consensus that the internet's wide prevalence brings convenience and possibilities. In China, dominated stimulation for the retail business and catering services primarily, internet technology has played a significant role in routine affairs that are governed by the relevant government department and community office. As long as the community network system and the platform are permissive to the basic services for management and construction, the future process appeals to profound academic research and practical attempts from a spiritual culture perspective. In this regard, the subdistrict exhibition hall works as a starting point for the exhibition of local characters and affairs by sustaining culture display installation and devises. The general recognition of virtual community is rooted in social community platforms, however, it should go further. Instead, to develop a new role of information and neighborhood communication, the virtual community platform based on exhibition space will provide a window for citizens and urban departments to understand each other's situations.

The Linkage with Sustainability

Since the concept of "Organic Renewal" (Wu 2011) purposed in 1994, the relevant theoretical and practical research has been advancing in exploration, which attracts a growing number of professions and experts to be involved in the interdisciplinary urban projects. Entering the new century, China has staged a phase of comprehensive transformation and upgrading of material and non-material cities, ecology, and culture. In fact, the purpose of urban regeneration is to reshape the community public area for the inheritance and innovation of culture to achieve sustainability in the urbanization process instead of re-identifying the constructed city space casually. To create a sustainable city, one needs to strengthen public space's functional equipment and turn a vital part of developed and interactive virtual connections into their natural world.

References

Granger, R., Sykes, H.: Urban Regeneration, India. SAGE Publications, Thousand Oaks (2016)

Pugalis, L., Liddle, J.: Austerity era regeneration: conceptual issues and practical challenges. Part 1(6), 333–338 (2013)

Ye, L.: Urban regeneration in China: policy, development, and issues. Local Econ. 26(5), 337–347 (2011)

Fang, K.: Contemporary Regeneration in the Inner City of Beijing: Survey Analysis and Investigation. China Construction Industry Publishing House, Beijing (2000).(in Chinese)

Li, X., Zhang, F., Hui, E.C., Lang, W.: Collaborative workshop and community participation: a new approach to urban regeneration in China. Cities, 102, Article 102743. Chinanews (2020). https://m.chinanews.com/wap/detail/chs/zwsp/9047301.shtml

Central Commerce of Government Procurement-Beijing. https://www.ccgp-beijing.gov.cn/

Chen, T., Hui, E.C., Wu, J., Lang, W., Li, X.: Identifying urban spatial structure and urban vibrancy in highly dense cities using georeferenced social media data. Habitat Int. 89, 102005 (2019)

Keane, M.: China's New Creative Clusters: Governance, Human Capital and Investment. (n.p.): Taylor & Francis, Abingdon on Thames (2013)

Yue, G.A., Wang, X.X., Wang, X.J.: Research on Contemporary Chinese Human Relationship. Nankai University Press, Tianjin (2002).(in Chinese)

Hoyem, H.: Urban renewal practices in Xi'an Drum tower Muslim district. World Archit. 6, 56–58 (2001). (in Chinese)

Brown, B., Perkins, D.D., Brown, G.: Place attachment in a revitalizing neighborhood: individual and block levels of analysis. J. Environ. Psychol. 23(3), 259–271 (2003)

Wu, L.: Rehabilitating the Old City of Beijing: A Project in the Ju'er Hutong Neighbourhood. UBC Press, Canada (2011)

Binqing, Z.H.A.I., Ng, M.K.: Urban regeneration and its realities in urban China. Urban Planning Forum. 2, 75–82 (2009)

'Blooming': A Design Concept for Period Poverty in Rural Areas of China

Jingchun Zeng, Bingjian Liu[✉], Xu Sun, and Jiang Wu

University of Nottingham Ningbo China, Ningbo, China
bingjian.liu@nottingham.edu.cn

Abstract. Period poverty has a significant impact on the lives of women and girls. Through this study, it is identified that traditional culture has significant impact on period poverty in rural areas of China. This article analyzes the causes of the period poverty in the world, especially in Asia, combining the different situations to evaluate current Chinese situations and causes. Through the interviews with volunteers who offer free pads to the students in rural areas and questionaries carried out in people living in cities, the gap between the females in different areas and potential solutions are identified. In addition, a design solution named 'blooming' is developed in order to explore the possibilities to reduce the period poverty. The evaluation of the design shows that it can provide the under-age girls free sanitary products and physiological knowledge at the same time, and encourage the public to donate for the period poverty. However, it needs further user testing in the local environment to ensure it is acceptable and adjustable.

Keywords: Product design · Period poverty · Culture · China · Under-age girls

1 Introduction

Period poverty is a global issue. Period poverty can be defined as the inadequate access to menstrual hygiene tools and educations, including the washing facilities, sanitary products, or waste management [1]. It is reported by the International Federation of Gynecology and Obstetrics [2] that about 10% of young females in the world cannot afford the period protection. In addition, up to 500 million women and girls are experiencing the period poverty in the world. It is difficult for them to find a proper place to change their sanitary products [3]. In developed countries, such as United States, about two-thirds of low-income women could not afford the menstrual hygiene products [4]. Capatides [5] also states that American women are 38% more likely to live in poverty than men because of the fee of menstrual products. And in developing countries, period poverty is more common. For instance, in Guatemala, the situation of period poverty is very serious [6]. And in Pakistan, the majority of females are suffering from period poverty and period shaming, since some traditional thoughts make menstruation as a symbol of impurity and dirt [7].

Apart from low-income women, teenagers are also significantly influenced by period poverty. It was reported by Zhang [8] that the period poverty has bad effect on a woman's

© Springer Nature Switzerland AG 2021
P.-L. P. Rau (Ed.): HCII 2021, LNCS 12772, pp. 408–422, 2021.
https://doi.org/10.1007/978-3-030-77077-8_31

lifelong wellbeing and development. For teenagers, due to the lack of basic physiological knowledge, they usually have the issue of period shaming and do not know how to handle the period. Therefore, during period they intend to choose to avoid school. In America, there are about one in five girls have missed classes because of no period products [9].

During the special period of COVID-19, new challenges were brought to the issue of period poverty. In China, during the COVID-19 pandemic, few people noticed that the sanitary products are extremely scarce for the female nurses and doctors. It was reported by Chen [10] that because of the lack of sanitary products, they used the adult diapers or plastic wraps as the substitutes. In early 2020, Liang Yu Stacey initiated the "Reassurance for Sisters Fighting the Virus" online campaign, which were widely supported to help the doctors and the nurses. And then it was extended to the project "Stand By Her", to reduce the period poverty for the under-age girls in rural areas [8]. In 2020, a topic related to the period poverty gained more than 1.38 billion views on Weibo [11]. The period poverty became one of the most popular topics in 2020.

In this study, the causes of period poverty are analyzed from multiple perspectives and a design solution is proposed to address the needs of teenagers in rural area of China. In the design process, the feedbacks of experts were collected to evaluate the effectiveness of the solution. It is found that it is possible to reduce the period poverty through proper product design. However, due to the constraints caused by COVID-19, field study with target users becomes impossible which influences the evaluation of the design. It is expected that in the future, the design concept can be further developed based on in-depth research with target users.

2 Literature Review

Publications related to period poverty are reviewed to investigate the causes and impacts to female's health and development. In particular, situations in the context of China, the country with biggest population, were further studied.

2.1 Causes of Period Poverty

High price of the menstrual hygiene products, period-shaming, the lack of the physiological knowledge and the menstruation taboo are the main reasons of period poverty. The lack of access to effective menstrual hygiene products, inadequate social support and the presence of taboos mainly influenced the period poverty [12]. What's more, period poverty is always accompanied by period shaming. It is reported by Zhang [13] that because of the lack of physiological knowledge, girls are ashamed to communicate with their families. In this section, the causes of the period poverty are analyzed from various perspectives.

One of the basic reasons for the period poverty is the high price. Many females take the cost of purchasing sanitary products as a hurdle. According to FIGO [2], a fifth of UK parents think it is difficult for them to afford sanitary products for their daughters. However, the cost of manufacturing a period pad is very cheap. It was reported by Tencent News [14] that through the research, the maximum net profit ration of selling menstrual products can reach 20%. The other cause of the high price is the tampon tax.

Nowadays, though the period products are the necessities, many countries make the tax of the menstrual products as high as normal goods. According to BBC News [15], the sanitary products have 10% Goods and Services tax (GST). And in Slovakia, the tax of the sanitary products reaches 20% of the basic good rate.

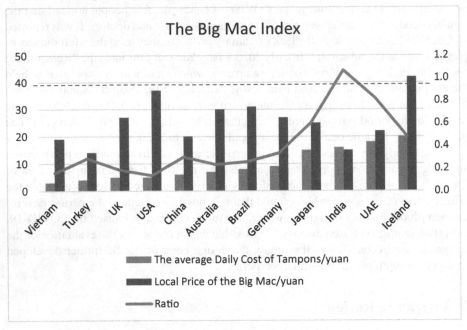

Fig. 1. The Big Mac Index [14] (Color figure online)

The Fig. 1 shows how expensive the menstrual products are in different countries, based on the local price of the Big Mac. The red dotted line indicates that the price of a hamburger equals the daily cost of tampons. According to the data, only India is beyond the dotted line. Though Iceland has the most expensive price of a tampon, the females in India are facing the largest pressure to afford the menstrual products [14].

Some experts think the myths, sociocultural restrictions and taboos would severely influence the period poverty and period shaming [16]. People in many countries still hold the opinions that having the period is a symbol of impurity and dirt, women should be ashamed of it. It is very common in some Asia countries. Pad Man [17] describes the phenomenon that most of the Indians still believe the period is dirty and humiliating, because of some traditional thoughts. Chothe et al. [16] hold the same opinion, due to the inadequate education and unhealthy social customs and norms, the Indian girls may not pay attention to menstrual hygiene. And because of some myths and taboos, girls are ashamed of having the period. According to Montgomery et al. [18], menstruation has become the gender-specific barrier to school participation.

Lacking the basic physiological knowledge may worsen the period poverty. On one hand, the women do not know how to protect themselves. On the other hand, they will feel stressful, afraid, and ashamed about having the period. According to the study of

Belayneh, Mareg and Mekuriaw [19], females would suffer from mental, physical and emotional problems, because of the lack of adequate perception towards menstruation. Miiro et al. [12] found that among 359 female students in Uganda, 23.8% of them lack the knowledge of periods.

2.2 Impact on Health and Development

Period poverty will bring negative effect to women's health and their personal development. When having period, some females will use the used cloths or pads with low quality and some students will use the books or their socks, which are very dirty and dangerous to their body. According to a news report of Sina [20], because of using unqualified period products, 38% of users have serious gynecology department diseases and 80% of users will feel uncomfortable during the period. These females would face high risk of having a skin irritation, vaginal itching or white or green discharge. What's worse, the use of dirty material instead of proper period products might make them lose the ability to give birth to a child [21]. To the school-aged girls, period poverty can increase their absence rate in school. For instance, according to a study of WHO [22], in the former Yugoslav Republic of Macedonia, 90% of female students in rural areas will avoid school for 4–5 days because their period. Therefore, period poverty will discourage the girls to accept the education, which would worsen the local poverty and development.

2.3 Situations in China

According to the study of Zhang [13], an internal study by the nonprofit group White Shell Project showed that 5% of girls in rural areas of China have no access to the sanitary products, while 13% feel ashamed of asking their parents for money to buy them. It is reported by Zhang [8] that China has the similar or even worse situation than the other countries. As a result of lacking the basic menstrual knowledge and the common menstruation taboo, the period poverty in rural areas is even worse. In China, especially in many rural areas, many girls are living with their grandparents. According to the study of Li and Luo [23], some left-behind children are ashamed to tell their grandparents about having the period. They have no idea about what is menstruation and what they need to do. According to the study of Li and Luo [24], their low self-esteem, shame and insecurity will bring long time unhealthy influence on their life and emotion. Furthermore, the lack of education would be the barrier to their life and the development of local economy, and the period poverty would lead a vicious circle in rural areas. Based on the information from publications, the vicious circle of period poverty in rural areas was summarized and shown in Fig. 2.

2.4 Current Situations

Period poverty has raised attention in the society and a number of solutions have been developed from different perspectives, such as, reducing the tax fee, developing the physiological education, finding new materials and offering free pads to women.

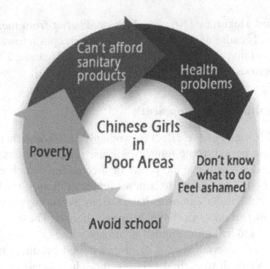

Fig. 2. The vicious circle in period poverty

Reduce the Tax Fee

Reducing the tampon tax can directly decrease the price of the menstrual hygiene products. According to the study of Buchholz [25], Poland, the Czech Republic and Lithuania decreased the "tampon tax" to 5%. And other countries also decreased the tampon tax. Germany slashed the taxes form 19% to 7% and Luxembourg made the tax of period products as low as 3%. However, for the under-age girls in poverty, though the price of the sanitary products decreases, they still feel ashamed to buy them because of the lack of physiological knowledge. According to the study of Lui and Chen [26], the under-age girls in rural areas of China are ashamed of having the period and even shamed for being a girl. Though decreasing the tampon tax can reduce the period poverty to a large extent, the hygiene knowledge and the sex education are still the problem for the girls in rural areas.

Develop the Education

Providing physiological education to children could have positive effect on the economic growth and productivity of an area. It is reported by Montgomery et al. [18] that educating girls can develop the health of females and delay the sexual debut and marriage. In addition, Jewitt and Ryley [27] point out that girls' education could help prevent the sexual/reproductive harms including HIV/AIDS. According to a study of WHO [22], the United Nations Children's Fund (UNICEF) supported the Ministry of Education to develop the education materials related to the menstrual hygiene management, including the materials for the disabled children. The education intervention provides the opportunities for girls to communicate with their friends and other support sources [28]. Recently in China, many organizations began to offer classes of hygiene knowledge and the sex education to the under-age girls in rural areas and they found the under-age girls are ashamed of having the period. According to Li and Luo [23], the nonprofit group White Shell Project offer the free sanitary products and teach them the physiological knowledge at the same time by playing games and having workshops. They point out that because of lacking hygiene knowledge and sex education, girls do not attach importance to using the clean sanitary products, which would bring lots of illness. They also reported that many girls are ashamed to communicate with their families because of having the period. Due to this fact, how to make the hygiene knowledge and sex education more acceptable and easier to understand still need to be explored.

New Materials or New Products

Finding new materials of the menstrual hygiene products, to make them more healthy and cheaper can be one of the solutions to reduce the issue of period poverty. According to Miiro et al. [12], among all the interviewees, 75.5% of the girls are interested in trying the local pads if they are cheaper or reusable. In other words, if a new and cheaper material is used in the sanitary products, it would be accepted by the public. In India, Arunachalam Muruganantham created a low-cost sanitary napkin machine, to provide clean and cheap period products to the local women and bring the job opportunities to them. Sahoo and Panda [29] point out that Mr. Arunachalam Muruganantham was not only raising the awareness among the period poverty but also making females in India independent and confident.

On the other hand, designing new products to wash and dry the sanitary pads for the females in poverty, to make the sanitary products reusable can also be a solution to the issue of period poverty. In 2014, Mariko, et al. [30] developed a product called Flo, which is toolkit that allow girls to wash, dry and reuse the sanitary pads. It aims to solve the issue of no place to dry the pads and the issue of using dirty cloths. Based on the environment of rural areas, this product can be easily operated by users with no power. It also can be the place to keep the clean pads. The reusable menstrual hygiene products can reduce the financial burden on girls to some degree [28].

Offer Free Menstrual Products

Many countries are trying to reduce the period poverty. According to Shearing [31], the government of England provide free period products for students in state schools and colleges. And in 2020, Scotland became the first country to provide free menstrual products to the public.

In 2020, many social organizations appeared to help the low-income women in rural areas in China. They encourage the public to donate the money, and they will use the donation to offer free menstrual products to the females in rural areas, especially the under-age girls. According to Zhang [8], the "Stand By Her" project helped more than 6.000 girls from 33 schools across China, and raised more than 368,700 RMB. Li and Luo [23] also reported that girls felt pressure to accept the sanitary products, because of the pattern of the pads and words on the package. However, because of the poor transport and the period shaming in rural areas, the way to send and offer the sanitary products might need further developed.

3   User Studies

According to Zhang [8], "Stand By Her", as one of the most popular and largest-scale projects in China, is trying to develop the physiological education and offer free menstrual hygiene products in rural areas. In this study, two volunteers from the project "Stand By Her" were interviewed to know more detailed information about the real situations in rural areas. Through the interviews, volunteers described the real situation about some rural areas in Guizhou province. There are some schools that lack the access to clean water and hot water, which means girls have no access to a proper place to change their pads. In addition, many of the girls have no idea about what period is and what they can do to it. Although some girls know the period products, they still have no access to it, due to the high price. Instead, some of them put rough paper with low quality on their underpants. During the period, they feel ashamed, embarrassed, stressful, and afraid. Most of them choose to stay at home instead of go to school. The volunteers also introduced the way they help the under-age girls. Because of the poor traffic condition, they have to send the menstrual hygiene products to the teachers in the school three times or four times a year by post. And then, the teacher will collect the packages and distribute the products to the girl students. The volunteers will go to the local school to hold workshops to introduce the physiological knowledge to the girls in the summer or winter holidays. All the expense in the project is collected from the social platforms, which is donated by the public. It was reported by Chen [10] that since the 10th of February 2020, Yu Liang provided the progress and the details of the projects daily by Weibo, to ensure the accountability and transparency of "Stand by Her".

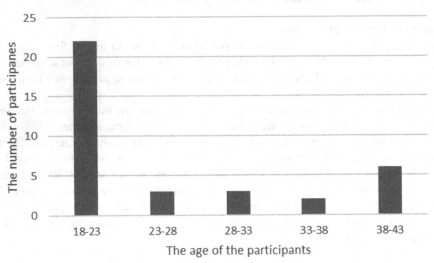

Fig. 3. The basic information of the participants

Due to the significant difference between rural and urban areas in China, to explore the public attitudes in urban area towards the period poverty, a questionnaire was carried out in 36 females living in cities, aged between 18 to 43 (Fig. 3).

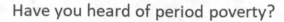

Have you heard of period poverty?

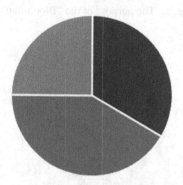

■ No   ■ Yes, but jut heard of it   ■ yes, and I read lots of news about it

Fig. 4. The result of the questionnaire

According to Fig. 4, among 36 participants, only 25% of them know what the period poverty is and 41.67% of them never heard about it. This result shows the majority of females in urban areas do not know the situations in rural areas. There is a big gap between the urban and rural females. However, although the majority of the participants know little about the period poverty, 97.22% of them are willing to donate to help reducing this issue in rural areas. Meanwhile, some of the participants raised their concern that their personal information could be breached by donating on the internet. If the donations are collected by well-known public platforms, such as Tencent, these worries would disappear.

4 Proposed Design Solution

4.1 Design Concept

Based on the literature review and the user research, a design solution was developed by the authors in order to explore the possibilities to reduce the period poverty. Figure 5 shows the purpose of this project. This design aims to break the vicious circle of the period poverty in rural area by offering free menstrual hygiene products and enhancing user awareness by teaching the under-age girls physiological knowledge in the school.

The concept is called "blooming", which indicates the beautiful age of the girls in poverty and the love between people. (Fig. 6) The main idea of this project is connecting the people living in urban cities and girls in rural areas. In the urban areas, there will be a machine set in the public toilet in urban areas, to encourage people donate for the period poverty. Due to the uncertainty of having the period, women in urban areas would meet

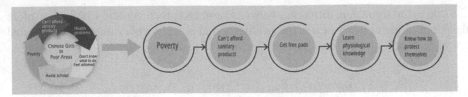

Fig. 5. The purpose of the "Blooming"

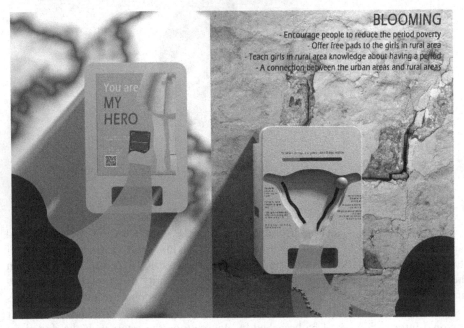

Fig. 6. The design concept of the "Blooming"

embarrassing situations of no sanitary product. And it is the time they can have great empathy with the girls in rural areas. Due this fact, this machine also has the function of selling sanitary product.

The Machine in Urban Areas

To encourage the public to donate for the period poverty, the author uses the idea of interactive screen. A picture of a girls with a single sock and a dirty skirt would attract the public's attention. And a sentence near the girl demonstrates how serious the period is in China. After people donating for the period poverty by scanning the code, the content of the screen will change. The girl will wear a pair of socks and clean skirt. Ans a big smile will appear. (Fig. 7).

The Machine in Rural Areas

Based on the finding of the user studies, the machine designed to offer the free sanitary products and teach the basic physiological knowledge at the same time. This project

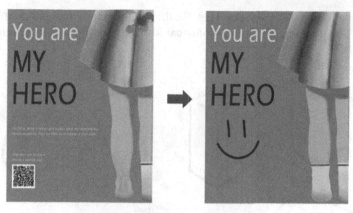

Fig. 7. The changes in different interfaces

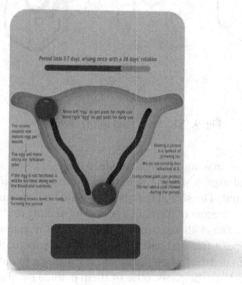

Fig. 8. The final products for the under-age girls in rural areas

could simulate the process of the ovary releasing an "egg". Girls could get the daily use pads or night use pads by moving the different "egg" down. Some slogans demonstrate the process of having a period and tell the girls there is no need to be ashamed of it, as shown in Fig. 8.

4.2 Modelling and Evaluation

To explore the shape and form of the machine, sketches and physical models were done to find the best solution, which could explain the physiological knowledge correctly, and make the product understandable, attractive, and acceptable for the under-age girls.

In the first round of the sketches (Fig. 9), the author mainly focused on the organic shapes and how to combine the physiological knowledge with the distribution of the sanitary pads.

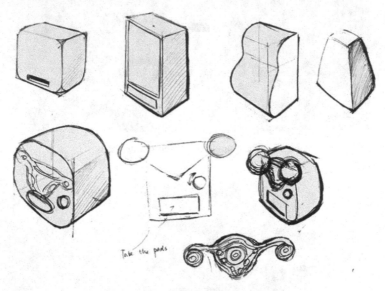

Fig. 9. The first round of the sketches

In the first round of making physical models (Fig. 11), the author tried to take advantage of the visual aspect and the feeling to make the physiological knowledge more easily to understand. The soft materials, like balloons, were used to simulate the ovaries. Tell the girls the process of forming a period by making the "egg" going through the numbered "circles". The cloth was used to simulate the soft endometrium. And when the girls pulling the rope, a free pad will come out. What's more, the author also tried to explain the method to use the pad on the product by using a foldable model. Through the user testing, among 10 participants, 60% of them pointed out that it was difficult for them to make the "egg" move through the circles. After talking with doctors, to ensure the knowledge is correct, the scale of the ovaries needs to be smaller and the ovaries is not as soft as balloons. According to the feedback, the way to simulate the process of forming a period needs to be developed, and new materials need to be explored to represent the ovaries. The industrial design experts also gave some advices that it might be better if the introduction of how to use the pad is combined with the package of the sanitary products (Fig. 10).

In the second round of sketches (Fig. 11), the author explored more interesting appearance of the products and took the capacity and the volume of this product into consideration.

The physical models of the ovaries were also made into 1:1 scale by foam (Fig. 12), to introduce the physiological knowledge correctly. However, according to the feedback from the user testing, considering the ovaries may not be accepted by the under-age girls,

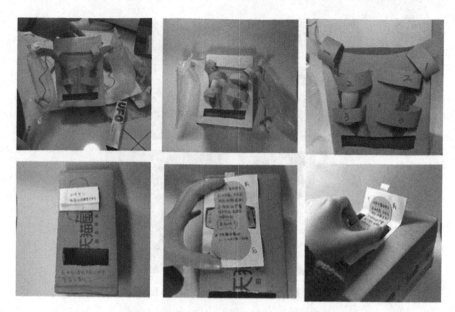

Fig. 10. The first round of making models

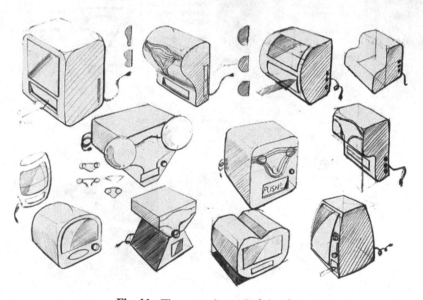

Fig. 11. The second round of sketches

the models of the ovaries did not be used in the final design. To make the final products more beautiful and attractive, the shape of the uterus needs to be more abstract.

When design the mechanism of the product, the local environment and conditions were considered, for instances, the lack of workers, the life of the product, and the cost of manufacturing. With these considerations, this product was designed to be operated

Fig. 12. The second round of models

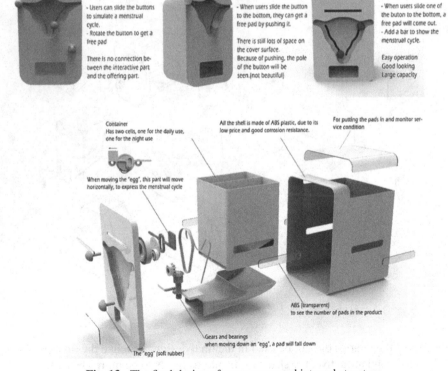

- Users can slide the buttons to simulate a menstrual cycle.
- Rotate the button to get a free pad

There is no connection between the interactive part and the offering part.

- When users slide the button to the bottom, they can get a free pad by pushing it.

There is still lots of space on the cover surface.
Because of pushing, the pole of the button will be seen.(not beautiful)

- When users slide one of the buton to the bottom, a free pad will come out.
- Add a bar to show the menstrual cycle.

Easy operation
Good looking
Large capacity

Container
Has two cells, one for the daily use, one for the night use

All the shell is made of ABS plastic, due to its low price and good corrosion resistance.

For putting the pads in and monitor service condition

When moving the "egg", this part will move horizontally, to express the menstrual cycle

ABS (transparent)
to see the number of pads in the product

Gears and bearings
when moving down an "egg", a pad will fall down

The "egg" (soft rubber)

Fig. 13. The final design of appearance and internal structure

totally by physical movement, which means it can be operated without power. In the development process, suggestions from industrial experts were taken into account to make sure the internal mechanical design is feasible for the design purpose. The final design appearance and internal structure is shown in Fig. 13.

5 Conclusion

The period poverty is a serious global issue and many women suffer from it. In this study, the causes and current solutions for the period poverty globally, and specially in China, are presented. The current solutions show their effectiveness in specific context and solved the problem to some extent. However, along with the situation changes and new technology becomes available, it is necessary to explore new solutions, particularly for the context of China, where traditional thoughts and culture still have significant impact on period issue.

In this study, the authors tried to use public resource to reduce period poverty through product design approach. Through interviews and survey, it is found that the public in urban area of China have strong willingness to help the female in rural areas. Based on this finding, the authors developed a product system called 'blooming' to bridge the denotator in cities and females in rural areas. The feedback from users and experts showed that this design can provide an innovative solution to provide target users with menstrual products with the support of the public. However, longitudinal evaluations are needed to test if the concept can work properly in real environment.

References

1. Alvarez, A.: Period Poverty (2019). https://www.amwa-doc.org/period-poverty/. Accessed 15 Feb 2021
2. International Federation of Gynecology and Obstetrics: Month After Month: Period Poverty. https://www.figo.org/news/month-after-month-period-poverty. Accessed 15 Feb 2021
3. UNICEF: International Women's Day: 10 quick facts on girls. https://www.unicef.org/media/media_81135.html. Accessed 15 Feb 2021
4. Carroll, L.: Even in the U.S., Poor Woman Often Can't Afford Tampons Pads (2019). https://www.reuters.com/article/us-health-menstruation-usa/even-in-the-u-s-poor-women-often-cant-afford-tampons-pads-idUSKCN1P42TX. Accessed 15 Feb 2021
5. Capatides, C.: What is Period Poverty? (2019). https://www.cbsnews.com/news/what-is-period-poverty/. Accessed 15 Feb 2021
6. Wang, V.: 3 Organizations Ending Period Poverty in Guatemala (2021). https://borgenproject.org/tag/period-poverty/. Accessed 15 Feb 2021
7. Randolph, K.: Combating Period Poverty in Pakistan (2021). https://borgenproject.org/tag/period-poverty/. Accessed 15 Feb 2021
8. Zhang, J.: Period Poverty in China and Current Campaigns (2020). https://borgenproject.org/period-poverty-in-china/. Accessed 15 Feb 2021
9. Rifenburg, L.: Nearly 1 in 5 American Girls Have Missed School Due to Lack of Period Protection1: Always® Joins Forces with Gina Rodriguez & Feeding America® to Help #EndPeriodPoverty and Keep Girls in School (2018). https://www.businesswire.com/news/home/20180807005135/en/Nearly-1-in-5-American-Girls-Have-Missed-School-Due-to-Lack-of-Period-Protection1-Always%C2%AE-Joins-Forces-with-Gina-Rodriguez-Feeding-America%C2%AE-to-Help-EndPeriodPoverty-and-Keep-Girls-in-School. Accessed 15 Feb 2021

10. Chen, C.: "Stand By Her:" Chinese Feminist Rhetoric during the COVID-19 Pandemic (2020). https://www.digitalrhetoriccollaborative.org/2020/07/13/stand-by-her-chinese-feminist-rhetoric-during-the-covid-19-pandemic/. Accessed 15 Feb 2021
11. Zhao, L.: The Unspeakable Pain of Period Poverty and Shame in China (2020). https://radiichina.com/menstrual-period-poverty-shame-china/. Accessed 15 Feb 2021
12. Miiro, G., et al.: Menstrual health and school absenteeism among adolescent girls in Uganda (MENISCUS): a feasibility study. BMC Women's Health **18**(1), 1–13 (2018)
13. Zhang, W.: Campaign for Affordable Menstrual Products Gains Ground in China (2020). https://www.sixthtone.com/news/1006124/campaign-for-affordable-menstrual-products-gains-ground-in-china. Accessed 15 Feb 2021
14. Tencent: Neglected "menstrual poverty": how much do Chinese women spend on sanitary napkins all their lives? (2020). https://new.qq.com/omn/20200903/20200903A09VID00.html. Accessed 15 Feb 2021
15. BBC: 'Tampon tax' paid around the world (2015). https://www.bbc.com/news/world-32883153. Accessed 15 Feb 2021
16. Chothe, V., et al.: Students' perceptions and doubts about menstruation in developing countries: a case study from India. Health Promot. Pract. **15**(3), 319–326 (2014)
17. Pad Man Directed by R. Balki [DVD]. U.S., Calif.: Sony Pictures Entertainment (2018)
18. Montgomery, P., et al.: Menstruation and the cycle of poverty: a cluster quasi-randomised control trial of sanitary pad and puberty education provision in Uganda. Plos One **11**(12), e0166122 (2016)
19. Belayneh, Z., Mareg, M., Mekuriaw, B.: How menstruation is perceived by adolescent school girls in Gedeo Zone of Ethiopia? Obstet. Gynecol. Int. **2020**, 1–6 (2020)
20. Sina: Period poverty is destroying Chinese women! (2020). https://k.sina.com.cn/article_3688920760_dbe076b800100qxv3.html. Accessed 15 Feb 2021
21. Rapp, A., Kilpatrick, S.: Changing the Cycle: Period Poverty as a Public Health Crisis (2020). https://sph.umich.edu/pursuit/2020posts/period-poverty.html. Accessed 15 Feb 2021
22. World Health Organization: Tackling the Taboo of Menstrual Hygiene in the European Region (2018). https://www.euro.who.int/en/countries/kyrgyzstan/news/news/2018/11/tackling-the-taboo-of-menstrual-hygiene-in-the-european-region. Accessed 15 Feb 2021
23. Li, S., Fan, N.: In addition to "sanitary napkin poverty", the physiological knowledge of girls in backward areas is more "poor" (2020). https://www.thepaper.cn/newsDetail_forward_8995567. Accessed 15 Feb 2021
24. Li, W., Luo, D.: What those "menstrual poverty" girls are missing exactly (2020). https://news.ifeng.com/c/7zV7o0ZrsFC. Accessed 15 Feb 2021
25. Buchholz, K.: Where the "Tampon Tax" is Highest and Lowest in Europe (2020). https://www.statista.com/chart/18192/sales-tax-rates-on-feminine-hygiene-products-in-europe/. Accessed 15 Feb 2021
26. Lui, L., Chen, R.: Period Poverty in China (2020). https://varsity.com.cuhk.edu.hk/index.php/2020/12/period-poverty-in-china/. Accessed 15 Feb 2021
27. Jewitt, S., Ryley, H.: It's a girl thing: menstruation, school attendance, spatial mobility and wider gender inequalities in Kenya. Geoforum **56**, 137–147 (2014)
28. Hennegan, J., et al.: A qualtative understanding of the effects of reusable sanitary pads and puberty education: implications for future research and practice. Reprod. Health **14**(1), 78 (2017)
29. Sahoo, S., Panda, A.: Arunachalam Muruganantham: the man who sparked a revolution against all odds. Parikalpana KIIT J. Manag. **12**(1), 98 (2016)
30. Mariko, H., et al.: Flo-Tool Kit for Girls Living in Poverty (2014). https://marikoproduct.com/Flo. Accessed 15 Feb 2021
31. Shearing, H.: Period poverty: Schools urged to order free menstrual products (2020). https://www.bbc.com/news/uk-51167487. Accessed 15 Feb 2021

The Vista of Information Communication Technology in the Ageing Society: A Perspective from Elderly's Basic Needs

Liang Zhang[1,2]([✉]), Xiaolei Ma[3], Ningxuan Zhang[4], Huajun Cao[5], Chao Ai[5], Jingyu Zhang[1,2], Wenwei Xu[5], and Kan Zhang[1,2]

[1] Key Laboratory of Behavioral Science, Institute of Psychology, Chinese Academy of Sciences, Beijing 100101, China
zhangl@psych.ac.cn
[2] University of Chinese Academy of Sciences, Beijing 100049, China
[3] University College London, London WC1E 6BT, UK
[4] School of Psychology, University of Glasgow, Glasgow G12 8QQ, Scotland, UK
[5] Institute of Strategic Research, Huawei Technologies Co., Ltd., Shenzhen 518129, China

Abstract. This study aimed to explore the elderly's basic needs which are indispensable for developing age-friendly Information Communication Technology (ICT) products. Seventeen interviewees who were aged from 54–90 yrs participated in the online/offline interviews. By qualitative and quantitative analysis, we showed the implication and contributory factors of the elderly's basic needs of "Health" and "Longevity." Physical (normal sensory function, no disease, etc.), psychological (inner peace, good mood, etc.) and environmental factors (companionship, etc.) all play important roles for elderly health and longevity. Among them, psychological factors are the most important, rather than physical factors. We found the typical problems in using and accepting ICT products, such as Technophobia and Learnability. The results suggested ICT products would play a more vital role in a future aging society. The age-friendly design is needed according to psychological and physical aging features and based on the elderly's basic needs.

Keywords: Ageing society · Information Communication Technology · Health · Longevity · Basic needs · Technophobia

1 Introduction

The increase in the elderly population has become a global trend. According to the WHO reports, citizens over 60 years old reached 1 billion in 2020 ("Ageing," 2021). This number will increase to 1.4 billion by 2030 and 2.1 billion by 2050, about 22% for the whole world population (WHO (2016b); WHO 2018). On the other hand, life expectancy has been rising since the 1960s (WHO 2016a). The increase in life expectancy not only happens in developed countries but also in developing countries. The growth rate of the elderly over 80 has exceeded that of the younger elderly between 65 and 80

© Springer Nature Switzerland AG 2021
P.-L. P. Rau (Ed.): HCII 2021, LNCS 12772, pp. 423–440, 2021.
https://doi.org/10.1007/978-3-030-77077-8_32

(United Nations 2019). It means that not only the total number of older people in the world has increased rapidly, the age distribution structure of the elderly has also changed at a fast pace.

A massive demographic structure shift will bring unprecedented challenges to society, without a doubt. For example, there is a tremendous demand for daily life assistance or careers because of the decline of their physical functions. Yang et al. (2012) found a robust negative correlation between the care needs of the elderly and the family caregivers' life quality. It isn't easy to find a balance between work and family support.

To reduce the burden of providing for the elderly, information and communications technology (ICT) has been introduced. From the careers' side, adopting ICT in home-care has significantly increased the caring quality (Rantanen et al. 2017; Martínez-Alcalá et al. 2016). For the users, Lewis and Neider (2017) suggested that ICT could help the senior users enhance health monitoring and solve social isolation with another avenue accessing people. Knowing the usefulness of ICT in improving life quality, a few commercialized products and mobile applications specially designed for the older population have been available on the markets, i.e., smartphones (Malwade et al. 2018; Berenguer et al. 2017). However, the whole population's senior customers' ratio is much lower than younger customers among ICT users (Berenguer et al. 2017). Despite the popularity, the variety of these commercial products is far from enough to satisfy the senior population's actual needs. Therefore, it is essential to investigate the elder's needs and concerns to maximize the potential of ICT in elder support.

Psychological researchers have promoted the ideas of successful aging: health, longevity, psychological factors and social factors (Bowling and Dieppe 2005). Among these needs, Health and Longevity are the basic of all the needs. However, it is unclear the definitions and extensions of the two needs. According to the concept of "Health" defined by WHO, it includes physical health, mental health and healthy social functioning. However, aging exerts negative impacts on all these aspects. For example, aging works as an essential risk factor for diseases while reducing physical ability (Partridge et al. 2018). With the decline of physical ability, it becomes harder for seniors to visit relatives and friends, which will shrink their social network and lead to social isolation. This situation often creates a vicious circle link to physical and mental health, increasing the risk of impaired ability to perform daily activities and mental discomfort (Jang et al. 2016). Besides, the gap between healthy life expectancy and life expectancy is getting larger while both of them are increasing (Murray et al. 2015). It also suggests that significant problems are existing in health and later life quality.

This study presented a comprehensive perspective of the elderly's basic needs, which is indispensable for developing age-friendly ICT products. The present research aimed at describing the elderly's basic needs, "Health" and "Longevity," and more importantly, the typical problems for the needs, by qualitative research of a group of Chinese elderly. We combined the usage of semi-structural interviews and questionaries. The present results would provide the primary information for future ICT product development in the aging society.

2 Methods

2.1 Participants

The study was based in Beijing, China, in July 2020. We designed the interview outline "the Outline of Interview on Needs of the Elderly" and the questionnaire "The Scale of Basic Needs of the Elderly" according to scientific literature analysis. We got in touch with some elderly and conducted an online or offline interview to find out what their daily lives looked like. Interviews were conducted to understand what the old generation do after retirement and what they need to improve the quality of life. Through conversations with them, we tried to figure out what technology problems they have met every day, and behind that, what kind of elderly needs we ignored before. The deficiency of education is one of the reasons that could cause problems in accepting and using techniques. To exclude that reason, seventeen elders with a high level of education volunteered to participate in the interviews. Their ages were ranged from 54 yrs to 90 yrs (Table 1). Those participants were all well-educated and heavy users of ICT products. The physical and mental aging mainly caused the problems they met after retirement.

Table 1. Study participants' information.

Participants number	Sex	Age	Previous/current employer	Work status
1	Female	83	Professor	Retired
2	Female	77	Professor	Retired
3	Male	83	Professor	Retired
4	Male	81	Professor	Retired
5	Male	77	Professor	Retired
6	Male	81	Professor	Retired
7	Male	83	Professor	Retired
8	Male	54	Professor	Expert
9	Female	65	Doctor	Expert
10	Male	79	Professors	Retired
11	Male	68	Officer	Retired
12	Female	78	Officer	Retired
13	Female	85	Professor	Retired
14	Male	79	Doctor	Retired
15	Male	90	Professor	Retired
16	Male	74	Officer	Retired
17	Male	90	Officer	Retired

2.2 Tools

This consultation uses a combination of semi-structured interviews and questionnaires, involving the following two tools:

Interview Outline – "The Outline of Interview on Needs of the Elderly." The interview outline is based on the classic Behavioral Event Interview (BEI, see the Appendix for details). Besides, we interviewed additional questions according to the participants' background. For example, for the two participants who are professionals in aging psychology and gerontology, the questions included representative events in the health and longevity and descriptions of typical problem events/persons.

Questionnaire – "The Scale of Basic Needs of the Elderly." The questionnaire was prepared regarding older persons' primary physical, psychological, and social conditions (Kozma et al. 1980; Li et al. 2003; the WHOQOL Group 1995). The final scale contained 61 conceptual dictionaries (See the Appendix for details).

Interviewer. According to the project's needs, we organized six interview experts and set up three interview groups with interview supervisors. Each group included a senior interviewer and an experienced research assistant.

Before the interview research implementation, the experts systematically trained the interview team to ensure standardization and scientific implementation.

2.3 Interview Process

The implementation process of this interview is divided into the following four phases (Fig. 1):

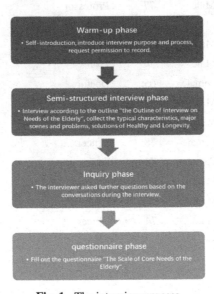

Fig. 1. The interview process.

The total length of each interview and questionnaire was about 1.5 h. The interview location is based on the situation of the respondents, including on-site and online interviews. As a result of the COVID outbreak, most interviews are done online.

Three respondents participated in an on-site interview, 12 respondents participated in an online interview. Two senior respondents were unable to participate for a long time due to their ages and health status and finished the questionnaires. We carried out the interviews according to standardized procedures to ensure no systemic errors in the data sources.

2.4 Data Analysis

All the interviews were audio-recorded and transcribed. Representative quotes were translated into English and applied for illustration purposes in this paper. Besides the interviews, we also collected data from the questionnaire. All informants' names are anonymized.

Two interviewers conducted the initial coding, and the emerged themes were discussed and iteratively refined among all the authors. As themes began to emerge, we steered the questions around the emerged themes in subsequent interviews.

3 Results

3.1 Quantitative Analysis

Interview Coding. We used template analysis to extract features and sbasic according to the frequency mentioned in the coding process. The coding information includes conceptual categories (health, longevity), problem categories (positive description, negative description, recommendation), factors (mental state, physical condition, life status, social association, additional support, other) and performance (illness, self-identification, etc.). In each item, we indicate the original meaning and corresponding original text.

Frequency Results. Based on three categories: positive description, negative description and suggestion, we extracted keywords and ranked the keywords according to their frequency. We used the word clouds below to demonstrate (Fig. 2).

Questionnaire. To describing the elderly's basic needs, Health and Longevity, we adopt the questionnaire "The Scale of Basic Needs of the Elderly" to get the relevant descriptions of the two needs. A total of 13 valid questionnaires were collected, and all valid questionnaires were analyzed; and the following are the top 10 relevant descriptions for "health" and "longevity," respectively (Fig. 3).

According to the most relevant health descriptions, we divided the influence factors into the following categories. Physical: "Normal sensory function", "Excellent physical condition" and "Not Disease" implied that overall physical health is important to elderly people, and they need the body to function well to support their daily life. Psychological: "Inner peace" is the most related indicator of all, besides, "Freedom to make own

a. Frequency results of "Health."

b. Frequency results of "Longevity."

Fig. 2. a. Frequency results of "Health." b. Frequency results of "Longevity."

decisions" indicated that the sense of self-control is significant for the elderly. Together with "Fulfilling life", "Enjoyable to live", "Good mood" and "positive emotions," the six indicators suggested the significance of mental status in "Health." Environmental: "Live without difficulties" showed their concerns about the surroundings. The elderly frequently worried about their financial status, the convenience of the living environment and the accessibility to medical services.

In terms of "longevity," specific indicators of "Health" contribute to it similarly, e.g., "Inner peace" also sbasic the highest correlation of "Longevity." However, the elderly emphasized "no major diseases" and "Act energetically" in physical indicators. For the psychological part, stable social support are more prominent, and the elderly want to "Feel companionship and love in life."

3.2 Typical Problems and Responses

This section presented the problems and challenges the elder met in this digital age and proposed some suggestions and solutions from their perspective.

Technophobia. For most older people, due to the decline of cognitive function and learning ability, it is difficult to adapt to new technology and even lead to Technophobia. Technophobia refers to the negative perception of new technologies and negative emotional feedback (Brosnan 2002), but the content varies with time. Technophobia originated in the era of the industrial revolution. In the 19th century, people who didn't trust mechanical production and carried on disruptive activities as luddites were regarded as technophobic. Technophobia is mainly related to advanced technology such as computers, robots, and artificial intelligence in contemporary society. In our study, we also

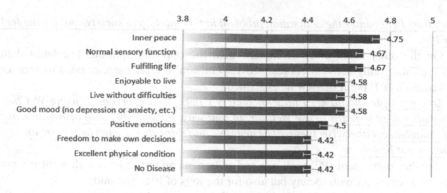

a.Ten relevant descriptions of Health

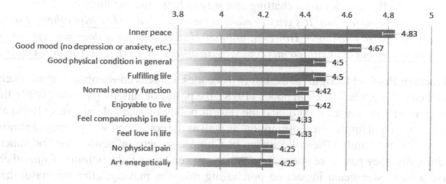

b.Ten relevant descriptions of Longevity

Fig. 3. a. Ten relevant descriptions of Health b. Ten relevant descriptions of Longevity

found that one of our informant (P8) mentioned the word "technophobia." He indicated that:

"Technophobia" shouldn't be ignored. It's much easier for young people to adapt to new technology; older people generally have Technophobia. Technical isolation is the norm in the elderly, and the elimination of technical isolation is vital for older people to live well.

What he said was most evident in the cases of P4, the participant said:

A series of minor troubles in my life, I can't use Alipay or WeChat very well, but anyway, I won't use it cause it's not necessary to me.

But for some elderly, it's inevitable for them to use new technology, especially during the quarantine. For example, the new teaching form of live broadcasting is supposed to be convenient and efficient. However, it made more troubles than the traditional ways in those senior teachers and professors. Like P1 said:

I adapt to new things slow; for example, some educational institutions ask me to do a live broadcast. It's troublesome to get a taxi to the institution, but I still go there because I am worried about using the technology at home. I can only use the most stupid method every time I encounter the adaptation problem in this intelligent society, making me feel terrible.

On the other hand, other informants held the opposite opinion. The latest data that WeChat's daily active users reached 1.09 billion in 2021 corresponded to another participant's (P7) point of view he explained:

Older people should keep up with society's pace, and everyone is using WeChat, so we also need to learn to use WeChat. In that way, the elderly could also gain some self-confidence. Otherwise, they will be negative and think they are left behind by society, which is not beneficial.

Another participant (P2) took a friend of hers as an example. She thought it's not only for keeping up with society but also for the joys of life. She said:

Although she turned 90 years old, she still advanced with the times. She can handle computers, WeChat, online shopping, etc. She can have fun herself on the Internet.

For herself, P2 took online chatting as a way to help ease loneliness:

Now we have WeChat. It's easy to make a phone call and chat with others. I think it's a way to ease loneliness. However, another kind of loneliness does not refer to no communication but thinks differently compared to others. In short, it's all about mentality.

Defects in Product Design. In the last two decades, China's consumption environment changed rapidly. The one-child policy (1978), the policy of enriching people (1979), the policy of private houses (2000), and the reform policy of medical expenses (1998) all made a profound impact on consumption, as well as the consumption decisions of almost every Chinese family. The collectivism of Chinese society influenced the consumers profoundly: they pay more attention to prestige when buying; the opinions from others have a more significant impact on purchasing decision making; after purchase, they value the evaluation and comments from others more; Advertising is more influential; the market effect of authoritative media is more prominent; word of mouth is more important to brands and companies.

Taking the population aged between 50 and 90 in 1–3-tier cities of China as a sample, China Urban Pension Consumption Insight Report 2019 found that the factors affecting the decision making are: quality > function > safety > price > brand. The older adults paid great attention to the quality, function and safety of pension products, all of which exceed 40%. It required the enterprises to discover the substantial needs of the elderly. As P16 said:

There is a consuming psychology problem that the consumer may say it's good but never use in daily life. From the perspective of the enterprises, products can not be made based on the former thoughts.

With the development of online shopping, it requests higher identifying and decision-making ability of consumers while purchasing. Older adults are more unwilling to be bothered by buying these products. P13 is one of the elderly consumers who met the problems of distinguishing false information on the Internet.

But often, the clothing looks perfect on the Internet. However, it became ill-fitting and unattractive when you tried it on.

Compared to other age groups (such as children), the elderly product market is still in a primary stage. The supply of products and services in the elderly market is unable to meet the needs of the elderly.

Intelligent Medical Service. As mentioned before, artificial intelligence is not intelligent for the elderly, but they have an increasing need for aging disease management. Therefore, quite a few of the participants mentioned the problem of Intelligent Systems in hospitals nowadays. For P16:

As the smartphone and computers, we might be able to try them, but most elderly can't use them at all. They will feel abandoned. You need a reservation to go into the hospital, but they don't know how to reserve, and they have to ask for help.

This kind of helplessness may lead to a sense of worthlessness. In elderly's emotional experience, various "loss" brings loneliness: the loss of physical and mental health, the loss of economic independence, the loss of family and social relations, and the loss of the purpose of survival. And for the middle-aged and elderly, loneliness is a risk factor for depression, which eventually affects health. Cacioppo et al. found that loneliness in the elderly can predict the occurrence of depression symptoms through a 5-year longitudinal study (Cacioppo et al. 2010).

In terms of longevity, the elderly are concerned about another medical problem, emergency assistance. They've been heard a lot from friends and society about the accidents of older people. About 16% of the elderly in China had fallen at least once in one year. In an urban area, the fall rate of young elderly is about 11%, that of 70–80 years old is about 16%, and that of 80 years old rise to about 20%. One of our informants (P6) had the same experience:

I fell once seriously, and I called 120, but no one answered, then I felt dizzy and asked the passengers to call the family. Finally, my family sent me to the hospital.

That reminded her of a device that was installed in her bedroom by the community.

There is a system in Beijing that is supplied by the community for free. You can put it in front of the bed. It is said that the help message could be directly sent to the hospital if you press the button, but I never try it.

Coincidentally, another interviewee had interests in the same product.

I think a button will be good. If there is something urgent happens, it's too complicated to use a mobile phone.

Besides, some enterprises have discovered the needs of the elderly and provided this service.

A system can help to buy, taking you to the hospital or anything urgent, with just a click of the button. I try it once to find a cleaner. But the price is high, more expensive than the market price, not necessary for me. But if I encounter difficulties, the price will not be a problem.

It's simple techniques to develop such a product to accomplish this information transmission. The hardest part is to do the following medical service and make it as simple as just a click on the button for the elderly.

4   Discussion

The present study described the elderly's basic needs of "Health" and "Longevity" and abstracted the top 10 relevant descriptions respectively by quantitative analysis of the questionnaire. Through interviews, We listed the typical problems they met in daily

ICT products using, e.g., Technophobia. Based on these findings, we will discuss the underlying mechanism and alternatives of future ICT products of the elderly, mainly focusing on needs, not deficiencies, and the whole elder group, not individuals.

By a quantitative analysis of the elderly's basic needs of "Health" and "Longevity," we found that the associated factors are physical, psychological, and environmental. Although most previous studies of aging focused more on disease and physically healthy, our studies have found that mental health, such as "Inner peace," "Good mood," plays a crucial part in the life of the elderly.

Based on the interviews, we used qualitative methods to make a comprehensive description of the ICT problems and difficulties from the perspective of the Chinese elderly. Different life experiences make everyone's level and type of Technophobia different. With the fast-changing technology, the Technophobia faced by the elderly now mainly includes the use of the Internet and the use of portable digital devices such as mobile phones. In our study, some older people also face the difficulties of using self-service deposit and withdrawal machines in the bank or making online hospital appointments. Although Technophobia exists at all ages, as some empirical studies have suggested, it's more common in the elderly. Two surveys in Ireland in 2005 and 2008 (sample sizes 160 and 150, respectively) found that about 50% of older people had medium-high levels of Technophobia (Hogan 2005; Hogan 2008).

Technophobia also contributed to the "digital divide" in the elderly (Nimrod 2018). The digital divide is often defined as the disparity between those with access to all forms of internet information and communication technologies and those without (Dijk 2017). The digital divide is also a widespread problem in China. 67% of the elderly in the United States would use the Internet (Anderson and Perrin 2017). Among EU countries, the number of Internet users among the elderly is 61% (Organization for Economic Cooperation and Development (OECD) 2017). In China, the proportion of the elderly who often surf the Internet is only 5.0%, while the proportion of urban elderly is 9.2% (Zhang et al. 2019).

With the rapid increase of dependence on science and technology in contemporary life, it is of great significance to reduce the Technophobia and digital divide in the elderly to improve the quality of life in their later years.

As mentioned before, there are fewer products specially designed for the elderly compared to other age groups. White Book on the Consumption Habits of the Elderly in China 2017 shows that the most expensive part of the elderly at all ages is daily life, accounting for almost 70%. With the aging process, the elderly spend more on their health and medical care, while social entertainment and other aspects gradually reduce. In the future, the elderly mainly consider increasing expenditure in the following four areas: disease management (43%), nutrition (29%), tourism (25%), daily expenditure of food and catering (22%). Cognitive aging is one important reason to limit the elder's daily activities and reduce their independence. For example, perceptually, the vision and hearing of the elderly generally decreased or lost. (Berk 2014). With aging, it is more difficult for the elderly to fall asleep. They have less sleep time and fewer dreams. 20–40% of the elderly suffer from insomnia several nights each month (Papalia et al. 2013). A marked decrease in working memory may appear (Wingfield et al. 1988). Cognitive intervention training can improve the cognitive ability of the elderly (Corbett et al. 2015) and effectively delay its quality of life reduction (Wolinsky et al.). But more importantly, redesigning products and environments to conform to the physical and psychological characteristics of the elderly and using assistive technology helps make up for the deficiency of cognitive aging in the elderly.

Assistive technology helps the elderly with low ability and improves their physical function. For example, a microcomputer chip placed on the medicine bottle can regularly remind the elderly to take medicine. "smart homes" have been designed by architects to help the elderly being safe and independent, such as straps connected to the tracks on the ceiling, to facilitate the mobility of the elderly between rooms (Berk 2014). Assistive technology help maintain the independence of the elderly. In our research, the interviews suggested that the emergency assistant device like an emergency button in the bedroom is of great importance to the elderly.

Our study has several limitations that need to be addressed in future studies. Firstly, it includes 17 interviewees only, who have a well-educated background, middle or upper-class social status and currently lives in Beijing. Thus, the collected data might not fully uncover people's needs in other backgrounds, i.e., lower-income and diverse cultures.

Also, the majority of interviewees are in their 70s and 80s. Only one of our interviewees are in their 50s and two in their 60s. It's important to mention that the elderly are a very diverse group. In terms of age, the elderly can be divided into the young elderly (65–74 years old), the middle elderly (75–84 years old), and the old elderly (85 years old and above) (Papalia et al. 2013). People in different brackets are very likely to have different demand structures.

In conclusion, the present research obtained veritable primary data from the elderly population (aged 56–90, majorly in the 70s and 80s) for the future development of the ICT. The interview was not directly started from the existing problems of ICT products but focused on the health and longevity issues, which were primarily concerned by the elderly. In this way, first, we could understand the substantial needs of the elderly, and second, we can be aware of the potential demand and market in the field of health and longevity with ICT application. The study suggested that ICT does have a distinct possibility in the aging society, but there is still a lot to be improved.

Acknowledgment. This research was supported by the National Key Research and Development Plan (Grant No. 2018YFC0831001). We are particularly grateful for the support of the Huawei-CAS program "Decoding the visions in the aging society" The authors thank Yufang Liao, Yuqing Meng, Huihui Zhang, Xiaowei Luo and Yichen Zhao for their contribution to the data collection and analysis.

Appendix

Interview Outline

China has entered the stage of rapid aging. The number of older people aged 60 and over in China is about 18% of the total population, expanding. However, there are more and more elderly groups and the rapid development of science and technology, whether from the perspective of scientific research or IT enterprises, the younger generation does not understand the substantial needs of the elderly. Therefore, the Institute of Psychology of CAS hopes to conduct in-depth communication through interviews to aggregate and meet the substantial needs of more elder users to make their life better, happier and more comfortable. The following questions will not be judged as right or wrong, nor be aimed at individuals. We just want to understand you from your perspective of view.

Health

Do you know any one of the elderly that you think he/she lives healthy? Can you describe his/her life with one or two examples?

What experiences make you feel healthy?

What difficulties does the elderly face in terms of health? Do you have any suggestions or solutions for these difficulties?

Please rate each item base on your knowledge about the relationship between the items and the concept of Health. 1 = completely unrelated, 5 = highly related.

No.	Item	Completely unrelated	Slightly unrelated	Uncertain	Slightly related	Highly related
1	Normal sensory function	1	2	3	4	5
2	Having the freedom to make own decisions	1	2	3	4	5
3	Feeling in control of your future	1	2	3	4	5
4	Being able to do what you want to do	1	2	3	4	5
5	Others respect your freedom	1	2	3	4	5
6	Having something to look forward to	1	2	3	4	5
7	Being able to make further accomplishments	1	2	3	4	5
8	Gaining the recognition you deserve in your life	1	2	3	4	5
9	Feeling satisfied with the accomplishments you made	1	2	3	4	5
10	Feeling satisfied with how you use your time	1	2	3	4	5
11	Feeling satisfied with your activity level	1	2	3	4	5
12	Having enough things to do every day	1	2	3	4	5
13	Feeling satisfied with opportunities for community participation	1	2	3	4	5
14	Having no fear of death	1	2	3	4	5
15	Having no fear of the pain before death	1	2	3	4	5
16	Having a sense of companionship in your life	1	2	3	4	5
17	Feeling the love in your life	1	2	3	4	5
18	Having the opportunities to love	1	2	3	4	5
19	Having the opportunities to being loved	1	2	3	4	5
20	Having positive emotions	1	2	3	4	5
21	Feeling extremely satisfied with life	1	2	3	4	5
22	Feeling lucky	1	2	3	4	5
23	Having no worries	1	2	3	4	5
24	Feeling no loneliness or alienation	1	2	3	4	5
25	Feeling no worries or unhappiness	1	2	3	4	5
26	Having no worries about the future	1	2	3	4	5

(continued)

(*continued*)

No.	Item	Completely unrelated	Slightly unrelated	Uncertain	Slightly related	Highly related
27	Feeling as happy as you did when you were young	1	2	3	4	5
28	Feeling satisfied when you look back on your life	1	2	3	4	5
29	Feeling enjoyable to live	1	2	3	4	5
30	Live without difficulties	1	2	3	4	5
31	Being in better health condition than the peers	1	2	3	4	5
32	Being in the excellent physical condition	1	2	3	4	5
33	No disease	1	2	3	4	5
34	It is in a good mood without depression or anxiety etc	1	2	3	4	5
35	Having no physical pain	1	2	3	4	5
36	Fulfilling life	1	2	3	4	5
37	Feeling inner peace	1	2	3	4	5
38	Act energetically	1	2	3	4	5
39	Having faith or religious support	1	2	3	4	5
40	Live where you like	1	2	3	4	5

Longevity

Do you know any one of the elderly that you think he/she is long-lived?

Which aspects of life help you find out if a person is long-lived?

What difficulties does the elderly face in terms of longevity?

Do you have any suggestions or solutions for these difficulties?

Please rate each item base on your knowledge about the relationship between the items and the concept of Longevity. 1 = completely unrelated, 5 = highly related.

No.	Item	Completely unrelated	Slightly unrelated	Uncertain	Slightly related	Highly related
1	Normal sensory function	1	2	3	4	5
2	Having no fear of death	1	2	3	4	5
3	Feeling companionship in life	1	2	3	4	5
4	Feeling the love in life	1	2	3	4	5
5	Good physical condition in general	1	2	3	4	5
6	Being in better health condition compared with one year ago	1	2	3	4	5
7	No disease	1	2	3	4	5
8	Being in better health condition than the peers	1	2	3	4	5
9	Regular socializing (visiting relatives or friends)	1	2	3	4	5
10	Feeling no restrictions on daily activities (e.g., climbing stairs, shopping, etc.)	1	2	3	4	5
11	Feeling no restrictions on other activities	1	2	3	4	5
12	Feeling enjoyable to live	1	2	3	4	5
13	Live without difficulties	1	2	3	4	5
14	It is in a good mood without depression or anxiety etc	1	2	3	4	5
15	No physical pain	1	2	3	4	5
16	Fulfilling life	1	2	3	4	5
17	Feeling inner peace	1	2	3	4	5
18	Acting energetically	1	2	3	4	5
19	Live where you're like	1	2	3	4	5
20	Receiving appropriate treatment	1	2	3	4	5
21	Having faith or religious support	1	2	3	4	5

References

Aging (2021). https://www.who.int/health-topics/ageing#tab=tab_1. Accessed 4 Feb 2021

Kozma, A., Stones, M.J.: The measurement of happiness: development of the Memorial University of Newfoundland Scale of Happiness (MUNSH). J. Gerontol. **35**(6), 906–912 (1980). https://doi.org/10.1093/geronj/35.6.906

Anderson, M., Perrin, A.: Tech adoption climbs among older adults (2017). https://www.pewint ernet.org/2017/05/17/tech-adoption-climbs-among-older-adults/

Berenguer, A., Goncalves, J., Hosio, S., Ferreira, D., Anagnostopoulos, T., Kostakos, V.: Are smartphones ubiquitous? An in-depth survey of smartphone adoption by seniors. IEEE Consum. Electron. Mag. **6**, 104–110 (2017). https://doi.org/10.1109/MCE.2016.2614524

Berk, L.E.: Development Through the Lifespan: From Youth to Old Age (4th Edition, translated by Chen). China Renmin University Press (2014). (Chinese version)

Bowling, A., Dieppe, P.: What is successful aging and who should define it? BMJ (Clin. Res. Ed.) **331**(7531), 1548–1551 (2005). https://doi.org/10.1136/bmj.331.7531.1548

Brosnan, M.: Technophobia: the psychological impact of information technology. Routledge, London (2002)

Corbett, A., Owen, A., Hampshire, A., Grahn, J., Ballard, C.: The Effect of an online cognitive training package in healthy older adults: an online randomized controlled trial. J. Am. Med. Direct. Assoc. **16**(11), 990–997 (2015)

Cacioppo, J.T., Hawkley, L.C., Thisted, R.A.: Perceived social isolation makes me sad: 5-year cross-lagged analyses of loneliness and depressive symptomatology in the Chicago health, aging, and social relations study. Psychol. Aging, **25**, 453–463 (2010)

Dijk, J.: Digital divide: impact of access. In: The International Encyclopedia of Media Effects, pp. 1–11 (2017). https://doi.org/10.1002/9781118783764 wbiemc0043

GBD 2013 DALYs and HALE Collaborators, et al.: Global, regional, and national disability-adjusted life years (DALYs) for 306 diseases and injuries and healthy life expectancy (HALE) for 188 countries, 1990–2013: quantifying the epidemiological transition. Lancet (London England) **386**(10009), 2145–2191 (2015). https://doi.org/10.1016/S0140-6736(15)61340-X

Hogan, M.: Technophobia amongst older adults in Ireland. Irish J. Manag. **27**(1), 57–77 (2005). 2005 Special Issue

Hogan, M.: Age differences in technophobia: an Irish study. In: Barry, C., Conboy, K., Lang, M., Wojtkowski, G., Wojtkowski, W. (eds.) Information Systems Development: Challenges in Practice, Theory and Education, pp. 117–130. Springer, New York (2008). https://doi.org/10.1007/978-0-387-68772-8_10

Jang, Y., et al.: Risk factors for social isolation in older Korean Americans. J. Aging Health **28**(1), 3–18 (2016). https://doi.org/10.1177/0898264315584578

Lewis, J., Neider, M.: Designing wearable technology for an aging population. Ergon. Des. Q. Hum. Factors Appl. **25**(3), 4 (2017). https://doi.org/10.1177/1064804616645488

Li, L., Wang, H.M., Shen, Y.: Chinese SF-36 health survey: translation, cultural adaptation, validation, and normalisation. J. Epidemiol. Community Health **57**, 259–263 (2003)

Malwade, S., et al.: Mobile and wearable technologies in healthcare for the ageing population. Comput. Methods Programs Biomed. **161**, 233–237 (2018). https://doi.org/10.1016/j.cmpb.2018.04.026

Martínez-Alcalá, C.I., Pliego-Pastrana, P., Rosales-Lagarde, A., Lopez-Noguerola, J.S., Molina-Trinidad, E.M.: Information and communication technologies in the care of the elderly: systematic review of applications aimed at patients with dementia and caregivers. JMIR Rehabil. Assist. Technol. **3**(1), e6 (2016). https://doi.org/10.2196/rehab.5226

Nimrod, G.: Technophobia among older internet users. Educ. Gerontol. **44**(2–3), 148–162 (2018). https://doi.org/10.1080/03601277.2018.1428145

Organization for Economic Cooperation and Development: OECD digital economy outlook 2017 (2017). https://www.oecd-ilibrary.org/science-and-technology/oecd-digital-economy-outlook-2017_9789264276284-en;jsessionid=5nbu6fmksr718.x-oecd-live-03

Papalia, D.E., Olds, S.W., Feldman, R.D.: Developmental Psychology: From Early Adulthood to Old Age (10th edition, translated by Li, etc.). Posts and Telecom Press (2013). (Chinese version)

Partridge, L., Deelen, J., Slagboom, P.E.: Facing up to the global challenges of ageing. Nature **561**(7721), 45–56 (2018). https://doi.org/10.1038/s41586-018-0457-8

Pwc: 2017 White Paper of the Consumption Habits of China's Elderly (2017). (Chinese version)

Rantanen, P., Parkkari, T., Leikola, S., Airaksinen, M., Lyles, A.: An in-home advanced robotic system to manage elderly home-care patients' medications: a pilot safety and usability study. Clin. Ther. **39**(5), 1054–1061 (2017). https://doi.org/10.1016/j.clinthera.2017.03.020

The WHOQOL Group: World Health Organization Quality of Life Assessment (WHOQOL): position paper from world health organization. Soc. Sci. Med. **41**, 1403–1409 (1995)

United Nations: World population ageing, 2019 highlights, p. 5, New York (2019)

World Health Organization (WHO): Ageing and health (2018). https://www.who.int/news-room/fact-sheets/detail/ageing-and-health. Accessed 4 Feb 2021

World Health Organization (WHO): Life expectancy increases by 5 years, but inequalities persist (2016a). https://www.who.int/news/item/19-05-2016-life-expectancy-increased-by-5-years-since-2000-but-health-inequalities-persist. Accessed 4 Feb 2021

World Health Organization (WHO): Multisectoral action for a life course approach to healthy ageing: draft global strategy and plan of action on ageing and health. SIXTY-NINTH WORLD HEALTH ASSEMBLY Provisional agenda item 13.4 A69/17 (2016b)

Wingfield, A., Stine, E. A.L., Lahar, C.J., Aberdeen, J.S.: Does the capacity of working memory change with age? Exp. Aging Res. **14**(2), 103–107 (1988)

Yang, X., Hao, Y., George, S., Wang, L.: Factors associated with health-related quality of life among Chinese caregivers of the older adults living in the community: a cross-sectional study. Health Qual. Life Outcomes **10**(1), 143 (2012). https://doi.org/10.1186/1477-7525-10-143

Zhang, Q., Li, J., Dang, J., Luo, X.: 2019 Blue Book on Ageing: A Report on the Development of the Quality of Life of the elderly in China. Social Science Academic Press (2019). (Chinese version)

Valuing Social Media Affordances

Xingchen Zhou and Pei-Luen Patrick Rau(✉)

Department of Industrial Engineering, Tsinghua University, Beijing 100084, BJ, China
rpl@mail.tsinghua.edu.cn

Abstract. Various social media products concentrate differently on social media affordances to meet the needs of users. When designing social media products, understanding the value of each social media affordance is crucial to realizing commercial success. This study aims to expand the limited understanding of social media affordances from the perspective of users' monetary valuations. An *in situ* investigation was conducted among 39 users to estimate the value of eight social media affordances. We tracked participants' daily social media usage and assessed how they valued each affordance every day for two weeks. We contrasted the difference between willingness to accept (WtA) and willingness to pay (WtP) when making monetary valuations. Furthermore, we examined how perceived social capital and social media addiction influenced users' valuations of each affordance. The results showed that affordances like Conversation and Instrument were most valued. Affordances like Identity, Presence, and Reputation were least valued, but they were associated with addiction. These findings can be used as guidelines on what affordances should be concentrated on when designing the commercial strategies of social media products. They also identified which affordances should be controlled to prevent users from suffering social media addiction.

Keywords: Social media · Affordances · Monetary valuation · Social capital · Addiction

1 Introduction

Social media is playing an increasingly important role in many different domains of the world and it has brought about many changes. It is used in public affairs, commercial innovation, organization management and many other fields [1, 2]. With the proliferation of social media to various domains, the affordances of social media have expanded to meet the different needs of users. In addition to the basic social affordances like messaging, information sharing, and group chatting, many social media platforms have extended their services to non-social functions. For example, WeChat, the biggest social media platform in China, released its wallet function in 2013; it has now become one of the most widely used transactional tools in China.

Different social media products (e.g., Facebook, Twitter, YouTube, and TikTok) may fulfill different affordances. Understanding how users value social media affordances could help with designing new social media products and their marketing strategies. Thus, in this study, we investigated how users valued different social media affordances,

© Springer Nature Switzerland AG 2021
P.-L. P. Rau (Ed.): HCII 2021, LNCS 12772, pp. 441–453, 2021.
https://doi.org/10.1007/978-3-030-77077-8_33

especially the insufficiently studied non-social affordances of social media, with the aim of creating guidelines on the development of new social media products and commercial models.

While pursuing commercial success, many social media products are competing for users' time. Accordingly, the excessive use of social media has developed into a new problem [3, 4]. People with pathological levels of social media usage have suffered mental disorders [5]. Much of the existing research has revealed the association between users' characteristics and social media addiction [5, 6], but little attention has been paid to the association between addiction and social media affordances. Understanding how social media affordances are related to addiction will contribute to the design of healthier products, which may benefit users' well-being.

This study focuses on the monetary valuation of social media affordances. We primarily want to answer two questions. First, *how do users value each social media affordance*? Finding out the most highly valued affordance and revealing the value difference of each affordance is important for the design of a new social media product and its commercial model. Second, *how does daily social media use, addiction, and perceived social capital influence users' valuations of each affordance*? We explored the associations between users' behavior and attitude toward social media (usage behaviors, perceived social value, and addiction) and their valuation of each affordance, aiming to reveal how each affordance influenced addictive behavior and usage patterns. These findings will help find a balance between the commercial benefits of social media products and the well-being of social media users.

2   Related Works

2.1   Social Media Affordances

Affordances mean the possible actions users can take through using a technology [7]. Accordingly, social media affordances "are action possibilities permitted by social media features" [8]. How these affordances meet users' psychological needs is a key factor for a product's success. A clear definition and a reasonable classification of social media affordances will improve our understanding of how social media can meet users' needs, which can guide the design and improvement of new social media products [9].

Taking Facebook as an example, affordances have been classified into three categories: recent data and impression management, longer term presentations of a user's self-image, and archiving meaningful facets of a user's life [9]. This classification has two limitations. First, the affordances of Facebook cannot cover all social media affordances. Other social media applications (like YouTube and WeChat) may provide affordances that are not well supplied by Facebook. Second, Facebook itself has developed with the market. New affordances have been embedded but not yet included in the three categories. Dawot and Ibrahim provided a classification for general social media rather than specific social media products [10]. They also categorized social media into three main categories of affordances, namely, the individual, conversation, and community. Individual affordance focuses on self-identification, whereas the conversation affordance focuses on generating social content. Community affordance aims to build connections and support each other's activities [10]. However, this classification is still too general to guide the design of social media features and functions in detail.

Table 1. Eight social media affordances

Affordance	Description
Conversation	To communicate with other users in social media, both individually and within groups
Groups	To form communities and sub-communities. To help manage relationships and the way one shares content such as posting an update to different groups and building groups to do teamwork
Identity	To present one's identity such as expressing one's feelings, thoughts, likes and dislikes, and sharing one's location, profession, and real name
Instrument	To provide services that assist in daily living such as making payments, ticket bookings, and other public services
Presence	To know if other people are available, such as knowing whether others are in the virtual world or the real world
Relationships	To connect with others such as for obtaining a job from a group and finding people with the same interests
Reputation	To identify the social standing of people such as having fans and followers on social media and earning fame
Sharing	To exchange, distribute, and receive content such as sharing photos, paintings, articles, files, and other resources

Compared to Dawot et al.'s and Zhao et al.'s classification, the honeycomb model proposed by Kietzmann, Hermkens, McCarthy, and Silvestre contains more details [11]. In the honeycomb model, a framework of seven affordances is proposed: identity, conversation, sharing, presence, relationships, reputation, and groups. Different social media are defined according to how they focus on each affordance (the description of each affordance is shown in Table 1). The honeycomb model has come to be accepted as a model that contains most of the possible social media affordances.

However, all the aforementioned affordance classifications are mainly focused on social features (e.g., social activities and social communities) of social media. They ignore the non-social features that are embedded in many social media products to meet market needs. To date, only a small amount of research has tried to discuss the influence of non-social affordances (e.g., the affordance of transactions on WeChat) on users' behaviors. In this study, in addition to the social affordances included in the functional honeycomb proposed by Kietzmann et al. [11], we introduce the affordance we name as Instrument. Instrument affordances allow users to take actions that assist in daily affairs, to obtain public services, and to conduct other non-social activities (see Table 1).

2.2   Valuation of Social Media

With the prevalent use of social media, many service providers are considering the possibility of translating the value of social media into economic returns. A key point to making profits is to improve users' willingness to pay for social media services. Investigations show that how much a user is willing to pay (WtP) for social media services is highly related to their perceived value [12, 13].

Perceived social capital is a key indicator of how users perceive social value from social media. In a social group, social capital is regarded as the resource of social actions [14]. In online social media communities, users perceive social capital: they can use online relationships as a resource to realize their personal goals such as finding a job [15]. Perceived social capital may indirectly influence users' WtP for social media via the effect of perceived social value [13].

In addition to WtP, willingness to accept (WtA) is another measure to describe users' judgments of social media values. Valuing in the opposite direction, biases were found between WtP and WtA [16]. Previous research asserts that WtA is normally greater than WtP [16]; however, the WtA/WtP ratio will be influenced by the product or services targeted [17]. Understanding both WtP and WtA, and their disparity is beneficial for the generalization of valuation results and for avoiding possible estimation errors [18]. Thus, in this study, we focused on both WtP and WtA when valuing social media affordances, aiming to make the results fit practical contexts, and to examine the reliability of estimations.

In previous studies, when estimating the value of social media, all services were always treated as a whole; no details were provided on how users valued different affordances [13, 19]. More detailed valuations of each social media affordance will help service providers improve their services or design a business model for new products [20]. Thus, in this study, we valued social media on the basis of affordances.

Each social media affordance may satisfy a different need of the user, and how the needs are satisfied may influence the valuation. According to motivation theory, the value of social media can be classified into two groups: utilitarian values and hedonic values. The utilitarian value of social media involves how it can improve a user's performance (extrinsic benefits), and the hedonic value concerns how people can obtain emotional benefits (intrinsic benefits) [21]. The combined effect of the utilitarian and hedonic value of each social media affordance may influence its monetary valuation.

2.3   Addiction and Social Media Use

Along with the popularity of social media came the emergence of problematic social media usage behaviors. Social media addiction is becoming a problem for many users, and it is widely regarded as a new type of behavioral addiction [3, 4, 22]. Excessive social media use will lead to detrimental effects on mental health [3]. For example, overuse of social media in a workplace causes feelings of overload, invasion and uncertainty of online social interaction [23].

Social media addiction is closely related to users' daily social media usage behaviors (e.g., how much time a day they spend on social media). Researchers have found that the more time people spend on social media, the more their well-being will be undermined [24–26]. However, in the social media application markets, many companies are competing to occupy users' time, because they believe that more usage will ultimately lead to monetary returns [27].

It is possible that addiction to social media is closely related to social affordances. The online connections developed in social media make users more sensitive to comparisons with their peers, which easily leads to envy of others [6, 28]. Nowadays, people are trying different ways to help addicts with their social media addiction [29]. Understanding the associations of social media affordances and addiction is crucial for finding coping methods. Determining the affordances related to addiction can help in the creation of guidelines on both the future designs of social media products and addiction treatments.

3 Method

3.1 Investigation Design

An *in situ* study was designed to investigate users' monetary valuations of social media affordances. To obtain a comprehensive understanding of users' monetary valuations of social media affordances, we measured both how much they were willing to pay for these affordances (willingness to pay, WtP) and how much they wanted to get if they were asked not to use it (willingness to accept, WtA), considering that WtP and WtA were found to be different for the valuation of products (Horowitz, 2002). To ensure the reliability of valuations and to determine the effect of users' daily use on their valuations, investigations were conducted repeatedly for two weeks. Daily data logs of users' actual usage time and their monetary valuations were recorded. Both WtP and WtA were measured once a day for a total of seven times respectively in two weeks.

At the beginning of this study, users' perceived social capital in the social media they were using was measured to observe their valuation of social features. Users were tested for social media addiction to examine possible associations between problematic use and different social media affordances.

3.2 Participants

Participants in this study were recruited from an international class in Tsinghua University. They received a course credit for finishing the investigation. Considering that the affordance, Instrument, which although not common in traditional social media design was now widely used by Chinese users [30] and so their experience of this could influence their valuations, we recruited international students who had only started to experience these affordances for a few months. Hence, we were able to obtain valuations from new users.

In total, 39 participants were included in this study. They were international students who came from 19 different countries, such as France, Italy, Japan, Thailand, Brazil, Pakistan, Azerbaijan, South Korea, the UK and the US, and they all had stayed in China for more than three months. The ages of the participants ranged from 21 to 30 (M = 24.33, SD = 2.29). Thirty-one of them were male and eight were female.

3.3 Procedures

Informed consent was collected before the study began. The participants were requested to fill a pre-study questionnaire to collect demographic information, including nationality, age, gender, addiction to social media, and their perceived social capital from social media. We then recorded participants' daily use of social media and their monetary valuations for the eight social media affordances. Participants' daily social media use was recorded by time management applications (Moment for iOS, and Quality Time for Android). All participants submitted their daily data log and valuations of the eight social media affordances to an online questionnaire platform at around 10 p.m.

The investigation comprised two stages. Each stage lasted seven days. In the first stage, participants' willingness to pay (WtP) for each affordance was measured once a day for a total of seven times. In the second stage, the same method was used to measure how much money the participants would want if they were required not to use social media (WtA). After two weeks, every participant wrote a report on their reasons for their monetary valuations and to explain what they thought was the most valuable affordance of social media.

3.4 Data Collection and Analysis

We adopted the scale invented by Vock et al. to measure users' perceived social capital [13]. It was measured based on three criteria: trust, reciprocity and voluntarism. Our data showed that the internal consistency of each criteria of perceived social capital was satisfactory (with all Cronbach's αs larger than 0.8), and the Pearson correlations between each criteria and the average score of perceived social capital was large (trust: $\rho = 0.81$, $p < 0.001$; reciprocity: $\rho = 0.67$, $p < 0.001$; voluntarism: $\rho = 0.86$, $p < 0.001$), showing good validity of this measure.

The scale used to measure participants' level of addiction to social media was adapted from Young's internet addiction scale [31] by changing the word internet into social media. This scale has been used to measure social media addiction in previous studies [29]. Our data also showed good internal consistency of this measure (Cronbach's $\alpha > 0.86$).

Participants' daily valuations of social media affordances were measured by directly answering questions about their willingness to pay for certain social media affordances (e.g., "How much will you pay for the use of the Instrument affordance of social media?") and their willingness to accept payment for not using certain affordances of social media (e.g., "How much will you expect to get for not using the Instrument affordance of social media?").

We used R to make the statistical analysis. Repeated measure analyses of variance (ANOVAs) were conducted to determine the differences between WtP and WtA, and the differences among monetary valuations of various social media affordances, with both the valuation type (WtP versus WtA) and affordance as within-group factors. Generalized eta-square (η^2_g) was used to denote the effect size.

We used multilevel linear models (MLMs) to analyze the effects of daily social media use, addiction, and perceived social capital on users' monetary valuations. The MLMs controlled for the non-independence of samples. The data in our sample exhibited a multilevel structure with daily assessment (level 1) nested within participants (level 2). We built models for the monetary valuation of each social media affordance. All models included fixed effects of the assessment day, the addiction level, the daily social media use, and the perceived social capital; all MLMs included a random intercept to indicate that the monetary valuations varied between participants.

Considering that participants may have used different standards when they made the monetary valuations, which could cause standardization problems in the analysis, we divided the monetary valuation of each affordance by the sum of all affordances and used the value to denote the relative importance. Thus, the data we used in the analysis were not exact values measured in units. Instead, we used percentages to show the relative importance.

4 Results

4.1 Monetary Valuations of Different Affordances

The results of the two-way within-group ANOVA showed that the valuation pattern (WtA versus WtP) had no significant influence on participants' monetary valuation of social media affordances ($F_{1,38} = 2.18$, $p = 0.15$, $\eta^2_g = 0.00$), and neither did the interaction effect of the valuation pattern and the affordance type ($F_{7,266} = 1.45$, $p = 0.18$, $\eta^2_g = 0.01$). Considerable differences existed among various affordances ($F_{7,266} = 26.99$, $p < 0.001$, $\eta^2_g = 0.36$). Table 2 presents the results of post hoc comparisons with a Bonferroni correction and Fig. 1 shows the mean value of participants' monetary valuations of each social media affordance, illustrating that among all the eight affordances of social media, participants thought the Conversation affordance was most valuable (around 30% of the total value of social media). The second tier comprised Instrument and Groups. The third tier contained Relationship and Sharing. Identity, Presence, and Reputation were in the fourth tier.

We triangulated the results in the personal reports with participants' daily monetary valuations and found they were in accordance. Personal reports showed that 33 out of the 39 participants regarded Conversation as the most valuable function of social media. One participant claimed that he valued Conversation most for "it permits me to stay in contact with families and friends… and the main goal of all the social media is to keep people connected." Instrument received the second highest valuation. The remaining six participants thought it most valuable for "it is really useful and has become an absolute requirement in China." Reputation was least valued and 12 participants felt it useless because "reputation in a virtual world is intangible and superficial". In all, when assigning monetary valuations of social media affordances, participants tended to emphasize the utilitarian values of affordances like Instrument and Conversation.

The records of participants' daily usage behaviors of each affordance also supported the findings of monetary valuations. Every day, we recorded the first two most highly used affordances. We found 91.3% of the records showed that Conversation was used most within a day whereas the other 8.7% refer to Sharing. As for the second most used affordance, Sharing constituted 48.4% of the total number and Instrument constituted 6.7%. These results showed that Conversation and Sharing were used most frequently. Users

Table 2. Results of post-hoc comparisons with a Bonferroni correction.

	1	2	3	4	5	6	7
2	<0.001						
3	<0.001	<0.001					
4	0.007	1.00	<0.001				
5	<0.001	<0.001	1.00	<0.001			
6	<0.001	0.706	<0.001	0.040	<0.001		
7	<0.001	<0.001	1.00	<0.001	1.00	<0.001	
8	<0.001	0.228	<0.001	0.014	0.002	1.00	0.001

Note. 1 = Conversation, 2 = Groups, 3 = Identity, 4 = Instrument, 5 = Presence, 6 = Relationship, 7 = Reputation, 8 = Sharing. Considering that pairwise comparisons were conducted 28 times, the alpha level was reduced to 0.05/28

did not spend that much time on Instrument, even though they gave it high valuations (see Fig. 1).

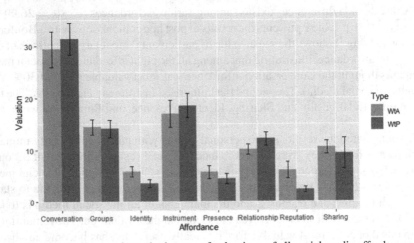

Fig. 1. Mean values and standard errors of valuations of all social media affordances.

4.2 Effects of Addiction, Perceived Social Capital, and Daily Use

The results of the effects of addiction, perceived social capital, and daily use on participants' WtA and WtP for social media affordances are presented in Tables 3 and 4. For WtP, the results of the MLM showed that daily use of social media (h) had a positive effect on the valuation of the affordance Groups (B = 1.18, SE = 0.52, p < 0.05). Addiction had a positive effect on affordances like Identity (B = 1.56, SE = 0.75, p

< 0.05), Presence (B $= 2.60$, SE $= 0.90$, p < 0.01), and Reputation (B $= 1.39$, SE $= 0.53$, p < 0.05). However, perceived social capital showed no significant effects on the monetary evaluation of social media affordances.

Table 3. Willingness to pay

	1	2	3	4	5	6	7	8
Intercept	**48.23***	1.41	2.74	19.38	1.95	**13.72***	0.44	10.82
Day	0.37	**0.53***	0.18	0.34	0.13	**−0.49***	**0.17***	−0.22
Daily use	1.68	**1.18***	−0.12	−0.75	0.29	−0.42	0.12	−0.54
Addiction	0.49	−1.70	**1.56***	−0.74	**2.60****	0.64	**1.39***	0.87
Social capital	−5.69	3.37	−1.10	0.34	−1.61	−0.22	−0.79	−0.58

Note. 1 = Conversation, 2 = Groups, 3 = Identity, 4 = Instrument, 5 = Presence, 6 = Relationship, 7 = Reputation, 8 = Sharing
* p < 0.5, ** p < 0.01, *** p < 0.001.

Table 4. Willingness to accept

	1	2	3	4	5	6	7	8
Intercept	29.21	10.00	11.17	13.31	7.80	10.21	8.71	12.49
Day	−0.18	−0.22	0.14	0.04	0.12	−0.06	0.39	−0.42
Daily use	−0.67	−0.24	0.00	0.00	−0.21	0.00	**1.14****	0.43
Addiction	5.20	−1.55	1.53	−3.18	0.17	−0.66	−1.02	−0.09
Social capital	−2.98	3.00	**−2.83***	3.16	−0.89	0.65	−1.58	0.51

Note. 1 = Conversation, 2 = Groups, 3 = Identity, 4 = Instrument, 5 = Presence, 6 = Relationship, 7 = Reputation, 8 = Sharing
* p < 0.5, ** p < 0.01, *** p < 0.001.

The results of the effects of addiction, perceived social capital, and daily use on participants' WtA for social media affordances were different. Participants' addiction showed no significant effects on their WtA value of social media affordances. Daily usage time of social media showed a positive effect on WtA for Reputation (B $= 1.14$, SE $= 0.35$, p < 0.01), whereas perceived social capital showed a negative effect on WtA for Identity (B $= -2.83$, SE $= 1.36$, p < 0.05).

5 Discussion

Social media platforms combine various affordances to meet the needs of different end-users. How a social media platform focuses on certain affordances is determined by its target users, and thus the design of affordances is related to the commercial underpinnings of social media platforms [32]. This study contrasted users' valuations of different affordances. The results will contribute to reasonable tradeoffs when designing a business model of social media platforms. Our findings suggest that, among the eight social media affordances investigated in this study, Conversation was most valued, which showed that users allocated the most value to social media because it provided channels to communicate with others. Providing a good communication experience might be the key way for social media products to gain commercial success.

Our study introduced the affordance Instrument. Even though this affordance was rarely investigated in previous studies of social media affordances [8], it was actually commonly accepted as a non-social feature of many social media products [30]. According to the results of our investigation, Instrument was a highly valued affordance of social media, which could explain why social media products like WeChat and Facebook produced commercial benefits through their non-social life services (e.g., transactional services).

How much people use a social media product is determined by how the affordances of the product satisfy their psychological needs [8]. However, usage only reflects how much time users would like to spend on a certain social media product. It does not reflect how much money users are willing to spend. The results of our investigation showed that daily use of social media did not directly influence users' valuations of most social media affordances. The valuations of different social media affordances are quite stable within a period despite the fluctuations in daily usage time.

Our results showed that users' addiction to social media will influence their valuations on affordances like Identity, Presence, and Reputation. In our investigation, users with higher addiction to social media valued these affordances more. However, these three affordances were still less valued compared with the other affordances (see Fig. 1), which shows that users were not willing to pay for these affordances. A product on which people spend time, but for which they are not willing to pay much was called Wasting Time Goods (WTGs) in a previous article [19]. We found the affordances of Identity, Presence, and Reputation were quite similar to the WTGs, and this finding pointed to a paradox in the market: when companies want to improve commercial benefits by getting users addicted to their products through facilitating these three affordances, they actually may be getting only users' time, rather than monetary rewards.

The WTG characteristics of some social media affordances raised a marketing challenge: how to convert users' time to monetary rewards. Methods like persuasive technology were applied in social media or other digital applications to induce customers to make purchases without thorough consideration [33]. These technologies that encourage possibly blind consumption are controversial. We should admit that in this study, the valuation of each social media affordance was recorded every day, and the participants had time to thoroughly reflect on their valuations. Thus, the results we got may ignore the influence of persuasive triggers and customers' irrational consumption behaviors, which is a limitation of the data collection method. The results of our study reflect users' long-term valuations of different social media affordances.

The valuation differences of social media affordances may also result from different psychological needs they satisfy. We roughly classified users' needs into two types:

utilitarian needs and hedonic needs. How much an affordance satisfies these needs reflects the hedonic/utilitarian value of the affordance. Generally, the fulfillment of hedonic needs is related to addiction [34]. However, the hedonic value of social media is not necessarily related to purchase intention [35]. In our study, affordances like Identity, Presence, and Reputation were found to be related to social media addiction, but they were valued at a relatively low level. A possible reason for this could be that in the users' eyes, expressing feelings/thoughts (Identity), knowing the presence of others (Presence), and getting followers (Reputation) brought hedonic values for which they were not willing to pay much. Affordances like Conversation and Instrument can fulfill utilitarian needs, and they were highly valued.

The valuation of social media affordances may also change when they are embedded in different social media applications. Xu et al. found that in utilitarian systems extrinsic motivators are more important, whereas in hedonic systems, intrinsic motivators are more critical factors [36], which means an affordance satisfying hedonic needs may be valued higher in hedonic social media applications. In our study, we asked the participants to evaluate affordances based on all social media applications they were using; we did not ask them to specify a certain application, which may ignore the influence of social media product types. When utilizing our findings for future studies, this limitation should also be considered.

6 Conclusion

This study investigated users' monetary valuations of eight social media affordances. The results showed that users valued more affordances that fulfilled utilitarian needs and valued less affordances that fulfilled hedonic needs. Affordances like Conversation and Instrument were the most highly valued among all eight social media affordances. Affordances like Identity, Presence, and Reputation were valued low, but they were positively related to users' social media addiction. These findings illustrate that companies' pursuit of social media users' time by getting them addicted may not lead to commercial success; although, it may cause compulsive usage problems. Understanding the value of each social media affordance and the association between each affordance and addiction will contribute to better designs of future social media products and will provide guidance for ways to improve commercial strategies while also protecting users' well-being.

References

1. Bertot, J.C., Jaeger, P.T., Hansen, D.: The impact of polices on government social media usage: issues, challenges, and recommendations. Gov. Inf. Q. **29**, 30–40 (2012)
2. Huang, Z., Benyoucef, M.: From e-commerce to social commerce: a close look at design features. Electron. Commer. Res. Appl. **12**, 246–259 (2013). https://doi.org/10.1016/j.elerap.2012.12.003
3. Andreassen, C.S.: Online social network site addiction: a comprehensive review. Curr. Addict. Rep. **2**(2), 175–184 (2015). https://doi.org/10.1007/s40429-015-0056-9

4. Ryan, T., Chester, A., Reece, J., Xenos, S.: The uses and abuses of Facebook: a review of Facebook addiction. J. Behav. Addict. **3**, 133–148 (2014). https://doi.org/10.1556/JBA.3.201 4.016

5. Błachnio, A., Przepiorka, A., Pantic, I.: Association between Facebook addiction, self-esteem and life satisfaction: a cross-sectional study. Comput. Hum. Behav. **55**, 701–705 (2016). https://doi.org/10.1016/j.chb.2015.10.026

6. Tandoc, E.C., Ferrucci, P., Duffy, M.: Facebook use, envy, and depression among college students: is facebooking depressing? Comput. Hum. Behav. **43**, 139–146 (2015). https://doi.org/10.1016/j.chb.2014.10.053

7. Gibson, J.J.: The Ecological Approach to Visual Perception: Classic Edition. Psychology Press, Hove (2014)

8. Karahanna, E., Xu, S.X., Xu, Y., Zhang, N. (Andy): The needs–affordances–features perspective for the use of social media. MIS Q **42**, 737–756 (2018). https://doi.org/10.25300/MISQ/2018/11492

9. Zhao, X., Salehi, N., Naranjit, S., Alwaalan, S., Voida, S., Cosley, D.: The many faces of Facebook: experiencing social media as performance, exhibition, and personal archive. In: Proceedings of the SIGCHI Conference on Human Factors in Computing Systems - CHI 2013, Paris, France, p. 1. ACM Press (2013). https://doi.org/10.1145/2470654.2470656

10. Dawot, N.I.M., Ibrahim, R.: A review of features and functional building blocks of social media. In: 2014 8th Malaysian Software Engineering Conference (MySEC), pp. 177–182 (2014). https://doi.org/10.1109/MySec.2014.6986010

11. Kietzmann, J.H., Hermkens, K., McCarthy, I.P., Silvestre, B.S.: Social media? Get serious! Understanding the functional building blocks of social media. Bus. Horiz. **54**, 241–251 (2011). https://doi.org/10.1016/j.bushor.2011.01.005

12. Hsiao, K.: Why internet users are willing to pay for social networking services. Online Inf. Rev. **35**, 770–788 (2011). https://doi.org/10.1108/14684521111176499

13. Vock, M., van Dolen, W., de Ruyter, K.: Understanding willingness to pay for social network sites. J. Serv. Res. **16**, 311–325 (2013). https://doi.org/10.1177/1094670512472729

14. Nahapiet, J., Ghoshal, S.: Social capital, intellectual capital, and the organizational advantage. Acad. Manag. Rev. **23**, 242–266 (1998)

15. Lovejoy, K., Saxton, G.D.: Information, community, and action: how nonprofit organizations use social media*. J. Comput.-Mediat. Commun. **17**, 337–353 (2012). https://doi.org/10.1111/j.1083-6101.2012.01576.x

16. Horowitz, J.K., McConnell, K.E.: A review of WTA/WTP studies. J. Environ. Econ. Manag. **44**, 426–447 (2002)

17. Rotteveel, A.H., Lambooij, M.S., Zuithoff, N.P.A., van Exel, J., Moons, K.G.M., de Wit, G.A.: Valuing healthcare goods and services: a systematic review and meta-analysis on the WTA-WTP disparity. Pharmacoeconomics **38**(5), 443–458 (2020). https://doi.org/10.1007/s40273-020-00890-x

18. Koń, B., Jakubczyk, M.: Is the literature on the WTP-WTA disparity biased? J. Behav. Exp. Econ. **82**, 101460 (2019). https://doi.org/10.1016/j.socec.2019.101460

19. Sunstein, C.R.: Valuing Facebook. Behav. Public Policy **4**, 370–381 (2020)

20. Staiano, J., Oliver, N., Lepri, B., de Oliveira, R., Caraviello, M., Sebe, N.: Money walks: a human-centric study on the economics of personal mobile data. In: Proceedings of the 2014 ACM International Joint Conference on Pervasive and Ubiquitous Computing - UbiComp 2014 Adjunct, Seattle, Washington, pp. 583–594. ACM Press (2014). https://doi.org/10.1145/2632048.2632074

21. Xiang, J.Y., Jing, L.B., Lee, H.S., Choi, I.Y.: A comparative analysis on the effects of perceived enjoyment and perceived risk on hedonic/utilitarian smartphone applications. Int. J. Netw. Virtual Organ. **15**, 120 (2015). https://doi.org/10.1504/IJNVO.2015.070422

22. Kuss, D.J., Griffiths, M.D.: Online social networking and addiction—a review of the psychological literature. Int. J. Environ. Res. Public Health **8**, 3528–3552 (2011). https://doi.org/10.3390/ijerph8093528
23. Bucher, E., Fieseler, C., Suphan, A.: The stress potential of social media in the workplace. Inf. Commun. Soc. **16**, 1639–1667 (2013). https://doi.org/10.1080/1369118X.2012.710245
24. Kross, E., et al.: Facebook use predicts declines in subjective well-being in young adults. PLoS ONE **8**, e69841 (2013). https://doi.org/10.1371/journal.pone.0069841
25. Sagioglou, C., Greitemeyer, T.: Facebook's emotional consequences: why Facebook causes a decrease in mood and why people still use it. Comput. Hum. Behav. **35**, 359–363 (2014). https://doi.org/10.1016/j.chb.2014.03.003
26. Verduyn, P., et al.: Passive Facebook usage undermines affective well-being: experimental and longitudinal evidence. J. Exp. Psychol. Gen. **144**, 480–488 (2015). https://doi.org/10.1037/xge0000057
27. Hsu, C.-L., Lin, J.C.-C.: Effect of perceived value and social influences on mobile app stickiness and in-app purchase intention. Technol. Forecast. Soc. Change **108**, 42–53 (2016). https://doi.org/10.1016/j.techfore.2016.04.012
28. Steers, M.-L.N., Wickham, R.E., Acitelli, L.K.: Seeing everyone else's highlight reels: how Facebook usage is linked to depressive symptoms. J. Soc. Clin. Psychol. **33**, 701–731 (2014). https://doi.org/10.1521/jscp.2014.33.8.701
29. Zhou, X., Rau, P.-L., Yang, C.-L., Zhou, X.: Cognitive behavioral therapy-based short-term abstinence intervention for problematic social media use: improved well-being and underlying mechanisms. Psychiatr. Q. 1–19 (2020). https://doi.org/10.1007/s11126-020-09852-0
30. Qu, Y., Rong, W., Ouyang, Y., Chen, H., Xiong, Z.: Social aware mobile payment service popularity analysis: the case of WeChat payment in China. In: Yao, L., Xie, X., Zhang, Q., Yang, L.T., Zomaya, A.Y., Jin, H. (eds.) APSCC 2015. LNCS, vol. 9464, pp. 289–299. Springer, Cham (2015). https://doi.org/10.1007/978-3-319-26979-5_22
31. Young, K.S.: Internet addiction: symptoms, evaluation and treatment. Innov. Clin. Pract. Source Book **17**, 351–352 (1999)
32. Bucher, T., Helmond, A.: The affordances of social media platforms. Sage Publications (2018)
33. Fogg, B.J.: Persuasive technology: using computers to change what we think and do. Ubiquity. **2002**, 2 (2002)
34. Davis, C., Loxton, N.J.: A psycho-genetic study of hedonic responsiveness in relation to "food addiction." Nutrients **6**, 4338–4353 (2014)
35. Pöyry, E., Parvinen, P., Malmivaara, T.: Can we get from liking to buying? Behavioral differences in hedonic and utilitarian Facebook usage. Electron. Commer. Res. Appl. **12**, 224–235 (2013). https://doi.org/10.1016/j.elerap.2013.01.003
36. Wu, J., Lu, X.: Effects of extrinsic and intrinsic motivators on using utilitarian, hedonic, and dual-purposed information systems: a meta-analysis. J. Assoc. Inf. Syst. **14**, 153–191 (2013). https://doi.org/10.17705/1jais.00325

A Step Towards Inclusive Design and Cross-cultural Communication: Rethinking the Design of Public Bus Services in Hefei Based on the Behaviour of International Student Users

Chunxiao Zhu[(✉)] [iD] and Honglei Lu[iD]

Anhui University, Hefei 230601, China
zcxdesign@ahu.edu.cn

Abstract. This study adopts a combination of design research methods, including shadowing and customer journey maps, to study the service process of ground public transportation in Hefei from two dimensions of time and space. The researchers observed and captured various visible, identifiable and accessible physical contact points between people and objects and people in the process of using the facilities related to bus stations, as well as the international student users' travel. The impact of the interactive environment on user behavior was studied, the contact points that have serious impact on user experience were discovered, and the travel chain and behavior flow of international student users were established. Based on the research results, this article proposes to optimize the inclusive design of Hefei city bus service from three dimensions: ontology, behavior and value, and constructs a multi-level, multi-channel and all-process product-information-environment-service system of "mobile touchpoints - travel context" to realize user pleasure and cross-cultural communication. In addition, this paper also proposes strategies to improve the inclusive design of the service system from the perspective of different stakeholders, including the government, bus operators, designers and society, to create a positive, positive and friendly inclusive environment, which is important for building a harmonious society.

Keywords: Inclusive design · Cross-cultural communication · Public bus service design · International student users

1 Introduction

1.1 Research Background

City public bus system is a social beneficial project that meets the basic travel needs of the people and is also the basic support for the normal functioning of the city. In recent years, the government has also made attempts to balance the demand and supply of public transportation, and various government departments and related agencies have actively organized relevant personnel to study and formulate transportation development plans and guidelines. In December 2012, China's State Council issued the "Guidance

© Springer Nature Switzerland AG 2021
P.-L. P. Rau (Ed.): HCII 2021, LNCS 12772, pp. 454–467, 2021.
https://doi.org/10.1007/978-3-030-77077-8_34

of the State Council on the Priority Development of Public Transportation in Cities" pointing out that public transportation should be given top priority in transportation development, coordinating the effective connection between overall urban planning and public transportation planning, optimizing line network structure, improving operation speed, and ensuring driving safety. In July 2016, the Ministry of Transportation issued the "Thirteenth Five-Year Plan for Urban Public Transport Development", pointing out the need to summarize the experience of public transport city construction and enrich the connotation of public transport city construction; deepen the reform of public transport management, fare setting, land development and other institutional mechanisms; establish an intelligent system to improve traffic guidance; and ensure the sustainable development of public transport through the construction of regulations and standards and the support of financial and tax policies. In 2019, China's two sessions of the government work report also pointed out the need to build a comprehensive transportation system, strengthen investment in transportation infrastructure, optimize the market environment, lead the development of transportation innovation, and enhance the people's sense of access and happiness in transportation. With the support of national strategic policies, city bus service companies are also actively responding to the national call to continuously carry out and improve innovative activities in bus services to enhance passenger satisfaction and enable passengers to lead a green and low-carbon lifestyle. City bus intelligent scheduling system, dynamic monitoring system and real-time information service levels continue to improve and enhance, business shuttle, fast direct special line, holiday special line, high-speed rail special line and other special public transport services have also gradually emerged. This series of initiatives, although greatly improve the level of public transport services, but the "bus priority" strategy is not as effective as it should be. Currently, most cities in China have only 20% public transport share [1], and especially in large and medium-sized cities (with a resident population of 500,000 to 5 million), the share of public transport has shown difficulties in growth in recent years.

With the rapid development of globalization and the integration of knowledge economy, cross-cultural communication and cooperation has become an irreversible trend. In recent years, Hefei City has implemented a comprehensive guiding document to carry out the introduction of foreign talents under the new situation and issued one implementation opinion and seven supporting rules or measures. The number of foreign talents coming to Hefei has been growing steadily, and the proportion of high-level foreign talents remains high. In 2018, the number of foreigners temporarily entering Hefei reached more than 70,000, up 12.68% year-on-year, while more than 5,000 foreigners applied for various visa documents, up 6.01% year-on-year [2]. On November 8, 2020, the International Talent Exchange and Project Cooperation Conference held in Hangzhou released the results of the theme events: 2019 "Charming China - The Most Attractive Chinese Cities in the Eyes of Foreign Talents" theme. The top 10 most attractive Chinese cities in the eyes of expatriates are Shanghai, Beijing, Shenzhen, Hangzhou, Guangzhou, Hefei, Nanjing, Chengdu, Qingdao and Suzhou [3], with Hefei ranking 6th and entering the top 10 list for the third consecutive year. However, with the proliferation of expatriates, it has brought various problems and challenges to Hefei's city public transportation service system, but at the same time, it has also highlighted the importance and relevance of research on the design of more inclusive public transportation services in the city.

In the context of promoting the construction of "Beautiful China", cities need to improve their own image in order to enhance their comprehensive competitiveness and residents' happiness. The image of a city is influenced by many factors, among which the public service system determines the vitality and attractiveness of a city. City bus system is an important part of the public service system, and the economic development and cultural heritage of a city can be seen from its bus routes. With demographic changes, increasing aging of society, and increasing awareness of human rights of people with disabilities, etc. giving rise to a paradigm shift in public service design, inclusive design has become a design theory approach that has received widespread attention from society and industry [4]. Therefore, from the perspective of inclusive design, this paper takes the group of international students who studying and living in Hefei as the object of user study, and through the research and analysis of their behavioral characteristics and touch points with public bus services, proposes strategies and suggestions for optimizing the design of city public bus services, which will improve the travel experience of Hefei citizens, neighboring residents and foreigners, enhance the cultural inclusiveness of the city and improve the It is of great significance and value to improve the travel experience of Hefei citizens, neighboring residents and foreign students, thus enhancing the cultural inclusiveness of the city and improving the infectiousness of its image.

1.2 Inclusive Design Overview

Inclusive design is a design approach and process that allows mainstream products and services to be used by as many people as possible without specialized planning. Inclusive design is a universal design approach in which designers ensure that products and services are designed to meet the needs of their audiences as much as possible, regardless of the age or ability of the users [5]. Compared to accessible design, inclusive design tries to encompass the disabled, the elderly and the able-bodied [6], designing for as many people as possible and opposing design exclusion [7] while placing more emphasis on its values of equality and sustainability. Inclusive design is centered on human-centered design, which balances basic and advanced human needs [8], while taking function, convenient, desirability, and sustainability into account. The basic principles of inclusive design include: 1) putting people at the center of design; 2) recognizing the diversity and differences of users; 3) providing choice, i.e., offering alternatives when a single design cannot satisfy all users; 4) providing flexible spaces and products; 5) creating convenient, comfortable, and positive spatial environments [9].

The inclusive design of city bus system revolves around bus users, recognizes the diversity and differences of users. When the facilities and services of the bus system cannot meet the needs of users, it can provide other convenient options and create a friendly, comfortable and accessible riding environment, thus improve the travel satisfaction of bus users and attracting more groups to travel by public transportation.

1.3 Service Design Overview

Service design is an interdisciplinary study that combines tools and methods from different fields and belongs to a new way of thinking, and becoming an independent specialized academic genre [10]. The first to combine the terms design and service was Shostack,

G. Lynn's paper Designing Services, which was published in 1984 in the Harvard Enterprise Review. The term Service Design appeared in 1991 in the book Total Design by Mr. and Mrs. Bill Hollins, in which they proposed that service design was not limited to product design theory, but also incorporated management concepts and methods. The concept of service design has been gradually enriched.

According to Wikipedia, service design is the planning and organization of people, facilities, communication, and service components to improve service quality and the interaction of service providers with customers and their experiences [11]. Moritz defined service design in terms of design, which refers to the design of a comprehensive experience of services and the design of processes and strategies to deliver services [12]. Hollins et al. state that service design can be tangible or intangible, may involve artifacts or other things and include communication, context and behavior, and must be consistent, easy to use and strategically applied, whether shaped or accessed [13]. The British National Standards Institute established BS7000-3:1994 Design Management System Guide to Managing Service Design to provide guidance to all design organizations and all service forms at all levels of service design management. The standard defines service design as a phase of service shaping that meets the reasonable and predictable needs of potential service users and makes economical use of available resources [14]. After conducting a lot of research on cognitive psychology, social behavior and service design practice, Richard Chase proposed the primary principles of service design, which mainly include: giving customers control over the service process, splitting the pleasure, integrating dissatisfaction and strong closure [15].

With the development of information society and network technology, service design has moved to a broader and more far-reaching field. It is fundamentally changing people's lifestyles. In the experience economy, experience-centric service (ExS) should be given attention [16]. If the transportation, transportation environment, auxiliary facilities, transportation information, and different service users, service providers, and service operators are placed together in the macro context of transportation service system, the paradigm changes to "service organization and experience-centered" in the mode of travel activities. For users, good city bus service design will bring good experience (including products, system and environment involvement, usage and feedback, etc.), create a good and convenient travel environment for users, reduce travel costs and improve the quality of life. For cities, good bus service design can establish a good image of the city in the minds of users and enhance the city's tolerance and infectivity. For companies, good service design can create unique business opportunities and points of interest. In summary, good service design allows stakeholders to achieve shared value.

2 Method

The ultimate goal of the service is to understand the user better, so that the developed product can meet the user experience and provide better service to the user. A company that strives for excellence in service must provide consistent service quality at "Any time, Any where, Any one" in order to build a good corporate identity and brand image. "Any one" refers to the service person who is in contact with the customer, "Any where" refers to the customer's touch points, and "Any time" means that customers can receive the same quality of service at any point in any time [17]. Effective touch points make customers more accessible to your organization, while ineffective touch points keep customers away [18].

Customer perception and experience at any touch point is an important factor that must be considered to enhance or maintain the brand value of the company's image [12]. With regard to the definition of the concept of "touch points", the broad definition of touch points refers to all communications that encompass all human and physical interactions between the organization and the customer during the lifecycle of the customer relationship [19]. The UK National Council defines touch point as a tangible object or interaction that combines the overall experience of a service [20], while from the company's perspective, the touch point is every interaction between the company and the customer. In terms of brands, touch points are the various points of connection where brands appear in public and generate customer experiences [21]. In summary, the touch point is the total experience of all communication, interaction and connection throughout the life cycle of the relationship with the customer [22]. In the service design process, it is a key issue to accurately capture and express the service touch points, connect the relationship between the service provider and the service receiver, and accurately apply them in the service design to guide or satisfy the needs of the users.

Therefore, this study adopts shadowing and behavior mapping to study the service flow of city bus in Hefei in both time and space dimensions, to observe and capture various visible, identifiable and reachable physical touch points between people-objects and people-people in the process of using the related bus stop facilities, as well as the riding experience of international student users, and to study the influence of the interactive environment on user behavior. Discover the touch points that have the most serious impact on user experience, and establish the travel chain and behavioral flow of international student users.

1. Shadowing. Shadowing involves researchers immersing themselves in the lives of customers, front-line staff, or people behind the scenes in order to observe their behavior and experiences. Compared with other research methods, shadowing is an effective way to develop a truly holistic view of how the service is operating, as it provides an intimate understanding of the real-time interactions that take place between the various groups and touch points involved. Shadowing is also a useful technique for identifying those moments where people may say one thing, and yet do another [23].

2. Customer journey maps. A customer journey map provides a vivid but structured visualization of a service user's experience. The touchpoint where users interact with the service are often used in order to construct a "journey"-an engaging story based upon their experience. This story details their service interactions and accompanying emotions in a highly accessible manner.

A customer journey map provides a high-level overview of the factors influencing user experience, constructed from the user's perspective. Basing the map on user insights allows it to chart both formal and informal touch points. "Personalising" the map - incorporating photographs along with personal quotes and commentary - can make it an even more immersive user-focused experience. The overview the map provides enables the identification of both problem areas and opportunities for innovation, whilst focusing on specific touch points allows the service experience to be broken down into individual stages for further analysis [24].

3   Results

3.1   Fieldwork Results

The bus stops on the eastern section of Huangshan Road in Hefei was selected as a pilot study for this field study. Huangshan Road is an east-west arterial road in Hefei, Anhui Province, China, starting from the eastern foothills of Dashu Mountain in the west and reaching Ningguo Road in the east, with a total length of about 10 km. Along the road are the top three universities in Hefei, including University of Science and Technology of China (West Campus, Central Campus, North Campus and East Campus), Anhui University (Longhe Campus) and Hefei University of Technology (South Campus), which is the main study and living area for international students in Hefei. As it runs through many educational places and residential areas, there is a large flow of people, especially the bus stop located on the section from Hezuohua Road to Susong Road are the most frequently used bus stops by the international students. Figure 1 shows the pedestrian flow map and the distribution of bus stops in this area.

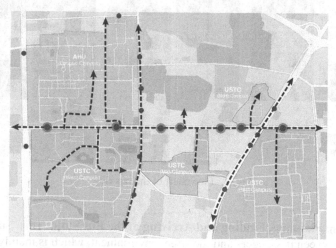

Fig. 1. Distribution of pedestrian flow and bus stops.

The following characteristics and problems of public bus system in the eastern section of Huangshan Road were found through the field study.

1. The number of bus stops is relatively large and basically covers the main crowded areas, which can meet people's travel needs, but the functions are simple.
2. The bus stop guidance system is not perfect, and there are no bus stop directional signs on the road and at the entrance of the university.

3. The shape of the bus stop is traditional and old-fashioned, with weak sense of culture and lack of suitable cultural elements to show the characteristics of the city.
4. The appearance of the bus design is not uniform. The current Hefei city buses have different shapes, and even the buses in the same line are have different shape, color and pattern.

3.2 User Research Results

The research team used the method of shadowing to observe the bus riding behavior of 15 international students by means of follow-up photography. The field researchers do not subjectively interfere with the behavioral paths of the observed users, but only track and record the behavioral and action details of both users and bus staffs during the pre-, mid-, and post-ride phases, which is used to conduct the analysis of the problematic points behind the behavior and to map out the customer journey map. Figure 2 shows a typical ride flow diagram summarized from the behavioral paths of 15 passengers.

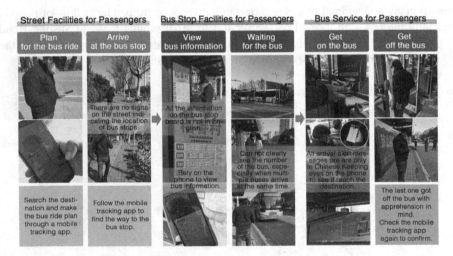

Fig. 2. Flowchart of the bus ride.

Phase 1: Trip Planning, Finding and Arriving at the Bus Stop. This stage is the interaction between passengers and the street environment, which is mainly concerned with the services provided to passengers by the street environment. The 15 international students who participated in this study used a tracking app on their cell phones to look up their bus routes, determine which bus stop they wanted to go to, and then followed the app's prompts to the bus stop. 10 passengers initially went in the opposite direction of the station and walked some distance before realizing the mistake and turning back in the right direction. There is no corresponding bus stop location signage on the street to provide directions and the stop is still not visible at only 30 m away from the bus stop. Some bus stops were not designed to be visible enough in the environment and blended in with it, resulting in passengers not easily recognizing them and missing them. There were three participants missed the bus stop they had planned to go to and turned back.

Phase 2: Checking the Bus Information and Waiting for the Bus. This stage is the interaction between passengers and bus stop facilities, which mainly involves the service of the bus stop facilities to passengers. From the pedestrian's perspective, although the name of the bus stop is displayed in both Chinese and English, the English label font is too small and not easy to identify. The information on the bus stop signs for each line is dense and in Chinese only, which makes it difficult for international students to understand and they have to ask passers-by or use mobile tracking apps to confirm the route. The service facilities at the bus stops selected for this study are not sufficiently intelligent, resulting in passengers not being able to know waiting times and vehicle locations directly at the stops and having to rely on mobile apps to obtain the corresponding information. There are not enough seats set up on the bus stop for passengers to rest while waiting for bus, many passengers were observed leaning against the side posts of the bus stop signs to rest. The auxiliary facilities at bus stops are inadequate, for example, there are no cell phone charging devices or beverage vending machines for passengers to use. The study observed that several study participants were very anxious because their cell phones were running out of power, reflecting the fact that international students are far more dependent on their cell phones than ordinary citizens when travelling on bus due to the lack of inclusion in the design of the existing bus service system. When waiting for a bus, most passengers will peek out to see if the target bus arrives, this behavior has certain safety risks, and when multiple vehicles arrive at the same time, it is difficult to see the information of the bus behind, which may lead to miss the ride.

Phase 3: Getting On and Off the Bus. This phase is the interaction between the passenger and the bus system, which is mainly concerned with the bus service to the passenger. The bus provides a variety of ways to pay for the ticket, passengers can choose to pay by swiping the Hefei City Pass card, coins, scanning the ride code in mobile phone Alipay or WeChat and scanning the QR code posted on the bus directly with their mobile phones, due to the widespread use of mobile phone payment in China, it was observed that all international students passengers participating in this study used mobile phone payment and generally had a very smooth experience in the payment of tickets. The voice prompts and electronic screen text prompts inside the bus are in Chinese only, which is incomprehensible to international students. In this study, most of them were glued to their mobile tracking apps to determine whether they had reached their destinations. When approaching the destination station, they were observed to get up early to reach the window near the exit door and look out, trying to see in advance whether the name of the bus stop outside was their destination, but from the perspective of the passengers on the bus, they could not see the English station name at all and could only look at the mobile tracking app again and again, and finally, they becoming the last passengers to get off the bus with apprehension.

While observing and outlining passenger paths using Shadowing, 10 international students were randomly selected for interviews (Table 1), with the aim of understanding the travel habits of the international students in Hefei as well as the barriers to travel by bus and the experience of the Hefei city bus service. The interviews reflect that international students have more negative than positive opinions about Hefei city bus service, and the negative opinions mostly point to the lack of inclusive information prompt language (no

English prompt), lack bus stop indication system on the road, imperfect bus stop service facilities, and bus driver service quality need to be improved.

Table 1. Information record table of interviewed passengers.

No.	Nationality	Barriers	General feeling	Transportation options
1	Pakistani	Most of the information instructions are not in English, hard to understand Some facilities are not intelligent, don't know how long to wait	Bus stops are not designed with cultural characteristics	Taxi, Electric Bicycle
2	Ethiopia	The information on the station sign is not in English	Intelligent Some bus drivers are not welcoming and do not speak English, making it difficult to communicate	Subway, Taxi, Bus
3	Pakistani	No clear arrival reminders inside the bus (no English) The arrival voice reminder is inaudible and unintelligible	Not smart enough	Subway, Bus, Taxi
4	Nigeria	It is difficult to find bus stops, sometimes the two directional stops of the same bus station name are far apart, or even only one way	Not convenient for foreigners to use	Subway, Electric Bicycle, Walking
5	Kenya	The information on the station sign is not clear and do not know the direction of the bus	Overall okay, but not inclusive enough	Subway, Taxi

Finally, the Customer journey map was used to summarize the subconscious "doing" and conscious "saying" behaviors of the interviewees and the "observing" content of the researcher to explore the problems of the existing bus system in terms of service design, the obstacles affecting user satisfaction and the needs of international students, so as to provide opportunities and ideas for improving the cultural inclusion of Hefei city bus services (Fig. 3).

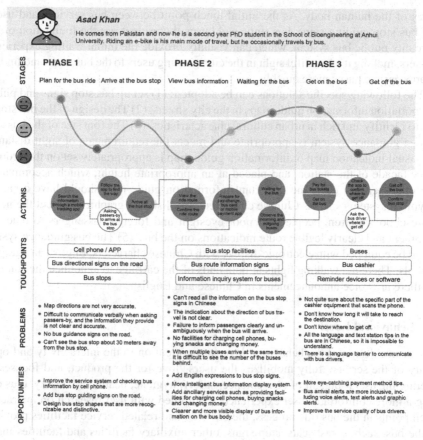

Fig. 3. Customer journey map of international students taking bus.

4   Discussion

In response to the above-mentioned studies, the design of more culturally inclusive bus services should not only focus on the cognitive rules and constraints of expatriate users, but also consider their travel activities and the transition interface between bus vehicles, auxiliary facilities and bus services, as well as the functional composition of the service system on shared transportation facilities. Therefore, from a service design perspective, in order to build a holistic service experience, inclusive urban bus services can be organized and innovated in the following areas: bus stop facility systems, information accessible guidance signage systems, real-time traffic information alert services and bus styling. This paper proposes the optimization direction of inclusive design of Hefei city bus service from three dimensions: ontology, behavior and value.

4.1   Ontology Level

Ontology-level service design focuses on the service and the design itself, communicating with the user about the physical properties of the service itself through the different senses of the human body. As the initial touch point between bus services and users, road bus stop guiding signs, bus stops and buses themselves are the foundation of the entire city public bus system, which can visually provide the initial waiting experience for users, making it a beautiful sight in the city, guiding users to the bus stops and finding the appropriate buses more quickly.

The following specific solutions can be adopted: (1) set up bus stop signs and public transportation information guide maps in the city streets. (2) The design of the bus stop is easy to identify and rich in urban cultural characteristics. (3) The font size of the bus stop signage guidance system is appropriate and meets the requirements of sight distance; The visual indication map or information guide map is appropriately set on the ground, top or façade of the station, and placed at an appropriate height, which accompanied with other sensory cues; the important information guide map should have a variety of symbol systems such as Chinese characters, English and graphics to meet the needs of preschool children, people with poor eyesight and foreign passengers to read. (4) Prominent and clearly legible route indications on the bus. (5) The bus guidance system should be equipped with electronic display with Chinese characters, English and graphic symbols. There are walking lights at both ends of the carriage to announce the stations, and there are voice announcements in Chinese and English.

4.2 Behavioral Level

The service design of the behavioral layer pays attention to the interactivity and oper-ability of the service, fully mobilizes the users' love for the product, and focuses on meeting the users' pursuit of convenience, safety, hygiene, health and beauty, thus cre-ating a more comfortable user experience. Combined with user research on interactive touch points in the bus ride process, the bus stop and related service facilities provided by the bus, such as rest seats, stop signs, other auxiliary facilities and facilities inside the bus interact most closely with the user and determine the main feelings of the user's bus ride experience.

(1) Building more intelligent, systematic and inclusive public transportation smart travel apps or programs and smart bus stop signs, providing multilingual modes for passengers to choose from. These smart technologies can push travel advice based on geographic location, allowing passengers to get the right information about the right place at the right time. (2) Provide a full range of services to passengers by improving auxiliary facilities at bus stops, such as charging equipment, automatic change equip-ment and beverage vending machines. (3) Improving the level of service in the bus to further enhance the inclusiveness and humanity of bus service, such as the intelligence of collection facilities, the visualization of payment information, the internationalization of driver service, and the humanization of arrival information.

4.3 Value Level

The value layer of service design is to make people pay more attention to the story and cultural connotation behind the service, and to arouse the emotional resonance of users. City bus service is an important medium for international students to feel the humanistic care and inclusiveness of a city. By optimizing the design of hardware facilities and software service processes, we build a "product-information-environment-services" system based on the travel experience of international students to realize the whole process of user pleasure and cultural dissemination, and expand the service attributes of the city bus system as a travel mode.

In addition to the above key points of inclusive design of city bus services in Hefei, the optimization strategy of inclusive design to enhance the service system should also include the involvement of different stakeholders and user participation. (1) Government. The government can merge the inclusive design concept and city environmental culture construction into the design of city bus transportation, so that it can reduce the cost of later transformation and thus avoid the waste of resources. At the same time, the government should advocate and encourage pilot lines that combine inclusive design principles with artificial intelligence, big data and other technologies to promote the implementation of inclusive design concepts by taking a point-by-point approach. (2) Bus operators. Bus operators should improve their service awareness and provide humane services to different groups; they can also establish effective feedback mechanisms and channels to collect user feedback as much as possible for improving various aspects of inclusive design. (3) Design. Designers should fully understand and apply inclusive design methods to enable users to use safely and comfortably, revisit the range of users, incorporate inclusive groups into the design objects, and further explore the market for inclusive groups. (4) Society. It is important to reach a consensus on inclusiveness among all social actors, strengthen the promotion of an inclusive environment through the media, education and street communities, correct misunderstandings about inclusiveness, enhance social equity and humanistic care, and jointly create a positive, positive and friendly inclusive environment, which is of great practical significance for building a harmonious society.

5 Conclusions

The development of the city and the improvement of people's quality of life have brought about an upgrade of the consumer experience, however, the study found that the service experience provided by the Hefei city bus system has not been improved in terms of inclusiveness, and there are still a lot of problems for passengers in the process of riding the bus, especially for foreign passengers. The design of bus service not only affects the passenger experience, but also represents the culture and image of the city as a city card. Therefore, it is important to rethink the service design of city public bus, not only to improve the travel experience of foreign students and other foreign groups, but also to enhance the cultural inclusiveness of the city and improve the infectious effect of the city's image. In addition, it is also significant to strengthen cultural exchanges and enhance mutual understanding.

Through a series of user studies, this paper proposes a direction for optimizing the inclusive design of Hefei city bus service in three dimensions: ontology, behavior and value. It also means building a "product-information-environment-services" system with multiple levels, channels and processes of "mobile touch points - travel context". Although the three levels of service design optimization proposed above are far from a comprehensive solution for city bus service system and the different design needs of different expatriate groups, but they provide new innovative opportunities for the next step of more culturally inclusive bus service design application and research.

References

1. Zhang, C., Juan, Z., Luo, Q., et al.: Performance evaluation of public transit systems using a combined evaluation method. Transp. Policy **45**, 156–167 (2016)
2. Li, Y.: 2018 "Charming China the most attractive Chinese cities in the eyes of foreign talents" theme campaign released. Int. Talent Exch. **31**(05), 12–18 (2019)
3. Li, Y.: Gathering talents from all over the world and promoting the vitality of science and innovation--Note on "Charming China--the most attractive Chinese cities in the eyes of foreign talents" in 2019. Int. Talent Exch. **32**(11), 6–11 (2020)
4. Zhao, C.: Application of inclusive design methodology in the urban traffic furniture design. Packag. Eng. **38**(2), 8–14 (2017)
5. Design Council. Inclusive Design Education Resource. https://www.designcouncil.info/inclusivedesignresource/. Accessed 20 Jan 2021
6. Hu, F., Zhang, X.: Design for aging: development and evolution of the design concept involving the elderly since 1945. J. Nanjing Inst. Art (Art Des.) **40**(6), 33–44+235 (2017)
7. Dong, H.: Inclusive design: China and UK compared. Design **33**(15), 56–58 (2020)
8. Dong, H.: Inclusive Design: Chinese Archives. Tongji University Press, Shanghai (2019)
9. Howard, F.: The Principles of Inclusive Design. (They Include You.). CABE Publication, London (2006)
10. Zhao, J.: Design Psychology. Beijing Polytechnic University Press, Beijing (2004)
11. Wikipedia. Service Design. https://en.wikipedia.org/wiki/Service_design. Accessed 15 May 2009
12. Moritz, S.: Service Design: Practical Access to an Evolving Field. Stefan Moritz, London (2005)
13. Hollins, B., Blackman, C., Shinkins, S.: Design and its management in the service sector – updating the standard (Practice based research). Design management: branding, TEXVN (2008)
14. BSI. Guide to Managing Service Design. BS7000-3:1994 Design Management System. British Standard Institute (1994)
15. Chase, R.B.: Its' time to get to first principles in service design. Managing Serv. Qual. **14**(2/3), 126–128 (2004)
16. Luo, S., Zou, W.: Status and progress of service design. Packag. Eng. **39**(24), 43–53 (2018)
17. Huang, S.F.: Customer experience in critical moments. https://www.bethelink.com/epaper/2009.01/sale.htm. Accessed 10 Jan 2021
18. MCorp Consulting (n.d.). Touchpoints Drive Experience and Attitudes. https://www.mcorpconsulting.com/approach/touchpoints.asp. Accessed 18 Jan 2021
19. Brigman, K.: Defining Customer Touchpoints. https://www.imediaconnection.com/content/4508.imc. Accessed 25 Jan 2021
20. Design council. Service design glossary. https://www.designcouncil.org.uk/about-design/Types-of-design/Service-design/What-is-service-design/. Accessed 25 Jan 2021
21. Spengler, C., Wirth, W.: Maximizing the impact of marketing and sales activities. IO new management. https://www.accelerom.com/fileadmin/pdf/Accelerom_Maximising-impact-marketing-sales_io-new-management_2009.pdf. Accessed 25 Jan 2021
22. Teng, C.-l.: Touch the service touchpoints. Zhuangshi **53**(06), 13–17 (2010)

23. Alves, R., Jardim Nunes, N.: Towards a taxonomy of service design methods and tools. In: Falcão e Cunha, J., Snene, M., Nóvoa, H. (eds.) IESS 2013. LNBIP, vol. 143, pp. 215–229. Springer, Heidelberg (2013). https://doi.org/10.1007/978-3-642-36356-6_16
24. Stickdorn, M., Schneider, J.: This is Service Design Thinking. Wiley, Hoboken (2012)

Author Index

Printed in the United States
by Baker & Taylor Publisher Services